Beyond Schools

Islamic History and Civilization

STUDIES AND TEXTS

VOLUME 154

The titles published in this series are listed at *brill.com/ihc*

Beyond Schools

Muḥammad b. Ibrāhīm al-Wazīr's (d. 840/1436) Epistemology of Ambiguity

By

Damaris Wilmers

BRILL

LEIDEN | BOSTON

The Library of Congress Cataloging-in-Publication Data is available online at http://catalog.loc.gov
LC record available at http://lccn.loc.gov/2018030043

Typeface for the Latin, Greek, and Cyrillic scripts: "Brill". See and download: brill.com/brill-typeface.

ISSN 0929-2403
ISBN 978-90-04-37835-3 (hardback)
ISBN 978-90-04-38111-7 (e-book)

This book is printed on acid-free paper and produced in a sustainable manner.

Contents

Acknowledgements IX

Introduction 1

1 The Lives and Intellectual Environment of Ibn al-Wazīr and Ibn al-Murtaḍā 15

1 Muḥammad b. Ibrāhīm b. al-Wazīr's (d. 840/1436) Biography 15

1.1 *Sources on Ibn al-Wazīr's Life* 15

1.2 *Ibn al-Wazīr's Family and Upbringing* 17

1.3 *Ibn al-Wazīr's Education and Intellectual Development* 20

1.3.1 Theology, Legal Theory and Other Classics of Zaydi Learning 21

1.3.2 Sunni Hadith Studies 30

1.3.3 Studies in Mecca 33

1.3.4 Productive Conflict 35

1.3.5 Scholarship in Solitude 38

1.3.6 Teaching and Students 41

2 Aḥmad b. Yaḥyā b. al-Murtaḍā (d. 840/1436) as a Scholar 44

2.1 *Teachers, Education and Students* 46

2.2 *Ibn al-Murtaḍā's Works* 49

2.3 *Intellectual Controversy between Ibn al-Wazīr and Ibn al-Murtaḍā* 55

3 Conclusion 58

2 Ibn al-Wazīr's Works 60

1 *Al-Amr bi-l-ʿuzla* 61

2 *Al-ʿAwāṣim wa-l-qawāṣim* 63

3 *Al-Āyāt al-mubīnāt* 72

4 *Āyāt al-aḥkām al-sharʿiyya* 74

5 *Al-Burhān al-qāṭiʿ fī ithbāt al-ṣāniʿ* 76

6 *Al-Ḥusām al-mashhūr* 80

7 *Al-Istiẓhār bi-l-dalīl al-samʿī fī ʿadam wuqūʿ al-ṭalāq al-bidʿī* 84

8 *Īthār al-ḥaqq ʿalā l-khalq* 87

9 *Kitāb al-Qawāʿid* 98

10 *Kitāb fī l-tafsīr* 103

11 *Majmaʿ al-ḥaqāʾiq wa-l-raqāʾiq fī mamādiḥ rabb al-khalāʾiq* 104

12 *Manẓūma shiʿriyya fī uṣūl al-fiqh* 109

13 *Masāʾil arbaʿa tataʿallaq bi-l-muqallad wa-l-mustaftī* 112
14 *Masʾalat ikhtilāf al-Muʿtazila wa-l-Ashʿariyya fī ḥamd Allāh ʿalā l-īmān* 116
15 *Masāʾil mustakhrajāt* 120
16 *Masāʾil shāfiyāt* 120
17 *Masāʾil sharīfa* 122
18 *Mukhtaṣar mufīd fī ʿulūm al-ḥadīth* 123
19 *Muthīr al-aḥzān fī wadāʿ shahr Ramaḍān* 124
20 *Nuṣrat al-aʿyān* 125
21 *Qubūl al-bushrā bi-l-taysīr lil-yusrā* 126
22 *Al-Rawḍ al-bāsim* 129
23 *Al-Taʾdīb al-malakūtī* 135
24 *Taḥrīr al-kalām fī masʾalat al-ruʾya* 136
25 *Takhṣīṣ āyāt al-jumʿa* 138
26 *Tanqīḥ al-anẓār fī maʿrifat ʿulūm al-āthār* 140
27 *Tarjīḥ asālīb al-Qurʾān ʿalā asālīb al-Yūnān* 142
28 Additional Works Ascribed to Ibn al-Wazīr 148

3 Central Concepts of Ibn al-Wazīr's Epistemological Thought 151
1 Definitions of Knowledge 151
1.1 *Necessary* (ḍarūrī) *and Acquired* (muktasab) *Knowledge* 152
1.2 *A Shift in Distinction: from Necessary and Acquired to Necessary and Conjectural Knowledge* (ʿilm ẓannī) 155
2 Definitions of the Means to Possess Knowledge 161
2.1 *A Shift in the Definition: from* Naẓar *as Philosophical Speculation to* Naẓar *as Pious Contemplation* 161
2.2 *Shifting the Emphasis: Original Human Disposition* (fiṭra) *and Intellect* (ʿaql) 167
3 The Proof of God's Existence (*ithbāt al-ṣāniʿ*) 174
3.1 *Proving God's Existence by Inference* (istidlāl) 175
3.2 *Proving God's Existence from Necessity* (ḍarūra) 178
4 The Argument from the Absence of Evidence (*dalālat nafy al-dalāla*) 185
4.1 *Absence of Evidence as an Argument for Certainty* 188
4.2 *Absence of Evidence as an Argument for Ambiguity* 189
5 Conclusion 195

4 Central Concepts of Ibn al-Wazīr's Theological Thought 198
1 God's Wisdom (*ḥikma*) as the Key to Harmonization 200
1.1 *Ibn al-Wazīr's Harmonization Regarding God's Wisdom* 202

1.1.1 Mitigated Rational Discernment and God's Wisdom 206
1.1.2 God Is Perfect Through His Wisdom 213
1.1.3 The Hiddenness of Wise Purposes 216
1.2 *Ibn al-Murtaḍā's Concept of God's Wisdom* 220
1.3 *Conclusion* 223
2 Harmonized Doctrine: God's Names (*asmāʾ*) and Attributes (*ṣifāt*) 224
2.1 *Ibn al-Wazīr's Harmonization Regarding God's Names and Attributes* 224
2.2 *Ibn al-Murtaḍā's Concept of God's Names and Attributes* 227
2.3 *Conclusion* 229
3 Harmonized Doctrine: God's Will (*irāda*) 229
3.1 *Ibn al-Wazīr's Harmonization Regarding God's Will* 229
3.1.1 Will and Love 231
3.1.2 Will and Motive 234
3.2 *Ibn al-Murtaḍā's Concept of God's Will* 237
3.3 *Conclusion* 240
4 Harmonized Doctrine: Human Actions (*afʿāl al-ʿibād*) and Free Will (*ikhtiyār*) 241
4.1 *Ibn al-Wazīr's Harmonization Regarding Human Actions and Free Will* 242
4.1.1 Action and Capacity 243
4.1.2 Action and Motive 247
4.2 *Ibn al-Murtaḍā's Concept of Human Actions* 253
4.3 *Conclusion* 256
5 Conclusion 257

5 The Structure of Legal Authority in Ibn al-Wazīr's Thought 260
1 The Theory of Infallibilism and the Probability of *Ijtihād* 260
1.1 *Ibn al-Wazīr's Concept of Infallibilism and* al-Ashbah 263
1.2 *Ibn al-Murtaḍā's Concept of Infallibilism and* al-Ashbah 267
2 The Possibility of *Ijtihād* and the Existence of *Mujtahids* 271
2.1 *Ibn al-Wazīr's Position on the Existence of* Ijtihād 273
2.2 *Ibn al-Murtaḍā's Concept of the Existence of* Ijtihād 276
3 *Taqlīd* and Concepts of Following 279
3.1 *Ibn al-Wazīr's Concept of* Taqlīd *and Following* 279
3.2 *Ibn al-Murtaḍā's Concept of* Taqlīd *and Following* 287
4 The Requirements (*shurūṭ*) for *Ijtihād* 290
4.1 *Ibn al-Wazīr's and Ibn al-Murtaḍā's Concepts of the Requirements for* Ijtihād 291

5 Divisibility (*tajazzuʾ*) of *Ijtihād* and the Discerning Student (*al-ṭālib al-mumayyiz*) 312
5.1 *Ibn al-Wazīr's Position on the Divisibility of* Ijtihād 314
5.2 *Ibn al-Murtaḍā's Position on the Divisibility of* Ijtihād 317
6 Extrapolation of Principles (*takhrīj*) 322
6.1 *Ibn al-Wazīr's Concept of* Takhrīj 324
6.2 *Ibn al-Murtaḍā's Concept of* Takhrīj 329
7 The *Muqallid*'s Commitment to a Legal School (*iltizām*) 335
7.1 *Ibn al-Wazīr's Concept of* Iltizām 336
7.2 *Ibn al-Murtaḍā's Concept of* Iltizām 339
8 Conclusion 345

6 Conclusion 350

Bibliography 367
Index of Pre-modern Authors 384
Index of Geographical Names 387
Index of Pre-modern Books 388
Index of Quran Citations 391
Index of Arabic Terms 392

Acknowledgements

I would need many pages to name every single one of those to whom I am grateful for their contribution to this book in idea, content and form. The few that I do mention stand for the many. To begin with, I would like to express my sincere gratitude to Prof. Dr. Jens Scheiner, without whom my project would not have come to a conclusion. His commitment to see the person of the researcher thrive along with her work is extraordinary and bears witness to his dedication to the ideal of a good teacher and mentor. I am deeply grateful for the many hours that he devoted to my work with precision and love for detail and structure as well as for the constructive discussions and feedback. My deepest thanks also to Prof. Dr. Sebastian Günther for taking me on at such a late stage of my dissertation, for giving me the opportunity to take part in the work of the *Courant-Forschungszentrum "Bildung und Religion"* during a crucial period of my project, and for actively supporting the publication of my book.

Without Prof. Dr. Sabine Schmidtke, my mentor during the first and major part of my project, my dissertation would not have had a beginning. The broadness and depth of her work as well as her eagerness to share her vast resources provided me with a roadmap for the country of Zaydī intellectual history through which I had previously wandered in dazzled fascination. Just as I never left the office of Dr. Hassan Farhang Ansari without a clearer understanding of the path I was following, whether or not it was worth pursuing or where else to turn. Further, I want to thank my colleagues from the *Research Unit Intellectual History of the Islamicate World* of the *Freie Universität Berlin* for their inspiration, especially Dr. Eva-Maria Lika for her eager encouragement and exchange about many aspects of the life and work of a doctoral student, for hosting me whenever I was in Berlin, and for reading and commenting on my favorite chapter in the whole thesis. In the same vein, I want to thank the participants of the *Area-3: Offenbarung, Ratio und Identität* meetings of the *Courant-Forschungszentrum "Bildung und Religion"* at the *Georg-August Universität Göttingen* for contributing to the final version of my thesis with their excellent questions, remarks and interest in spite of my absence when the fruit of their own labor was discussed. Many thanks to the *Evangelische Studienwerk e.V. Villigst* for their financial and moral support, for eagerly providing me with the opportunity to go on numerous productive research trips.

I am very grateful to Dr. Leigh Chipman for commenting on a major part of my thesis, for directly and indirectly improving my language and for her encouraging remarks. Many thanks also to Prof. Dr. Thomas Eich for critically reading a chapter and for other helpful advice. Words are not enough to thank my dear friend and brother Tayyib ʿAydān of the *Markaz al-Turāth wa-l-buḥūth al-yamanī*, who opened the gates for me not only to the library of the *Markaz* but also to the living world of letters of Zaydī Yemen and introduced me to all those who like Muḥammad ʿIzzān and ʿAbd al-Karīn Jadbān—knowingly or unknowingly—led me to think that the study of Ibn al-Wazīr's thought is relevant beyond an interest in intellectual history. If nothing had come of my thesis, all the effort would have been worth it for the friendship that I gained. I want to thank the al-Wazīr family of the *Markaz al-turāth wa-l-buḥūth al-Yamanī*, especially Zayd al-Wazīr and his son Nabīl for their encouragement and for providing me with hitherto unpublished editions of important manuscripts. I also want to thank the employees at the *Dār al-Makhṭūṭāt* in Ṣanaʿaʾ as well as the *Ministry of Culture* for providing me with digitizations of numerous manuscripts in a time when reconstruction in the buildings, catalogization of the collections and political unrest in the country made the access to these manuscripts very inconvenient. My thanks also to all those who made the many hours of waiting for permissions and the actual digitizations much more interesting. Like all who study Yemen's intellectual history, I am also indebted to the *Muʾassasat al-Imām Zayd b. ʿAlī al-thaqāfiyya* for their diligent efforts to make the riches of Yemen's cultural heritage accessible by their continuous manuscript digitization campaign.

From the early days of my studies, I want to thank my Arabic teacher ʿAbd al-Ghafūr Ṣabūnī for awakening in me the passion for his beautiful language, Müfit for working his way through ancient texts with a number of ignorant novices just out of shared passion, Dan-Paul Josza and all who participated in his seminar for introducing me to Muʿtazilī thought and Samet Serani for our endless discussions. I am deeply grateful to my parents, Helma and Adolf Pottek, who always encouraged and supported me in my studies, and to my entire family and friends who amazed me with their incessant interest and encouragement through words, thoughts and prayers in spite of my frequent physical or mental absence. This applies most of all to my marvelous husband, friend and brother of my soul Burkhard, whose confidence in me and the meaningfulness of my work was so tangible that I could hold on to it whenever I lost sight of its purpose. Beyond that his eagerness to discuss my findings, read chapters and be my constant IT consultant was an equally tangible help.

Introduction

One of the most vehement challenges to the identity of the Yemeni Zaydiyya has been posed by what Cook has termed "Sunnisation of Zaydism."[1] Although Cook formed this term with regard to the duty to command right and forbid wrong in Zaydi theology and law, it was subsequently used to refer to Zaydi accommodation to Sunni thought in general. This process of "Sunnisation" is associated with a trend toward traditionism within Zaydi Yemen and gained momentum in the politics of the 12th/18th century Zaydi imamate, culminating in the reform project of the traditionist scholar (*muḥaddith*) Muḥammad b. ʿAlī l-Shawkānī (d. 1250/1834).[2] One figure who is commonly associated with the early Sunnisation of Zaydism as well as Yemeni traditionism is Muḥammad b. Ibrāhīm b. al-Wazīr (d. 840/1436).[3] The present study investigates Ibn al-Wazīr's thought vis-à-vis the ideas of his Zaydi contemporaries, in order to determine the causes of the rupture with the prevalent Zaydi tradition and enhance understanding of the Sunnisation process at its alleged outset.

The essential trait of the Sunnisation process is the increasing significance of the Sunni canonical hadith compilations, as opposed to Zaydi texts, as authoritative sources in matters of theology and law. This is why Sunnisation is inextricably linked with traditionism, which is opposed to the idea of legal schools. Haykel, a leading scholar on traditionism within the Yemeni Zaydiyya from the 12th/18th century onwards, identifies epistemological questions at the heart of the traditionist reform. According to him, the trend toward traditionism was motivated by the greater certainty of God's will which traditionist scholars could attain from the Sunni hadith compilations in contrast to the works and views of Zaydi imams and scholars of theology and law.[4] Although Ibn al-Wazīr doubtlessly championed the authoritativeness of the Sunni hadith compila-

1 Cook, *Commanding Right* 247.

2 Other Yemenī scholars associated with this development are al-Ḥasan al-Jalāl (d. 1084/1683), Ṣāliḥ b. al-Mahdī al-Maqbalī (d. 1108/1696), Muḥammad b. Ismāʿīl b. al-Amīr (d. 1182/1769) and Muḥammad b. ʿAlī al-Shawkānī (d. 1250/1834); cf. Haykel, *Revival and Reform*; Haykel, ʿUlamāʾ ahl al-ḥadīth, Haider, *Shīʿī Islām* 103, 113, and footnote 3 below.

3 Haykel, *Revival and Reform* 10–11; Haykel, Dissolving the *Madhāhib* 338; Haykel and Zysow, What Makes a *Madhhab*? 343; Madelung, Introduction. Part VI: Theology 457; King, Zaydī Revival 408; Schwarb, Muʿtazilism 381, footnote 51; Schwarb, Guide to Zaydī *Kalām* 157, footnote 7, 158, footnote 8; vom Bruck, Regimes of Piety 193. The process of "Sunnisation of Zaydism" has continued to this day and has received renewed attention in studies about the developments in post-revolutionary Yemen, i.e. after 1962.

4 Haykel, *Revival and Reform* 10.

 | DOI:10.1163/9789004381117_002

tions and the certainty of their soundness, I argue that his epistemological program went far beyond the role he played in the Sunnisation of Zaydism. It was hallmarked by a high ambiguity tolerance in multiple fields of Islamic theology and law, restricting the core Islamic beliefs on which certainty was required to the least common denominator between conflicting schools. Thereby the commonality of knowledge became the distinctive factor in matters of certain and core doctrine, whereas the individual religious experience and practice prevailed in matters of secondary doctrine and law, effectively championing ambiguity as a God-given characteristic in a kind of Islamic universalism. In other words, while Ibn al-Wazīr's version of traditionism brought him greater certainty in some questions, it also deemphasized the requirement of certainty in others. He doubted the modes of knowing the answers to these questions and was therefore content with ambiguity. A central feature of his thought may thus be called an "epistemology of ambiguity," comprising both theology and legal theory.[5]

The increasing attention given to the Yemeni Zaydiyya in recent decades has centered on its gradual adoption of Muʿtazili doctrine between the 3rd/9th and 4th/10th centuries, as well as its reception of the Bahshami-Muʿtazili school during the 6th/12th and 7th/13th centuries.[6] Although Zaydi law has received some minor attention in a field dominated by the study of theological systems, its analysis has been similarly restricted to its early history. Hence, as Schwarb writes, "subsequent periods remain largely unexplored"[7] in both theology and legal theory.[8] The few studies that treat the intersection of Zaydi law and theology refer to a time from the 12th/18th century onwards.[9] Research on

5 Although the Arabic term for ambiguity (*tashābuh*) is significant in both Ibn al-Wazīr's theological and legal thought, my use of the term comprises *tashābuh* as well as other terms that broadly imply what the term 'ambiguity' signifies in the English language, namely something that can be understood in two or more different ways.

6 The essential studies on the history of the Zaydiyya are Madelung, *Der Imam al-Qāsim*; Strothmann, *Das Staatsrecht der Zaiditen*; van Arendonk, *Les Debuts de L'Imamat Zaidite au Yemen*. Members of the research unit "Intellectual History of the Islamicate World" have contributed decisively to the current state of research on the Yemeni Zaydiyya. For an overview see, for example, Ansari and Schmidtke, The Literary-Religious Tradition; Schmidtke, History of Zaydī Studies, which provides a list of the important contributions to Zaydi studies from Yemeni scholars (193–194); Thiele, *Theologie in der jemenitischen Zaydiyya* 6–7.

7 Schwarb, Guide to Zaydī *Kalām* 157.

8 Among the few studies that treat Zaydi legal theory are Ansari and Schmidtke, Muʿtazilī and Zaydī Reception and a to date unpublished article by Schwarb, Zaydī-Muʿtazilī Traditions of Uṣūl al-Fiqh. 4th/10th–10th/16th Centuries, to which I unfortunately did not get access.

9 Cf. Haykel and Zysow, What Makes a *Madhhab*?; Ghanem, The Development of the Hādawī Doctrine.

the "Sunnisation" process has concentrated on the thought and program of al-Shawkānī along with their ramifications in Yemeni society to this day. However, in most publications, politico-theological questions such as the imamate have received a share of attention disproportionate to other theological matters.[10] Therefore, the present study focuses mainly on theology and legal theory at a point in history which, according to Schwarb, is remarkable for its "multiple rival intellectual traditions and contemporaneous scholarly trends."[11]

As Zysow in his groundbreaking thesis has convincingly argued, Muslims look on Islamic law from a primarily epistemological perspective. "Certainty and probability were the fundamental categories with which they approached every question of law."[12] Similarly, it has been argued that differences between theological systems are insuperable as long as their epistemological precepts remain incongruous.[13] Starting from these premises, I argue that the nexus of theology and legal authority can be described by epistemology and that it is ultimately Ibn al-Wazīr's epistemology which sets him at odds with some of his Zaydi contemporaries.

In this context, a word on the use of terms is due. Islamic epistemology has been studied with regard to the use of the terms *ʿilm*, *maʿrifa* and *yaqīn*, all three denoting knowledge. Whereas *ʿilm* came to be the focus of discussions among speculative and traditionalist theologians and jurists, *yaqīn* received special attention in the context of Sufism, more strictly referring to certainty.[14] *Maʿrifa* apparently connoted particular aspects of either term.[15] But although, as we shall see, Ibn al-Wazīr has a clear tendency to Sufism, and although his

---

10 Recent research on the identity of the Yemeni Zaydiyya and its "Sunnisation" approaches the question mostly from the socio-political angle; cf. Dorlian, Les reformulations identitaires; King, Zaydī Revival; vom Bruck, Regimes of Piety; Bonnefoy, Les identités religieuses. Schwarb's investigation of 20th century Zaydi Quran commentary is an exception; cf. Schwarb, Muʿtazilism esp. 380. The neglect of theology in the research on the process of Sunnisation is largely due to the fact that traditionists like al-Shawkānī tended to reject the discussion of theological matters. One result was the elimination of theological studies from teaching curricula; see for example Haykel, *Revival and Reform* 11; Subḥī, *al-Zaydiyya* 444–447; Schwarb, Guide to Zaydī *Kalām* 184.

11 Schwarb, Guide to Zaydī *Kalām* 157.

12 Zysow, *Economy of Certainty* 1.

13 Ghaneabassiri, Epistemological Foundation 95.

14 For the Sufi use of the term *yaqīn* in contradistinction to the use of *ʿilm* among "legal-traditionalist theologians," see for example Rosenthal, *Knowledge Triumphant* 168; for the prominence of *ʿilm* in the thought of speculative theologians like ʿAbd al-Jabbār al-Hamadhānī, see Peters, *God's Created Speech* 47–56.

15 For *ʿilm* and *maʿrifa* see Rosenthal, *Knowledge Triumphant* 113; for *yaqīn* and *maʿrifa* among a Sufis, see ibid., 156; for *ʿilm* and *maʿrifa* in the Muʿtazili thought of ʿAbd al-Jabbār, see for example Peters, *God's Created Speech* 56.

biography and quest for certainty features similarities to those of scholars like al-Ghazālī who are famous for their occupation with the different degrees of *yaqīn*,[16] his discussion and classification of knowledge focused primarily on the term *ʿilm*. This focus may be seen as an indicator as to the group of scholars among which Ibn al-Wazīr must be classed, or at least the group to which the bulk of his work was addressed. Although he uses the term *yaqīn* to denote certainty, he does not explicitly distinguish it from what he considers *ʿilm*, and *maʿrifa* for that matter, in the strict sense.

Broader Intellectual Milieu

The influence of speculative theology in the form of Muʿtazili teachings on the Yemeni Zaydiyya is already manifest in the theology of its founder and first imam al-Hādī ilā l-ḥaqq Yaḥyā b. al-Ḥusayn (d. 298/911). Likewise, the Zaydi community at the Caspian Sea adopted Muʿtazili theology to a large extent. However, the reception followed different Muʿtazili schools: while the Basran school (later called Bahshamiyya after Abū Hāshim al-Jubbāʾī (d. 321/933)) dominated at the Caspian Sea, the Yemeni Zaydiyya predominantly followed the teachings of the Baghdad school. This changed in a period of intellectual exchange when the two imamates acknowledged each other's legitimacy in the 4th/10th and 5th/11th centuries and a massive transfer of manuscripts was initiated.[17] In the 6th/12th century, the Yemeni imam al-Mutawakkil ʿalā llāh Aḥmad b. Sulaymān (d. 566/1170) promoted unity with the Caspian Zaydiyya and the establishment of Basran Muʿtazili theology in the Yemeni Zaydiyya.[18] This unity was as relevant on the level of Zaydi law as it was on the theological level. Imam al-Mutawakkil argued for the recognition of the legal interpretations of Caspian imams based on the theory of infallibilism.[19] *Kull mujtahid muṣīb* means that all legal interpretations must be accepted equally as long as

16 See for example Bakar's chapter on "The Place of Doubt in Islamic Epistemology: al-Ghazālī's Philosophical Experience" in his *History and Philosophy* 39–60.

17 The Caspian and the Yemeni Zaydiyya were politically united for the first time under the Caspian imam Abū Ṭālib al-akhīr (d. 520/1126) in 511/1117; cf. Schwarb, In the Age of Averroes 265.

18 For a more detailed account of the transition from Baghdadi to Basran teaching, i.e. Bahshami theology and the role of Imam al-Mutawakkil, see Schwarb, In the Age of Averroes 266–276.

19 In the Caspian Zaydiyya, the theory of infallibilism was accepted in the 4th/10th century; cf. Haykel and Zysow, What Makes a *Madhhab*? 336.

they resulted from the process of *ijtihād*. The theory of infallibilism has been considered a central characteristic of the Zaydiyya ever since.[20]

Parallel to the reception of Bahshami theology, aspects of the Baghdadi doctrine continued to exist within the teachings of the Yemeni Muṭarrifiyya, a pietist and conservative movement that referred back to the theology of al-Hādī ilā l-ḥaqq and rejected the unity with the Caspian Zaydiyya. Although the Muṭarrifiyya was fought and largely brought to extinction under the reign of Imam al-Manṣūr bi-llāh ʿAbdallāh b. Ḥamza (d. 614/1217), responses to their doctrines continued to have an impact on Zaydi theology.[21]

Besides the Muʿtazili schools of Baghdad and Basra, another Muʿtazili school influenced the theological landscape in Yemen from the 6th/12th century onwards, namely the school of Abū l-Ḥusayn al-Baṣrī (d. 436/1044).[22] What little is known about the rivalry between Abū l-Ḥusayn al-Baṣrī's and the Basran/Bahshami school in the Yemeni Zaydiyya includes Imam al-Muʾayyad bi-llāh Yaḥyā b. Ḥamza's (d. 749/1346) endorsement of Abū l-Ḥusayn al-Baṣrī's doctrines.[23]

However, not all Zaydis advocated the fusion of Zaydi and Muʿtazili theology. In the 7th/13th century, a group of scholars around Sayyid Ḥumaydān b. Yaḥyā (d. early 7th/13th century) attempted to demonstrate the discrepancy between the teachings of the Zaydiyya's founding figures and the Muʿtazila,

20 Cf. Madelung, *Der Imām al-Qāsim* 210; Madelung, Zaydiyya; vom Bruck, Regimes of Piety 186, esp. footnote 2.

21 Schwarb, In the Age of Averroes 275; Ansari and Schmidtke, Literary-Religious Tradition (II) 102. On the Muṭarrifiyya, see also Gochenour, *The Penetration of Zaydī Islam* 186–201; Madelung, Muṭarrifiyya.

22 According to Fakhr al-Dīn al-Rāzī in his heresiographical digest *Kitāb Iʿtiqādāt firaq al-muslimīn wa-l-mushrikīn* (*The Beliefs of the Sects of Muslims and Polytheists*) and subsequent research, the only two surviving Muʿtazili schools up to Fakhr al-Dīn al-Rāzī's time and beyond are those going back to Abū Hāshim al-Jubbāʾī and Abū l-Ḥusayn al-Baṣrī. The only known exception is the above-mentioned Muṭarrifiyya; cf. Schwarb, In the Age of Averroes 257.

23 Cook, *Commanding Right* 246–247, 218, footnote 115; Madelung, *Der Imām al-Qāsim* 221–222; Ansari, Maḥmūd al-Malāḥimī. The first known proof of the presence of Abū l-Ḥusayn's doctrine in the Yemeni Zaydiyya took the form of a refutation. The foremost proponent of Bahshami doctrine in the Yemeni Zaydiyya of the time, al-Ḥasan b. Muḥammad al-Raṣṣāṣ (d. 584/1159) refuted central aspects of Abū l-Ḥusayn al-Baṣrī's doctrine as rendered in a major theological work of his follower, Rukn al-Dīn Maḥmūd b. Muḥammad al-Malāḥimī (d. 536/1141); cf. Schwarb, In the Age of Averroes 273–274. A refutation of Abū l-Husayn al-Baṣrī's theology by the Jewish theologian Yūsuf al-Baṣīr (d. between 428/1037 and 430/1039) may have been introduced into the Yemeni debates about the same time; cf. Ansari et al., Yūsuf al-Baṣīr's Rebuttal 37.

as well as to expose many Muʿtazili positions as essentially heretical.[24] Nevertheless, Muʿtazili theology continued to thrive in the Yemeni Zaydiyya after its decline in the Caspian Zaydiyya from the 6th/12th century onwards, and its broad extinction in most regions of the Islamic world after the 7th/13th century.[25]

Beyond the Zaydi realm, Sunnism had been present in Yemen for a few centuries and the Sunni domain increasingly intersected with traditionally Zaydi territories. From the beginning of the 7th/13th to the mid-9th/15th century, Shafiʿi and to a lesser extent Hanafi scholarship flourished under the Rasulid dynasty in Yemen's west and parts of the highlands.[26] Sanaa itself had only shifted from Rasulid to Zaydi hegemony in the mid-8th/14th century, albeit with several Rasulid attempts to retake it. Theologically, the Rasulids increasingly chose Ashʿari teachings over traditionalism.[27] Furthermore, the Rasulids of the late 8th/14th and early 9th/15th centuries enhanced the flourishing of various Sufi orders, some leaning towards the theology of al-Ashʿarī, others towards the teachings of Ibn al-ʿArabī from al-Andalus.[28]

Beyond the Yemeni territory, the Hejaz strongly influenced Yemeni scholarship and had been an intermediate point in the transmission of knowledge from the Caspian to the Yemeni Zaydiyya for centuries.[29] Many Zaydis travelled to Mecca on pilgrimage as well as for studies. The sharifs of Mecca, who had been predominantly Zaydis since the 4th/10th century, turned increasingly towards Sunnism from the late 8th/14th century onwards. They completely abandoned Zaydism at the beginning of the 9th/15th century.[30]

---

24 Ibid., 218–219.

25 The remnants of the Caspian Zaydiyya are known to have fully converted to Imāmī Shīʿism in 933/1526. Although the Caspian Zaydiyya apparently continued to exist beyond the 6th/12th century, their activities between the late 6th/12th and the 10th/16th century are largely obscure; cf. ibid., 218; Schmidtke, History of Zaydī Studies 197.

26 The first ruler of the Rasulid dynasty, Nūr al-Dīn ʿUmar b. ʿAlī b. Rasūl (r. 626/1229–646/1249), had originally functioned as a governor for the Ayyubids but later claimed the title of a sultan and was recognized by the Abbasid caliph al-Mustanṣir (d. 639/1241) in Baghdad. The Rasulids extended their rule in western Yemen and parts of the Yemeni highlands between 626/1229 and 858/1454. The Shafiʿi Ayyubids had ruled Yemen's southern parts and some of its western regions since the middle of the 6th/12th century; cf. Madelung, Islam im Jemen 173.

27 Smith, Politische Geschichte 144; Madelung, Rasulids; Madelung, Islam im Jemen 174–175; Schwarb, In the Age of Averroes 273.

28 An example of a prominent Yemeni mystic who was also an Ashʿari theologian and great historian is ʿAfīf al-Dīn al-Yāfiʿī (d. 768/1367); cf. ibid., 147; Madelung, Zaydiyya; van Ess, *Der Eine und das Andere* 970–975.

29 Cf. Schwarb, In the Age of Averroes 270–271, footnote 94; Zayd, *Tayyārāt* 159.

30 Mortel, Zaydī Shīʿism 455, 468.

In sum, the broader intellectual milieu of the Yemeni Zaydis increasingly called for involvement with different theological as well as legal schools. As Grünschloss illustrates in his deliberations on interreligious hermeneutics, involving oneself with the religious (or confessional, as I take it) "other" challenges the perception of the self just as much as that of the other.[31] In consequence, the Zaydiyya needed to (re-)define their theological and legal identity as well as their relationship to other Islamic schools of thought and law. Notably, this definition had to be achieved through a branch of Islam that preserved the teachings of two Muʿtazili theological schools, namely the Basran school or Bahshamiyya and the school of Abū l-Ḥusayn al-Baṣrī, when the Muʿtazila had become extinct almost everywhere else in the Muslim world.

However, the inner-Zaydi reaction to increasing theological and legal diversity did not start at the time of Ibn al-Wazīr. Some Zaydi scholars are known to have studied non-Zaydi hadith and *fiqh* literature from the 6th/12th century onwards,[32] and Zaydi theologians had already grappled with the challenge of Ashʿari theology in the 7th/13th century,[33] although mainly to consolidate their Zaydi positions.[34] Nevertheless, it was this occupation with Sunni literature, according to Ansari and Schmidtke, that initiated the process of the "Sunnisation of Zaydism."[35] However, from the late 8th/14th and early 9th/15th century onwards, the need to meet the challenges of an increasingly multilayered intellectual and textual landscape became especially urgent, all the more so since the theory of infallibilism, as a central characteristic of the Zaydiyya, was theoretically not restricted to Zaydi *mujtahids*.

These challenges could be met by pursuing different approaches. Ibn al-Wazīr found a unique approach to these challenges, if not unique in view of the whole history of the entire Muslim world, then at least unique for his time and his immediate surrounding. In order to appreciate this uniqueness, Ibn al-Wazīr's approach should be studied for its own sake and then compared to different approaches to the same challenges, as exemplified by that

31 Grünschloss, *Der eigene und der fremde Glaube* 31.

32 For a list of pre-9th/15th-century Zaydi scholars who studied with Sunni teachers, see Schwarb, Guide to Zaydī *Kalām* 158, footnote 8.

33 Cf. ibid., 160.

34 Cf. Haykel, *Revival and Reform* 9; Schwarb, Muʿtazilism 381; Ansari and Schmidtke, The Literary-Religious Tradition (II) 105–106; Ansari and Schmidtke, Between Aleppo and Saʿda 161.

35 In their recent publication, Ansari and Schmidtke locate the beginning of what they call the "Sunnification" in the mid-7th/13th century, manifest in a teaching license issued to the influential Yemeni Zaydi scholar ʿAbdallāh al-ʿAnsī (d. 667/1269) in 644/1246; ibid., 108.

of Ibn al-Wazīr's contemporary and eminent Zaydi scholar Aḥmad b. Yaḥyā b. al-Murtaḍā (d. 840/1436).

Research on Ibn al-Wazīr

Although a number of scholars of Yemeni intellectual history have acknowledged Ibn al-Wazīr's brilliance as well as his significance, few have attempted to investigate his thought beyond brief references. Ibn al-Wazīr's significance has commonly been equated with his role in the Sunnisation of the Zaydiyya mainly because of his unprecedented vindication of Sunni textual sources.[36] Although his contribution to Zaydi accommodation of Sunnism cannot be denied, reducing him to the range of his sources ignores *how* his conclusions from these sources answered pressing questions of his intellectual context. This lack of inquiry into Ibn al-Wazīr's thought is especially true of European research. An exception is Hoover's recent article on Ibn al-Wazīr's position on the duration of hell-fire, "Withholding Judgement on Islamic Universalism." Hoover shows that Ibn al-Wazīr, instead of opting for either of the doctrinal positions he discusses, chooses the path of cognitive uncertainty and, in Hoovers words, "withholds judgment."[37] Among Arabic-speaking researchers, Ḥajar's monograph from 1984 is of particular interest, as it investigates Ibn al-Wazīr's success in harmonizing contending theological schools.[38] From about the same time (1985), al-Ḥarbī's doctoral thesis investigates Ibn al-Wazīr's use of his sources with the major goal of determining Ibn al-Wazīr's school affiliation.[39] However, both works investigate only very few of Ibn al-Wazīr's works, partly because only few of them had been edited or published by the early 1980s. After the publishing of Ibn al-Wazīr's most famous work *al-ʿAwāṣim wa-l-qawāṣim*, it became the source of a number of biographies on Ibn al-Wazīr. Similarly, various editions of Ibn al-Wazīr's works are introduced with a brief biography. The section Haykel devotes to Ibn al-Wazīr in his article on the hadith scholars of the Yemeni Zaydiyya takes up essential aspects of Ibn al-

36 See for example Madelung, Zaydī Attitudes 143; Haykel, *Revival and Reform* 10, 41, 91, 108; Haykel, Reforming Islam 338; Haykel and Zysow, What Makes a *Madhhab*? 343; Brown, *Canonization* 214, 314; Schwarb, Muʿtazilism 831; Schwarb, Guide to Zaydī *Kalām* Studies 157–158.

37 Hoover, Withholding Judgement 208.

38 Ḥajar, *Ibn al-Wazīr wa-manhajuhu al-kalāmī* (*Ibn al-Wazīr and His Theological Program*).

39 The thesis was published in 2009 as al-Ḥarbī, *Ibn al-Wazīr wa-ārāʾuhu l-ʿitiqādiyya* (*Ibn al-Wazīr and his Doctrinal Positions*).

Wazīr's life and thought.[40] However, Haykel's goal of ranging Ibn al-Wazīr with later traditionist scholars and his profound erudition in al-Shawkānī's thought and later Salafism lead to an emphasis on a few points that reflect al-Shawkānī's priorities in what Haykel and Zysow elsewhere call the popularization of Ibn al-Wazīr's program.[41]

What many studies on Ibn al-Wazīr have in common is the attempt to discern whether or not he is a Zaydi scholar in either a theological or a legal sense or both, or to associate Ibn al-Wazīr's individual positions with one of the existent schools of thought. This was already done by Ibn al-Wazīr's contemporaries, followed by generations of Zaydi scholars as well as recent Muslim and Western scholarship in general. Al-Ḥarbī's thesis is a good example of this attempt. Whereas some, like ʿIzzān or al-Akwaʿ, claim that Ibn al-Wazīr embodies central features of the Zaydiyya,[42] others, like Haykel, conclude that Ibn al-Wazīr has left the school altogether and fallen in with another, namely the traditionist school that received the attribute of being Sunni.[43] Some, however, like al-Ṣubḥī, have recognized Ibn al-Wazīr's unique position outside of the school system,[44] a view I agree with entirely; to my mind, that unique position featured a syncretistic version of a universalist Islam.[45] Whether or not he thereby fell in with or even founded the school of Yemenī traditionists is a subject for further comparative research. The present study offers a starting point for such comparison with later Yemeni traditionists. However, an understanding of Ibn al-Wazīr's approach within his immediate context must come first.

---

40 Haykel, ʿUlamāʾ ahl al-ḥadīth 2–5.

41 Haykel and Zysow, What Makes a *Madhhab*? 343. One example of the emphases that I cannot affirm from the comprehensive reading of Ibn al-Wazīr's work is the rejection of Sufism, which Haykel calls a common characteristic of all the "traditionist scholars" he discusses. Furthermore, Haykel points out Ibn al-Wazīr's criticism of the Muʿtazila and Ashʿariyya, and fails to identify what I attempt to reveal below as the goal behind the criticism, namely the emphasis on an essential harmony; cf. Haykel, ʿUlamāʾ ahl al-ḥadīth (Ahl al-Hadith Scholars) 1, 4.

42 ʿIzzan, al-Tasāmuḥ al-madhhabī. However, al-Akwaʿ maintains that the Zaydi doctrine of *ijtihād*, coming into its own in Ibn al-Wazīr, at the same time led Ibn al-Wazīr to Sunnism. Furthermore, al-Akwaʿ holds that Ibn al-Wazīr pretended to be more Zaydi than he really was out of fear; cf. al-Akwāʿ (intr.), *al-ʿAwāṣim* i, 80.

43 Haykel, *Revival and Reform* 10–11; Haykel, ʿUlamāʾ ahl al-ḥadīth 1, 4.

44 Al-Ṣubḥī, *al-Zaydiyya* 500.

45 I use the term "syncretistic" and "syncretism" as defined by Grünschloss in his portrayal of Berner's syncretism model. Accordingly, syncretism describes "all processes where the boundaries and therefore the state of competition with other systems are eliminated: formerly heterogenous elements are then defined as elements of a new, comprehensive system;" cf. Grünschloss, *Der eigene und der fremde Glaube* 48. Ibn al-Wazīr legitimizes his syncretism by relating the new system to a purported original state of Islam.

Why Compare Ibn al-Wazīr to Ibn al-Murtaḍā?

Ibn al-Murtaḍā was a contemporary of Ibn al-Wazīr and is comparable to Ibn al-Wazīr in both theology and legal theory for the following reasons: First of all, Ibn al-Murtaḍā was a prolific theologian with immense output and influence even at the time of Ibn al-Wazīr. Neither Muslim nor non-Muslim research doubts the connection between Ibn al-Murtaḍā and Muʿtazili teaching. Al-Ṣubḥī is only one of the many scholars who mention Ibn al-Murtaḍā as a major representative of the Zaydi-Muʿtazili current within the Zaydiyya.[46] For Cook, Ibn al-Murtaḍā personifies what he calls the Zaydi-Muʿtazili symbiosis.[47] Van Ess points out Ibn al-Murtaḍā's lack of originality as well as his vast erudition, and mentions that early European researchers on the Muʿtazila profited greatly from Ibn al-Murtaḍā's conservatism.[48] On the topics of legal theory and the structure of legal authority Ibn al-Murtaḍā is an equally interesting character in the comparison of Ibn al-Wazīr's thought with his scholarly environment. Not only did Ibn al-Murtaḍa write a major compendium on Zaydi law that has been a reference for Zaydi believers ever since,[49] he also authored systematic treatises on Zaydi legal theory in which he had much to say on questions of legal interpretation, adherence and affiliation. Most importantly, Ibn al-Murtaḍā did not receive major criticism for his ideas nor was his loyalty to the Zaydiyya questioned in any of the above-mentioned disciplines. Therefore, Ibn al-Murtaḍā can be taken as representative of the dominant intellectual current within the Yemeni Zaydiyya of the 8th/14th–9th/15th centuries. Lastly, the greater part of works by and on Ibn al-Murtaḍā has remained uninvestigated and unedited. With regard to theology, for example, the reasoning behind Ibn al-Murtaḍā's positions has received little attention. The main interest in Ibn al-Murtaḍā can be accounted for by his representation of earlier Muʿtazila in his heresiographical works as well as his rendering of their theological positions in the form of assertions in his shorter theological treatises, as van Ess explains.[50] Concerning legal theory, almost everything that Ibn al-Murtaḍā wrote remains uninvestigated. An exception to this is Haykel and Zysow's article "What Makes a *Madhhab* a *Madhhab*?" in which they draw conclusions on the state of the Zaydiyya as a legal school from the 11th/17th century onwards, partly based on the recep-

46 Al-Ṣubḥī, *al-Zaydiyya* 341–393.
47 Cook, *Commanding Right* 242.
48 Cf. van Ess, *Der Eine und das Andere* 989; and below.
49 Cf. Haykel, Reforming Islam 338.
50 Van Ess, *Der Eine und das Andere* 986–995.

tion of Ibn al-Murtaḍā's legal encyclopedia.[51] Schwarb, in his investigation of a seminal theological commentary on a part of one of Ibn al-Murtaḍā's works, along with its position in 9th/15th–12th/18th century Zaydi curricula, again confirms Ibn al-Murtaḍā's leaning on Bahshami tradition. Schwarb also refers to Ibn al-Murtaḍā's grappling with Ashʿari theology, indicating the urgency for Zaydis of the 9th/15th century to face the challenges of Sunnism.[52] No study known to me has explored what Ibn al-Murtaḍā's positions were in matters of theology and legal theory with regard to his epistemology, let alone discussed its implications for the division of Islamic unity into multiple schools of law and thought.

A few modern researchers do offer helpful discussions of Ibn al-Murtaḍā's life, work and thought. Al-Kamālī in his monograph as well as al-Ṣubḥī in his entry on Ibn al-Murtaḍā restrict themselves to Ibn al-Murtaḍā's theological thought. Yet al-Kamālī laments the lack of research especially on Ibn al-Murtaḍā's theological doctrine.[53] Al-Mākhidhī, in his introduction to Ibn al-Murtaḍā's *Minhāj al-wuṣul* on legal theory, touches upon Ibn al-Murtaḍā's theological as well as legal thought.[54] However, none of them draws conclusions on an overarching epistemological approach or its implication for the broader problem of theological and legal division in the Muslim community, let alone relates it with Ibn al-Wazīr's thought on this matter.

Although my main focus is on Ibn al-Wazīr, investigating Ibn al-Murtaḍā's life, work and approach in regard to the questions Ibn al-Wazīr wrestles with will accomplish three things: Firstly, it will put Ibn al-Wazīr's views into perspective. Secondly, it will fill out the scanty picture we have of the intellectual situation of the 8th/14th–9th/15th century Yemeni Zaydiyya in general, and the rivalry between the Bahshamiyya and the school of Abū l-Ḥusayn al-Baṣrī, the two Muʿtazili schools—along with the respective impact they may have had on the "Sunnisation of the Zaydiyya"—in particular. Thirdly, and as an important result of the former, we will see how two ways of relating to the confessional other, and responding to questions of theological and legal diversity—questions which the Islamic community has had to face in other regions and times and which it has to face still today—correlate with two distinct concepts of knowledge.

51 Haykel and Zysow, What Makes a *Madhhab*?
52 Schwarb, Guide to Zaydī *Kalām*; see also, Cook, Commanding Right 242.
53 Al-Kamālī, *al-Imām al-Mahdī* 16; al-Ṣubḥī, *al-Zaydiyya* 340–393.
54 Al-Mākhidhī (ed., intr.), *Minhāj al-wuṣūl* 7–204.

Outline

In chapter 1, I give an account of Ibn al-Wazīr's life and intellectual development. The goal of this chapter is to outline the various influences on Ibn al-Wazīr's thinking as well as to illustrate the intellectual milieu he lived in. To this end, a briefer biography of Ibn al-Murtaḍā will also be presented. I will show that both Ibn al-Wazīr and Ibn al-Murtaḍā were exposed to the same theological and legal diversity from within and outside of the Zaydiyya. The sources I use in this chapter are mainly biographical dictionaries (*ṭabaqāt*), biographies and historical accounts of the Yemeni Zaydiyya, whereas the subsequent chapters are chiefly based on Ibn al-Wazīr's and, to a lesser degree, Ibn al-Murtaḍā's works.

Chapter 2 presents an introduction to Ibn al-Wazīr's works in form and content. The survey and summary of Ibn al-Wazīr's works is the foundation on which the subsequent analysis of the central concepts of his thought is built. Beyond that, it is intended as a starting point for further research on the aspects of Ibn al-Wazīr's thought that I do not cover here.

Chapters 3 to 5 are concerned with elaborating the findings from the bibliographical chapter. First, I discuss Ibn al-Wazīr's epistemology in chapter 3. I will show how a number of recurring concepts are logical constituents of this comprehensive although rather unsystematically presented theory of knowledge. I will also tackle Ibn al-Wazīr's concept of knowledge in the context of the dominant Zaydi-Muʿtazili current of his time. Besides the concept of knowledge itself, I will discuss and contrast Ibn al-Wazīr's and Ibn al-Murtaḍā's understanding of the means commonly associated with the occurrence of knowledge, namely *naẓar*, *ʿaql* and *fiṭra*. This is followed by two examples showing the difference between the concepts of knowledge. The first example, the proof of God's existence, illustrates the doctrinal implications of epistemological concepts. The second example, the "argument from the absence of evidence," is a basic logical principle that manifests the different approaches to certainty.

It could be argued that epistemology and theology do not represent two different disciplines of Muslim scholarship and should therefore not be treated in two different chapters. While it is true that the theory of knowledge forms no separate discipline in Muslim scholarship and many theological *summae* begin with an exposition of knowledge, the same applies to many works on legal theory.[55] The concept of knowledge may be seen as a link between theology and legal theory, and is therefore central in both disciplines discussed

55 This is true, for example, for some of most influential works on legal theory apart from Abū l-Ḥusayn al-Baṣrī's (d. 436/1044) *al-Muʿtamad fī uṣūl al-fiqh* (*The Reliable in Legal The-*

here. More importantly, Ibn al-Wazīr frequently discusses epistemological factors when grappling with theological as well as legal questions. Thus the first chapter in the main part of this study is dedicated to a separate discussion of epistemology.

In chapter 4, I reconstruct how Ibn al-Wazīr harmonizes the theological tenets of the Muʿtazila and the Ashʿariyya, how he arrives at the supposed core of each of the theological tenets argued about and what this core contains. This core can be considered tantamount to Ibn al-Wazīr's own understanding of the central tenets of Islamic faith.

In chapter 5, I analyze the main points of contention between Ibn al-Wazīr and his contemporaries with regard to legal theory, mainly by comparing Ibn al-Wazīr's positions with those expressed in Ibn al-Murtaḍā's writings. These main points of contention fall within the realm of *ijtihād* and *taqlīd*, the central constituents of the structure of legal authority. Therefore, I will demonstrate how Ibn al-Wazīr's concept of knowledge can be deployed for his view on the system of legal schools and contrasted with the ramifications of Ibn al-Murtaḍā's concept of knowledge in the system of legal schools.

In the summarizing chapter, I conclude that legal pluralism and the theological harmonization of schools of thought are two consequences sought by Ibn al-Wazīr through his epistemology. Ibn al-Wazīr restricts the realm of certainty to a minimum. Beyond this minimum, much is left to the discretion of the individual. This applies to the quest for theological as well as that for legal knowledge. It was an attempt which ran contrary to the prevalent trend of solidifying theological and legal affiliation as well as arguing over secondary matters of doctrine. Two relevant results of this latter trend were the epistemo-theological exclusion of several schools of thought as well as the rejection of a large part of the source material, namely the Sunni hadith compilations. Both of these trends can be seen as reactions to the increasingly multilayered intellectual and textual landscape in the Yemen of the 8th/14th and 9th/15th centuries. While Ibn al-Wazīr's approach promoted acceptance of the theology and law of Sunni Islam and therefore advanced the "Sunnisation of Zaydism,"

---

ory), namely ʿAbd al-Jabbār al-Hamadhānī's (d. 415/1025) *Kitāb al-ʿUmad* (*The Book of Main Issues*), Imām al-Ḥaramayn al-Juwaynī's (d. 478/1051) *al-Burhān fī uṣūl al-fiqh* (*The Evidence On Legal Theory*), Abū Ḥāmid al-Ghazālī's (d. 505/1111) *al-Mustaṣfā min ʿilm al-uṣūl* (*The Clarified from the Science of Principles*), Fakhr al-Dīn al-Rāzī's (d. 606/1209) *al-Maḥṣūl fī ʿilm al-uṣūl al-fiqh* (*What Can Be Obtained in the Science of the Principles of Jurisprudence*). Although ʿAbd al-Jabbār's *Kitāb al-ʿUmad* is not extant, Abū l-Ḥusayn in his *al-Muʿtamad* criticizes *al-ʿUmad* for the very fact that the definition of knowledge played such an important part in it; cf. Abū l-Ḥusayn al-Baṣrī, *al-Muʿtamad* i, 3.12.

it also anticipated an individualization of religious interpretation in a universalistic manner, irrespective of theological and legal schools, be they Zaydi or Sunni. This was effected by Ibn al-Wazīr's high ambiguity tolerance, his "epistemology of ambiguity."

CHAPTER 1

The Lives and Intellectual Environment of Ibn al-Wazīr and Ibn al-Murtaḍā

The main interest of this biographical chapter will be to understand Ibn al-Wazīr in his intellectual environment. Yemeni historiography of the 8th/14th and 9th/15th centuries in the Zaydi region mainly consists of biographies (*siyar* or *tarājim*) and biographical dictionaries (*ṭabaqāt*), focussing on the protagonists rather then the events of history. Understanding Ibn al-Wazīr in his intellectual environment, therefore, means reading the events of his life in relation to the events of the lives of his contemporaries. The focus will be on Ibn al-Wazīr's as well as Ibn al-Murtaḍā's education, intellectual development and scholarly output. What did they study and with whom? How did they react to the different elements of their education? What influenced the direction that their development took? How did their environment react to their ideas and output? Besides filling in the scanty picture we have of the intellectual environment in 8th/14th and 9th/15th century Zaydiyya, initial conclusions can be drawn regarding Ibn al-Wazīr's motivation for his syncretistic approach to the different schools of thought and his role in the "Sunnisation" process.

1 Muḥammad b. Ibrāhīm b. al-Wazīr's (d. 840/1436) Biography

1.1 *Sources on Ibn al-Wazīr's Life*

The main sources on Ibn al-Wazīr's life originate from his immediate family. Next to the biography (*tarjama*) written by the grandson of Ibn al-Wazīr's brother, Muḥammad b. ʿAbdallāh b. al-Hādī b. al-Wazīr (897/1492),[1] a chapter in the family history *Taʾrīkh Banī l-Wazīr* (*The History of the al-Wazīr Family*)

1 Muḥammad b. ʿAbdallāh b. al-Hādī not only wrote the *Tarjama* of Ibn al-Wazīr, but also provided the sequel of al-Hādī b. Ibrāhīm b. al-Wazīr's family history *Thabat Banī l-Wazīr* (*The List of the al-Wazīr Family*). Al-Ḥadī b. Ibrāhīm b. Muḥammad alias al-Hādī al-Ṣaghīr (d. 923/1517) wrote a follow-up to Muḥammad b. ʿAbdallāh's sequel, which in turn became the basis of Aḥmad b. al-Wazīr's (d. 985/1577) *Taʾrīkh Banī l-Wazīr*. On Muḥammad b. ʿAbdallāh b. al-Wazīr, see al-Shahārī, *Ṭabaqāt al-Zaydiyya* ii, 993–995; Ibn Abī l-Rijāl, *Maṭlaʿ al-budūr* iv, 331–332. On al-Ḥādī al-Ṣaghīr, see for example Ibn Abī l-Rijāl, *Maṭlaʿ al-budūr* iv, 459–461; al-Shawkānī, *al-Badr al-ṭāliʿ* Suppl. 223–224.

 | DOI:10.1163/9789004381117_003

by Aḥmad b. ʿAbdallāh b. al-Wazīr (d. 985/1577)[2] is dedicated to Ibn al-Wazīr. The two extensive biographical collections, Ibrāhīm b. al-Qāsim al-Shahārī's (d. 1152/1739) *Ṭabaqāt al-Zaydiyya al-kubrā* (*The Great Classes of the Zaydiyya*)[3] and Aḥmad b. Ṣāliḥ b. Abī l-Rijāl's (d. 1092/1681) *Maṭlaʿ al-budūr wa-majmaʿ al-buḥūr fī tarājim rijāl al-Zaydiyya* (*Where Full Moons Rise and Oceans Meet: Biographies of Zaydi Personalities*),[4] both draw their data on Ibn al-Wazīr chiefly from Muḥammad b. ʿAbdallāh's *Tarjama*. Ibn Abī l-Rijāl's emphatic preference for the family narrative may be one of the reasons his description of Ibn al-Wazīr's skill and rank depicts such an extremely outstanding scholar.[5]

From among the non-Zaydi authors, the richest accounts are found in the writings of two historiographers who were active in the Hejaz, namely Shams al-Dīn al-Sakhāwī's (d. 902/1497) *al-Ḍawʾ al-lāmiʿ li-ahl al-qarn al-tāsiʿ* (*The Light that Shines on the People of the Ninth Century*) and Muḥammad b. Aḥmad al-Fāsī's (d. 832/1429) *al-ʿIqd al-thamīn fī taʾrīkh al-balad al-amīn* (*The Precious Necklace: On the History of the Safeguarded Town*).[6] Al-Sakhāwī mentions ʿUmar b. Muḥammad b. Fahd (d. 885/1480) as a source who in turn wrote a supplement to al-Fāsī's work.[7] Al-Fāsī seems to have drawn his information from his thorough acquaintance with events in Mecca, where Ibn al-Wazīr received an important part of his education (as will be discussed later).

Among the later biographical accounts, Muḥammad b. ʿAlī l-Shawkānī's (d. 1250/1834) *al-Badr al-ṭāliʿ bi-maḥāsin man baʿd al-qarn al-sābiʿ* (*The Full Moon Rising: The Merits of Those Who Came after the Seventh Century*) is of particular interest. Biographical collections of the 14th/20th century like Ismāʿīl b. ʿAlī al-Akwaʿ's (d. 1429/2008) *Hijar ʿilm wa-maʿāqilihu fī l-Yaman* (*Abodes of Emigration for Knowledge and Its Strongholds in Yemen*), ʿAbd al-Salām b. ʿAbbās

2 I am using an unpublished partial edition of *Taʾrīkh Banī l-Wazīr*, which the editor, Zayd al-Wazīr, kindly made available to me prior to the completion and publishing of the whole work. Unfortunately, this edition has not yet been provided with page numbers. I am therefore using my own consecutive numbering, starting with the entry on al-Hādī b. Ibrāhīm al-Wazīr as page 1. On Aḥmad b. ʿAbdallāh b. al-Wazīr, see Ibn Abī l-Rijāl, *Maṭlaʿ al-budūr* i, 329–345; al-Shahārī, *Ṭabaqāt al-Zaydiyya* i, 153–158.

3 Ibid., ii, 896–903.

4 Ibn Abī l-Rijāl, *Maṭlaʿ al-budūr* iv, 138–160.

5 Ibid., iv, 142.

6 Al-Sakhāwī, *al-Ḍawʾ al-lāmiʿ*; al-Fāsī, *al-ʿIqd al-thamīn*. Additionally, Ibn Abī l-Rijāl refers to Ibn Ḥajar al-ʿAsqalānī's (d. 852/1449) *al-Durar al-kāmina fī aʿyān al-miʾa al-thāmina* (*The Hidden Pearls: Important Personalities of the First Eight Hundred Years*) as a source for Ibn al-Wazīr's life, which I could not verify. Ibn Abī l-Rijāl must have confused *al-Durar al-kāmina* with Ibn Fahd's *al-Durr al-kāmin* (see below); cf. Ibn Abī l-Rijāl, *Maṭlaʿ al-budūr* iv, 142.

7 Ibn Fahd, *al-Durr al-kamīn bi-dhayl al-ʿIqd al-thamīn* (*The Hidden Pearls: Supplement of The Precious Necklace*).

al-Wajīh's (b. 1376/1975) *Aʿlām al-muʾallifīn al-Zaydiyya* (*Outstanding Authors of the Zaydiyya*) and ʿAbdallāh Muḥammad al-Ḥibshī's (b. 1368/1949) *Maṣādir al-fikr al-Islāmī fī l-Yaman* (*The Sources of Islamic Thought in Yemen*) mostly rely on the above-mentioned earlier sources as well. Al-Wajīh's and al-Ḥibshī's works are of special value, because they combine biographical data with their bibliographical research. Most editions of Ibn al-Wazīr's works contain a biographical sketch in the introduction. These are useful where they represent a study in their own right, as in the case of al-Akwaʿ's (d. 1429/2008) introduction to Ibn al-Wazīr's *magnum opus*,[8] or where the authors illustrate their data with elements such as letters or poems not easily available elsewhere, as in the case of ʿAbd al-Raḥmān b. Yaḥyā al-Iryānī's (d. 1419/1998) introduction to Ibn al-Wazīr's first known work on theology.

In summary, the Yemeni sources seem to draw mostly on the two family accounts as well as on letters and poems scattered throughout the extensive manuscript collections in Yemeni libraries. In some instances, Ibn al-Wazīr's own remarks provided information for historiographers and later researchers.[9]

1.2 *Ibn al-Wazīr's Family and Upbringing*

Muḥammad b. Ibrāhīm b. al-Wazīr was born into the ancient and today still well known al-Wazīr[10] family as the youngest of three sons, followed by one daughter. His family descends from the cousin and son-in-law of the prophet Muhammad, ʿAlī b. Abī Ṭālib, as attested by his genealogy.[11] Ibn al-Wazīr was born in Rajab 775/January 1374[12] in a center of Zaydi learning (*hijra*) called Ẓahrawayn,

8 Al-Akwaʿ (intr.), *al-ʿAwāsim* i. Al-Akwāʿ's introduction was published separately in Beirut in 1997. However, I used the version introducing *al-ʿAwāṣim*.

9 For a remark from Ibn al-Wazīr on his own spiritual development, see for example Ibn al-Wazīr, *al-ʿAwāṣim* i, 201–202. Al-Akwāʿ made use of Ibn al-Wazīr's autobiographical comments in his introduction to *al-ʿAwāṣim*.

10 Ibn al-Wazīr's ancestor Muḥammad b. al-Mufaḍḍal al-ʿAfīf was given a leading administrative position (*al-wazīr*, or elsewhere *al-amīr*) after having given up his claim to the imamate to the advantage of his rival, the great scholar al-Manṣūr bi-llāh ʿAbdallāh b. Ḥamza (d. 614/1217). Henceforth, the family was called al-Wazīr; cf. al-Hādī b. Ibrāhīm, *Thabat Banī l-Wazīr* 5–10; al-Jirāfī, *al-Muqtaṭaf* 129. To trace the fame of the family one need only survey the indices of the Grand Mosque in Ṣanaʿāʾ or, for the role played by members of the family throughout the events of the last century, see von Bruck, *Islam, Memory and Morality*.

11 For the genealogy, see al-Ṣubḥī, *al-Zaydiyya* 437; al-Shahārī, *Ṭabaqāt al-Zaydiyya* ii, 896; al-Shawkānī, *al-Badr al-ṭāliʿ* ii, 81; Ibn Abī l-Rijāl, *Maṭlaʿ al-budūr* iv, 138; al-Sakhāwī, *al-Ḍawʾ al-lāmiʿ* vi, 272.

12 Muḥammad b. ʿAbdallāh, *Tarjama* f. 126b; Ibn Abī l-Rijāl, *Maṭlaʿ al-budūr* iv, 138; al-Ṣubḥī, *al-Zaydiyya* 368; al-Ḥibshī, *Maṣādir* 133; al-Ziriklī, *al-Aʿlām* v, 300–301; ʿAfīf, *al-*

located approximately 100 km northwest of Sanaa.[13] In line with the family's history and standing, Ibn al-Wazīr was "raised to be a scholar"[14] with his father Ibrāhīm b. ʿAlī (d. 782/1380)[15] and elder brother al-Hādī (d. 822/1419)[16] as his principle teachers in his youth. His father was a scholar in many disciplines, especially known for his poetry and his piety.[17] Al-Hādī, the eldest of the brothers (b. 758/1357–1358),[18] became a second father to Ibn al-Wazīr and his brother Ṣalāḥ (d. after 840/1436)[19] after the death of their father Ibrāhīm b. ʿAlī in 786/1384.[20]

Al-Hādī b. Ibrāhīm, having studied with a number of influential Zaydi scholars in Saʿda and Sanaa, was known for his mastery of "circulating books of *kalām*" besides other classical fields of Zaydi learning such as legal theory, lin-

Mawsūʿa al-yamaniyya iv, 3157; al-Shawkānī, *al-Badr al-ṭāliʿ* ii, 81. Only al-Sakhāwī, most probably relying on Ibn Fahd, would have 765/1363–1364 as the year of birth; cf. al-Sakhāwī, *al-Ḍaw' al-lāmiʿ* vi, 272. Aḥmad b. ʿAbdallāh does not mention a date of birth at all.

13 The history of the so-called *hijra* is something uniquely Yemeni. Making use of the well-known concept of emigration (*hijra*) from the abode of injustice (*dār al-ẓulm*), the concept of a *hijra* as a protected abode for scholars was developed in the 5th/11th century when members of the Zaydi sect of the Muṭarrifiyya sought refuge among the tribes from their Zaydi contemporaries as well as the Ismāʿīli Sulayḥids of lower Yemen. The Yemeni tribes would protect the scholars in their fortresses in exchange for spiritual guidance, education and mediation. Later on, the concept was used beyond the Muṭarrifiyya; cf. Gochenour, *The Penetration of Zaydī Islam* 148–243; al-Akwaʿ, *Hijar al-ʿilm*; Madelung, Yemenite Hijra; Madelung, Muṭarrifiyya; Schwarb, In the Age of Averroes 267.

14 Al-Shahārī, *Ṭabaqāt al-Zaydiyya* ii, 897.

15 Aḥmad b. al-Wazīr, *Taʾrīkh Banī l-Wazīr* 47, 54. Ibn Abī l-Rijāl and al-Shahārī date it in the year 782/1380; cf. Ibn Abī l-Rijāl, *Maṭlaʿ al-budūr* i, 151–155; al-Shahārī, *Ṭabaqāt al-Zaydiyya* i, 78–79. In the predecessor of *Taʾrīkh Banī l-Wazīr*, *Thabat Banī l-Wazīr*, Hādī b. Ibrāhīm b. al-Wazīr does not mention the date of either birth or death; cf. al-Hādī b. Ibrāhīm b. al-Wazīr, *Thabat Banī l-Wazīr* 100–101. An edited, not yet published version of the *Thabat* was given to me by Nabīl al-Wazīr, another very helpful member of the Wazīr family and of the Markaz al-Turāth wa-l-buhūth al-yamanī.

16 Al-Shahārī, *Ṭabaqāt al-Zaydiyya* ii, 1181; al-Ḥibshī, *Maṣādir* 132.

17 Aḥmad b. al-Wazīr, *Taʾrīkh Banī l-Wazīr* 44; al-Akwaʿ, *Hijar al-ʿilm* 1347.

18 Cf. Aḥmad b. al-Wazīr, *Taʾrīkh Banī l-Wazīr* 11; Ibn Abī l-Rijāl, *Maṭlaʿ al-budūr* iv, 461.

19 Ibn Abī al-Rijāl notes that Ṣalāḥ b. Ibrāhīm died after 810/1407 but does not mention a source for that date. However, in *Taʾrīkh Banī l-Wazīr*, a story is told of a meeting between Ṣalāḥ and Imam al-Mahdī Ṣalāḥ al-Dīn b. ʿAlī b. Abī l-Qāsim (d. 849/1445). When they met, Ṣalāh b. Ibrāhīm was an old man and Ṣalāḥ b. ʿAlī was already imam. But since Ṣalāḥ b. ʿAlī only became imam in 840/1436, Ṣalāḥ b. Ibrāhīm must have died after 840/1436; cf. Aḥmad b. al-Wazīr, *Taʾrīkh Banī l-Wazīr* 21.

20 Ibid., 19.

guistics, law and hadith.[21] He himself was a prolific scholar of Zaydi-Muʿtazili theology, a fervent defender of the *ahl al-bayt* in general[22] and early Zaydī imams like the founder of the Yemeni Zaydiyya in particular.[23] Yet, he also received teaching licenses from Sunni scholars like Nafis al-Dīn al-ʿAlawī in Taʿizz[24] and Ibn Ẓahīra in Mecca[25] and was associated with such scholars as Imam al-Nāṣir Salāḥ al-Dīn Muḥammad (d. 793/1391) who was known for promoting the dissemination of the Sunni hadith compilations.[26] This exposure to Sunni texts and thought was not unusual for his time. Ibn Abī l-Rijāl mentions al-Hādī's written and personal correspondence with scholars beyond the boundaries of region, school of law and theology, including for example with the Shafiʿi poet and jurist Ismāʿīl Abū Bakr al-Muqrī (d. 837/1433–1434).[27] Al-

21 On al-Hādī, see Aḥmad b. al-Wazīr, *Taʾrīkh Banī l-Wazīr* 2–17; al-Wajīh, *Aʿlām* 1069–1073; Ibn Abī l-Rijāl, *Maṭlaʿ al-budūr* iv, 462–470; al-Shahārī, *Ṭabaqāt al-Zaydiyya* iii, 1181–1185; al-Shawkānī, *al-Badr al-ṭāliʿ* ii, 316–317.

22 Aḥmad b. al-Wazīr notes that even those older than al-Hādī referred to him with regard to the genealogies of the *ahl al-bayt*; cf. Aḥmad b. al-Wazīr, *Taʾrīkh Banī l-Wazīr* 4.

23 Among his works are commentaries like the one on al-Raṣṣāṣ' *Khulāṣa*, entitled *Durrat al-ghawāṣ naẓm Khulāṣat al-Raṣṣāṣ* (*The Diver's Pearls: Al-Raṣṣāṣ Khulāṣa in Verse*), which is concerned with arguments for God's unicity and justice dominant in speculative theology. The titles of two other theological works, namely *Kifāyat al-qāniʿ fī maʿrifat al-ṣāniʿ* (*The Satisfying Amount of Knowledge of the Creator*) and *al-Suyūf al-murhafāt ʿalā man alḥada fī l-ṣiffāt* (*The Sharpened Swords to Him Who Deviates Concerning the Attributes* [*of God*]) indicate a similar focus. *Hidāyat al-rāghibīn ilā madhhab ahl al-bayt al-ṭāhirīn* (*Right Guidance for Him Who Desires the Madhhab of the Pure Ahl al-Bayt*) and *Nihāyat al-tanwīh fī izhāq al-tamwīh* (*The Utmost Praise for the Destruction of Distortion*) are theological defenses of the privileged position occupied by the *ahl al-bayt* in Zaydi thought. Similarly, *Riyāḍ al-absār fī dhikr al-aʾimma l-aqmār wa-l-ʿulamāʾ al-abrār wa-shiʿatihim al-akhyār* (*Meadows of Vision: An Account of the Moonlike Imams, Pious Scholars and Their Excellent Followers*) as well as a refutation of the Shiʿi-critical book on the history of the Maliki Abū Bakr b. al-ʿArabī (543/1148) called *al-Tafṣīl fī l-tafḍīl* (*The Elaboration of Favoring* [*the Ahl al-Bayt*]) both defend the position of the Prophet Muḥammad's progeny. Cf. al-Ḥibshī, *Maṣādir* 132–133; Ibn Abī l-Rijāl, *Maṭlaʿ al-budūr* iv, 463 al-Shahārī, *Ṭabaqāt al-Zaydiyya* ii, 1183–1184; al-Wajīh, *Aʿlām* 1070–1072.

24 Al-Shahārī falsely associates the Hanafi Nafīs al-Dīn al-ʿAlawī with the Shafiʿi school of law; cf. al-Shahārī, *Ṭabaqāt al-Zaydiyya* ii, 1183. See in contrast Ibn Abī l-Rijāl, *Maṭlaʿ al-budūr* iv, 464; al-Ḥibshī, *Maṣādir* 132.

25 Ibn Abī l-Rijāl, *Maṭlaʿ al-budūr* iv, 462–463.

26 Al-Hādī b. Ibrāhīm authored two biographical defenses of Imam al-Nāṣir Ṣalāḥ al-Dīn with the titles *Kāshifat al-ghumma ʿan ḥusn sīrat imām al-aʾimma* (*The Remover of Worries from the Excellence of the Biography of the Imam of Imams*) and *Karīmat al-ʿanāṣir fī sīrat al-Imām al-Nāṣir* (*The Most Precious Element: The Biography of Imam al-Nasir*); cf. al-Ḥibshī, *Maṣādir* 492; Ibn Abī l-Rijāl, *Maṭlaʿ al-budūr* iv, 463–464; al-Wajīh, *Aʿlām*, 1072. More on Imam al-Nāsir Ṣalāḥ al-Dīn below.

27 Ibn Abī l-Rijāl, *Maṭlaʿ al-budūr* iv, 463–465. For al-Muqrīʿ, see al-Ḥibshī, *Maṣādir* 220. Al-

Hādī was known beyond Yemen even as far as Egypt, so that the Egyptian historian and scholar of hadith, Ibn Ḥajar al-ʿAsqalānī (d. 852/1449) and a member of the ruling houses (*amīr*) of Mecca[28] are said to have commended his character and learning.[29] However, in contrast to his brother Ibn al-Wazīr, al-Hādī b. Ibrāhīm did not challenge prevailing Zaydi notions in theology or legal theory. On the contrary, a whole tribe in the Hejaz apparently left the Shafiʿi school in favor of adherence to the *ahl al-bayt* on al-Hādī's account.[30]

Nonetheless, the intimate relationship between the eldest, al-Hādī b. Ibrāhīm, and the youngest brother, Ibn al-Wazīr, and their deep mutual influence is not least obvious in their continuous exchange of poems and letters. Ibn al-Wazīr is known to have taken his brother's advice and often calls al-Hādī his father and his master (*sayyidī*). The other members of the family, the middle brother Ṣalāḥ,[31] their sister Fāṭima (d. after 840/1436) and their mother Ḥawriyya bt. Ḥamd b. Ṣalāḥ b. al-Hādī b. Imām Ibrāhīm b. Tāj al-Dīn (n.d.) are well known for their learning and piety as well.[32]

1.3 *Ibn al-Wazīr's Education and Intellectual Development*

Ḥajar, in his analysis of Ibn al-Wazīr's theological thought, divides Ibn al-Wazīr's life into three stages characterized as follows: a.) Growing up and studies; b.) Teaching, writing and debate; c.) Asceticism and isolation. Whereas he can limit the first stage roughly to the first 25 years of Ibn al-Wazīr's life, Ḥajar

---

Shawkānī commends the latter not so much for the content of his scientific observations as for the unusual poetic manner of conveying them; cf. al-Shawkānī, *al-Badr al-ṭāliʿ* i, 142–143.

28 The *amīr*'s name is al-Ḥasan b. ʿIjlān b. Rumaytha (d. 827/1424), as documented in a poem by the gatekeeper of the Kaʿba Abū Shayba; cf. Ibn Abī l-Rijāl, *Maṭlaʿ al-budūr* iv, 465; Aḥmad b. al-Wazīr, *Taʾrīkh Banī l-Wazīr* 8.

29 Ibn Abī l-Rijāl, *Maṭlaʿ al-budūr* iv, 465; al-Shahārī, *Ṭabaqāt al-Zaydiyya* ii, 1185.

30 Cf. Aḥmad b. al-Wazīr, *Taʾrīkh Banī l-Wazīr* 8; Ibn Abī l-Rijāl, *Maṭlaʿ al-budūr* ii, 121.

31 For his brother Ṣalāḥ see ibid., 18. Zayd al-Wazīr mentions in a footnote that there are glosses in another hand in the copy of *Taʾrīkh Banī l-Wazīr* which determine 810/1407 as the date of death. But according to Zayd al-Wazīr, Ṣalāḥ's date of death must have been after 840/1436, because of a report of Ṣalāḥ's meeting with Imam al-Mahdī Ṣalāḥ b. ʿAlī, whose call to allegiance (*daʿwā*) occurred in that year. Ibn Ḥajar and another comment in the margins suggest a date after 822/1419, because al-Hādī would have included him in his *Thabat* had he died before him.

32 His mother is mentioned in the section about his eldest brother al-Hādī. His sister has her own entry in *Taʾrīkh Banī l-Wazīr* but not in *Maṭlaʿ al-budūr*. Yet, the dates of birth and death of both seem to be unknown; cf. Aḥmad b. al-Wazīr, *Taʾrīkh Banī l-Wazīr* 10 (for his mother), 45–47 (for his sister); al-Akwaʿ, *Hijar al-ʿilm* 26; Ḥajar, *Ibn al-Wazīr wa-manhajuhu* 52–57; al-Ḥarbī, *Ibn al-Wazīr wa-ārāʾuhu* 35.

admits that the boundary between the second and third stages is rather vague. However, Ibn al-Wazīr's own accounts and the intellectual content of his work suggest a much higher degree of overlap. The only marked crossover from one stage to another can be detected in the shift from the perceived incertitude of speculative theology to the peace of mind that goes along with the prophetic traditions. This crossing over must have taken place at an early stage of his education, since his first known works already clearly show him as a strong proponent of the prophetic traditions, wary of the methods of speculative theology.[33] According to Ḥajar, Ibn al-Wazīr spent the last twenty years of his life preoccupied with the path of an ascetic, no longer given to intellectual exchange. But the survey of his works in the next chapter shows that arguably his most brilliant work on theology, *Īthār al-ḥaqq*, was written in the last twenty years of his life. I suggest looking at Ibn al-Wazīr's life as a whole, with a unique turn early on that determined the fruits of his life's labours.

1.3.1 Theology, Legal Theory and Other Classics of Zaydi Learning

The disciplines of Ibn al-Wazīr's education covered a multitude of sciences. Besides the memorization of the Quran, his early years were dominated by the study of works in two important disciplines generally called "the two principles" (*uṣūlān*) in Zaydi literature, namely theology (*uṣūl al-dīn* or *kalām*) and legal theory (*uṣūl al-fiqh*). Furthermore, Ibn al-Wazīr is said to have memorized works in substantive law (*fiqh*) and stylistics and the theory of imagery (*ʿilm al-maʿānī wa-l-bayān*) in part or in toto.[34] From his home in *hijrat* Ẓahrawayn he moved to Saʿda, the traditional heartland of Zaydi learning, sometime after his brother al-Hādī moved there in 780/1378.[35] In Saʿda, Ibn al-Wazīr studied *uṣūl al-fiqh* and *fiqh* with Qadi ʿAbdallāh b. al-Ḥasan al-Diwārī (d. 800/1379)[36] and Arab language and linguistics (*ʿarabiyya*), lexicography (*lugha*), literature (*adab*) and exegesis (*tafsīr*) with Qadi Muḥammad b. Ḥamza b. Muẓaffar

---

33 Cf. summary of *al-Burhān al-qāṭiʿ* below, ch. 2 sec. 5.

34 Al-Akwaʿ (intr.), *al-ʿAwāṣim* i, 14–15. In my translation of *ʿilm al-maʿānī wa-l-bayān* as "stylistics and the theory of imagery," I follow Heinrichs in his *EI* article about one of the most influential Arab rhetoricians, Yūsuf b. Abī Bakr al-Sakkākī (d. 626/1229). *ʿIlm al-maʿānī wa-l-bayān* is a sub-discipline of rhetoric. The difficulty of the translation and definition of the term has already been discussed by Bonebakker; cf. Heinrichs, al-Sakkākī; Bonebakker and Reinert, al-Maʿānī wa-l-bayān.

35 Cf. al-Shahārī, *Ṭabaqāt al-Zaydiyya* i, 591.

36 Qadi al-Diwārī was probably Ibn al-Wazīr's most prominent teacher; cf. al-Ḥibshī, *Maṣādir* 132; al-Shahārī, *Ṭabaqāt al-Zaydiyya* i, 891, i, 89; Aḥmad b. al-Wazīr, *Taʾrīkh Banī l-Wazīr* 42; Muḥammad b. ʿAbdallāh, *Tarjama* f. 133b.

(796/1393–1394)[37] as well as with his older brother al-Hādī.[38] Al-Diwārī was probably one of Ibn al-Wazīr's early and most important teachers in *kalām, uṣūl al-fiqh* and *fiqh*, as the qadi spent most of his life teaching and writing on these subjects in the al-Hādī mosque in Saʿda.[39]

No teaching licenses (*ijāzāt*) are known to have existed at that time. According to Yaḥyā b. al-Ḥusayn in *Ghāyat al-amānī*, Saʿda in those days was governed by a group of influential Zaydi scholars around the al-Diwārī family.[40] Yet al-Diwārī's influence reached far beyond that, as illustrated in the events concerning Imam al-Manṣūr bi-llāh ʿAlī b. Ṣalāh al-Dīn's (d. 840/1436) call to allegiance (*daʿwa*) in 793/1390–1391. ʿAlī b. Ṣalāḥ al-Dīn only received the oath from the scholars of Sanaa after a delegation of scholars from Saʿda headed by al-Diwārī spoke out for him.[41] It stands to reason, therefore, that while in

37 Al-Shahārī, Zabāra and al-Wajīh mention 796/1393–1394 as the year of death, whereas al-Ḥibshī gives 836/1432–1433 and Ibn Abī Rijāl 808/1405–1406. Qadi Muḥammad b. Ḥamza b. Muẓaffar was known for his expertise in exegesis. According to the sources, Ibn al-Wazīr was his most prominent student; cf. al-Wajīh, *Aʿlām* 895–897; Ibn Abī l-Rijāl, *Maṭlaʿ al-budūr* iii, 290–292; Zabāra, *Aʾimmat al-Yaman* i, 286; al-Shahārī, *Ṭabaqāt al-Zaydiyya* ii, 965; al-Ḥibshī, *Maṣādir* 26 f.

38 Muḥammad b. ʿAbdallāh, *Tarjama* f. 133b.

39 Prominent among al-Diwārī's works is a four-volume work on Zaydi *fiqh*, commenting on al-Amīr ʿAlī b. al-Ḥusayn's (d. 7th/13th century) major work on Zaydi *fiqh, Kitāb al-Lumaʿ fī fiqh ahl al-bayt* (*The Book of Shimmers on the Jurisprudence of the Ahl al-Bayt*); cf. al-Shahārī, *Ṭabaqāt al-Zaydiyya* i, 590; al-Ḥibshī; *Maṣādir* 214; Ibn Abī l-Rijāl, *Maṭlaʿ al-budūr* iii, 227. On al-Amīr al-Husayn, see for example al-Wajīh, *Aʿlām* 675–677. Furthermore, al-Diwārī authored two commentaries on major works of Zaydi-Muʿtazili theology, namely on Aḥmad b. al-Ḥasan b. Muḥammad al-Raṣṣāṣ' (d. 621/1224) *al-Khulāṣa l-nāfiʿa* (*The Useful Summa*). For Raṣṣāṣ's *Khulāṣa*, see al-Ḥibshī, *Maṣādir* 118; for al-Diwārī's two commentaries, see ibid., 131. In legal theory, al-Diwārī wrote a commentary on Aḥmad b. Muḥammad b. al-Ḥasan al-Raṣṣāṣ's (d. 656/1285) *Jawharat al-usūl* (*The Gem of Principle*) called *Sharḥ Jawharat al-uṣūl* (*A Commentary on the Gem of Principles*); cf. al-Ḥibshī, *Maṣādir* 180. Al-Shawkānī mentions that the Zaydi scholars ceased to write commentaries on al-Raṣṣāṣ's *Jawhara*, because they could not produce anything superior to the work of al-Diwārī; cf. al-Shawkānī, *al-Badr al-ṭāliʿ* i, 382. Indeed, al-Raṣṣāṣ's *Jawhara* is one of the works most commented on in this field. To this day, it remains a foundational work in Zaydi *uṣūl al-fiqh*, as does al-Diwārī's commentary on it; cf. al-Maḥatwarī, *Uṣūl al-fiqh* 19. The great number of commentaries testifies to the *Jawhara's* importance; cf. al-Ḥibshī, *Maṣādir* 178. Ibn al-Wazir refers to al-Diwārī only a few times. He never mentions that al-Diwārī had been his teacher. Yet whenever he refers to al-Diwārī, he refers to the latter's commentary on al-Raṣṣāṣ's *Khulāṣa*, making a direct influence by al-Diwārī appear even more likely. It is hard to imagine that he would have been taught al-Diwārī's commentaries by anyone but the author in such a local and temporal proximity.

40 Yaḥyā b. al-Ḥusayn, *Ghāyat al-amānī* 555–556.

41 Ibid., 538–539; al-Wajīh, *Aʿlām* 571; Zabāra, *Aʾimmat al-Yaman* 314; al-Kamālī, *al-Imām al-Mahdī* 74. Similarly al-Diwārī was crucial for his remaining in power on several other

Saʿda, Ibn al-Wazīr would have studied with al-Diwārī and his associates, of whom Ibn al-Wazīr's brother al-Hādī b. Ibrāhīm was a particularly close one.[42] Al-Diwārī and Ibn al-Wazīr's brother al-Hādī were also powerful supporters of Imam al-Nāṣir Ṣalāḥ al-Dīn, who is known for his profound erudition and the dissemination of the prophetic Sunna and the Sunni hadith collections.[43] It is unlikely that Ibn al-Wazīr would have been left untouched by this, as evident in his own support of Imam al-Nāṣir and his son and successor ʿAlī b. Ṣalāḥ al-Dīn.

Fortunately, more data exists concerning the next stage of Ibn al-Wazīr's education. The focus of his studies in later years can be concluded from the titles given in teaching licenses (*ijāzāt*) and biographical sources. The sources tell us that his focus on theology and legal theory was still prevalent during the next stage of his studies in Sanaa. When exactly he left Saʿda is unclear. But he must have done so before 793/1390–1391, since that is the year of death of his teacher ʿAlī b. ʿAbdallāh b. Abī l-Khayr, who lived and taught in Sanaa.[44] Ibn al-Wazīr seems to have moved to Sanaa of his own accord or at least without his elder brother al-Hādī, who remained in Saʿda until 802/1399.[45] An account of a night vision Ibn al-Wazīr had on a mountain close to Sanaa when he was around 15 years of age further indicates that he lived in Sanaa from the early 790s/late 1380s onwards.[46]

The historical accounts suggest that the intellectual environment in Sanaa was not as purely Zaydi as it had been in Saʿda. It is likely that Ibn al-Wazīr began to question prevalent Zaydi teachings in this more diverse environment, and that his teacher Ibn Abī l-Khayr played an important role in this development. According to Aḥmad b. ʿAbdallāh, it was Ibn Abī l-Khayr who encouraged a focus on hadith studies for the simple reason that Ibn al-Wazīr had

---

occasions; cf. Yaḥyā b. al-Ḥusayn, *Ghāyat al-amānī* 538–550; al-Shawkānī, *al-Badr al-ṭāliʿ* i, 381–382.

42 Al-Hādī b. Ibrāhīm is mentioned as Diwārī's master student; cf. al-Shahārī, *Ṭabaqāt al-Zaydiyya* i, 591; Aḥmad b. al-Wazīr, *Taʾrīkh Banī l-Wazīr* 3. Al-Hādī b. Ibrahim wrote about Qadi al-Diwārī's life and works, lauded him in his poems and was a close associate of the whole al-Diwārī family. Al-Hādī married the daughter of the qadi, al-Mahdiyya bint ʿAbdallāh al-Diwārī. ʿAbdallāh al-Diwārī's son Aḥmad travelled to Mecca with al-Hādī after they had left Saʿda in 802/1399; cf. Ibid., 10; Ibn Abī l-Rijāl, *Maṭlaʿ al-budūr* iii, 77.

43 According to Yaḥyā b. al-Ḥusayn, Imam al-Nāṣir was among the leading traditionists of his time, so that scholars would come from countries like Egypt in order to hear hadith from him; cf. Ibn al-Ḥusayn, *Ghāyat al-amānī* 537.

44 Al-Shahārī, *Ṭabaqāt al-Zaydiyya* ii, 761–765; Ibn Abī l-Rijāl, *Maṭlaʿ al-budūr* iii, 274; al-Ḥibshī, *Maṣādir* 180.

45 Ibid., 555–556.

46 Cf. Ibn al-Wazīr, *Majmaʿ al-ḥaqāʾiq* 395; Ibn al-Amīr, *Fatḥ al-khāliq* 210.

already excelled in the other sciences and exhausted what they held for him.[47] According to al-Shawkānī, Ibn Abī l-Khayr, being a scholar of the *uṣūlān*, taught Ibn al-Wazīr a number of classics of contemporary Zaydi-Muʿtazili learning; namely, ʿAbd al-Jabbār's (d. 415/1025)[48] *Sharḥ al-usūl al-khamsa* (*Commentary on the Five Principles*), Aḥmad b. al-Ḥasan al-Raṣṣāṣ's (d. 621/1224) *al-Khulāṣa l-nāfiʿa bi-l-adilla l-qāṭiʿa fī fawāʾid al-tābiʿa* (*The Useful Summa: Certain Proofs and the Resulting Benefits*)[49] and Aḥmad b. Muḥammad b. al-Ḥasan al-Raṣṣāṣ's (d. 656/1285) *Jawharat al-usūl wa-tadhkirat al-fuḥūl* (*The Gem of Principles and the Reminder of Masters*).[50] Ibn Abī l-Khayr's own work comprised commentaries on the latter writings.[51]

However, beyond Zaydi-Muʿtazili doctrine, Ibn Abī l-Khayr was the one with whom Ibn al-Wazīr studied the writings of a detractor of the Muʿtazili influence on Zaydi doctrine, Ḥumaydān b. Yaḥyā al-Qāsimī (d. after 653/1255).[52] Ibn Abī l-Khayr also introduced Ibn al-Wazīr to the works of a Kufan scholar of Zaydi *fiqh*, history (*taʾrīkh*) and hadith, namely Muḥammad b. Manṣūr al-Murādī (d. 290/903),[53] to whom Ibn al-Wazīr refers approvingly in his major work *al-ʿAwāṣim* as well as in his *Kitāb al-Qawāʿid* (*Book of Principles*). In Ibn al-Wazīr's view, al-Murādī's *ʿUlūm Āl Muḥammad* (*The Sciences of Muhammad's*

47 Aḥmad b. al-Wazīr, *Taʾrīkh Banī l-Wazīr* 29; Ibn Abī l-Rijāl, *Maṭlaʿ al-budūr* iv, 145.

48 ʿAbd al-Jabbār al-Hamadhānī was one of the most important teachers of the Basran branch of the Muʿtazila. He is often accorded the title *qāḍī l-quḍāt*, as he was appointed chief judge in Buyid Rayy. In the above-mentioned *Sharh al-uṣūl al-khamsa*, one of his principle works in speculative theology, he comments on the five Muʿtazili principles; cf. Peters, *God's Created Speech* 13–14. For more on ʿAbd al-Jabbar, see also Stern, ʿAbd al-Djabbār b. Aḥmad.

49 For the location of copies of these works, see for example al-Ḥibshī, *Maṣādir* 118.

50 Al-Shawkānī, *al-Badr al-ṭāliʿ* ii, 81.

51 In the field of the *uṣūlān*, Ibn Abī l-Khayr's major works are commentaries on works of Zaydi-Muʿtazili scholars such as Aḥmad b. al-Ḥasan al-Raṣṣāṣ's *Khulāṣa* and Aḥmad b. Muḥammad al-Raṣṣāṣ's *Jawhara*; cf. al-Ḥibshī, *Maṣādir* 130, 180.

52 Al-Akwaʿ classes Ḥumaydān among the scholars of the 7th/14th century; cf. al-Akwaʿ, *Hijar al-ʿilm* 1343–1344. See also al-Shahārī, *Ṭabaqāt al-Zaydiyya* i 413–416; al-Ṣubḥī, *al-Zaydiyya* 397–434. Ibn al-Wazīr refers to him on several occasions when discussing Muʿtazili views; see for example Ibn al-Wazīr, *Tarjīḥ* 34, 88.

53 Muḥammad b. Manṣūr al-Murādī was the head of one of the four Zaydi schools in the Kufa of the 3rd/10th and 4th/11th centuries. Besides being a "gewaltiger Sammler des Rechts der Prophetenfamilie," he rejected Muʿtazili theology, compiled Aḥmad b. ʿĪsā's (d. 247/861) *Amālī* and was used as a source for Muḥammad b. ʿAlī al-ʿAlawī's (d. 445/1053) *al-Jāmiʿ al-kāfī*. For more on al-Murādī, see Madelung, *Der Imām al-Qāsim* 80; Sezgin, *Taʾrīkh al-turāth* iii, 333–335, al-Sabḥāni, *Buḥūth* vii, 391–392. In Ibn al-Wazīr's biography, Muḥammad b. ʿAbdallāh al-Wazīr mentions al-Murādī's *al-Jumla wa-l-ulfa* (*Totality and Harmony*), or *al-Ulfa wa-l-jumla* as it is elsewhere called, as one of the books Ibn al-Wazīr read with Ibn Abī l-Khayr; cf. Muḥammad b. ʿAbdallāh, *Tarjama* f. 134a.

Family) represents the first book of Zaydi hadith and features transmissions from al-Bukhārī's famous hadith collection.[54]

A commentary on the Maliki Abū ʿAmr b. ʿUmar b. al-Ḥājib's (d. 646/1248–1249) *Mukhtaṣar Muntahā l-suʾl wa-l-amal* (*Digest of The Utmost of Demand and Wish*) called *Mishkāt anwār al-ʿuqūl* (*The Lamp for the Lights of the Intellect*) is among Ibn Abī l-Khayr's writings in jurisprudence and among the things Ibn al-Wazīr would have learned from him. For Ibn al-Ḥājib's *Mukhtaṣar al-muntahā* this is documented by Muḥammad b. ʿAbdallāh b. al-Hādī in his biography of Ibn al-Wazīr,[55] though no actual *ijāza* is preserved. Although Ibn al-Ḥājib was a Maliki scholar, many a Zaydi's writing on legal methodology was patterned on Ibn al-Ḥājib's work in the field. Ibn al-Wazīr refers to him frequently.[56] Other writings that are essential to Zaydi *uṣūl al-fiqh* studied by Ibn al-Wazīr were Imam Abī Ṭālib Yaḥyā al-Hārūnī's (d. 424/1033) *al-Mujzī fī uṣūl al-fiqh* (*The Sufficient [Amount] in Uṣūl al-Fiqh*) and Imam al-Manṣūr ʿAbdallāh b. Ḥamza's (d. 614/1217) *Ṣafwat al-ikhtiyār fī uṣūl al-fiqh* (*The Prime Choice in Uṣūl al-Fiqh*).

According to Muḥammad b. ʿAbdallāh, Ibn al-Wazīr studied the essential work on Zaydi *fiqh*, *al-Jāmiʿ al-kāfī* (*The Sufficient Collection*) of Imam Muḥammad b. ʿAlī al-ʿAlawī al-Ḥasanī (d. 445/1053–1054) with his teacher Ibn Abī l-Khayr. Moreover, several writings by his grandfather Yaḥyā b. Manṣūr b. al-ʿAfīf b. al-Mufaḍḍal (d. 788/1386)[57] were transmitted to him by the same teacher.[58]

Mysticism (*taṣawwuf*) is another field that Ibn al-Wazīr became acquainted with through Ibn Abī l-Khayr. Ibn Abī l-Khayr authored a number of works on mysticism[59] and was affiliated with a Sufi tradition that passed on the symbolic cloak (*khirqa*). According to Madelung, Ibn Abī l-Khayr founded the first Zaydi Sufi order.[60] An anecdote narrated by Ibn al-Wazīr illustrates his teacher's atti-

54 See for example Ibn al-Wazīr, *al-ʿAwāṣim* viii, 278.

55 Muḥammad b. ʿAbdallāh, *Tarjama* f. 133b.

56 In the case of the prolific Zaydi scholar Ibn al-Murtaḍā, the editor of one of his most important writings on *uṣul al-fiqh*, Aḥmad ʿAlī Muṭahhar al-Mākhidhī, goes so far as to say that Ibn al-Murtaḍā practices "*taqlīd* of this exalted scholar [Ibn al-Ḥājib] where the method of writing is concerned"; al-Mākhidhī (ed., intr.), *Minhāj al-wuṣūl*, 157.

57 Yaḥyā b. al-Manṣūr b. Muḥammad al-ʿAfīf was especially known for his scholarship in *kalām*; cf. al-Hādī b. Ibrāhīm, *Thabat Banī l-Wazīr* 33; Aḥmad b. al-Wazīr, *Taʾrīkh Banī l-Wazīr* fs. 184–189; Ibn Abī l-Rijāl, *Maṭlaʿ al-budūr* iv, 513–515.

58 Muḥammad b. ʿAbdallāh, *Tarjama* f. 133b.

59 According to Yaḥyā b. al-Mahdī, student of al-Kaynaʿī (see below), Ibn Abī l-Khayr authored around 40 works; cf. Al-Ḥibshī, *Maṣādir* 328.

60 Madelung, Introduction. Part VI: Theology 457. Ibn Abī l-Khayr was the most important teacher of the ascetic shaykh and co-founder of a Sufi order Ibrāhīm b. Aḥmad al-Kaynaʿī (d. 793/1390–1391) to whom he passed on the symbolic cloak of Sufi affiliation (*khirqa*), after he had passed it on to another Sufi in 790/1388. Ibn Abī l-Khayr himself received

tude towards the persuasive power of *kalām*-arguments and his typically Sufi way of responding: Once Ibn al-Wazīr confronted his teacher with the challenges concerning the existence of God that some philosophers brought forth. These caused Ibn Abī l-Khayr to doubt all evidence that was propounded in *ʿilm al-kalām*. Ibn al-Wazīr reports that Ibn Abī l-Khayr's supplication to God was answered by a divine inspiration (*ilhām*) in the form of a nightly vision. The proofs advanced in this vision were based on miracles to be perceived in nature.[61] Both Ibn Abī l-Khayr's attitude towards *kalām*-arguments and his way of responding resonate with Ibn al-Wazīr's reasoning, as we shall discuss in subsequent chapters.

In short, it is very probable that Ibn al-Wazīr's stance of being critically disposed towards speculative theology and favorably receptive to traditionalism and Sufism was formed at an early stage of his life. And it is equally likely that Ibn Abī l-Khayr played a major role in this regard. Hence, already in his teens and his twenties, Ibn al-Wazīr would have been familiar not only with an extensive amount of what the different disciplines of Zaydi teaching held, but also with the range and limits of Zaydi contribution to the study of traditions and reports (*ʿilm al-ḥadīth*). Where *kalām* is concerned, it can be ascertained that he had been introduced to criticism of the prevalent Muʿtazili teaching from within the Zaydiyya in the writings of Ḥumaydān b. Yaḥyā al-Qāsimī and possibly Ibn Abī l-Khayr himself, who had strong reservations, at least, concerning a proof of God that relied on logical presuppositions alone.

But this did not stop Ibn al-Wazīr's study of classical Zaydi literature. The content of the *ijāza* he received from al-Nāṣir b. Aḥmad b. al-Imām al-Muṭahhar (d. 802/1399–1400)[62] around the year 800/1397–1398 supports this claim. Unfortunately, the *ijāza* does not state a date or place. However, Muḥammad b. ʿAbdallāh al-Wazīr suggests that it must have been issued two or more years

---

the *khirqa* from his teacher Yūsuf al-Kurānī (d. 769/1367). Al-Kurānī traces his authority in the teaching of remembrance (*dhikr*) back to ʿAlī b. Abī Ṭālib and the Prophet Muḥammad through the line (*tarīqa*) of al-Ḥasan al-Baṣrī. For the complete line, see al-Shahārī, *Ṭabaqāt al-Zaydiyya* ii, 763. Most sources attest to Ibn Abī l-Ḳhayr's Sufism; cf. al-Ḥibshī, *Maṣādir* 328; al-Wajīh, *Aʿlām* 692–694; Ibn Abī l-Rijāl, *Maṭlaʿ al-budūr* iii, 275; al-Shahārī, *Ṭabaqāt al-Zaydiyya* ii, 761–765. On al-Kaynaʿī, cf. *Maṭlaʿ al-budūr* i, 120; Ibn al-Qāsim, *Ṭabaqāt al-Zaydiyya* i, 64–65; al-Wajīh, *Aʿlām* 45; al-Shawkānī, *al-Badr al-ṭāliʿ* i, 4; Madelung also discusses al-Kaynaʿī's relationship to Ibn Abī l-Khayr; cf. Madelung, Zaydī Attitudes 131.

61 Ibn al-Wazīr, *Tarjīḥ* 105; cf. Ibn Abī l-Rijāl, *Maṭlaʿ al-budūr* iii, 281.

62 On al-Nāṣir b. Aḥmad, see al-Shawkānī, *al-Badr al-ṭāliʿ* suppl., 219; al-Wajīh, *Aʿlām* 1057; Ibn Abī l-Rijāl, *Maṭlaʿ al-budūr* iv, 442; al-Shahārī, *Ṭabaqāt al-Zaydiyya* ii, 1167; Zabāra, *Aʾimmat al-Yaman* i, 291; al-Ḥibshī, *Maṣādir* 562.

before al-Nāṣir's death 802/1399–1400 in Sanaa's al-Ajdham Mosque where al-Nāṣir taught.[63] That Ibn al-Wazīr was residing and studying there at the time is confirmed in *Ṭabaqāt al-Zaydiyya al-kubrā* and *Maṭlaʿ al-budūr*.[64] Al-Nāṣir b. Aḥmad attests to having transmitted the entire content of the Khizāna al-Mahdiyya, the library of the Zaydi imam al-Mahdī Muḥammad b. al-Muṭahhar.[65] Examples of the theological works Ibn al-Wazīr studied with him are generic for Zaydi learning of that time, mirroring the proximity between Zaydi scholarship and Muʿtazili doctrine: ʿAbd al-Jabbār's *Sharḥ al-uṣūl al-khamsa*, Ibn Mattawayh's (d. 5th/11th c.) *Tadhkira fī aḥkām jawāhir wa-aʿrāḍ* (*The Reminder: On the Characteristics of Substances and Accidents*),[66] Aḥmad b. Ḥasan al-Raṣṣāṣ's (d. 621/1224) *Khulāṣa* and its commentary *al-Ghiyāṣa sharḥ al-Khulāṣa* (*Pearl Diving: A Commentary on The Summa*) by Muḥammad b. Aḥmad Ḥanash (d. 719/1319).[67] It must be noted that all these authors represent the Bahshami school of Muʿtazili teaching. Even though the latter two scholars, al-Raṣṣāṣ and Ḥanash, belong to the Yemeni Zaydiyya, they are known for their Bahshami-Muʿtazili leanings as well.

Al-Nāṣir b. Aḥmad's *ijāza* also provides us with a list of what Ibn al-Wazīr studied in the fields of *fiqh* and hadith: *Majmūʿ* (*Collection*), the collection of writings on questions of substantive law by the eponym of the Zaydiyya, the imam Zayd b. ʿAlī (d. 122/740); the extensive *fiqh* work *Amālī* (*Expectations*) by Aḥmad b. ʿĪsā b. al-Imām Zayd b. ʿAlī (d. 247/861–862); Imam Aḥmad b. Sulaymān b. Muḥammad b. al-Muṭahhar's (d. 566/1170) collection of three thousand traditions concerning legal issues, *Uṣūl al-ahkām fī l-ḥalāl wa-l-ḥarām* (*The Principles of Rulings on the Allowed and the Prohibited*);[68] Imam al-Mahdī Muḥammad b. al-Muṭahhar b. Yaḥyā's (d. 728/1380–1381) treatise on abrogation, *ʿUqūd al-ʿuqyān fī l-nāsikh wa-l-mansūkh min al-Qurʾān* (*Necklaces of Pure Gold:*

63 Muḥammad b. ʿAbdallāh, *Tarjama* f. 141a. Zayd al-Wazīr confirms this estimation in a footnote in *Taʾrīkh Banī l-Wazīr*; cf. Aḥmad b. al-Wazīr, *Taʾrīkh Banī l-Wazīr* 39.

64 Al-Shahārī, *Ṭabaqāt al-Zaydiyya* ii, 1167; Ibn Abī l-Rijāl, *Maṭlaʿ al-budūr* iv, 442.

65 Al-Shahārī, *Ṭabaqāt al-Zaydiyya* ii, 1167; cf. Ibn al-Wazīr, *al-ʿAwāṣim* ii, 195.

66 Abū Muḥammad b. al-Ḥasan b. Aḥmad b. Mattawayh was a principle student of ʿAbd al-Jabbār. The exact date of birth or death is not known. Schmidtke suggests the end of the 5th/11th century; cf. Schmidtke (ed., intr.), *An Anonymous Commentary*. Schwarz suggests 414–415/1024 as the year of death; cf. Schwarz, Maimonides' Mutakallimun? 159. See also Ibn al-Murtaḍā, *Ṭabaqāt al-Muʿtazila* 119; Madelung, Ibn Mattawayh.

67 Al-Shahārī mentions two separate works on the *Khulāṣa*, as does al-Ḥibshī; cf. al-Shahārī, *Ṭabaqāt al-Zaydiyya* ii, 1098–1103; al-Ḥibshī, *Maṣādir* 126. Ḥanash's *Ghiyāṣa* was published at an unknown date by the Muʿassasat Imām Zayd.

68 Cf. al-Ḥibshī, *Maṣādir* 617. On Imam Aḥmad b. Sulaymān, see Ansari and Schmidtke, Literary-religious tradition 168, 202, 204; Ansari and Schmidtke, Muʿtazilī and Zaydī Reception 95, footnote 17.

The Abrogation and the Abrogated in the Quran),[69] and his *al-Sirāj al-wahhāj fī ḥaṣr masāʾil al-Minhāj* (*The Blazing Lamp: A Compilation of the Questions in The Path*), which may be a commentary on his *al-Minhāj al-jalī fī sharḥ majmūʿ Imām Zayd b. ʿAlī* (*The Clear Path: A Commentary on Imam Zayd b. ʿAlī's Collection*), which, in turn, is a commentary on the above-mentioned *fiqh* collection of the eponym of the Zaydiyya.[70] Furthermore, Ibn al-Wazīr got a license for a certain *Sharḥ Nukat al-ʿibādāt wa-jumal al-ziyādāt* (*A Commentary on the Issues of Worhip and the Generals of Additional Subjects*), a commentary on a widely used *fiqh* treatise of Qadi Jaʿfar b. Aḥmad b. ʿAbd al-Salām (d. 573/1177–1178) by, apparently, an anonymous writer.[71]

Besides being a scholar of theology and *fiqh*, al-Nāṣir b. Aḥmad was known as a mystic who lived as a hermit and devoted all of his time to teaching. Many sources mention only Ibn al-Wazīr, of his many students, by name. This indicates that Ibn al-Wazīr was al-Nāṣir b. Aḥmad's most important student and that al-Nāṣir b. Aḥmad had at least some lasting influence on him.[72]

The titles in this *ijāza* and those listed previously for Ibn Abī l-Khayr show two things: Firstly, up to this point Ibn al-Wazīr's education focussed on Zaydi writings that were widely studied among the students of Zaydi *kalām*, *uṣūl al-fiqh* and *fiqh*. Though the study of prophetic reports had not formed a major part of his education, it had not been altogether absent either. Yet this is only the case for Zaydi compilations. There is no indication that he had been intro-

---

69 Cf. al-Ḥibshī, *Maṣādir* 643.

70 Zabāra mentions the commentary in *Aʾimmat al-Yaman* 211. See also al-Ḥibshī, *Maṣādir* 642.

71 Al-Ḥibshī mentions a commentary of Qadi Jaʿfar's work by an anonymous commentator, of which several copies are known to exist; cf. al-Ḥibshī, *Maṣādir*, 197. The existence of several copies from the 8th/14th and early 9th/15th centuries indicates that it was a widely used text at the time of Ibn al-Wazīr. This of course is only the case if the writing mentioned by al-Ḥibshī is the one al-Nāṣir b. Aḥmad lists in his *ijāza* to Ibn al-Wazīr. Al-Nāṣir b. Aḥmad does not give the name of the commentator either. Qadi Jaʿfar's *Nukat wa-l-jumal*, as al-Nāṣir b. Aḥmad calls it, is a treatise on the rulings of Zayd b. ʿAlī's legal school; cf. Muḥammad b. ʿAbdallāh, *Tarjama* f. 140b. Qadi Jaʿfar was appointed by the above-mentioned Imam al-Mutawakkil ʿalā llāh Aḥmad b. Sulaymān and lived during the time of ʿAbdallāh b. Ḥamza. He was very active in combating the Mutarrafiyya and in spreading the teachings of the Bahshami variety of the Muʿtazila. His most prominent student was al-Ḥasan al-Raṣṣāṣ; cf. Thiele, Propagating Muʿtazilism 541; al-Ḥibshī, *Maṣādir* 110. On Qadi Jaʿfar, see Ibn Abī l-Rijāl, *Maṭlaʿ al-budūr* i, 617–624; al-Shahārī, *Ṭabaqāt al-Zaydiyya* i, 273–278; Ibn Fanad, *Maʾāthir al-abrār* ii, 769–774; al-Wajīh, *Aʿlām* 278–282; Madelung, Djafar b. Abī Yaḥyā; al-Akwaʿ, *Hijar al-ʿilm* 955–959.

72 Al-Nāṣir b. Aḥmad was taught by the above-mentioned Zaydi Sufis Ibn Abī l-Khayr and Ibrāhīm al-Kaynaʿī. Cf. reference on al-Nāṣir above (footnote 62) and 30n78 below.

duced to the Sunni hadith collections. However, it is likely that he was familiar with them to a certain extent, since scholars such as Imam al-Nāṣir Ṣalāḥ al-Dīn, of whom Ibn al-Wazīr was a supporter, were known for propagating the Sunni hadith compilations. Their absence from Ibn al-Wazīr's *ijāzas* until this point indicates that they had not become an essential part of Zaydi education and were therefore not considered worth mentioning.

What is strikingly absent from records of the teaching Ibn al-Wazīr had received up to this point are writings from the school of thought competing with the Bahshami teaching, namely the school of Abū l-Ḥusayn al-Baṣrī. As in the case of the Sunni hadith compilation, this does not mean that he did not receive such teaching, but rather that it was not considered important enough to be quoted in any of the lists found in the *ṭabaqāt* or *tarājim*—even though by this time, not only had Abū al-Ḥusayn's writings become part of the Zaydi curriculum in the field of *uṣūl al-fiqh*[73] but, beyond *uṣūl al-fiqh*, Abū l-Ḥusayn's theological views had already penetrated Zaydi Yemen in the early 7th/13th century. As the research of Ansari, Madelung and Schmidtke has shown, manifestations of Abū l-Ḥusayn's Muʿtazili thought were part of the teaching tradition in the Yemeni Zaydiyya of the early 7th/13th century, introduced mainly through the writings of Rukn al-Dīn Maḥmūd b. al-Malāḥimī al-Khwārazmī (d. 536/1141). The conflict between the two Muʿtazili schools remained active in the 8th/14th century and beyond.[74] However, none of this is documented in the accounts of Ibn al-Wazīr's education, indicating that the Bahshamiyya found wider acceptance than Abū l-Ḥusayn's school in Ibn al-Wazīr's lifetime.

The sources state that Ibn al-Wažir excelled in the scholarship of the abovementioned disciplines. Already during his years as a student he functioned as a reference for his peers in the *uṣūlān*. This is reported about Muḥammad b. Dawūd al-Nahmī (n.d.), who met Ibn al-Wazīr while both were pupils of Ibn Abī l-Khayr.[75] Muḥammad b. ʿAbdallāh states that al-Nahmī accompanied Ibn al-Wazīr constantly, referred to him and gave credit to his fellow student's views in *kalām*, highlighting that Ibn al-Wazīr persuasively undermined a number

73 The earliest extant copy of Abū l-Ḥusayn al-Baṣrī's *Kitāb al-Muʿtamad fī uṣūl al-fiqh* in Yemen dates from the year 550/1155–1156; cf. Ansari and Schmidtke, Muʿtazilī and Zaydī Reception 100.

74 For the influence of Abū l-Husayn and Ibn al-Malāḥimī on the Yemeni Zaydiyya, see for example Ansari and Schmidtke, Muʿtazilī and Zaydī Reception 100; Madelung and Schmidtke (eds., intr.), *Abū l-Ḥusayn al-Baṣrī's Taṣaffuḥ al-adilla*; Ansari, Maḥmūd al-Malāḥimī al-Muʿtazilī 48–58; Ibn al-Malāḥimī, *Kitāb al-Muʿtamad*; Ibn al-Malāḥimī, *Kitāb al-Fāʾiq*; Ibn al-Malāḥimī, *Tuḥfat al-mutakallimīn*; Ansari and Thiele, A Unique Manuscript 73–74.

75 Muḥammad b. ʿAbdallāh, *Tarjama* f. 134a; al-Shahārī, *Ṭabaqāt al-Zaydiyya* ii, 970.

of views held by the speculative theologians. Muḥammad b. ʿAbdallāh records that Ibn al-Wazīr challenged a view here attributed to the eponym of the Bahshamiyya, Abū Hāshim al-Jubbāʾī (d. 321/933),[76] according to which anyone claiming to know God save by their own way of logical argument is an unbeliever.[77] This indicates that Ibn al-Wazīr vocalized his criticism, already at an early stage of his career, of at least some of Bahshami doctrines that were prevalent among the Zaydis of his day. This very view is evidence of the initial point of much of Ibn al-Wazīr's criticism towards speculative theologians in general, and the Bahshami Muʿtazila in particular.

Furthermore, it must be noted that Ibn al-Wazīr's early years featured a considerable influence of Sufi scholars, or those leaning towards mysticism. Besides his two above-mentioned teachers Ibn Abī l-Khayr and al-Nāṣir b. Aḥmad, Imam al-Nāṣir Ṣalāḥ al-Dīn and Qadi al-Diwārī are known for having encouraged Sufism in Zaydi lands.[78] This confirms my assumption that Ibn al-Wazīr's tendency towards mysticism and life in seclusion was not merely a later reaction to scholarly conflict as Ḥajar suggests. Rather, his studies in his early and later youth in Sanaa already featured a strong influence of a Zaydi version of Sufism.

1.3.2 Sunni Hadith Studies

Many acknowledged that Ibn al-Wazīr reached a stage of learning in general and *ijtihād* in particular that equalled the eponyms of Sunni schools of law.[79] According to Ibn Abī l-Rijāl, a major factor in Ibn al-Wazīr's outstanding rank was his profound erudition in the texts of revelation, and particularly in the prophetic traditions. Ibn Abī l-Rijāl quotes an outstanding scholar of the time, Aḥmad b. Muḥammad al-Azraqī (d. around 850/1446), to this effect:

> No one in our time has reached the [level of] *ijtihād* that the Sayyid ʿIzz al-Dīn Muḥammad b. Ibrāhīm [Ibn al-Wazīr] has attained. We have done well in everything, but what he has attained we cannot, because of his

76 Abū Hāshim ʿAbd al-Salām was the son of Abū ʿAlī al-Jubbāʾī. Though none of his works survived and little is known about his life, his views are transmitted by his students; cf. Gardet, al-Jubbāʾī.

77 Muḥammad b. ʿAbdallāh, *Tarjama* f. 134a.

78 Madelung states that Imam al-Nāṣir b. Ṣalāḥ al-Dīn was a close associate of Ibrāhīm al-Kaynaʿī. According to al-Kaynaʿī, no one was better informed about the practices and disciplines of the ascetics than the imam. Furthermore, al-Kaynaʿī was apparently invited to Ṣāʿda by Qadi al-Diwārī in order to spread his blessings and his teachings; cf. Madelung, Zaydī Attitudes 133.

79 Ibn Abī l-Rijāl, *Maṭlaʿ al-budūr* iv, 143–145.

> knowledge of the traditions, the transmitters and his deep penetration into the texts of revelation.[80]

It was in the early years of the 9th/15th century that Ibn al-Wazīr's education focused mainly on the study of prophetic traditions and the Sunni hadith collections. Ibn al-Wazīr himself states that after having studied the *uṣūlān*, a major principle of these very sciences was decisive in intensifying his occupation with hadith. This principle said that those who emulate others in doctrinal questions are unbelievers (*man qallada fī l-iʿtiqād kafara*).[81] By his own account, this principle was not only his reason for an in depth study of those non-Zaydi positions which the Zaydiyya deemed misguided, but also convinced him that a wide knowledge of the prophetic traditions was a collective duty (*farḍ kifāya*) in order to base one's own opinions on the sources rather than on the opinions of others.[82]

Curiously, it may have been ʿAlī b. Muḥammad b. Abī l-Qāsim (d. 837/1433–1434),[83] Ibn al-Wazīr's most famous opponent, who enhanced Ibn al-Wazīr's desire to study the Sunni hadith collections. Ibn Abī l-Qāsim lived in Sanaa, where he taught, wrote and issued legal opinions.[84] The sources state that Ibn al-Wazīr received another *ijāza* for Ibn Ḥājib's *Muntahā* among other works in theology and exegesis from Ibn Abī l-Qāsim.[85] If it is accurate that Ibn Abī l-Qāsim taught his students from the six Sunni hadith collections, as al-Ḥibshī indicates, we can assume that some of Ibn al-Wazīr's views on hadith developed under Ibn Abī l-Qāsim's before the year 808/1406, when their difference of opinion culminated in Ibn al-Wazīr's legendary scholarly output, *al-ʿAwāṣim*.[86] However, a great part of *al-ʿAwāsim* is dedicated to refuting Ibn Abī l-Qāsim's claim of the unreliability of the Sunni hadith collections. Furthermore, Ibn Abī l-Qāsim's staunch Zaydism is attested in the biographical sources. In Ibn Abī l-Rijāl's words, Ibn Abī l-Qāsim "prohibited al-Sayyid Muḥammad [Ibn al-Wazīr]

---

80 Ibid., iv, 145. For al-Azraqī, see ibid., i, 410.

81 Ibn al-Wazīr, *al-ʿAwāṣim* i, 202.

82 Ibn al-Wazīr, *al-Rawḍ al-bāsim* 6.

83 Ibn Abī l-Rijāl, *Maṭlaʿ al-budūr* iii, 310–318.

84 Ibn Abī l-Qāsim's most famous work is his exegetical *Tajrīd al-Kashshāf al-muzīd fīhi min al-nuqaṭ al-liṭāf* (*Disentangling The Revealer Extended by a Few Subtle Points*). He also authored books in Arabic grammar, such as for example a commentary on Ibn al-Ḥājib's *Kāfiyya* (*The Sufficient*); cf. al-Ḥibshī, *Maṣādir* 27; Ibn Abī l-Rijāl, *Maṭlaʿ al-budūr* iii, 311; al-Wajīh, *Aʿlām* 717; al-Shahārī, *Ṭabaqāt al-Zaydiyya* ii, 780.

85 Ibn Abī l-Rijāl, *Maṭlaʿ al-budūr* iii, 311; al-Shawkānī, *al-Badr al-ṭāliʿ* i, 485.

86 Al-Ḥibshī, *Maṣādir* 27.

from engaging any other [than the books of the Āl Muḥammad]."[87] It is therefore more likely that Ibn al-Wazīr's interest developed in opposition to Ibn Abī l-Qāsim's vehement partisanship for the sources and teachings of the Zaydiyya, rather than through Ibn Abī l-Qāsim's encouragement.

Whether or not Ibn al-Wazīr's zeal for prophetic traditions intensified through the teaching of Ibn Abī l-Qāsim, it evidently caused his brother al-Hādī to send him to the Hanafi jurist Nafīs al-Dīn al-ʿAlawī (d. 825/1422)[88] in Taʿizz. In a letter of recommendation, al-Hādī indicates that Ibn al-Wazīr's passion for and emphasis on the study of the prophetic tradition had evoked the disapproval of fellow Zaydi scholars.[89]

At this stage, Ibn al-Wazīr had already written at least *al-Burhān al-qāṭiʿ fī ithbāt al-ṣāniʿ* (*The Certain Proof: Establishing* [*the Existence of*] *the Creator*), arguing for the knowledge of God on the basis of the signs in the revelational sources.[90] According to al-Ḥarbī, by this time Ibn al-Wazīr had also already authored his *al-Ḥusām al-mashhūr* (*The Unsheathed Sword*) in defense of the imamate of al-Manṣūr. In the latter work, Ibn al-Wazīr challenges prevalent interpretations of the two major requirements of a Zaydi imam, partially based on his interpretation of knowledge, as I will show below. However, al-Ḥarbī's date (805/1402–1403) is rendered unlikely by data given in the content itself. On the first folio of the manuscript, Ibn al-Wazīr mentions a letter that had been send to Imam al-Manṣūr ʿAlī in the year 826/1423.[91] Since the place where the letter's author should have been named is blank in all copies I viewed, the occasion of the treatise cannot be verified unambiguously. In any case, the dating of the treatise before or after Ibn al-Wazīr's studies with the Hanafi jurist does not disprove the apparent assumption that, by this time, Ibn al-Wazīr's criticism of prevalent Muʿtazili notions in the Yemeni Zaydiyya was already well established in the field of *kalām*. This can be concluded from *al-Burhān*

87 Ibn Abī l-Rijāl, *Maṭlaʿ al-budūr* iii, 311. Cf. ibid., iii, 310; al-Shahārī, *Ṭabaqāt al-Zaydiyya* ii, 779, 780.

88 Nafīs al-Dīn authored several works in the *arbaʿīn* genre. Furthermore, he authored a work on Sufism, called *Irshād al-sālikīn fī-l-tasawwuf* (*Guidance for the Followers of the Sufi Path*). Nafīs al-Dīn studied *hadīth* and *fiqh* in Mecca, and later studied and taught in the famous Ṣulayḥī school in Zabīd before moving to Taʿizz permanently; cf. al-Sakhāwī, *al-Ḍawʾ al-lāmiʿ* iii, 259; al-Shawkānī, *al-Badr al-ṭāliʿ* i, 265; al-Ḥibshī, *Maṣādir* 56, 330.

89 Al-Akwaʿ (intr.), *al-ʿAwāṣim* i, 25–26.

90 Ibn al-Wazīr himself mentions the 4th or 5th of Rajab 801 (13th or 14th of March 1399) as the time of completion; cf. Ibn al-Wazīr, *al-Burhān al-qāṭiʿ* MS 1) f. 114b.

91 Cf. Ibn al-Wazīr, *al-Ḥusām al-mashhūr* MS 1) f. 182b; MS 2) f. 103a. Another indication that *al-Ḥusām al-mashhūr* was authored later are cross-references to *al-ʿAwāṣim* on fs. 105b and 107a.

al-qāṭiʿ taken together with the above-mentioned comment of Ibn al-Wazīr's fellow student, Muḥammad al-Nahmī, who supported Ibn al-Wazīr in his criticism of prevailing theological notions and al-Hādī's letter to the Taʿizzī jurist and traditionist Nafīs al-Dīn al-ʿAlawī. It was thus not rooted in his subsequent intensified immersion in the study of hadith of other schools.

The educational focus is evident in an *ijāza* that Ibn al-Wazīr received from his Taʿizzī teacher. It is dated Tuesday, 8th Dhū l-Qaʿda 806 (May 18, 1404) in the house of Nafīs al-Dīn in Taʿizz. Besides an extensive appraisal of Ibn al-Wazīr, Nafīs al-Dīn mentions Ibn al-Wazīr's explicit wish to study the prophetic traditions. Corresponding to Ibn al-Wazīr's wish and Nafīs al-Dīn's expertise, special focus was laid on the major Sunni hadith collections as well as on comparative works like the *Jamʿ bayn al-Ṣaḥīḥayn* (*Comparison Between the Ṣaḥīḥayn*) by a student of the Ẓāhirī Ibn Ḥazm al-Andalusī (d. 456/1064), namely Muḥammad b. Abī Naṣr Futūḥ al-Ḥumaydī al-Andalusī (d. 488/1095).[92] Next in line were works on narrator biographies (*ʿilm al-rijāl*) including Yūsuf b. ʿAbd al-Raḥmān al-Mizzī's (d. 742/1342) *Tahdhīb al-kamāl fī asmāʾ al-rijāl* (*The Refinement of the Complete: On the Names of Narrators*) and its abridgment *Tadhhīb tahdhīb al-kamāl* (*Gilding The Refinement of the Complete*) by Muḥammad b. Aḥmad b. ʿUthmān al-Dhahabī (d. 748/1348), as well as historiographical works of ʿAlī b. Muḥammad b. al-Athīr (d. 630/1233).[93] Furthermore, Nafīs al-Dīn reports that he gave another, less extensive *ijāza* to Ibn al-Wazīr and his brother al-Hādī on Jumādā l-ākhira 19th 806/January 3, 1404.[94] Nafīs al-Dīn informs us that, besides his brother al-Hādī, Ibn al-Wazīr had a certain Hanbali Ṣāliḥ b. Qāsim b. Sulaymān al-Maʿmarī as a travelling and studying companion.

1.3.3 Studies in Mecca

Ibn al-Wazīr intensified his Sunni hadith studies on his three subsequent journeys to Mecca. Apparently, the first time was shortly after his sojourn in Taʿizz in 807/1404.[95] In Mecca, Ibn al-Wazīr studied with a number of famous Meccan scholars, among them the Maliki judge and historian Muḥammad b. Aḥmad

92 Cf. Muḥammad b. ʿAbdallāh al-Wazīr, *Tarjama* f. 142b. On al-Ḥumaydī, see Miranda, al-Ḥumaydī; Goldziher, *Die Zahiriten* 172. According to Fierro, Abū Naṣr Futtūḥ al-Ḥumaydī played a major role in the invention of the genre; cf. Fierro, Local and Global Ḥadīth Literature 68, 73.

93 Cf. Muḥammad b. ʿAbdallāh, *Tarjama* fs. 141a–b; al-Shahārī, *Ṭabaqāt al-Zaydiyya* ii, 899–900.

94 Al-Shahārī, *Ṭabaqāt al-Zaydiyya* iii, 900.

95 Muḥammad b. ʿAbdallāh, *Tarjama* f. 141a; Aḥmad b. al-Wazīr, *Taʾrīkh Banī l-Wazīr* 40, footnote 235; al-Shahārī, *Ṭabaqāt al-Zaydiyya* ii, 899; al-Akwaʿ (intr.), *al-ʿAwāṣim* i, 31.

al-Fāsī (d. 832/1429)[96] and the Shafiʿi chief judge Muḥammad b. ʿAbdallāh b. Ẓahīra (d. 817/1414).[97] According to the author of his biography, Ibn al-Wazīr apparently received teaching licenses in the disciplines of *fiqh, hadīth, tafsīr, lugha, al-maʿāni wa-l-bayān, uṣūl al-fiqh* and *kalām* in Muḥarram 807/July 1404.[98] A famous anecdote illustrates how firm Ibn al-Wazīr's views on the *madhhab* must have been already at that time. When the famous judge Ibn Ẓahīra asked Ibn al-Wazīr whether he would consider becoming a follower of the Shafiʿi *madhhab*, Ibn al-Wazīr is said to have replied indignantly that if emulation (*taqlīd*) was permitted to him he would emulate his forefathers Imam al-Hādī ilā l-ḥaqq (d. 298/911) and Imam al-Qāsim b. Ibrāhīm (d. 264/860).[99] This episode shows that Ibn al-Wazīr's immersion in the disciplines of Sunni learning in general and hadith in particular was not motivated by a desire to challenge the Zaydiyya in its entirety, nor to leave the school of his forefathers altogether in order to become a Sunni.

The list of Ibn al-Wazīr's non-Zaydi teachers in Mecca encompass three Shafiʿi, two Maliki and one Hanafi jurist, as well as one jurist of uncertain affiliation, all of whom were mainly occupied with the transmission of prophetic traditions.[100] It is not entirely clear with whom Ibn al-Wazīr extended his studies in non-Zaydi theology. Most sources, like Muḥammad b. ʿAbdallāh al-Wazīr and those that use him as a major source, mention the extension of his theo-

96 Cf. al-Sakhāwī, *al-Ḍawʾ al-lāmiʿ* vii, 18–20; al-Ziriklī, *al-Aʿlām* v, 331; al-Shawkānī, *al-Badr al-ṭāliʿ* ii, 114.

97 Cf. al-Fāsī, *al-ʿIqd al-thamīn* ii, 53–59; al-Sakhāwī, *al-Ḍawʾ al-lāmiʿ* viii, 92–96; al-Shawkānī, *al-Badr al-ṭāliʿ* ii, 196.

98 Muḥammad b. ʿAbdallāh, *Tarjama* f. 141a.

99 According to Aḥmad b. al-Wazīr, Ibn Ẓahīra was not the only one to pose such a question and receive such an answer; cf. Aḥmad b. al-Wazīr, *Taʾrīkh Banī l-Wazīr* 31. Similarly, Ibn Abī l-Rijāl, *Maṭlaʿ al-budūr* iv, 142; al-Shahārī, *al-Ṭabaqāt al-Zaydiyya* ii, 901; al-Shawkānī, *al-Badr al-ṭāliʿ* ii, 90.

100 Besides Ibn Ẓahīra, Muḥammad b. Aḥmad b. al-Raḍī Ibrāhīm al-Ṭabarī (d. 809/1406) and ʿAlī b. Aḥmad b. Muḥammad b. Salāma al-Sulamī al-Makkī (d. 828/1425) were both Shafiʿī. On al-Ṭabarī, see al-Fāsī, *al-ʿIqd al-thamīn* i, 282–285; al-Sakhāwī, *al-Ḍawʾ al-lāmiʿ* vi, 287–288. On al-Sulamī al-Makkī, see al-Fāsī, *al-ʿIqd al-thamīn* vi, 139–142; al-Sakhāwī, *al-Ḍawʾ al-lāmiʿ* v, 183. Besides al-Fāsī, there was the Maliki ʿAlī b. Masʿūd b. ʿAlī b. Aḥmad al-Ansārī al-Khazūmī (d. 813/1410); cf. al-Fāsī, *al-ʿIqd al-thamīn* vi, 267–268; al-Sakhāwī, *al-Ḍawʾ al-lāmiʿ* vi, 38–39. Jār Allāh b. Ṣāliḥ b. Aḥmad b. Abī Maʿālī al-Shaybānī (d. 815/1413) was a Hanafi jurist; cf. al-Fāsī, *al-ʿIqd al-thamīn* iii, 407; al-Sakhāwī, *al-Ḍawʾ al-lāmiʿ* iii, 52. Muḥammad b. Ḥusayn b. Muḥammad b. al-Quṭb al-Qasṭalānī (d. 811/1408) was a Meccan traditionist of unknown affiliation; cf. al-Fāsī, *al-ʿIqd al-thamīn* ii, 8–9. For lists of the teaching licenses Ibn al-Wazīr received from Meccan teachers, see for example Muḥammad b. ʿAbdallāh, *Tarjama* f. 141a; Abī l-Qāsim, *Ṭabaqāt al-Zaydiyya* ii, 899; al-Shawkāni, *al-Badr al-ṭāliʿ* ii, 82.

logical studies in general.[101] The little that is intelligible from a teaching license issued by Ibn Ẓahīra indicates that he was at least one source for the study of non-Zaydi and non-Muʿtazili doctrine. And indeed, Ibn Ẓahīra is the only one of Ibn al-Wazīr's Meccan teachers who is known for his scholarship in theology alongside other disciplines.[102] Be that as it may, Ibn al-Wazīr would have been deeply familiar with the ideas and sources of many different schools of thought and law by this time.

1.3.4 Productive Conflict

Coming back from his first pilgrimage around the beginning of 808/1405, Ibn al-Wazīr wrote a long poem in which he praised the Quran, prophetic Sunna and the Prophet Muḥammad. In the poem, Ibn al-Wazīr describes his spiritual and scientific quest for certainty, which was only satisfied after having returned to the sources of revelation. This poem apparently provoked Ibn al-Wazīr's former teacher Ibn Abī l-Qāsim to write the famous, now lost letter which in turn caused Ibn al-Wazīr to write his *magnum opus al-ʿAwāṣim wa-l-qawāṣim* late in 808/1406.[103]

The content of the controversy between Ibn al-Wazīr and his teacher Ibn Abī l-Qāsim is known in great detail. This dispute clearly went to the core of Ibn al-Wazīr's beliefs. Ibn Abī l-Qāsim's family background and his progeny were staunchly Zaydi-Hādawī. He, his brothers and his sons were known as fervent defenders of the Zaydi branch of Muʿtazili theology as well as the Prophet's posterity.[104] The major source for details of the controversy is Ibn al-Wazīr's *magnum opus al-ʿAwāṣim* as well as its abridgment, *al-Rawḍ al-bāsim*. But beyond Ibn al-Wazīr's own account and despite the absence of Ibn Abī l-Qāsim's letters, most sources leave little doubt that Ibn Abī l-Qāsim accused Ibn al-Wazīr of having completely left not only the path of al-Hādī ilā l-ḥaqq, the eponym of the Yemeni Zaydiyya, but also the path of the *ahl al-bayt*. A major cause for this accusation was Ibn al-Wazīr's claim to *ijtihād*, which will be investigated in detail in subsequent chapters.[105] Although the facts indicate that the chal-

101 Muḥammad b. ʿAbdallāh, *Tarjama* f. 141a.

102 Ibn Ẓahīra was a judge, *faqīh*, *mujtahid* and grammarian in addition to his occupation in the learning and teaching of sciences of transmission. See also footnotes 99 and 100 above.

103 Ibn al-Wazīr, *al-Rawḍ al-bāsim* 14, 16; cf. al-Akwaʿ (intr.), *al-ʿAwāṣim* i, 37. The first 14 lines of the poem are preserved in Ibn al-Wazīr's biography; cf. Muhammad b. ʿAbdallāh's biography, *Tarjama* fs. 139b–140a.

104 Ibn Abī l-Rijāl, *Maṭlaʿ al-budūr* iii, 310; al-Shahārī, *Ṭabaqāt al-Zaydiyya* ii, 778–780; al-Shawkānī, *al-Badr al-ṭāliʿ* i, 485; al-Ḥibshī, *Maṣādir* 27.

105 Aḥmad b. al-Wazīr, *Taʾrīkh Banī l-Wazīr* 33; Ibn Abī l-Rijāl, *Maṭlaʿ al-budūr* iv, 148.

lenge directly initiating the controversy came from Ibn Abī l-Qāsim, it is likely that Ibn al-Wazīr, for his part, was challenged by Ibn Abī l-Qāsim's vehement partisanship for the Zaydiyya. Commands like the one mentioned by Ibn Abī l-Rijāl, namely that Ibn al-Wazīr may not use any books other than those of the *ahl al-bayt*, must have been deeply disturbing for one who had become familiar with the intellectual, theological and legal diversity of Islam, and who took the prohibition against emulation in matters of doctrine as well as the correctness of all *mujtahids* seriously.[106]

Although the controversial poem is generally summarized as a love poem for the Prophet Muḥammad, it was probably Ibn al-Wazīr's attitude towards the common practice of *taqlīd* that offended Ibn Abī l-Qāsim. A few lines will suffice to anticipate the conflict between Ibn al-Wazīr and all those who restricted the Zaydiyya to the persons, doctrine and rulings of the *ahl al-bayt*:

> Look to the fairness of the *ahl al-bayt*,
> they were not extreme or fanatic in any resolution.
> They disagreed with their fathers and sought to discover,
> what is correct, seeking the most rightly guided.
> I took them as models. Then every idiot
> from the troop of riffraff denied me my model (*qudwa*).
> (…)
> All are brothers, and religion is one,
> in the legal rulings, every *mujtahid* is correct, as is him who is guided
> in these rulings; and in the *uṣūl* [*al-dīn*], my doctrine is that
> upon which no Muslim (*muwaḥḥid*) disagrees.[107]

Although Ibn al-Wazīr expresses his criticism of *taqlīd* rather cautiously in this poem, he insists on his right to investigate in matters of law independently of legal affiliation, based on the principle of permissible legal disagreement already practiced by the early authorities. Furthermore, the poem bespeaks Ibn al-Wazīr's agenda in the harmonization of contending theological schools, namely restricting himself to agreed upon general Islamic tenets. This implies two things: Firstly, the bulk of criticism that Ibn al-Wazīr received was aimed at his challenge to the prevalent notion of legal authority at a doctrinal level. He insisted on practicing his own *ijtihād* and claimed to apply the doctrine of the *ahl al-bayt* in so doing. This apparently infuriated his contemporaries

106 Cf. Ibn al-Wazīr, *al-ʿAwāṣim* i, 201–202; Ibn Abī l-Rijāl, *Maṭlaʿ al-budūr* iii, 311.
107 Al-Akwaʿ (intr.), *al-ʿAwāṣim* i, 34–35.

more than his early criticism of speculative theology had done. And secondly, Ibn al-Wazīr's method of harmonization developed in the midst of conflict on doctrinal grounds, and was probably the cause of, as well as the reaction to, criticism of his contemporaries.

Despite al-Ḥādī's defense of his brother's views, which supposedly had been dreadfully misunderstood, Ibn Abī l-Qāsim and others with him saw the principles of the Zaydiyya threatened. Letters were exchanged, meetings held and books were written: *al-ʿAwāṣim* in 808/1406 and its abridgment al-*Rawḍ al-bāsim* in 817/1414, indicating that the conflict lasted for a number of years. Eventually Ibn al-Wazīr and Ibn Abī l-Qāsim made peace with each other, years later. Convincing evidence for this reconciliation, attested by a number of sources, is seen in Ibn Abī l-Qāsim's sending his son Ṣalāḥ (d. 849/1445)[108] to study under Ibn al-Wazīr. However, most sources do not mention when the rapprochement took place. A note written by Muḥammad b. ʿAbdallāh b. al-Wazīr and recorded in a collection of Ibn al-Wazīr's writings mentions "eight hundred thirty and something" (i.e. in the late 1420s or early 1430s) as the year of reconciliation.[109]

Yet again, the periods where peace reigned and those where conflict prevailed do not seem to have been so easily distinguishable. We can gather this from a poem in which Ibn al-Wazīr scolded his teacher for the fickleness of attitude towards himself.

> You knew my value, then you denied it.
> By God! What has led you away from your first state?[110]
> Every day you have an opinion of me,
> you went too far in your words about the evil of what seems.
> Yesterday praise, and today the evil of insult,
> I wish I knew how I will appear tomorrow.[111]

The poem clearly speaks of a continuous vacillation in their relationship. Beyond Ibn Abī l-Qāsim's charge, most sources report the extensive intellectual

108 Yaḥyā b. al-Ḥusayn, *Ghāyat al-amānī* 573–582; al-Sakhāwī, *al-Ḍawʾ al-lāmiʿ* iii, 323; al-Shawkānī, *al-Badr al-ṭāliʿ* suppl., 107; Zabāra, *Aʾimmat al-Yaman* i, 321–322; al-Ziriklī, *al-Aʿlām* iii, 207; Kaḥḥāla, *Muʿjam al-muʾallifīn* v, 21–22; al-Ḥibshī, *Maṣādir* 675; al-Wajīh, *Aʿlām* 505; al-Ḥusaynī, *Muʾallafāt al-Zaydiyya* iii, 96.

109 *Majmūʿ Muḥammad b. Ibrāhīm*, f. 511. Again, Ibn al-Wazīr's biography written by the same author does not mention the date.

110 The phrase used here is "*fa-mā ʿadā bi-llāh mimmā badā*," referring to a famous saying by ʿAlī b. Abī Ṭālib to ʿAbdallāh b. Abbās, asking him what made him turn away from the obedience he had showed at first.

111 Aḥmad b. ʿAbd al-Allāh, *Taʾrīkh Banī l-Wazīr* 34; Ibn Abī l-Rijāl, *Maṭlaʿ al-budūr* iv, 149–150.

attacks that Ibn al-Wazīr had to face.[112] A number of poems attest to al-Hādī b. Ibrāhīm's attempts to calm down his brother as well as his critics, and to Ibn al-Wazīr's docile replies to his beloved advocate. However, al-Hādī's attempts to clear up some of what he considered misunderstandings seem not to have been entirely convincing.[113]

The bibliographical sources provide little data on Ibn al-Wazīr from this time onwards. As most of his writings do not mention a date, these do not easily provide the reader with a guideline to the events and developments of Ibn al-Wazīr's life. We know that he wrote a book on the science of hadith, called *Tanqīh al-anẓār fī ʿulūm al-athār* (*Rectifying the Perceptions in the Science of Traditions*) in 813/1411, and the abridgment of *Awāṣim*, his *al-Rawḍ al-bāsim fī l-dhabb an sunnat Abī l-Qāsim* (*The Smiling Meadows: A Rebuffal of the Sunna of Abū l-Qāsim*) in 817/1414. Ibn al-Wazīr travelled to Mecca at least once after the controversies had ensued. But there is no indication that he wanted to leave his Zaydi environment permanently. Aḥmad b. al-Wazīr mentions that Ibn al-Wazīr set out on pilgrimage three times.[114] Little is known of the two later pilgrimages. One was never concluded because a conflict between the sharifs and the people of a village 400 km south of Mecca forced him to return. Al-Hādī wrote a poem to his brother Ibn al-Wazīr in 818/1416, in which he consoles him for not having been able to complete his pilgrimage. Zayd al-Wazīr, editor of *Ta'rīkh Banī l-Wazīr*, thinks it was his second Hajj,[115] while al-Arna'ūt, editor of *al-Awāṣim*, considers it number three.[116] Nothing else is known about this last pilgrimage, other than that a number of miracles (*karāmāt*) occurred in Mecca and on the way there, just as they are reported to have occurred throughout Ibn al-Wazīr's life and especially during the times that he spent in solitude.[117]

1.3.5 Scholarship in Solitude

Most sources contain a section or a comment on Ibn al-Wazīr's life in solitude or seclusion (*ʿuzla*). Works such as Ibn al-Wazīr's *al-Amr bi-l-ʿuzla fī ākhir al-*

---

112 See for example the excerpts of other attacks and defenses in verse preserved in ibid., iv, 140–141.

113 Al-Hādī's poem summarizing his defense is called *Jawāb al-nāṭiq bi-l-ḥaqq al-yaqīn al-shāfī li-ṣudūr al-muttaqīn* (*The Answer of Him Who Says the Truth Healing the Hearts of the Pious*); cf. al-Ḥibshī, *Maṣādir* 132; ʿAlī b. Muḥammad al-ʿAmrān (ed.), *al-Rawḍ al-bāsim* 12, footnote 2. Ibn al-Wazīr's comments on the attacks on him are numerous. See for example Ibn al-Wazīr, *al-Rawḍ al-bāsim* 13.

114 Aḥmad b. al-Wazīr, *Ta'rīkh Banī l-Wazīr* 40.

115 The conflict took place in Ḥalī b. Yaʿqūb; cf. ibid.

116 Al-Arna'ūt (ed.), *al-ʿAwāṣim* i, 52.

117 Cf. Aḥmad b. al-Wazīr, *Ta'rīkh Banī l-Wazīr* 35–41.

zamān (*The Command of Solitude at the End of Times*) leave no doubt that Ibn al-Wazīr's regret at having been involved in doctrinal (and political) strife led him to turn away from public life.[118] Most sources mention that he spent periods of time in solitude in mosques in Sanaa and the surrounding region, as well as in mountains and wadis in the Ibb region. Yet none of them tell us when that would have been.[119] Ḥajar suggests that the last twenty years of Ibn al-Wazīr's life were dominated by his reclusiveness. Haykel likewise restricts Ibn al-Wazīr's retreat into solitude to the latter part of his life.[120] Although Ḥajar understandably gives Ibn al-Wazīr's remarks in *Tarjīḥ* as a main reason for his assumption, I suggest that these very same remarks indicate a less distinct division between the different phases of Ibn al-Wazīr's life.[121] It is true that Ibn al-Wazīr states that he spent a number of years (*sinīn ʿadīda*) in seclusion from people and their continuous strife, preferring to commit the rest of his life to preparing to face his Creator. And the dates given for most of Ibn al-Wazīr's visions and dreams in his *Dīwān* (*Collection of Poems*) indicate that he had most of them within the last decade of his life. Yet there is no convincing reason why "*sanīn adīda*" should necessarily mean 20 years, nor that he should have chosen the lifestyle of an ascetic or a mystic only at an advanced age. Indeed, a mystic attitude towards God and a tendency to withdraw from society is already apparent in poems Ibn al-Wazīr wrote and visions that he had during his youth. Two events are narrated for the time that he spent studying in Sanaa: First, the poem recorded in his *Dīwān* from the time when he "had just reached adulthood" and realized that he had no friend in the city: He went out to Nuqum which holds a Mosque he is said to have frequented during his times of solitude.[122] The second is a night vision that he had "in his youth," recorded by

118 See for example aspects four and eight in Ibn al-Wazīr's *al-Amr bi-l-ʿuzla* 307. For similar thoughts, see Ibn al-Wazīr, *Tarjīḥ* 61, 67.

119 Ibn al-Wazīr seems to have frequented the Wahb Mosque in Sanaa's south, the Nuqum Mosque between Sanaa and Nuqum, the al-Rawna Mosque 13 km northeast of Sanaa and the al-Akhdhar Mosque, now called Khaḍīr, close to al-Shaʿūb Gate in the east of Sanaa. A school on Jabal Saḥammur close to Yarīm in the Ibb governorate was apparently named al-Wazīr School in memory of Ibn al-Wazīr's sojourn there; cf. Aḥmad b. al-Wazīr, *Taʾrīkh Banī l-Wazīr* 35 (main text and footnote 227); Ibn Abī l-Rijāl, *Maṭlaʿ al-budūr* iv, 150; al-Shawkānī, *al-Badr al-ṭāliʿ* ii, 92; al-Sakhāwī, *al-Ḍawʾ al-lāmiʿ* vi, 272; al-Akwaʿ, *Hijar al-ʿilm* 1371.

120 Haykel, 'Ulamāʾ ahl al-ḥadīth 4.

121 Ḥajar, *Ibn al-Wazīr wa-manhajuhu* 44–45.

122 See Ibn al-Wazīr, *Majmaʿ al-ḥaqāʾiq* 395; Ibn al-Wazīr, *Dīwān* laq. 56l; cf. Ibn al-Amīr, *Fatḥ al-khāliq* 221. According to Aḥmad b. al-Wazīr, the Mosque of Nuqum was one of the places where Ibn al-Wazīr experienced miraculous events (*karāmāt ṣūfiyya*). The occurrence of other miracles during his pilgrimages and in Mecca is recorded in the family history; cf. Aḥmad b. al-Wazīr, *Taʾrīkh Banī l-Wazīr* 35–37.

his relative in his biography.[123] At the age of eighteen, Ibn al-Wazīr wrote a poem to his brother al-Hādī in which he warns him against political involvement and insists on the preferability of asceticism. Al-Hādī lauds his brother's words as well as his deeds, indicating that Ibn al-Wazīr already practiced the life of an ascetic.[124] Furthermore, Ibn al-Wazīr received the sign of Sufi affiliation (*khirqa*) according to al-Shahārī. Apparently, it was the Shaykh ʿUmar b. Muḥammad al-ʿIrābī (d. 827/1424) who passed on the *khirqa* to Ibn al-Wazīr.[125] Since al-ʿIrābī moved to Mecca in 811/1408–1409 and, more importantly, Ibn al-Wazīr mentions al-ʿIrābī in *al-ʿAwāṣim*, written in 808/1406, as "our shaykh (*shaykhunā*),"[126] it is likely that Ibn al-Wazīr received the *khirqa* and was familiar with ascetic practices already in the first half of his life.

Besides, the very request that caused Ibn al-Wazīr to mention the years spent in seclusion also caused him to write a book of considerable theological insight, namely *Tarjīḥ asālīb al-Qurʾān ʿalā asālīb al-Yunān* (*The Preponderance of the Methods of the Quran Over the Methods of the Greeks*). And we know that his last great theological work, *Īthār al-ḥaqq ʿalā l-khalq* (*Preferring the Truth to Man*), was written in 837/1433–1434. Both writings are rife with theological subtlety and discuss intricate questions of speculative theology, something that Ibn al-Wazīr was loath to do while living in seclusion.[127] By his own account, lethargy (*khumūl*), sadness (*ḥuzn*) and hopelessness (*yaʾs*) often threatened to overcome him while living in solitude.[128] He found relief in a deeper "commitment of all his affairs to God" (*tafwīḍ, tawakkul*) bountifully expressed in the collection of his poems.[129] Yet it seems that the desire to benefit students and seekers, awakened by the request that provoked the writing of *Tarjīḥ*, initiated another phase of productivity.[130] I would therefore suggest that the last phase of Ibn al-Wazīr's life was not entirely dominated by his reclusiveness, but rather that he alternated between solitude and scholarly activity throughout his life. Furthermore, the periods spent in isolation during his later adulthood resulted in a richer understanding of the different responsibilities of a scholar and teacher,

123 Muḥammad al-Wazīr, *Tarjama* f. 137a.

124 Cf. vom Bruck, Regimes of Piety 206–207; Zabāra, *Aʾimmat al-Yaman* iii, 484.

125 Al-Shahārī, *Ṭabaqāt al-Zaydiyya* ii, 902. On al-ʿIrābī, see al-Fāṣī, *al-ʿIqd al-thamīn* vi, 360; al-Sakhāwī, *al-Ḍawʾ al-lāmiʿ* vi, 131–132.

126 Ibn al-Wazīr, *al-ʿAwāṣim* viii, 297.

127 Cf. Ibn al-Wazīr, *Tarjīḥ* 61, 63.

128 Ibid., 62–63; see also Ibn al-Wazīr, *Majmaʿ al-ḥaqāʾiq* 401; Ibn al-Wazīr., *Dīwān* laq. 69l, in which he laments his solitude.

129 Cf. Ibn al-Wazīr, *Tarjīḥ* 63.

130 Cf. ibid.

and what a Muslim believer needs to know and do. Such a nuanced understanding finds expression, for example, in his defense of a life in seclusion, namely Ibn al-Wazīr's *al-Amr bi-l-ʿuzla*, or in his exposition of the general tenets that supposedly unite all Muslim schools and individuals. This understanding was already implied in the early poem quoted above as well as in *al-ʿAwāṣim*, and was masterfully elaborated in his late *Īthār al-ḥaqq*.

1.3.6 Teaching and Students

It is uncertain when Ibn al-Wazīr began teaching. Zaydi Yemen knew of no official *madrasas* until the 10th/16th century.[131] And even then, Zaydi scholars were not paid, rendering it difficult to trace the circumstances of employment. The only sources on Ibn al-Wazīr's students are *ijāzas* and biographical accounts, of which the former are especially hard to find. If al-Akwaʿ's account is accurate and Ibn al-Wazīr did indeed teach Imam al-Nāṣir Ṣalāḥ al-Dīn, he must have started teaching at quite a young age.[132] Imam al-Nāṣir died in 793/1391, when Ibn al-Wazīr had not even reached the age of twenty. It is more likely that al-Akwaʿ is correct in naming the late imam's son, al-Manṣūr ʿAlī b. Ṣalāḥ al-Dīn, among Ibn al-Wazīr's students since Ibn al-Wazīr supported al-Manṣūr and seemed to have had considerable knowledge regarding al-Manṣūr's education. This is apparent in Ibn al-Wazīr's written defense of Imam al-Manṣūr.[133] It is documented, however, that Ibn al-Wazīr's fellow students listened to his opinions from an early age on. Prologues and comments in a number of his writings reveal that he was sought after as a teacher even after he received criticism from a number of his contemporaries, although in many cases his critics were actually urging him to justify his supposedly deviant arguments. As men-

---

131 The first Zaydi imam to build *madrasas* in the *hijras* of Kawkabān, Sanaa, Thulāʾ and Dhamar was Imam al-Mutawakkil Sharaf al-Dīn (r. 912/1506–965/1558); cf. Madelung, Islam im Jemen 175.

132 None of the sources apart from al-Akwaʿ claim that he was a student of Ibn al-Wazīr; cf. al-Akwaʿ (intr.), *al-ʿAwāṣim* i, 102. On Imam al-Nāṣir, see Yaḥyā b. al-Ḥusayn, *Ghāyat al-amānī* 523–538; al-Shahārī, *Ṭabaqāt al-Zaydiyya* ii, 1023–1026; al-Wajīh, *Aʿlām* 972; al-Ziriklī, *al-Aʿlām* vi, 287; al-Ḥibshī, *Maṣādir* 655–657; Zabāra, *Aʾimmat al-Yaman* 261.

133 Besides Ibn al-Wazīr's reference to his no longer extant biography of Imam al-Manṣūr, his *al-Ḥusām al-mashhūr* boasts the imam's erudition in the main sources Quran and Sunna. This impression is confirmed by the accounts of Yaḥyā b. al-Ḥusayn, where it was his statesmanship and his strong support of a number of scholars that helped to defeat his enemies and extend the area under his control. Though similar and more extensive achievements can be ascribed to Imam al-Nāṣir's father, the former lacked his father's learning; cf. Yaḥyā b. al-Ḥusayn, *Ghāyat al-amānī* 538–573; al-Sakhāwī, *al-Ḍawʾ al-lāmiʿ* v, 232, 324; al-Shawkānī, *al-Badr al-ṭāliʿ* i, 487; Zabāra, *Aʾimmat al-Yaman* i, 280–312; al-Ziriklī, *al-Aʿlām* v, 8.

tioned above, even the son of the belligerent teacher Ibn Abī l-Qāsim, Ṣalāḥ, was sent to study with Ibn al-Wazīr by his own father.[134]

The sources are not in accord concerning most of the names and biographical data of a number of Ibn al-Wazīr's students. However, a name all sources associate with Ibn al-Wazīr is the Shafiʿi al-Ḥasan b. Muḥammad al-Shaẓabī (d. 834–835/1430–1431). Al-Shaẓabī studied under Ibn al-Wazīr in Sanaa and later taught a number of disciplines in Taʿizz.[135] Furthermore, Ibn al-Wazīr probably taught his brother's grandson and author of a major source on the life of Ibn al-Wazīr, Muḥammad b. ʿAbdallāh b. al-Hādī (d. 897/1492).[136] Other students mentioned in connection to Ibn al-Wazīr are either his own son ʿAbdallāh b. Muḥammad (d. 840/1436) or his nephew ʿAbdallāh b. al-Hādī (d. 840/1436), or both of them.[137] Even more obscure are the names of Qadi ʿAbdallāh b. Muḥammad al-Nahwī (n.d.)[138] and ʿAbdallāh b. Muḥammad al-Ḥamzī (n.d.).[139]

134 Cf. Aḥmad b. al-Wazīr, *Taʾrīkh Banī l-Wazīr* 34. On Ṣalāḥ b. ʿAlī, who functioned as an imam briefly but then took to scholarship, see Yaḥyā b. al-Ḥusayn, *Ghāyat al-amānī* 573–582; al-Sakhāwī, *al-Ḍawʾ al-lāmiʿ* iii, 323; al-Shawkānī, *al-Badr al-ṭāliʿ* suppl., 107; Zabāra, *Aʾimmat al-Yaman* i, 321–322; al-Ziriklī, *al-Aʿlām* iii, 207; Kaḥḥāla, *Muʿjam al-muʾallifīn* v, 21–22; al-Ḥibshī, *Maṣādir* 675; al-Wajīh, *Aʿlām* 505; al-Ḥusaynī, *Muʾallafāt al-Zaydiyya* iii, 96.

135 Cf. al-Ḥibshī, *Maṣādir* 26; Ibn Abī l-Rijāl, *Maṭlaʿ al-budūr* ii, 101; al-Shahārī, *Ṭabaqāt al-Zaydiyya* i, 341; al-Wajīh, *Aʿlām* 346; al-Sakhāwī, *al-Ḍawʾ al-lāmiʿ* iii, 125.

136 Born in 810, this nephew of Muḥammad b. Ibrāhīm is known for his skill as a writer and penman in verse and prose with handwriting like "chains of gold," besides being a distinguished scholar; cf. Ibn Abī l-Rijāl, *Maṭlaʿ al-budūr* iv, 331–332; al-Sakhāwī, *al-Ḍawʾ al-lāmiʿ* viii, 120; al-Shawkānī, *al-Badr al-ṭāliʿ* suppl., 202; al-Akwaʿ, *Hijar al-ʿilm* 429–450.

137 Although Aḥmad b. al-Wazīr and al-Akwaʿ name Ibn al-Wazīr's son among his students, the other biographical sources state that it was in fact the son of his brother al-Hādī, likewise called ʿAbdallāh, who was taught by Ibn al-Wazīr. However, Ibn Abī l-Rijāl and al-Shahārī mention no ʿAbdallāh b. Muḥammad b. Ibrāhīm (Ibn al-Wazīr) at all, whereas Aḥmad b. al-Wazīr has no entry on a son of al-Hādī called ʿAbdallāh. There are other overlaps in the biographical data on the two cousins, as for example their year of death (840/1436) and their focus on Zaydi *fiqh*. Therefore it may well be that the two cousins were confused in person or in details; cf. Aḥmad b. al-Wazīr, *Taʾrīkh Banī l-Wazīr* 42–45; Ibn Abī l-Rijāl, *Maṭlaʿ al-budūr* iii, 153; al-Shahārī, *Ṭabaqāt al-Zaydiyya* i, 649; al-Akwaʿ, *Hijar al-ʿilm* 1377; al-Ḥibshī, *Maṣādir* 384.

138 Aḥmad b. al-Wazīr states nothing but his name; cf. Aḥmad b. al-Wazīr, *Taʾrīkh Banī l-Wazīr* 42.

139 What is said about the above-mentioned ʿAbdallāh b. Muḥammad al-Naḥwī seems also to be the case for ʿAbdallāh b. Muḥammad al-Ḥamzī. Al-Shawkānī has an entry that appears to be a blend of both ʿAbdallāhs, namely ʿAbdallāh b. al-imām al-Muṭahhar b. Muḥammad b. Sulaymān al-Ḥamzī. However, he does not mention that an ʿAbdallāh b. Muḥammad studied with Ibn al-Wazīr. Yet Aḥmad b. al-Wazīr al-Wazīr says that he was one of Ibn al-Wazīr's particularly close followers; cf. Aḥmad b. al-Wazīr, *Taʾrīkh Banī l-Wazīr* 42; al-Shawkānī, *al-Badr al-ṭāliʿ* i, 399.

FIGURE 1 Annex of Farwa b. Musayk al-Murādī Mosque, Sanaa
PHOTOGRAPH BY THE AUTHOR

Although disseminating knowledge was an important part of Ibn al-Wazīr's life, continuous teacher-student relationships apparently did not play a central role in his scholarly activities. When the plague that had devastated lower Yemen for some months hit the northern towns and killed tens of thousands in 840/1436, Ibn al-Wazīr died, leaving one son and an intellectual legacy that was not immediately palpable in any circle of students or followers.[140] He was buried in the annex of the al-Ru'ya Mosque, now known as Farwa b. Musayk al-Murādī Mosque, located in the south of Yemen's capital (figure 1 above).[141] His relationship to the Shāfiʿī al-Shaẓabī next to his Zaydi pupils further attests to Ibn al-Wazīr's negligent attitude towards *madhhab* boundaries. Although Ibn al-Wazīr is often referred to as an independent *mujtahid* who founded his own school,[142] this school was apparently not characterized by immediate trans-

140 According to Muḥammad b. ʿAbdallāh, Ibn al-Wazīr died on the same day as Imam al-Manṣūr; cf. Muḥammad b. ʿAbdallāh, *Tarjama* f. 143a. For an account of the plague years, see Aḥmad b. al-Ḥusayn, *Ghāyat al-amānī* 572–574.

141 Cf. al-Akwaʿ, *Hijar al-ʿilm* 1371.

142 See for example Aḥmad b. al-Wazīr, *Taʾrīkh Banī l-Wazīr* 28.

missions of opinions in the sense of a legal or a theological school. This phenomenon is in line with Ibn al-Wazīr's life task of counteracting divisions into rivaling schools of legal and theological thought.

2 Aḥmad b. Yaḥyā b. al-Murtaḍā (d. 840/1436) as a Scholar

A scholar is hardly understood unless seen against the background of his contemporaries. As anticipated in the introduction, Ibn al-Murtaḍā represents not only a mainstream current in Zaydi theology and law,[143] but also the group of speculative theologians whose star has long been on the wane in other regions of the Islamic World, namely the Bahshami Muʿtazila.

Little is known of the first years of Ibn al-Murtaḍā's life. The major source for data on Ibn al-Murtaḍā is *Kanz al-ḥukamāʾ wa-rawḍat al-ʿulamāʾ* (*The Treasure of Sages and the Garden of Scholars*), his biography written by his son al-Ḥasan b. Aḥmad (d. 840/1438).[144] Ibn al-Murtaḍā's birth took place in Alhān Ans, part of the district of Dhamar in the south of Sanaa. As to the date of his birth the sources mention a number of dates between 764/1363 and the less likely 775/1373.[145] Born into the same extended family that Ibn al-Wazīr belonged to, Ibn al-Murtaḍā grew up as a scholar. After the death of his parents he was taught by his uncle Imam al-Mahdī ʿAlī b. Muḥammad (d. 773/1371–1372),[146]

143 On Ibn al-Murtaḍā, see Yaḥyā b. al-Ḥusayn, *Ghāyat al-amānī* ii, 538; al-Shawkānī, *al-Badr al-ṭāliʿ* i, 122; Zabāra, *Aʾimmat al-Yaman* i, 312; al-Ḥibshī, *Maṣādir* 661–674; al-Shahārī, *Ṭabaqāt al-Zaydiyya* i, 226–233; al-Wajīh, *Aʿlām* 206–213; Blackburn et al., Al-Mahdī li-Dīn Allāh Aḥmad 2.

144 Cf. al-Ḥibshī, *Maṣādir* 493.

145 Ibn Murtaḍā's son al-Ḥasan reports 764/1363 as the year of birth, yet he acknowledges that it might well have been a few years earlier or later; cf. l-Ḥasan b. Aḥmad, *Kanz al-ḥukamāʾ* 148. Al-Ḥibshī agrees with him, as do al-Ṣubḥī and Zabāra; cf. al-Ḥibshī, *Maṣādir* 583; al-Ṣubḥī, *al-Zaydiyya* 340; Zabāra, *Aʾimmat al-Yaman* 312. Al-Shawkānī marks 775/1373 as Ibn al-Murtaḍā's year of birth, as does al-Ziriklī; cf. al-Shawkānī, *al-Badr al-ṭāliʿ* ii, 8; Ziriklī, *al-Aʿlām* vi, 269. A third position, again held by Zabāra, contradicts itself. He says that Ibn al-Murtaḍā was 24 when he received the *bayʿa*, which was in 793/1390–1391 The concluded year of birth (769/1367–1368) contradicts what Zabāra records as the age at his death in 840/1436, namely 76 years. This age would mean that he was born in 674. It is confirmed by all sources that Ibn al-Murtaḍā received the *bayʿa* in 793 when he would have been 29 and therefore in compliance with one of the conditions of the imamate. More arguments are provided by al-Kamālī, *al-Imām al-Mahdī* 69–70.

146 The date of birth given by al-Shawkānī (775/1873–1874) calls the influence of Ibn al-Murtaḍā's uncle, Imam al-Mahdī ʿAlī, into question. However, besides the data rendered by Ibn al-Murtaḍā's son, several factors speak for the likelihood of an earlier date and of a relationship between uncle and nephew. For one thing, Ibn al-Murtaḍā expressed his

his brother al-Hādī b. Yaḥyā (d. 785/1383–1384)[147] and his sister Dahmā' bt. Yaḥyā b. al-Murtaḍā (d. 837/1433–1434) in his hometown of Dhamar.[148] Dahmā' probably also taught him in Thulā', where she spent a considerable amount of time.[149]

Basic information relevant to Ibn al-Murtaḍā's later life and scholarship can be summarized as follows: After Imam al-Nāṣir Ṣalāḥ al-Dīn's death in 793/1390–1391, Ibn al-Murtaḍā received the oath of allegiance (*bay'a*) in Sanaa from a number the city's scholars. This *bay'a* was the reaction to the news of plans made by a group of Sa'da's most prominent scholars around Qadi al-Diwārī to appoint the son of the late imam, 'Alī b. Ṣalāḥ al-Dīn.[150] The sources leave no doubt that not all scholars agreed with the choice, a main reason being 'Alī b. Ṣalāḥ al-Dīn's young age and inability to meet all the intellectual requirements for the imamate.[151] Ibn al-Murtaḍā, for his part, proved the scholar, yet not the warrior and statesman an imam was required to be.[152] Consequently, the military conflict that arose between the armed groups of the two candidates in Sanaa's south (Bayt Baws) was terminated after thirteen days by a truce and a subsequent arbitration tribunal of leading scholars. The arbitration in favor of 'Alī b. Ṣalāḥ al-Dīn was not complied with, which resulted in more fighting and ended with Ibn al-Murtaḍā's arrest.[153]

From the time of his imprisonment, the instances of his political involvement decreased, whereas his scholarly productivity increased. Ibn al-Wazīr's brother, al-Hādī b. Ibrāhīm, played a crucial role in ensuring proper treatment of Ibn al-Murtaḍā and his release seven years later.[154] Apparently, Ibn al-Murtaḍā received ink and paper and authored a number of books while in prison. After a second uprising in Sa'da, he relinquished the reign to his ally Imam al-Hādī al-Mu'ayyad (d. 836/1432–1433) and settled in Thulā' where he remained until 816/1413–1414. At the time, Thulā' was a famous center of

---

appreciation for his uncle and mentions him among the Zaydi imams who were *mujtahids*; cf. Ibn al-Murtaḍā, *Muqaddima* 231. Furthermore, Ibn al-Murtaḍā took on his uncle's former title "al-Mahdī li-Dīn Allāh" when he himself became imam, as al-Mākhidhī points out; cf. al-Mākhidhī (ed., intr.), *Minhāj al-wuṣūl* 29.

147 Al-Shawkānī, *al-Badr al-ṭāli'* ii, 321.

148 Al-Ḥasan b. Aḥmad, *Kanz al-ḥukamā'* 108.

149 For more on Dahmā' b. Yaḥyā, see al-Ḥasan b. Aḥmad, *Kanz al-ḥukamā'* 58; al-Ḥibshī, *Maṣādir* 221.

150 Yaḥyā b. al-Ḥusayn, *Ghāyat al-amānī* 539.

151 Cf. ibid., 538.

152 For the details of the dispute between the contending scholars, see especially al-Ḥasan b. Aḥmad, *Kanz al-ḥukamā'* 111–113.

153 Ibid., 546.

154 Ibid., 553.

learning and home of the prolific Qadi Yūsuf b. Aḥmad ʿUthmān (d. 832/1429). According to Yaḥyā b. al-Ḥusayn, Qadi Yūsuf had supported Ibn al-Murtaḍā's *daʿwa* in 793/1390–1391 and had received Aḥmad b. Yaḥyā after his release in 801/1398. That Qadi Yūsuf's love for the *ahl al-bayt* was given as the reason for supporting Ibn al-Murtaḍā indicates that Ibn al-Murtaḍā was readily identified with Zaydi scholarship and that his imprisonment by the imam did not call that into question.[155] In 816/1414, Ibn al-Murtaḍā moved to Jabal Miswar were he remained until 836/1432–1433, with an intermediate sojourn in the mountainous Ḥarāz. When the plague reached the Yemeni highlands in 840/1436, Ibn al-Murtaḍā lived in Ẓafīr, a fortress in the region of Ḥajja he had taken over from his former ally Imam al-Hādī al-Muʾayyad after the latter's death. Ibn al-Murtaḍā, like his former opponents Ibn al-Wazīr and Imam al-Manṣūr, died of the plague in that year.[156]

2.1 *Teachers, Education and Students*

Ibn al-Murtaḍā's uncle, brother and sister were scholars of *kalām*, *uṣūl al-fiqh* and other disciplines typical for a scholarly Zaydi family.[157] His father had guided Ibn al-Murtaḍā into the sciences of the Arabic language, of which Ibn al-Murtaḍā was considered an extraordinary scholar throughout his whole life.[158] He began studying *kalām* with his brother and later continued with Qadi Abū Muḥammad b. Yaḥyā b. Muḥammad al-Madhhajī (d. early 9th/15th century).[159] Al-Madhhajī gave him teaching licenses in the field of *kalām* for al-Raṣṣāṣ's *Khulāṣa*, *Sharḥ al-uṣūl al-khamsa* (*A Commentary on the Five Principles*) by the

155 Besides the title of qadi, Yūsuf b. Aḥmad more accurately carries the epithet *al-faqīh* (the jurist). Considered one of the important *mudhākirūn*, he probably played an active role in consolidating the *corpus* of Zaydi substantial law. This is illustrated, for example, by the high number of *ijāzas* (at least five or six) he received for Imam Yaḥyā b. Hamzā's (d. 749/1346) important compendium of Zaydi substantial law, *al-Intiṣār ʿalā ʿulamāʾ al-amṣār* (*The Triumph Over the Scholars of the Region*). *Al-Faqīh* Yūsuf's subsequent abridgment of *al-Intiṣār*, namely *al-Istibṣār al-muntazaʿ min al-Intiṣār* (*The Insight Gained from The Triumph*) is likewise influential. He also wrote a commentary on al-Muʾayyad bi-llāh Aḥmad b. al-Ḥusayn al-Hārūnī's (d. 411/1020) *Ziyādāt* and one on al-Amīr ʿAlī b. al-Ḥusayn's (d. around 670/1270) *Lumaʿ*; cf. al-Shahārī, *Ṭabaqāt al-Zaydiyya* iii, 1275–1279; Ibn Abī l-Rijāl, *Maṭlaʿ al-budūr* iv, 521–523; al-Shawkānī, *al-Badr al-ṭāliʿ* ii, 350; al-Ḥibshī, *Maṣādir* 219.

156 Yaḥyā b. al-Ḥusayn, *Ghāyat al-amānī* 573.

157 Al-Mākhidhī (ed., intr.), *Minhāj al-wuṣūl*, 33.

158 Al-Ḥasan b. Aḥmad, *Kanz al-ḥukamāʾ* 108; al-Shawkānī, *al-Badr al-ṭāliʿ* i, 122.

159 Al-Shahārī, *Ṭabaqāt al-Zaydiyya* ii, 1109–1110; Ibn Abī l-Rijāl, *Maṭlaʿ al-budūr* iv, 403. Both biographers point out especially that al-Madhhajī taught Ibn al-Murtaḍā al-Raṣṣāṣ's *Khulāṣa*.

Zaydi-Muʿtazili Aḥmad b. al-Ḥusayn al-Qazwinī al-Manakdīm (d. 425/1034), *al-Ghurar wa-l-ḥujūl fī qāwaʿid sharḥ al-uṣūl al-khamsa* (*Blazes and Anklets: Principles of A Commentary on the Five Principles*) by al-Qāsim b. Aḥmad al-Muḥallī (d. 8th/14th c.),[160] Ibn Mattawayh's (d. after 415/1025) *Tadhkira* and *al-Muḥīṭ bī-l-taklīf* (*The Encompassing [Treatment] of That which God Makes Incumbent*) of ʿAbd al-Jabbār al-Hamadhānī (d. 415/1025).[161] In *uṣūl al-fiqh*, al-Madhhajī taught him Aḥmad b. Muḥammad al-Raṣṣāṣ's *Jawhara* as well as Abū al-Ḥusayn l-Baṣrī's *al-Muʿtamad fī uṣūl al-fiqh* and Ibn al-Ḥājib's *Muntahā l-suʾl*.[162]

Like Ibn al-Wazīr, Ibn al-Murtaḍā was a student of the above-mentioned Ibn Abī l-Khayr (d. 793/1391) under whom he intensified his understanding of Ibn Mattawayh's *Tadhkira*.[163] Al-Mākhidhī states in his introduction to Ibn al-Murtaḍā's *Minhāj al-wuṣūl* that Ibn al-Murtaḍā studied *al-Muḥīṭ*, *al-Muʿtamad* and *Muntahā l-suʾl* a second time with Ibn Abī l-Khayr.[164] Another teacher of considerable interest is Imam al-Nāṣir Ṣalāḥ al-Dīn (d. 793/1391). As already mentioned, Imam al-Nāṣir was well known for teaching and propagating the use of the Sunni hadith compilations.[165] Moreover, Ibn al-Murtaḍā learned *al-Kashshāf* from Aḥmad b. Muḥammad al-Najrī al-Nassākh (n.d.).[166] With al-Ḥusayn b. Alī l-ʿAdwī (n.d.) he studied Ibn Hishām's prophetic biography as well as writings on Arabic linguistics.[167] Another teacher Ibn al-Murtaḍa had in common with Ibn al-Wazīr was the Nafīs al-Dīn al-ʿAlawī (d. 825/1422) from Taʿizz. Ibn al-Murtaḍā studied the hadith compilations of al-Bukhārī and Muslim, as well as a number of other writings with him.[168]

As to Ibn al-Murtaḍā's students, a few famous individuals are mentioned in *Ṭabaqāt al-Zaydiyya*, with a reference to a much greater number of less significant names: Firstly, there is Imam al-Muṭahhar b. Muḥammad b. Sulaymān (d. 879/1474), to whom Ibn al-Murtaḍā passed on his theological and jurisprudential writings.[169] Another pupil of Ibn al-Murtaḍā, *al-faqīh* Yaḥyā b. Aḥmad

160 On *al-Ghurar wa-l-ḥujūl*, see al-Ḥibshī, *Maṣādir* 131.

161 ʿAbd al-Jabbār's *Muḥīṭ* is also among his principle works on speculative theology and has had a strong influence in Bahshami-Muʿtazili thought; cf. Peters, *God's Created Speech* 10.

162 Al-Shahārī, *Ṭabaqāt al-Zaydiyya* i, 227.

163 Al-Kamālī, *al-Imām al-Mahdī* 73; al-Ḥasan b. Aḥmad, *Kanz al-ḥukamāʾ* 58.

164 Al-Mākhidhī (ed., intr.), *Minhāj al-wuṣūl* 34.

165 Yaḥyā b. al-Ḥusayn, *Ghāyat al-amānī* 537.

166 Ibn Abī l-Rijāl, *Maṭlaʿ al-budūr* i, 458–459, al-Shahārī, *Ṭabaqāt al-Zaydiyya* i, 206.

167 Al-Ḥasan b. Aḥmad, *Kanz al-ḥukamāʾ* 109.

168 Al-Kamālī, *al-Imām al-Mahdī* 73; al-Ḥasan b. Aḥmad, *Kanz al-ḥukamāʾ* 58; for the wording of an *ijāza* issued in 795 in Taʿizz, see ibid., 148.

169 Imam al-Muṭahhar was a teacher of the author of *Maʾāthir al-abrār*, i.e. Ibn Fanad; cf. al-Shahārī, *Ṭabaqāt al-Zaydiyya* ii, 1130–1134.

b. Mughram (d. 865/1460–1461), was also taught by the above-mentioned Imam al-Muṭahhar. Both teachers are said to have given Ibn Mughram *ijāzas* for important works of Ibn al-Murtaḍā, like *al-Baḥr al-zakhkhār* and its *Muqaddima* (*Introduction*).[170] ʿAlī b. Muḥammad al-Najrī (d. around 840/1436) wrote another commentary on his teacher's *Kitāb al-Azhār*, namely *Sharḥ al-Najrī*. He followed Ibn al-Murtaḍā in the *furūʿ* and gave teaching licenses for Ibn al-Murtaḍā's works and his own commentary to his own students.[171] ʿAlī al-Najrī's younger brother, ʿAbdallāh b. Muḥammad al-Najrī (d. 877/1472–1473), though probably no immediate student of Ibn al-Murtaḍā, was yet associated with some of Ibn al-Murtaḍā's most influential students alongside his brother ʿAlī al-Najrī.[172] ʿAbdallāh al-Najrī wrote a commentary on a part of Ibn al-Murtaḍa's introduction (*Muqaddima*) to his *al-Baḥr al-zakhkhār* which was to become "the backbone of Zaydi *kalām* studies."[173] Another student worth mentioning is Zayd b. Yaḥyā al-Dhamārī (d. unknown).[174] Al-Dhamārī was the link between Ibn al-Murtaḍā and Ibn Miftāḥ, writer of the most important commentary on Ibn al-Murtaḍā's *Kitāb al-Azhār*, or rather on Ibn al-Murtaḍā's own commentary on *Kitāb al-Azhār*, called *Taʿlīq Ibn Miftāḥ* (*Ibn Miftāḥ's Commentary*) or *Sharḥ al-Azhār al-muntazaʿ al-mukhtār min al-Ghayth al-midrār al-mutafattiḥ li-kamāʾim al-Azhār* (*Commenting on The Blossoms: A Chosen Extract from The Abundant Rain Opening Up the Perianths of The Blossoms*).[175] A final student mentioned by name is Yaḥyā b. Aḥmad b. Muẓaffar (d. 875/1470–1471).[176]

170 Cf. ibid., iii, 1206–1207.

171 Ibid., ii, 789–790. According to Schwarb, ʿAlī b. Muḥammad al-Najrī died in 844/1441; cf. Schwarb, Guide to Zaydī *Kalām* 161, footnote 16.

172 Cf. ibid., 161. The biographical sources are silent concerning ʿAbdallāh al-Najrī's Yemeni teachers besides his brother ʿAlī and his father Muḥammad b. al-Qāsim al-Najrī (d. 852/1448). Yet ʿAbdallāh al-Najrī is known to have been in close contact with Imam al-Muṭahhar b. Muḥammad and Yaḥyā b. Aḥmad b. Muẓaffar. On ʿAbdallāh al-Najrī, see for example Ibn Abī l-Rijāl, *Maṭlaʿ al-budūr* iii, 129–133; al-Shawkānī, *al-Badr al-ṭāliʿ* i, 436–438; al-Ḥibshī, *Maṣādir* 29, 137, 226, 385, 425, 586.

173 Ibid., 155. ʿAbdallāh al-Najrī's *Kitāb Mirqāt al-anẓār al-muntazaʿ min Ghāyāt al-afkār al-kāshif li-maʿānī al-muqaddimat al-Baḥr al-zakhkhār* (*The Book of the Ascent of Opinions Chosen From The End of Thoughts Revealing the Meaning of the Introduction to The Overflowing Sea*) was written in 853/1449–1450. The *Kitāb Mirqāt al-anzār* constituted the central part of Zaydi *kalām*-studies from the mid-9th/15th until the end of the first century of Qāsimī rule (early 12th/18th century).

174 Al-Shahārī, *Ṭabaqāt al-Zaydiyya* i, 458. The data on the content of al-Dhamārī's studies with Ibn al-Murtaḍā is restricted to Ibn al-Murtaḍā's own works, as it is in the case of Ibn Mughram.

175 Cf. ibid., i, 229.

176 Ibid., iii, 1205–1206.

A survey of Ibn al-Murtaḍā's main teachers and the content of his education shows that his educational upbringing was in many ways congruent with Ibn al-Wazīr's. Not only were they students of the same teachers, they moreover studied many of the same books in Zaydi *kalām* with Bahshami-Muʿtazili influence. These similarities hold true for Zaydi *uṣūl al-fiqh* as well as in respect to Sunni hadith compilations. Since a large number of Ibn al-Murtaḍā's teachers died before his claim to the imamate (793/1390–1391), no potential shift in educational focus in later years can be concluded from the input he received. Zaydi-Muʿtazili *kalām* and *uṣūl al-fiqh* was as much a part of his early education as were the studies in Sunni hadith. Whether or not Ibn al-Murtaḍā and Ibn al-Wazīr studied together cannot be established due to the lack of temporal specification of the teaching periods with the respective scholar.

Where students are concerned, a greater number is documented for Ibn al-Murtaḍā. The teacher-student relationships as well as the content of teaching indicate that Ibn al-Murtaḍā was part of an ongoing teaching tradition, and that his *Muqaddima* to his *al-Baḥr al-zakhkhār* in Zaydi theology (beside other disciplines) as well as his *Kitāb al-Azhār* in Zaydi *fiqh* formed a vital part of this tradition.

2.2 *Ibn al-Murtaḍā's Works*

The list of Ibn al-Murtaḍā's literary output is extensive. Al-Ḥibshī lists sixty titles,[177] among which Ibn al-Murtaḍā's works in theology, legal theory, positive law and heresiography are most famous.

In the field of theology, Ibn al-Murtaḍā's *Kitāb al-Qalāʾid fī taṣḥīḥ al-ʿaqāʾid* (*The Book of Necklaces: Affirming the Doctrines*)[178] is well known, wherein he renders the doctrinal positions of different schools of thought and later compares them, pointing out the differences in the understanding of the five fundamental doctrines between the Zaydi and the Muʿtazili teaching. This writing is considered one of the most important sources for the study of Zaydi doctrine because of its brevity.[179] Al-Kamālī compares its importance for Zaydi

177 Cf. al-Ḥibshī, *Maṣādir* 661–675. An in-depth analysis of Ibn al-Murtaḍā's works may reveal false ascriptions or numerous titles of the same work. Yet, as my main focus is not on Ibn al-Murtaḍā, it will suffice to mention the magnitude of Ibn al-Murtaḍā's productivity and some of his most important works.

178 For *Kitāb al-Qalāʾid*, see Ibn al-Murtaḍā, *Muqaddima* 52–89. *Al-Qalāʾid* contains six separate books.

179 The number of copies of commentaries of *al-Qalāʾid* and Ibn al-Murtaḍā's own commentary, i.e. *al-Durar al-farāʾid*, indicate its importance. For a list of the copies and commentaries, see al-Ḥibshī, *Maṣādir* 592.

theology with the importance of Ibn al-Murtaḍā's *Kitāb al-Azhār* for Zaydi *fiqh*.[180] Beyond the Zaydiyya, the *Kitāb al-Qalāʾid* already functioned as a source for research on the Muʿtazila in the early 20th century, as van Ess tells us.[181] Ibn al-Murtaḍā himself expounds on *al-Qalāʾid* in its commentary *al-Durar al-farāʾiḍ fī sharḥ kitāb al-Qalāʾid* (*Rare Pearls: Commenting on The Book of Necklaces*).[182] In *Riyāḍat al-afhām fī laṭīf al-kalām* (*Excercise for the Intellects: Subtleties of Kalām*)[183] and its commentary *Dāmigh al-awhām fī sharḥ Riyāḍat al-afhām* (*Triumph over Errors: A Commentary on Exercise for the Intellects*), Ibn al-Murtaḍā discusses his theological methodology and epistemology as well as some aspects of natural theology.[184] *Riyāḍat al-afhām* was used as a source for the study of Muʿtazili theology along with *Kitāb al-Qalāʾid*.[185]

In legal theory, Ibn al-Murtaḍā authored *Fāʾiqat al-uṣūl fī ḍabṭ maʿānī Jawharat al-uṣūl* (*The Superior in [the Science] of Principles: Capturing the Meaning of The Gem of Principles*), a commentary on al-Raṣṣāṣ's famous *Jawhara*.[186] His *Miʿyār al-ʿuqūl fī ʿilm al-uṣūl* (*The Standard for Intellects in the Science of Principles*) is divided into an introduction and 11 chapters, comprising the common questions of legal theory.[187] Its commentary *Minhāj al-wuṣūl ilā sharḥ Miʿyār al-ʿuqūl* (*The Path to Arriving at the Commentary of The Standard for Intellects*) is widely read still today.[188]

---

180 Cf. al-Kamālī, *al-Imām al-Mahdī* 116.

181 Van Ess refers to Max Horten's *Die Philosophische Systeme der spekulativen Theologie im Islam* from 1910, using the *Kitāb al-Qalāʾid* to examine Shahrastānī's presentation of the Muʿtazila. Van Ess, in his citation of the title of Horten's work, has turned "Systeme" into "Probleme"; cf. van Ess, *Der Eine und das Andere* 989.

182 *Al-Durar al-farāʾid* is the second of nine parts of Ibn al-Murtaḍā's commentary on his *Muqaddima* to *al-Baḥr al-zakhkhār* called *Ghāyāt al-afkār* (*The End of Thoughts*). For the discussion of Ibn al-Murtaḍā's positions in *al-Durar al-farāʾid*, I use Dāwūd b. Aḥmad al-Ḥayyī commentary called *Sharḥ al-Qalāʾid al-muntazaʿ min al-Durar al-farāʾid fī sharḥ Kitāb al-Qalāʾid* (*A Commentary on The Necklaces Drawn from Rare Pearls: Commenting on The Book of Necklaces*). Al-Ḥayyī's representation of Ibn al-Murtaḍā's reasoning coincides with Ibn al-Murtaḍā's positions in other works. For *al-Muntazaʿ min al-Durar al-farāʾid*, see Ahlwardt, *Verzeichnisse* x, 310. On al-Ḥayyī, cf. al-Ḥibshī, Maṣādir 151; al-Wajīh, *Aʿlām* 420.

183 Cf. al-Ḥibshī, *Maṣādir* 669.

184 Several copies of *Dāmigh al-awhām* are apparently located in the Dār al-Makhṭūṭāt; cf. al-Ḥibshī, *Maṣādir* 667–668. For *Riyāḍat al-afhām*, see Ibn al-Murtaḍā, *Muqaddima* 99–158.

185 Horten's monograph consists of a rearranged translation of the two works; cf. van Ess, *Der Eine und das Andere* 989.

186 Cf. al-Ḥibshī, *Maṣādir* 671.

187 Ibn al-Murtaḍā, *Muqaddima* 159–204; cf. al-Ḥibshī, *Maṣādir* 673.

188 Cf. al-Ḥibshī, *Maṣādir* 674; The last edition of the work is al-Mākhidhī's from 1992.

In positive law, Ibn al-Murtaḍā's most annotated writing[189] remains to date a major source of Zaydi *fiqh* in Yemen: his *Kitāb al-Azhār fī fiqh al-aʾimma al-athār* (*The Book of Blossoms: The Jurisprudence of the Pure Imams*).[190] In *Kitāb al-Azhār*, Ibn al-Murtaḍā compiled and rectified the legal rulings handed down from the eponym of the Yemeni Zaydiyya, al-Hādī ilā l-ḥaqq, and thereby consolidated the latter's *madhhab*.[191] The similarly famous *al-Baḥr al-zakhkhār al-jāmiʿ li-madhāhib ʿulamāʾ al-amṣār* (*The Overflowing Sea Compiling the Opinions of the Scholars of the Regions*) extends to the *fiqh* of scholars of other schools of law. However *al-Baḥr al-zakhkhār* is introduced with a section on the speculative theologians as well as their classes (*maqālāt*) as the first of six separate books in which legal theory and theology figure prominently. These six introductory books are called *Muqaddimat al-Baḥr al-zakhkhār* or *Dībāja*.[192]

Prominent among Ibn al-Murtaḍā's heresiographical works on Muslim sects is *al-Munya wa-l-amal fī sharḥ al-milal wa-l-niḥal* (*Desire and Hope: A Commentary on Denominations and Creeds*),[193] a commentary on his *al-Milal wa-l-niḥal* (*Denominations and Creeds*) that discusses confessional groups within and outside the borders of Islam.[194] *Kitāb al-Milal wa-l-niḥal*, in turn, is the first part of Ibn al-Murtaḍā's *Muqaddima* to *al-Baḥr al-zakhkhār*.[195] According to Arnold, van Ess and Stern, the part of *al-Munya wa-l-amal* (and *al-Milal wa-l-niḥal*) that is concerned with the Muʿtazili classes is hardly more than a reworking of al-Ḥakim al-Jishumī's (d. 464/1101) *Sharḥ ʿUyūn al-masāʾil*,[196] which in

189 Al-Kamālī counts at least 24 commentaries and glosses; cf. al-Kamālī, *al-Imām al-Mahdī* 122.

190 *Kitāb al-Azhār* has been edited and printed a few times since 1913, with the fourth and to date last edition by al-Faḍl b. Abī l-Saʿd ʿUsayfirī and ʿAbd al-Wāsiʿ b. Yaḥyā Wāsiʿī from 1993. Its commentaries and glosses are numerous; cf. al-Ḥibshī, *Masādir* 662–664.

191 Al-Ḥasan b. Aḥmad, *Kanz al-ḥukamāʿ* 123–124. For the reception of *Kitāb al-Azhār*, see al-Ḥibshī, *Muʾallafat ḥukkām* 94.

192 *Al-Baḥr al-zakhkhar* was edited and printed a number of times, with the first edition in 1949 in Cairo and the last one by Muḥammad Tāmir and Muḥammad Bahrān in 2001.

193 Cf. Ibn al-Murtaḍā, *Muqaddima* 16–31.

194 Cf. Al-Ḥibshī, *Maṣādir* 590, 594. The last chapter of *al-Munya wa-l-amal* concerning the generations of Muʿtazili scholars was printed by Harrasowitz in 1902 as *Bāb dhikr al-Mutazila min kitāb al-Munya wa-l-amal fī sharḥ kitab al-Milal wa-l-niḥal*, Thomas Arnold (ed.).

195 Cf. Arnold (ed., intr.), *Bāb dhikr al-Muʿtazila* 1.

196 Al-Muḥassin b. Muḥammad b. Karāma al-Barūqānī alias al-Ḥākim al-Jishumī (elsewhere al-Jushamī) (d. 484/1101) was an influential student of ʿAbd al-Jabbār in the second generation, as well as a Hanafi convert to Zaydism from Bayhaq. His conversion is probably a major reason why his works were widely received among the Yemeni Zaydiyya. On al-Jishumī, his heresiographical works and his reception among the Yemeni Zaydiyya, cf. van

turn had ʿAbd al-Jabbār's *Ṭabaqāt al-Muʿtazila* as its main source. Apparently, Ibn al-Murtaḍā focused mainly on the early Muʿtazili sects with little attention to either the developments since al-Jishumī's death, or to Ibn al-Murtaḍā's contemporary environment.[197] Hence, heresiography is another discipline in which Ibn al-Murtaḍā's Muʿtazilism is evident.

Furthermore, Ibn al-Murtaḍā dedicated a considerable number of writings to the sciences of the Arabic language and a few to mysticism (*ʿilm al-tarīqa*). According to al-Ḥibshī, Ibn al-Murtaḍā's commentary on his Sufi-styled book on ethics in *al-Baḥr al-zakhkhār*, called *Thamarāt al-akmām* (The *Fruits of the Perianth*, alluding to the sleeves of the Sufi cloak) became popular among Yemeni Sufis.[198] On the other hand, his *al-Qamar al-nawwār fī-l-radd ʿalā al-murakhkhisīn fī l-malāhī wa-l-mizmār* (*The Shining Moon: A Refutation of Those Who Concede Entertainment and Flute Play*) was written in refutation of Sufi practices. Other disciplines of his proficiency in which he contributed to Zaydi scholarship were the prophetic Sunna, the science of inheritance (*ʿilm al-mawārīth* or *ʿilm al-faraʾiḍ*), history (*taʾrīkh*) and logic (*manṭiq*).[199]

Not much can be extracted from the primary sources as to when Ibn al-Murtaḍā wrote which book. The major source for dating his works is again *Kanz al-ḥukamāʾ*. Al-Kamālī, in his analysis of Ibn al-Murtaḍā's thought, relied mostly on *Kanz al-ḥukamāʾ* for the biographical and bibliographical data.[200]

As the sources indicate, Ibn al-Murtaḍā was prominent from his early days on for his scholarship in the sciences of Arabic. His first book, *al-Kawkab al-ẓāhir fī sharḥ Muqaddimat Ibn Ṭāhir* (*The Clear Star: A Commentary on Ibn Ṭāhir's Introduction*), was dedicated to linguistics. According to his son, Ibn al-Murtaḍā wrote it before he was twenty, hence between 783/1381 and 784/1383.[201] According to al-Kamālī, the *Kitāb al-Qalāʾid* on the positions of the theological schools was the next book Ibn al-Murtaḍā wrote, although Ibn al-Murtaḍā's son mentions that he wrote another theological work, along with its commentary, before *Kitāb Qalāʾid*.[202] Al-Kamālī assumes, on the basis of the report in *Kanz al-ḥukamāʾ*, that Ibn al-Murtaḍā turned to the study of *kalām* after having

---

Ess, *Der Eine und das Andere* 761–770; Madelung, *Der Imam al-Qāsim* 188; Madelung, al-Ḥākim al-Djushamī; Schwarb, In the Age of Averroes 252.

197 Cf. Arnold (ed., intr.), *Bāb dhikr al-Muʿtazila* 66; van Ess, *Der Eine und das Andere* 988–995; Stern, ʿAbd al-Djabbār b. Aḥmad. On al-Jishumī's heresiographical works, cf. van Ess, *Der Eine und das Andere* 761–770.

198 Cf. al-Ḥibshī, *al-Ṣūfiyya wa-l-fuqahāʾ* 65–66; Madelung, Zaydī Attitudes 135.

199 Cf. al-Ḥasan b. Aḥmad, *Kanz al-ḥukamāʿ* 147–148.

200 Cf. al-Kamālī, *al-Imām al-Mahdī* 113–116.

201 Al-Ḥasan b. Aḥmad, *Kanz al-ḥukamāʾ* 108.

202 Ibid., 146.

mastered the various disciplines of Arabic linguistics. He summarized the theological works he studied and compiled their meaning "in two and a half notebooks."[203] The first recorded titles of works Ibn al-Murtaḍā studied in *kalām* are al-Raṣṣāṣ's (d. 621/1224) *Khulāṣa*, Ḥanash's (d. 719/1319) *al-Ghiyāṣa* and al-Manakdim's (d. 425/1034) *Sharḥ al-uṣūl al-khamsa*, representing a Bahshami-Muʿtazili current in the Zaydiyya. Ibn al-Murtaḍā's *Kitāb al-Qalāʾid* is indeed rather short, possibly the length of two and a half notebooks. Without claiming to be an in-depth analysis, a resemblance to a commentary of *al-Uṣūl al-khamsa* suggests itself upon the reading of *Kitāb al-Qalāʾid*. And in those instances where Ibn al-Murtaḍā mentions his own choice, it is often in line with what he ascribed to ʿAbd al-Jabbār or the Bahshami variety of the Muʿtazila.[204] Therefore, it is likely that Ibn al-Murtaḍā's account of the theological schools with respect to the five principles (*al-uṣūl al-khamsa*), along with his own opinion, were already established at an early stage of his career. Likewise his views on legal theory: According to his son, his first writing on legal theory was the versified summary of Aḥmad b. Muḥammad al-Raṣṣāṣ's *Jawhara*, called *Fāʾiqat al-uṣūl*.[205] It is uncertain at what point he authored *Miʿyār al-ʿuqūl*. According to *Kanz al-ḥukamāʾ*, all this happened before Ibn al-Murtaḍā's political career even started, hence before 793/1390–1391.[206]

It is quite certain that a large part of the six years of Ibn al-Murtaḍā's captivity (794/1392–801/1389) were spent in scholarly activity. At least three of his writings resulted from this period, most prominently *Kitāb al-Azhār* and its commentary *Sharḥ al-Azhār*.[207] During his years in Thulāʾ (801/1399–816/1413), Ibn al-Murtaḍā wrote at least his great *fiqh* work *al-Baḥr al-zakhkhār*.[208] During his sojourn in Jabal Miswar (816/1413–836/1432–1433) he authored *Ghāyāt al-afkār*, a commentary on the introduction of *al-Baḥr al-zakhkhār*, completed *al-Durar al-farāʾiḍ*, commenting on his earlier *Kitāb al-Qalāʾid*, and began to write *Dāmigh al-awhām*.[209] In an intermezzo of what must have been a few years between 816/1413 and 836/1432–1433, Ibn al-Murtaḍā lived in Ḥarāz where he authored a large part of his writings. He completed *Dāmigh al-awhām* and wrote *Minhāj al-wuṣūl*. Al-Ḥasan b. Aḥmad additionally mentions that Ibn

203 Ibid., 109.

204 For Ibn al-Murtaḍā's *Kitāb al-Qalāʾid*, see Ibn al-Murtaḍā, *Muqaddima* 52–98; cf. al-Ḳamālī, *al-Imām al-Mahdī* 114.

205 Al-Ḥasan b. Aḥmad, *Kanz al-ḥukamāʾ* 109.

206 Ibid., 109.

207 Ibid., 123.

208 Ibid., 130.

209 Ibid., 131; cf. al-Shahārī, *Ṭabaqāt al-Zaydiyya* i, 230–231.

al-Murtaḍā wrote the following works while in Ḥarāz: *Tāj ʿulūm al-adab wa-qānūn kalām al-ʿarab* (*The Crown of the Sciences of Poetry and the Rules of Arabic Speech*) and *Iklīl al-tāj wa-jawharat al-wahhāj* (*The Crown's Corona and the Glittering Gem*) in the field of Arabic linguistics, *al-Qisṭās al-mustaqīm fī ʿilm al-ḥadd wa-l-burhān al-qawīm* (*The Trustworthy Scales in the Science of Definition and the Sound Proof*) in logic, and *al-Qāmūs al-fāʾiḍ fī ʿilm al-farāʾiḍ* (*The Plentiful Lexicon in the Science of Inheritance*) in inheritance.[210] Upon his return to Jabal Miswar at an unknown date before 836/1432–1433, Ibn al-Murtaḍā authored the above-mentioned *al-Qamar al-nawwār* against leniency towards mystical practices.[211] None of the sources give specific information about Ibn al-Murtaḍā's literary productivity after he took over the fortress Ẓafīr in Hajja in 836/1432–1433.[212]

When comparing to the account of the chronology of Ibn al-Wazīr's works, the following must be noted: When Ibn al-Wazīr wrote his first known criticism of contemporary speculative theology in general and the proof of God's existence in particular, *al-Burhān al-qāṭiʿ*, in 801/1399, Ibn al-Murtaḍā would already have authored his great work on Hādawī-Zaydi *fiqh*,[213] *Kitāb al-Azhar*. It is also likely that his central work on speculative theology *Kitāb al-Qalāʾid* had already appeared. Although it is not clear how well known Ibn al-Murtaḍā's *al-Baḥr al-zakhkhār, Riyāḍat al-afhām* and *al-Durar al-farāʾid* would have been at the time when Ibn al-Wazīr wrote *al-ʿAwāṣim*, it is quite likely that he knew of Ibn al-Murtaḍā's positions. After all, he visited and questioned Ibn al-Murtaḍā during the latter's sojourn in Thulāʾ. Concerning the consolidation of the Zaydi *madhhab*, Ibn al-Murtaḍā's *Kitāb al-Azhar* would have been indicative enough of his views.

If *Tarjīḥ* was authored at a later stage of Ibn al-Wazīr's life, as the second part of the work indicates, Ibn al-Wazīr would have been familiar with all of Ibn al-Murtaḍā's theological positions at the time of writing. Ibn al-Murtaḍā was well known as a scholar of theology and law by then. Therefore, from a historical point of view, it is very likely that Ibn al-Wazīr reacted at least partly to Ibn al-Murtaḍā's doctrinal influence described in *Tarjīḥ*, as well as to his influence on the structure of legal authority manifest in the trend to consolidation of the Zaydi *madhhab*.

---

210 Al-Ḥasan b. Aḥmad, *Kanz al-ḥukamāʾ* 132.
211 Ibid., 133; cf. al-Kamālī, *al-Imām al-Mahdī* 115.
212 Al-Ḥasan b. Aḥmad, *Kanz al-ḥukamāʾ* 132.
213 Those within the Zaydiyya who claim to follow the legal doctrine of the founder of the first Zaydi state in Yemen, al-Hādī ilā l-ḥaqq, are called Hādawiyya.

2.3 *Intellectual Controversy between Ibn al-Wazīr and Ibn al-Murtaḍā*

In the rivalry between Ibn al-Murtaḍā and al-Manṣūr ʿAlī b. Muḥammad around the succession of Imam al-Nāṣir in the year 793/1390–1391, Ibn al-Wazīr was clearly opposed to Ibn al-Murtaḍā. According to Haykel, Ibn al-Wazīr's support for al-Manṣūr ʿAlī was motivated by political and family matters.[214] One such reason may have been that Ibn al-Wazīr endorsed the endeavor of al-Manṣūr's father, Imam al-Nāṣir, to disseminate the Sunni hadith compilations. The discussion of Ibn al-Wazīr's defense of Ibn al-Murtaḍa's rival (see chapter 2 section 6 below), although probably of a much later date (after 826/1423), will shed light on the initial reasons. What we do know is that the nature of the controversy between Ibn al-Wazīr and Ibn al-Murtaḍā was obviously doctrinal at a later stage. Remarks in Ibn al-Wazīr's writings point to Ibn al-Murtaḍā as a representative of a current within the Zaydiyya which Ibn al-Wazīr attempted to challenge.[215] A keen exchange of polemical poems between the two scholars provides evidence that their controversy went to the core of both scholars' beliefs. After Ibn al-Wazīr declared that the "principles of my religion are God's book, not the accidents" (*uṣūl dīnī kitāb Allāh lā l-ʿarāḍ*),[216] Ibn al-Murtaḍā replied by accusing Ibn al-Wazīr of opposing the principles of religion altogether:

O you who contradicts the principles of religion,
  and said: I have no purpose of knowing them,
that is the saying of one whose foot has slipped
  from the path of truth, or whose heart is diseased.[217]

Since Ibn al-Wazīr mentions this poetical dispute in his *al-ʿAwāṣim*, it must have taken place before 808/1406, the year when *al-ʿAwāṣim* was completed.[218] It is also clear that their controversy had doctrinal grounds when they met after Ibn al-Murtaḍā pretended to the imamate a second time. After his imprisonment, when Ibn al-Murtaḍā found refuge in Thulāʾ with Qadi Yūsuf, Ibn al-Wazīr visited him for some time and probed into Ibn al-Murtaḍā's view of the imamate

214 Cf. Haykel, ʿUlamāʾ ahl al-ḥadīth 5.

215 Ibn al-Wazīr, *Tarjīḥ* 8–9.

216 Ibid., 68; cf. Ibn al-Wazīr, *al-ʿAwāṣim* iii, 422. For an explanation of the verses, see ch. 2 sec. 27. and ch. 3 sec. 3.1. below.

217 The poem is quoted in al-Kamālī, *al-Imām al-Mahdī* 43. For what is either a similar poem or perhaps another part of the above poem and its theological context, see ch. 3 sec. 3.1. below.

218 Cf. Ibn al-Wazīr, *al-ʿAwāṣim* iii, 422, 441.

in 25 queries.[219] Apparently, Ibnal-Wazīr was neither convinced of nor satisfied with Ibn al-Murtaḍā replies.[220] In a similar incident with Ibn al-Murtaḍā's ally of the second uprising, Imam al-Hādī al-Mu'ayyad, Ibn al-Wazīr left his opponent after having investigated his arguments during a prolonged visit and joint journeys, with the following lines:

> If I desired, I could make the eyes cry by censuring,
> and ignite fire in the hearts by subtle issues.
> Yet, a desirer of God I have become,
> the concern with trifles has been divorced from me.[221]

Evidently, Ibn al-Wazīr was satisfied, because he had acquainted himself with Imam al-Hādī l-Mu'ayyad's positions and did not disagree on the core beliefs. There is no mention of any controversy between them afterwards.

Both incidents must have taken place sometime between 802/1399, when Ibn al-Murtaḍā came back to Thulā' after his second uprising, and 816/1413 when he went to Jabal Miswar. Aḥmad b. al-Wazīr writes that the theological controversy between Ibn al-Murtaḍā and Ibn al-Wazīr broadened and intensified after the latter's views had become more outspoken in the course of his controversy with his teacher Ibn Abī l-Qāsim, and after Ibn al-Wazīr had discovered that Ibn al-Murtaḍā was, or was becoming, a Zaydi with a strong Muʿtazili leaning.[222] That means it would have had to be after Ibn al-Wazīr had written *al-ʿAwāṣim* in 808/1406. However, I suggest that both scholars were well aware of each other's theological positions before that time, based on the assumption that Ibn al-Murtaḍā's views regarding theology and legal theory were already well established and partially expressed prior to his pretension to the imamate in 793/1390–1391. Furthermore, biographical and bibliographical sources tell us of the continuous exchange of letters between Ibn al-Wazīr and Ibn al-Murtaḍā throughout many years.[223] If al-Akwaʿ is correct in assuming that Ibn al-Murtaḍā wrote his *al-Qamar al-nawwār* against leniency towards Sufi

219 Aḥmad b. al-Wazīr, *Ta'rīkh Banī l-Wazīr* 31.

220 For Ibn al-Wazīr's response to Ibn al-Murtaḍā's unsatisfactory argumentation, see al-Akwaʿ (intr.), *al-ʿAwāṣim* i, 49.

221 Cf. Aḥmad b. al-Wazīr, *Ta'rīkh Banī l-Wazīr* 31; Ibn Abī l-Rijāl, *Maṭlaʿ al-budūr* iv, 147. According to the editor of *Ta'rīkh Banī l-Wazīr*, the second part of the quoted verse is found only in the margins of one copy of the family chronicles. However, Muḥammad b. ʿAbdallāh has recorded the entire poem; cf. Muḥammad b. ʿAbdallāh, *Tarjama* fs. 138b–139a.

222 Cf. Aḥmad b. al-Wazīr, *Ta'rīkh Banī l-Wazīr* 33–34.

223 Ibid., 34.

practices to refute Ibn al-Wazīr's *Qubūl al-bushrā*,[224] their controversy would still have been relevant between 816/1413 and 836/1432–1433 and it would have involved issues of legal theory.[225]

In Ibn al-Wazīr's fruitful controversy with his former teacher Ibn Abī l-Qāsim, on the other hand, the case was apparently different. Aḥmad b. al-Wazīr and Ibn Abī l-Rijāl tell us that Ibn al-Wazīr had Ibn al-Murtaḍā as a major comrade-in-arms in the struggle for the validity of *ijtihād* after the establishment of the legal schools. Ibn Abī l-Qāsim apparently rejected its validity, referring even to non-Zaydi scholars who had argued against the practice of *ijtihād* after the time of "Muḥammad b. Idrīs [al-Shāfiʿī]."[226] Both sources present Ibn al-Wazīr and Ibn al-Murtaḍā as working hand in hand on the question of *ijtihād*. Yet even if both spoke out for the possibility and significance of *ijtihād*, the grounds on which they did so reveal the epistemological differences which were also at the root of their doctrinal controversy, as we shall see in subsequent chapters.

The controversy between Ibn al-Wazīr and Ibn al-Murtaḍā ended through the mediation of one ascetic who was a friend to both, namely Muḥammad b. ʿAlī b. Ismāʿīl al-Kinānī (d. unknown).[227] This reconciliation probably took place late in their lives. In the glosses of one MS of the *Taʾrīkh Banī l-Wazīr*, the year 839/1435 is suggested. The remark is probably not on the original, as it appears in none of the manuscripts that Ibn Abī l-Rijāl used.[228] However, an entry recorded in a collection of writings by or related to Ibn al-Wazīr mentions the same year.[229] Beyond these indications, it is likely that their conflict would have lasted until a very late stage since Ibn al-Wazīr challenged ideas that would have been in line with what Ibn al-Murtaḍā held throughout all of his writings.

224 Cf. al-Akwaʿ (intr.), *al-ʿAwāṣim* i, 50.

225 As I shall discuss below, *Qubūl al-bushrā* treats leniency as a legal maxim in general, and in Zaydi law in particular. Legal maxims are located at the intersection of legal theory and law.

226 Ibid., 33; Ibn Abī l-Rijāl, *Maṭlaʿ al-budūr* iv, 148–149.

227 Apparently, al-Kinānī appealed to their common sense, placidity, kinship and lineage; cf. ibid., 34. Ibn Abī l-Rijāl suggests that al-Kinānī died before the beginning of the 9th/15th century. This is of course unlikely, given his mediative role at the end of the two scholars' lives; cf. Ibn Abī l-Rijāl, *Maṭlaʿ al-budūr* iii, 345–346; al-Shahārī, *Ṭabaqāt al-Zaydiyya* ii, 901.

228 Ibn Abī l-Rijāl, who took different MSS of *Taʾrīkh Banī l-Wazīr* as his sources, does not mention the date.

229 Cf. *Majmūʿ Muḥammad b. Ibrāhīm*, 511. The remark was apparently recorded by the grandson of al-Ḥadī al-Wazīr, Muḥammad b. ʿAbdallāh. However, the biography of Ibn al-Wazīr that Muḥammad b. ʿAbdallāh authored and that I used as a source does not contain these informations.

3 Conclusion

An account of Ibn al-Wazīr's life, education and personal controversies within his context reveals the picture of a man whose life, thought and work developed in the intellectual environment of Yemen and the Hejaz, where different schools of thought and law had a bearing on the political and social climate. While Ibn al-Wazīr participated in political decisions and contributed to the related doctrinal controversies to a certain degree, he actively sought to understand the argumentation of opponents, and retreated where the issues at stake were marginal. He endeavored to acknowledge the various theological and legal influences that were already present in his immediate Zaydi environment, and the more so in the broader context of Yemen and the Hejaz. However, this endeavor involved criticism of the state of scholarship in the Yemeni Zaydiyya of his day, which was wary of acknowledging the diversity. But his criticism apparently did not involve the origins of the Zaydiyya, nor was it expressed comprehensively until his views met with the broad indignation of his Zaydi contemporaries.

Ibn al-Wazīr often chose retreat from social activity and turned to ascetic and mystical forms of worship. He chose this path early on in his life and pursued it until his death, albeit to varying degrees of social activity, alternating scholarly productivity with phases of retreat.

One might expect that the content of Ibn al-Wazīr's studies were a decisive factor for the prominent position he took in the criticism of prevalent Muʿtazili manifestation of Zaydi thought in *kalām* and *uṣūl al-fiqh*. Yet if compared to the contents of the studies of his contemporary, Ibn al-Murtaḍā, who was influential in his time and took decisively Muʿtazili views, it becomes evident that the content of Ibn al-Wazīr's education was by no means extraordinary. Ibn al-Murtaḍā not only studied the same works to a large extent, but also received licenses for these same works from the same teachers. It is very likely that both scholars studied other works in common as well. The choice of what was mentioned is probably based on what was considered most important in the eyes of historiographers. This choice itself reflects the dominant teaching in the Zaydiyya of the time. It is, for example, noteworthy that none of the sources mentions theological works by the Muʿtazili school of Abū l-Ḥusayn al-Baṣrī, although the dissemination of Abū l-Ḥusayn al-Baṣrī's thought in Zaydi Yemen is documented prior to the 8th/14th century. In contrast, the Muʿtazili school of the Bahshamiyya is strongly represented in the recorded education of Ibn al-Wazīr and Ibn al-Murtaḍā.

Be that as it may, Ibn al-Wazīr was influenced by the study with non-Zaydi teachers in general, and of prophetic traditions in particular, in a way Ibn al-

Murtaḍā was not. The intensive extension of his knowledge in prophetic traditions seems not only to have quietened his soul, as he himself says,[230] but also to have furnished him with the sources he needed to cultivate and express the views that he had already developed earlier in his education and that had moved him to deepen his studies of the prophetic traditions in the first place.

Ibn al-Murtaḍā's case lies differently. Although he studied Sunni hadith and was familiar with theology and legal theory of other schools of thought and law, his scholarly and spiritual activity did not seem to have diverged from the contemporary mainstream. Even if Ibn al-Wazīr built upon ideas that were already present among the Zaydiyya of his day, many contemporaries strongly reacted to his conclusions. In contrast to that, Ibn al-Murtaḍā's pretension to the imamate was not rejected for doctrinal reasons. On the contrary, many lauded and preferred him because he represented the Zaydi ideal of a scholar imam, member of the *ahl al-bayt* and well-versed in the important disciplines of Zaydi learning. Ibn al-Murtaḍā's legal and theological works became a beacon of Zaydi learning in his time and much beyond. His teacher-student relationships, although not differing much from Ibn al-Wazīr's experience where input is concerned, are an argument for the claim that Ibn al-Murtaḍā stood in an established teaching tradition that referred back to authorities like the eponym of the Yemeni Zaydiyya al-Hādī ilā l-ḥaqq. Ibn al-Murtaḍā even enhanced this tradition by his own contributions.

In sum, Ibn al-Wazīr and Ibn al-Murtaḍā were exposed to the same intellectual, theological and legal diversity. Even though a degree of inclusivist approach to non-Zaydi texts and concepts cannot be denied in the life and work of Ibn al-Murtaḍā, this does not go beyond what is almost inevitable, according to Grünschloss, whenever one scholar has to grapple with the belief system of the religious (or confessional) other.[231] The factors for the diverging reactions to the intellectual, theological and legal diversity are not perfectly clear. Possibly, Ibn al-Wazīr spent more time in the intellectually more heterogenous Sanaa, whereas Ibn al-Murtaḍā had little personal contact with other schools of thought and law in the Zaydi *hijras* he occupied. Moreover, Ibn al-Murtaḍā apparently never travelled to Mecca to learn from any of the non-Zaydi scholars of the Hejaz. However, no external element in Ibn al-Wazīr's development renders him more prone to initiate or endorse a "Sunnisation" of the Zaydiyya than his contemporaries, since Sunni texts and teachers as well as alternatives to the Bahshami-Muʿtazili theology were already present in the Zaydi heartland.

---

230 Cf. Ibn al-Wazīr, *al-ʿAwāṣim* i, 201–203.

231 Grünschloss, *Der eigene und der fremde Glaube* 313.

CHAPTER 2

Ibn al-Wazīr's Works

This section provides a survey of Ibn al-Wazīr's works and serves as the basis for analysis of Ibn al-Wazīr's thought in the subsequent chapters. Although a number of Ibn al-Wazīr's writings have been discussed by mostly Muslim scholars, many others have been neglected beyond a mere mention. To my knowledge, an overview of his complete works has not been published yet. Therefore, this survey will also provide a basis for further research on Ibn al-Wazīr, for example in the important areas of Sufism and hadith studies, which I have only touched upon.

The description of each work commences with a brief explanation of external features, such as the date and number of copies along with their locations. Extant and accessed copies of each manuscript, as well as printed editions, if available, will be listed. After a short description of the structure, i.e. chapters and section topics, of each book, its subject will be discussed at slightly greater length.[1] In the frequent case of no apparent internal structure, I have attempted to order the writing into semantic fields without changing too much of the original. Where access to a given work was impossible, the description and analysis may be limited to the data given in catalogues and bibliographical sources.

The descriptions are arranged in alphabetical order. Bibliographical accounts like al-Ḥibshī's *Maṣādir* opted for an arrangement according to genre. However, many books, like *al-ʿAwāṣim*, incorporate more than one discipline, intertwining them in the line of argument for different topics. Others, like *al-Āyāt al-mubīnāt*, which is a list of Quranic verses with infrequent comments, may formally belong into the category of *ʿulūm al-Qurʾān*, as al-Ḥibshī suggested,[2] but the choice of verses as well as the content of the comments render the writing a highly theological one. Another option would have been to arrange Ibn al-Wazīr's works chronologically. Yet only very few writings are provided with a date of completion. Furthermore, the thick pattern of references and cross-references makes it extremely difficult to track a development, especially since they frequently refer to works which we know were completed at a later date. Therefore a chronological ordering could only be extremely ten-

1 The length of the descriptions is not proportional to the length of the original work. Rather, I attempted to summarize the contents as well as possible while yet preserving the main propositions and train of thought.

2 Cf. al-Ḥibshī, *Maṣādir* 28.

 | DOI:10.1163/9789004381117_004

tative. With regard to both genre and chronology, Ibn al-Wazīr's works elude classification. Beyond merely being a problem of research, this phenomenon is symptomatic of Ibn al-Wazīr's integrative thought and method. It is among Ibn al-Wazīr's original features that he fuses genres, and that he claims to have reached conceptions of the religious sciences that are consistent and timeless.

1 *Al-Amr bi-l-ʿuzla*

Ibn al-Wazīr's *al-Amr bi-l-ʿuzla fī ākhir al-zamān* (*The Command of Solitude at the End of Times*) is extant in several copies in the library of Sanaa's Grand Mosque as well as in a number of private libraries.[3] One version in the Grand Mosque as well as copies found in the Ambrosiana in Milan and the British Museum list varying titles: *Anīs al-akyās fī l-iʿtizāl ʿan al-nās* (*The Intimately Known of the Fine Points on Isolation from People*) or *ʿIddat al-akyās fī l-iʿtizal ʿan al-nās* (*A Number of Fine Points on Isolation from People*).[4] It is commonly listed under the titles belonging to mysticism (*taṣawwuf*). Al-Shawkānī does not mention a title for this "writing in praise of celibacy (*ʿuzba*) and solitude (*ʿuzla*)."[5]

No date of completion is indicated, neither in any of the consulted versions nor in the biblio- and biographical sources.[6] Yet a comment in the second chapter in the context of *ijtihād* clearly refers to *Kitāb al-Qawāʿid*, indicating that it was written sometime after the *Book of Principles*.[7] It is very likely that Ibn al-Wazīr wrote *al-Amr bi-l-ʿuzla* at a later stage of his life. Although none of the biographical sources tells us when exactly he went into isolation, the content of *al-Amr bi-l-ʿuzla* provides some indication. Some of the advantages of seclusion from people refer to the temptations of fame as well as to the nuisance of being sought for help and inquiry. Both suggest that Ibn al-Wazīr was already advanced in age when he wrote the work, unless he referred to other, senior scholars without mentioning it.

---

3 MS Sanaa, Dār al-Makhṭūṭāt, colls. 21 and 118, 698; cf. Ruqayḥī iii, 1301–1303, which gives the year 1281/1864–1865 for the second copy. The third copy is from 957/1550. Al-Ḥibshī and al-Wajīh also mention copies in the private libraries of Zabāra as well as Muḥammad al-Kibsī; cf. al-Ḥibshī, *Maṣādir* 332; al-Wajīh, *al-Aʿlām* 826.

4 Cf. Al-Ḥibshī, *Maṣādir* 332.

5 Al-Shawkānī, *al-Badr al-ṭāliʿ* ii, 91.

6 Ibn Abī l-Rijāl, like most other sources, simply mentions the title; cf. Ibn Abī l-Rijāl, *Maṭlaʿ al-budūr* iv, 151.

7 Ibn al-Wazīr, *al-Amr bi-l-ʿuzla* 307.

Of the two copies of the MS used here, one is relatively old, dating from 1035/1626, whereas the other copy was apparently completed in 1350/1932. The older one has a number of collation remarks and comments from later centuries (1223/1809) indicating that it was well read. Both copies were part of collections that mainly contained writings of Ibn al-Wazīr and thematically related authors.[8] *Al-Amr bi-l-ʿuzla* was edited by Ibrāhīm Bājis ʿAbd al-Majīd and printed at the Dār Ibn al-Qayyim in al-Dammām, Saudi Arabia, in 1412/1991.

Content

The treatise is divided into a prologue, an introduction with a long section discussing scriptural evidence, and three main chapters (*fuṣūl*). The benedictions in the short prologue give prominence to the clarifying nature of the Prophet Muḥammad's legal endeavor. According to him, this clarification consisted in explaining what benefits (*maṣāliḥ*) and causes of evil (*mafāsid*) particularly pertain to all times and all legally responsible individuals (*mukallafūn*). Further, the Prophet clarified the means to gain the benefits and to ward off harms. Ibn al-Wazīr's wording indicates the probable nature of finding those means. He emphasizes the necessity of prefering that which is more likely to lead to the desired end—the preponderant (*al-rājiḥ*).[9]

In the introduction, Ibn al-Wazīr informs the reader about the purpose of his brief treatise: factors which render the retreat into solitude (*ʿuzla*) preferable in certain times. He points out that these factors are in agreement with Quran and Sunna. Ibn al-Wazīr generally points to the one reason for choosing solitude: bringing one's heart into unity with God and His will.[10] He then lists a number of conditions for such a retreat, which can be summarized as the absence of any duties that an individual would violate if he went into solitude.

The next four pages are devoted to four Quranic narrations relating how Quranic figures spent a time in solitude (*ʿuzla*), followed by a number of prophetic reports about the same topic.[11] The main chapter follows these prophetic reports. Ibn al-Wazīr supports these narrations and reports with a series of

8 Both copies originate from the private library of Muḥammad al-Kibsī. Only the older one has pagination, although infrequent. I will henceforth quote from the older copy. Writings of other authors contained in the collection include for example Ṣāliḥ b. al-Mahdī al-Maqbalī's (d. 1108/1696) *al-ʿAlam al-shāmikh fī tafḍīl al-ḥaqq ʿalā l-abāʾ wa-l-mashāyikh* (*The Lofty Banner: Preferring the Truth over the Fathers and Chiefs*). For *al-ʿAlam al-shāmikh*, see al-Ḥibshī, *Maṣādir* 153.

9 Ibn al-Wazīr, *al-Amr bi-l-ʾuzla* 293.

10 Ibid., 293.

11 Ibid., 294–298.

Quranic verses, from which a number of lessons (*fawāʾid naẓariyya*) can be drawn. Ibn al-Wazīr arranges these in the form of seventeen aspects.[12]

The second chapter is devoted to distinguishing isolation as a means (*wasīla*), rather than an end (*maqṣad*) in itself.[13] Accordingly, the value of the period of isolation is determined by the way it is employed to arrive at its end: worshipping God.

The third chapter deals with the duty of *jihād*.[14] Q 9:36 and 41 are two Quranic verses portraying the duty of *jihād* as a general command for everyone and in every circumstance. The particular verse that Ibn al-Wazīr employs to qualify the general duty is Q 9:91, in which the weak, the sick and the poor are excluded from the obligation of *jihād*. The vital point of the chapter comes down to the fact that a preference of those who fight for God's cause as opposed to those who remain behind is only valid where those remaining behind have no excuse (*ʿudhr*) in the sense of weakness, sickness or lack of means.[15] Whereas *jihād* is a duty of the able, it is (only) a merit (*faḍīla*) in the eyes of the incapable.

The so-called principles which dominate Ibn al-Wazīr's reasoning are very general ones and are also applicable in the fields of theology and, especially, of legal theory. Where tension between demands, duties and principles exists, an individual must do what appears the most probable to him (*rājiḥ*). The ends determine the means. Whatever is likely to lead to harm, needs to be shunned, even though it may be good in itself. Furthermore, Ibn al-Wazīr directly refers to the texts of revelation and, without discussing opinions of other scholars, enhances the focus on spiritual and epistemological subjectivity.

2 *Al-ʿAwāṣim wa-l-qawāṣim*

Al-ʿAwāṣim wa-l-qawāṣim fī l-dhabb ʿan sunnat Abī l-Qāsim (*Defenders and Breaking [Arguments]: The Rebuffal of the Sunna of Abū l-Qāsim*) is Ibn al-Wazīr's most famous work.[16] He completed it in 808/1406. Yet many references

12 Ibid., 299–309.

13 Ibid., 309.

14 Ibid., 310.

15 Q 4:95 for example speaks of "those with an incapacity" (*ūlī l-ḍarar*) as excused; cf. Ibn al-Wazīr, *al-Amr bi-l-ʿuzla* 311. Citations from the Quran verses follow M.A.S. Abdel Haleem's translation.

16 See for example al-Akwā (intr.), *al-ʿAwāṣim* i; and al-Ḥarbī, *Ibn al-Wazīr wa-ārāʾuhu*, who identifies Ibn al-Wazīr almost entirely with his *ʿAwāṣim*. For Ibn Abī l-Rijāl, "he who studies it does not need to study anything else," because of the comprehensiveness with which it

to later works of his own as well as to other authors indicate that he continuously revised it. For example, Ibn al-Wazīr's last work, *Īthār al-ḥaqq*, which was completed in 837/1433–1434, is quoted in vol. 8, 383 of *al-ʿAwāṣim*.[17] The original consists of four volumes and is preserved in numerous complete as well as partial MSS in several libraries inside and outside of Yemen. The oldest extant copy is probably from 1083/1672–1673 and located in the Dār al-Makhṭūṭāt.[18] *Al-ʿAwāṣim* was edited by Shuʿayb Arnaʾūt and printed in 9 volumes for the first time in 1405/1985 and several times afterwards.

Al-ʿAwāṣim triggered the bulk of the criticism Ibn al-Wazīr received during his lifetime. This *magnum opus* incorporates and discusses the positions of various schools of thought and interweaves a large number of disciplines. Al-Ḥibshī, and after him Rizq Ḥajar, call it an "encyclopedia of *kalām*."[19] Al-Shawkānī counts it among the outstanding writings of Yemeni scholarship, "containing useful lessons in various sciences that cannot be found elsewhere."[20] Describing *al-ʿAwāṣim* as a "refutation of the Zaydiyya," as al-Shawkānī does, is nevertheless a far too restricted and biased view of the work, as we shall see.[21]

Content

The work is written in the polemical *ilzām*-style widespread in Muslim *kalām*: Ibn al-Wazīr's express aim is to refute his opponent based on his opponent's challenges.[22]

---

apparently treats a large range of topics; cf. Ibn Abī l-Rijāl, *Maṭlaʿ al-budūr* iv, 150. Biographies written on Ibn al-Wazīr's life and work frequently refer to him as *ṣāḥib al-ʿAwāṣim wa-l-qawāṣim*, especially outside of Yemen as in the case of Ṣadīq Ḥasan Khān; cf. Ṣadīq Ḥasan Khān, *al-Tāj al-mukallal* 332–339; al-Ḥarbī, *Ibn al-Wazīr wa-ārāʾuhu* 97.

17 Furthermore, Ibn al-Wazīr quotes Ibn Ḥajar's *Talkhīṣ al-ḥabīr* (ix, 278), *Fatḥ al-bārī* (viii, 341) as well as *Sharḥ al-nukhba* (ix, 127, 260), which were completed after 808/1406, 813/1411 and 818/1416 respectively. The details of references to later writings by other authors were gathered from the editor's introduction to *al-Rawḍ al-bāsim*; cf. al-ʿAmran (ed., intr.), *al-Rawḍ al-bāsim* 58–59.

18 Copies are documented for the Dār al-Makhṭūṭāt and Maktabat al-Awqāf in Ṣanaʿāʾ, as well as several private libraries. More copies can be found in the Maktabat Shaykh al-ʿAbīkan in Riyāḍ and the Maktabat Markaz al-baḥth al-ʿilmī in the University of Umm al-Qura; cf. Ruqayḥī, 688–690; al-Ḥarbī, *Ibn al-Wazīr wa-ārāʾuhu* 96; al-Ḥibshī, *Maṣādir* 134; al-Wajīh, *Aʿlām* 829.

19 Al-Ḥibshī, *Maṣādir* 134; Ḥajar, *Ibn al-Wazīr wa-manhajuhu* 17.

20 Al-Shawkānī, *al-Badr al-ṭāliʿ* ii, 91.

21 Ibid., ii, 82.

22 On *ilzām*, see Peters, *God's Created Speech* 74.

The first volume of the original MS corresponds to volumes 1 to 3 (to page 299) of the edited version. It commences with an appeal to turn to the prophetic Sunna as the main source of evidence in all religious questions. The virtues of the Prophet, the *ahl al-bayt* and the Prophet's companions are emphasized. The appraisal of the virtues of the Muslim community requires that those disagreeing in doctrinal issues apart from the five pillars may not be called unbelievers. Indeed, to charge a person with unbelief (*takfīr*) and strife between Muslims is prohibited, and the first part of this volume is a strong appeal to avoid strife along with methods for compliance with this appeal. This section sets the stage for most of Ibn al-Wazīr's further endeavor and indeed his entire agenda. Ibn al-Wazīr explains his concept of knowledge as a means of preserving unity. He refers to the Muslim community at the time of the Prophet, when faith was based on the knowledge that necessarily follows from the perception of his miracles and preternatural phenomena, as well as being informed about his attributes along with circumstantial evidence (*qarīna*) in his surroundings.[23] Ibn al-Wazīr emphasizes a view which regards that kind of knowledge which is apparent to all human beings as the basis of faith, supposedly free of doubt and confusion and manifest in the general tenets of Islam (*jumal*).[24] This view is what he calls the "middle between the two groups" (*al-wasaṭ bayn al-farīqayn*), which most likely refers to the extreme Muʿtazila and Ashʿariyya.[25]

In the next section, the question is whether the duty of independent legal interpretation (*ijtihād*) is still valid, or its performance is no longer within the abilities of believers. Ibn al-Wazīr discusses the arguments of both sides. On the one hand, there are those who negate the question and consider *ijtihād* beyond the abilities of believers after the establishment of the schools of law. This group is called *muʿassirūn*, i.e. "those who render *ijtihād* exceedingly difficult." On the other hand, there are those who consider the duty valid and "render *ijtihād* easily attainable," called *muyassirūn*. Ibn al-Wazīr clearly ranges

23 Ibn al-Wazīr, *al-ʿAwāṣim* i, 206–207.

24 Ibid., i, 211. *Jumal*—the things as a whole, broadly defined, understood integrally—is not to be confused with the concept of the general (*ʿāmm*, pl. *ʿumūm*) in legal methodology, which has the particular (*khāṣṣ*, pl. *khuṣūṣ*) as its counterpart. *Jumal* in this context pertains to knowledge and is not well defined; it refers to the external meanings of passages, the whole of a text, or a broad tenet.

25 This middle ground was actually held by another group of Muʿtazilis, namely Abū l-Qāsim al-Kaʿbī al-Balkhī and his followers. Al-Balkhī is an authority to whom Ibn al-Wazīr refers more than once in his attempt to champion Muʿtazili views that he could agree with. On Abū l-Qāsim al-Balkhī, see the doctoral thesis of Omari as well as its reworked version, Abū l-Qāsim al-Balkhī al-Kaʿbī's doctrine 39–57.

himself with the latter. His arguments treat the requirements of a *mujtahid*, as well as the implications of *taqlīd*.[26]

The second prominent controversial question in Volume I is whether reports of those who interpret the sources differently—or erroneously, according to the Zaydiyya—i.e. *ahl al-taʾwīl*, should be accepted and incorporated into the working material of a religious scholar. Again, Ibn al-Wazīr explains the distinction between those who reject transmission from the *ahl al-taʾwīl* on the one hand, and those for whom the scientific contributions of the *ahl al-taʾwīl* are valid on the other hand. Ibn al-Wazīr especially questions the claim of certainty for rejection, before he goes on to discuss the affirming party.[27] A consensus—among which influential Zaydi and Muʿtazili scholars of the earlier generation are particularly mentioned[28]—apparently accepts information from those whose wrong interpretation of the sources leads them to grave sin (*fussāq taʾwīl*). Extensive evidence from reason and revelation is given.

The matter is different concerning those whose wrong interpretations lead to more than grave sin, namely to unbelief (*kuffār taʾwīl*). Although the same arguments apply as in the case of *fussāq taʾwīl*, only five Zaydi authorities insist on consensus in the matter. Ibn al-Wazīr affirms the acceptance, yet leaves the matter in the realm of the merely probable where different positions coexist (*maḥall naẓar wa-ijtihād*).[29]

A specific accusation towards Ibn al-Wazīr discussed at the end of Volume I reveals how Ibn al-Wazīr's position in these questions of legal theory specifically challenged Zaydi doctrine: For the Zaydiyya, the Prophet's progeny theoretically occupied a privileged role in all matters of religious knowledge. Ibn al-Wazīr often seemed to prefer statements of those considered *fussāq taʾwīl* by the Zaydiyya to positions of the *ahl al-bayt*.[30] Was this a methodical preference, revealing his rejection of the Zaydiyya as a whole? Ibn al-Wazīr strongly denied this. Rather, his occasional preference for the information of scholars other than *ahl al-bayt* manifests the principle that "the specialists of each discipline should be preferred in their field" (*taqdīm ahl kull fann fī fannihim*).[31] This preference of specialists is manifest in Ibn al-Wazīr's strong reliance on the six main Sunni hadith compilations, especially those of al-Bukhārī and Muslim,

26 Cf. Muḥammad b. ʿAbdallāh, *Tarjama* f. 167a.

27 Cf. ibid., f. 167b.

28 Ibn al-Wazīr lists twelve Zaydi and Muʿtazili scholars in support; cf. Ibn al-Wazīr, *al-ʿAwāṣim* ii, 317–330.

29 Cf. ibid., ii, 402.

30 See for example ibid., iii, 21.

31 Ibid., ii, 429.

whose value he upholds in spite of the concession that not all of the traditions mentioned in their compilations are sound.[32]

In a last extensive section, Ibn al-Wazīr defends the traditionists (*ahl al-ḥadīth* or *muḥaddithūn*) against a number of accusations. Some of these refer to beliefs such as the assumption that the traditionists consider Muḥammad's companions infallible (*ʿiṣma*). Others justify the acceptance of particular transmitters, who would not be accepted by the Zaydiyya for doctrinal reasons. Many of these justifications are closely related to the position vis-à-vis the *ahl al-taʾwīl*.[33] Ibn al-Wazīr points out that although many members of the Zaydiyya and Muʿtazila reject the six Sunni hadith compilations, they still rely upon them heavily, either directly or by adopting them indirectly from others.[34]

The second volume of the original MS corresponds to vol. 3, 300 to vol. 5, 263 of al-Arnaʾūt's edition. Throughout the work, Ibn al-Wazīr defends central theological beliefs of the traditionists against accusations that would render them beyond the limits of sound and certain doctrine. Aḥmad b. Ḥanbal, for example, supposedly did not defend anthropomorphism (*al-tashbīh wa-l-tajsīm*).[35] Ibn al-Wazīr supports his theological reasoning with transmissions from a group of the *ahl al-bayt* who hold to the agreed-upon matters of general knowledge (*ahl al-jumal*).[36] Ibn al-Wazīr follows this with the reasoning of these so-called *ahl al-jumal* in the vital theological matters of God's unicity, prophethood, and the rest of the central doctrines[37] in contradisctinction to prominent Bahshami-Muʿtazili arguments.[38]

Ibn al-Wazīr further explains and defends the reasons for desisting from speculative theology by the example of Mālik b. Anas as well as other jurists and traditionists who rejected *kalām*.[39] One reason pertains to the question of whether or not *kalām* leads to the highest certainty about the existence of God.[40] Another reason refers to the validity of *kalām* as a necessary means to refute the philosophers and innovators.[41]

---

32 Ibid., iii, 65, 89.

33 Ibn al-Wazīr discusses 14 of 27 wrong assumptions in reference to the traditions; Ibn al-Wazīr, *al-ʿAwāṣim* iii, 142; cf. Muḥammad b. ʿAbdallāh, *Tarjama* f. 168a.

34 Ibid., iii, 299.

35 Cf. ibid., iii, 300.

36 Ibid., iii, 409.

37 Here again Ibn al-Wazīr discusses the poem which caused him much opposition; cf. ibid., iii, 422.

38 Ibid., iii, 441.

39 Ibid., iii, 453.

40 Ibid., iv, 33.

41 See for example ibid., iv, 58, 87.

After the defense of this first group of traditionists, Ibn al-Wazīr continues to discuss another group. Unlike the first group, this second group combines reasoning based on revelation with the rational sciences. Ibn Taymiyya would be an example for this group.[42] In this context, the *ahl al-ta'wīl* are discussed again, along with the arguments of different schools for or against *takfīr* of them. Ibn al-Wazīr discusses the question of whether the consensus of the *ahl al-bayt* can be used as the standard for judging *ahl al-ta'wīl*, referring to Zaydī authorities such as the imams al-Manṣūr bi-llāh ʿAbdallāh b. Ḥamza and al-Mu'ayyad bi-llāh Yaḥyā b. Ḥamza to support his point.[43]

The next controversial doctrine discussed in volume two is the createdness of the Quran.[44] Although Ibn al-Wazīr defends the uncreatedness of the Quran (*ʿijāz*), he alludes only to his own position. More importantly, he argues against *takfīr* in the controversies on this question, and supports his argument with quotations from early Zaydi and Muʿtazili authorities. Insistence on the *jumal* is repeatedly determined to be the way to avoid charges of unbelief. The forefathers or early generations (*salaf*) are an often-cited example for the support of such *jumal*. But the early Zaydi theologian al-Qāsim b. Ibrāhīm al-Rassī is also claimed for the defense of this view.[45]

A considerable part of the volume is dedicated to the question of whether or not God can be seen in the Hereafter (*mas'alat al-ru'ya*). In this case, it is the eponym of the Shafiʿi school that becomes the means by which the opponents of the speculative theologians are defended against the charge of anthropomorphism.[46] In two chapters, Ibn al-Wazīr ranges himself with those who affirm the possibility of seeing God in the Hereafter, without speculating on how (*bi-lā kayf*).[47] Again, he expends most of his efforts on defending the views of those who differ from the predominant Zaydi-Muʿtazili view, rather than elucidating his own.[48]

In the next section, Ibn al-Wazīr discusses a number of other doctrinal issues in which a misunderstanding of the Sunni and traditionists' approach apparently prevails. Ibn al-Wazīr touches upon compulsion (*jabr*) and goes into the

---

42 Ibid., iv, 119.

43 Ibid., iv, 196–197.

44 Ibid., iv, 342.

45 Ibid., iv, 396. Another example of a member of *ahl al-bayt* who insists on the restriction to the *jumal* is Ibn al-Wazīr's relative, Imam Yaḥyā b. Manṣūr b. al-ʿAfīf b. Mufaḍḍal (d. around 680/1281–1282) in his *Jumal al-islām wa-uṣūl dīn Muḥammad*; cf. ibid., iii, 411; Ibn al-Wazīr, *Tarjīḥ* 30.

46 Ibid., v, 5.

47 Cf. ibid., v, 74.

48 Ibid., v, 72, 74, 107, 208–238.

difference between hoping for God's mercy (*rajāʾ*) and deferment of judgement (*irjāʾ*), associated with school of the Murjiʾa.[49] Faith is also discussed in this context: Is the utterance of the creed a necessary condition of faith or only an independent duty, subsequent to internal conviction as fasting or praying are?[50] Other questions include the necessity of thankfulness towards God; the question of whether reason knows of the duty to be thankful and whether it is able to discern good and evil independently (*al-taḥsīn wa-l-taqbīḥ bi-l-ʿaql*); and the consensus of the Islamic community that no deficient attribute can be ascribed to the Divine.[51] However these questions are answered, the opponents are not charged with deliberate unbelief (*kufr taṣrīḥ*).

In the third and longest volume of *al-ʿAwāṣim*—corresponding to vol. 5, 264—vol. 8, 11 of the edition—Ibn al-Wazīr resumes his vindication of Sunni doctrine from the accusation of denying the human being any part in their actions and conduct.[52] In this volume, Ibn al-Wazīr's predominant method is to show that the doctrines of the Ashʿariyya and the Muʿtazila do not differ in essence. In other words, they do not disagree on the matters known by necessity, the *jumal*.[53]

The first central matter treated in this volume is the human being's free choice (*ikhtiyār*).[54] Ibn al-Wazīr employs Muʿtazili, Shiʿi and Sunni texts in order to uncover the error of the prevailing opinion about the Ashʿariyya and the resulting *takfīr* expressed by his opponent. The root of the question of *ikhtiyār* is determined by the various doctrines on the divine will (*irāda, mashīʾa*)[55] and the closely related issue of the divine decree (*al-qaḍāʾ wa-l-qadar*).[56] Although Ibn al-Wazīr insists that the divine decree is among those matters of *kalām* which human reason should not attempt to penetrate, he broadly discusses the different positions on the issue along with the respective proofs and backgrounds. Ibn al-Wazīr's major emphasis is on demonstrating that the Ashʿari insistence on the divine decree is not equal to championing the idea of absolute voluntarism. The understanding Ibn al-Wazīr develops in

49 Ibid., v, 255.
50 Ibid., v, 245.
51 Ibid., v, 258–259.
52 Ibid., v, 264.
53 Al-Akwaʿ says that if anyone wanted to know the two groups in full, he should read this volume, adding that one would have to be an extremely knowledgable scholar, since he himself did not succeed in giving order or structure to its contents; cf. al-Akwaʿ (intr.), *al-ʿAwāṣim* i, 94.
54 Ibid., v, 271.
55 Ibid., v, 272.
56 Gardet, al-Ḳaḍāʾ wa l-Ḳadar.

his discussion of related evidence and opinions would supposedly be agreeable to the Ashʿariyya as well as the Muʿtazila.

Subsequently, Ibn al-Wazīr argues that there is a broad consensus in the Muslim community to the effect that human beings' reward and punishment (*al-waʿd wa-l-waʿīd*) for their actions correspond to divine measures of justice. Of course, the Ashʿari idea of acquisition (*kasb*) must be discussed in this context. The various positions of Muʿtazili and Ashʿari groups in respect to *kasb* are put forth to show that the attitudes toward the idea differed in both schools. Apparently, the Muʿtazila did not entirely reject the idea as a whole.[57]

Another controversy which arises from the doctrine of the divine will is the question of whether or not God charges his creatures with doing what is impossible (*taklīf mā lā yuṭāq*). With few exceptions, Ibn al-Wazīr endeavors to discharge the Ashʿari doctrine of an allegation concluded from the Ashʿari view of divine voluntarism according to which God needs no motive (*dāʿī*) for actions. The points of contention between the Muʿtazila and the Ashʿariyya are especially drawn out in volume three of *al-ʿAwāṣim*, so that Ibn al-Wazīr's biographer writes: "Whoever desires to know the two schools entirely and belongs to those who are studious, knowledgeable and equitable should occupy himself with it."[58]

In volume four (vol. 8, 11—vol. 9, 404 in the edition) Ibn al-Wazīr again endeavors to dissociate the views held by the traditionists from a number of doctrines that amount to unbelief: anthropomorphism (*tajsīm*), the theory of coerced human actions (*jabr*) and the deferment of judgement (*irjāʾ*).[59] These doctrinal issues were used to explain why transmissions by the traditionists were rejected, at least by later Zaydiyya and Muʿtazila, exemplified in the challenges of Ibn al-Wazīr's teacher Ibn Abī l-Qāsim throughout the entire work. Yet another doctrine of particular interest in the Zaydi rejection of the transmissions of Sunni traditionists is extensively treated in the fourth volume of *al-ʿAwāṣim*: the theory of the imamate.[60] Ibn al-Wazīr illustrates with arguments, traditions and quotations of opinions that many traditionists are supposedly either close the Zaydiyya or the Muʿtazila on different aspects of the imamate. Those who apparently allow the imamate of an unjust ruler do so only out of necessity and only so long as the injustice does not exceed a particular level.[61] The level of injustice that determines whether or not a ruler should be endured

57 Cf. Ibn al-Wazīr, *al-ʿAwāṣim* vii, 56.
58 Muḥammad b. ʿAbdallāh, *Tarjama* f. 130b.
59 Cf. ibid., f. 131a. Ibn al-Wazīr takes up the same topic again at the end of volume three.
60 Ibn al-Wazīr, *al-ʿAwāṣim*, viii, 11.
61 Ibid., viii, 163.

according to the traditionists is closely connected to the performance of the five pillars of Islam.[62] Where the traditionists differ from the Zaydis, namely concerning genealogy, they do not differ from the Muʿtazila: neither restrict the imamate to the members of *ahl al-bayt*. In the same vein, Ibn al-Wazīr treats the matter of social intercourse with questionable rulers, which was yet another point of criticism towards the traditionists.[63]

Furthermore, Ibn al-Wazīr discusses the different kinds of interpretation (*taʾwīl*).[64] The context is once again the accusation that the traditionists hold views that anthropomorphize God. According to Ibn al-Wazīr, this false ascription is due to a misunderstanding of interpretation. A major distinction between the permitted kind of interpretation and the kind advised against pertains to the relation between the ambiguous (*mutashābih*) and the metaphorical (*majāz*). Ibn al-Wazīr discusses this relationship along with its epistemological implications for diverging doctrinal conclusions, to the effect that many interpretations may co-exist.[65]

In the last part of the fourth volume, Ibn al-Wazīr provides the reader with his exposition of a collection of traditions that are decisive for further doctrinal issues at the center of the controversy between the speculative theologians and the traditionists.[66] Significantly, Ibn al-Wazīr repeatedly states that he does not claim certainty (*qaṭʿ*) for his expositions, but rather allows for other interpretations.

The doctrinal issues subsequent to anthropomorphic statements about God are those of promise, threat and hope in God's goodness (*waʿd, waʿīd* and *rajāʾ*).[67] The last concept, i.e. *rajāʾ*, is much emphasized time and again. The certainty of God's ultimate goodness functions as a counterbalance to the many doctrinal matters that must be relinquished to the realm of conjecture.

Notably, Ibn al-Wazīr concludes *al-ʿAwāṣim* with a topic that is already salient in the introduction of the book. Although al-Ḥibshī's characterization of *al-ʿAwāṣim* as an "encyclopedia of *kalām*" registering multiple positions of numerous Islamic groups appears accurate,[68] there is one main theme that renders significance to the discussion of different topics: The larger part of doctrinal matters cannot be known for certain. Natural differences between

---

62 Ibid., viii, 168.
63 Ibid., viii, 203.
64 Ibid., viii, 262.
65 Ibid., viii, 264–325. See also al-Ṣubḥī, *al-Zaydiyya* 362–363.
66 Ibid., viii, 336.
67 Cf. Muḥammad b. ʿAbdallāh, *Tarjama* f. 131b.
68 Al-Ḥibshī, *Maṣādir*, 134.

created beings bear on the differences in understanding. An example of this are the different emphases placed on either the fear of God or the hope for His mercy. In one particular tradition, a quarrel between the angels is reported: Shall God have mercy on the murderer of one hundred men or shall he punish him? Neither of the two groups of angels occupying opposite positions was rebuked.[69] Ibn al-Wazīr relates this to opposing views among human beings. Consequently, charges of unbelief, rejection of transmissions and division of the Muslim community cannot be justified by reference to the discussed doctrines. A satisfaction with a general understanding of the broad tenets (*al-iktifāʾ bi-l-jumal*) keeps the community together. But, according to Ibn al-Wazīr, *al-iktifāʾ bi-l-jumal* is hard to maintain using any source other than the texts of the Quran and prophetic Sunna and necessary knowledge that is general. Methodologically, direct reference to these sources is especially endangered by the practice of *taqlīd*, not only in legal matters, but also in theological questions where individuals affiliate with scholars and schools who represent different doctrinal systems.

3 *Al-Āyāt al-mubīnāt*

The short title of Ibn al-Wazīr's treatise *The Clear Verses* gets a different twist when linked to the longer title: *al-Āyāt al-mubīnāt li-qawlihi taʿalā {yuḍill man yashāʾ wa-yahdī man yashāʾ}* (*The Verses That Elucidate the Divine Saying "He Leads Astray Whom He Wills and Guides Whom He Wills"*).[70] The verse in question is part of Q 16:93.[71] Al-Ḥibshī calls the treatise *al-Āyāt al-bayyināt* with a similar meaning. Al-Ḥarbī considers *al-Āyāt al-mubīnāt* clearer, yet has found the other title in the catalogues as well.[72] Ibn Abī l-Rijāl's information on the work confirms the first title.[73] Al-Ḥibshī mentions two separate works with the same title, but under different categories and in different locations.[74] He failed to either realize or to point out their identity. No indication as to the time of writing of the original can be found.

69 Ibn al-Wazīr, *al-ʿAwāṣim* ix, 376.
70 Ibn al-Wazīr, *al-Āyāt al-mubīnāt*, MS Sanaa, Maktabat Muḥammad al-Kibsī, coll. 89, 291.
71 The same phrase recurs in Q 14:4.
72 Al-Ḥarbī, *Ibn al-Wazīr wa-ārāʾuhu*, 88 (footnote 2).
73 Ibn Abī l-Rijāl, *Maṭlaʿ al-budūr* iv, 153.
74 One MS with the title *Āyāt al-bayyināt* is mentioned in the category of Quranic sciences (*ʿulūm al-Qurʾān*); cf. al-Ḥibshī, *Maṣādir* 28; another one is in the category of theology (*ʿilm al-kalām*); cf. ibid., 134. Al-Wajīh lists only one MS titled *al-Āyāt al-mubīnāt*, which is to be found in a collection of al-Kibsī's library; cf. al-Wajīh, *al-Aʿlām* 826.

Content

ʿAlī l-ʿAmrān, editor of the latest version of *al-Rawḍ al-bāsim*, ranks *al-Āyāt al-mubīnāt* among those "epistles and responses to the innovators among the Muʿtazila and the Ashʿariyya that can neither be counted, nor can that which they comprise be responded to."[75] As the longer title indicates, Ibn al-Wazīr's *al-Āyāt al-mubīnāt* is a list of Quranic verses that attest to Ibn al-Wazīr's understanding of Q 16:93.[76] The verse was of central importance in the disagreement between the Muʿtazila and the Ashʿariyya concerning predestination and free will. Although it is placed well in the category of theology, it contains none of the disputation style prevalent in many other theological writings by Ibn al-Wazīr. Briefly stating his position on the question of right guidance and leading astray, he immediately starts to list numerous Quranic verses to confirm his view. He begins with the second Sura and systematically works his way through the Quran from beginning to end. Ibn al-Wazīr finds support for his understanding of Q 16:93 in a number of verses from 43 other Suras. Explanations of the verses are rare and, if existent, very brief, hardly ever more than one line. It appears that Ibn al-Wazīr meant this piece of writing to be a source for a related discussion he conducted elsewhere.

The first statement of the work sets the stage for the subsequent understanding of the verse. Ibn al-Wazīr leaves no doubt that he is among those who defend both God's justice and human free will. Right guidance and leading astray must refer to a point in time after the human being has chosen his path. Reminiscent of one typical Muʿtazili explanation of the verse in question, Ibn al-Wazīr insists that the concept of misguidance signifies a punishment which occurs after sinning.[77] After this initial statement, Ibn al-Wazīr starts listing the Quranic verses. Similarly to the first statement, Ibn al-Wazīr interprets the "seal" which God "set on the heart of the unbelievers" according to Q 2:7 to signify punishment.[78] A little later, the verse about guidance and misguidance in Q 14:4 is commented upon briefly and clearly to the same effect, namely that the leading astray occurs "after it is deserved" (*baʿd al-istiḥqāq*).[79] Ibn al-Wazīr points out that Q 14:4 concludes with the divine name 'the All-Wise' (*al-ḥakīm*).

---

75 Al-ʿAmrān (ed., intr.), *al-Rawḍ al-bāsim* 35.

76 The manuscript used for the present study was copied in Shaʿbān 1035/May 1626. Ibn al-Wazīr, *al-Āyāt al-mubīnāt* 291, colophon. It is part of a collection from the library of Muḥammad al-Kibsī (p. 284 to p. 292).

77 Ibn al-Wazīr, *al-Āyāt al-mubīnāt* 284.

78 Ibid., 284.

79 Ibid., 285.

God's wisdom in the "leading astray" or the "right guidance" is that He does this for a particular purpose. Ibn al-Wazīr does not go into what this purpose signifies in detail.

Another example is taken from Q 39:57–59: An individual facing perdition laments his fate and asserts that he would have been among the righteous had he been guided by God. In response, there is an appeal to the signs which God did indeed send for guidance, but which were unheeded. For Ibn al-Wazīr, this response is clear evidence against undeserved leading astray of the unbelievers. Had God wanted to mislead or prevent guidance, so Ibn al-Wazīr's argument goes, He would have done so from the beginning.[80]

Besides a confirmation of the above-mentioned argument that there can be no initial "leading astray" before it is deserved, another aspect is of interest here. Ibn al-Wazīr insists that guidance is for all (*qad hadā l-jamīʿ*).[81] An example from Q 41:17 that talks about the tribe of Thamūd[82] explains Ibn al-Wazīr's stance: all mankind had the choice of following the guidance and were (or are) either rewarded or punished according to their choice. If, then, the verse that "He guides whom He wills" refers to a time before the choice, all would have been given guidance.

The last verse that apparently yields an argument for guidance is Q 100:11. God will be informed about (*khabīr*) the supposedly sinful secrets of the hearts on the Day of Judgement. Logically, this has consequences for the question of responsibility.[83]

In conclusion, this brief work is of great interest for the study of Ibn al-Wazīr's thought. It is a clear and brief expression of Ibn al-Wazīr's own position and method concerning a central issue in dispute between the two dominant theological schools, the Muʿtazila and the Ashʿariyya. Ibn al-Wazīr's method, the direct reference to Quranic verses, bears on the whole work's character as an expression of his own view.

4 *Āyāt al-aḥkām al-sharʿiyya*

Ibn al-Wazīr's *Collection of Quranic Verses Pertaining to Religious Law* received much attention in spite of its brevity. It is listed in numerous biographical

80 Ibn al-Wazīr, *al-Āyāt al-mubīnāt* 289.

81 For the corresponding concept of *luṭf*, see Leaman, Luṭf.

82 Thamūd is the name of an ancient Arab tribe, which disappeared before the rise of Islam and is presented as a godless people; cf. Shahid, Thamūd.

83 Ibn al-Wazīr, *al-Āyāt al-mubīnāt* 291.

and bibliographical sources. Another version of the title reads *Ḥaṣr āyāt al-aḥkām*. One or two copies of the MS are apparently to be found in the Dār al-Makhṭūṭāt.[84] According to al-Wajīh, the original is located in the Maktabat al-Awqāf.[85] The copy used for the present study dates from the year 1034/1625. It originates from a collection of the private library of al-Kibsī's, which is probably the same that al-Wajīh mentions. Muḥammad b. al-Ḥusayn b. al-Qāsim (d. 1067/1657)[86] used the work as a major source for his commentary on the legally significant verses of the Quran (*āyāt al-aḥkām*). His book is called *Muntahā l-marām fī sharḥ āyāt al-ahkām* (*The Utmost Desire: Explaining the Legal Verses*) and was edited and printed by the Dār al-yamaniyya in Sanaʿāʾ in 1986.

Content

Āyāt al-aḥkām is not a rich source of information on the thought of Ibn al-Wazīr. It is hardly more than a list of Quranic verses. In contrast to the other collections of Quranic verses concerning particular topics, Ibn al-Wazīr does not comment on a single one of the listed verses. His list commences with Surat al-Baqara (Q 2). Surat al-Kawthar (Q 108) provides the last legally applicable verse. There are, however, interesting insights into Ibn al-Wazīr's epistemology that can be indirectly gathered from the writing.

It is noteworthy, for example, that those verses which Ibn al-Wazīr lists as verses of rules (*āyāt al-aḥkām*) amount to only 236. Different ways of counting exist. Yet there is agreement among later jurists that there are 500 Quranic verses from which legal rules can be derived.[87] Ibn al-Wazīr lowers the number of required verses without weakening the importance of the Quran as a major source. This is emphasized especially in his *Tarjīḥ asālīb al-Qurʾ ān*. In *Āyāt al-aḥkām*, Ibn al-Wazīr refers to the *Tarjīḥ* with the aim of warding off the potential challenge that he would not take the Quran as a source of knowledge seriously enough.[88] On the contrary, according to Ibn al-Wazīr, the whole of the

84 The information provided as to location varies; cf. al-Ḥarbī, *Ibn al-Wazīr wa-ārāʾuhu*, 94; al-Ḥibshī, *Maṣādir*, 27–28; al-Wajīh, *al-Aʿlām*, 828. Al-Akwaʿ mentions *Āyāt al-aḥkam* without locating it; cf. al-Akwaʿ (intr.), *al-ʿAwāṣim* i, 74.

85 Cf. al-Wajīh, *al-Aʿlām* 828.

86 Al-Shawkānī, *al-Badr al-ṭāliʿ* suppl., 197.

87 Cf. Pakatchi and Harris, Āyāt al-aḥkām.

88 Ibn al-Wazīr does not mention his *Tarjīḥ* explicitly by title. Rather, he refers to a "separate book" which he "committed to the strengthening of the principle of taking the Qurʾān as the greatest foundation as well as the means of distinction in ambiguous issues"; cf. Ibn al-Wazīr, *Āyāt al-aḥkām* 267.

Quranic text needs to be known, as a foundation for the deduction of legal rules from particular verses.[89] But why then does he not require the same amount of verses others do? A concept ever present with Ibn Wazīr permeates the introductory sentences of *Āyāt al-aḥkām*. One must distinguish, he writes, between two kinds of verse: One the one hand, there are verses in which the connection between indicator and that indicated (*madlūl*) is so obvious that everyone agrees about it. On the other hand, there are verses upon which the scholars disagree as to whether they point to a particular matter of legal interest at all.[90] These need only be known by scholars who base their arguments on them. It is not certain whether they are of legal significance. Therefore, they are dispensable for the legal discourse of which all active legal interpreters must be aware. Unfortunately, Ibn al-Wazīr does not explain how he distinguishes between the two kinds of inference in the first and second sets of Quranic verses. Further, Ibn al-Wazīr writes that it is impossible to limit all the material of which one supposes or allows legal rules to be inferred.[91] In other words, where matters are binding, as the *āyāt al-aḥkām* in this case, one should restrict oneself to a minimum. This minimum is defined by the agreement that exists among the scholars.

5 *Al-Burhān al-qāṭiʿ fī ithbāt al-ṣāniʿ*

The full title is usually given as *al-Burhān al-qāṭiʿ fī ithbāt al-ṣāniʿ wa-jamīʿ mā jāʾat bihi l-sharāʾi* (*The Conclusive Proof of* [*the Existence of*] *the Creator and All That is Put Forth by the Revealed Law*). Yaḥyā b. al-Ḥusayn (d. 1099/1698) quotes the title of a book that might be identical with *al-Burhān al-qāṭiʿ* as *Kitāb al-Burhān fī uṣūl al-adyān* (*The Book of Proof: On the Principles of Religions*).[92] Ibn Abī l-Rijāl has *Kitāb al-Burhān al-qāṭiʿ fī maʿrifat al-ṣāniʿ* (*The Book of Conclusive Proof: On the Knowledge of the Creator*).[93] According to the bibliographical sources as well as the catalogues, the oldest copy of the MS exists in the Dār al-Makhṭūṭāt and was copied in the year 957/1550.[94] Neither the digitized copy received from the Dār al-Makhṭūṭāt in Sanaa, nor the one from the Muʾassasat

89 Ibn al-Wazīr, *Āyāt al-aḥkām* 267.
90 Ibn al-Wazīr, *Āyāt al-aḥkām* 267.
91 Ibid., 267.
92 Cf. al-Akwaʿ (intr.), *al-ʿAwāṣim* i, 74.
93 Ibn Abī l-Rijāl, *Maṭlaʿ al-budūr* iv, 151.
94 Cf. al-Ḥibshī, *Maṣādir* 135.

al-Imām Zayd were headed originally.[95] After the colophon of the preceding work, the scribes state that "now follows *al-Burhān al-qāṭiʿ*." The catalogue of the Dār al-Makhṭūṭāt mentions that the title is a reconstruction. However, it must have already been established by the time of al-Shawkānī, since he mentioned the above title in full.[96] It is possible that the title was not known to Yaḥyā b. al-Ḥusayn and hence he rendered it slightly differently. Ibn al-Wazīr, however, makes mention of *al-Burhān al-qāṭiʿ* along with references to its contents a few times in *al-ʿAwāṣim*.[97] *Al-Burhān al-qāṭiʿ* was edited and printed in 1349/1930–1931 in Cairo.

This is one of the rare cases in which a writing of Ibn al-Wazīr can be dated with a degree of certainty. The author mentions the day on which he completed his work as the fourth or fifth of Rajab 801, corresponding to the 13th or 14th of March 1399.[98] This completion date, being prior to the writing of Ibn al-Wazīr's *magnum opus*, is further confirmed by his detailed reference to the content of *al-Burhān al-qāṭiʿ* along with its title in more than one instance in *al-ʿAwāṣim*.

Content

Like most of Ibn al-Wazīr's writings, the content of *al-Burhān al-qāṭiʿ* is not divided into clearly defined chapters headed by titles and subtitles. The suggested arrangement of the content is based firstly on the accentuations given to the respective topics by the copier (or author) of the MS by means of the size and color of the letters.[99] Secondly, the content is arranged into units of meaning according to the connection the treated topics have in the discourse in general, and in Ibn al-Wazīr's works in particular. Ibn al-Wazīr remarks in *al-ʿAwāṣim* as well as in *al-Burhān al-qāṭiʿ* itself that the treatise is a reproduction and extension of Fakhr al-Dīn al-Rāzī's (d. 606/1209) *Kitāb al-Arbaʿīn fī uṣūl al-dīn* (*The Book of Forty: On the Principles of Religion*).[100] However, Ibn al-Wazīr

95 MS 1) Sanaa, Dār al-Makhṭūṭāt, coll. 3133, (1185/1745); MS 2) Sanaa, Muʾassasat al-Imām Zayd, CD coll. 1407, (1350/1931), originating from the private library of Muḥammad al-Kibsī.

96 Al-Shawkānī, *al-Badr al-ṭāliʿ* ii, 91.

97 Ibn al-Wazīr, *al-ʿAwāṣim* i, 207; iii, 436.

98 Ibn al-Wazīr, *al-Burhān al-qāṭiʿ*, MS 1) f. 114b; likewise in other versions of the MS. See also Ibn Abī l-Rijāl, *Maṭlaʿ al-budūr* iv, 151, and other biographical sources.

99 Size and color in one MS, and only size in another. I do not feel bound by the order and hierarchy of significance given to the various topics in the index of the edited version. Indeed, the arrangement under headings in that edition seems arbitrary and is apparently determined by the length of discussion of each item in *Burhān al-qāṭiʿ* as well as by personal interest. Both arrangements, mine and that of the edition, remain arbitrary to the same extent, as neither strictly follows the order of items and sub-items suggested by the size and colors of the letters in the MSS.

100 Ibn al-Wazīr, *al-ʿAwāṣim* i, 207; Ibn al-Wazīr, *Burhān al-qāṭiʿ* 18, 30.

only reproduces a few of the forty issues treated by al-Rāzī and imbues them with his own meaning.[101]

After a short prologue, Ibn al-Wazīr involves the reader in an ongoing argument, which can be divided into eight subsections. The prologue sets the stage for the subsequent argumentation. Ibn al-Wazīr emphasizes that a matter (be it a report, a claim, etc.) uncertain in itself necessarily becomes conclusive when corroborated by multitudinous pieces of evidence, even if these are likewise not conclusive in themselves. This corroboration generally happens by means of transmission, witness or sensual perception and is of the same value as uninterrupted transmission (*tawātur*).[102]

In the first subsection Ibn al-Wazīr illustrates this kind of corroboration on the example of the prophets. Contextual evidence (*qarīna*, pl. *qarāʾin*) in the form of the prophets' circumstances testifies to the truthfulness of their message. The truthfulness is not established by *tawātur* transmission. Some of Ibn al-Wazīr's examples for the evidence of the circumstances of different prophets are their unusual uprightness (*ʿadāla*), their abandoning of the path of their forefathers, their poverty, and the realization of their purposes (*ḥuṣūl aghrāḍihim*).[103]

In the second subsection, Ibn al-Wazīr explains the nature of prophetic miracles (*muʿjizāt*). They are divided into those perceived by the senses (*ḥissiyya*) and those determined to be miracles by reason (*ʿaqliyya*). The miracles concluded by perception are divided into three types: those outside the being (*khārij ʿan dhātihi*) of Muḥammad, those within him (*fī dhātihi*), and thirdly, the miraculous nature of his attributes.[104] The latter seems to be the most important for Ibn al-Wazīr, as he expands on it most and later uses it as a basis for another argument.[105]

In the third subsection, Ibn al-Wazīr summarizes the rational arguments for miracles as *qarāʾin* that are apparent in the circumstances of Muḥammad (*aḥwāl*). Muḥammad's truthfulness thereby attains the rank of necessary knowledge (*ḍarūrī*) in accordance with the reasoning of a number of prominent scholars.[106]

101 Cf. al-Rāzī, *al-Arbaʿīn*.

102 Ibn al-Wazīr, *al-Burhān al-qāṭiʿ* 7.

103 Ibn al-Wazīr lists a number of other arguments for the truthfulness of Muḥammad's prophethood, resulting from the consideration of his circumstances (*aḥwālihi*); cf. ibid., 8–17.

104 Ibid., 19.

105 Cf. ibid., 22–33.

106 Ibn al-Wazīr refers to Imam al-Mu'ayyad bi-llāh al-Hārūnī, Imam Yaḥyā b. Ḥamza, Ibn al-

In the fourth subsection, the same concept is illustrated in the case of a solitary report (*aḥad*).[107] A solitary report that is corroborated by contextual evidence (*qarāʾin*) leads to necessary knowledge. Ibn al-Wazīr identifies the individual conjectural report with a single conjectural and contextual unit of evidence (*qarīna*).

The fifth subsection is devoted specifically to miracles as a vital part of the verification of prophethood.[108] This is illustrated by the discussion of four rational arguments as well as four instances from revelation. Reason, according to Ibn al-Wazīr, would permit the authentication of prophethood without miracles, if the purpose (*qaṣd*) of prophecy was solely action in compliance with the prophecy. Action can be based on conjecture. Revelation, however, requires that the claimant's truthfulness be known in order for the purpose of prophecy to be accomplished. Therefore reason's conjecture needs corroboration by miracles. The authentication of prophecy without miracles would otherwise be invalid.

The sixth subsection discusses what reason and revelation say concerning the degree of certainty arrived at by *qarāʾin*.[109] After quoting Quranic verses and prophetic traditions, Ibn al-Wazīr basically repeats the line of argument mentioned above, namely that the corroborative effect of an accumulation of contextual evidence amounts to necessary knowledge, without determining the amount or number.

The subsection that follows is shaped by (hypothetical) questions as a prelude to explanations of Ibn al-Wazīr's views. Firstly, Ibn al-Wazīr explains the difference between conjecture and knowledge. Conjecture leaves room for doubt, whereas knowledge is signified by the absence of doubt. This distinction pertains to ordinary things (*ʿādiyyāt*). In other words, the distinction is obvious to all. There is either necessary knowledge or conjecture. This is the defining distinction whenever conjecture and knowledge occur.[110] An ensuing longer passage is devoted to the ways to know God. Most of these are effected by considering creation, the miracles and the circumstances of the prophets. This knowledge is informed by a *tawātur* of meaning.[111]

Ḥājib and Fakhr al-Dīn al-Rāzī, al-Nazzām, Imām al-Ḥaramayn al-Juwaynī and al-Ghazālī, while many others deny it; cf. ibid., 36.

107 Ibid., 36.

108 Ibid., 38–43.

109 Ibid., 43–49.

110 Ibid., 49.

111 Ibid., 49–51.

This is followed by a long eighth subsection arguing for the collective truthfulness of the prophets. In the eight arguments discussed in the section, Ibn al-Wazīr puts major emphasis on the corroborative conclusiveness of contextual evidence.[112] Furthermore, the arguments point at how the prophets arrived at and handed down knowledge of God and creation by means other than the speculative investigation suggested in the "four claims" (*al-daʿāwā l-arbaʿa*) of the theologians.[113]

The last passage resembles a conclusion of the eight subsections and contains an affirmation of philosophical speculation (*naẓar*) in the context of theological knowledge. However, *naẓar* with regard to the knowledge of God is redefined and applied to two areas: firstly, the wisdom and order that is apparent in created things and beings; secondly, the narratives of the prophets and their circumstances (*aḥwāl*).[114] Ibn al-Wazīr concludes with his notorious statement that probing too much into the nature of unclear matters leads to the denial of necessary matters on the basis of probabilities.

6 *Al-Ḥusām al-mashhūr*

Ibn al-Wazīr's *al-Ḥusām al-mashhūr fī l-dhabb ʿan al-imām al-Manṣūr* (*The Unsheathed Sword: Defense of Imam al-Manṣūr*) is, according to its subtitle, the completion (*takmīl*) of Qadi Jaʿfar b. ʿAbd al-Salām's (d. 753/1177–1178) *Wāḍiḥat al-manāhij wa-faḍīḥat al-Khawārij* (*Clear Paths and the Disgrace of the Khawārij*).[115] This additional title is probably the reason why al-Ḥibshī

112 Ibid., 52–57.

113 Ibid., 57–64.

114 Ibid., 66–76.

115 On Qadi Jaʿfar, see Ibn Abī l-Rijāl, *Maṭlaʿ al-budūr* i, 617–624; al-Shahārī, *Ṭabaqāt al-Zaydiyya* i, 273–278; al-Ḥibshī, *Maṣādir* 110–112; Madelung, Jaʿfar b. Abī Yaḥyā, Shams al-Dīn Abū 'l-Faḍl; Madelung, *Der Imām al-Qāsim* 204, 212–216; Thiele, *Propagating Muʿtazilism* 541; al-Wajīh, *Aʿlām* 278–282. The title under which Qadi Jaʿfar's work is known in the bibliographical sources varies slightly without change of meaning: *Ibāna l-manāhij fī nasīḥat al-Khawārij*; cf. al-Ḥibshī, *Maṣādir* 111; al-Wajīh, *Aʿlām* 280. Ibrāhīm al-Wazīr erroneously thought *Wāḍiḥat al-manāhij* to be a no longer extant writing of Ibn al-Wazīr's; cf. Ibrāhīm al-Wazīr (intr.), Author's biography, in *al-ʿAwāṣim* i, 103. Al-Ḥibshī lists two similar titles for Qadi Jaʿfar in the category of *kalām*, namely *Īḍāḥ al-minhaj fī fawāʾid al-miʿrāj* and *Ibānat al-manāhij fī naṣīḥat al-Khawārij*; cf. al-Ḥibshī, *Maṣādir* 110. I consulted neither of these MSS, yet from another version of the title of Ibn al-Wazīr's *al-Ḥusām al-mashhūr*, namely *al-Ḥusām al-mashhūr fī-l-radd ʿalā l-Khawārij*, I gather that *al-Ḥusām al-mashhūr* was a response to Qadi Jaʿfar's *Ibānat al-manāhij*. Ibn al-Wazīr mentions the title of the

thought the "completion of *Wāḍiḥat al-manāhij*" to be a separate work called *al-Ḥusām al-mashhūr fī l-radd ʿalā l-Khawārij* (*The Unsheathed Sword: A Refutation of the Khawārij*) and located it in the field of theology, whereas he inaccurately considered *al-Ḥusām al-mashhūr* to be a work on history.[116] Al-Ḥarbī claims to know that *al-Ḥusām al-mashhūr* was written in 805/1402–1403. This is questionable, not only because of the lack of evidence—he does not refer to his source for this information—but two other details also render this date unlikely: Firstly, both copies consulted for the present study contain a reference to *al-ʿAwāṣim*, which was written in 808/1406, on the last pages just before the colophon. In spite of the difficulty of using references from and to *al-ʿAwāṣim* as a source for chronology, there is another detail indicating that *al-Ḥusām al-mashhūr* was written long after *al-ʿAwāṣim*. In the prologue of *al-Ḥusām al-mashhūr*, Ibn al-Wazīr explains his motivation for writing his treatise: In the year 826/1423, a treatise reached the said imam, the main concern of which was the requirements for the imamate. Unfortunately, both copies have a lacuna where the name of the author of the letter should have appeared.[117] However, we can conclude that Ibn al-Wazīr could not have written his treatise in support of the imam in the year 805/1402–1403, but that it originates from after 826/1423 instead. Al-Ḥarbī's source is most likely to have been *Ghāyat al-amānī* which mentions a similar writing of Ibn al-Wazīr for that year. The date was probably assumed because it followed close on the year of the expulsion of the two imams, al-Hādī and al-Mahdī Ibn al-Murtaḍā, from Saʿda by Imam al-Manṣūr 802/1399.[118] The year 805/1402–1403 itself is marked in *Ghāyat al-amānī* by another extension of al-Manṣūr's imamate. Both events caused a new

book which he completed (*takmīl*) as being *Wāḍiḥat al-manāhij wa fāḍiḥat al-Khawārij*; cf. Ibn al-Wazīr, *al-Ḥusām al-mashhūr* MS 1), f. 103a.

116 Cf. Al-Ḥibshī, *Maṣādir*, 143 (*al-Ḥusām al-mashhūr fī l-radd ʿalā l-Khawārij*), 493 (*al-Ḥusām al-mashhūr fī-l-dhabb ʿan dawlat al-Manṣūr*). Al-Ḥibshī gives no details as to the location of the former work and dates the copying of the latter MS to the year 1158/1745, which corresponds to one of the MSS with the addition "completion of *Wāḍiḥat al-manāhij*" in the Dār al-Makhṭūṭāt in Sanaa. Cf. MS 1) Dār al-Makhṭūṭāt, coll. 3313, fs. 182a–191a, quote f. 182a. The foliation seems to have changed repeatedly because the *Fihris* gives varying numbers. There is also pagination in red which seems to be an even later addition. The second copy consulted for this study is another MS (MS 2) from Dār al-Makhṭūṭāt, coll. 3158, fs. 102a–113b. It must have been copied before 1343/1924–1925, since that is the date mentioned in the collation mark. The following quotes will refer to the earlier copy (MS 1) unless I explicitly refer to MS 2.

117 Ibn al-Wazīr, *al-Ḥusām al-mashhūr* f. 182b. This indicates that they were copied from the same source.

118 Yaḥyā b. al-Ḥusayn, *Ghāyat al-amānī* 554–557.

series of challenges to the legitimacy of al-Manṣūr's imamate. Ibn al-Wazīr's brother al-Hādī apparently authored writings in al-Manṣūr's defense in that year.[119] However, what al-Ḥarbī mentions is unlikely to be the present writing because of a remark in the glosses of MS (2) that Ibn al-Wazīr's refutation of the Kharijites is identical with his "defense of Imam al-Manṣūr."[120] Yet, Ibn al-Wazīr refers to a biography of Imam al-Manṣūr in *al-Ḥusām al-mashhūr*.[121] Since it is not mentioned in any of the catalogues, its identity with the historical defense cannot be verified.

Content

The content is best divided into two major parts. For Ibn al-Wazīr, the second and greater part is the conclusion of the first part. Folios 182b–185b are dedicated to the different kinds of *ijtihād* in general, and Imam al-Manṣūr's status as a *mujtahid* in particular. This is followed by part two, which occupies fs. 185b–191a and discusses what is required of an imam.

Part one is structured by a number of assumptions along with Ibn al-Wazīr's responses, which partly merge into three sub-chapters. It starts with the affirmation that knowledge (*ʿilm*) is required as a condition of the imamate. The question is whether or not Imam al-Manṣūr possesses the knowledge required of an imam. Ibn al-Wazīr begins by singling out "the true [kind of] knowledge" (*al-ʿilm al-ḥaqq*) as opposed to the kind of knowledge that should be derivative of the former. The former kind of knowledge is linked to the reflection of the certain textual sources, the Quran and Sunna, as well as of the conditions of the early generations without *taqlīd*.[122] The other kind of knowledge is that which is occupied first and foremost with derivative questions of substantive law. But speculative theology would also have to fall under this category. A significant distinction he makes is that between certain and uncertain knowledge: the first is that necessary knowledge of which important elements are the texts of revelation and the basic doctrines. The second is broader and could be used to signify a range of things like understanding, skill, information or scientific discipline. Furthermore, the existence of a considerably high degree of probability still allows one to speak of knowledge, and not just any kind of knowledge, but knowledge sufficient to make legal decisions and, indeed, to practice *ijtihād*. This definition of knowledge allows Ibn al-Wazīr to divide the degrees of *ijtihād*

119 Ibid., 559–560.

120 Ibn al-Wazīr, *al-Ḥusām al-mashhūr* MS 2) f. 113b.

121 Ibn al-Wazīr refers the reader to his biography of al-Manṣūr for a more detailed list of writings that the imam studied; cf. ibid., f. 185a.

122 Ibid., f. 183b.

and employ its lowest form. The lowest form of *ijtihād* is a hidden (*khafī*) and therefore conjectural matter which cannot be judged objectively other than from the material it uses as a source.[123]

Subsequently, the two criteria for the validity of al-Manṣūr's *ijtihād* are established. Firstly, his consultation of the major sources: since *ijtihād* and *taqlīd* belong to the realm of conjecture, it must be concluded that al-Manṣūr's inferences from the sources might very well be a form of *ijtihād*. Secondly, the source material he knows and consults: as Ibn al-Wazīr shows in a tentative list of sources imparted to Imam al-Manṣūr and authorized by *ijāzāt*, al-Manṣūr has mastered the Quran and prophetic Sunna to a considerable degree. The quality of his sources, therefore, determines the validity of his *ijtihād*. After discussing the definitions of knowledge advanced by a number of Zaydi, Imāmī and Muʿtazili scholars,[124] Ibn al-Wazīr proceeds to his conclusion, which is the prelude to the discussion of whether the imam must be a *mujtahid*. Firstly, no one can deny that al-Manṣūr is a *mujtahid* in the most basic meaning of the word. Secondly, even if al-Manṣūr's claim to the imamate were not valid if based on the absolute *ijtihād*, the other functions that he would be permitted to conduct according to the opinion of some would allow him to perform the role of an imam. Thirdly, the requirement of *ijtihād* for the imamate is uncertain.

Providing evidence for this last conclusion is the concern of the second part of the treatise. After an extensive discussion of the opinions of several scholars from *ahl al-bayt* in support of Ibn al-Wazīr's view, he goes on to argue from the Quran, supporting this by a number of traditions and opinions in one chapter.[125] This is followed by a chapter elucidating the meaning of tyrant (*jāʾir*): The primary sources are very clear about the moral status of an imam. He may not be unjust. By contrast, the sources are silent concerning the kind of

123 Ibid.

124 The scholars quoted as sources in his argument are an interesting choice: Next to Ibn Ḥājib (d. 646/1248) and his *Mukhtaṣar al-muntahā* (*Abridgement of the Utmost Limit*), al-ʿAllāma al-Ḥillī (d. 726/1325) as well as al-Muʾayyad bi-llāh al-Hārūnī figure greatly. The Imāmī al-Ḥillī scholar is quoted from his commentary on Ibn al-Ḥājib's *Mukhtaṣar al-muntahā*. One of the many feats of al-Ḥillī was the establishment of *ijtihād* as a major instrument of Imāmī jurisprudence. Al-Muʾayyad bi-llāh al-Hārūnī's *Ziyādāt* (*Additions*) and *al-Ifāda* (*The Benefit*) are both works mentioned repeatedly throughout Ibn al-Wazīr's writings. See for example ibid., f. 183a.

125 Ibn al-Wazīr repeatedly refers back to an instance from the succession struggle after Muḥammad's death where propositions emphasized both candidates' (i.e. Saʿd b. ʿUbāda by the *anṣār* and Abū Bakr by the *muhājirūn*) justice and leadship abilities rather than their outstanding knowledge. See for example ibid., fs. 186b–187b.

knowledge expected of an imam.[126] A final chapter discusses the origins of the discourse on the imamate and its requirements, drawn from two sources: texts of revelation and reason.[127]

The core argument in part two of *al-Ḥusām al-mashhūr* goes as follows: There is disagreement among the scholars within the Zaydiyya, as well as between the Zaydiyya and other schools, as to whether or not *ijtihād* is a requirement for the imamate. Furthermore, the primary sources are not explicit about it. This necessitates that the topic be detached from the realm of core doctrine. The purported consensus on the topic is only a tacit one, falling short of the certainty necessary to make a general rule. In contradistinction to the requirement of *ijtihād* for an imam, the Quran focuses on the necessity that an imam be a just and strong leader rather than an unjust ruler.

Drawing the line back to part I, the knowledge that is required of an imam—knowledge of the textual sources—is part of the *taklīf* of all Muslims. Accordingly, the role of the imam is open to all Muslims as far as the requirement of knowledge is concerned, because all Muslims have knowledge. Analogously, every *mukallaf* is able to practice some form of *ijtihād*, be he *muqallid* or not.[128] In line with this is Ibn al-Wazīr's understanding of rebellion (*khurūj*) against an unjust ruler. Those proposing it as well as those rejecting it are equally supported in their decision as long as they base their views on conjectural conclusions arrived at by investigation of the indicators.[129] To Ibn al-Wazīr it is no doctrinal issue where certain judgments are required.

7 *Al-Istiẓhār bi-l-dalīl al-samʿī fī ʿadam wuqūʿ al-ṭalāq al-bidʿī*

This response to a legal inquiry is also called *Bayān al-madhhab al-manṣūr fī ḥukm al-ṭalāq al-maḥẓūr* (*The Explanation of the Supported Opinion: The Case of the Prohibited Divorce*).[130] The first title, *The Exposition of the Scriptural Evidence for the Ineffectiveness of the Irregular Divorce*, is given as the first part of the name in the consulted manuscripts. It is uncertain from what year the writing dates. Only al-Wajīh mentions the writing as part of a collection in the

126 Ibid., f. 189b.

127 Ibid., f. 190a.

128 For the relation between the "correct *taqlīd*" (*al-taqlīd al-saḥīḥ*) and the "lowest levels of *ijtihād*" (*adnā marātib al-ijtihād*), see ibid., f. 191b.

129 Cf. ibid., f. 190a.

130 Al-Wajīh erroneously writes *maqṣūr* (restricted) instead of *manṣūr* (supported); cf. al-Wajīh, *al-Aʿlām* 829. All accessed MSS render the latter name. A "restricted opinion" would lack meaning in any case.

private library of Muḥammad b. Muḥammad al-Kibsī. One of the copies used for the study at hand is from that same library. It is uncertain, however, whether it is the same collection that al-Wajīh speaks of since the number of pages he counts (36) does not correspond to the number counted in the said copy (24, with 35 lines per page). The copies used for the present study are from the years 1032/1622 and 1350/1932 respectively.[131]

Content

Al-Istiẓhār was written as a response to an inquiry addressed to Ibn al-Wazīr. The inquirer apparently asked which of the two prevalent opinions concerning the irregular divorce (*ṭalāq al-bidʿa*) was the correct or rather the apparent (*ẓāhir*) one.[132] *Ṭalāq al-bidʿa* is the counterpart of *ṭalāq al-sunna*, the "regular divorce."[133] *Ṭalāq al-sunna* describes the repudiation expressed by a man towards his wife between her menses, i.e. during the time of purity (*ṭahāra*), under the condition that the couple had no sexual intercourse. Another condition of the regular divorce is that the husband utters the statement of repudiation three times, with intervals each as long as one cycle of menstruation and purity.[134] The question of *ṭalāq al-bidʿa* is whether or not the unilateral declaration of the husband is effective (*waqaʿa*) while the women is menstruating or between the menses if they have not abstained from sexual intercourse? Furthermore, is a divorce definite, if the husband utters the triple statement of repudiation all at once? Apparently both procedures concerning the validity of irregular divorce were in practice in the time of Ibn al-Wazīr.

Two aspects of Ibn al-Wazīr's response are worth mentioning here: Firstly, by his own account Ibn al-Wazīr wrote his response while he lived as a hermit in the Yemeni wilds. What arguments and quotes he mentions in his discussion must therefore have been provided from memory.[135] Secondly, Ibn al-Wazīr formulates his response as a basis for the legal activity of a student of the religious disciplines who has achieved the ability to weigh evidence, determine preponderance (*tarjīḥ*) and reach his own decision (*al-nāẓir al-mumayyiz*). Expressly, Ibn al-Wazīr does not intend to write a legal opinion (*fatwā*), which a supposed legal inquirer would be called to apply by *taqlīd*.[136]

---

131 Both copies were made available to me in digitized form by a Yemeni friend, whom I would like to thank for his support. The quotes will refer to the earlier copy (that of al-Kibsī's collection), mainly because it provides pagination.

132 Ibn al-Wazīr, *al-Istiẓhār* 107.

133 Cf. Mir-Hosseini, *Marriage on Trial* 36.

134 Cf. ibid., 37.

135 Ibn al-Wazīr, *al-Istiẓhār* 107.

136 Ibid., 107.

The structure of the writing is as follows: after presenting the two opposing sides of the question, Ibn al-Wazīr proceeds to list the arguments (*ḥujaj*) of those rejecting the effectuality of an irregular repudiation. Later, these are followed by the arguments of their opponents. The reason he provides for starting with this group is that their position is grounded on the apparent (*ẓāhir*) meaning of the texts. It is apparently defended by the majority of the Imāmiyya, the Nāṣiriyya[137] of the Caspian Zaydiyya, as well as most of the Ẓāhiriyya.[138] The first three of sixteen arguments in favor of this position are grounded in reason. Firstly, this kind of repudiation is prohibited for its own sake. The prohibition of actions which are prohibited in and of themselves is unrestricted (*muṭlaq*).[139] This determines the general rule. In other words, potential examples where *ṭalāq al-bidʿa* was effective describe exceptions. Secondly, divorce is a legal issue. The revealed law is not silent about it, wherefore rational understanding does not occupy center stage in the interpretation and application of the ensuing legal rule. The primary source text and its apparent meaning determine the outcome of the legal ruling to a much higher degree.[140] Thirdly, the presumption of continuity (*istiṣḥāb*) applies in the question of the irregular divorce. The validity of the latter is doubtful, whereas the soundness of the state of being married is certain. This certain matter continues to apply until evidence is provided that is stronger than what is rendered by mere possible, exceptional rulings.[141]

The remaining thirteen arguments consist of traditions of the Prophet Muḥammad and ʿAlī b. Abī Ṭālib transmitted by Sunni, Imami and Zaydi authorities. The apparent meaning in all of them amounts to the fact that an irregularly divorced woman is returned to her husband.[142] Whereas the first three rational arguments above determine why the apparent meaning of the text is decisive in the question of the irregular divorce, the remaining arguments provide this apparent meaning of the text itself.

---

137 The school of the Nāṣiriyya goes back to the prolific Imam al-Ḥasan b. ʿAlī al-Uṭrush al-Nāṣir lil-ḥaqq who was active in Gīlān and Daylamān. The rivaling Zaydi school at the Caspian Sea, the Qāsimiyya, goes back to Imam al-Qāsim b. Ibrāhīm. Al-Nāṣir's doctrinal views did not differ much from al-Qāsim's, although he was critical of Muʿtazili teachings. In positive law, al-Nāṣir was close to the Kufan Zaydi tradition as well as to the Imāmiyya. The irregular divorce is taken as a sign of this closeness. Like the Imāmiyya, the irrevocable triple repudiation of the wife is not considered lawful by al-Nāṣir and his followers; cf. Madelung, Zaydiyya.

138 Ibn al-Wazīr, *al-Istiẓhār* 107, 118; cf. Mir-Hosseini, *Marriage on Trial* 37.

139 Ibn al-Wazīr, *al-Istiẓhār* 107–110.

140 Ibid., 110–111.

141 Ibid., 111.

142 See for example ibid., 111, 113, 116, 117, 118.

The opposing side argues that a number of reasons demand that one turn away from the apparent meaning. Ibn al-Wazīr can recall eleven arguments from memory. Of these eleven arguments, the first sets the stage for the other ten: The Quranic verse prohibiting reunion of a couple after the third repudiation, i.e. Q 2:230, is taken to apply to irregular as well as regular divorce. The second argument discusses the meaning of return (*murājaʿa*) used in many traditions to describe the sending back of the wife to her husband.[143] The remaining nine arguments consist of traditions which go back to the Prophet Muḥammad or ʿAlī b. Abī Ṭālib.[144] Most of these traditions are rendered in al-Amīr al-Ḥusayn b. Badr al-Dīn's (d. 662/1264) standard work on Zaydi hadith, *Shifāʾ al-uwām* (*Quenching the Thirst*).[145] Rather than challenging the content, Ibn al-Wazīr queries the soundness and strength of these traditions formally.

The presentation of the two sides of the question is followed by four lessons (*fawāʾid*) that can be drawn from it. Ibn al-Wazīr frequently challenges the soundness of traditions that are used for arguments that conflict with his own opinion. Furthermore, he refers to the opinions of scholars of different Zaydi (Nāṣiriyya, Hādawiyya) and non-Zaydi affiliations (Imāmiyya, Ẓāhiriyya).[146]

Ibn al-Wazīr concludes with a quote of ʿUmar b. al-Khaṭṭāb, which is used to argue against the instant effectiveness of a thrice uttered repudiation: "Verily the people have begun to hasten in the matter in which they are required to observe respite."[147]

In conclusion, it can be said that Ibn al-Wazīr provided the different opinions along with their evidence. His own preference was in favor of the apparent meaning of the texts of revelation.

8 *Īthār al-ḥaqq ʿalā l-khalq*

Īthār al-ḥaqq is one of Ibn al-Wazīr's greatest works. Few who write about Ibn al-Wazīr fail to comment on it.[148] Some versions have an extended title,

143 Ibid., 118.

144 Ibid., 123–126.

145 For al-Amīr al-Ḥusayn and his *Shifāʾ al-uwām*, see al-Ḥibshī, *Maṣādir* 50; al-Wajīh, *Aʿlām* 390.

146 Cf. Ibn al-Wazīr, *al-Istiẓhār* 127–130. Ibn al-Murtaḍā's accounts of Zaydi positions do not always agree with Ibn al-Wazīr's, as for example concerning the recompense (*ʿiwaḍ*) paid to the husband by the wife; cf. Ibn al-Murtaḍā, *al-Baḥr al-zakhkhār* vii, 260–261.

147 Ibid., 130. See also *Sahīh Muslim*, The Book of Divorce, hadith 3491.

148 Ibn Abī al-Rijāl, for example, gives prominence to the discovery that Ibn al-Wazīr indeed

Īthār al-ḥaqq ʿalā l-khalq fī radd al-khilāfāt ilā l-madhhab al-ḥaqq min uṣūl al-tawḥīd (*Preferring the Truth to Man: Bringing Deviations Back to the Path of Truth Concerning the Principles of God's Unicity*).[149] Written in 837/1433–1434, *Īthār al-ḥaqq* was probably Ibn al-Wazīr's last work.[150] The references to *Īthār al-ḥaqq* in *al-ʿAwāṣim*[151] is, as mentioned repeatedly, more likely to be an indication of a continuing adjustment of *al-ʿAwāṣim* than of an early dating of *Īthār al-ḥaqq*. Numerous references to *Tarjīḥ asālīb al-Qurʾān* confirm that *Īthār* was written much later than 808/1406.[152] A number of copies of the MS are extent in the libraries belonging to the Grand Mosque in Sanaa as well as private libraries. The number of MSS as well as the span of years of completion—ranging from 846/1443 to 1212/1797–1798—show the work's popularity.[153] In 1318/1900–1901, *Īthār al-ḥaqq* was edited and printed in Cairo for the first time, with several later editions to follow. It was most recently printed at the *Dār al-kutub al-ʿilmiyya*, Beirut, in 1987. The copy consulted for the present study (see figure 2 below) is from the year 846/1443, only 9 years after the original was authored.[154]

Content

Īthār al-ḥaqq is Ibn al-Wazīr's most comprehensive work on theological matters. Similar to most of Ibn al-Wazīr's writings, structure and content are not very neatly arranged. Al-Shawkānī calls the style "queer" (*gharīb al-uslūb*), although he appreciates the content.[155] The tone is less polemic than in his other writings on theology and legal methodology. This probably reflects not only Ibn al-Wazīr's advanced age at the time of writing—he was around 62 by then—but also the work's express purpose, namely to bring together quarreling groups within the Islamic community[156] and to "prefer the truth before man,"

wrote introductions to many Suras, as Ibn al-Wazīr claims to have done; cf. Ibn Abī al-Rijāl, *Maṭlaʿ al-budūr* iv, 152–153.

149 Al-Ḥibshī lists the longer title, as does the first edition. The MS from the *Dār al-Makhṭūṭāt* used for the present study gives only the shorter version.

150 Muḥammad b. ʿAbdallāh, *Tarjama* f. 133b; al-Akwaʿ (intr.), *al-ʿAwāṣim* i, 73. However, the *Dīwān* contains poems that were written in 838/1435 and 839/1435–1436 and are thus younger than *Īthār al-ḥaqq*.

151 Ibn al-Wazīr, *al-ʿAwāṣim* viii, 142, (to *Īthār*, 425), 383 (to *Īthār*, 382).

152 Ibn al-Wazīr, *Īthār al-ḥaqq* i, 53, 91, 97, 100, 109, 156, 179.

153 Cf. *Fihris al-Makhṭūṭāt al-yamaniyya*, 259–260; al-Ḥibshī, *Maṣādir* 134–135; al-Wajīh, *Aʿlām* 826; Ahlwahrdt, *Verzeichnisse* ii, 579–580.

154 Ibn al-Wazīr, *Īthār al-ḥaqq*, MS Sanaa, Dār al-Makhṭūṭāt, no. 579. It encompasses 361 pages including the title page.

155 Al-Shawkānī, *al-Badr al-ṭāliʿ* ii, 91.

156 Ibn al-Wazīr, *Īthār al-ḥaqq*, 9.

FIGURE 2 Īthār al-ḥaqq ʿalā l-khalq fs. 74b–75a (Sanaa, Dār al-makhṭūṭāt)

i.e. ignore his school background, as the title indicates.[157] The content is divided into an introduction, prolegomena consisting of five chapters, a main text, and a brief epilogue. The original work consists of two volumes, with volume two starting apparently arbitrarily in the middle of the main text, after the discussion of the divine names and attributes.

In the lengthy introduction of the book, Ibn al-Wazīr explains the important elements of his undertaking. First, he distinguishes between two kinds of knowledge: the useful and the harmful. Examples from revelation, the traditions and authorities in *kalām* testify to his claim.[158] He discusses the means of obtaining knowledge, i.e. the original human disposition (*fiṭra*) and philosophical speculation (*naẓar*), and conducts a redefinition of *naẓar*.[159]

157 Ibid., 33.
158 Ibid., 10.
159 Cf. ibid., 15.

The first part of the introduction is permeated by two topics in a rather unsystematic manner. First are the seven major tenets that can be known by the uncorrupted *fiṭra*. If human nature has shifted away from its original state of completeness and is corrupted, it can be cured. This cure is what Ibn al-Wazīr intends to provide in his present work.[160] The seven tenets concern: 1. Things known by necessity (*al-ʿulūm al-ḍarūriyya*); 2. God's existence (*thubūt al-rabb*); 3. God's unicity; 4. God's completeness in His beautiful names (*kamāluhu bi-asmāʾihi l-ḥusnā*); 5. The existence of the prophecies as a whole (*thubūt al-nubūwāt*); 6. Belief in all the prophets without distinction; 7. Renunciation of innovations by addition or omission.[161] The other topic permeating the discussion is the preoccupation of some groups of theologians with the subtleties of the premises of doctrinal issues. In this context, the *fiṭra* is again contrasted with *naẓar* as regards the epistemological implications of both concepts.[162]

The second part of the introduction is an appeal to laymen and inquirers after knowledge.[163] In light of the reprehensibility of ignorance (*jahl*) taught by the Zaydi sect,[164] Ibn al-Wazīr defines the reprehensible kind of ignorance.[165] He explains why, in consequence, *ʿilm al-kalām* cannot be the means of finding a way out of that ignorance. This is what caused Ibn al-Wazīr to look for another way that leads to certainty (*yaqīn*),[166] one not involving the emulation of a *kalām* school (*taqlīd*).[167] Confidence in the ability of the *fiṭra* as well as fairness in the study of the scholars' arguments irrespective of school affiliation are two of the five important characteristics of those who want to gain knowledge.[168]

The next brief passage of the introduction contains a more detailed distinction between the knowledge required for religion and that knowledge which is not required.[169] Of the needful kinds of knowledge some require study, like

160 Ibid., 15, 26.

161 Ibid., 21.

162 Ibid., 17–18.

163 Ibid., 18.

164 Ibn al-Wazīr refers to al-Muʾayyad bi-llāh al-Hārūnī in his *al-Ziyādāt*; cf. ibid., 18.

165 Ibn al-Wazīr's definition of the reprehensible kind of ignorance is the exact negative of Abū l-Qāsim al-Balkhī's definition of knowledge (*ʿilm*); cf. Omari, The Theology of Abū al-Qāsim al-Balkhī 162.

166 Ibn al-Wazīr, *Īthār al-ḥaqq*, 20.

167 Ibid., 22–23.

168 Ibid., 27–28.

169 For those sciences which are not needed, yet not reprehensible, Ibn al-Wazīr refers to Muḥammad b. Ibrāhīm al-Anṣārī alias Ibn al-Afkānī's (d. 749/1348) list of 40 sciences in his *Irshād al-qāṣid ilā asnā l-maqāṣid* (*Guidance for the One Headed for the Most Sublime Goal*). Ibn al-Wazīr mentions a number of such permitted, yet nonessential sciences, like astrol-

the sciences of the traditions or exegesis. Whereas disagreement is natural in some, like substantive law or linguistics, disagreement is reprehensible in others, like the seven tenets in listed above. Accordingly, as repeatedly stated, these tenets along with their premises ought to be acknowledged rather than investigated.[170]

The chapters of the prolegomena are vaguely in line with the seven tenets, with chapter one treating the first tenet (i.e. knowledge), chapters two and three addressing the second tenet (i.e. God's existence), chapter four covering tenets three to six (i.e. God's unicity, prophecy and the prophets) and chapter five addressing tenet seven (i.e. innovations).

In the first chapter, Ibn al-Wazīr establishes that knowledge does exist (*ithbāt al-ʿulūm*). Two groups of people deny the existence of knowledge: some philosophers and Sufi monists (*Ittiḥādiyya*).[171] Ibn al-Wazīr attempts to demonstrate how even they employ some kinds of knowledge as a basis for action.[172] In this context, Ibn al-Wazīr discusses the virtues of beneficial knowledge and those who have it.[173]

The second chapter establishes the ways to the knowledge of God (*al-ṭuruq ilā llāh*). Whereas chapter two establishes this in general (*ʿalā sabīl al-ijmāl*), chapter three goes into detail.[174] Ibn al-Wazīr introduces three ways (*dalālāt*) that lead to the necessary knowledge of God.[175]

In chapter four, Ibn al-Wazīr presents God's unicity (*tawḥīd*) as necessary knowledge.[176] Those who affirm the existence of knowledge (*ʿulūm*) and divinity (*rubūbiyya*), discussed in previous chapters, disagree as to how the argument for *tawḥīd* can be established. Clearest among those is the proof of the prophecies (*ithbāt al-nubuwwāt*), and especially the uniqueness of Muḥam-

---

ogy, natural sciences, natural magic, chemistry, engineering, medicine and also the knowledge of the subtleties of theology (*ʿilm al-laṭīf*); cf. ibid., 34–35. For the the development of the term *ʿilm* from an indivisible abstract to *ʿilm* as the sum of all things known, divisible into separate *ʿulūm*, as for example the scientific disciplines, see Rosenthal, *Knowledge Triumphant* 41–45.

170 Ibn al-Wazīr, *Īthār al-ḥaqq* 36.

171 Ibn al-Wazīr mentions the extent of the monist "error" in order for his reader not to think that truth can only be that which is not denied by anyone. He denies that monists, going back to Muḥyī l-Dīn Muḥammad b. ʿAlī b. al-ʿArabī (d. 638/1240), are entitled to the name "Sufism"; cf. ibid., 37–39.

172 Ibid., 39; cf. Gutas, Certainty, Doubt, Error 284.

173 Ibn al-Wazīr, *Īthār al-ḥaqq* 44.

174 Ibid., 45.

175 Ibid., 45–54.

176 Ibid., 64.

mad's prophecy.[177] The characteristics of prophethood and its distinction from magic play a major role among the topics of this chapter.[178]

Chapter five leads to the main part of the writing. It is called "chapter on prudence towards the innovations of Muslims" and introduces[179] Ibn al-Wazīr's concept of innovations as "obscure matters of detail" (*masāʾil mubhama tafṣīliyya*) in the latter part of the chapter.[180] Said innovations are either additions to (*ziyāda*) or omission from (*naqṣ*) the Islamic core beliefs. Both kinds of innovation can have roots in reason as well as revelation. Indeed, mastery of both is one of two ways to avoid innovations.[181] The other way is to live as one who abstains from all partisanship (*tamadhhub*), emulation, school affiliation or fanaticism and relies solely on Quran and Sunna, "as if he had lived before the time of the advent of schools."[182]

Of the two kinds of innovations, Ibn al-Wazīr first addresses cases where an innovation was added to the Islamic core beliefs (*ziyādāt*). Ibn al-Wazīr repeats that rational reasons for innovations of that kind are mostly rooted in the intensive occupation with matters that the human mind cannot understand. Such innovators err in their distinction between the self-evident and the ambiguous issues (*al-muḥkam wa-l-mutashābih*) in revelation, as well as the known (*ʿilm*) and the conjectural (*ẓann*).[183] The confusion between the conjectural and the known goes back to the criteria of knowledge which Ibn al-Wazīr lists and discusses.[184]

Innovations based on omission (*naqṣ*) predominantly originate in the refusal to take the texts (*nuṣūṣ*) at their face value (*ẓawāhiruhā*) and often follow from the emulation of certain theologians or school doctrine.[185] Ibn al-Wazīr illustrates this issue based on the divine names, some of which are interpreted metaphorically by different schools in order to circumnavigate, for example, the reprehensible identification (*mumāthala*) of divine attributes with human ones.[186] The insufficiency of believing in metaphorical meanings also becomes

177 Cf. ibid., 76–83. See also the summary of *Tarjīḥ* below, ch. 2 sec. 27.

178 Ibn al-Wazīr refers to al-Muʾayyad bi-llāh's writings, most probably the imam's *Kitāb Ithbāt al-nubuwwa* (*The Book on Proofing Prophecy*), which, according to Ibn al-Wazīr, was shaped after al-Jāḥiẓ's book on prophecies; cf. Ibn al-Wazīr, *Īthār al-ḥaqq* 66.

179 Ibid., 84–157.

180 Ibid., 157–415.

181 Ibid., 122.

182 Ibid.

183 Ibid., 101–103.

184 Ibid., 117–120.

185 Ibid., 123.

186 Ibid., 89, 114–129.

evident in the reprehensibility of such an abstraction where prophethood or angels are concerned.[187]

Besides addition and omission, a third phenomenon is considered to be the root of innovations: the exercise of too much freedom in the employment of expressions in the exegesis (*tafsīr*) of the Quran and Sunna (*taṣarruf*).[188] Although *taṣarruf* is the result of the two former phenomena *ziyāda* and *naqṣ*, a separate discussion seems justified as *taṣarruf* in exegesis frequently leads to invalid *takfīr*.[189]

The last part of the general presentation of the obscure matters (*mubham*) is a schematic exposition. Ibn al-Wazīr distinguishes between the personal exegesis which goes back to narration (*riwāya*) by the companions and followers, on the one hand,[190] and seven kinds of scientific exegesis (*dirāya*), on the other hand.[191] Emphasis is put on explaining the controversial nature of some kinds of scientific exegesis and the epistemological implications.[192]

The rather extensive prolegomena are followed by an exposition of a number of controversial matters of detail (*al-masāʾil al-tafsīliyya al-mukhtalafa fīhā*) which were discussed in a general manner in the prolegomena. Concerning these, Ibn al-Wazīr seeks to establish the sound core.[193] The first concerns the divine names, the second God's wisdom, will and love as well as human actions. God's names figure first, because they are the only way by which God's essential self (*dhāt*) can be known, albeit in a general way.[194]

After establishing the central tenets and how they can be preserved from innovations in the first volume, the second volume of *Īthār al-ḥaqq* is an exposition of Ibn al-Wazīr's views on "divine wisdom, will, love, human actions and all that is related to it."[195] The related areas concern unbelief and grave sin (*al-kufr wa-l-fisq*), as well as the promise and the threat (*al-waʿd wa-l-waʿīd*).[196] Ibn

187 Ibid., 129–130.

188 Ibid., 133.

189 Ibid., 136–145. Frequently mentioned examples of *kalām* scholars who acknowledge human limitations in their doctrine are the Bagdhādī Muʿtazili Abū l-Qāsim al-Balkhī, the Shiʿi Muʿtazili Ibn Abī l-Ḥadīd and the Zaydi Muḥammad b. Manṣūr al-Murādī. The latter, for example, is quoted as reporting the prohibition on uttering *takfīr* in the foundations of religion (*uṣūl al-dīn*) for that very reason; cf. Ibn al-Wazīr, *Īthār al-ḥaqq* 138.

190 Ibid., 146–148.

191 Ibid., 149.

192 Ibid., 149–156.

193 Ibid., 157.

194 Ibid., 177–180.

195 Ibid., 181.

196 Ibid.

al-Wazīr commences with what he considers the foundation of all the following concepts, i.e. divine wisdom (*ḥikma*), and defines what he means by it.[197] In what follows, Ibn al-Wazīr discusses the implications for divine justice (*ʿadl*). The question is whether or not good and evil are objective entities and may thus be discerned by human reason (*al-taḥsīn wa-l-taqbīḥ al-ʿaqlī*). Ibn al-Wazīr relates his concept of divine wisdom to the way God makes good on his promise and his threat in a just, yet not always comprehensible way.[198]

In nine studies, Ibn al-Wazīr goes on to define and expound the divine will (*irāda, mashīʾa*).[199]

The theological problem is rooted in a supposed scriptural discrepancy between God's hatred of sin and the affirmation of His power to have everything that he intends executed. After affirming common ground between the schools, Ibn al-Wazīr's line of argument focuses on the idea that God's will is directed towards two different kinds of intentions (*murād*) manifest in connection with the command.[200]

The question of the origin of human actions (*afʿāl al-ʿabd*) is intricately interwoven with the question of divine will and consequently with divine wisdom. Again, Ibn al-Wazīr essentially claims a concurrence between Muʿtazili and Ashʿari positions. He himself is the representative of the middle ground, based on doctrine of the *salaf*.[201] After mentioning and discussing 14 different positions towards human actions—eight of the Muʿtazila, four of the Ashʿariyya and *ahl al-sunna* and two of the Jabriyya[202]—Ibn al-Wazīr establishes the limits of what can be known with certainty. He excludes from this the idea of compulsion (*jabr*)[203] and discusses agency in the context of motives (*dawāʿī*),[204] human choice[205] and his particular understanding of God's anticipation of and reaction to this choice (*taqdīr*).[206]

In contrast to what was generally held by the Muʿtazila and Zaydiyya, Ibn al-Wazīr argues that none of the *ahl al-sunna* and the Ashʿaris supported the view that human actions are coerced.[207] The same must be said about the obli-

197 Ibid., 181–183.
198 Ibid., 200–228.
199 Ibid., 228.
200 Ibid., 250–251.
201 Cf. ibid., 290.
202 Ibid., 282–285.
203 Ibid., 287–324.
204 Ibid., 287.
205 Ibid., 314–315.
206 Ibid., 312–313, 323–324; cf. Ibn al-Wazīr, *al-ʿAwāṣim* vii, 5–165.
207 Al-Ashʿarī (d. 324/935–936) is the only acknowledged exception. Ibn al-Wazīr admits this

gation to do the impossible (*taklīf mā lā yuṭāq*). Ibn al-Wazīr employs numerous Quranic verses and traditions and shows how the concept is contrary to the doctrine of divine wisdom.[208] The arguments ascribed to a number of Ashʿaris[209] can be exposed as void. Both elements of the term are discussed: the obligation (*taklīf*)[210] as well as the impossible (*mā lā yuṭāq*).[211] In conclusion, Ibn al-Wazīr insists that only that kind of "obligation to do the impossible" is inconceivable which necessitates severe punishment in case of omission (*tark*).[212] Ibn al-Wazīr's distinction between a term and its possible meanings allows him to harmonize the doctrine of different theological schools, in this case that of al-Ghazālī and Fakhr al-Dīn al-Rāzī on the one hand, and an undefined group of Muʿtazilis and Zaydiyya and *ahl al-bayt* on the other.[213]

In this context, Ibn al-Wazīr discusses the question of whether the children of unbelievers can be punished for the sins of their fathers. Negating this, Ibn al-Wazīr mentions a number of possible explanations for Quranic passages and traditions that imply the possibility of such punishment.[214] However, the more prevalent and stronger arguments refer back to divine wisdom.[215] Although the Muʿtazila explicitly reject the doctrine of substitutionary punishment, based on their doctrine of divine justice,[216] Ibn al-Wazīr bases his views mainly on the consensus of the *salaf*, which supposedly agreed on God's wisdom on the whole (*fī l-jumla*).[217]

The question of whether unaided human reason can discern good and evil (*al-taḥsīn wa-l-taqbīḥ al-ʿaqlī*) is also closely linked to divine wisdom. Indeed, those who deny this ability also argue against divine wisdom. The majority of the Ashʿari school is famous for this, although Ibn al-Wazīr notoriously ascribes the negation to only a few "extremists" (*ghulāt*) among the Ashʿariyya. As is often the case, Fakhr al-Dīn al-Rāzī is the instrument of Ibn al-Wazīr's harmonization between a moderate Ashʿari position and the genuinely Muʿtazili

in his quotation of Ibn al-Ḥājib, according to which al-Ashʿarī allowed that God obliges the believer to do the impossible; cf. Ibn al-Wazīr, *Īthār al-ḥaqq*., 324.

208 Ibid., 325, 339.

209 The scholar discussed here is first and foremost al-Ghazālī; cf. ibid., 325.

210 Ibid., 332–337. The discussion of al-Ghazālī's positions refers to *Iḥyāʾ ʿulūm al-dīn* (*Revival of the Religious Sciences*) and more explicitly to his *Iqtiṣād fī l-iʿtiqād* (*The Median in Belief*).

211 Ibid., 328–331.

212 Ibid., 333.

213 Cf. ibid., 325. See also Gimaret, Taklīf.

214 Ibn al-Wazīr, *Īthār al-ḥaqq*, 340, 342.

215 Ibid., 342.

216 Cf. Gimaret, Muʿtazila.

217 Ibn al-Wazīr, *Īthār al-ḥaqq* 339.

tenet of *al-taḥsīn al-ʿaqlī*. According to Ibn al-Wazīr, agreement exists that the human reason is able to recognize the moral value of a number of qualities and attributes. In his discussion, Ibn al-Wazīr focuses on the ability of the human *fiṭra* to discern good and evil, the role of revelation in completing that knowledge[218] and the part that God's wisdom plays in cases of seeming contradictions.[219]

Following the discussion of *al-taḥsīn wa-l-taqbīḥ*, Ibn al-Wazīr resumes the discussion of promise and threat (*al-waʿd wa-l-waʿīd*), emphasizing God's forgiveness (*ʿafw*), his mercy, and the good purposes.[220] It is the insistence on God's nature as expressed in the beautiful names, the good opinion of Him (*ḥusn al-ẓann*), that allows the believer to hope for God's forgiveness. Ibn al-Wazīr again refers to God's wisdom.[221]

Promise and threat is another occasion for Ibn al-Wazīr to defend an intermediary position between two extremes. These extremes are here represented in the Waʿīdiyya, i.e. the people of the threat (*waʿīd*), and the Murjiʾa, those who defend the deferment of judgment (*irjāʾ*).[222] In a sub-chapter, Ibn al-Wazīr argues against a recurring assumption which equates *irjāʾ* with *rajāʾ* (hope in God's mercy) and erroneously ranges the *ahl al-sunna* as a whole with the Murjiʾa.[223] Although Ibn al-Wazīr does not approve of the Murjiʾī doctrine, he still considers the Murjiʾa merely as innovators who are within the group of believers.[224]

The concept of *walāya* and *barāʾa*, literally the duty of association and dissociation, is a term discussed in this context. The underlying question is whether or not a Muslim can, or even must, declare a fellow Muslim an unbeliever under particular circumstances. Beyond the theological implications of *takfīr*, the acceptance of religious information was open to debate. In line with that concern, *Īthār al-ḥaqq* is another instance where Ibn al-Wazīr emphasizes the

218 Ibid., 343.

219 Ibid., 344.

220 Ibid., 358–361; likewise ibid., 185, 224, 346.

221 Ibid., 366–367; likewise ibid., 227.

222 For the Murjiʾa, see Madelung, Murjiʾa. The Waʿīdiyya refers predominantly to the Muʿtazila because of their requirement that God strictly deliver on His threats (and promises); cf. ʿAbd al-Jabbār, *al-Mughnī* xiv, 337.

223 Ibn al-Wazīr, *Īthār al-ḥaqq* 365–370.

224 A quote of Shaykh Mukhtār al-Muʿtazilī's *al-Mujtabā* (*The Chosen Among Many*) shows that not all early Muʿtazila excluded the Murjiʾa from the creed; cf. Ibn al-Wazīr, *Īthār al-ḥaqq* 366. See also Ibn al-Wazīr's reference to al-Ḥākim al-Jishumī's *Sharḥ ʿuyūn al-Masāʾil* (*The Explanation of the Question's Essences*), where the latter apparently argued in favor of *rajāʾ*; ibid., 366–367.

distinction between an explicit unbeliever (*kāfir ṣarīḥ*) and one whose beliefs are wrong because of an error in interpretation of the main sources (i.e. *kuffār taʾwīl, mutaʾawwilūn* (those who interpret) or *ahl al-taʾ wīl*), and positions, both with regard to association and dissociation. Ibn al-Wazīr affirms that the explicit unbelievers doubtlessly deserve the full range of the results of unbelief. The reason for this is the explicit textual command that they do. However, *mutaʾawwilūn* remain within the group of Muslims.[225]

Besides Ibn al-Wazīr's position, three other views incorporate the question of *kufr taʾwīl* into the scope of permissible disagreement.[226] However, to him, the apparent meaning (*ẓāhir*) of the broadly authenticated transmission (*mutawātir*) as a whole represents the only matter on which disagreement leads to *takfīr*.[227] There is no *takfīr* based on derived knowledge. What some term matters of certainty (*qawāṭiʿ*) not pertaining to necessary knowledge are no exception.[228] Exclusion based on an error in interpretation would not only lead to broad *takfīr*, but also stand in conflict with other important principles like *taklīf mā lā yuṭāq* or the principle that God intends religion to be easy.[229]

This also finds expression in the last subchapter on grave sin (*fisq*). In most cases, grave sins must explicitly be declared to be such in the *tawātur*-transmission. However, some schools include actions in the list of grave sins that are derived from the explicit command.[230] According to Ibn al-Wazīr, the grounds for acceptance of the *mutaʾawwilūn* is the clear distinction between the necessary (*ḍarūrī*) and the conjectural (*ẓannī*). The person in question erred in what he took to be conjectural. Other schools of thought, like the Muʿtazila and some Shiʿi groups, insist on a third separate category: knowledge which is certain (*qaṭʿ*), yet not necessary.[231] If one who commits a grave sin because of his wrong interpretation of certain yet not necessary matters (*qawāṭiʿ*) is equated with a grave sinner in the necessary matters, this results in his condemnation.[232] Ibn al-Wazīr, in turn, puts those who erred in the correct understanding of grave sins on a par with *mujtahids* in the conjectural matters of law. He mentions the corresponding cases where *mujtahids* come to con-

225 Ibid., 371–374.

226 Cf. ibid., 376. Ibn al-Wazīr refers to the *salaf*, early *ahl al-bayt*, as well as Muʿtazila. His source is the often cited *al-Jumla wa-l-ulfa* of the early Zaydi authority Muḥammad b. al-Manṣūr al-Murādī (d. 290/903).

227 Ibid., 377.

228 Ibid., 386.

229 Ibid., 393–400.

230 Cf. ibid., 408.

231 Ibid., 409.

232 Cf. ibid., 376–378, 407–409; Ibn al-Wazīr, *al-ʿAwāṣim* i, 84–86, 328–329.

flicting conclusions in matters of *ḥadd*-punishment. The *ḥudūd* are explicitly defined as a whole in the Quran. As such they are a matter of certainty. But there is disagreement as to their application. According to the position defended by Ibn al-Wazīr, the pardon in all such cases applies as long as the striving was the result of a mistaken but honest attempt to do right.[233]

Ibn al-Wazīr's brief epilogue of his *Īthār al-ḥaqq* clearly reflects the harmonizing approach dominant in the whole work. He finishes with a laudation of *ahl al-bayt* and the companions alike. Both groups are particularly singled out in the *tawātur* transmission as well as in consensus.[234] Beyond that, all scholars and laymen should be valued and honored "equally" to the aforementioned group. This reflects Ibn al-Wazīr's general approach and especially his idea of the source of true knowledge: no group is singled out by special access to knowledge. Although *ahl al-bayt* and companions enjoy a special status, each believer should respect every fellow believer irrespective of position. Ultimately, every Muslim must himself ascertain that his own positions are in line with the divine book and the prophetic Sunna. And every believer is responsible for the knowledge that he has by necessity.[235]

9 *Kitāb al-Qawāʿid*

The *Book of Principles* is referred to under various titles. The *Dār al-Makhṭūṭāt* in Sanaa owns one MS that is titled *Kitāb al-Qawāʿid.*[236] Al-Ḥarbī lists the copy under the name *al-Qawāʿid fī uṣūl al-fiqh* (*The Principles of Uṣūl al-Fiqh*), while al-Wajīh mentions *Kitāb* [*al-*]*Qawāʿid min qadīm* (*The Book of Long Standing Principles*) as well as *al-Qawāʿid fī l-ijtihād* (*The Principles of Ijtihād*).[237] Al-Ḥibshī knows only of the latter title.[238] In fact, *al-Qawāʿid fī l-ijtihād* is the additional title given in the colophon of one of the two abridgments of *Kitāb al-Qawāʿid,* likewise to be found in the *Dār al-Makhṭūṭāt.*[239] The copy that found its way to the Mu'assasat al-Imām Zayd b. ʿAlī is called *Qawāʿid min qadīm,* although their catalogue has *Qawāʿid man qad tamma jamaʿa* [*sic*]. This slightly obscure title is probably due to a repetition of the word "*jamaʿa*" (here: com-

233 Ibn al-Wazīr, *Īthār al-ḥaqq* 414.
234 Ibid., 416–417.
235 Ibid., 417.
236 MS Sanaa, Dār al-Makhṭūṭāt, coll. 3158.
237 Al-Ḥarbī, *Ibn al-Wazīr wa-ārā'uhu* 99; al-Wajīh, *Aʿlām,* 829.
238 Al-Ḥibshī, *Maṣādir,* 181.
239 MS Sanaa, Dār al-Makhṭūṭāt, colls. 1772, 3088.

FIGURE 3 Kitāb al-Qawāʿid (Qawāʿid min qadīm) 32 (Sanaa, Muʾassasat al-Imām Zayd b. ʿAlī al-thaqafiyya)

piled by) in the first and second line of the title (see figure 3 above). Additionally, the script of the title shows hardly any diacritical marks. This last MS seems to be the oldest extant copy (1204/1799).[240]

The high number of copies in libraries inside and outside Yemen bespeaks the interest in its subject, namely the structure of legal authority. Ibn al-Wazīr is most likely to have written the original before *Qubūl al-bushrā*, as the latter

240 This is the copy I will quote henceforth. It is paginated. A comparison with the copy from *Dār al-Makhṭūṭāt*, coll. 3158 showed that the content is identical apart from minor discrepancies. The colophon of the latter gives no indication of the date of completion.

has a reference to it. The context of this reference is the discussion of the transfer of adherence from one *madhhab* to another (*tanaqqul*). In *Qubūl al-bushrā*, the reference mentions that "a separate book" (*kitāb mufrad*) was written on the the topic. No title is mentioned, which would also explain the variety of titles supposedly given to the treatise at a later stage. It most likely refers to *Kitāb al-Qawāʿid* since, to my knowledge, Ibn al-Wazīr's discussion of this topic is much more extensive in his *Book of Principles* than it is in *Masāʾil arbaʿa* or anywhere else.

Content

Kitāb al-Qawāʿid is divided into a prologue followed by prolegomena and the five principles to which the title refers. In the prologue, Ibn al-Wazīr commences by lamenting intellectual corruption, and the spread of the practice of emulation (*taqlīd*) as a token of that corruption. Ibn al-Wazīr calls for a search for truth and certainty. Both can be arrived at in one of only two ways: firstly, by individual investigation; secondly, by maintaining a good opinion (*ḥusn al-ẓann*) of others engaged in the quest for understanding, irrespective of affiliation. From the outset, Ibn al-Wazīr clarifies what he considers to be the only source capable of rendering the "tranquility of the soul" (*sukūn al-nafs*) the seeker of knowledge aims at, namely the prophetic Sunna. In the remaining part of the prologue, Ibn al-Wazīr outlines his own history in the writing of the book. Wrongly accused of having abandoned the early imams and *ahl al-bayt*, he set out not to vindicate himself in the eyes of his accusers, but rather to clarify the principles and causes that provide the background of his teaching. His express purpose is to show that his views realize rather than violate the *madhhab* of the early imams and preserve the eager student from falling prey to intellectual degradation.[241]

In the prolegomena, Ibn al-Wazīr warns the pursuer of knowledge against five impediments to the understanding of clear proofs and obvious arguments. The first impediment describes someone who prejudges a book he is about to read, concluding from the name of the author that the latter is incapable of conveying any truthful or useful knowledge. The second impediment deals with an investigator who considers his own reason too weak to discern the sound and the false, even though his conscience and mind give him clear indications as to a particular conclusion. The third impediment discusses one who discards an entire book on the basis of having found a number of weak points in it. The fourth impediment is effective if a student or scholar rejects or accepts

241 Ibn al-Wazīr, *Kitāb al-Qawāʿid* 64.

a statement, ruling or evidence, because of the evaluation of the one who conveyed the statement to him. Fifth and last is the case of an investigator who is predetermined to consider something correct or false prior to a thorough investigation. In the context of these five impediments to thorough understanding, Ibn al-Wazīr embarks on the discussion of his five principles.

Principle I is concerned with the true meaning of following another (*al-mutābaʿa lil-ghayr*).[242] Ibn al-Wazīr makes a distinction between three kinds of following (*ittibāʿ*) the Prophet Muḥammad, *ahl al-bayt* or early imams in legal matters: following in a way of a formal outward imitation (*al-ittibāʿ fī l-ṣūra*), following with regard to the meaning of doctrines (*al-ittibāʿ fī l-maʿnā*) or following in form and in meaning (*fī l-ṣūra wa-l-maʿnā*). Whereas the first kind of following is invalid, the second kind is praiseworthy, while the third is likewise praiseworthy although not always possible. The first and objectionable kind of following is manifest in the practice of emulating the dead (*taqlīd al-mayyit*, pl. *amwāt*). Consequently, the greater part of the treatise deals with establishing the impermissibility of emulating dead scholars. Ibn al-Wazīr claims for himself the true and permissible kind of following: that which takes someone as an example in the widest sense.

The discussion is divided into four parts. The first and second explicitly deal with the prohibition of emulation of the dead. First, its impermissibility is argued for.[243] Then, the conditions of its restricted permissibility (according to some scholars) is discussed.[244] Part three reiterates the impermissibility of merely outward compliance (*al-ittibāʿ fī l-sūra*).[245] And part four anticipates principle II: the restraint put on a student able to discern legal qualifications to practice *taqlīd*.[246] This first principle takes predominance over the other four not only in terms of the space it occupies, but with regard to the variety of topics it contains. Furthermore, the ramifications of the "wrong kind of following" are discussed.

Principle II treats the restraint put on a student capable of discerning legal qualifications, i.e. the prohibition to practice *taqlīd* (*taqlīd al-ṭālib al-mumayyiz lā yajūz*) and the related concept of divisibility of *ijtihād* (*tajazzuʿ al-ijtihād*).[247] The separate discussion of the "discerning student" as well as a prolonged proof for the divisibility of *ijtihād* given under principle I render principle II rather

242 Ibid., 66.
243 Ibid., 67.
244 Ibid., 74.
245 Ibid., 80.
246 Ibid., 81.
247 Ibid., 131.

short. It is not even a page long and simply contains some autobiographical explanations of how Ibn al-Wazīr was forced to discover that *ijtihād* must be divisible.[248]

This brief report is immediately followed by principle III: the performance of a *sunna* or pious deed (*qurba*) is preferable to precaution (*iḥtiyāt, al-aḥwat*).[249] Ibn al-Wazīr emphasizes the duty to act according to anything considered *sunna*, i.e. that which is rewarded if performed, but not punished if omitted.[250] This emphasis is especially formulated in opposition to the tendency to act according to precaution. Along these lines Ibn al-Wazīr emphasizes the reward associated with *sunna*, as opposed to focusing on the avoidance of punishment associated with precaution. On the following pages, Ibn al-Wazīr discusses what he considers the recommendable kinds of precaution as well as what moderation in precaution would amount to.[251]

Principle IV provides a full discussion of the requirements (*shurūṭ*) for *ijtihād*.[252] His notion on the ease of *ijtihād* apparently contrasts with another prevalent notion, namely that *ijtihād* can no longer be performed.[253] The requirements discussed—but not yet agreed to—are knowledge of theology (*ʿilm al-kalām*), Quran, prophetic traditions, Arabic linguistics and legal methodology, as well as of stylistics and imagery (*ʿilm al-maʿānī wa-l-bayān*).

The fifth and last principle taken up in *Kitāb al-Qawāʿid* treats the prophetic traditions or, more precisely, the soundness of the Sunni *Ṣaḥīḥ* compilations.[254] However, in Ibn al-Wazīr's introduction to the last principle as well as in the issues he chose for discussion in the two sub-chapters of principle V, it becomes apparent that the defense of the Ṣaḥīḥan is the result of a number of epistemological conclusions rather than a statement in favor of a particular *madhhab*. Accordingly, the first subchapter discusses the practical legal implications of accepting religious information of *kuffār* and *fussāq taʾwīl*. The second subchapter extends the evidence advanced in the first and discusses the implicit acceptance of *kuffār* and *fussāq taʾwīl*. Some Zaydis reject transmissions of such *mutaʾawwilūn*, yet accept reports of unknown origin (*majhūl*) or interrupted transmission (*mursal*) from transmitters who accept *kuffār* and *fussāq taʾwīl*.[255] What is more, they themselves do not engage in the science neces-

248 Ibid.
249 Ibid.
250 Cf. Krawietz, *Hierarchie der Rechtsquellen* 115–116.
251 Ibn al-Wazīr, *Kitāb al-Qawāʿid* 132.
252 Ibid., 134.
253 Ibid.
254 Ibid., 141.
255 Ibid., 142. However, others accept *majhūl* traditions as well as *ahl al-taʾwīl*, as for example

sary for authenticating and ranking transmissions, in contrast to those whose transmissions they reject, namely the traditionists.[256] The last principle is an attempt by Ibn al-Wazīr to show his contemporaries that their evaluation of the traditionists is based on wrong assumptions. Furthermore, they neglect early Zaydi scholars who would still provide grounds for valid hadith criticism. After all, these early Zaydi scholars themselves were majorly involved in it—an issue in which Ibn al-Wazīr practices the endorsed kind of following.[257]

10 *Kitāb fī l-tafsīr*

The Book on Exegesis is one of Ibn al-Wazīr's writings of which nothing but the title seems to be extant.[258] Al-Wajīh suggests that *Kitāb al-tafsīr* may be identical to a certain *Kitāb fī tafsīr ʿulūm al-Qurʾān* (*Book on the Sciences of the Quran*). Otherwise, the title might refer to a *Kitāb al-tafsīr min al-kalām al-nabawī* (*Book on the Exegesis of the Words of the Prophet*) which is mentioned by Ibn Abī l-Rijāl as well as by al-Wajīh and al-Ḥibshī, but is apparently equally lost.[259] Only al-Ḥarbī claims to have found it,[260] but its supposed location in the Dār al-Makhṭūṭāt could not be verified. Al-Ḥibshī and al-Wajīh both mention two books on exegesis, referring them both back to Ibn Abī l-Rijāl. But Ibn Abī l-Rijāl only lists one book on exegesis, the *Exegesis of Words of the Prophet*.[261] It is very likely, therefore, that the two are identical. Ibn al-Wazīr himself only refers to his "prophetical exegesis" (*tafsīr nabawī*) in *Īthār al-ḥaqq*.[262] It is not certain whether he meant a separate writing, as Ibn Abī l-Rijāl suggests. Ibn al-Wazīr may have also referred to his exegesis of the Prophet's words on several occasions in *Īthār la-ḥaqq* and elsewhere.

al-faqīh ʿAbdallāh al-ʿAnsī (d. 667/1269), from whose *al-Durar al-manẓūma* Ibn al-Wazīr frequently quotes in this context.

256 Ibid., 146–147.

257 Ibn al-Wazīr refers to *al-ʿAwāṣim* for a more extensive discussion of the same point; cf. ibid., 148.

258 Al-Ḥibshī, *Maṣādir* 28; al-Wajīh, *Aʿlām* 829.

259 Ibn Abī l-Rijāl, *Maṭlaʿ al-budūr* iv, 151.

260 Al-Ḥarbī, *Ibn al-Wazīr wa-ārāʾuhu*, 92.

261 Cf. al-Akwaʿ (intr.), *al-ʿAwāṣim* i, 74; al-Ḥibshī, *Maṣādir* 28; al-Wajīh, *Aʿlām* 827.

262 Ibn al-Wazīr, *Īthār al-ḥaqq* 154.

11 *Majmaʿ al-ḥaqāʾiq wa-l-raqāʾiq fī mamādiḥ rabb al-khalāʾiq*

From a literary point of view, the collection of Ibn al-Wazīr's poems (*Dīwān*) falls into the category of fine literature, especially poetry (*adab*). However, topics of theology, personal piety and asceticism dominate the content of almost all poems contained in Ibn al-Wazīr's collection. The title *Majmaʿ al-ḥaqāʾiq wa-l-raqāʾiq fī mamādiḥ rabb al-khalāʾiq* (*Collection of Truths and Subtleties: The Praiseworthy Characteristics of the Lord of Created Beings*) referred to in many sources is most likely a later addition. Some sources list it simply as *Dīwān al-Murtaḍā* (*Poem Collection of the One* [*God*] *Approves of*) or *Dīwān shiʿrihi* (*Collection of His* [*Ibn al-Wazīr's*] *Poems*).[263] This indicates that *Majmaʿ al-ḥaqāʾiq* is only the first part of the entire collection of poems.[264] Ibn Abī l-Rijāl explicitly says that *Majmaʿ al-ḥaqāʾiq* is part of Ibn al-Wazīr's "extensive collection of poems."[265] No reference to the longer title can be found in any of Ibn al-Wazīr's writings. He himself refers to his *Collection of Poems and Qasīdas* (*Dīwān wa-qasāʾid*) at the beginning of the writing. However, the longer title sounds like a summary of the prologue. It is uncertain when the collection was compiled. The prologue indicates that Ibn al-Wazīr himself had compiling in mind.[266] An indicator of the time of writing is found elsewhere: a number of poems are introduced by a verse or two, informing the reader that the poem originated in a night vision and was expanded later. The dates of those visions are recorded. The latest vision in *Majmaʿ al-ḥaqāʾiq* dates from Muḥarram 834/September 1430.[267] The extended version records a last poem for the year 839/1435–1436, which was shortly before his death.[268]

At least two copies are found in the library of the Grand Mosque in Sanaa[269] as well as in several private libraries.[270] The two copies used for the present study are from Shawwāl 1035/June 1626 (MS 1) and Dhū l-Qaʿda 1247/April 1832 (MS 2) respectively. Both originate from private libraries.[271] While both copies

263 Al-Ḥibshī, *Maṣādir* 424.

264 Al-Akwaʿ lists both titles separately; cf. al-Akwaʿ (intr.) *al-ʿAwāṣim* i, 76. See also al-Akwaʿ, *Hijar al-ʿilm* 1375; al-Wajīh, *Aʿlām* 828.

265 Ibn Abī l-Rijāl, *Maṭlaʿ al-budūr* iv, 154.

266 Ibn al-Wazīr, *Majmaʿ al-ḥaqāʾiq* 373; Ibn al-Wazīr, *Dīwān* laq. 7r.

267 Ibn al-Wazīr, *Majmaʿ al-ḥaqāʾiq* 388; Ibn al-Wazīr, *Dīwān* laq. 39l.

268 Ibid., laq. 87r.

269 Cf. al-Wajīh, *Aʿlām* 282: Dār al-Makhṭūṭāt; al-Ḥibshī, *Maṣādir*, 424; al-Ḥarbī, *Ibn al-Wazīr wa-ārāʾuhu* 98.

270 Cf. al-Akwaʿ, *Hijar al-ʿilm* 1375.

271 *Majmaʿ al-ḥaqāʾiq* was digitized by the Muʾassasat al-Imām Zayd (CD 279); the digitization of the *Dīwān* is likely to originate from the same source.

mention the title *Majmaʿ al-ḥaqāʾiq* on the first page and are concluded with a colophon, the younger copy (MS 2) is more extensive than the compilation of MS 1 and has *Dīwān Muḥammad b. Ibrāhīm al-Wazīr* written on the cover. MS 1 extends over 31 pages with an average of 30 lines, whereas MS 2 counts 229 pages averaging 12 lines.[272] Be that as it may, the additional poems speak in favor of the above-mentioned remark that Ibn al-Wazīr's *Dīwān* is more extensive than *Majmaʿ al-ḥaqāʾiq*. For the sake of clarity, the younger copy (MS 2) will be called *Dīwān* henceforth.[273] The *Dīwān* is extensively commented on by Muḥammad b. Ismāʿīl al-Amīr al-Ṣanʿānī in his *Fatḥ al-khāliq fī sharḥ Majmaʿ al-ḥaqāʾiq wa-l-raqāʾiq fī mamādiḥ rabb al-khalāʾiq* (*The Victory of the Maker: A Commentary on A Collection of Truths and Subtleties: The Praiseworthy Characteristics of the Lord of Created Beings*).[274]

Content

The Yemeni theologian often mentioned along with Ibn al-Wazīr and his appeal to the prophetic traditions, i.e. Ibn al-Amīr al-Ṣanʿānī, considers *Majmaʿ al-ḥaqāʾiq* too extensive to respond to appropriately.[275] The broadness he speaks of allows for a bias in favor of some of the issues addressed. Such bias is discernible in some of the brief comments on the subject matter of the *Dīwān*. Al-Ḥarbī, for example, turns the poetry collection into a poetic call to the Sunna and the refutation of the innovators (*mubtadiʿūn*).[276] Although al-Ḥarbī thereby describes aspects of the collection accurately, other biographers seem to grasp its broadness more properly. Ibn Abī l-Rijāl, for example, mentions divine issues (*ilāhiyyāt*), intimate dialogues with God, fear and hope, trust in God and admonitions in prose as major themes of the work.[277] The *Dīwān* is probably most fittingly described by Ibn al-Amīr al-Ṣanʿānī, who calls it the "extract of his [Ibn

272 Next to the number of lines, the apparently great difference in extent is put into perspective by the fact that each verse in MS 1 incorporates two verses of MS 2.

273 A printed digest is supposed to exist, edited by Ismāʿīl Jirāfī and ʿAlī b. al-Muʾayyad and printed in Cairo 1961 with the title *Madāʾiḥ ilāhiyya* (*Panegyrical Poems on the Divine*). Yet, apart from an entry in the catalogue of the library of the Centre français d'archéologie et de sciences sociales de Sanaa (CEFAS), no attestation to the book could be found. In the CEFAS catalogue, Ibn al-Wazīr's younger relative, Ibrāhīm b. Muḥammad b. al-Wazīr, is erroneously mentioned as the author.

274 *Fatḥ al-khāliq* was completed in Ṣafar 1108/September 1696; cf. Ibn al-Amīr, *Fath al-khāliq* 322.

275 Ibn al-Amīr, *Fatḥ al-khāliq* 4.

276 al-Ḥarbī, *Ibn al-Wazīr wa-ārāʾuhu* 93.

277 Ibn Abī al-Rijāl, *Maṭlaʿ al-budūr* iv, 154; and similarly al-Ḥibshī, *Maṣādir* 424, and al-Shawkānī, *al-Badr al-ṭāliʿ* ii 91.

al-Wazīr's] two writings *al-ʿAwāṣim* and *Īthār*."[278] However, an introduction to the prologue and a tentative classification of the poems appear feasible.

After a prologue in praise of God and His Prophet, Ibn al-Wazīr goes on to explain his motivation for compiling his poetry. Along with quotations from Quran and Sunna he emphasizes the significant role of praising God in order to approach him (*min al-muqarribāt*). Realizing this significance caused Ibn al-Wazīr to write down the panegyrical poems granted (*wahaba*) to him. He especially points out those praises that manifest a perfect trust in God's plan (*tawakkul ʿalā llāh*) and expectancy of God's benevolence (*rajāʾ*), expressing an undefined but determined good opinion of God (*ḥusn al-ẓann*). He contrasts this with "some of his Muʿtazili contemporaries and neighbors who exaggerate in the disparagement of the strength of these two principles [i.e. *tawakkul* and *ḥusn al-ẓann*] of Islam and the path of the important scholars as well as the early generation of the Prophet's family,"[279] although they belong to the fundamentals of Islam as well as the different schools (*madhāhib*) including the Prophet's family (*ʿitra*). His poems are based on the multiple testimonies to *tawakkul* and *ḥusn al-ẓann* found in Quran and Sunna. Therefore, he can speak of proofs (*barāhīn*) contained in his poems, which, he hopes, will last beyond his death and benefit not only his own standing before God, but also the understanding of his fellow Muslims.[280]

The number of poems counted as far as *Majmaʿ al-ḥaqāʾiq* (MS 1) extends is approximately 85. The *Dīwān* contains another 42 poems.[281] The poems can be roughly classified into four groups. While many have no heading other than "[Ibn al-Wazīr] May God be pleased with him, said," the ones that do have a heading are not arranged according to content. Sometimes a poem without a title concludes with a thought which is then taken up by the following title and further elaborated in subsequent verses. Sometimes no immediate connection is noticeable. Some headings are repeated much later in the collection with a slight variation.

A chronological order is also not obvious. A number of poems refer to visions Ibn al-Wazīr had, all but one of which are dated. The first was written just after Ibn al-Wazīr had entered adulthood. Yet, the first vision listed in the *Majmaʿ al-ḥaqāʾiq* as well as the *Dīwān* is from the year 827/1423–1424;[282] a later one from

278 Ibn al-Amīr, *Fatḥ al-khāliq* 4.

279 Ibn al-Wazīr, *Majmaʿ al-ḥaqāʾiq* 374; Ibn al-Wazīr, *Dīwān* laq. 8l.

280 Ibn al-Wazīr, *Majmaʿ al-ḥaqāʾiq* 373; Ibn al-Wazīr, *Dīwān* laq. 8l.

281 The number is only tentative, because MS 1 and MS 2 do not always admit the same set of verses to be a separate poem.

282 Ibn al-Wazīr, *Majmaʿ al-ḥaqāʾiq* 385; Ibn al-Wazīr, *Dīwān* laq. 33r.

834/1430–1431,[283] and at the end, there is a poem recording the date Jumādā l-ākhira 832/March 1429.[284] The more extensive version, i.e the *Dīwān*, ends with a vision from Ramaḍān 838/April 1435,[285] listing the latest one chronologically (from 839/1435–1436) as the second but last.[286] Yet, generally speaking, the extended collection of the *Dīwān* does quote the later dates at a later point. Chronology therefore seems to have played some role.

As to the four groups, the most important group of poems treats those topics announced in the introduction: Fourteen poems alone are explicitly dedicated to the issue of trusting perfectly in God's plan (*tawakkul*) and entrusting one's affairs to him (*tafwīḍ*),[287] fourteen to hoping for His goodness and mercy (*rajāʾ*).[288] Similarly, numerous poems contain appeals to Ibn al-Wazīr's fellow Muslims to think well of God and people (*ḥusn al-ẓann*), to thank God (*shukr*), to implore Him (*taḍarruʿ, ṭalab, suʾāl*) or to dwell on God's pleasure (*riḍā*), his forgiveness (*ʿafw*) and wisdom (*ḥikma*). Ibn al-Wazīr often emphasizes the harmonizing effect of a focus on these divine characteristics in cases where the doctrines of different schools are in disagreement.[289]

Most of the poems are formulated as lessons for the reader and are testimonies of Ibn al-Wazīr's position. The very first poem is of this kind. The title and its extent is likely a major reason why researchers like al-Ḥarbī subsumed the entire poem collection under the category of calls to the prophetic Sunna and a refutation of innovators.[290] In these verses, Ibn al-Wazīr refers to five predominant theological innovations for which he finds no basis in Quran and Sunna, and contrasts them with God's superior wisdom and the proper human response. The subsequent pages are dedicated to a discussion of these innovations. The principles that Ibn al-Wazīr does find established in the textual sources are God's benevolent characteristics which are obvious in concepts like "the good is the first," "the purpose of the evil is merely the good" and "mercy precedes wrath."[291]

II. While some poems are phrased in an exhortative manner, addressing the reader, others are directly addressed to God in the second person. Of the poems

283 Ibn al-Wazīr, *Majmaʿ al-ḥaqāʾiq* 388; Ibn al-Wazīr, *Dīwān* laq. 39l.
284 Ibn al-Wazīr, *Majmaʿ al-ḥaqāʾiq* 392; Ibn al-Wazīr, *Dīwān* laq. 48l.
285 Ibn al-Wazīr, *Dīwān* laq. 119l.
286 Ibid., laq. 87r.
287 Cf. Ibn al-Wazīr, *Majmaʿ al-ḥaqāʾiq* 373, 378, 382, 383, 384, 385, 386, 387, 388, 389, 397, 399, 401, 403; Ibn al-Wazīr, *Dīwān* laqs. 8l, 17r, 25r, 26l, 30r, 32r, 36r, 37l, 39r, 42l, 62r, 66r, 70r, 75r.
288 Cf. Ibn al-Wazīr, *Majmaʿ al-ḥaqāʾiq* 378, 383, 386, 389, 396, 399; Ibn al-Wazīr, *Dīwān* 18r, 27l, 34r, 34l, 43l, 59r, 66r, 100r.
289 Cf. Ibn al-Wazīr, *Majmaʿ al-ḥaqāʾiq* 377; Ibn al-Wazīr, *Dīwān* laq. 14l.
290 Ibn al-Wazīr, *Majmaʿ al-ḥaqāʾiq* 374, Ibn al-Wazīr, *Dīwān* laq. 9r.
291 Ibn al-Wazīr, *Majmaʿ al-ḥaqāʾiq* 386; Ibn al-Wazīr, *Dīwān* laq. 34r.

that can be termed dialogues between Ibn al-Wazīr and God, many have no explicit title. The scholar addresses God in praise of His virtues, in benedictions for mercy and wisdom, or for help in need.[292] Ibn al-Wazīr emphasizes the limitations of human beings' knowledge and understanding of their affairs and appeals to God for forgiveness and favor in highly emotional terms.[293] The man who trusts God's plans perfectly (*tawakkul*) and thinks well of Him beyond his own understanding (*ḥusn al-ẓann*) is aware of his own limitations and seeks to encounter God in his need. On the other hand, if man claims an ability to make sense of the ambiguous, his strife to explain prompts him to think God incapable of undeserved kindness or purposeless in his actions.[294]

III. Another set of poems is framed by autobiographical information as to date, location and cause of composing. Usually, Ibn al-Wazīr saw (*ra'aytu*) the first few lines of the poems in a night vision, dream or mystical experience, and added to them later. Poems of this kind broach similar subjects as his other poems, namely the passionate love of God and the abandoning of the self to him.[295] In other instances, however, it was a particular thought or insight caused by an experience that triggered the writing.[296] Besides the poem that he had apparently written "just after reaching adulthood,"[297] the dates of other temporally identified poems range between 827/1414 and 839/1436, hence in the latter part of Ibn al-Wazīr's life.

IV. The last group, consisting of approximately ten poems, are responses to other scholars. In most cases, Ibn al-Wazīr first quotes the verses he wants to respond to, followed by his own verses. Two poems are dedicated to the refutation of the Abbasid poet Abū Nuwās (d. 814–815/1412–1413),[298] one to the poet Ibn Ṭabāṭabā l-ʿAlawī (d. 322/934)[299] and one to Ibn al-Wazīr's teacher Ibn Ẓahīra (d. 817/1414).[300] Beyond these refutations in *Majmaʿ al-ḥaqā'iq*, the *Dīwān* adds responses to poems of Abū Ṭayyib al-Mutanabbī (d. 354/965),[301]

---

292 See for example Ibn al-Wazīr, *Majmaʿ al-ḥaqā'iq* 394, Ibn al-Wazīr, *Dīwān* laq. 53r.

293 See for example Ibn al-Wazīr, *Majmaʿ al-ḥaqā'iq* 388.

294 Ibn al-Wazīr, *Majmaʿ al-ḥaqā'iq* 400; Ibn al-Wazīr, *Dīwān* laqs. 14r–l; cf. Ibn al-Amīr, *Fatḥ al-khāliq* 76–77.

295 Cf. Ibn al-Wazīr, *Majmaʿ al-ḥaqā'iq* 385, 388, 392, 394; Ibn al-Wazīr, *Dīwān* laqs., 32r, 33r, 39l, 48l, 53l, 76l, 80l, 89l, 121l.

296 Ibn al-Wazīr, *Majmaʿ al-ḥaqā'iq* 395; Ibn al-Wazīr, *Dīwān* laq. 56l; cf. Ibn al-Amīr, *Fatḥ al-khāliq* 221.

297 Ibn al-Wazīr, *Majmaʿ al-ḥaqā'iq* 395; Ibn al-Wazīr, *Dīwān* laq. 56l.

298 Ibn al-Wazīr, *Majmaʿ al-ḥaqā'iq* 385; Ibn al-Wazīr, *Dīwān* laqs. 31l–32r.

299 Ibn al-Wazīr, *Majmaʿ al-ḥaqā'iq* 394; Ibn al-Wazīr, *Dīwān* laq. 54l.

300 Ibn al-Wazīr, *Majmaʿ al-ḥaqā'iq* 401; Ibn al-Wazīr, *Dīwān* laq. 71r.

301 Ibn al-Wazīr, *Dīwān* laq. 88l.

the mystic Muḥyī l-Dīn Muḥammad b. al-ʿArabī (d. 638/1240),[302] the Muʿtazili Abū l-Qāsim Maḥmūd al-Zamakhsharī (d. 583/1144)[303] and the physician and philosopher Abū ʿAlī l-Ḥusayn b. Sīnā (d. 428/1037).[304] Less specific, yet significant for the understanding of the context of Ibn al-Wazīr's thought, are the responses to unspecified verses of "some strangers,"[305] "some Sufis,"[306] "some Muʿtazilis"[307] or simply questions directed towards him.[308] In these poems, Ibn al-Wazīr contrasts his theological positions with those of his contemporaries or of scholars widely read in his day. In one instance, Ibn al-Wazīr debates the mutual but largely false accusations between the theological schools. This is then followed by a poem expressing Ibn al-Wazīr's affirmation of all schools.[309]

The last 33 pages of the *Dīwān* contain refutations of some kind. Ibn al-Amīr does not really consider them as belonging to the "praises of the Divine" (*mamādiḥ ilāhiyya*).[310] Although written in verse, scholarly argumentation and the justification of Ibn al-Wazīr's position is much more apparent than in the preceding poems. The *Dīwān* concludes with a poem originating in a vision, in which Ibn al-Wazīr consolidates his desire and intention for continuous defense (*dhabb*) of the Prophet.[311]

12 *Manẓūma shiʿriyya fī uṣūl al-fiqh*

Ibn al-Wazīr's *Treatise in Verse on Legal Theory* is only mentioned in one of the biographical and bibliographical sources, namely al-Wajīh's *Aʿlām*.[312] Yet it con-

302 Ibn al-Wazīr, *Dīwān* laq. 103r.
303 Ibn al-Wazīr, *Dīwān* laq. 118r. Al-Zamakhsharī was a Muʿtazili who apparently refused to takes sides in the tension between the Bahshamiyya and Abū l-Ḥusayn al-Baṣrī's school. His poetry originated with al-Mutanabbī. On al-Zamakhsharī, see Madelung, al-Zamakhsharī; Schmidtke (ed., transl.), *A Muʿtazilite Creed of az-Zamakhshari*.
304 Ibn al-Wazīr, *Dīwān* laq. 119l.
305 Ibn al-Wazīr, *Majmaʿ al-ḥaqāʾiq* 376; Ibn al-Wazīr, *Dīwān* laq. 14r; cf. Ibn al-Amīr, *Fatḥ al-khāliq* 72.
306 Ibn al-Wazīr, *Majmaʿ al-ḥaqāʾiq* 377; Ibn al-Wazīr, *Dīwān* laqs. 15l–16r.
307 Ibn al-Wazīr, *Majmaʿ al-ḥaqāʾiq* 400; Ibn al-Wazīr, *Dīwān* laq. 67l.
308 An example is Ibn al-Wazīr's response to students who wanted to study logic with him; cf. ibid., laq. 92r.
309 Ibn al-Wazīr, *Majmaʿ al-ḥaqāʾiq* 400; Ibn al-Wazīr, *Dīwān* laq. 67l; cf. Ibn al-Amīr, *Fatḥ al-khāliq* 243–244. For related topics, see also *Majmaʿ al-ḥaqāʾiq* 374–376; Ibn al-Wazīr, *Dīwān* laqs. 9r–14l.
310 Cf. Ibn al-Amīr, *Fatḥ al-khāliq* 315.
311 Ibn al-Wazīr, *Dīwān* laqs. 121l–122r.
312 Al-Wajīh, *Aʿlām* 829.

tains valuable information on the thought of Ibn al-Wazīr as it is probably his most concise and systematic writing on all the classical questions of Islamic legal theory. However, the authorship is not entirely certain, as the *Manẓūma* appears in only one relatively recent collection.[313] It is not mentioned elsewhere and has no explicit internal reference, other than a remark in the margins according to which it was written by "the great scholar and pride of the Banū l-Wazīr, Muḥammad."[314] Yet the collection also contains a few writings which are clearly not authored by Ibn al-Wazīr. Furthermore, the *Manẓūma* did not make its way into Ibn al-Wazīr's *Dīwān* although the *Dīwān* is where Ibn a-Wazīr's most important poems are collected. However, the content bespeaks the authenticity of Ibn al-Wazīr's authorship. The copy of the *Manẓūma* was completed in 1350/1931.[315] It covers 8 pages with an average of 27 lines per page.

Content

The *Manẓūma* is divided into a prologue, an introduction, four preliminary poems and 27 chapters (*fuṣūl*). All is versified, including the initial praise of God and the Prophet. The chapters of the *Manẓūma* are arranged similar to the order in Zaydi[316] and other works on legal theory.[317] Indeed, in the intro-

---

313 MS Sanaa, Maktabat Muḥammad al-Kibsī, coll. 49; cf. al-Wajīh, *Maṣādir turāth* i, 219.

314 Ibn al-Wazīr, *Manẓūma* laq. 111r. There is another Muḥammad of the Āl al-Wazīr that could have been meant, namely the writer of the first version of the family biography *al-Faḍāʾil fī taʾrīkh al-sāda l-aʿlām Āl al-Wazīr* (*The Virtues: On the History of the Outstanding Masters of the House of al-Wazīr*), Muḥammad b. al-ʿAfīf al-Wazīr. *Al-Faḍāʾil* was extended by several of Muḥammad's descendants. The last version, compiled by a grandson of Ibn al-Wazīr's brother al-Hādī, Aḥmad b. ʿAbdallāh al-Wazīr, became famous under the title *Taʾrīkh Banī al-Wazīr*; cf. al-Ḥibshī, *Maṣādir* 487. It is unlikely, however, that the remark in the margins of the *Manẓūma* should have meant the earlier Muḥammad. He was not particularly known for his productivity in legal theory.

315 Ibn al-Wazīr, *Manẓūma shiʿriyya* laq. 114l.

316 See for example al-Manṣūr bi-llāh's (d. 614/1217) *Ṣafwat al-ikhtiyār* and Ṣārim al-Dīn b. al-Wazīr's (d. 914/1508) *Fuṣūl al-luʾluʾiyya*. Of the MS of al-Manṣūr bi-llāh's *Ṣafwat al-ikhtiyār*, numerous copies exist, cf. Schwarb, *Handbook*, MS no. 362. According to Ansari and Schmidtke, *Ṣafwat al-ikhtiyār* was the "first deliberate attempt by an imam to formulate a specifically Zaydī legal methodology." Cf. Ansari and Schmidtke, Muʿtazilī and Zaydī Reception 103. The earlier works of the Zaydi imam al-Nāṭiq bi-l-ḥaqq Abū Ṭālib al-Hārūnī (d. 424/1033) *al-Mujzī fī uṣūl al-fiqh* and *Jawāmiʿ al-adilla fī uṣūl al-fiqh* (*Comprehensive Proofs in Uṣūl al-Fiqh*) reflect the view of the Muʿtazili Abū ʿAbdallāh al-Baṣrī on legal theory; cf. ibid., 94. See also Ṣārim al-Dīn, *al-Fuṣūl al-luʾluʾiyya* 430–433 (index of topics).

317 The reception of the *al-Muʿtamad* of the Muʿtazili Abū l-Ḥusayn al-Baṣrī (d. 436/1044) is only one testimony to the fact that legal methodology generally defies the boundaries of legal as well as theological schools. For the reception of Abū al-Ḥusayn's *al-Muʿtamad* see Ansari and Schmidtke, Muʿtazilī and Zaydī Reception 90–109.

ductory verses, Ibn al-Wazīr refers his reader to Imām al-Ḥaramayn al-Juwaynī (d. 478/1085), of whose legal doctrine the *Manẓūma* is little more than a reformulation.[318] The following four preliminary poems provide definitions (*taʿrīf*) of the basic operative elements of *uṣūl al-fiqh* (i.e. the root (*aṣl*) and the branch (*farʿ*)), as well as the epistemological values attainable by the various operations (i.e. knowledge (*ʿilm*) and ignorance (*jahl*), conjecture (*ẓann*) and doubt (*shakk*)), and finally of the discipline of legal theory (*uṣūl al-fiqh*) in general.

Ibn al-Wazīr's concern with epistemology is noteworthy. The fact that the preliminary poem of the *Manẓūma* is devoted to the different kinds of knowledge (*aqsām al-ʿulūm*)[319] is in line with Ibn al-Wazīr's general concern with knowledge, and with the common practice among scholars of *uṣūl al-fiqh* to preface their works with an epistemological introduction.[320]

The next chapters present a list of the hermeneutical principles with which legal theory is occupied.[321] The order, accurately repeated in subsequent chapters, again follows the order rendered in classical treatises of *uṣūl al-fiqh*: 1. speech (*kalām*); 2. the literal and the metaphorical along with their respective subdivision, namely; 3. literal figures of speech (*aqsām al-ḥaqīqa*); and 4. metaphorical figures of speech (*aqsām al-majāz*); 5. the command (*amr*); 6. that which should be considered part of speech and what should not; 7. the prohibition (*nahy*); 8. the relationship between the general (*ʿāmm*) and the particular (*khāṣṣ*); 9. the particular (*khāṣṣ*) on its own; 10. connected particularization (*takhṣīṣ bi-l-muttaṣil*); 11. unconnected particularization (*takhṣīṣ bi-l-munfaṣil*); 12. the ambiguous (*mujmal*) and the clarified (*mubayyan*); 13. clarification (*bayān*); 14. the text (*naṣṣ*); 15. the apparent (*ẓāhir*) and the interpreted (*muʾawwal*); 16. the deeds of the Prophet; 17. abrogation (*naskh*); 18. consensus (*ijmāʿ*); 19. the reports (*akhbār*); 20. analogy (*qiyās*); 21. impermissibility and permissibility (*ḥaẓar wa-ibāḥa*); 22. presumption of continuity (*istiṣḥāb*); 23. the order of evidence (*tartīb al-adilla*); 24. requirements of the legal interpreter and the inquirer (*muftī wa-mustaftī*); 25. *taqlīd* and 26. *ijtihād*.

Some of these chapters are worth pointing out as they speak in favor of the likelihood of Ibn al-Wazīr's authorship. The indications that this poetical treatise is at least in line with Ibn al-Wazīr's thinking commence already in

318 Ibn al-Wazīr, *Manẓūma* laq. 111r.

319 Ibn al-Wazīr, *Manẓūma* laq. 111l.

320 Cf. Rosenthal, *Knowledge Triumphant* 195, 213. An exception to this was Abū l-Ḥusayn al-Baṣrī, who considered epistemology to belong to the subtleties of *kalām*; cf. Abū l-Ḥusayn al-Baṣrī, *al-Muʿtamad* i, 3. Ibn al-Wazīr did not seem to have agreed with him in this, whereas other *kalām* topics that should have no part in *uṣūl al-fiqh* according to Abū l-Ḥusayn were not touched upon in the *Manẓūma*.

321 Ibn al-Wazīr, *Manẓūma*, laq. 111l.

the prologue in praise of God and his Prophet. Among the divine attributes that are singled out for praise is God's mercy. God is to be praised because He is the provider of wisdom, reason and favor.[322] Furthermore, there is a list of the requirements of a *mujtahid* that does not mention speculative theology as a requirement.[323] Furthermore, the author of the *Manẓūma* insists on knowing the proofs that lead to the different opinions. Likewise redolent of Ibn al-Wazīr's thinking, as we shall see later, are the last two lines of the verses on the requirements: the necessity of *ijtihād* for everyone who is capable of it.

The *Manẓūma* represents the only systematic illustration of Ibn al-Wazīr's legal methodology available to us. Although *uṣūl al-fiqh* figures majorly in many other writings, discussions of many, but not all elements of legal theory are scattered throughout these writings.

13 *Masāʾil arbaʿa tataʿallaq bi-l-muqallad wa-l-mustaftī*

This short treatise called *Four Questions Related to the One Who is Emulated and the Legal Inquirer* is not mentioned in any of the bibliographical sources. The time of authorship is hard to determine. It was probably a relatively early writing. Some of Ibn al-Wazīr's positions in legal methodology, which later became rather distinct beacons of his argumentation, are hardly pronounced yet. The MS consulted for the present study issues from the year 1032/1622. It extends over eight pages with an average of 34 lines.[324]

Content

After a short prologue, Ibn al-Wazīr discusses four questions that concern the relationship between an emulator asking for a legal opinion (*mustaftī muqallid*) and the legal interpreter (*mujtahid, muqallad*), i.e. his imam. The four questions were posed to him by some of his students. The interest in the questions issued from their prominence in the books on legal theory circulating in Ibn al-Wazīr's lifetime.[325] Significantly, Ibn al-Wazīr points out that an active subject of law does not need profound knowledge of either the essential rules of philosophi-

322 Ibid., laq 111r.

323 Ibid., laq 114l.

324 Ibn al-Wazīr, *Masāʾil arbaʿa* 131–138; MS Sanaa, Maktabat Muḥammad al-Kibsī, coll. 89; cf. al-Wajīh, *Maṣādir al-turāth* 232.

325 In their What Makes a *Madhhab*?, Haykel and Zysow confirm the centrality of the four questions in the discourse around the identity of the Zaydi *madhhab* far beyond Ibn al-Wazīr's lifetime.

cal speculation (*naẓar*) or the principles of verifying traditions. In other words, the information sought is attainable by all. It belongs to those issues where the Creator and Lawmaker (i.e. God) encourages, desires and indeed expects general understanding.[326]

Discussing question I, namely whether a non-*mujtahid* has to adhere (*yaltazim*) to one particular imam,[327] Ibn al-Wazīr presents six positions along with their respective proponents. There are those who declare adherence binding and others who do not. The first two positions represent the two opposing extremes: incumbency of *iltizām* on the one hand,[328] and the claim that *iltizām* is an unacceptable innovation on the other.[329] The subsequent positions are nuances of the permission to transfer from one school or imam to another.[330] Ibn al-Wazīr explains that the reason for the differences goes back to the different stances toward four questions concerning a particular principle (*aṣl*) of *uṣūl al-fiqh*, namely the legal quality of *taqlīd* in its most basic form: Is the original quality of *taqlīd* permissibility, or does the permissibility apply only to some forms after particularization? Is the proof on which the permissibility claim relies a general or a particular proof? Is the emulator permitted to act without knowledge or conjecture, and is he allowed to act against his conjecture? Or is the emulator equal to the *mujtahid* in his obligation to act according to his own conjecture?[331]

The ensuing discussion touches upon a number of issues implied in the different positions towards the question of adherence. First, Ibn al-Wazīr debates the four arguments (*ḥujaj*) of some who declare that neither adherence to one imam or school nor the investigation of evidence is binding. Their sole indicator is the leniency of the respective rulings. This position stands for the complete acceptance of unquestioning *taqlīd*. It applies to both sets of principle questions concerning the legal quality of *taqlīd* as well as the significance of conjecture.[332]

---

326 Ibn al-Wazīr, *Masāʾil arbaʿa* 131.

327 Ibid., 131.

328 Examples of proponents of this view are Imam al-Manṣūr bi-llāh ʿAbdallāh b. Ḥamza, Imam al-Manṣūr's teacher al-Ḥasan al-Rassas and al-Raṣṣāṣ's grandson, Aḥmad b. Muḥammad al-Raṣṣāṣ, as well as Ibn al-Wazīr's teacher and transmitter of the said disagreement, ʿAlī b. Abī al-Khayr. Ibn Abī l-Khayr claims that this view was held by the majority of jurists; cf. Ibn al-Wazīr, *Masāʾil arbaʿa* 131.

329 Examples are the Baghdadi Muʿtazili Abū l-Qāsim al-Balkhī, Ibn ʿAbd al-Salām, Ibn ʿAbd al-Barr and a number of Zaydis, as for example Imam Yaḥyā b. Ḥamza; cf. ibid., 131.

330 Ibid., 131.

331 Ibid., 132.

332 Ibid., 132–135.

Another topic touched upon is that of precaution (*iḥtiyāt*), which Ibn al-Wazīr discusses in two studies (*bahthān*). A distinction must be made between acts of worship (*ʿibādāt*), where the intention must entirely conform to divine intention behind the action, and mundane matters. In mundane matters, the cautious, hence more severe, ruling can be chosen. A second distinction concerns individual rights (*ḥuqūq al-makhlūqīn*) and demands of public well-being (*ḥuqūq Allāh*). If statements and evidence in the case of public well-being are contradictory and conjecture does not tend towards one of them, the *muqallid* can chose the ruling of anyone who acknowledges that there is neither a duty to perform nor to omit. Where the individual rights are concerned, the layman must refer to a judge in the case of a lawsuit or can chose the ruling of a scholar, who releases him from his legal obligations. In brief, the basis of every action and every choice for a particular ruling should be based on the *muqallid*'s conjecture as a result of an investigation. In ambiguous matters, where evidence is equally indecisive on either side (*haythu yaḥṣul shakk mustawī l-ṭarafayn*), caution is desirable. However, the most appropriate application of caution consists in the omission of *taqlīd*. For Ibn al-Wazīr, choosing the most cautious ruling is not identical to choosing the prohibition over permission or the more severe ruling over the lighter one.[333]

Question II asks whether or not it is permissible to follow more than one imam in a single case.[334] Ibn al-Wazīr basically refers to the response to question I. Those, who consider strict adherence (*iltizām*) binding, prohibit that more than one imam be followed, and *vice versa*.

Question III refers to the issue of the *ahl al-bayt*'s collective prerogative to being emulated. Is transfer of following (*tanaqqul*) permitted only among the positions of *ahl al-bayt*?[335] In this passage, Ibn al-Wazīr establishes that the prevalence of *ahl al-bayt* holds true in a number of issues. Prominent among them are the pronouncement of *tafsīq* and *takfīr* and other matters where certainty is required (*ijmāʿ qaṭʿī, masāʾil qaṭʿiyya*). Similarly, preeminence is conceded to their consensus in suppositional matters.[336] This preeminence is based on the praise they received among the Prophet and his companions and followers.[337] Even though Ibn al-Wazīr grants them this extraordinary status, he does not restrict *ijtihād, taqlīd* or adherence to them. Being a descendant of the Prophet's daughter Fāṭima has not been made a requirement for *ijtihād*, nor

333 Ibid., 136.
334 Ibid.
335 Ibid.
336 Ibid., 137.
337 Ibid.

does descent from the Prophet outweigh evidence.[338] Investigation of the evidence with the aim of arriving at an informed starting point for weighing the given positions against each other (*rujḥān*) remains the postulate of all matters of probability, hence all matters of *ijtihād*. The highest probability (*al-ẓann al-aqwā*) is the ultimate goal.[339] The dominant role in matters requiring certainty that Ibn al-Wazīr concedes to *ahl al-bayt* seems to speak for an early origin. This observation may be qualified by the fact that *Masāʾil arbaʿa* is not at all specific, up until the time that the consensus of *ahl al-bayt* may be considered valid. If the consensus of *ahl al-bayt* is only valid up until the spread of Islam, the argument of *ijmāʿ ahl al-bayt* can only be of very limited applicability.

Question IV treats the divergence between the texts of an imam and the rulings of his school's *muṣaḥḥiḥūn*.[340] What if a layman adheres to the *madhhab* of an imam and finds that some later authorities of the imam's school (*muṣaḥḥiḥūn*) bring forth rulings that diverge from the explicit textual sources of the imam in question?[341] Ibn al-Wazīr answers the question with the repeated reference to and insistence on the "most probable according to individual conjecture" (*ittibāʿ al-ẓann al-aqwā*) as a heuristic method. The weightier argument must be found and followed, and the possibility of weighing the evidence in the case of supposed evenness must be sought (*ṭalab al-rujḥān*). Ibn al-Wazīr enumerates mechanisms for arriving at the most probable: a) investigating the indicators of the case in question (*al-naẓar bi-l-adilla*); b) weighing the indicators of the different parties (*tarjiḥ dalīlihim*), i.e. the imam and the *muṣaḥḥiḥūn* of his school, with the possible inclusion of c) contextual evidence (*bi-l-qarīna*). Ibn al-Wazīr insists: "With these scales, weigh everything that you receive in these issues!"[342]

---

338 Ibn al-Wazīr's choice of examples indicates the background of his addressees in law and theology: Abū Ḥanīfa (d. 148/767), a non-Arab, was a known and referred to mufti during the time of the Zaydi eponym Zayd b. ʿAlī (d. 122/740); likewise the Muʿtazili theologian ʿAbd al-Jabbār al-Hamadhānī (d. 415/1025), who did not refer to his contemporaries and representatives of the Zaydi legal school, the Hārūnī brothers Imam al-Muʾayyad bi-llāh Aḥmad b. al-Ḥusayn (d. 411/1020) or Imam al-Nāṭiq bi-l-ḥaqq Abū Ṭālib (d. 424/1033). Hence, with these examples, Ibn al-Wazīr points out that important landmarks in their intellectual past did not confer prerogatives of leadership in matters of *ijtihād* to members of the Prophet's progeny; cf. ibid., 137.

339 Ibid., 138.

340 *Muṣaḥḥiḥūn* are scholars of a particular legal school that extract the principles underlying their imam's (or more than one imam's) legal positions. Subsequently, the *muṣaḥḥiḥūn* bring the diverging legal opinions into harmony with these principles. They are also called *muḥaṣṣilūn*; cf. Haykel and Zysow, What Makes a *Madhhab*? 9, and below.

341 Ibn al-Wazīr, *Masāʾil arbaʿa*, 138.

342 Ibid., 138.

If the above-mentioned procedures are followed, the origin of the ruling that is embraced is of no consequence. The ruling can originate from the imam himself, the *muṣaḥḥiḥūn* of his school or some other origin. The implications for adherence are obvious: even an emulator that holds to strict adherence (*iltizām*) must abandon the school of his imam in a particular ruling, if he arrives at the conviction that that particular ruling is most likely to be weak. In his insistence that everyone must follow what seems most probable to him after investigation, Ibn al-Wazīr goes as far as affirming the unlikely case that a *muqallid* emulates his deceased imam even if this imam prohibited *taqlīd al-mayyit*, if the *muqallid* himself came to the conclusion that it is permissible.[343]

Ibn al-Wazīr concludes with an appraisal of the *salaf*. In the discussion of these four questions, the significance that Ibn al-Wazīr grants the informed conjecture of the legal subject and his participation in the legal activity becomes evident.

14 *Masʾalat ikhtilāf al-Muʿtazila wa-l-Ashʿariyya fī ḥamd Allāh ʿalā l-īmān*

Alternative titles for *The Issue of the Disagreement Between the Muʿtazila and the Ashaʿriyya Concerning the Praise of God for Faith* are *Risāla fī taqrīr raḥmat Allāh taʿālā ʿalā l-īmān* (*Epistle Establishing Faith as God's Mercy*),[344] *Baḥth fī ḥamd Allāh ʿalā l-īmān wa-ikhtilāf al-Muʿtazila wa-l-Ashʿariyya* (*A Study on the Praise of God for Faith and the Disagreement the Muʿtazila and the Ashaʿriyya*),[345] and *al-Ikhtilāf fī ḥadd Allāh ʿalā l-īmān* (*The Disagreement on the Limitation* [*sic*] *of God for Faith*).[346] Al-Wajīh suggests the identity of *al-Ikhtilāf* with a *Risāla fī taqrīr ḥamd Allāh*, although he mentions them as two distinct works. Possibly, there is confusion as to the titles because the original had none, or had various titles. The uncertainty of the title rather than the diversity of works is further supported by the suggestion that the word *ḥadd* in *al-Ikhtilāf* is a reading mistake. No date of completion of the original is explicitly given. However, on the last page, Ibn al-Wazīr refers the reader to his *al-ʿAwāṣim* for further detail, indicating that *Masʾalat ikhtilāf al-Muʿtazila wa-l-Ashʿariyya* may have been written

343 Ibid.
344 Al-Wajīh, *Aʿlām* 828; al-Ḥibshī, *Maṣādir* 134; al-Ḥarbī, *Ibn al-Wazīr wa-ārāʾuhu* 93.
345 Al-Ḥibshī, *Maṣādir* 135; Ibn Abī l-Rijāl, *Maṭlaʿ al-budūr* iv, 154.
346 Cf. al-Wajīh, *Aʿlām* 826.

after 808/1406. Of the two copies used for this study, one was completed in 1035/1626.[347] The other copy from the *Dār al-Makhṭūṭāt* does not mention a date of completion.[348]

Content

As the title says, *Masʾalat ikhtilāf al-Muʿtazila wa-l-Ashʿariyya* is devoted to the question of the origin of faith and, more generally, the origin of human actions. The writing is divided into a long introduction and two following sections. In the introduction, Ibn al-Wazīr explains his motivation for writing the treatise and establishes two doctrines concerning the question of the createdness of human actions, which he then elaborates in the two following sections.

Ibn al-Wazīr was asked to explain the differences between the doctrine of faith in Muʿtazili and Ashʿariyyi teaching. According to Ibn al-Wazīr, the abyss that is supposed to exist between the two groups is due to contentiousness inhibiting an accurate understanding of their respective positions. Ibn al-Wazīr repeatedly refers to the Prophet Muḥammad's admonition not to quarrel.[349] Investigation would show that ultimately, there is no essential difference in the understanding of faith, but rather a difference in expression (*fī l-iʿbārāt, lafẓī*).

Ibn al-Wazīr establishes two tenets on which supposedly both schools and the Muslim community at large agree (*ijmāʿān*): I. God deserves praise for the occurrence of faith in human beings. II. Human beings have free choice (*ikhtiyār*) in their actions. According to Ibn al-Wazīr, the differences came about in the course of polarization. The general tenet that God is to be thanked for all graces (*niʿam*) is apparently not doubted. The choice that the human being has in acting according to divine command and prohibition is likewise affirmed by all, according to Ibn al-Wazīr, until "the saying appeared that human actions are created."[350] The Jabriyya took this in an extreme way and denied human beings any agency in their actions, faith included. The Ashʿariyya likewise employed the expression that "actions are created" extensively. In reaction, the Muʿtazila identified everyone phrasing this statement with one who denied that human beings have free choice (*ikhtiyār*). By calling such people unbelievers, they neglected to refer back to the intention of those who expressed the phrase as a tenet. Exaggeration on the Ashʿari side has led some Muʿtazilis to go far beyond

347 Ibn al-Wazīr, *Masʾalat al-ikhtilāf*, MS Sanaa, Maktabat Muḥammad al-Kibsī, coll. 89, 363–371. I was given access to a digitized version of the MS by a Yemeni friend, whom I want to thank for this help. The references below refer to this copy.

348 Ibn al-Wazīr, *Masʾalat al-ikhtilāf*, MS Sanaa, Dār al-Makhṭūṭāt, coll. 2990.

349 Ibn al-Wazīr, *Masʾalat al-ikhtilāf* 363.

350 Ibid., 363.

the limits of their own school, ending up with the opposite, namely that "God must be thankful towards human beings for their faith."[351]

After describing the general problem, Ibn al-Wazīr briefly shows how both sides—the Muʿtazila and the Ashʿariyya—actually do advocate the same position: The Muʿtazila acknowledge that God deserves praise and thanksgiving for all things. An example of this advocacy is found in the preamble of an important Muʿtazili writing of "the teacher and source of the Muʿtazili and Zaydi doctrine for the theologians in our time and country,"[352] i.e. Aḥmad b. Ḥasan al-Raṣṣāṣ's (d. 621/1224) *Khulāṣa*. According to Ibn al-Wazīr, the due al-Raṣṣāṣ paid God for His being the director (*qawwām*) of all things and guide to Islam (*hadānā lil-Islām*) was not questioned by any Muʿtazili theologian after him. Correspondingly, the Ashʿariyya affirm that there is an element of free choice in faith for which human beings are responsible and deserve reward or punishment accordingly.

In the two subsequent sections, Ibn al-Wazīr elaborates these supposedly agreed-upon tenets. Elucidating the first tenet (I), Ibn al-Wazīr puts forward four arguments from reason and three from the Quran (Q 49:17, Q 5:3 and Q 4:94). In all of these arguments, the emphasis is put on God's favor in creating what helps people to have faith (i.e. ability, reason, motives, prophets, revelation, etc.). These things are seen as derivations from the root of favor and hence to be ascribed to God. In contradistinction, sin and disobedience are described as deviations from the root and not ascribed to God accordingly.[353]

In elucidating the second tenet (II), Ibn al-Wazīr makes an effort to absolve those accused of negating this tenet, i.e. the Jabriyya and the Ashʿariyya, from the allegations advanced by the Muʿtazilis. The Zaydi Muʿtazili Aḥmad b. Abī Hāshim known as al-Manakdim (d. 425/1034) is used as an example of one who mitigates the disagreement between the Muʿtazili and the Ashʿari doctrine of human actions.[354] Ibn al-Wazīr goes on to buttress his assumption with the writings of an Ashʿari authority, namely Fakhr al-Dīn al-Rāzī (d. 606/1209) in his *Nihāyat al-ʿuqūl fī dirāyat al-uṣūl* (*The Goal of Intellects Concerning the Knowledge of the Principles*). Ibn al-Wazīr draws a not-unlikely relationship to the thought of Abū l-Ḥusayn al-Baṣrī (d. 436/1045) on two issues.[355] Firstly,

351 Ibid., 363–364.
352 Ibid., 364.
353 Ibid., 364–366.
354 The quote is taken from the beginning of chapter two of al-Manakdim's commentary on ʿAbd al-Jabbār's *al-Uṣūl al-khamsa* on justice.
355 For the reception of Abū l-Ḥusayn al-Baṣrī by Fakhr al-Dīn al-Rāzī, see for example Madelung (ed., intr.), *Kitāb al-Fāʾiq*, 4–5; Madelung, Late Muʿtazila; Madelung, Abū l-

he attempts to square al-Rāzī's understanding of compulsion (*jabr*) with that of Abū l-Ḥusayn.[356]

Secondly, Ibn al-Wazīr attempts to harmonize the views of al-Rāzī and other Ashʿaris with that of Abū l-Ḥusayn's concerning the effectiveness of human capacity (*qudra muʾaththira*).[357] Again, the assumed disagreement is said to pertain only to the mode of expression. At times drawing on Muʿtazili reasoning, Fakhr al-Dīn al-Razī and other Ashʿaris even go further than Bahshami Muʿtazilis in that they, like Abū l-Ḥusayn, insist that the connection between the human being and his freely chosen action is one of necessity (*ḍarūrā*) rather than merely being known by inference (*istidlālī*). Necessity has a higher epistemic value than inference. In consequence, Ibn al-Wazīr expresses his great astonishment that supposed opponents of the Muʿtazila should be accused of negating free choice, although they support and go beyond what he calls "extreme Muʿtazilism."[358]

In the subsequent pages, more examples are provided from the writings of Ashʿaris that allegedly parallel Abū l-Ḥusayn's views,[359] such as Abū Bakr Muḥammad al-Baqillānī (d. 402/1013) and Imām al-Ḥaramayn al-Juwaynī (d. 478/1085). Ibn al-Wazīr emphasizes the important agreement that goodness (*ḥusn*) and evil (*qabḥ*) are attributes of actions rather than their essence and that human beings are responsible for their actions in the sense that their power has an effect on these attributes.[360]

In conclusion, *Masʾalat al-ikhtilāf* must be considered a masterpiece of synthesis. Furthermore, what suggests itself on reading this short theological treatise is that according to Ibn al-Wazīr, the scholars most conducive to harmonization of Ashʿari and Muʿtazili thinking are Fakhr al-Dīn al-Rāzī and Abū l-Ḥusayn al-Baṣrī.

Ḥusayn al-Baṣrī's Proof for the Existence of God; Ansari and Schmidtke, Muʿtazilī and Zaydī Reception. See also the relationship of their respective positions on human action in Hoover, *Ibn Taymiyya's Theodicy* 140.

356 Cf. Ibn al-Wazīr, *Masʾalat al-ikhtilāf* 367.

357 Ibid., 367–368.

358 Ibn al-Wazīr mentions Ibn al-Ḥājib (d. 646/1248–1249) along with Fakhr al-Dīn al-Rāzī; ibid., 368. For the difference between Abū l-Ḥusayn and the Bahshamiyya, see al-Ḥayyī, *al-Muntazaʿ min al-Durar al-farāʾid* f. 82b and below.

359 Cf. Ibn al-Wazīr, *Masʾalat al-ikhtilāf* 370.

360 Imām al-Ḥaramayn al-Juwaynī is mentioned as an example; cf. ibid., 371. See also Ibn al-Wazīr, *al-ʿAwāṣim* v, 53–65, 265–268.

15 *Masāʾil mustakhrajāt*

The full title is given as *Masāʾil mustakhrajāt min qawlihi taʿālā* {*ʿĀlim al-ghayb wa-l-shahāda*} (*Questions Extracted from the Word of the Sublime* {*He is the Knower of the Unseen and the Seen*}). Al-Ḥibshī places this treatise in the category of the sciences of the Quran.[361] Unfortunately, I could not get access to the treatise. However, it is likely that it was mainly concerned with the theological implications of the relevant Quranic verse, namely Q 13:9, which reads {He knows what is not seen as well as what is seen; He is the Great, the Most High}. If it is indeed a theological exposition of the verse, it might be similar or even identical to *Masāʾil sharīfa min qawlihi taʿālā* {*ʿĀlim al-ghayb wa-lā yuẓhir ʿalā ghaybihi aḥadan*}, discussed below. There are several reasons for this assumption: Titles were often a later ascription, the topics are similar, and Ibn al-Wazīr would have mentioned more than one Quranic verse in each work. It is possible that only the one verse chosen for the title varied. A copy is to be found in the Dār al-Makhṭūṭāt, MS no. 53. No date of authorship nor of completion is mentioned.

16 *Masāʾil shāfiyāt*

The full title of this short work, *Masāʾil shāfiyāt wa-bi-l-maṭālib wāfiyyāt fī-mā yataʿallaq bi-āyāt karīma Qurʾāniyya tadull ʿalā llāh al-mabʿūd wa-ṣidq anbiyāʾihi l-muballighīn ʿanhu*, succinctly describes its contents: *Issues that Cure and Fully Meet the Requests Related to the Noble Verses of the Quran that Point to the Worshipful God as well as the Truthfulness of His Prophets Who Give Account of Him*. A few copies are known to exist in the libraries of the Grand Mosque in Sanaa.[362] The writing is most probably identical with two manuscripts mentioned elsewhere: 1. *al-Āyāt al-dālla ʿalā llāh wa-ʿalā ṣidq anbiyāʾihi*, of which al-Wajīh found a copy in the library of the Ministry of Religious Endowments dating from 957/1550–1551,[363] and 2. *Baḥth ʿan mā dhakaruhu llāh taʿālā fī l-Qurʾān al-karīm min al-āyāt al-dālla ʿalayhi ʿizz wa-jall wa-ṣidq anbiyāʾihi min al-khawāriq*,

361 Al-Ḥibsī, *Maṣādir*, 28.

362 Cf. al-Wajīh, *al-Aʿlām* 829; cf. ʿAlī al-ʿAmrān (ed., intr.), *al-Rawḍ al-bāsim* 35. Al-Ḥarbī mentions the same number of folios from the collection. Neither apparently consulted the work, although al-Ḥarbī quotes the first line after the *basmala*. It is also possible that both considered *al-Āyāt al-mubīnāt* to be a part of the *Masāʾil shāfiyāt*; cf. al-Ḥarbī, *Ibn al-Wazīr wa-ārāʾuhu* 100.

363 Al-Wajīh, *al-Aʿlām* 826.

mentioned by al-Ḥarbī.[364] Al-Wajīh's identification of *Masāʾil shāfiyāt* with a *Mukhtasar fī ʿilm al-ḥadīth* (*Synopsis of the Sciene of Hadith*) in a collection of al-Kibsī is erroneous. In contrast to al-Wajīh's assumption, *Masāʾil shāfiyāt* should not be classified as a writing in the science of hadith, but rather as a brief doctrinal treatise. It is unknown when Ibn al-Wazīr finished the writing.

The copy used here is a digitized version from the *Dār al-Makhṭūṭāt*. No date of completion is mentioned in the colophon. Yet the copy is likely to originate from around 1158/1745, judging from other works comprised in the same codex.[365]

Content

As the full title mentions, the work provides Quranic verses in evidence of God and His prophets. In the two lines after the *basmala*, Ibn al-Wazīr asserts the sufficiency of the Quranic evidence.[366] Subsequently, he systematically works his way through the first nineteen Suras of the Quran, at times quoting a passage or a phrase from the relevant Sura. At other times, he simply mentions the story and draws a brief conclusion in support of his main thesis: Things transcending the natural are employed to prove God's existence as well as the truthfulness of those He sent to convey His word to human beings. For this the Quran gives ample evidence. In the second Sura of the Quran, Ibrāhīm asks God to give him more evidence after he witnesses the revival of the dead, so that his heart may be at rest (*iṭmiʾnān*). God asks why Ibrāhīm does not have faith. Ibn al-Wazīr concludes from this that faith is a confirmation (*taṣdīq*) in the realm of conviction (*iʿtiqādāt*), not in the realm of deeds. God subsequently gives further signs that lead to more certainty. These signs are clearly within the realm of rational activity.[367] Thus, the signs and miracles in creation which are mentioned in the Quran should be the source and subject of rational endeavor. Reason plays a large part in religious knowledge. More specifically,

---

364 Al-Ḥarbī, *Ibn al-Wazīr wa-ārāʾuhu* 90. He refers to *Maṭlaʿ al-budūr* which mentions *Ḥaṣr al-āyāt al-dālla ʿalayhi taʿālā wa-ʿalā ṣidq anbiyāʾihi wa-awliyāʾihi min al-khawāriq* (*Collection of Verses that Point to God the Exalted and to the Truthfulness of His Prophets and Friends by Way of Things that Surpass the Ordinary*). Ibn Abī al-Rijāl does not mention the alternative title *Masāʾ il shāfiyāt*; cf. Ibn Abī al-Rijāl, *Maṭlaʿ al-budūr* iv, 153.

365 MS Sanaa, Dār al-Makhṭūṭāt, coll. 3133. The editor of *al-Rawḍ al-bāsim* mentions fs. 92–114. Yet the text amounts only to 9 pages (fs. 92a–96a; or pages 183–191 according to the newer pagination which I will henceforth quote). In the said collection, *Masāʾ il shāfiyāt* is followed by a copy of *al-Āyāt al-mubīnāt* which is not mentioned as part of that collection, neither in the catalogue nor in any of the bibliographical sources.

366 Ibn al-Wazīr, *Masāʾil shāfiyāt* 184.

367 Ibid., 185.

Ibn al-Wazīr speaks of the "conditions or circumstances of creation" (*aḥwāl*) which need to be pondered. An indication of what Ibn al-Wazīr terms *aḥwal*-proof elsewhere is found in the discussion of Q 11:6. The verse speaks of all the beasts of the earth. None of them was created without God being the one who gives them substance and sustenance. The circumstances of these creatures (*aḥwāl al-khalq*) should be pondered, leading to the knowledge of the truthfulness of God and his message.[368] Besides the miracles within the realm of nature, there is the miracle of the Quran itself which indicates the existence of God and the truthfulness of His messenger. This is also treated in the Quran.[369]

Another noteworthy aspect of *Masāʾil shāfiyāt* reveals Ibn al-Wazīr's involvement with Sufism. Addressing Sufis in a passage in *Masāʾil shāfiyāt*, he explains as follows: In Q 2:144, the direction of prayer, the *qibla*, is determined as being toward Mecca. This determination comes about as a response to Muḥammad's turning his face towards heaven. God wants to give Muḥammad and his followers another direction which supposedly pleases them more. In this verse, Ibn al-Wazīr finds support for his teaching of human freedom in relation to God's wisdom and decree.[370] For one thing, human beings seem to have the choice between several actions within the decrees of God. To explain this, Ibn al-Wazīr uses the term *taqdīr* which must be understood as some kind of presupposition or prescience. Furthermore, Ibn al-Wazīr's comment on Q 2:144 illustrates his view of God's divine wisdom and motive behind every act and decree. This apparently is not impaired or questioned by the believer's favoring one over the other. Lastly, Ibn al-Wazīr states that the command which is more pleasant to the believer is also more beneficial for him.

In sum, the main features of this work are the importance Ibn al-Wazīr places on miracles to prove the veracity of prophethood, and that he argues for his positions in his preferred manner of rendering proof: directly from scripture.

17 *Masāʾil sharīfa*

According to al-Ḥibshī, a copy of *Masāʾil sharīfa mustakhraja min qawlihi taʿālā* {*ʿĀlim al-ghayb wa-lā yuẓhir ʿalā ghaybihi aḥadan*} (*Noble Questions Extracted from the Word of the Sublime* {*He is the One Who Knows What is Hidden and He*

368 Ibid., 190.

369 See for example ibid., 190, 191.

370 Ibn al-Wazīr, *Masāʾil shāfiyāt* 185.

Does not Disclose it.})[371] can be found in the Dār al-Makhṭūṭāt. He ranks *Masāʾil sharīfa* in the category of theology as well as science of the Quran.[372] Unfortunately, I did not get access to the MS. However, the title and al-Ḥibshī's account indicate that *Masāʾil sharīfa* is an exposition of Q 72: 26–27a.[373]

18 *Mukhtaṣar mufīd fī ʿulūm al-ḥadīth*

The Beneficial Compendium on the Sciences of Hadith was written as an "improvement" (*taslīḥ*) of the Shafiʿi Ibn Ḥajar al-ʿAsqalānī's (d. 852/1449) *Nukhbat al-fikr* (*The Top of Thinking*). Accordingly, it was also called *Taslīḥ Nukhbat al-fikr*.[374] Al-Ḥibshī simply gives a description as the title: *Risāla taʿaqqaba fīhā ʿalā risālat al-ḥāfiẓ Ibn Ḥajar al-ʿAsqalānī fī ʿilm al-athār* (*Epistle Following Ibn Ḥajar al-ʿAsqalānī's Treatise on the Science of Traditions*).[375] Al-Ḥarbī, who mentions the latter title as well as *Mukhtaṣar fī ʿulūm al-ḥadīth*, did not realize that the content is identical.[376] Besides the libraries of the Grand Mosque, copies of the manuscript are extant in the Königliche Staatsbibliothek zu Berlin[377] as well as the private library of Muḥammad al-Kibsī.[378]

The introduction of the *Mukhtaṣar* informs the reader of an approximate time of writing. Ibn al-Wazīr states that he wrote his *Mukhtaṣar* after he had read Ibn Ḥajar's *Nukhbat al-fikr*. According to Ibn al-Wazīr, Ibn Ḥajar wrote his masterpiece on hadith during his journey to Mecca in the year 817/1414–1415.[379] Hence Ibn al-Wazīr's *Mukhtaṣar* must have been written after that year. The MS used for the study at hand originates from the collection of writings of Ibn al-Wazīr found in the library of Muḥammad al-Kibsī. The copy was completed in 1034/1625.

371 Ibn Abī l-Rijāl adds part of the following verse, "except unto a messenger of His choosing;" cf. Ibn Abī al-Rijāl, *Maṭlaʿ al-budūr*, vol. 4, 154.

372 al-Ḥibshī, *Maṣādir*, 28 (Quranic sciences), 135 (theology).

373 Q 72:26–27a reads {He is the One who knows what is hidden. He does not disclose it except to a messenger of His choosing}.

374 Ibn Abī l-Rijāl, *Maṭlaʿ al-budūr* iv, 153; al-Wajīh, *Aʿlām* 827.

375 Al-Ḥibshī, *Maṣādir* 57. Likewise al-Ḥarbī, *Ibn al-Wazīr wa-ārāʾuhu* 94.

376 This is apparently due to the fact that both titles are mentioned in the catalogue of the Dār al-Makhṭūṭāt; cf. al-Ḥarbī, *Ibn al-Wazīr wa-ārāʾuhu* 99.

377 Ahlwardt, *Verzeichnisse*, no. 1117, Glaser 234, fs. 120–124.

378 This is the same writing that al-Wajīh took to be identical with *Masāʾil shāfiyāt*; see above.

379 Ibn al-Wazīr, *Mukhtaṣar* 187.

Content

In his *Mukhtaṣar*, Ibn al-Wazīr strongly affirms the Shafiʿi traditionist. The points that need amendment are apparently minor and due to limitations that are common to all human beings.[380]

The main text of the treatise begins by listing and explaining the different categories of traditions along with their conditions and epistemic value, starting with the uninterrupted tradition (*mutawātir*) and its counterpart, the solitary tradition (*aḥad*).[381] Among the different categories of hadith treated in the following passage, the controversies around the acceptance of traditions that either have gaps in the line of transmission (*mursal*) or feature transmitters whose doctrinal orientation is unknown or not impeccable according to the teaching of one's own school (*majḥūl*), receive special attention.[382] These controversies represent an important dividing line between the Zaydi and Sunni sciences of hadith as well as a hindrance to mutual acceptance of traditions.[383] It is in this context that Ibn al-Wazīr provides Ibn Ḥajar's nomenclature with additions. He adduces Zaydi and Muʿtazili authorities to stress his point in favor of the principles set down by Ibn Ḥajar, as for example in the controversy around the acceptance of *majhūl* traditions. In this case, Ibn al-Wazīr refers to Imam ʿAbdallāh b. Ḥamza, Imam Yaḥyā b. Ḥamza, and al-Ḥasan al-Raṣṣāṣ among others.[384]

The subsequent passage is dedicated to the different kinds of licenses for transmission (*ijāza*).[385] Ibn al-Wazīr concludes his brief *Mukhtaṣar* with a list of the different categories by which transmitters are either disqualified (*jarḥ*) or qualified (*taʿdīl*) as trustworthy sources.[386]

19 *Muthīr al-aḥzān fī wadāʿ shahr Ramaḍān*

The Stimulant of Sadness Concerning Bidding the Month of Ramadan Fare-well is a short collection of poems. Only few sources mention it. Ibn Abī l-Rijāl refers to

380 Ibid., 187.
381 Ibid., 187.
382 Ibid., 188.
383 For a comparison between hadith science in the Zaydiyya and among the Sunni traditionists, see al-ʿIzzī, *ʿUlūm al-ḥadīt*; for the question of the acceptance of *majhūl* traditions, see Ibn al-Wazīr, *Mukhtaṣar*, 109–110.
384 Ibid., 189.
385 Ibid., 190.
386 Ibid., 191.

the collection in the glosses of his *Maṭlaʿ al-budūr*.[387] One copy is found in the Maktabat al-Awqāf dated to the year 807/1404.[388] There is said to be another copy in the Dār al-Makhṭūṭāt.[389] The MS used for the study at hand is part of a collection from the private library of al-Kibsī. 1359/1940 is mentioned as the year of completion of the copy.[390]

Content

With 5 to 15 lines each, the 16 poems in this collection are relatively short. All are shaped in the form of dialogues between Ibn al-Wazīr and his soul, his heart or an undefined addressee. As regards content, the main theme is repeated throughout: the benefits of staying awake in contemplation during the nights of the month of Ramaḍān. The addressee, be it soul, heart or human counterpart, is encouraged to endure, and is promised the help that is due to those who love God. At the outset of the collection, Ibn al-Wazīr refers his soul to the prophetic practice transmitted in a tradition that is mentioned in all six Sunni hadith collections. According to this tradition, a person who stays awake during the nights of Ramaḍān in contemplation is forgiven all previous sins.[391] Ibn al-Wazīr repeatedly encourages his addressee not to fear the strains involved in vigils, with reference to the mitigating effect of love.[392] The "Night of Power" (*laylat al-qadr*) is especially singled out because of the multiple effectiveness that is ascribed to prayer during that night. As the "Night of Power" usually occurs within the last five nights of the third portion of Ramaḍān, the reason that this poetic emphasis on personal piety and mystic experiences is named "bidding Ramaḍān farewell" is not far to seek.[393]

20 *Nuṣrat al-aʿyān*

The complete title of the writing is *Nuṣrat al-aʿyān ʿalā shirr al-ʿumyān fī l-radd ʿalā Abī l-ʿAlāʾ al-Maʿarrī* (*Assistance for the Eyes Against the Evil of Blindness: A*

---

387 Cf. Ibn Abī l-Rijāl, *Maṭlaʿ al-budūr* iv, 151, footnote 1.

388 Ruqayhī, *Fihrist* 1385–1386.

389 Al-Ḥibshī does not specify which library, Dār al-Makhṭūṭāt or Maktabat al-Awqāf; cf. al-Ḥibshī, *Maṣādir* 332; al-Wajīh, *Aʿlām* 829.

390 Ibn al-Wazīr, *Muthīr al-ahzān* laq. 126l.

391 Ibid., laq. 108r; Ibn al-Wazīr explicitly refers to the tradition in Ibn al-Wazīr, *al-ʿAwāṣim* ix, 136.

392 Ibn al-Wazīr, *Muthīr al-ahzan* laq. 108r.

393 Ibid., laq. 109r.

Refutation of Abū l-ʿAlāʾ al-Maʿarrī).[394] Unfortunately, the writing is apparently lost.[395] However, some information can be gathered from the biographical and bibliographical sources: In *Nuṣrat al-aʿyān*, Ibn al-Wazīr rebuts the blind Syrian poet Abū l-ʿAlāʾ al-Maʿarrī (d. 449/1058). According to al-Ḥibshī, Ibn al-Wazīr refers to al-Maʿarrī's verses on *taqlīd* of the legal schools.[396] But that is questionable since al-Maʿarrī was also a critic of *taqlīd* and the system of legal schools.[397] The first few verses reproduced by Ibn Abī l-Rijāl indicate that Ibn al-Wazīr's main concern was with al-Maʿarrī's stance on prophecy, which was at least questionable from an orthodox point of view. According to Muḥammad b. ʿAbdallāh, Ibn al-Wazīr's biographer, Ibn al-Wazīr compares al-Maʿarrī's physical blindness with the spiritual one which supposedly led to the disparagement of the prophets.[398] Whoever does that, Ibn al-Wazīr writes, thereby devaluates the imams of Islam, "destroying the *furūʿ* by destroying the foundations."[399] From these lines alone it is imaginable that Ibn al-Wazīr would have criticized al-Maʿarrī's degradation of the prophets. As regards al-Maʿarrī's stance towards *taqlīd*, Ibn al-Wazīr might have criticized the way rather than the fact that al-Maʿarrī spoke out against it.

21 *Qubūl al-bushrā bi-l-taysīr lil-yusrā*

An alternative name for *The Acceptance of the Good News Concerning the "Making Easy of the Path to Ease"* is *Qubūl al-bushrā fī taysīr al-yusrā*, with basically the same meaning.[400] The title refers to Q 92:7 which reads {We shall smooth his way unto ease}. In addition to several copies of the MS in the Dār al-Makhṭūṭāt, a number of copies can be found in private libraries.[401] The copies of the MS consulted here were copied in 1158/1745 and in 1151/1738.[402] A number of reference works state that *Qubūl al-bushrā* was edited and printed in Egypt

394 *Naṣr al- aʿyān* is an alternative title to *Nuṣrat al-aʿyān*; cf. Ibn Abī al-Rijāl, *Maṭlaʿ al-budūr* iv, 150.

395 Cf. al-Akwaʿ (intr.), *al-ʿAwāṣim* i, 75; al-Ḥarbī, *Ibn al-Wazīr wa-ārāʾ uhu* 100; al-Ḥibshī, *Maṣādir* 424; al-Wajīh, *Aʿlām* 129.

396 Al-Ḥibshī, *Maṣādir* 424.

397 On al-Maʿarrī, see Smoor, al-Maʿarrī.

398 Cf. Muḥammad b. ʿAbdallāh, *Tarjama* fs. 133a–133b.

399 Ibn Abī l-Rijāl, *Maṭlaʿ al-budūr* iv, 150. *Nuṣrat al-aʿyān* seems to have been extant at the time of Ibn Abī l-Rijāl, since he quotes from it.

400 Ibn Abī al-Rijāl, *Maṭlaʿ al-budūr* iv, 151.

401 Cf. al-Ḥibshī, *Maṣādir* 222; al-Wajīh, *Aʿlām* 829; al-Ḥarbī, *Ibn al-Wazīr wa-ārāʾ uhu* 98.

402 MS 1) Sanaa, Dār al-Makhṭūṭāt, coll. 3133; MS 2) Sanaa, Muʾassasat al-Imām Zayd, CD 3.

in the year 1349/1931–1932. The fact that there are references to *Qubūl al-bushrā* in *al-ʿAwāṣim*[403] allows for the possibility that it was written before 808/1406, the year *al-ʿAwāṣim* was completed. In addition, *Qubūl al-bushrā* contains a reference to *Kitāb al-Qawāʿid*.[404]

Content

Some sources classify *Qubūl al-bushrā* within the discipline of substantive law (*fiqh*). Others consider it a work on asceticism and mystics.[405] Yet a thorough analysis of its content allows for a classification within the realm of legal theory as well. Although the examples from substantive law take much more space, the vital points under discussion belong within the realm of legal theory or the overlapping genre of legal maxims (*qawāʿid*).[406] Another indication in support of this is al-Akwaʿ's supposition that Ibn al-Murtaḍā wrote his *al-Qamar al-nuwwār fī l-radd ʿalā l-murakhkhiṣīn fī-l-malāhī wa-l-mizmār* in response to *Qubūl al-bushrā*, criticizing Ibn al-Wazīr's legal methodology and the resulting leniency towards Sufi practices.[407]

The writing consists of an introduction followed by a number of substantially different sections illustrating the main argument. In the introduction, Ibn al-Wazīr sets the stage: God in His wisdom and mercy intended the law brought by his messenger to bring ease to faithful human beings. Yet some of these human beings render law much more difficult than it was intended to be. Apparently, this applies to some of Ibn al-Wazīr's Zaydi contemporaries, who claimed that Imam al-Hādī ilā l-ḥaqq's rulings were especially strict and cautious (*aḥwaṭ*).[408]

The first section contains a list of Imam al-Hādī ilā al-ḥaqq's legal opinions in several areas of substantive law. In all of these, al-Hādī apparently ruled much more leniently than many other scholars of the Zaydiyya and other schools.[409] These examples illustrate that "the sound concession of a scholar can be more excellent than precaution."[410]

In later chapters, Ibn al-Wazīr continues to illustrate the point by referring to lenient rulings of Hādawī-Zaydi scholars, but also more broadly from the

---

403 Ibn al-Wazīr, *al-ʿAwāṣim* i, 199, 298.
404 Ibn al-Wazīr, *Kitāb al-Qawāʿid* 316.
405 *Fihris al-Makhṭūṭāt al-raqamiyya*, no. 3.
406 For legal maxims in the Zaydiyya, see al-Siyāghī, *Uṣūl al-madhhab al-Zaydī* 27–28.
407 Al-Akwaʿ (intr.), *al-ʿAwāṣim* i, 50.
408 Ibn al-Wazīr, *Qubūl al-bushrā* 256.
409 The examples extend from p. 254 to p. 270 in the quoted copy.
410 Ibid., 263.

Zaydiyya in general. Indeed, more than a quarter of the treatise is taken up by individual rulings.

The section of examples is followed by a defense of the principle that "making legal concessions (*rukhṣa*) is generally preferable."[411] After a general explanation, Ibn al-Wazīr lists five circumstances that render concessions desirable (*mustaḥabb*). This is followed by a discussion of Quranic verses advanced by the proponents of said principle,[412] and a section that is devoted to discussing 146 prophetic traditions in support.[413]

There is, of course, an opposing view. The arguments and evidence from Quran, Sunna and reason for the view that "shunning concessions is more excellent" are brought forth and refuted subsequently.[414] A major principle of the opposing view equates precaution (*iḥtiyāṭ, al-aḥwaṭ*) in legal matters with the stricter ruling in cases of doubt, for example where matters are ambiguous. In order to refute his opponent's claims, Ibn al-Wazīr refers to the understanding and implications of the problem of ambiguous matters (*mutashābihāt, mushtabihāt*): 1. Ambiguous matters are reprehensible (*makrūh*) not prohibited (*muḥarram*).[415] 2. "Ambiguous" is an additional, not an essential qualification of legal issues (*aḥkām*).[416] 3. "Ambiguous" is employed as a classification of matters actually belonging to another class of doubt.[417]

Discussing the arguments of his opponents, Ibn al-Wazīr demonstrates how the ruling of each different ambiguous question depends on the nature of the ambiguity. It is determined by an investigation of the indicators leading to a conclusion of preponderant probability. But this is precisely what is forestalled by elevating the equation of precaution, strictness and truth to a general principle. Ibn al-Wazīr laments that this causes most *muqallids* to neglect the investigation of the indicators, to oppose the clear texts and sound proofs, and "to establish customs that ignore the known and unknown evidence."[418] In the last pages and much in the manner of the introduction, Ibn al-Wazīr concludes with a summary of the vital points. He follows this up with a final set of examples from Zaydi authorities and those accepted by the Zaydiyya, all pointing to the same fact: the easiness of the divine law is known from this law as well as from what is known about God by necessity. Hence, ease and rendering the

411 Ibid., 270.
412 Ibid., 272.
413 Ibid., 290.
414 Ibid., 305–335.
415 Ibid., 322.
416 Ibid., 330.
417 Ibid., 331.
418 Ibid., 270.

easier ruling should be the preponderant notion. A thorough understanding of preponderance is vital, so that a distinction within the category of the ambiguous matters is possible. A last remark refers the reader to Ibn Taymiyya's *Taysīr al-ʿibādāt ʿalā ahl al-ḍarūrāt* for further details.[419]

22 *Al-Rawḍ al-bāsim*

The full title of this lengthy work indicates that it is an abridgment of his *magnum opus* bearing partly the same title: *al-Rawḍ al-bāsim fī l-dhabb ʿan sunnat Abī l-Qāsim* (*The Smiling Meadows: A Rebuffal of the Sunna of Abū l-Qāsim*).[420] It is safe to say that the abridgment was written in 817/1414, nine years after the principal work. Apparently, the date is indicated in one copy in the author's own handwriting as Shaʿbān 3rd 817/October 17th 1414.[421] A further indicator that Ibn al-Wazīr must have written the abridgment before or during 817/1414 is found on page 213 of the work itself. Ibn al-Wazīr uses a eulogy to his teacher Ibn Ẓahīra that is only used as long as the person in question is alive: "May God grant those who benefit from him the enjoyment of his continuing life."[422] Ibn Ẓahīra died during Ramaḍān 817/November 1414.[423] The cross-references, on the other hand, do not help to place *al-Rawḍ al-bāsim* in a chronological order. Most of these cross-references are found in *al-ʿAwāṣim*, which must have been written before its own abridgment.

Besides authors of biographical collections and commentators, Ibn al-Wazīr himself refers to the fact that *al-Rawḍ al-bāsim* is the abridgment of *al-ʿAwāṣim*.[424] Interestingly, there are other biographers who do not mention *al-Rawḍ al-bāsim* at all. These include Aḥmad b. ʿAbdallāh al-Wazīr, author of the family history *Taʾrīkh Banī l-Wazīr*, as well as Ibn Abī l-Rijāl.[425] Discrepancies between the two works, for example in the rendering of prophetic reports, could be explained by the suggestion that Ibn al-Wazīr wrote the abridgment during a

---

419 Ibid., 334–341.

420 Cf. al-Wajīh, *Aʿlām* 828.

421 The editor of *al-Rawḍ al-bāsim* refers to the MS that was used as a source for previous editions; cf. al-ʿAmrān (ed., intr.), *al-Rawḍ al-bāsim* 58. See also al-Akwaʿ (intr.), *al-ʿAwāṣim* i, 74.

422 Ibn al-Wazīr, *al-Rawḍ al-bāsim* 213.

423 Al-Fāsī, *al-ʿIqd al-thamīn* ii, 53–59; al-Sakhāwī, *al-Ḍawʾ al-lāmiʿ* viii, 92–96.

424 Cf. Ibn al-Wazīr, *al-ʿAwāṣim* i, 225; Ibn al-Wazīr, *al-Rawḍ al-bāsim* 15, 19; al-Ḥibshī, *Maṣādir* 134; al-Shawkānī, *al-Badr al-ṭāliʿ* ii, 82, 91.

425 Muḥammad b. ʿAbdallāh al-Wazīr only mentions *al-Rawḍ al-bāsim* in a passing remark and not in the list with other major writings; cf. Muḥammad b. ʿAbdallāh, *Tarjama* f. 144b.

period he spent in isolation. In several instances, he indicates that the books he quotes from were not present with him at the time of writing.[426]

There are a number of extant copies. The oldest one is from the year 956/1550.[427] Another copy dates from 1178/1766 and is found in the Dār al-Makhṭūṭāt. Yet another from the same library (dating from 1336/1918) is apparently a copy of the former. This is what the editor of the 1419/1999 edition of *al-Rawḍ al-bāsim*, ʿAlī b. Muḥammad al-ʿAmrān, states. He used both copies as sources for this edition.[428] The digitizations I received from the Dār al-Makhṭūṭāt are taken from a copy of the Ramaḍān 1137/May 1725 edition.[429] In addition to several copies in private libraries, the Dār al-Kutub al-Miṣriyya in Cairo apparently possesses a copy from 1319/1901–1902.[430] The book was edited and printed for the first time in 1385/1964 by the Maṭbaʿat al-Salafiyya in Cairo. Besides the MS copies, I made use of ʿAlī b. Muḥammad al-ʿAmrān's edition from 1998. The number of copies, frequency of references and literary reactions to the work reflect its significance.

Content

Although *al-ʿAwāṣim* is the accumulation of Ibn al-Wazīr's scholarly productivity and *al-Rawḍ al-bāsim* only the abridgment, it is the latter that found response in two refutations. The first known refutation bears the title *al-ʿAḍb al-ṣārim fī l-radd ʿalā ṣāḥib al-Rawḍ* (*The Sharp Sword: A Refutation of the Writer of The Meadows*). Al-Ḥibshī mentions that it was written by Ibn al-Wazīr's grandson, without specifying which one.[431] Al-Wajīh says the author is unknown, as does al-Ḥarbī.[432] Another well-known rebuttal of *al-Rawḍ al-bāsim* bears the title *al-ʿIlm al-wāṣim fī l-radd ʿalā hafawāt al-Rawḍ al-bāsim* (*Blaming Knowledge: Refutation of the Errors of The Smiling Meadows*). It was written by Aḥmad b. Ḥasan b. Yaḥyā l-Qāsimī (d. 1375/1956) and edited and printed in 1429/2008

426 Ibn al-Wazīr, *al-Rawḍ al-bāsim* 15, 276, 278.

427 Cf. Ruqayḥī, *Fihrist* ii, 638; al-Wajīh, *Aʿlām* 828; al-ʿAmrān (ed., intr.), *al-Rawḍ al-bāsim* 97.

428 Cf. Ibid., 92–96.

429 The Dār al-Makhṭūṭāt possesses another copy, of which the date cannot clearly be identified; cf. *Fihris al-makhṭūṭāt al-yamaniyya* 321–322.

430 Cf. Al-Hibshī, *Maṣādir* 134; al-Wajīh *Aʿlām*, 828. Several copies from private libraries in Yemen were digitized by the Mu'assasat al-Imām Zayd; cf. *Fihris al-makhṭūṭāt al-raqmiyya*, MS 724, CD 72; MS 1976, CD 195.

431 Cf. al-Ḥibshī, *Maṣādir* 134.

432 Al-Wajīh, *Aʿlām* 828. Al-Ḥarbī mentions 1214/1799–1800 as the year of writing. If, however, al-Ḥibshī is correct in suspecting a grandson of Ibn al-Wazīr's to be the writer, al-Ḥarbī's date is likely to refer to the time of copying rather than of authoring; cf. al-Ḥarbī, *Ibn al-Wazīr wa-ārā'uhu* 59.

in Sanaa.[433] Considering the fact that *al-ʿAwāṣim* was written first, one may ask why *al-Rawḍ al-bāsim* became the focus of criticism rather than the more extensive and apparently more famous *al-ʿAwāṣim*. One possible reason is the fact that *al-Rawḍ al-bāsim* features considerable improvement in structure and setup. Whereas *al-ʿAwāṣim* discussed the arguments, evidence, and examples in the order in which they were advanced in the letter from Ibn al-Wazīr's teacher and opponent ʿAlī b. Muḥammad b. Abī l-Qāsim, *al-Rawḍ al-bāsim* renders them in coherent clusters without following the order provided by the opponent. The editor al-ʿAmrān points out, for example, that Ibn al-Wazīr takes up the defense of the doctrine of the eponyms of the four Sunni schools of law coherently in one section of *al-Rawḍ al-bāsim*.[434] In *al-ʿAwāṣim*, in contrast, the link between the defenses of the eponyms of the four Sunni schools is not immediately apparent, as they are spread throughout the entire work.[435] Moreover, *al-ʿAwāṣim* contains more examples and additional lessons (*fawāʾid*) not immediately related to Ibn Abī l-Qāsim's challenges. In the abridgment, Ibn al-Wazīr furthermore omitted points of challenge he did not consider worth responding to because of their supposed internal contradictions.[436] *Al-Rawḍ al-bāsim* is simply easier to read and comprehend. According to the author, this was his intention in writing the abridgment so that potential readers would not be dissuaded from studying the book by its lengthiness.[437] A further and probably decisive reason for refuting *al-Rawḍ al-bāsim* instead of *al-ʿAwāṣim* is the fact that Ibn al-Wazīr expresses his own views much more markedly in the later writing. The main goal of *al-ʿAwāṣim* was to "commit the opponent to the consequences of the doctrines of his own school" in the manner of *ilzām*.[438] He wanted to disprove Ibn Abī l-Qāsim's accusations and rectify prevalent notions on the existing schools of thought. Although Ibn al-Wazīr employs the method of *ilzām* in *al-Rawḍ al-bāsim* as well,[439] it seems to be written as a more emphatic statement of his own views.[440]

---

433 Al-Muʾayyidī, *al-ʿIlm al- wāṣim* 2008.

434 Al-ʿAmrān (ed., intr.), *al-Rawḍ al-bāsim*, 67; cf. Ibn al-Wazir, *al-Rawḍ al-bāsim* i, 295–326, 308.

435 See, for example, the defense of Aḥmad b. Ḥanbal against the accusation of anthropomorphism, Ibn al-Wazīr, *al-ʿAwāṣim* iii, 300, 331, or of al-Shafiʿi's understanding of the "vision of God" in ibid., v, 5.

436 Ibn al-Wazīr, *al-Rawḍ al-bāsim* 230.

437 Cf. ibid., 19.

438 Ibn al-Wazīr, *al-ʿAwāṣim* i, 225.

439 Cf. Ibn al-Wazīr, *al-Rawḍ al-bāsim* 27.

440 Ibn al-Wazīr, *al-ʿAwāṣim* i, 225.

The text of Ibn al-Wazīr's *al-Rawḍ al-bāsim* commences with an appraisal of the prophetic Sunna, and its role in Ibn al-Wazīr's own life and scholarly development. An excerpt from a long poem in honor of the traditions and the traditionists emphasizes his point. He explains how this passion for the prophetic traditions caused opposition, manifest in the letter from his former teacher Ibn Abī l-Qāsim. After briefly describing the contents of the letter, Ibn al-Wazīr explains his reasons for and methods in writing *al-Rawḍ al-bāsim* and its longer precursor, *al-ʿAwāṣim*.[441] After this introduction, he sets out to respond to the claims of his opponent. More clearly than in *al-ʿAwāṣim*, it becomes evident that the challenges of Ibn al-Wazīr's opponent and the group of scholars he apparently stood for all converged in one question: Are the traditions collected in the six Sunni hadith compilations, and especially the two collections of al-Bukhārī and Muslim (*Ṣaḥīḥān*), trustworthy enough to be relied upon in doctrinal as well as in legal matters? Whereas Ibn al-Wazīr's critic negates the question, Ibn al-Wazīr answers in the positive.

The validity of the *Ṣaḥīḥān* traditions along with the other four collections is substantiated by means of the following questions of doctrine and legal methodology. First, Ibn al-Wazīr shows that it is possible to make conclusive statements on the uprightness of transmitters in general.[442] In contrast, Ibn Abī l-Qāsim is depicted as denying the trustworthiness of the transmitters of hadith and subsequently the use of the prophetic traditions (as preserved by the traditionists) as a whole. But Ibn al-Wazīr argues that the hadith collections are necessary for the performance of the duty of *ijtihād*,[443] as well as all other sciences, indeed of religious knowledge as a whole. From the challenges of his opponent Ibn Abī l-Qāsim, Ibn al-Wazīr infers the following claim: the disappearance of knowledge has made *taqlīd* a necessity. Of course, this can only be rejected, as it would reduce the entire system of Islamic science to absurdity.[444] A more specific refutation of Ibn Abī l-Qāsim's claims follow: As part of this discussion, Ibn Abī l-Qāsim challenges the acceptance of prophetic traditions which have not been transmitted by an immediate eyewitness (*mursal*) as well as such that were transmitted by an unknown person at one stage of transmission (*majhūl*).[445] Ibn al-Wazīr in turn argues for the acceptance of both *mursal* and *majhūl* traditions in reference to Muʿtazili and Zaydi sources. In response to his opponent's general challenge of the rectitude (*ʿadāla*) of a number of

441 Ibn al-Wazīr, *al-Rawḍ al-bāsim* 14–15.

442 Ibid., 19.

443 Ibid., 20.

444 Ibid., 60.

445 Ibid., 31–52.

transmitters, Ibn al-Wazīr insists that minor sins do not nullify uprightness.[446] Thus, according to Ibn al-Wazīr, the traditions rendered in the Sunni hadith compilations cannot be rejected on the basis of these claims. On the contrary, the state of traditions and their transmitters can be discerned easily.[447]

In the following, the same principle is in effect: Ibn al-Wazīr acquits those who prove the trustworthiness of the transmitters in question (*muʿaddilūn*) from the charges of holding doctrines such as compulsion (*jabr*), anthropomorphism and deferral of judgment (*irjāʾ*).[448]

After the discussion of transmitter status, the next section is dedicated to the traditions of the Sunni hadith compilations themselves. According to Ibn al-Wazīr, most of them are sound (*ṣaḥīḥ*). The rank of only a few is questionable. However, the doubts regarding their soundness do not reach the degree of probability necessary to reject them.[449] Ibn al-Wazīr continuously challenges his opponent in respect of the degree of knowledge or certainty that can or must be reached.

This may be recognized in the following section about *taqlīd* and *ijtihād*:[450] From the moment a student is able to weigh instances of textual evidence against each other (*tarjīḥ*) and discern the most probable or preponderant (*al-rājiḥ*), he has the duty to decide and act on the basis of his discernment. *Ijtihād* in one or a number of questions is possible for a student of one or more disciplines.[451]

After a general discussion of the above points, Ibn al-Wazīr sets about to examine them in more detail. A large section is dedicated to the defense of individual transmitters, among them the eponyms of the four Sunni schools of law.[452] Beyond doctrinal differences, one criticism against the traditionists expressed in the second letter from Ibn Abī l-Qāsim was their reluctance or resistance to engaging in speculative theology. Ibn al-Wazīr's opponent equated this reluctance with being simple-minded (*balah*).[453] But what characteristic is it, asks Ibn al-Wazīr, that restricts knowledge among the Muʿtazila? Ibn al-Wazīr discusses the indications of stupidity and intelligence. For him, *ʿilm al-kalām* is no sign of intelligence or quality of knowledge. He disputes a histor-

446 Ibid., 52.

447 Ibid., 78.

448 Ibid., 85, 94, 110. Most of the *muʿaddilūn* are companions who are all trustworthy according to Ibn al-Wazīr.

449 Ibid., 159.

450 Ibid., 207–229.

451 Ibid., 216.

452 Ibid., 229–307.

453 Ibid., 326.

ical event in which *kalām* had been considered to be the decisive characteristic of intelligence and subsequently of excellence (*faḍl*), with the result that the status of a particular imam, i.e. al-Mahdī l-Ḥusayn b. al-Qāsim b. ʿAlī al-ʿIyānī (d. 404/1013),[454] was elevated above that of the Prophet Muḥammad. According to Ibn al-Wazīr, the elevation of *kalām* above everything (any other kind of knowledge or science) is the reason al-ʿIyānī "departed from the Zaydi school and even the Islamic schools altogether."[455] The traditionists, however, can be proved to be thoroughly skilled in the knowledge of the prophetic Sunna. Professionalism in their own discipline is the benchmark of intelligence and excellence, rather than derived knowledge as defined by the principles of the logicians. A recurring argument insists that the experts of each of the Islamic sciences need to be honored and praised for laying the groundwork others can benefit from in their specific discipline.[456]

In what follows, Ibn al-Wazīr defends the traditionists against a number of other doctrinal impeachments: they do not allow the obligation of the impossible (*taklīf mā lā yuṭāq*);[457] they do not hold that the innocent children of unbelievers are to be punished for their parents' sins,[458] nor do they condone the imamate of an unjust ruler.[459] Ibn al-Wazīr intends to prove that the traditionists do not rank among those whose unbelief is clearly expressed (*kufr ṣarīḥ*) and whose transmission would have to be rejected in consequence.[460] As stated and discussed repeatedly, the opponent is mistaken when he surmises the doctrines of compulsion (*jabr*) and deferral of judgement (*irjāʾ*) in the traditions of the Sunni hadith compilations.[461]

After having defended the traditionists from accusations of holding doctrines erroneous to the degree of clear unbelief, Ibn al-Wazīr endeavours to prove that the transmissions of those whose interpretation have lead to errors (*mutaʾawwilūn*) may still be employed as sources for religious knowledge and argumentation. First, Ibn al-Wazīr discusses the arguments of proponents and opponents of the acceptance of such traditions. He demonstrates that most Zaydis accept the traditions and reports of *mutaʾawwilūn*, especially if their

454 Al-Ḥibshī, *Maṣādir* 610–613.

455 Ibn al-Wazīr, *al-Rawḍ al-bāsim* ii, 328. Others, like the anti-Muʿtazili scholar Ḥumaydān b. Yaḥyā (d. after 653/1255), judged al-ʿIyānī similarily; cf. al-Ḥibshī, *Maṣādir* 611.

456 Ibn al-Wazīr, *al-Rawḍ al-bāsim* 340.

457 Ibid., 367.

458 Ibid., 368.

459 Ibid., 379–413.

460 Ibid., 354.

461 Ibid., 415–446.

interpretation results in sin (*fisq*) and not in unbelief (*kufr*).[462] Similarly to the Zaydiyya, the traditionists apparently broadly accept the reports of those whom they consider *fussāq ta'wīl* and *kuffār ta'wīl*, under the condition that the latter do condemn lying.[463]

In closing, Ibn al-Wazīr examines three groups mentioned explicitly by Ibn Abī l-Qāsim as examples of the untrustworthiness of the Sunni hadith collections: the Mujbira, the Murji'a and three of the companions (Muʿāwiya b. Abī Sufyān, al-Mughīra b. ʿUthmān and ʿAmr b. al-ʿAṣ). He argues that the Ashʿariyya are falsely accused of holding a predeterminist doctrine like the Mujbira. This accusation is supposedly only the result of strife between the Ashʿariyya and the Muʿtazila. In the course of this strife, the Muʿtazila likewise have been ascribed beliefs which they do not really hold. Consequently, Ibn al-Wazīr himself insists on the use of those traditions that can be affirmed by two (or more) contending groups directly or indirectly.[464] Restricting the requirements for the acceptable to a minimum makes it possible to find points of agreement. In the case of Muʿāwiya, for example, there is only one agreed-upon way: a group of companions who attest the soundness of his transmission, especially in legal issues (*siḥḥat al-riwāya*). This group of companions is accepted by the Shīʿites and the Sunnis alike.[465] Other examples of traditions by the three companions in question follow. Apparently, there should be agreement on the soundness of these latter traditions.[466]

The last few pages contain advice in prose and in verse: Ibn al-Wazīr wants to urge his fellow believers not to be discouraged from reliance on Quran and Sunna. The work ends as it begins, with a warning against deep immersion in *kalām* which supposedly results in strife and innovations.[467]

23 *Al-Ta'dīb al-malakūtī*

The Heavenly Discipline is mentioned by all consulted biographical and bibliographical sources. Unfortunately, it does not seem to be extant, at least not *in toto*.[468] This writing on "marvels and wonders" (*al-ʿajā'ib wa-l-gharā'ib*) was

462 Ibid., 481.
463 Ibid., 483.
464 Ibid., 523.
465 Ibid.
466 Ibid., 524–590.
467 Ibid., 594.
468 Al-Akwaʿ states that a few pages probably belonging to *al-Ta'dīb al-malakūtī* have been found; cf. al-Akwaʿ (intr.), *al-ʿAwāṣim* i, 73.

apparently not very long,[469] yet its loss is regrettable in respect to any further study of the influence Sufism had on Zaydi thought during the time of Ibn al-Wazīr and his teacher Ibn Abī l-Khayr.

24 *Taḥrīr al-kalām fī masʾalat al-ruʾya*

The full title is sometimes given as *Taḥrīr al-kalām fī masʾalat al-ruʾya wa-tajwīdihi wa-dhikr mā dāra bayna l-Muʿtazila wa-l-Ashʿariyya* (*Record of Speech Regarding the Vision Along with its Amelioration and a Reference to the Discussion Between the Muʿtazila and the Ashʿariyya*),[470] which is a quotation from the prologue. There are several copies of the work in the Dār al-Makhṭūṭāt[471] as well as in the private library of al-Kibsī. The two copies accessed for the present study were completed in the years 1034/1625 and 1158/1745 respectively.[472] The work itself could not be dated yet. It is very likely, however, that it was written before the year 822/1420, the year Ibn al-Wazīr's brother al-Hādī died. Ibn al-Wazīr wrote *Taḥrīr al-kalām* at his brother's request. When informing the reader of this detail, Ibn al-Wazīr does not add any benediction to his brother's name that would have indicated his having died.

Content

As stated in the prologue, Ibn al-Wazīr wrote this brief treatise in compliance with a request advanced by his brother al-Hādī b. Ibrāhīm, asking him to clarify the positions taken in respect to the issue of seeing God (*ruʾya*). The controversy applied especially to the Muʿtazila and the Ashʿariyya. Al-Hādī had written a refutation of the Ashʿari theologian Muḥammad b. ʿAbd al-Karīm al-Shahrastānī's (d. 548/1153–1154) theological work, *Nihāyat al-aqdām fī ʿilm al-kalām* (*The End of Steps in the Science of Theology*).[473] Ibn al-Wazīr informs the reader that he will comply with his brother's request by presenting

469 Al-Ḥibshī, *Maṣādir* 332; al-Ḥarbī, *Ibn al-Wazīr wa-ārāʾuhu* 90; Ibn Abī l-Rijāl, *Maṭlaʿ al-budūr* iv, 151; al-Ṣubḥī, *Kuttāb al-Zaydiyya* 207; al-Wajīh, *Aʿlām* 827; Muḥammad b. ʿAbdallāh, *Tarjama* f. 133a.

470 Cf. Ibn Abī l-Rijāl, *Maṭlaʿal-budūr* iv, 153–154.

471 Cf. al-Ḥibshī, *Maṣādir* 135; al-Wajīh, *al-Aʿlām* 827; al-Ḥarbī, *Ibn al-Wazīr wa-ārāʾ uhu* 91. I found a copy of *Taḥrīr al-kalām* in Dār al-Makhṭūṭāt, MS coll. 3133 not mentioned elsewhere; cf. *Fihris al-makhṭūṭāt al-yamaniyya* 272.

472 MS 1) copied in Ramaḍān 1034/June 1625 is part of an MSS collection from the library of Muḥammad al-Kibsī, coll. 89. MS 2) copied in 1185/1757 originates from Dār al-Makhṭūṭāt. In what follows, source information will refer to the earlier copy, which is paginated.

473 Ibn Abī l-Rijāl, *Maṭlaʿal-budūr* iv, 153.

what information is generally available on the topic, extending it with additional insights and omitting marginal or exceptional views.[474] Firstly, he reproduces al-Shahrastānī's Ashʿari arguments from *Nihāyat al-aqdām* concerning the vision of God based on the prophet Moses' request to see God in Q 7:143. Secondly, al-Hādī's views are rendered as representative of the Muʿtazila. After presenting both schools' positions, Ibn al-Wazīr clarifies them and sometimes adds a comment about his own view.

The argument and accordingly the response consists of four parts: Firstly, al-Shahrastanī argued that Moses knew of the possibility of seeing God and therefore asked to see Him. In response to the first argument, al-Hādī claimed that Moses did not ask for himself but for his people, who did not believe him.[475] Moses knew that seeing God is impossible (*mustaḥīl*) even before he asked. He knew it by rational evidence, since being visible would have required a physical body. However, a physical body cannot be ascribed to God. Furthermore, Moses knew it before he asked because in this rational question, no revelation is necessary. Testifying to his Muʿtazilism, al-Hādī stated that revelation came as a confirmation of the rational investigation.

According to the following argument from the Ashʿari side, God's answer shows that His refusal refers merely to the incapability of the one requesting the vision, rather than the utter impossibility of the matter. The Muʿtazili counterargument runs that God's answer gives evidence for the impossibility of the matter not with regard to the inquirer (i.e. Moses), but with regard to the object of inquiry: God told Moses to look at the mountains, and said he would see Him when the mountains were still. Then God sent down his glory, and the mountains collapsed. Accordingly, they could not be called "still mountains" anymore. The impossibility of calling them so indicates the impossibility of seeing God, as the seeing was linked to the still mountains.[476]

Thirdly, it is argued that if Moses had asked to see God's face or form rather than asking to see God in a general manner, the answer would have been different. The corresponding Muʿtazili argument claims that Moses knew the answer to the question, but his people did not. Hence, Moses asked God so that they would be convinced of the truthfulness of his message. God's answer was not more precise ("I have no form, face etc.") in order to force the people to employ their rational faculties to discover the reason for the prohibition. There is no necessary connection (*mulāzama*) between the rejection of seeing (*nafy*

474 Ibn al-Wazīr, *Taḥrīr al-kalām* 341.

475 Ibid., 342.

476 Ibid.

al-ruʾya) on the one hand, and the possibility of seeing on the other. Yet, the reference of negation (*nafy*) to impossibility is prevalent and customary (*ʿurfī*).[477]

The fourth argument claims that it is inappropriate for a prophet to ask for anything impossible. If he did ask, the object must have been possible. The counterargument runs that the intention of the inquiry after this known impossibility renders it acceptable even for a prophet. The intention was to free his people from disbelief. Hence, Moses could have asked for what he knew was impossible.[478]

In *Taḥrīr al-kalām*, Ibn al-Wazīr mainly reproduces the arguments of the two theological schools dominant in his time and context. His comments are little more than qualifications of the reasonings expressed before. In one case, Ibn al-Wazīr makes a remark on the question of whether the impossibility lies on the part of the inquirer or of the object of inquiry. Ibn al-Wazīr merely states that God may interrelate the possible, of which He knows that it will not occur, with the impossible in itself. The condition is that the impossible bears resemblances to the possible that will not occur.[479] Later, Ibn al-Wazīr responds to the question of how a negation is to be understood. He points out that the customary use (*ʿurfī*) of the negation is only as valid as the other two possible uses—linguistic (*lughawī*) and legal (*sharʿī*)—are.[480] Yet, Ibn al-Wazīr's reluctant way of commenting reiterates the emphasis on the investigation of proofs and arguments of different schools irrespective of affiliation. Together with the mitigation of contrasting positions, it allowed potential inquirers to trace each side's arguments and come to a conclusion that allowed for agreement with both. However, Ibn al-Wazīr's reluctance in expressing his own views may also have been influenced by his high respect for his brother.

25 *Takhṣīṣ āyāt al-jumʿa*

Takhṣīṣ āyāt al-jumʿa (*The Particularization of the Verses on Friday*) is not mentioned in many biographical or bibliographical sources.[481] In spite of the little attention this short treatise received in the secondary literature, the relatively large number of copies indicate a considerable interest in the matter. Several public and private libraries possess manuscripts of the writing.[482] *Takhṣīṣ*

477 Ibid., 344.
478 Ibid.
479 Ibid., 342.
480 Ibid., 343.
481 al-Ḥarbī, *Ibn al-Wazīr wa-ārāʾ uhu* 91; Ibn Abī al-Rijāl, *Maṭlaʿ al-budūr* iv, 154.
482 Cf. al-Wajīh, *Aʿlām*, 827; al-Ḥarbī, *Ibn al-Wazīr wa-ārāʾuhu* 91.

āyāt al-jumʿa is possibly identical or at least very similar in content to *Iqāmat al-jumʿa min dūna imām* (*The Performance of Friday* [*Prayers*] *Without Imam*) and *Suʾāl fī imāmat al-jāmiʿ wa-iʿtirāḍat baʿḍ al-nās ʿalayhi* (*A Question Concerning Friday Prayers and the Objections of Some People*) mentioned by al-Wajīh,[483] *Risāla fī iqāmat al-jumʿa bi-ghayr imam* (*Treatise on the Performance of Friday* [*Prayers*] *Without Imam*) listed by al-Ḥibshī,[484] and *Risāla fī ʿadam ishtirāṭ al-imām al-aʿẓam fī ṣalāt al-jumʿa* (*Treatise Concerning* [*the Fact*] *that* [*the Presence*] *of the Main Imam is No Condition for Friday Prayers*) briefly referred to by al-Akwaʿ without further detail.[485] Their identity is likely since titles were often later additions. The copy consulted for the present study is part of the collection of Ibn al-Wazīr's works in Muḥammad al-Kibsī's library and was completed in 1035/1626.[486] Unfortunately, no date of completion is known for the original writing.

Content

Takhṣīṣ āyāt al-jumʿa refers to Q 62:9, wherein believers are exhorted to leave everything behind once they hear the call to the communal Friday prayer. Ibn al-Wazīr's writing originates in a response to an inquiry advanced to him by several students of *fiqh*.[487] The question was whether or not the said Quranic verse was to be particularized by a prophetic tradition starting with the words "Know that God has prescribed to you the Friday." Throughout the whole writing, Ibn al-Wazīr shows that the general implication of the Quranic verse cannot be particularized by this specific tradition.[488] The issue evolved around a central point of controversy in doctrine and law between the Zaydiyya and Sunni schools, i.e the Zaydi obligation to strive against an unjust imam (*khurūj ʿalā l-imām al-jāʾir*) along with its legal implications. Contrary to a prominent opinion among Ibn al-Wazīr's contemporaries,[489] he defended the view that the duty of prayer applies irrespective of an imam. Consequently, praying behind an unjust imam or, by implication, a non-Zaydi imam, would be permissible in Ibn al-Wazīr's understanding.

---

483 Cf. al-Wajīh, *Aʿlām* 826, 828.

484 Cf. al-Ḥibshī, *Maṣādir* 222.

485 Al-Akwaʿ (intr.), *al-ʿAwāṣim* i, 76.

486 MS Sanaa, Maktabat Muḥammad al-Kibsī, coll. 89; cf. al-Wajīh, *Maṣādir al-turāth* 233.

487 Ibn al-Wazīr, *Takhṣīṣ* 352.

488 Cf. ibid., 352.

489 As usual, Ibn al-Wazīr refers to Zaydi authorities such as the imams al-Muʾayyad bi-llāh al-Hārūnī, al-Manṣūr bi-llāh ʿAbdallāh b. Ḥamza and al-Muʾayyad bi-llāh Yaḥyā b. Ḥamza in support of his argument; cf. ibid., 359.

At the outset of the writing, Ibn al-Wazīr emphasizes the central role the texts (*nuṣūṣ*) have in the acquisition of knowledge as well as in legal argumentation. Along with it, he provides a hierarchy of sources in which the *salaf* figure prominently.[490] In contradistinction to the later generations (*khalaf*), the *salaf* apparently referred to the texts of revelation. They thereby provide evidence for subsequent generations to reconstruct their line of argument and to arrive at the conclusion they themselves consider preponderant. Relying on scholars of later generations, however, results in less replicable ways of argumentation. This leaves laymen or students unaware of the evidence and possible lines of reasoning. Determination of preponderance among the indicators (*tarjīḥ*) is thereby obstructed. But *tarjīḥ* is the decisive mechanism in the acquisition of legal understanding as well as a major religious duty.[491]

The significance of *Takhṣīṣ āyāt al-jumʿa* lies in the fact that it is a call to the revival of *ijtihād*, rather than in the fact that in it, Ibn al-Wazīr does not agree with many of his contemporaries. Weighing evidence (*tarjīḥ*) is equated to the study and comprehension of law (*tafaqquh*).

26 *Tanqīḥ al-anẓār fī maʿrifat ʿulūm al-āthār*

Ibn al-Wazīr's treatise on the science of hadith, *Rectifying the Perceptions in the Science of Traditions*, is one of the few writings of Ibn al-Wazīr that al-Shawkānī mentions by name.[492] Next to the copies in libraries of the Grand Mosque,[493] al-Wajīh lists a number of copies in various private libraries.[494] *Tanqīḥ al-anẓār* has been edited and printed in 1999. Unfortunately, the editors Muḥammad Ṣubḥī b. Ḥasan Ḥallaq and Amīr Ḥusayn do not indicate the origin of the MS they used for the edition. However, it seems to be older (1008/1601) than the copies at the Grand Mosque (1158/1745). Besides the large number of extant copies and the broad scope of dates—from 870/1456[495] to 1350/1932[496]—the extensive reception of the book is further documented in its most important

490 Ibid., 351.
491 Ibid., 351.
492 Al-Shawkānī, *al-Badr al-ṭāliʿ* ii, 91.
493 MS Sanaa, Dār al-Makhṭūṭāt, coll. 3313, fs. 137b–181a. See also al-Ḥibshī, *Maṣādir* 57.
494 Cf. al-Wajīh, *Aʿlām* 827.
495 The very early date is found on the copy in the Staatsbibliothek Berlin. The date given here, however, is the collation date since the other one was not legible. It is likely to have been sometime in the same year or a little earlier.
496 This late date refers to the abridgment of the *Mukhtaṣar* found in a collection of different MSS of the Muʾassasat al-Imām Zayd.

commentary, namely *Tawḍīḥ al-afkār li-maʿānī Tanqīḥ al-anẓār* (*Clarifying the Thoughts on the Concepts of Rectifying the Perceptions*) by Ibn al-Amīr al-Sanʿānī (d. 1182/1768), which was edited and published in 1997. *Tanqīḥ al-anẓār* is one of those rare writings that can be dated with a high degree of certainty. According to Ibn Abī l-Rijāl, it was completed in 813/1411.[497] There are numerous references to *al-ʿAwāṣim*. *Tanqīḥ al-anẓār* is one of Ibn al-Wazīr's most systematic writings due to its focus on the terminology of the science of hadith.

Content

The relatively brief prologue contains an appraisal of the prophetic traditions. Then, Ibn al-Wazīr goes on by dedicating his compendium to students of *ʿilm al-ḥadīth* who need to master the following information and technical terminology.

The book is divided into three parts in which the three different categories of traditions are discussed: sound (*ṣaḥīḥ*), good (*ḥasan*) and weak (*ḍaʿīf*). Subsequently, a fourth part treats several questions of a more polemic nature. Part I is concerned with the most basic categorizations of traditions, followed by the discussion of sound traditions (*ṣaḥīḥ*) and the conditions for soundness. This chapter deals with the vindication of the Sunni hadith compilations. The basis for this vindication is found in the epistemological value they represent, which is manifest in their soundness. The debate revolves around the question which collections of traditions contain the soundest traditions. Furthermore, Ibn al-Wazīr deals with the criteria for traditions not found in the *Ṣaḥīḥān* of al-Bukhārī and Muslim. Here he considers the possibility of judging on the soundness of hadiths in general (*taṣḥīḥ*). A brief discussion is added concerning the transmission of traditions from books (*wijāda*).

Part II is dedicated to the group of traditions considered good (*ḥasan*) along with the conditions of goodness advanced by the compilers of the Sunni hadith collections. Subsequently, Ibn al-Wazīr treats the usefulness of *aṭrāf* works[498] as well as ambiguities in the classification of traditions as sound and good.

Part III deals with the different sub-categories of the weak tradition (*ḍaʿīf*). Of special interest is the afterthought which Ibn al-Wazīr deemed necessary to emphasize at the end of part III: a scholar or student of hadith should not consider a tradition weak too readily and without detailed information. This is especially true if the qualification as weak is merely rendered by one's own

---

497 Ibn Abī l-Rijāl, *Maṭlaʿ al-budūr* iv, 151. See also al-Ḥarbī, *Ibn al-Wazīr wa-ārāʾuhu* 93.

498 Cf. Ibn al-Wazīr, *Tanqīḥ al-anẓār* 92. For the genre of *aṭrāf*, see Brown, *Canonization* 105.

teacher or imam. Even if it is considered weak, the classification should be based on the line of transmitters (*isnād*) rather than the content (*matn*).[499]

Part IV is not designated as such by Ibn al-Wazīr. Moreover, whereas parts I–III dealt with the three different categories of traditions, part IV is separate from the other parts. Here, Ibn al-Wazīr discusses a number of controversies around the transmitters.[500] What are the criteria for accepting a transmission and how certain can one be as to the qualification of a transmitter? And what weight is ascribed to professional skill in proportion to rectitude (*ʿadāla*) and doctrinal soundness?[501] In this last part, the relation to the acceptance of the Sunni hadith compilations and the transmissions of the totality of the companions is evident—one of the most controversial issues between the Zaydiyya and the Sunni legal schools.

A significant feature of Ibn al-Wazīr's *Tanqīḥ al-anẓār* is that he mentions the opinions of his Zaydi predecessors on the principles of *ʿilm al-ḥadīth* along with those of traditionists of other schools. Furthermore, he discusses the technical terms of *ʿilm al-ḥadīth* and distinguishes them from their use in *uṣūl al-fiqh*, wherever they overlap. Consequently, the importance of this work and the significance Ibn al-Wazīr concedes to the study of hadith must be seen in light of the theory of *ijtihād*. An informed use of the prophetic Sunna as well as an awareness of the whole range of different opinions on a given topic is a major requirement for the performance of *ijtihād* independent of school affiliation.

27 *Tarjīḥ asālīb al-Qurʾān ʿalā asālīb al-Yūnān*

The Preponderance of the Methods of the Quran Over the Methods of the Greeks is another of Ibn al-Wazīr's relatively widely known writings. In *al-ʿAwāṣim*, he himself refers to it as *Tarjīḥ dalāʾil al-Qurʾān ʿalā dalāʾil al-Yūnān*,[502] as well as by the more common name *Tarjīḥ asālīb al-Qurʾān*.[503] The explicit references in *al-ʿAwāṣim* to *Tarjīḥ* are numerous. Additionally, Ibn al-Wazīr has quoted a number of poems, also found in *Tarjīḥ*. *Tarjīḥ*, in turn, contains a few references to *al-ʿAwāṣim*. These references, however, appear like additions at the end of passages that point the reader to *al-ʿAwāṣim* for further details.[504] But the

499 Ibn al-Wazīr, *Tanqīḥ al-anẓār* 158.
500 Ibid., 187.
501 Ibid., 205.
502 Ibn al-Wazīr, *al-ʿAwāṣim* i, 214.
503 Ibid., iii, 420, 436; iv, 10, 50, 61; v, 59, 60, 86, 90, 34; viii, 263, 328.
504 Ibn al-Wazīr, *Tarjīḥ* 44, 53.

most compelling indicator for the time of writing comes from the text of *Tarjīḥ* itself. On page 54, Ibn al-Wazīr refers to an inquiry he received from a young student. Besides the development of his own intellectual journey, Ibn al-Wazīr refers to himself as an old man with considerable experience.[505] Accordingly, the *Tarjīḥ* must have been written long after *al-ʿAwāṣim*. The biographical and bibliographical sources that mention the work do not refer to a time of writing.[506]

There are copies of the MS in Sanaa's Grand Mosque as well as in a number of private libraries.[507] *Tarjīḥ* was first printed in Egypt in 1349/1930[508] and then again in Beirut in 1984.[509] The MS consulted for this study mentions the date Rajab 1204/March 1790 as the date of copying.[510] Different versions seem to exist, judging from the fact that the copies listed in the catalogue of the Dār al-Makhṭūṭāt, the Maktabat al-Awqāf as well as the one mentioned by Ibn Abī l-Rijāl give varying information for the *explicit*, varying from one another as well as from the MS and the printed copy used for this study.[511] At least one abridgment of the *Tarjīḥ* was written. Al-Ḥibshī mentions a *Mukhtaṣar Tarjīḥ asālīb al-Qurʾān* by al-Nāṣir b. ʿAbd al-Ḥāfiẓ al-Mahallā (d. 1037/1627).[512]

Content

Al-Shawkānī considers *Tarjīḥ* to be a highly useful book with an innovative style.[513] This innovative style might be the reason why it is rather difficult to discern a structure in the writing. The original text of *Tarjīḥ* itself is divided into two parts which are structured by five unequal chapters (*faṣl*), not all of them numbered. Between the second chapter of the first part and the first chapter

505 Ibid., 54, 67.

506 See for example Ibn Abī al-Rijāl, *Maṭlaʿ al-budūr* iv, 151; al-Shawkānī, *al-Badr al-ṭāliʿ* ii, 91.; as well as the footnote below.

507 Cf. al-Ḥibshī, *Maṣādir*, 134; al-Wajīh, *Aʿlām* 827; *Fihris al-Makhṭūṭāt al-yamaniyya* 276.

508 Muḥammad b. Ibrāhīm al-Wazīr, *Tarjīḥ asālīb al-Qurʾān ʿalā asālīb al-Yūnān*, Egypt: Maṭbaʿat al-Maʿāhid 1349/1930. It is based on a manuscript from Shawwal 1129/September 1717.

509 Muḥammad b. Ibrāhīm al-Wazīr, *Tarjīḥ asālīb al-Qurʾān ʿalā asālīb al-Yūnān*, Beirut: Dār al-kutub al-ʿilmiyya 1984.

510 This MS is part of a digitized collection obtained by Princeton University as part of the Yemeni Manuscript Digitization Initiative, see http://arks.princeton.edu/ark:/88435/zk51vh52r (28 February 2015). The MS is found in the inventory of the Muʾassasat al-Imām Zayd b. ʿAlī al-thaqāfiyya, CD 314.

511 Ibn Abī al-Rijāl mentions a poem in the conclusion; cf. Ibn Abī al-Rijāl, *Maṭlaʿ al-budūr* iv, 151. The catalogue of the Maktabat al-Awqāf quotes a reference to *al-ʿAwāṣim*; cf. Ruqayhī, *Fihrist* ii, 569.

512 Al-Ḥibshī, *Maṣādir* 134, 144.

513 Cf. al-Shawkānī, *al-Badr al-ṭāliʿ* ii, 91.

of the second part, an extensive parenthesis gives the impression of an introduction to the context of the whole book. The parenthesis takes the form of a request that was addressed to Ibn al-Wazīr after he had written the first two chapters. After explaining the circumstances of his reply, he responds to the inquiry in the following three chapters of the second part.

Chapters one and two of the first part were initially intended as a short treatise in itself (*mukhtaṣar*) in open response to a contemporary trend that was manifest in one or more real or imaginary opponents (*khaṣm*) who apparently attempted to weaken unmediated reliance on the Quranic text in favor of the Greek sciences. It is probable that Ibn al-Wazīr refers to Ibn al-Murtaḍā. In the glosses of two copies of *al-ʿAwāṣim*, "al-Mahdī Aḥmad b. Yaḥyā or Aḥmad b. Yaḥyā [Ibn al-Murtaḍā], author of *al-Azhār*," is mentioned in the context of Ibn al-Wazīr's provocative verses (quoted below). Furthermore, "Aḥmad b. Yaḥyā [Ibn al-Murtaḍā]" is mentioned in the glosses where Ibn al-Wazīr refers to a contemporary who contradicted his own insistence on the sufficiency of the Quran to prove God's unicity.[514] Ibn al-Wazīr portrays the argument of his opponents as follows: Although the unambiguous matters in the Quran appear obvious, the true meaning is hidden and a certain procedure needs to be followed for it to be understood.[515] Those who respond to the outward meaning of the Quranic text (*ẓāhir*) with acceptance and faith are disdained. Attainment of knowledge of the ambiguous matters (*mutashābihāt*) of the Quran is claimed instead. To Ibn al-Wazīr, denying others' ability to understand the outward meaning while claiming an understanding of the ambiguous meaning for oneself contradicts reason as well as revelation.

Chapter one is dedicated to invalidating the claim that the Quran falls short of rendering the proofs for God's divinity (*rubūbiyya*) and unicity (*tawḥīd*) as well as the truthfulness of the prophecies.[516] Ibn al-Wazīr's argumentation is based on the discussion of a number of Quranic verses, followed by rational arguments, prophetic traditions and consensus. Among the authorities in favor of Ibn al-Wazīr's argument, ʿAlī b. Abī Ṭālib figures most prominently. The discussion of a number of quotes from the *Nahj al-balāgha* is followed by various opinions. It focuses on the positions of several scholars from various theological and legal schools. Some of the Zaydiyya and early Shiʿa are worth mentioning as they reappear throughout: Muḥammad b. Manṣūr al-Murādī (d. 290/903) in his *al-Jumla wa-l-ulfa*, Muḥammad b. ʿAlī al-ʿAlawī al-Ḥasanī (d. 445/1053) in his *al-Jāmiʿ al-kāfī*, al-Ḥākim al-Jishumī (d. 484/1101) in his *Sharḥ al-ʿUyūn*,

514 Ibn al-Wazīr, *al-ʿAwāṣim* iii, 422.
515 Ibn al-Wazīr, *Tarjīḥ* 8–9.
516 Ibid., 9.

Shaykh Mukhtār b. Maḥmūd al-Ẓāhidī al-Muʿtazilī (d. 658/1260) in his *Kitāb al-Mujtabā*, and Imam Yaḥyā b. Ḥamza (d. 749/1348) in *al-Tamhīd*. Ibn al-Wazīr also mentions other scholars of the Imami Shiʿa, the Ashʿariyya and some traditionists.[517]

In chapter two, Ibn al-Wazīr introduces the concept of the general tenets (*jumal*), according to which an integral understanding of certain truths is sufficient (*kifāyat al-jumal*). He attempts to show, in numerous examples and quotations, that the whole of *ahl al-bayt* spoke out against the immersion in the subtleties of theology, preferring the concept of *kifāyat al-jumal* instead.[518] Next to a general reference to the time of the *salaf*, ʿAlī b. Abī Ṭālib, the early Imāmiyya and Zaydiyya,[519] Caspian imams like the Hārūnī brothers al-Mu'ayyad bi-llāh Aḥmad b. al-Ḥusayn (d. 411/1020)[520] and Abū Ṭālib Yaḥyā b. al-Ḥusayn (d. 424/1033)[521] figure most prominently in Ibn al-Wazīr's detailed references. Their reasoning, as presented by Ibn al-Wazīr, generally tends towards an aversion to probing into that which does not necessarily need to be known. Deferment of conclusive judgement in cases of uncertainty in inessential matters of theology is portrayed as recommended or even incumbent.[522] Examples of the Hārūnī brothers, famous for their productivity in all essential fields of Zaydi scholarship, are supposed to show that the Zaydiyya was not always identified with speculative theology. Ibn al-Wazīr claims that in spite of the high productivity of the Hārūnī brothers, they did not advance much into speculative theology. The main part of theology produced in their vicinity was said to originate from foreign disciples and to be based on ʿAbd al-Jabbār in terms of its content. Correspondingly, other theological writings of Zaydi scholars do not refer to the early Zaydis themselves but rather to Muʿtazili scholars.[523]

The rest of the chapter is devoted to the classical *kalām* argument that philosophical speculation (*naẓar*) is vital to finding answers to the challenges of

517 Ibid., 18.

518 Ibid., 24.

519 Cf. ibid., 27–28. Among others, Ibn al-Wazīr names ʿAlī b. al-Ḥusayn (d. between 92/710 and 95/714), the eponym of the Zaydiyya Zayd b. ʿAlī (122/740), Jaʿfar al-Ṣādiq (148/765), Aḥmad b. ʿIsā (d. 247/861) and even al-Qāsim b. Ibrāhīm (d. 264/860), grandfather of the eponym of the Zaydiyya. According to Madelung in his *al-Imām al-Qāsim*, the latter made a decisive step towards integrating Muʿtazili concepts into Zaydi doctrine.

520 al-Wajīh, *Aʿlām* 100–103.

521 Ibid., 1121–1123.

522 See for example Ibn al-Wazīr, *Tarjīḥ* 26, 28.

523 Ibid., 32. This interpretation of Zaydi history diverges considerably from what modern research reveals. Madelung, for example, describes the relationship between "den späten Muʿtaziliten und einigen der kaspischen Zaiditenimamen im 4. (10.) und 5. (11.) Jh." as "besonders eng;" cf. Madelung, Islam im Jemen 175.

heretics.[524] Ibn al-Wazīr refutes this in two points, discussing the means of attaining knowledge and the first proofs against heretics.[525]

The second part starts again with the *basmala* and the *ḥamdala*. It was the result of a question that was directly presented to Ibn al-Wazīr by an inquirer. The apparently young inquirer (*mustarshid* or *walad*) wanted to know Ibn al-Wazīr's reason for abandoning the methods of speculative theology. This abandonment was manifest in a poem written by Ibn al-Wazīr. In a long passage, Ibn al-Wazīr explains his adverse reactions to the inquiries and methods of speculative theology as well as his emotional journey in search of satisfying sources in the quest for certainty.[526] Before venturing to answer the inquirer, he recollects himself, seeks forgiveness for his hostile conduct and praises the inquirer for honest searching and good manners.[527]

The response contains a direct appeal to the inquirer as well as a substantial section in which Ibn al-Wazīr explains the theological implications of the first verse of the poem that triggered the inquirer's irritation. In the appeal, Ibn al-Wazīr emphasizes experience and the search for peace as a major guideline in the quest for knowledge.[528] The section is divided into one passage in which Ibn al-Wazīr explains the meaning of his verses, followed by three chapters in which he discusses the doctrines implied in that meaning. The relevant verses read: "The principles of my religion are God's book, not the accidents (*aʿrāḍ*), in other principles I have no interest."[529] Ibn al-Wazīr's intention in theses verses can be summarized as pointing to what he consideres the principles of religion: the inimitability of the Quran (*iʿjāz*) and the perfection of creation (*iḥkām khalq al-makhlūqāt*). The "accidents" in the first line refer to the proof of God's existence based on the real existence of accidents (*dalīl al-akwān*), as shall be discussed below.[530]

The three chapters of the second part address three major topics: proof of God's existence, the ambiguous matters in the Quran and the distinction between metaphorical and literal meanings. The first chapter is divided into two points of discussion. In point one, Ibn al-Wazīr discusses how the proof of God's existence is independent of the proof of the modes of spatial presence of accidents (*ṭarīq al-akwān, dalīl al-akwān*).[531] Leaning heavily on Shaykh

524 Ibn al-Wazīr, *Tarjīḥ*, 44.
525 Ibid., 44–49.
526 Ibid., 61.
527 Ibid., 63.
528 Ibid., 64–67.
529 Ibid., 68; cf. Ibn al-Wazīr, *al-ʿAwāṣim* iii, 422.
530 Ibn al-Wazīr, *Tarjīḥ*, 68–77.
531 Ibid., 78.

Mukhtār, Ibn al-Wazīr instead sees the *aḥwāl*-proof as especially effective in the human perception of their own conditions, details and varieties (*dalīl al-anfus*). Similarly, perceiving the processes, movements and mechanisms in the organic and inorganic world around (*dalīl al-āfāq*), should lead to the same realization.[532] The arguments of other scholars from the Muʿtazili camp in support of Ibn al-Wazīr's position are discussed as well, as for instance the proof from compositeness (*dalālat al-tarkīb*) as rendered by ʿAbd al-Ḥamīd b. Abī l-Ḥadīd (d. 656/1258).[533]

In point two, Ibn al-Wazīr responds to the inquirer's question as to why Ibn al-Wazīr turned away from the *akwān*-proof. He does not explain all his reasons, other than that they were many, showed themselves increasingly throughout a long period of investigation, and were amplified by the disagreements and contradictions between the theologians' arguments.[534] On his own account, Ibn al-Wazīr lacks comprehensive understanding of all the arguments and refers the inquirer to Shaykh Mukhtār's *Kitāb al-Mujtabā*, where the latter discusses the arguments of the Muʿtazili schools of the Bahshamiyya and Baghdadiyya concerning the proof of God's existence.[535]

Chapter two is again addressed to the opponent to whom Ibn al-Wazīr initially responded. Indicating his return to the Quranic text for argumentation, he refutes two claims made by the opponent: Firstly, that he knows as much of God's essence and attributes as God himself knows.[536] Secondly, that he can understand and interpret the ambiguous matters (*taʾwīl al-mutashābihāt*) in the Quran.[537] Ibn al-Wazīr responds to both claims with a discussion of the ambiguous matters.[538] Here as elsewhere, the Quranic verse on which this debate is based is Q 3:7 and concerns the debate of whether or not those firmly grounded in knowledge (*al-rāsikhūn fī l-ʿilm*) are able to understand the meaning of the ambiguous verses in the Quran. Along with many Zaydi and other scholars, who, according to Ibn al-Wazīr,[539] do not think that *al-rāsikhūn fī l-ʿilm* are included in the knowledge of the ambiguities, Ibn al-Wazīr postulates that knowledge of the ambiguous matters and verses can only be of a general nature (*ʿalā l-jumla*). The knowledge that the human being is commanded to have

532 Ibid., 109–110.
533 Cf. ibid., 86.
534 Ibid., 116.
535 Cf. ibid., 117.
536 Ibid., 129.
537 Ibid., 140.
538 Ibn al-Wazīr adopts this thought from the commentators (*shurrāḥ*) of *Nahj al-Balagha*; cf. ibid., 129.
539 Cf. ibid., 141.

would thus refer to the clear or unambiguous matters (*muḥkamāt*) in which God explicitly addresses the human beings subject to divine law.[540] Hence, Ibn al-Wazīr perceives part of the problem in the confusion of the *muḥkamāt* and the *mutashābihāt*.[541]

Chapter three, the brief final chapter of the second part, is concerned with another misconception related to the confusion between the *muḥkamāt* and the *mutashābihāt*. Ibn al-Wazīr concludes his *Tarjīḥ* by demonstrating why the interpretation (*taʾwīl*) of metaphors belongs to the unambiguous rather than the ambiguous parts of the Quran. Thus, the ambiguous matters cannot justifiably be brought into the realm of the certainly understandable by calling them metaphors. Their meaning would then have to be understood by all who are gifted with an original human disposition (*fiṭra*).[542]

28 Additional Works Ascribed to Ibn al-Wazīr

There are a few other pieces which may have to be ranked in Ibn al-Wazīr's theological work although their identity and/or location cannot be verified. For example, *al-Tuḥfa l-ṣafiyya fī sharḥ al-abyāt al-ṣūfiyya* (*The Lucid Gem: A Commentary on the Mystic Verses*) is ascribed to either Ibn al-Wazīr or his brother al-Hādī. What can be said with near certainty is that it is a commentary on the latter's *al-Abyāt al-ṣūfiyya*.[543] Ibn Abī l-Rijāl as well as al-Wajīh mention alternative names for *al-Tuḥfa l-ṣafiyya*, namely *al-Nasamāt al-najdiyya fī l-niʿamāt al-wajdiyya* (*Breezes from the Nejd: Blessings of Ardor*)[544] and *Sharīʿat al-Furāt fī sharḥ al-Abyāt* (*The Drinking Place of the Euphrates: Commentary on The Verses*).[545] It is not known when Ibn al-Wazīr authored the writing, if he did at all. Copies of the manuscript are found in the Dār al-Makhṭūṭāt and the Maktabat al-Awqaf, as well as in private libraries.[546] Unfortunately, I did not get access to the writing for verification of the authorship or investigation of the content. Furthermore, al-Ḥarbī mentions a certain *Kitāb al-Radd ʿalā ṣāḥib*

540 Ibid., 159–163.
541 Ibid., 167–168.
542 Ibid., 189–192.
543 Al-Akwaʿ (intr.), *al-ʿAwāṣim* i, 73; al-Ḥibshī, *Maṣādir* 332.
544 Ibn Abī l-Rijāl, *Maṭlaʿ al-budūr* 153.
545 Al-Wajīh, *Aʿlām* 827.
546 According to al-Wajīh, the version in the Maktabat al-Awqāf carries the alternative title *Sharīʿat al-Furāṭ*. The oldest copy seems to be the one found in a collection in the Dār al-Makhṭūṭāt dating from 957/1550; cf. al-Wajīh, *Aʿlām*, 827. See also al-Ḥibshī, *Maṣādir* 332, who mentions a copy from 1179/1765–1766, and al-Ḥarbī, *Ibn al-Wazīr wa-ārāʾuhu* 91.

al-Nihāya wa-l-Maḥṣūl (*Refutation of the Author of The End and The Harvest*) referring to Fakhr al-Dīn al-Rāzī. According to al-Ḥarbī, Ibn al-Wazīr himself refers to the work in *Īthār al-ḥaqq* and *al-ʿAwāṣim*.[547] However, no reference to the refutation could be found in either of the two books. Al-Ḥarbī might have taken Ibn al-Wazīr's affirmative reference to Ibn al-Ḥājib's refutation of al-Rāzī's negation of *al-taḥsīn al-ʿaqlī* in vol. vii of *al-ʿAwāṣim* as a reference to a book of his own.[548] Another book, which only al-Ḥarbī knows of, is a certain *Kitāb al-Mubtadiʾ* (*Book on the Beginning*).[549] Neither the supposed reference in *al-ʿAwāṣim* nor any other information on the book could be verified.

Ibn al-Wazīr himself refers to a *qaṣīda* listed only by al-Ḥarbī as well: *al-Ijāda fī l-irāda* (*The Excellent Accomplishment: On the Will*) is a poem of 1200 lines and of much theological interest.[550] Fifty-four lines of the poem are quoted in *Īthār al-ḥaqq*.[551] Moreover, Ibn al-Wazīr mentions a brief treatise in which he collects and comments on the thoughts of Ibn Taymiyya and his pupil Ibn Qayyim al-Jawziyya. The default title of the writing is *Bayān al-ḥikma fī l-ʿadhāb al-akhrawī* (*The Elucidation of the Wisdom Behind Punishment in the Hereafter*). Ibn al-Wazīr's summary of the writing supposedly emphasizes the wise purposes that are intended behind the apparent evil of punishment.[552] Al-Ḥarbī suggests that the work is identical to *Ijāda fī l-irāda*.[553] However, this identification is unlikely. Firstly, Ibn al-Wazīr mentions both explicitly and separately.[554] Secondly, the *Ijāda* is a *qaṣīda*, whereas *Bayān al-ḥikma* is a collection of statements for example from Ibn al-Qayyim's *Ḥādī l-arwāḥ ilā bilād al-afrāḥ* (*Spurring Souls on to the Realm of Joy*) which is not written in verse. Yet, in all probability, the *Ijāda* is close to *Bayān al-ḥikma* where content is concerned. The contexts in which Ibn al-Wazīr mentions the *Ijāda* treat questions such as why God created the damned (*ashqiyāʾ*)[555] closely related to the question of punishment in the Hereafter.

A number of writings in response to legal questions are ascribed to Ibn al-Wazīr, namely *Risāla jalīla fī thalāth masāʾil: al-fiṭra, himā l-arāk, nikāḥ al-yatīmiyya* (*Splendid Epistle on Three Questions: Original Disposition, Protection*

547 Cf. al-Ḥarbī, *Ibn al-Wazīr wa-ārāʾuhu* 99.
548 Ibn al-Wazīr, *al-ʿAwāṣim* vii, 52.
549 Cf. Al-Ḥarbī, *Ibn al-Wazīr wa-ārāʾuhu* 99.
550 See for example Ibn al-Wazīr, *al-ʿAwāṣim* vi, 325, 342; Ibn al-Wazīr, *Īthār al-ḥaqq* 204.
551 Ibid., 202–204.
552 Ibid., 96.
553 al-Ḥarbī, *Ibn al-Wazīr wa-ārāʾuhu* 100.
554 Ibn al-Wazīr, *Īthār al-ḥaqq* 202–204. See also Hoover, Withholding Judgement 218–220.
555 Cf. Ibn al-Wazīr, *Īthār al-ḥaqq* 204.

of Arak Trees and the Marriage of an Orphan Girl),[556] *Risāla fī zakāt al-fiṭr* (*Epistle on the Almsgiving at the End of Ramadan*),[557] and *Jawāb Muḥammad b. Ibrāhīm ʿalā fuqahāʾ abyāt Ḥusayn fī taqdīr al-dirham wa-l-awqiya* (*Muḥammad b. Ibrāhīm's Response to the Jurists of Husayn's Verses on the Evaluation of the Dirham and the Awqiyya*).[558] Apparently, Ibn al-Wazīr wrote a *Mukhtaṣar fī ʿilm al-maʿānī wa-l-bayān* (*Brief Exposition on the Sciences of Stylistics and Imagery*) on the science of stylistics and imagery. However, according to the bibliographical literature, nothing but the title is extant.[559]

Numerous *qaṣīdas* of Ibn al-Wazīr are quoted in different sources. Much of the exchange that happened for example between Ibn al-Wazīr and his brother al-Hādī was written in verse. Furthermore, there is a separate refutation of the famous ʿAbbāsid poet and slanderer of ʿAlī b. Abī Ṭālib, Marwān b. Sulaymān b. Abī Ḥafsa (182/798).[560] Many of these poems are found in Ibn al-Wazīr's *Dīwān* or scattered throughout the collections of different writings in many Yemeni libraries. No itemization of all of them is attempted here due to their vast number. A number of other pieces ascribed to Ibn al-Wazīr in different bibliographical sources shall not be discussed because of the blatant errors of the ascription.[561]

Following on this survey of his works, an examination of the major concepts in Ibn al-Wazīr's thought is due.

556 Cf. al-Ḥarbī, *Ibn al-Wazīr wa-ārāʾuhu* 94; al-Ḥibshī, *Maṣādir* 221; al-Wajīh, *Aʿlām* 828.

557 Cf. al-Ḥarbī, *Ibn al-Wazīr wa-ārāʾuhu* 94; al-Wajīh, *Aʿlām* 828.

558 Cf. al-Ḥibshī, *Maṣādir* 221; al-Wajīh, *Aʿlām* 827.

559 Cf. al-Akwaʿ (intr.), *al-ʿAwāṣim* i, 76; al-Ḥarbī, *Ibn al-Wazīr wa-ārāʾuhu* 99; al-Ḥibshī, *Maṣādir* 384.

560 Ibn Abī l-Rijāl, *Maṭlaʿ al-budūr* iv, 154. On Ibn Abī Ḥafsa, see Bencheikh, Marwān al-Akbar b. Abī Ḥafṣa and Marwān al-Aṣghar b. Abī ʾl-Janūb.

561 An example of this would be a *Irshād al-nuqqād ilā tafsīr al-jihād* and other known pieces by Ibn al-Amīr al-Ṣanʿānī. Al-Wajīh probably ascribed it to Ibn al-Wazīr because it is found in al-Kibsī's collection of writings of Ibn al-Wazīr which al-Wajīh often referred to; cf. al-Wajīh, *Aʿlām* 826.

CHAPTER 3

Central Concepts of Ibn al-Wazīr's Epistemological Thought

1 Definitions of Knowledge

The definitions of knowledge (*ʿilm*) vary considerably among the theologians.[1] Ibn al-Wazīr introduces none of his books with a definition of knowledge. He was most often occupied with discussing the use and limits of knowledge rather than with defining it. Ibn al-Wazīr, like the Ashʿari scholar Fakhr al-Dīn al-Rāzī (d. 606/1209), required that the "knowledge of knowledge" must be necessary or intuitive.[2] In his *Burhān al-qāṭiʿ*—admittedly an extended reproduction of al-Rāzī's *Arbaʿīn*—Ibn al-Wazīr mentions that the distinction between knowledge and conjecture is self-evident and "common knowledge" (*al-ʿilm al-ʿādī*).[3] However, when explaining how to distinguish true knowledge from invalid convictions in *Īthār al-ḥaqq*, Ibn al-Wazīr mentions three necessary characteristics of knowledge, supposedly uniting the positions of "the scholars:" certain resolution (*jazm*), correspondence to outward realities (*al-muṭābaqa fī l-khārij*) and persistence in spite of raised doubt (*al-thabāt ʿinda l-tashkīk*).[4] Although the definitions of knowledge vary considerably, these three conditions generally recur in the definitions of other scholars, albeit with different expressions.[5]

1 For an excellent overview of definitions of knowledge as well as the attitudes towards defining knowledge among various Islamic groups, see Rosenthal, *Knowledge Triumphant* 46–69.

2 Ibid., 46. Others who were apprehensive of defining knowledge tended to come from Sufi or traditionalist circles. Rosenthal cites Abū Bakr b. al-ʿArabī (d. 543/1148) in his commentary on the *Jāmiʿ* of al-Tirmidhī as an example of traditionists who rejected a definition of knowledge because of its supposed clarity. Such definitions were too reminiscent of the need of speculative theologians to complicate the obvious in order to lead people astray; cf. Ibid., 50–51. This argument is one frequently referred to by Ibn al-Wazīr, although he rarely accuses the speculative theologians of deliberately leading people astray.

3 Ibn al-Wazīr, *al-Burhān al-qāṭiʿ* 49.

4 Ibn al-Wazīr, *Īthār al-ḥaqq* 120.

5 The exact terminology is, of course, a very important matter in definitions, as every term implies a different understanding. But since Ibn al-Wazīr does not stick rigidly to one term or definition, and since the three elements mentioned by him are generally the points of discussion, one may well say that his definition agrees with those of other scholars. For example, Ibn al-Malāḥimī (d. 536/1141) mentions the first two elements as Abū Hāshim's definition, calling them "the tranquility of the soul" (*sukūn al-nafs*) that "the believed thing is according to what

 | DOI:10.1163/9789004381117_005

What Ibn al-Wazīr termed *jazm* in the above definition is equivalent to what was also termed the "tranquility of the soul" (*sukūn al-nafs*), as both describe a state of resolve that an individual "finds within himself."[6] Bahshami-Muʿtazilis like ʿAbd al-Jabbār and with him Ibn al-Murtaḍā considered the "tranquility of the soul" the one essential characteristic of knowledge because they considered it the only criterion that distinguishes knowledge from emulation (*taqlīd*).[7] According to them, the object that one is convinced of on the authority of another may correspond to truth, but does not result in the tranquility of the soul. Ibn al-Wazīr was likewise aggrieved by the *taqlīd* of theological schools. Yet the distinctions he makes between the concept of knowledge and modes of knowing reveal that he sought to restrict the scope of what could be called items of certain knowledge by counterbalancing the subjective criterion of the "tranquility of the soul" with what he considered a more objective standard.

1.1 *Necessary* (ḍarūrī) *and Acquired* (muktasab) *Knowledge*

Among speculative theologians, knowledge is usually divided into two kinds: self-evident or necessary knowledge (*ḍarūrī*) and acquired or inferred knowledge (*muktasab, istidlālī*).[8] The broad definitions of both terms are challenged

---

it is firmly believed to be" (*anna muʿtaqadahu ʿalā mā iʿtaqadahu ʿalayhi*); cf. Ibn al-Malāḥimī, *Kitāb al-Muʿtamad* 13. Rosenthal shows that this and similar definitions were usually ascribed to the Muʿtazila; cf. Rosenthal, Knowledge Triumphant 63–64. For general elements of the concept of knowledge among theologians, see Shihadeh, Argument from Ignorance 173–174.

6 Cf. Peter, *God's Created Speech* 48. See also Ibn al-Wazīr, *Īthār al-ḥaqq* 120, for his use of *jazm*.

7 According to Peter, ʿAbd al-Jabbār did include in his definition of knowledge the coincidence between that about which the soul is in a state of tranquility, on the one hand, and the reality of that very thing, on the other hand. Yet the major emphasis was apparently on the tranquility of the soul; cf. Peter, *God's Created Speech* 43–45, 47–50. According to Ibn al-Malāhimī, ʿAbd al-Jabbār did not include the correspondence to truth in his definition; cf. Ibn al-Malāḥimī, *Kitāb al-Muʿtamad* 12. Different versions of ʿAbd al-Jabbār's definition seem to have existed. However, in Ibn al-Murtaḍā's thought, the emphasis on the tranquility of the soul is perceptible in that he says that tranquility of the soul is the only thing that distinguishes knowledge (*ʿilm*) from the other kinds of conviction (*iʿtiqād*), which include *taqlīd* according to some definitions. Furthermore, the knowing person knows that he knows by finding his soul in a state of tranquility; cf. Ibn al-Murtaḍā, Riyāḍat al-afhām 127, 130. See also Omari, The Theology of al-Balkhī 163. The other kind of conviction that was debated in this context is supposition (*ẓann*). A supposition, according to most Muʿtazila and especially those who belonged to the Bahshamiyya, was not characterized by the tranquility of the soul; cf. Reinhart, *Before Revelation* 155.

8 See for example Wensinck, *The Muslim Creed* 252; Abrahamov, Necessary Knowledge 20; Peter, *God's Created Speech* 53. An exception to this distinction is represented by the early Muʿtazili al-Jāḥiẓ (d. 255/868–869) along with the "People of Cognitions" (*ahl al-maʿārif*) associated with him; see below 165, 183.

only seldom. Necessary knowledge is knowledge that is not produced by human beings. Rather, it occurs in them independent of their choice. Necessary knowledge cannot coexist with doubt. It is God's production and not the result of philosophical speculation or inquiry.[9] Acquired knowledge, on the other hand, is arrived at by human efforts of speculation and inference according to the rules of reasoning.[10] The premises of the speculation must be based on prior knowledge. Yet a central feature of this kind of knowledge, according to Muʿtazili teaching, is that the result of the speculation and inference itself is not known beforehand. It must be preceded by the absence of knowledge, by doubt with regard to the matter in question.[11]

Although the lists of sources of necessary knowledge differ, there are a few common elements.[12] An essential element of necessary knowledge is formed by *a priori* or intuitive knowledge (*badīhī*). To this *a priori* knowledge belong self-consciousness or logical judgements such as the knowledge that a thing cannot be simultaneously true and false, or eternal and created. A second element of necessary knowledge occurs through the senses (*ḥissī*). Perception thus plays an important role in necessary knowledge. A third element is formed by experience. This element is not always seen as separate from sense perception. A last but not unimportant element of necessary knowledge is supplied by *tawātur* information. This refers mainly to divine revelation but also to other issues of non-empirical knowledge, especially of past events. In these cases, the truth of an item of information is determined by the methodological criteria of corroboration by different trustworthy sources.[13]

A major disagreement exists between the Ashʿariyya and the Muʿtazila concerning moral judgments as part of necessary knowledge. The question of the independent rational discernment of something as good or evil (*al-taḥsīn wa-l-taqbīḥ al-ʿaqlī*) is tantamount to the question of whether moral judgment is

9 Ibn al-Murtaḍā, Riyāḍat al-afhām 128–129; Abrahamov, Necessary Knowledge 21; Frank, *God's Created Speech* 405. An exception to this view was held by Imām al-Ḥaramayn al-Juwaynī (d. 478/1085), for example. Al-Juwaynī thought that speculation can result in necessary knowledge; cf. al-Juwaynī, *al-Shāmil* 111.

10 Ibn al-Murtaḍā, Riyāḍat al-afhām 131.

11 For a Muʿtazili definition of acquired knowledge, see Peters, *God's Created Speech* 55, 57–61; concerning the element of uncertainty prior to acquired knowledge, cf. ibid., 60. See also Ibn al-Murtaḍā, Riyāḍat al-afhām 136; Ṣubḥī, *al-Zaydiyya* 359.

12 See for example Abrahamov, Necessary Knowledge 22–22; Peter, *God's Created Speech* 53–55; Wensinck, *Muslim Creed*, 252–254.

13 An often-used example of the latter kind of *tawātur* knowledge is the existence of the city of Mecca. Although we have never been there, many witnesses have testified to its existence. Therefore its existence is not in doubt; cf. Weiss, Knowledge of the Past 88.

a natural ability or not.[14] Another central difference concerns the knowledge of God. A significant part of the Muʿtazila deems the knowledge of God's existence acquired knowledge. The necessity to acquire knowledge of God is the main reasoning behind the duty of philosophical speculation (*naẓar*). Ibn al-Murtaḍā represents the Bahshami branch of the Muʿtazila well when he writes:

> The knowledge of God is a duty (...). He is not known by necessity nor by emulation; hence the requirement of *naẓar*. Its incumbency is established because it takes the place of averting harm. The significance of what we say lies in that it is the first duty: No *mukallaf* is free of that duty at the beginning of being obliged to [practice] it, in contrast to the rest of the duties.[15]

Accordingly, there is little doubt that Ibn al-Murtaḍā, like the majority of Muʿtazili theologians as well as those of other schools, takes the distinction between necessary and acquired knowledge as a major basis for argumentation.[16]

Ibn al-Wazīr agrees with most of the mentioned elements of necessary knowledge. There is *a priori* or intuitive knowledge, which includes moral judgments on good and evil, as for example the evilness of lying, as well as logical judgments like the impossibility of the same thing being both eternal and created. Sense perception is a vital part of the whole of necessary knowledge. But this is hardly challenged by anyone. Starting with his first (known) book on theology, *al-Burhān al-qāṭiʿ*, it becomes evident that *tawātur* forms a crucial constituent of Ibn al-Wazīr's concept of necessary knowledge beyond the *tawātur* of revelation. Ibn al-Wazīr argues for the knowledge of the prophets' trustworthiness (and of course ultimately for that of their message) based on the necessity which occurs by way of corroboration: different pieces of evidence from sense perception and intellect that would be inconclusive by themselves together effect necessary knowledge.[17] In what follows, Ibn al-Wazīr does the same with regard to the solitary report (*aḥad*): A solitary report, inconclusive by itself, is elevated to necessary knowledge by contextual evidence (*qarīna*).[18]

14 The disagreement of course reflects a central difference between Muʿtazili and Ashʿari ontology. If the ability to make moral judgments is acquired, it depends on knowledge of God's revealed will. If it is immediately God-given, it is an intrinsic part of the human being, independent of revelation.

15 Ibn al-Murtaḍā, Riyāḍat al-afhām 138.

16 Ibid., 128.

17 Cf. Ibn al-Wazīr, *al-Burhān al-qāṭiʿ* 8–17, 38–43.

18 Cf. ibid., 36, 43–49. Including the solitary report in the possible sources of true knowledge

The necessary knowledge occurs because the intellect realizes by necessity that the circumstances corroborate the solitary information. Consequently, all central tenets of Islam in their broad and general form can be considered necessary knowledge. The interesting issue here is that something that is neither *naẓar* nor *a priori* knowledge yet leads to necessary knowledge, and this necessary knowledge is attainable by all. Therefore, it may be termed *al-ʿilm al-ḍarūrī al-ʿādī* (common necessary knowledge) according to Ibn al-Wazīr. The strong emphasis Ibn al-Wazīr puts on necessary knowledge is evident. But what about acquired knowledge?

1.2 *A Shift in Distinction: from Necessary and Acquired to Necessary and Conjectural Knowledge* (ʿilm ẓannī)

The division between necessary and acquired knowledge is a central question in Ibn al-Wazīr's epistemological argumentation. He rejects the distinction and argues that acquired (or inferred) knowledge cannot be considered knowledge in the true sense:

> Knowledge as a technical term: differentiation within it is not sound. And there is disagreement concerning its division into necessary and inferred (*istidlālī*) [knowledge]. The sound [opinion] is that it cannot be distinguished where it is established by necessity. And when this necessity ceases it can no longer be described as knowledge in the technical sense.[19]

According to Ibn al- al-Wazīr, knowledge without necessity may be called knowledge, as preponderant probability is often commonly called "knowledge." But it cannot be that kind of knowledge which constitutes what is commonly agreed upon by the necessity of its givenness. The acquired knowledge of the speculative theologians always includes an element of doubt, which needs to be overcome so that reflection can result in proper knowledge.[20] For Ibn al-Wazīr, this kind of knowledge cannot be part of the body of knowledge to which all believers must have access. Additionally, such so-called knowledge cannot be the basis of evaluating a Muslim's faith. Only the acknowledgement or rejection of necessary knowledge may determine who is a Muslim and

---

appears to be a feature common to those who reject the distinction between necessary and acquired knowledge. This is true, for example, for the Ẓāhirī Ibn Ḥazm (d. 456/1063) who excludes the solitary report that urges one to follow God from the realm of doubt and uncertainty; cf. Abrahamov, Necessary Knowledge 24–25.

19 Ibn al-Wazīr, *al-ʿAwāṣim* i, 211.

20 Cf. Peters, *God's Created Speech* 60.

who is not. This refers to Ibn al-Wazīr's continuous attempt to reduce mutual charges of unbelief.

The necessary characteristic of knowledge, "correspondence to outward realities" (*al-muṭābaqa fī l-khārij*), emphasizes this. Ibn al-Wazīr explains what this term means when he argues that the inner conviction of the certainty of a matter (*sukūn al-nafs*) is not enough, because "the heart of futile ones is at rest in its futility,"[21] and

> Conjectures (…) may be absolutely certain in the souls of those who have them, but they do not correspond to outward realities or the beliefs of the common Muslims (*iʿtiqādāt ʿawāmm al-muslimīn*).[22]

Hence, the subjective standard of inner conviction must be reinforced by an objective standard, if one is to claim true knowledge. Whatever conviction does not fulfill the requirements of necessary knowledge remains conjecture, even if its bearer perceives certainty in himself or tranquility in his soul.[23] Ibn al-Wazīr himself employs descriptions such as *sukūn al-nafs* in legal questions, where absolute certainty is not required.[24]

In the strict sense of the word, the term 'knowledge' applies only to necessary knowledge as far as Ibn al-Wazīr is concerned, i.e. knowledge that is bestowed by God and can neither be produced nor doubted and rebutted by human beings. Necessary knowledge denotes what is at times called *yaqīn* (certitude) and *ʿilm qaṭʿī* (certain knowledge) by Ibn al-Wazīr. However, there is another, less restricted sense in which the term "knowledge" can be employed and times attributed with conjecture, i.e. *ʿilm ẓannī* (conjectural knowledge). The significance of this other use of the term in Ibn al-Wazīr's thinking becomes evident in his *al-Ḥusām al-mashhūr*. The writing represents a defense of Ibn al-Murtaḍā's rival for the imamate, Imam al-Manṣūr bi-llāh ʿAlī. The legitimacy

21 Ibn al-Wazīr, *Īthār al-ḥaqq* 114.

22 Ibid., 120.

23 The problem of tranquility residing in the soul without any actual correspondence to the truth of the known thing was largely included in the defenses of different concepts of knowledge. Ibn al-Murtaḍā defended the decisiveness of the condition by saying that in such a case, there is no occurrence of tranquility in the soul resulting from the truth, but rather an act of appeasing it (*taskīn*). In such a case, tranquility in the soul does not result from truth. He does not explain, however, how one is to tell the difference; cf. Ibn al-Murtaḍā, Riyāḍat al-afhām 130. For al-Jāḥiẓ, this problem was a major leverage point in his argument against acquired knowledge; cf. al-Jāḥiẓ, al-Masāʾil wa-l-jawābāt fī l-maʿrifa 39–41.

24 Ibn al-Wazīr, *Kitāb al-Qawāʿid* f. 85b.

of al-Manṣūr's imamate was challenged by means of the argument that the imam does not possess sufficient knowledge. Ibn al-Wazīr effectively argues that the implication of this challenge is that the knowledge that is required of the imam should be acquired knowledge. He strives to show that this challenge is invalid by arguing that Imam al-Manṣūr possesses knowledge based on two arguments: 1. The imam is well versed in the texts of revelation; 2. The preponderant supposition (*al-ẓann al-rājiḥ*) is called knowledge. This tells us the following two things.

The first argument implies that thorough familiarity with the *tawātur* texts is tantamount to (necessary) knowledge. At the beginning of the discussion of what "spending all efforts to formulate an independent judgment on a legal or theological question" (*ijtihād fī l-ʿilm*) means, Ibn al-Wazīr writes:

> A group of men ignorant of the real meaning of true knowledge which the righteous forefathers possessed saw that our Lord, the Commander of the Faithful, al-Manṣūr bi-llāh, peace be upon him, is wholly engaged with contemplating what is beneficial (*maṣāliḥ*) and is dedicated to studying the noble Quran, the prophetic reports and the traditions of the companions like the righteous forefathers were, [yet he] does not plunge into the innovations that occurred in recent times after the extinction of the best of all times. What I mean is the plunging into the predestined events before they occur, which God's prophet hated.[25]

According to Ibn al-Wazīr, Imam al-Manṣūr has the knowledge required of an imam, unlike those who require of him another kind of knowledge:

> And when methods differed and creatures feuded, those who were not occupied with the sciences of the forefathers deemed those who were [occupied with them] void of knowledge. Just as those who were occupied with the sciences of the forefathers knew those ignorant of them [the sciences] to be blind to true knowledge. Thus, the ignorant ones combined the vilest ignorance with claims to the highest ranks of knowledge. How greatly strange that they consider knowledge what [really] is ignorance, and that they defame our Lord, the Commander of the Faithful, peace be upon him, for not being occupied with what they consider knowledge.[26]

25 Ibn al-Wazīr, *al-Ḥusām al-mashhūr* f. 103a.
26 Ibid., f. 103b.

Considering that the *tawātur* report is one—for Ibn al-Wazīr, the major—source of necessary knowledge, it makes perfect sense to ascribe knowledge to Imam al-Manṣūr on that basis. This is especially so in the light of Ibn Ibn al-Wazīr's view that the most obvious way of understanding the texts—that which occurs first in the mind and is indeed "common necessary knowledge"—is the most important method of employing them.[27] In another passage of *al-Ḥusạm al-mashhūr,* Ibn al-Wazīr refers to the ascetics who are known for having been given knowledge because they know what is most worthy of being known: the five pillars of Islam and *tawātur* reports.[28] Here Ibn al-Wazīr clearly argues on the basis of necessary knowledge. Imam al-Manṣūr has knowledge in the strict sense, because he knows what represents the most important part of necessary knowledge: the pillars of Islam, known by all, as well as *tawātur* transmission. Inferred or acquired knowledge, associated with speculative theology and other sciences that developed in later generations, cannot be made incumbent nor a prerequisite for the imam (or anyone else) as long as knowledge is to be understood in its strict sense.

The second argument is of another kind. It reveals the heart of Ibn al-Wazīr's epistemology. Although Imam al-Manṣūr may merely possess conjectural judgment on a number of questions, these are as good as knowledge as long as the indicators leading to those judgments are stronger than those leading to contrary judgments.

> Secondly, conjecture is called knowledge as the Exalted says {When you know them to be believers, do not send them back} [Q 60:10]. (…) Conjecture is called knowledge in language. This has been well put by the commentator of *Jamʿ al-jawāmiʿ* in a useful instruction, namely that the Quran finds fault with conjecture sometimes, and praises it at other times. The response to this is that it [conjecture] is an expression shared between doubt of equal (*mustawā*) or overruled (*marjūḥ*) likelihood on the one side. This is the dispraised kind when it relates to something where knowledge is incumbent. On the other side, there is the preponderant (*rājiḥ*) conjecture that emerges from evidence necessitating it (*al-mūjiba lahū*). This is the praised kind [of conjecture] which is called knowledge.[29]

27 Ibid., fs. 104a–105a.
28 Ibid., f. 104b.
29 Ibid., f. 104b.

Ibn al-Wazīr distinguishes between two meanings of the term conjecture (*ẓann*). On the one hand, there is conjecture that is not based on indicators. It is merely a claim or unfounded assumption, equivalent to the opposite of knowledge, i.e. ignorance (*jahl*).[30] On the other hand, sometimes conjecture may be based on indicators that render the object of the supposition "almost certain" (*ghālib al-ẓann*). This "almost certain" supposition is encouraged in the texts of revelation, and indeed often called knowledge, according to Ibn al-Wazīr. Consequently, Ibn al-Wazīr can assert that, whether the knowledge required of an imam by al-Manṣūr's detractors refers to necessary or to conjectural knowledge, Imam al-Manṣūr has what it takes.

At first sight, this equation seems to contradict Ibn al-Wazīr's insistence on necessary knowledge. But if reconsidered more closely, it becomes clear that the broadening of the term 'knowledge' is in perfect harmony with the other elements of Ibn al-Wazīr's thought. In *al-Burhān al-qāṭiʿ*, Ibn al-Wazīr tells the reader that the ever-present distinction between knowledge and conjecture is that knowledge is necessary whereas conjecture is not.[31] All necessary knowledge occurs in all people, scholars as well as laymen. It is given by God and leaves no room for doubt. All else is conjecture. Although Ibn al-Wazīr equates the speculative theologians' acquired knowledge with preponderant conjecture, and although he equates this preponderant conjecture at times with knowledge, the two differ tremendously from one another. This difference is rooted in the function that ambiguity has in each. In the case of acquired knowledge, ambiguity is a means to an end. In the case of knowledge as overwhelming probability, ambiguity is the end. It is the end that corresponds to the human limitation of knowing and of producing knowledge, which "every one finds in himself."[32]

Furthermore, this difference is manifest in the function that each of the two concepts can have in the broader context of theology and legal theory. Speculative theologians use acquired knowledge as a foundation of religious doctrines, much like necessary knowledge. The decisiveness of its content at a given time,

30 There are two different kinds of *jahl*. The one corresponding to reprehensible *ẓann* is signified by an unfounded conviction that a thing is what it is not. The other kind of *jahl* describes the mere absence of knowledge, which is not meant by the prohibition; cf. Ibn al-Wazīr, *Tarjīh* 26; Ibn al-Wazīr, *Īthār al-ḥaqq* 18. Ibn al-Wazīr is neither the first nor the only one to make this distinction; cf. Shihadeh, Argument from Ignorance 174. Ibn al-Wazīr refers to the Caspian imam al-Mu'ayyad bi-llāh in this distinction, according to whom only the first kind of *jahl* is meant by the rule that prohibits *jahl*. See also ʿAbd al-Jabbār's definition in Peter, *God's Created Speech* 43.

31 Ibn al-Wazīr, *al-Burhān al-qāṭiʿ* 49.

32 Ibn al-Wazīr, *al-ʿAwāṣim* i, 210.

the tranquility of the soul that is present at the time of conclusion, qualifies it as knowledge of the truth of its object. For the speculative theologians, the initial doubt is no longer effective. But for Ibn al-Wazīr, knowledge of the truth of a thing cannot occur unless it was always beyond doubt.[33] He does not distinguish between temporal and absolute absence of doubt. All true knowledge is necessary knowledge. Necessary knowledge exists only in "the general tenets" (*jumal*)—those things that are necessarily known by all (*al-ʿilm al-ḍarūrī al-ʿādī*).[34] The theologians' acquired knowledge is claimed for the details of matters. Indeed, one reason why acquired knowledge can be termed knowledge at all is that it is a particularization of the necessary knowledge that is general.[35] But Ibn al-Wazīr argues that what they claim to be knowledge is really only a preponderant probability, a conjecture that is likely to be true. In contrast to the claim theologians make for their acquired knowledge, preponderant probability can never be made the foundation of doctrine. Doctrine cannot rest on the subjective criteria of the tranquility of the soul of the individual, arrived at by inference. Ibn al-Wazīr argues that the term *ʿilm* for conjectural matters is used in the Quran for things that the human being is encouraged or obliged to refer to.[36] He should "know" them rather in the sense that he should be occupied or acquainted with them. But he does not have, or cannot arrive at, a certain knowledge of them. This inquiry has practical rather than theoretical purposes. Like in the realm of legal methodology, preponderant probability may inform action, not theory or certain knowledge. Representing the realm of theory, it is the *jumal* that are known for certain because of necessary knowledge, and because the subjective inner state of individual "certainty" is reinforced by the commonality of the knowledge. But the concrete matters that require detailed response are vast. It seems that there is in actual fact little of which the human being can have true knowledge in the strict sense of the word. Thus, concerning their epistemic value, Ibn al-Wazīr equates all matters other than the most basic Islamic doctrines with the legal matters of substantive law. They are only probable, theoretically always allowing the possibility of another position or of someone else's deeper insight. But since no more certainty than this high probability can be arrived at, it must be taken as the basis for judgments and actions and theological statements. To emphasize it once again: the epistemic value of all these does not go beyond overwhelming probability at best.

---

33 See also Ibn al-Wazīr, *Tarjīḥ* 97–98.

34 Ibid., i, 211.

35 See for example Ibn al-Murtaḍā, Riyāḍat al-afhām 131; Ibn al-Malāḥimī, *Kitāb al-Fāʾiq* 369, 389.

36 Cf. Ibn al-Wazīr, *al-ʿAwāṣim* iv, 40.

Abrahamov shows how necessary knowledge mainly has been used as a basis of proof in Islamic theology. He argues that those issues where it has been used as evidence on its own merit were the "basic issues of Islamic theology."[37] I suggest that these "basic issues of Islamic theology" are identical to what Ibn al-Wazīr calls "the general tenets" (*jumal*). Abrahamov focusses on those theologians who did distinguish between necessary and acquired knowledge. But I suggest that the same is true for those who did not make that distinction: necessary knowledge is used as evidence itself in the basic and general issues of Islamic theology. In contrast to those who do distinguish, Ibn al-Wazīr does not see that philosophical speculation can lead to anything but overwhelming probability in the non-basic issues of Islamic theology.[38]

2 Definitions of the Means to Possess Knowledge

2.1 *A Shift in the Definition: from* Naẓar *as Philosophical Speculation to* Naẓar *as Pious Contemplation*

Ibn al-Wazīr's third criterion for knowledge, i.e. persistence (of the conviction) in spite of raised doubt (*al-thabāt ʿinda l-tashkīk*), is aimed against the notion of *naẓar* as a first duty. The definition of *naẓar* established by the theologians requires prior doubt regarding, or ignorance of, the object of later knowledge.[39] Ibn al-Murtaḍā writes that *naẓar* must produce something that was not there before.[40] Furthermore, the certainty of the result of *naẓar* is determined by the way it is practiced. *Naẓar* implies that the connection between an indication (*dalīl*) and that which it indicates (*madlūl*) is followed in a particular way that

---

37 Abrahamov, Necessary Knowledge 24.

38 There is of course another question, but one which I will not answer in much detail, as to whether there are any objective standards for the border between the necessary and the probable. Ibn al-Wazīr does refer to common necessary knowledge in a number of quite concrete matters. He does consider the corroboration of a solitary report and contextual evidence as informing necessary knowledge equal to *tawātur*. The transition from assumption to necessity in *tawātur* is no new subject. Al-Ghazālī and others state that the exact point of transition cannot be determined; cf. Weiss, Knowledge of the Past 88–90. Weiss speaks of an "adequate" number of witnesses. The point at which conjecture turns to knowledge depends on the experience of the individual. Ibn al-Wazīr formulates something similar with reference to the *mutawātir* traditions. It is not far-fetched to assume that he determined the point where probability turns into necessary knowledge, for example in the case of contextual evidence, with similar vagueness. For more on the criteria of *tawātur*, see van Ess, *Erkenntnislehre* 412–413.

39 See, for example, Ibn al-Malāḥimī, *Kitāb al-Fāʾiq* 376.

40 Ibn al-Murtaḍā, Riyāḍat al-afhām 137.

generates knowledge (*tawallud*). The second condition that Ibn al-Murtaḍā mentions for a conviction to be called knowledge is that it was "generated by correct speculation," implying the existence of incorrect speculation.[41] Ibn al-Malāḥimī writes that for *naẓar* to generate knowledge it must be based on correct premises, as well as consist in the correct ordering of these premises.[42] As Peter shows for ʿAbd al-Jabbār's thought, the connections drawn between the indication and the indicated are not always necessary. Doubt may enter here as well.[43] According to Ibn al-Murtaḍā, one distinction between necessary and acquired knowledge is that the former "cannot be expelled from the soul by doubt or sophism" whereas the latter can.[44] Ibn al-Wazīr rejects this notion of *naẓar*:

> If the suspicion (*waswasa*) occurs at the foundations of the evidence then doubt [*shakk*] will bring knowledge to an end. This necessitates renewed speculation. This is the opinion of Abū Hāshim and his followers who do not require that speculation arrive at the necessary premises. Rather, they are content with the tranquility of the soul concerning the foundations of the evidence, [because they] are only concerned with [the issue of] suspicion on that level. If they hold that to be true, it represents a great decline. It follows that the foundations of the evidence, which are an expression of the premises, cannot possibly be known with absolute certitude without doubt. Consequently, there is doubt in the result. (…) If the consensus of Muslims has concluded that the one to whom suspicion occurs in spite of spending the greatest effort in *naẓar* is not charged with unbelief, it follows that it is not assumed that decisive indicators (*al-adilla al-qāṭiʿa*) lead to the kind of certitude that necessitates the tranquility of the soul. Or this is not possible because it [the certitude] is oftentimes absent in spite of the abundance of claims to it. Hence, *naẓar* is possible but what it generates is diverse.[45]

For Ibn al-Wazīr, the existence of doubt at any stage of the process of knowledge means that this doubt is inherent in the relationship between the subject

41 Ibid., 131.
42 Ibn al-Malāḥimī explains how different conclusions can result from inquiry into the same questions, if, for example, the ordering of the premises (*tartīb al-muqaddimāt*) was not done correctly; cf. Ibn al-Malāḥimī, *al-Muʿtamad* 53–54.
43 Cf. Peter, *God's Created Speech* 65–68.
44 Ibn al-Murtaḍā, Riyāḍat al-afhām 129.
45 Ibn al-Wazīr, *al-ʿAwāṣim* iv, 49–50.

and its object of *naẓar*. Doubt or forgetfulness may return at any time, requiring renewed *naẓar*.[46] And, more gravely according to Ibn al-Wazīr, this doubt exists at levels as fundamental as the foundations of the evidence (*arkān al-dalīl*), resulting in the doubting of the most essential things, like God's existence. But these are the foundations of all secondary doctrines for which certainty is claimed. Consequently, not only the definition of knowledge in the strict sense would be invalidated, but also the grounds on which the faith of a Muslim is evaluated. In short, the definition of *naẓar* is another reason why Ibn al-Wazīr thinks that knowledge based on inference cannot be termed knowledge in the strict sense of the word. The threefold description of knowledge above (*jazm* or *sukūn al-nafs*, *al-muṭābaqa fī l-khārij* and *al-thabāt ʿinda l-tashkīk*) therefore always refers to necessary knowledge. A summarizing comment on a passage about necessary knowledge and its circumstances in *al-ʿAwāṣim* illustrates how Ibn al-Wazīr views the connection between acquired knowledge and *naẓar*:

> In sum, they [the speculative theologians] have made the admission of doubts and sophisms now and later the measurement by which they distinguish their kind of knowledge from ignorance (*jahl*), from the conviction that results from emulation (*taqlid*) and from matters of the necessary knowledge which does not need to be sought by speculation or teaching. If you have considered all this you will have found that all that can be described by these characteristics is far from that knowledge which can be distinguished from other things by certain resolution (*jazm*) and decisiveness (*qaṭʿ*). This is so, because whatever may be discovered to be invalid now, has never been certain knowledge. There is no difference whatsoever between it and preponderant conjecture.[47]

Besides illustrating Ibn al-Wazīr's rejection of acquired knowledge as knowledge, the passage refers to another aspect of Ibn al-Wazīr's epistemology: the distinction between knowledge and conjecture. Ibn al-Wazīr is obviously not averse to inquiry into the sources nor to the inference of information. However, he rejects the idea that *naẓar* in the realm of acquired knowledge as defined by the theologians leads to anything other than probable knowledge. And this

---

46 The position of the speculative theologians here challenged by Ibn al-Wazīr corresponds to Ibn al-Murtaḍā, Riyāḍat al-afhām 132. Acquired knowledge, in contrast to necessary knowledge, may be disproved or become absent (*intifāʾ*) if doubt, suspicion, inattentiveness or forgetfulness enters at the level of the premises of the inquiry that lead to the knowledge; cf. Ibn al-Malāḥimī, *Kitāb al-Fāʾiq* 393.

47 Ibn al-Wazīr, *al-ʿAwāṣim* i, 209.

kind of knowledge is on a par with other results of intellectual endeavor and does not qualify as a standard for truth or faith.

In Ibn al-Murtaḍā's thinking, *naẓar* figures as the first duty of every believer, and it is clear that *naẓar* generates certain yet acquired knowledge. Its significance is illustrated by the amount of knowledge that is required of every believer. In *al-Durar al-farāʾid*, Ibn al-Murtaḍā determines what needs to be known by every *mukallaf*:

> The later scholars of our school (*aṣḥābunā min al-mutaʾakhkhirīn*) have restricted it [the required amount] to thirty issues, ten concerning divine unicity, ten concerning divine justice and ten concerning promise and threat. Those concerning divine unicity are divided into affirmation and negation (…).[48]

Another slightly mitigated list that insists on the necessity of detailed knowledge is followed by Ibn al-Murtaḍā's conclusion and the indication that the required knowledge in each area will be specified in the respective chapters:

> Know that the requisite amount in every question where knowledge is required is the knowledge of what is true in it and the evidence that it is indeed true. This evidence amounts to the ordering of the premises (*tartīb al-muqaddimāt*) in the way that leads to knowledge. [Acquiring] this amount [of knowledge] is an individual duty.[49]

It is obvious that knowledge generated by *naẓar* amounts to a considerable part of the knowledge required of every common *mukallaf*. After all, the essential doctrines like God's unicity and justice, and the promise and the threat, have to be known in detail and by way of rational inference.

Ibn al-Wazīr is not the first to reject the distinction between necessary and acquired knowledge. Nor was he the only thinker to include preponderant probability in a broader concept of knowledge. In *al-ʿAwāṣim*, he discusses three (and elsewhere two) groups of theologians who supposedly held views similar to his own on the present topic.[50] This is in line with Ibn al-Wazīr's constant attempt to show that neither all Zaydis nor all Muʿtazilis took *naẓar* to be the first duty. Not all were set on the idea that human beings are able to produce certain knowledge themselves.

48 Quoted from al-Ḥayyī, *al-Muntazaʿ min al-Durar al-farāʾid* f. 4b.

49 Ibid., f. 5a.

50 Ibn al-Wazīr, *al-ʿAwāṣim* iv, 30–44.

The common feature of these groups consists in the severing of the causative relation between *naẓar* and knowledge. Al-Jāḥiẓ, and the so-called People of Cognitions (*ahl al-maʿārif*) associated with him, insisted that all true knowledge is necessary.[51] According to them, the role of *naẓar* consists in the contemplation of the things known by necessity. For the acquisition of knowledge, *naẓar* is merely a relative condition (*sharṭ iʿtibārī*).[52] It means that *naẓar* may coincide with knowledge, yet does not generate it. This resounds with Ibn al-Wazīr's description of commendable *naẓar*. He often quotes al-Jāḥiẓ's *al-ʿIbar wa-l-iʿtibār* with reference to proving God's existence and unicity through contemplation (*naẓar*) of the order of the natural necessary phenomena in the universe. Like the contemplation of miracles and perceptible things, contemplation of the necessary things of religion like death also belongs to this category. Ibn al-Wazīr's *Dīwān* is full of examples of this kind of reflection.[53] Al-Mu'ayyad bi-llāh al-Hārūnī in his *Siyāsat al-murīdīn* is quoted as having urged the contemplation of death for the very reason that it is known to exist by necessity.[54] This kind of *naẓar* has as its goal to come nearer to God.

In his definition of the commendable kind of *naẓar*, Ibn al-Wazīr often refers to the no longer extant *Kitāb al-Mujtabā* by the Muʿtazili Shaykh Mukhtār. Apparently, the latter defined *naẓar* as "divesting the intellect of distractions" (*tajrīd al-ʿaql ʿan al-ghaflāt*)[55] or "divesting the heart" (*al-qalb*).[56] This expression implies that the function of *naẓar* is to remind the human being of that which he knows already by necessity, rather than to generate (*tawallud*) knowledge following a particular order of premises (*tartīb al-muqaddimāt*) as described by the theologians.

Ibn al-Wazīr further quotes Shaykh Mukhtār, who referred to his own teacher Rukn al-Dīn al-Malāḥimī as one who did not require the acquisition of knowledge from every common Muslim.[57] Due to the lack of direct access to Shaykh Mukhtār's views, it is impossible to say whether or not this interpretation of Ibn al-Malāḥimī originates with Shaykh Mukhtār. It may also emanate from Ibn al-Wazīr's habitual attempt to harmonize and argue against contemporary Muʿtazili views with support from earlier Muʿtazila. However, the reading of

51 See also Abrahamov, Necessary Knowledge 24.
52 Ibn al-Wazīr, *al-ʿAwāṣim* iii, 423.
53 See for example Ibn al-Wazīr, *Majmaʿ al-ḥaqāʾiq* 382, 386, 396; Ibn al-Wazīr, *Dīwān* laq. 25a, 34a, 59a.
54 See for example Ibn al-Wazīr, *al-ʿAwāṣim* iv, 35.
55 Ibn al-Wazīr, *Tarjīḥ* 49.
56 Ibn al-Wazīr, *Īthār al-ḥaqq* 15.
57 Ibn al-Wazīr, *al-ʿAwāṣim* iv, 71. Shaykh Mukhtār's quote of Ibn al-Malāḥimī as rendered by Ibn al-Wazīr can be found in al-Malāḥimī, *Kitāb al-Fāʾiq* 6.

Ibn al-Malāḥimī's *Kitab al-Muʿtamad fī uṣūl al-dīn* shows a picture that differs from the way Ibn al-Wazīr presents him. Ibn al-Malāḥimī spends considerable effort on arguing that *naẓar* according to a certain order of premises (*tartīb al-muqaddimāt*) leads to acquired knowledge, that this kind of *naẓar* is a duty, and that it is the first duty of every believer once the state of responsibility is reached (*taklīf*).[58]

In contrast, Ibn al-Wazīr ranges Ibn al-Malāḥimī's student Shaykh Mukhtār with al-Jāḥiẓ and the *ahl al-maʿārif* in that he considers *naẓar* merely a relative condition (*sharṭ iʿtibārī*) of knowledge.[59] But unlike those with whom Ibn al-Wazīr contends, Ibn al-Malāḥimī does not call those unable to reach knowledge in all the details of doctrine by *naẓar* unbelievers.[60] A general comprehension, reminiscent of Ibn al-Wazīr's *jumal*, suffices them as knowledge. But while Ibn al-Malāḥimī requires that this general knowledge be acquired, Ibn al-Wazīr considers it necessary.[61] Still, Ibn al-Wazīr might have found Ibn al-Malāḥimī's views on the issue less severe than those of contemporary opponents. In comparison, Ibn al-Murtaḍā concludes every section on one of the essential attributes of the Divine in *al-Durar al-farāʾid* with the details of what knowledge is required of the ordinary believer (*mukallaf*). These details would doubtless be counted among the subtleties of *kalām*, as for example that God is able (*qadīr*) in his essence, not by an ability.[62]

According to Ibn al-Wazīr, the difference between philosophical speculation of the theologians and his pious contemplation—the two different definitions of *naẓar*—consists in the nature of the knowledge that results from it. *Naẓar* in the sense of philosophical speculation, on the one hand, consists in an inferential activity on the basis of necessary knowledge leading to other kinds of knowledge.[63] These kinds of knowledge are based on the choice and the activity of the human being. *Naẓar* in the sense of pious contemplation, on the other hand, does not generate knowledge. It leads to approximation to God. It may

58 Ibn al-Malāḥimī, *Kitāb al-Muʿtamad* 79–82; Ibn al-Malāḥimī, *Kitāb al-Fāʾiq* 7–9. About *naẓar* and *tartīb al-muqaddimāt* according to reason, see ibid., 363.

59 Ibn al-Wazīr, *Tarjīḥ* 95–97.

60 Ibn al-Malāḥimī, *Kitāb al-Muʿtamad* 63.

61 For Ibn al-Malāhimī, like the majority of Muʿtazila, acquisition of knowledge beyond the necessary is a vital duty. Conjecture in questions like God's unicity, justice etc., although allowed in cases of incapability, could never fulfill *taklīf*; cf. Ibn al-Malāḥimī, *Kitāb al-Muʿtamad* 60–64.

62 Cf. al-Ḥayyī, *al-Muntazaʿ min al-Durar al-farāʾid* f. 22b.

63 Ibn al-Murtaḍā and some Zaydis, however, hold that there are kinds of acquired knowledge which do not have their root in necessary knowledge; cf. Ibn al-Murtaḍā, Riyāḍat al-afhām 133.

correlate with knowledge but it does not have knowledge as its goal. If knowledge occurs, it is necessary, is given by God, and depends on neither the choice nor the activity of the human being. But if no knowledge occurs, the purpose of *naẓar* is not frustrated.[64]

The process described by al-Jāḥiẓ as reflection on nature, for example, may also be termed *naẓar*. But it is far from being a means by which a truth is deliberately proved by a conscious process of ordering correct premises. Rather, it coincides with the necessary knowledge of the meaning of the world (*dalīl al-āfāq*), the miracles, or the observed self (*dalīl al-anfus*). It is tantamount to the knowledge occurring by way of the senses or intuition in the natural human disposition (*fiṭra*).[65]

2.2 *Shifting the Emphasis: Original Human Disposition* (fiṭra) *and Intellect* (ʿaql)

All concepts of *fiṭra* as the original human disposition go back to a Quranic verse as well as a prophetic report. Q 30:30 speaks of a particular constitution "with which God created man," and unto which Muhammad is to set his purpose.[66] According to tradition, the prophet Muhammad said that "every infant is born according to *fiṭra*, then his parents make him a Jew or a Christian or a Zoroastrian, just as an animal is born intact."[67] The concept of *fiṭra* was mainly discussed in the context of the legal status of children and unbelievers, as well as their destiny in the Hereafter.[68] Both contexts imply an idea of pre-natal originality as well as uprightness in the sense of monotheistic religion. This resulted in the notion that the original nature of every human being is identical with Islam.[69] Although the term does not figure majorly in Muʿtazili literature, the notion of identifying Islam with the original human nature supported a number of Muʿtazili doctrines that caused indignation among their Ashʿari counterparts. The notion underscores the Muʿtazili emphasis on human responsibility for evil, but undermines the Ashʿari stress on the sovereignty of divine will and

---

64 Ibn al-Wazīr, *al-ʿAwāṣim* iv, 39.

65 On the *dalīl al-āfāq* and the *dalīl al-anfus*, see Ibn al-Wazīr, *Tarjīḥ* 109–110; cf. this study, 147 above.

66 Q 30:30 reads {So [Prophet] as a man of pure faith, stand firm and true in your devotion to the religion. This is the natural disposition God instilled in mankind—there is no altering God's creation—and this is the right religion, though most people do not realize it}.

67 For the *fiṭra* tradition, see for example al-Bukhārī, *Ṣaḥīḥ* xxiii, hadith 441.

68 van Ess, *Zwischen Hadith und Theologie* 110–114; Gobillot, *La Fiṭra*.

69 On the identification of *fiṭra* with Islam, see for example Adang, Islam as the Inborn Religion 391–410; Holtzman, Human Choice 163–188.

guidance.[70] Furthermore, it stands to reason that, if every human being is born a Muslim, divine revelation is little more than a confirmation of what the original disposition of the human being already knows. This idea is reminiscent of the Muʿtazili concept of the relationship between reason and revelation.[71]

Griffel shows that the epistemological dimension of *fiṭra* was hardly discussed by early Muslim scholars up until the time of al-Ghazālī.[72] In Ibn al-Wazīr's thought, it is in the context of knowledge that the concept of *fiṭra* is most often referred to. How then does he answer the question that would be asked in a discussion of the epistemological dimension of *fiṭra*? I borrow from Griffel and ask: "What knowledge does the original disposition of humans include?"[73] And does Ibn al-Wazīr take the originally created *fiṭra* to be identical to the Islamic religion? And what does that mean for Ibn al-Wazīr's view on the relationship between human knowledge and revelation?

To answer these questions one must look at the function Ibn al-Wazīr assigned to *fiṭra*, and of course what *fiṭra* really is in his thought. Ibn al-Wazīr does not give a clear definition of his concept of *fiṭra* anywhere in his writings. He first mentioned *fiṭra* in his *Tarjīḥ* when championing the *ahl al-jumal* whose thirst for certain knowledge was satisfied with the general tenets (*al-iktifāʾ bi-l-jumal*). Another occasion for a discussion of *fiṭra* was the distinction between the ambiguous and the clear matters in the Quranic text.[74] Moreover, the concept is extensively employed in the passage on the distinction between necessary and acquired knowledge in the fourth volume of *al-ʿAwāṣim*. Beyond that, the concept of *fiṭra* is the single most important methodological argument in *Īthār al-ḥaqq*.

In *Tarjīḥ*, Ibn al-Wazīr defends *fiṭra* as the source of knowledge in two functions. Firstly, the original human disposition created by God in man is sufficient to understand the meaning of the Quranic text. Ibn al-Wazīr's opponent apparently claimed that the revealed texts contain a high number of ambiguities, requiring prior knowledge and skill for their interpretation before knowledge of the essential truths can be extracted from them.[75] Secondly, according to Ibn al-Wazīr, the original human disposition knows the major tenets that unite all Muslims in a general manner. These *jumal* include extra-Quranic knowledge, namely necessary knowledge.[76] Although it appears that the second function is

70 Macdonald, Fiṭra.
71 Cf. Peters, *God's Created Speech* 95–102, 404.
72 Griffel, Original Human Disposition 5.
73 Ibid., 5.
74 Ibn al-Wazīr, *Tarjīḥ* 44, 189–192.
75 Ibn al-Wazīr, *Tarjīḥ* 8–9.
76 Ibid., 189–192.

broader and therefore more essential than the first one, we must keep in mind that Ibn al-Wazīr's main concern in *Tarjīḥ* is man's ability to understand divine revelation. It is only natural, therefore, that he should have focused more on the Quranic text.

The answer to our first question (What knowledge does the original disposition of human beings include?) appears obvious at first. In both functions of *fiṭra* described in *Tarjīh*—understanding the meaning of the texts of revelation and knowing the major Islamic doctrines—but especially in the first one, the human *fiṭra* is sufficient to know the meaning of texts and principles. But at second glance, it does not really answer the question. This is because Ibn al-Wazīr does not discuss knowledge that is *included* in the *fiṭra* in the sense that it is possessed by it in its original state. The *fiṭra* does not already possess the content of revelation. Rather, the *fiṭra* is a faculty which understands and knows the meaning of the information provided in the Quran. In that sense, the answer to the second question concerning the identity of *fiṭra* and Islam would have to be answered in the negative. *Fiṭra* appears to be a kind of disposition towards understanding God's revelation, rather than a body of information that already contains the knowledge confirmed by the content of the Quran.

The second function—the knowledge of the *jumal*—promises to be more conducive to understanding what knowledge is included in the original disposition. In *Īthār al-haqq*, the reader is presented with seven major issues (*ashyā*ʾ) that constitute general necessary knowledge or the broad general tenets known by all (*jumal*). The first issue is all necessary knowledge, the second through the sixth are the major Islamic tenets and the last is an awareness of divergence from the five Islamic tenets (*ʿadam al-ziyāda wa-l-naqṣ*). *Fiṭra* is a term often used in *al-ʿAwāṣim* as well. In most instances, Ibn al-Wazīr refers to "human intellects in their original state" (*fiṭar al-ʿuqūl*)[77] according to which God created human beings. When distinguishing between the blameworthy and the praised kind of conjecture, Ibn al-Wazīr writes:

> Wherever it [conjecture] is dispraised, what is intended is the doubt relying upon which human intellects in their original state know to be blameworthy. Wherever it is praised, what is intended is the preponderant, acting according to which human intellects in their original state know to be good.[78]

77 Ibn al-Wazīr's use of the plural indicates that this disposition is a common feature of all human beings' intellects.

78 Ibn al-Wazīr, *al-ʿAwāṣim* iv, 53.

True to type, Ibn al-Wazīr reduces almost every doctrine and theological problem to a minimum. Then he claims essential agreement on this minimum in the sense of a lowest common denominator. This represents the corresponding "tenet" in its most general form, i.e. *jumal*. Somewhere within the discussion of each of these doctrines, he refers to *fiṭar al-ʿuqūl* to show that these *jumal* are naturally and necessarily agreed upon. They are agreed upon because they are received and necessarily understood by every human being that is liable to *taklīf*. Indeed, whoever does not understand them cannot be liable to *taklīf*, in contradistinction to the subtle and detailed matters of knowledge which which require prolonged study, yet do not result in necessary knowledge.

> Experience shows that the principle proofs (*awāʾil al-adilla*) are stronger than the cryptic studies for which the theologians claim dependency on them [the principle proofs]. That is why Shaykh Maḥmūd [Ibn al-Malāḥimī], Shaykh Mukhtār and others among the Muʿtazili scholars have affirmed that every *compos mentis* quickly grasps them. And whoever does not understand them, is no *mukallaf* whatsoever, as will soon be shown in the third aspect. Be that as it may, both groups have concluded that they [the principle proofs] are strong, sound and conceivable for human intellects in their original state.[79]

In short, it is the essential tenets in their general form that are immediately realized by the original disposition upon the grasp of the most principle proofs. Hence, necessary knowledge is tantamount to *jumal*: both are known by *fiṭra*.

Interestingly, Ibn al-Wazīr's definition of *fiṭra* corresponds in many ways to the common Muʿtazili definition of *ʿaql*. Indeed, an overlap of the concepts of *ʿaql* and *fiṭra* is not uncommon.[80] Ibn al-Murtaḍā in *Riyāḍat al-afhām* defines *ʿaql* as follows:

> We say: if it [*ʿaql*] was something other than the ten [knowledge items] it would be correct [to say] that it exist and not exist and the opposite [all at once]. The ten are knowledge of the self and its states,[81] [knowl-

79 Ibid., 78.

80 Hoover shows how Ibn Taymiyya uses the two almost interchangeably; cf. Hoover, *Ibn Taymiyyah's Theodicy* 39–44.

81 "Knowledge of the self and its states" means that one knows that one exists, that one is willing or needy etc.

> edge] by sense perception, by intuition,[82] [knowledge of] rational principles,[83] by experience like [knowing] that stone breaks glass, [knowledge] of the connection between the action and its actor, of important recent events,[84] of the speaker's obvious intentions, [knowledge] of the detestableness of the detestable and the existence of duty; Abū ʿAlī [al-Jubbāʾī includes knowledge] by *tawātur* report; Abū Hāshim [al-Jubbāʾī says] that this is not part of the cognitions of *ʿaql* until after *taklīf* by revelation,[85] because *ʿaql* is complete without it through the rational knowledge of the duty and the detestable.[86]

ʿAql, according to this definition, includes all kinds of information that is indisputable. This is very similar to Ibn al-Wazīr's concept of *fiṭra*, which includes all kinds of things known by necessity. Yet, a difference exists between the two concepts, which bears on the answer to the question of whether or not *fiṭra* (and *ʿaql* accordingly) is identical to Islam. The answer becomes evident at the outset of both scholars' lists of what is known by *fiṭra* or *ʿaql*. Ibn al-Wazīr, criticizing speculative theologians for the attempt to attain detailed and certain knowledge of divine things, writes:

> I considered all the disagreement that happens between the denominations of the unbelievers and Muslims. With all their diversity and branches, as a whole they all go back to seven things, which *can easily be understood* by the *fiṭra* (*mudrakuha bi-l-fiṭra qarīb*), God's natural disposition according to which He has created people.[87]

---

82 Examples of intuitive knowledge are that the whole is more than a part or that five is half of ten.

83 Rational principles refer to the knowledge that a thing must be either negated or affirmed, or that a thing cannot be existent and non-existent.

84 Such knowledge would entail the event of an earthquake or the death of the king of a country.

85 Abū Hāshim (d. 321/933), eponym of the Bahshamiyya, apparently distinguished between the *mutawātir* of religious transmission, which becomes necessary only after revelation, and *tawātur* of events that were not witnessed personally, as for example that al-Quds is located in Palestine. He considers the latter a matter of inquiry and inference; cf. ʿĀrif, *al-Ṣila* 93.

86 Ibn al-Murtaḍā, Riyāḍat al-afhām 132–133. The origin of this list of ten elements or things known by necessity that constitute *ʿaql* is not entirely clear. It does not originate with ʿAbd al-Jabbār, for whom *ʿaql* consisted of three major elements. It is possible that Ibn al-Murtaḍā borrowed it from al-Raṣṣāṣ. See the list by Aḥmad b. Yaḥyā Ḥābis al-Suḥūlī al-Saʿdī (d. 1061/1650–1651) in his *al-Īḍāḥ sharḥ al-Miṣbāḥ*; ʿĀrif, *al-Ṣila* 93–94.

87 Ibn al-Wazīr, *Īthār al-ḥaqq* 21; emphasis in italics mine.

To Ibn al-Wazīr, the original human disposition is a nature that God gave to human beings so that they would be able and predisposed to know those things of which the knowledge is necessary. But these items of necessary knowledge are not present in the *fiṭra*.

In contrast, Ibn al-Murtaḍā, when discussing the different definitions of *ʿaql*, writes:

> The intellect *is* the things known by necessity. The philosophers say: Rather, it is a simple substance. Some say it is a complex substance, and others that it is a particular nature. But we say: If it were something other than the ten [kinds of knowledge] (…).[88]

Both concepts (*fiṭra* and *ʿaql*) are identified with things known by necessity. But whereas Ibn al-Wazīr describes *fiṭra* as a disposition by which things known by necessity are naturally perceived as such, the Muʿtazili *ʿaql* goes beyond the disposition or capacity and identifies *ʿaql* with this kind of knowledge itself.

The Muʿtazili concept of *ʿaql* is distinct from Ibn al-Wazīr's concept of *fiṭra* regarding another aspect. Beyond the inherent possession of indisputable facts, *ʿaql* is the initial point from which another kind of knowledge springs. According to Ibn al-Murtaḍā, knowledge constituting *ʿaql* includes the knowledge of human beings' state of contingency. In reaction to a so-called warner (*khāṭir*), the *ʿaql* fears that there may be a Creator who requires something of the human being. The duty to know more about the possible Creator and respond appropriately thus arises immediately in the *ʿaql* of the human being. This duty to know more signifies the duty of philosophical speculation (*naẓar*), because *naẓar* generates true knowledge, and it is knowledge of the Creator and His demands that is required here.[89] Consequently, knowledge of the duty of *naẓar* is part of *ʿaql*, and *naẓar* itself is the means to perform this duty.

Ibn al-Murtaḍā's notions of the initial points of philosophical speculation are common in Muʿtazili *kalām*.[90] Reinhart shows how *ʿaql*, for Basran Muʿtazilis like ʿAbd al-Jabbār, is both a "collection of particular knowledges" and a

88 Ibn al-Murtaḍā, Riyāḍat al-afham 132, emphasis in italics mine. Tritton describes an identical argumentation as typically Muʿtazili, cf. Tritton, Some Muʿtazilī Ideas 617.

89 Ibn al-Murtaḍā, Riyāḍat al-afhām 137.

90 Ibn al-Murtaḍā connects the duty of *naẓar* also with the duty of averting harm, which is known by necessity. Possible harm is represented by the fear of the existence of a Creator who demands something of human beings; cf. Ibn al-Murtaḍā, Riyāḍat al-afham 138–139. For more on the duty of *naẓar* as part of the necessary knowledge contained in human reason, see Ibn al-Malāḥimī, *Kitāb al-Fāʾiq* 382–383; Reinhart, *Before Revelation* 155–156.

"kind of perceptiveness" to things known by necessity and by philosophical speculation, but not in a comprehensive or final way. Rather, *ʿaql* is described as a set of things known by all, and by virtue of which those who possess it become responsible for *taklīf*[91] and gain the capacity (*quwwa*) to perform what *taklīf* entails, namely to inquire rationally.[92] Consequently, *ʿaql* indeed contains all those things that constitute necessary knowledge very similar to the "necessary common knowledge" continually referred to by Ibn al-Wazīr and identified with the original human disposition.[93] But it also includes the means of expanding the known things by acquired knowledge.[94] If this were not so and there was only necessary knowledge, says Ibn al-Murtaḍā, *taklīf* would be meaningless.[95]

Thus another difference between Ibn al-Wazīr's concept of *fiṭra* and the Muʿtazili concept of *ʿaql* becomes manifest. This difference again refers to the distinction between necessary and acquired knowledge. Whereas Ibn al-Wazīr restricts *fiṭrā* knowledge to knowledge known by necessity, Basran Muʿtazilis include necessary as well as acquired knowledge. Some of what *ʿaql* includes or comes to include is brought into the realm of the kinds of certain knowledge of *ʿaql* through *naẓar*.[96] The knowledge of *ʿaql* entails the duty of speculation which again leads to a set of secondary cognitions, namely the *uṣūl al-adilla*: kinds of knowledge or doctrines that *follow* from *ʿaql* and are thereby as much part of *taklīf* as the necessary knowledge inherent in *ʿaql* itself.[97] In contrast, Ibn al-Wazīr's concept of *fiṭra*: It comes to realize only that knowledge which occurs without human initiative or influence and cannot add to what it knows. As we read in the above quote, *taklīf* is justified only on the grounds that every *compos mentis* quickly grasps the principle proofs that constitute the central Islamic tenets in their general form. Hence the validity of *taklīf* rests on necessary knowledge.

---

91 Reinhart, *Before Revelation* 151–157, quotes 152.

92 Ibid., 139.

93 Reinhart compares the Muʿtazili notion of *ʿaql* with the 'common sense' of every day language as well as the Stoic understanding of 'common notions;' cf. Reinhart, *Before Revelation* 152. On *ʿaql* as a set of kinds of knowledge, see also Peters, *God's Created Speech* 82; Ghaneabassiri, Epistemological Foundation 82–83.

94 See also ʿĀrif, who ascribes the origin of this definition of *ʿaql* as a capacity to Abū Hudhayl, as indeed does Reinhart. Later Muʿtazilis like ʿAbd al-Jabbār rejected the idea that *ʿaql* is a substance; cf. ʿĀrif, *al-Ṣila* 91–92; Peter, *God's Created Speech* 82–84.

95 Ibn al-Murtaḍa renders this as the majority opinion; cf. Ibn al-Murtaḍā, Riyāḍat al-afham 128.

96 Reinhart, *Before Revelation* 155–156.

97 See for example ʿĀrif, *al-Ṣila* 95.

To sum up: for Ibn al-Murtaḍā, representing the Bahshami position, *ʿaql* is identical to true knowledge, is "the sum of essential knowledge" as Tritton puts it.[98] Furthermore, *naẓar* along with what it generates is also part of and conceived by *ʿaql*. We must conclude then that according to this position *ʿaql* is also identical to Islam. Revelation would then be little more than a confirmation of what is already present in the human *ʿaql*.[99] In contrast, for Ibn al-Wazīr, *fiṭra* is only the predisposition to realize necessary knowledge and to perceive the central Islamic tenets. It is not identical to Islam. Necessary knowledge as well as the central Islamic tenets are both general knowledge. The *fiṭra* is predisposed to this general knowledge, and revelation does not exist merely to confirm what *fiṭra* is predisposed to or includes. Rather, it gives details of what *fiṭra* is predisposed to in general.

3 The Proof of God's Existence (*ithbāt al-ṣāniʿ*)

The proof of God's existence is a classical instance where the difference between views on necessary and acquired knowledge, as well as the different definitions of *naẓar*, become manifest.

It is also the topic of Ibn al-Wazīr's first known objections to prevalent Muʿtazili methods, namely in *al-Burhān al-qāṭiʿ*. And it was the foundations of the proof of God's existence that caused Ibn al-Wazir to write his *Tarjīḥ*.

Arguments for God's existence based on inference leading to acquired knowledge prevailed in scholastic Muʿtazili doctrine. Of course, it is based in one way or another on the knowledge human beings find in themselves by necessity: they cannot help but know that they are created. But only in a sequence of steps does inference lead to the knowledge of a creator. However, coexistence of self-evident and inferred proofs for God's existence is documented in the works of early Muslim theologians.[100] In Ibn al-Wazīr's time and environment, the so-called *akwān*-proof was apparently the dominant argument for the existence of God. We can gather this from the reaction to the above-quoted verses of Ibn al-Wazīr in which he rejected the discussion of

98 Cf. Tritton, Some Muʿtazilī Ideas 617.

99 This is of course no new insight. The elevation of *ʿaql* and supposed degradation of revelation has been a major point of argument for opponents of the Muʿtazila all along. However, the two pieces of secondary literature that analyze Ibn al-Murtaḍā's thought most comprehensively, namely al-Ṣubḥī in *al-Zaydiyya* and al-Kamālī in *al-Imām al-Mahdī*, do not mention his definition of reason.

100 See for example Abrahamov, *al-Qāsim b. Ibrāhīm on the Proof*; Abrahamov, al-Qāsim b. Ibrāhīm's Argument from Design 266–267; van Ess, Early Islamic Theologians 46–81.

accidents (*aʿrāḍ*) as a basis for proving God's existence. However, a major constituent of the *akwān*-proof is the real existence of *aʿrāḍ*, whose contingent nature supposedly indicates the contingent nature of substances, which in turn points to a creator.[101] Ibn al-Wazīr's versified indifference towards such accidents apparently caused considerable indignation among his students and peers.[102] The inquirer in Ibn al-Wazīr's *Tarjīḥ* claims that elite among contemporary scholars rely on the proof.[103] Furthermore, the prominence of the *akwān*-proof is manifest in Ibn al-Murtaḍā's writings. Although, Ibn al-Wazīr does not explicitly refer to Ibn al-Murtaḍā by name, it is likely that he had Ibn al-Murtaḍā in mind when he juxtaposed the proof based on the contingency of accidents as entitative beings (*dalīl al-akwān*) with the "proof by way of states" (*dalīl al-aḥwāl*).[104]

3.1 *Proving God's Existence by Inference* (istidlāl)

Al-Iryānī argues convincingly that Ibn al-Murtaḍā wrote the following verses in reply to Ibn al-Wazīr's controversial verses on the "principles of my religion" (*uṣūl dīnī*):

> O you, who objects to the principles of religion,
> saying that you have no intention to know them.
> If you knew them you would not say in objection
> 'the principles of my religion are the book of God, not the accidents'.
> This is the position of one whose foot has slipped
> from the path of truth, or whose heart is diseased.
> What is the way to know our Creator?
> You said 'by the Book,' but this position is refuted.
> For we do not believe it, unless the wisdom of him
> who establishes it gives a proof that arouses the intellect.[105]

101 For the poem see Ibn al-Wazīr, *Tarjīḥ* 68; Ibn al-Wazīr, *al-ʿAwāṣim* iii, 422 as well as 55 and 147 above.

102 See for example Ibn al-Wazīr, *al-ʿAwāṣim* iii, 422–423, 441; Ibn al-Wazīr, *Tarjīḥ* 68; Ibn al-Wazīr, *Dīwān* laq. 103l.

103 Ibn al-Wazīr, *Tarjīḥ* 77.

104 There are a number of terms for the two proofs. Madelung translates ʿAbd al-Jabbār's version of the *dalīl al-akwān*, namely the *ṭarīqat al-maʿānī*, as the "proof by entitative beings;" cf. Madelung, Proof for the Existence of God 276. A variety of titles could also be given to different forms of rendering Abū l-Ḥusayn's *dalīl al-aḥwāl*. But in both cases the different terms signify the same concepts.

105 Cf. al-Iryānī (intr.), *al-Burhān al-qāṭiʿ* 7.

Discussing *aʿrāḍ* is a major component of the *akwān*-proof, as is the premise that knowledge of God is acquired. Al-Ṣubḥī says of Ibn al-Murtaḍā that he did not explicitly pronounce his opinion on the matter of knowledge of God.[106] This may be true for the passage in *Riyāḍat al-afhām*, where the question of whether knowledge of God is necessary or acquired is posed explicitly. However, Ibn al-Murtaḍā clearly expresses his opinion on the question of *naẓar* as the first duty a little later on in the same work.

> *Naẓar* is the first duty of the *mukallaf*. It is said that it is no duty. [But] we say: The knowledge of God is incumbent because it is a grace (*luṭf*). (…) It [the knowledge] can only be accomplished by means of it [*naẓar*] because He [God] is not known by necessity nor by *taqlīd*. Hence, *naẓar* is obligatory and its duty affirmed, because it fulfills the function of averting harm. When we say 'first duty' we mean that no *mukallaf* is free of it at the beginning of his *taklīf* in contradistinction to the other duties.[107]

In this reasoning, the assumption that the knowledge of God is acquired is the main argument. In his *Kitāb al-Qalāʾid*, Ibn al-Murtaḍā clearly uses inference to arrive at the knowledge of the existence of the Creator. Starting from the premise of the necessary knowledge that the world is created, Ibn al-Murtaḍā proceeds to argue from the different modes of spatial existence of accidents,[108] which is precisely what the *dalīl al-akwān* is concerned with. A little later, the fact that a human action must have been performed by someone is used as a basis for arguing that created beings must have been created by someone. This is different from Ibn al-Wazīr's proof of God's existence by the observation of creation, because a sequence of deliberate reasoning based on an analogy between the seen and the unseen (*qiyās al-ghāʾib ʿalā l-shāhid*) is involved in Ibn al-Murtaḍā's development of the argument.[109] He considers both elements of the argument as clearly inferential (*istidlālī*), leading to acquired knowledge.[110] Necessary knowledge is the basis of the proof rather than the proof in itself.

---

106 Al-Ṣubḥī nevertheless lists Ibn al-Murtaḍā's theory of the knowledge of God as the second example that marks Ibn al-Murtaḍā as a Muʿtazili in many doctrinal matters; cf. al-Ṣubḥī, *al-Zaydiyya* 358.

107 Ibn al-Murtaḍā, Riyāḍat al-afhām 138.

108 Ibn al-Murtaḍā, Kitāb al-Qalāʾid 53.

109 See also al-Ḥayyī, *al-Muntazaʿ min al-Durar al-farāʾid* fs. 7b, 22a.

110 Ibn al-Murtaḍā, Kitāb al-Qalāʾid 52–53; cf. al-Ḥayyī, *al-Muntazaʿ min al-Durar al-farāʾid* f. 10a.

The argumentation attributed to Ibn al-Murtaḍā by his commentator al-Ḥayyī leaves no doubt that Ibn al-Murtaḍā demonstrates God's existence based on the *akwān*-proof and a sequence of inferences according to a particular well-established order:

> The principles of evidence (*qawāʿid al-dalīl*) are first of all, that it needs to be established that accidents (*aʿrāḍ*) are additional to the body. Then their [the accidents'] contingency (*ḥudūthuhā*) is proved. Further, [it is proved] that the body does not precede them [the accidents]; then [it is proved] that the existence of that which does not precede the contingent must be contingent like it. And after all this is established by apodictic proof, we know that the body is contingent. Then it is established that whatever is contingent requires the existence of a creator (*muḥdith*). (…) If we then know that the bodies have a creator, [we have] what was desired from this proof. Yet, know that talking about the first principle must come first, which is the establishment of the accidents.[111]

Ibn al-Murtaḍā's views on this question ranges him clearly within the Bahshamiyya[112] who argued with the duty of philosophical speculation according to a certain order of evidence to arrive at the certainty about God's existence, the *dalīl al-akwān* as well as the analogy between the seen and the unseen world. This reasoning is ascribed to the Zaydiyya as a whole.[113]

This way of reasoning for the existence of God is the major point where ʿAbd al-Jabbār's student Abū l-Ḥusayn al-Baṣrī initially deviated from his teacher and coined the proof for the existence of God termed *dalīl al-aḥwāl*, "the proof by way of states."[114] Abū l-Ḥusayn's teaching on the matter is preserved in Ibn al-Malāḥimī's *Kitab al-Muʿtamad* and *Kitāb al-Fāʾiq*. According to Ibn al-Malāḥimī, Abū l-Ḥusayn rejects the analogy between the seen and the unseen world upon which his Bahshami predecessors based their inference of the existence of a creator. Furthermore, Abū l-Ḥusayn challenges the real existence of the contingent accidents (*aʿrāḍ*) upon which the proof of the contingency of the substances was based. His argument is termed *dalīl al-aḥwāl* because he

111 Ibid., f. 6a.

112 According to al-Ḥayyī, Ibn al-Murtaḍā affirms that his contemporary Zaydis and indeed he himself endorse the proof of the createdness of the world that rests on the real existence (*maʿānī*) of the accidents of bodies; cf. al-Ḥayyī, *al-Muntazaʿ min al-Durar al-farāʾid* f. 6b.

113 Ibid., f. 5a–6b.

114 Cf. Madelung, Abū l-Ḥusayn al-Baṣrī's Proof 273–280; Ansari et al., Yūsuf al-Baṣīr's Rebuttal 28–29.

defines these accidents as states (*aḥwāl*) or characteristics (*aḥkām*) of the substances, rather than separate entities (*maʿānī*).[115]

3.2 *Proving God's Existence from Necessity* (ḍarūra)

The major difference between Abū l-Ḥusayn's thought and that of his Bahshami colleagues that is of most interest for the present question concerns the kind of knowledge arrived at. Whereas the knowledge of the existence of the creator is acquired by way of analogical inference in the Bahshami argument, Abū l-Ḥusayn holds that it occurs by necessity.[116] This is why it was so conducive to Ibn al-Wazīr's argumentation. True to type, Ibn al-Wazīr confirms the *dalīl al-aḥwāl* according to Abū l-Ḥusayn in a rather broad way.[117] He endorses it in general, yet his own examples illustrate that he was not concerned with the question of whether accidents are entities (*maʿānī*) or states (*aḥwāl*) of substances per se, but rather with the states (*aḥwāl*) in which all elements of creation find themselves or are perceived to be. His emphasis is on the claim that *naẓar* in the theologians' sense is not needed. In a general way, it is self-evident that all elements of creation are brought into being and are arranged in a perfectly fitting way, necessarily speaking of a creator as well as of the wisdom of same.

> If you consider these different wonders that are perceived by the senses—heaven and earth and all the living things that are dispersed in them—you know that they were created from the appearance of createdness in them, acknowledging their own incapability of producing a thing.[118]

In reply to the question whether or not he rejects *naẓar* completely, Ibn al-Wazīr negates this and writes at the end of *al-Burhān al-qāṭiʿ*:

115 For juxtapositions of the *akwān*-proof and the *aḥwāl*-proof in Muʿtazili literature, see for example Ibn al-Malāḥimī, *Kitāb al-Muʿtamad* 101–109, 157–158.

116 The late Muʿtazili Taqī l-Dīn al-ʿUjālī (or ʿAjālī) summarizes the difference between the Bahshami position and that of Abū l-Ḥusayn and others most concisely; cf. Taqī l-Dīn al-ʿUjālī, *al-Kāmil* 155. On Taqī l-Dīn al-ʿUjālī, see footnote 126 below.

117 Ibn al-Wazīr does not reject the analogy between the seen and the unseen as a whole. According to him, the meanings of things in the unseen can only be understood through meanings in the seen. But unlike the analogy between the seen and the unseen employed by the Bahshamiyya for the proof of God's existence on a merely rational base, Ibn al-Wazīr applies the comparison to the interpretation of what God says about Himself in revelation; cf. Ibn al-Wazīr, *Īthār al-ḥaqq* 89.

118 Ibn al-Wazīr, *Tarjīḥ* 86; cf. ibid., 81, 91–94.

> There are two issues: [*Naẓar*] upon the creatures [that are] of miraculous making and brilliant wisdom in the towering heavens and hills and valleys of the earth, the masterfully made animals with their tools and instruments, like the instruments for seeing, smelling (…). When you contemplate these things, you know by necessity just after contemplation that they have a knowing, wise, able creator. (…) The second issue where *naẓar* leads to knowledge are the stories of the prophets and their circumstances (*aḥwāluhum*).[119]

Later in his *Tarjīḥ*, Ibn al-Wazīr gives the concept of this proof its common name:

> This is called the method of the states (*tarīqat al-aḥwāl*). It is the most familiar and most beneficial for most common people, women and the uneducated from among the Bedouins and slaves, because it causes them to arrive at the knowledge of God directly.[120]

The miracles of the prophets, and indeed the existence of the Quran, are considered in much the same way: the wondrous character of prophetic miracles and the Quran and the necessary knowledge of every *compos mentis* that he is incapable of producing anything similar are proof of the miracle's divine nature.[121]

> This knowledge [of the miraculous nature of the Quran] occurs by way of knowing our own incapability of [producing] it, not by way of knowing the real essence of the speech (*kalām*). If we knew the true essence of the speech and we were not incapable of [producing] something like the Quran, it [the Quran] would not be miraculous. And if we were incapable of it and did not know it, it would be miraculous. Consequently, the issue is the incapability (*ʿajz*) rather than the knowledge of the essence of that of which one is incapable (*al-maʿjūz ʿanhu*). We know by necessity of our incapability of [producing] some characteristics of sounds and their states. So we know of our incapability to produce a sound like thunder. And we know that our knowledge of our incapability of it does not

119 Ibn al-Wazīr, *al-Burhān al-qāṭiʿ* 67.

120 Ibn al-Wazīr, *Tarjīḥ* 109.

121 Ibid., 75, 81, 92–93. The acknowledgement of the reality of miracles was another point that caused Bahshami scholars to criticize Abū l-Ḥusayn; cf. Madelung (ed., intr.), *Kitāb al-Muʿtamad*, 11.

> depend on our knowledge of the essence of the sound and its technical definition after we know the sound in a general manner (*ʿalā sabīl al-jumla*). Likewise, we know the attributes of God the Exalted after we know His essence in a general manner. People at the time of the prophet knew of the inimitability. Yet, they did not penetrate into it. This is a matter that is not grasped by the original human disposition. (…) You, may God support you, know and I know that before we learned of what the theologians say about the speech and the *akwān*, we did not know these things by our *fiṭra*. The ordering that leads to the knowledge of evidence and definitions did not occur to us. Whoever denies that does not deserve to be heeded.[122]

In short, Ibn al-Wazīr's proof of God's existence incorporates the *dalīl al-aḥwāl* as well as the argument from the design of the world or the teleological argument. The argument from design predicates the necessary knowledge of a wise creator due to the wonderful and perfect composition (*tarkīb*) of the world.[123] A decisive characteristic of all the indicators and proofs for the knowledge of God endorsed by Ibn al-Wazīr is that they are grasped by every human being's original disposition immediately. This puts them in sharp contrast to arguments like the *akwān*-proof, which asserts that knowledge must be acquired by means of complicated inferences.

Equally true to type, Ibn al-Wazīr refers to earlier Muʿtazili as well as Zaydi authorities as having argued for the existence of God from the design of creation and the contemplation of same. According to Madelung as well as Abrahamov, the Zaydi imam al-Qāsim b. Ibrāhīm al-Rassī (d. 246/860) used the argument from design along with proofs more reminiscent of Muʿtazili reasoning.[124] In his *Tarjīḥ*, Ibn al-Wazīr at one point provides a short summary of the

122 Ibn al-Wazīr, *Tarjīḥ* 92–93.

123 For the argument from design, see Abrahamov, *al-Qāsim b. Ibrāhīm on the Proof*; Abrahamov, al-Qāsim ibn Ibrāhīm's Argument from Design 259–284.

124 Al-Qāsim b. Ibrāhīm's *Kitāb al-Dalīl al-kabīr* focuses more on the argument from design, whereas the following *Kitāb al-Dalīl al-saghīr* introduces arguments that involve philosophical speculation; cf. Abrahamov, *al-Qasim b. Ibrahim on the Proof* 8. Abrahamov and Madelung disagree concerning the influence of Muʿtazili doctrine on al-Qāsim's argument from design. According to Abrahamov, the argument from design was used by Muʿtazilis contemporary to al-Qāsim and passed on to the Zaydiyya. Madelung doubts the connection between al-Qāsim's argument from design and the Muʿtazila, apart from al-Jāḥiẓ. The connection between the argument from design and al-Jāḥiẓ is apparently neither new nor far-fetched. The difference between al-Jāḥiẓ's argument and that of al-Qāsim, and Ibn al-Wazīr for that matter, is that the former seems to be inspired by Christian authors while

Bahshami reasoning from Ibn Mattawayh's *Tadhkira fī aḥkām jawāhir wa-aʿrāḍ*. However, he attempts to illustrate that this position belongs to the irregularities (*shudhūdh*) even among the *kalām* theologians by mentioning a number of scholars who argued for God's existence by proofs other than the *dalīl al-akwān*.[125] Most frequently, he refers to Ibn Abī l-Ḥadīd (d. 656/1258) in his commentary on the *Nahj al-balāgha*, Abū l-Ḥusayn al-Baṣrī (d. 436/1045), Rukn al-Dīn al-Malāḥimī (d. 536/1141), Shaykh Mukhtār al-Muʿtazilī (d. 658/1260), Taqī l-Dīn al-ʿUjālī (d. late 6th/12th or early 7th/13th c.)[126] and the Zaydi imam al-Mu'ayyad bi-llāh Yaḥyā b. Ḥamza (d. 749/1346).

The claim that the Bahshami argument is, by and large, merely an irregularity would be hard to sustain. Yet the fact that all of the above-mentioned scholars are associated with the Muʿtazili school of Abū l-Ḥusayn al-Baṣrī[127] implies that Ibn al-Wazīr's attempt, at least in relation to this question, can be seen as evidence that the struggle between the Ḥusayniyya and the Bahshamiyya

---

the latter two draw the argument directly from the Quran; cf. Abrahamov, *al-Qāsim b. Ibrahim on the Proof* 2–4; Madelung, *Der Imām al-Qāsim* 106 and above.

125 Ibn al-Wazīr, *Tarjīḥ* 79.

126 Little is known of Taqī l-Dīn al-ʿUjālī or al-ʿAjālī, elsewhere endowed with the *nisba* al-Najrānī, other than that he was a Sunni representative of the school of Abū l-Ḥusayn who studied with Ibn al-Malāḥimī. Ibn al-Wazīr quotes extensively from his *Kitāb al-Kāmil fī l-istiqṣā' fīmā balaghanā min kalām al-qudamā'* on the very topic of the advantages of the *dalīl al-aḥwāl* as against the *dalīl al-akwān*. Although deficient according to Madelung, an edition of the extant parts of Taqī l-Dīn al-ʿUjālī's *al-Kāmil* was prepared by Muḥammad al-Shāhid, Cairo: Wizārat al-Awqāf 1999; cf. Madelung (ed., intr.), *Kitāb al-Muʿtamad* 6–7; Madelung, Elsayed Elshahed: Das Problem der transzendenten sinnlichen Wahrnehmung (review) 129. The editor of *al-Kāmil*, al-Shahid, identifies al-ʿUjālī with Shaykh Mukhtār based on the alleged identity of *al-Kāmil* and *al-Mujtabā* which Ibn al-Wazīr often refers to. He challenges Madelung's placement of the two scholars, arguing mainly that Madelung wrongly identifies Shaykh Mukhtār with the author of a book called *al-Mujtabā* on legal methodology (not *kalām*) extant in a library in Cairo; cf. al-Shāhid (ed.), *al-Kāmil* 13–20; Ansari argues for Madelung's distinction from the content of an extant copy of *al-Kāmil*. To my mind, Madelung's and Ansari's conclusion is much more likely than al-Shāhid's. It is supported by the fact that Ibn al-Wazīr quotes both scholars on various separate occasions, in the same context and even in the same sentence; cf. for example Ibn al-Wazīr, *al-ʿAwāṣim* v, 60; Ibn al-Wazīr, *Tarjīh* 99–101. For the connection between Taqī l-Dīn al-ʿUjālī and Abū l-Ḥusayn al-Baṣrī, see also Shihadeh, Argument from Ignorance 214; Schwarb, In the Age of Averroes 261. Schmidtke is preparing an article on Taqī l-Dīn al-ʿUjālī's reception of Abū l-Ḥusayn al-Basrī; cf. Schmidtke, The Sunni transmission of Abū l-Ḥusayn al-Baṣrī's theological thought, (forthcoming).

127 According to Madelung, Ibn Abī al-Ḥadīd "stood close to the school of Abū l-Ḥusayn al-Baṣrī;" Madelung, ʿAbd al-Ḥamīd b. Abū l-Ḥadīd. Shaykh Mukhtār and Taqī l-Dīn al-ʿUjālī both refer to Ibn al-Malāḥimī and Abū l-Ḥusayn as their teachers (*shuyūkh*). This term does not imply an immediate teacher-pupil relationship. See also Madelung (ed., intr.), *Kitāb al-Muʿtamad* 6–7. For Yaḥya b. Ḥamza, see also footnotes 128, 155 and 171 below.

within the Yemeni Zaydiyya was still ongoing in the 9th/15th century.[128] And indeed, Abū l-Ḥusayn's proof of the existence of God has a characteristic of central import in Ibn al-Wazīr's entire thought, namely that God is known by necessity. In no other instance does Ibn al-Wazīr express his support of Abū l-Ḥusayn's thought as emphatically as in this question, calling the line of arguing with the *dalīl al-aḥwāl* "the Sunna of the prophets, the predecessors and righteous forefathers."[129] But Ibn al-Wazīr, unlike Abū l-Ḥusayn al-Baṣrī according to Ibn al-Malāḥimī, does not allow *naẓar* in its prevalent speculative function a role in the acquisition of certain knowledge at any point of the religious endeavor. On this point, only Shaykh Mukhtār of Abū l-Ḥusayn's school seems to agree with Ibn al-Wazīr. Although Ibn al-Malāḥimī affirms that knowledge of the existence of a creator is necessary, he spends considerable effort to prove that philosophical speculation does lead to certain knowledge, and is the first duty of every believer once he reaches adulthood. He insists repeatedly that the ordering of the premises according to reason (*tartīb al-muqaddimāt*) is the essential characteristic of proper *naẓar*.[130] Ibn al-Malāḥimī's argument is similar to the views expressed by Ibn al-Murtaḍā in *Riyāḍat al-afhām*.[131] This was the very feature of the speculative version of *naẓar* that Ibn al-Wazīr rejected so vehemently.

The main difference between Ibn al-Wazīr's employment of the proof and that of Ibn al-Malāḥimī is grounded in the initial point of *naẓar*. For Ibn al-Malāḥimī, the initial point for the performance of *naẓar* is not the general proof of the existence of a creator, as it is in Bahshami's, and indeed in Ibn al-Murtaḍā's, thought. Rather, it is the particular knowledge of the Creator himself (*bi-l-ta'yīn*), namely that the Creator is one of unicity and wisdom along with His other attributes (*ṣifāt*).[132] According to him, a human being knows by necessity of the existence of a creator. But *naẓar* is needed to acquire a detailed knowledge of who the Creator is. For Ibn al-Wazīr, the knowledge of the essence and the attributes of God, like His wisdom, His power or His knowledge, is part

128 For this struggle, see for example Ansari, Maḥmūd al-Malāḥimī al-Muʿtazilī fī l-Yaman. The competition between the two schools is documented until the 8th/14th century. According to Ansari in this blog entry, Abū l-Ḥusayn's thought became more accepted among the Yemeni Zaydiyya through the efforts of Imam al-Muʾayyad bi-llāh Yaḥyā b. Ḥamza (d. 747/1346). See also Madelung (ed., intr.), *Kitāb al-Muʿtamad* 8.

129 Ibn al-Wazīr, *Tarjīḥ* 85.

130 Cf. Ibn al-Malāḥimī, *Kitab al-Muʿtamad* 27, where he clearly presents this as Abū l-Ḥusayn's definition of *naẓar*.

131 Ibn al-Murtaḍā, Riyāḍat al-afhām 139–140.

132 Ibn al-Malāḥimī, *Kitāb al-Muʿtamad* 175–181, 252–253; Thiele, Jewish and Muslim Reception 111.

of the necessary knowledge occurring along with the knowledge of God's existence, albeit in a general manner (*mujmalan*). It is impossible to arrive at a detailed knowledge of God's essence and attributes[133] and no further speculation is needed.[134] We conclude that Ibn al-Wazīr's concept of knowing God was informed by the proof of God's existence employed by Abū l-Ḥusayn's school—but only to a certain degree.

As a consequence, the relationship between the proof of God's existence and the insistence on necessary knowledge in Ibn al-Wazīr's thought becomes more evident if we consider early Muʿtazilis who also argued for the existence of the Creator from the design of the world.[135] Al-Jāḥiẓ and his *ahl al-maʿārif* are a prominent example.[136] They negated the distinction between necessary and acquired knowledge, insisting, like Ibn al-Wazīr, that all true knowledge must occur by necessity.[137] According to them, philosophical speculation does not lead to certain knowledge because the mental activity of human beings is influenced by a variety of matters, among them the ego. People therefore arrive at a variety of conclusions. The results are a matter of chance rather than certain knowledge. In short, there are limits to the human ability to think. True knowledge must always be a gift from God and cannot be a result of an active performance of human reason.[138]

It is questionable whether Ibn al-Wazīr would have agreed with callingthe result of mental activity mere chance. The line of argument just described, however, corresponds to the connection Ibn al-Wazīr first draws in *Tarjīḥ* between necessary knowledge, the original human disposition, and the proof of God's existence along with His wisdom: The knowledge of God's existence must be absolutely certain. It must be necessary knowledge inviolable by an initial absence of knowledge, doubt or possible error in the process of proving it. This necessary knowledge is attainable by all, because all possess the *fiṭra* bestowed by God. The necessary knowledge that a Creator exists is effected by a *tawātur* of meaning from the observation of the design of creation, and later on, from

133 Ibn al-Wazīr, *Īthār al-ḥaqq* 178.

134 See also Ibn al-Wazīr, *Tarjīḥ* 49–50.

135 Van Ess, Early Theologians 64–81.

136 Ibn al-Wazīr often refers to them in this context. On al-Jāḥiẓ's argument from design see also Abrahamov, *al-Qasim b. Ibrahim*, 2–3; Gibb, Argument from Design 150–162; van Ess, Early Theologians 69–71. An example of al-Jāḥiẓ's way of arguing for the existence of the Creator God is based on pondering the wise way in which man was made, cf. al-Jāḥiẓ, *al-ʿIbar wa-l-iʿtibār* 78–79.

137 Cf. al-Jāḥiẓ, al-Masāʾil wa-l-jawābāt fī l-maʿrifa 33–47.

138 For a survey of early Muʿtazili scholars who objected to the proof of God's existence based on philosophical speculation, see Joseph van Ess, Early Theologians 64–81.

the miracles and circumstances of the prophets as well as revelation. For Ibn al-Wazīr, the original human disposition is a crucial source of, as well as an instrument in, true, certain and general knowledge in the sense of a recipient. The knowledge is necessary and therefore bestowed by God. Human reason or intellect, even if identified with *fiṭra*, is no reliable deliberate producer of certain knowledge by its performance of *naẓar* in the sense of the theologians.

In conclusion, the difference to Muʿtazili doctrine represented by Ibn al-Murtaḍā consists in the restrictions placed on deliberate and independent human access to certain knowledge. Necessary knowledge is bestowed by God, be it by intuition, from sense perception or from the pondering of surrounding phenomena and reports, strengthened by contextual evidence. The same is true for revelation. That is why Ibn al-Wazīr could refute the speculative theologians' argument that they need to engage in speculation in order to refute unbelievers and heretics. The latter would not attain more proof from argumentation and debate than was already available to them in creation. This poses the question as to whether Ibn al-Wazīr thought, like al-Jāḥiẓ and others, that those in whom no necessary knowledge of the creator occurred would be exempt from *taklīf*.[139] The answer is no. But this answer is not based on reason. It was the distinction between necessary and acquired knowledge that provided a rational explanation for punishment of ignorance or denial of Islamic doctrine.[140] For Ibn al-Wazīr, the punishment of unbelievers is rather one of those cases where revelation supplied the details of what the intellect only knew in a general manner.[141] It illustrates Ibn al-Wazīr's recurring insistence that only revelation can determine the particularities of what is naturally known only in a general form—precisely what *naẓar* is supposed to achieve, according to

139 The Muʿtazili court theologian of Caliph al-Maʾmūn, Thumāma b. al-Ashras (d. 213/828), for example, is thought to have stated that only those who are compelled to the knowledge of God, His messenger and the Quran can be obliged with *taklīf*. Thumāma is counted among the *ahl al-maʿārif* for whom only necessary knowledge is true knowledge; cf. van Ess, Early Theologians 72. The quote that leads to the conclusion about al-Jāḥiẓ's understanding of the limitations of human beings' mental abilities is taken from an epistle that cannot be ascribed to al-Jāḥiẓ with certainty. However, the reading of *al-ʿIbār wa-l-iʿtibār* or al-Jāḥiẓ's letters suggests that this idea was at least shared by him. For example, in the thirteenth epistle of his letters, he argues that if two people practiced proper *naẓar*, yet one is right and the other one wrong, both will be equally convinced that they are correct. Furthermore, people who come to supposedly certain conclusions later change their minds. Even more clearly, al-Jāḥiẓ writes that reason may be overpowered by nature and become weak in its reasoning; cf. al-Jāḥiẓ, *Rasāʾil al-Jāḥiẓ*, 39–43. The treatise ascribed to al-Jāḥiẓ is called *Kitab al-Dalīl wa-l-iʿtibār*; cf. van Ess, Early Theologians 65.

140 Cf. van Ess, *Erkenntnislehre* 16–17.

141 Ibn al-Wazīr, *Tarjīḥ* 44.

speculative theologians. For Ibn al-Wazīr, only revelation determines, for example, to whom the term 'unbeliever' applies in particular. Only what is explicitly mentioned as unbelief in revelation can be excluded or condemned. Knowledge of God's existence is necessary yet general. All Muslims agree on it and have access to it. It is not, and indeed cannot be, proved by the practice of inference according to a particular ordering of premises, which would render only those few who perform it properly within the realm of what is true.

The connection between necessary knowledge occurring in the original disposition of all human beings as the only true knowledge, on the one hand, and proving God's existence from the design of the world and human beings' self and surroundings, on the other hand, is obvious. What is important is the fact that, once again, Ibn al-Wazīr restricts the matter that can be known with certainty to a minimum and removed it to a place beyond direct human influence. All true knowledge is directly bestowed by God. Similar to Ibn Taymiyya and Ibn Qayyim, Ibn al-Wazīr allows for the possibility that other kinds of knowledge may be granted by God, too. Yet, such "special knowledge" is not merited by an act of speculation nor is there any certain way of attaining it.[142] Thus, Ibn al-Wazīr extended what can be known with certainty to the whole Muslim community and took away the grounds for mutual condemnation or charge of unbelief.

4 The Argument from the Absence of Evidence (*dalālat nafy al-dalāla*)

The so-called "argument from the absence of evidence" has been formulated and applied by Muslim theologians in several versions.[143] In Ibn al-Wazīr's writings, it permeates several debates in theology as well as legal methodology. The attitude taken towards it illustrates epistemological differences as to the

142 On Ibn Taymiyya's and Ibn Qayyim's concept of special knowledge granted by God, see Schallenbergh, Ibn Qayyim al-Jawziyya's Manipulation 102. Some Ashʿaris, like ʿAbd al-Qāhir al-Baghdādī (d. 429/1037) and al-Baqillānī (d. 403/1013), likewise assert that secondary or speculative knowledge may be transferred to necessary knowledge through an act of God without merit; cf. Abrahamov, Necessary Knowledge 22.

143 Phrases that were used to describe the same principle are *"al-istidlāl bi-l-ʿadam," "mā lam yaqum al-dalīl ʿalā thubūtihi yajib nafyuhu"* and *"mā lā ṭarīq ilayhi fa-wājib nafyuhu."* See for example Ibn al-Wazīr, *al-ʿAwāṣim* v, 29; Taqī l-Dīn al-ʿUjālī, *al-Kāmil* 322, Abū l-Ḥusayn al-Baṣrī, *Taṣaffuḥ al-adilla* 13. See also Thiele, Jewish and Muslim Reception 111–113. For an overview of the different corollaries of the argument along with the respective counter-arguments, see Shihadeh, Argument from Ignorance 192–200.

degree of certainty a human being can expect or can be obliged to attain at a fundamental level. Furthermore, the argument is of interest for Ibn al-Wazīr's broader intellectual context. Like in the example of the definition of *naẓar* or the proof of the existence of God, the attitude taken towards this argument illustrates the influence of two different Muʿtazili schools in the Zaydiyya of Ibn al-Wazīr's time. Lastly, the argument from the absence of evidence has received hitherto little attention in spite of its significance for research on epistemology.[144]

Essentially, the argument purports that whenever the existence of an entity or state of affairs is not evidenced either by necessity or comprehensive *naẓar*, the entity or state of affairs must be negated, lest necessary as well as acquired knowledge be invalidated. Elaborately, it is argued that firstly, necessary knowledge would be invalidated because not negating what human beings have no way (*ṭarīq*) of perceiving would lead to the possibility of imperceptible existences that human beings have no way of knowing. Human beings could no longer trust their senses. Secondly, acquired knowledge would be invalidated because not negating what human beings have no way (*ṭarīq*) of procuring evidence for would lead to the possibility of undiscernible errors in the premises (*muqaddimāt*) of evidence. Human beings could no longer trust their *naẓar*.[145] As a consequence of negating what cannot be proven, certainty exists about the non-existence of the entity or state of affairs. In contrast, those negating this principle basically hold that the non-existence of decisive evidence for a particular entity or state of affairs must result in a statement about its possible existence (*tajwīz*). Apodictic judgement is deferred (*tawaqquf*).[146] Whereas the first conclusion signifies an epistemic value of certainty, the second signifies probability.

Considering the importance that probability and ambiguity have in Ibn al-Wazīr's thought, it would be reasonable to expect Ibn al-Wazīr to be an opponent of this argument. While Ibn al-Wazīr's opponents did not explicitly reason with the argument from the absence of evidence in all of the following questions, the epistemological implications of the argument are of such a fundamental nature that the attitude taken towards it can be perceived throughout an individual's thought. Accordingly, Shihadeh's conclusion from his discus-

144 Exceptions to this lack of attention are Shihadeh's article "Argument from Ignorance" and van Ess's monograph on al-Ījī's epistemology, where it is referred to as "argumentum e silentio;" cf. Shihadeh, Argument from Ignorance; van Ess, *Erkenntnislehre*, 376–380.

145 Cf. Ibn al-Malāḥimi, *Kitāb al-Muʿtamad* 282–285; Taqī l-Dīn al-ʿUjālī, *al-Kāmil* 324–325.

146 Cf. ibid, 323.

sion of the Muʿtazili defenses of the argument can be confirmed, namely that "school members were motivated in their espousal of the argument from ignorance by a complex combination of commitments of theirs—ontological, epistemological, soteriological, theodicean and dialectical (…). Chief among these is arguably the notion that humans are under obligation to arrive at perfect knowledge of God (…)."[147] This confirmation is based on the claim that the counterposition is of a similarly essential character in Ibn al-Wazīr's thought.

Shihadeh shows how the attitude towards what he calls "argument from ignorance" shifted in the Ashʿariyya. Al-Juwaynī and after him—and more comprehensively—Fakhr al-Dīn al-Rāzī refuted different corollaries of the argument, not only as propounded by the Bahshami school of the Muʿtazila or Ibn al-Malāḥimī,[148] but also those versions of the argument brought forth by their own predecessors from among the Ashʿariyya.[149]

As far as the Muʿtazila are concerned, Shihadeh assumes Ibn al-Malāḥimī to be the last to defend the argument comprehensively, although Ibn al-Malāḥimī challenges the Bahshami way of reasoning for the argument. It is difficult to determine whether Ibn al-Malāḥimī expressed his own positions or those of his predecessor.[150] What remains of Abū l-Ḥusayn's *Taṣaffuḥ al-adilla* shows that he endorsed the argument. Yet, he substantiated it only in the passing, as it was not his major concern in the extant fragments. Significantly, he explicitly distinguishes between non-existence of proof (*lā ṭarīq ilayhi*) and failing to find proof (*faqd al-dalāla*).[151] Shihadeh shows how Taqī l-Dīn al-ʿUjālī, from whom both Ibn al-Wazīr and Shaykh Mukhtār quote extensively, already deviated from the support of the argument so thoroughly treated by Ibn al-Malāḥimī. Although Taqī l-Dīn al-ʿUjālī did not mention Ibn al-Malāḥimī in his refutation and referred to the Bahshamiyya exclusively, he discussed and rebutted the very argument Ibn al-Malāḥimī demonstrated so elaborately and endorsed Fakhr al-Dīn al-Rāzī's counter-argument instead.[152]

---

147 Ibid., 191.

148 Cf. ibid., 183–191.

149 This refers especially to al-Baqillānī; cf. Shihadeh, Argument from Ignorance 192.

150 In the defenses of Ibn al-Malāḥimī's predecessors, the argument is employed to defend the epistemological foundations of their own school. However, a thorough defense of the argument would have to show that its rejection results in the abolition of the very grounds of necessary as well as acquired knowledge for all of Islam and indeed mankind; cf. ibid., 185; Ibn al-Malāḥimī, *Kitāb al-Muʿtamad* 278–287.

151 Cf. Abū l-Ḥusayn al-Baṣrī, *Taṣaffuḥ al-adilla* 13–15.

152 Ibid., 214–217; cf. Taqī l-Dīn al-ʿUjālī, *al-Kāmil* 322–334. See also Madelung's review of Elshahed's Das Problem der transzendenten sinnlichen Wahrnehmung 129.

In *al-ʿAwāṣim*, Ibn al-Wazīr's quote from Shaykh Mukhtār's *al-Mujtabā* is among the first the former refers to in support of his own position.[153] Another rebuttal of the argument originates from the Zaydi imam Yaḥyā b. Ḥamza, whom Ibn al-Wazīr cites along with Fakhr al-Dīn al-Rāzī in his presentation and ensuing refutation of the argument.[154] In Imam Yaḥyā b. Ḥamza's *Kitāb al-Tamhīd* a whole section is devoted to the exposition of five "corrupt methods used by *kalām* theologians" (*masālik al-mutakallimīn al-fāsida*), resembling the "four weak methods and two wrong principles" ascribed to the *kalām* theologians by Fakhr al-Dīn al-Rāzī.[155] The argument from the absence of evidence per se (*mā lā dalīl ʿalayhi wajaba nafyuhu*) and one of its corollaries figure prominently among them. According to Shihadeh, no serious defense of the argument could be brought forward after Fakhr al-Dīn al-Rāzī's refutation.[156] Imam Yaḥyā b. Ḥamza's statements confirm the great influence of al-Rāzī's reasoning on this particular point beyond the Ashʿariyya. Yet, one century after Fakhr al-Dīn al-Rāzī, at the time and in the context of Imam Yaḥyā b. Ḥamza, there still seems to have been the need to refute the argument in a place where Muʿtazilism, and especially its Bahshami variety, was still influential when it had ceased to be so elsewhere.

4.1 *Absence of Evidence as an Argument for Certainty*

In Ibn al-Murtaḍā's shorter theological writings *Kitāb al-Qalāʾid* and *Riyāḍat al-afhām*, he does not defend the argument from the absence of evidence explicitly. However, we learn that the argument was present and applicable in his thought from his own commentary on *Kitāb al-Qalāʾid*, namely *al-Durar al-farāʾid*. For example, the following proof of the limitlessness of divine powerfulness (*qādiriyya*) is ascribed to him:

> The powerfulness of the Exalted is all-transcending, there is no way of proving (*ithbāt*) [the existence of] its restriction (*ḥāṣir*) to a certain kind

---

153 Ibn al-Wazīr, *al-ʿAwāṣim* v, 30.

154 Ibid., v, 30. According to Ibn al-Wazīr, a certain al-Buḥturī (d. unknown) ascribes the rejection of the argument from ignorance to Imam al-Qāsim b. Ibrāhīm (d. 264/860), grandfather of the founder of the Yemeni imamate al-Hādī ilā l-ḥaqq (d. 298/911).

155 Yaḥyā b. Ḥamza, *Kitāb al-Tamhīd* i, 32–41. Interestingly, Yaḥyā b. Ḥamza does not identify what is called the "argument from impediments" (*dalīl al-mawāniʿ*) with the argument from the absence of evidence. Whereas he rejects the latter in its most general form as one of five invalid methods of reasoning, the former figures among the accepted arguments against the visibility of God; cf. ibid., 286–293. For al-Rāzī's refutation of the four methods and two principles, see Shihadeh, Argument from Ignorance 207.

156 Ibid., 217.

> or number, in contradistinction to our power. The evidence that will follow, God willing, leads us to the limitation of what it [our power] is capable of. If then the transcendence of the Powerfulness of the Eternal One is proved as well as the non-existence of a way to prove a restriction, the restriction must be negated.[157]

The line of reasoning features typical points of the argument, like the reference to the invalidation of knowledge if one allowed the existence of the unprovable.

Where the visibility of God is concerned, Ibn al-Murtaḍā argues against it with the "argument from impediments" (*dalīl al-mawāniʿ*), clearly based on what Shihadeh calls "the classical-*kalām* argument from ignorance."[158] A summary of Ibn al-Murtaḍā's argument runs as follows:

> There is no evidence for God's visibility at a given point (God is not seen). There are eight impediments that could hinder the perception of God at any time. None of these impediments applies at that given point in time. Hence the possibility of seeing God must be negated for that moment. There is no difference between that and other moments. Hence, the possibility of seeing God must be negated for all times.[159]

Ibn al-Murtaḍā clearly argues from a position that expects that certain knowledge of the existence of a fact or entity must be attainable by either perception or rational evidence. However, as we know from the discussion of *naẓar*, the validity of evidence depends on a particular order of premises and inferences. If this knowledge is not thus attainable, a different certain knowledge of something else is concluded, namely of non-existence. Ibn al-Murtaḍā is therefore clearly in line with the teaching of the Bahshami school that expects to arrive at a certain result susceptible of proof.

4.2 *Absence of Evidence as an Argument for Ambiguity*

Beyond the different versions of the argument, its significance is manifest in the large number of questions in which it is employed. We came across Ibn al-Wazīr's challenges towards different corollaries of the argument in several instances: Firstly, the Muʿtazila apparently invoked the principle on many occasions. Taqī l-Dīn al-ʿUjālī provides a list of issues where the Bahshami Muʿtazila

157 Al-Ḥayyī, *al-Muntazaʿ min al-Durar al-farāʾid* f. 22b.

158 Shihadeh, Argument from Ignorance 179. For Ibn al-Malāḥimī's argument from impediments, cf. ibid., 189.

159 Al-Ḥayyī, *al-Muntazaʿ min al-Durar al-farāʾid* fs. 39b–43a.

apparently argues based on the absence of evidence.[160] Abū l-Ḥusayn and Ibn al-Malāḥimī remarked that they themselves also use the argument in many places.[161] And we know that Ibn al-Wazīr responded to many issues that were prevalent in Zaydi doctrine as a result of the influence of the Muʿtazila.

Secondly, the suggestion is based on Ibn al-Wazīr's reasoning itself. In *Tarjīḥ*, the argument from the absence of evidence is mentioned only briefly, yet at the fundamental level of the definition of knowledge. Ibn al-Wazīr challenges whether a conclusion be called knowledge if it is based on the absence of evidence (*ʿadam wujūd dalīl ʿalā dhālika illā ʿadam al-wijdān*) as it is always possible that evidence be found later.[162] The argument receives the longest and most explicit attention in the fifth volume of *al-ʿAwāṣim*, where Ibn al-Wazīr responds to his opponent's charge that the supporters of the *bi-lā kayf* notion teach anthropomorphism (*tajsīm*).[163] The refutation of the claim that human beings will be able to see God without asking for the details of this visibility (*bi-lā kayf*) is a typical instance of the deployment of the argument from the absence of evidence, as the argument is often deployed in connection with God's unicity and His attributes.[164] In this particular case, the opponent's argument claims that, because there is no valid way of proving a difference between bodies (*ajsām*), the difference must be negated. If God were visible and hence found in a place, He would have to have a body like human beings. A corollary of the argument that constitutes the second pillar of the reasoning says that likeness in one aspect necessitates likeness in all resulting aspects.[165] In this case, that would mean that likeness of the divine and the human in their substantial nature (*jismiyya*) necessitates likeness in all bodily characteristics, allegedly amounting to reprehensible anthropomorphism.[166]

In his defense of the *bi-lā kayf* position concerning the "vision of God" in *al-ʿAwāṣim*, Ibn al-Wazīr explicitly and extensively disputes the argument, drawing largely on Fakhr al-Dīn al-Rāzī's as well as Imam Yaḥyā b. Ḥamza's refuta-

160 Taqī l-Dīn al-ʿUjālī, *al-Kāmil* 322–323.

161 Shihadeh, Argument from Ignorance 176, 184; referring the reader to Abū l-Ḥusayn, *Tasaffuḥ al-adilla* 13.

162 Ibn al-Wazīr, *Tarjīḥ* 98.

163 Ibn al-Wazīr, *al-ʿAwāṣim* v, 27–66.

164 Cf. al-Ḥayyī, *al-Muntazaʿ min al-Durar al-farāʾid* fs. 22b, 39b–42a; Ibn al-Malāḥimī, *Kitāb al-Muʿtamad* 278–296; Ibn al-Wazīr mentions the Muʿtazila in general and Ibn Mattawayh's *Tadhkira* in particular; cf. Ibn al-Wazīr, *al-ʿAwāṣim* v, 29–39. See also Shihadeh, Argument from Ignorance; Thiele, Jewish and Muslim Reception 111–113.

165 Cf. Yaḥyā b. Ḥamza, *al-Tamhīd* i, 36–37.

166 See for example Ibn al-Wazīr, *al-ʿAwāṣim* v, 28–29.

tions.[167] Ibn al-Wazīr describes his opponent as holding that "whatever cannot be affirmed must be negated" (*mā lā dalīl ʿalayhi yajib nafyuhu*). He seeks to invalidate their line of argument and, like the two aforementioned scholars, only considers the positive existence of evidence as proof for a statement on the existence or non-existence of an entity or state of affairs:

> It is agreed upon that the substances are at variance with each other in their essence. And it is agreed upon that their likeness (*tamāthul*) is not known by necessary knowledge. Whoever wants to argue that it is, needs sound apodictic evidence. But they [those who claim the likeness] did not bring forward anything like that. Shaykh Ibn Mattawayh responded with the famous doctrine that is invalid according to the critics. It [the doctrine] says that 'whatever cannot be affirmed by evidence must be negated.' This is refuted by [the statement] that there is no evidence that the Eternal (*qadīm*) [existed] in eternity (*fī l-azal*), in spite of the necessity that He was there at that time. Accordingly, they would have to negate that He was there at that time, and [it is refuted] because it is not more likely than [saying] that whatever cannot be negated must be affirmed.[168]

Admittedly, it would be a grave misrepresentation of Ibn al-Wazīr's opponents if he left it with the mere allegation that they negate anything for which they happen not to have evidence. However, in what follows, Ibn al-Wazīr, heavily quoting from Yaḥyā b. Hamza and Fakhr al-Dīn al-Razī, reacts to the reasoning that not applying the argument from the absence of evidence leads to an invalidation of necessary as well as acquired knowledge. According to the two scholars' line of argument, necessary knowledge is not invalidated, because the connection of dependence between the presence of imperceptible things on the one hand and the argument from the absence of evidence on the other is denied.[169] Likewise, acquired knowledge is not invalidated as long as only positive premises based on necessary knowledge are accepted, as is the case according to Fakhr al-Dīn al-Razī and Yaḥyā b. Ḥamza.[170]

---

167 Cf. Ibn al-Wazīr, *al-ʿAwāṣim* v, 30. This confirms Shihadeh's claim of the great influence of al-Rāzī's *Nihāyat al-ʿuqūl* beyond Ashʿarism; cf. Shihadeh, Argument from Ignorance 206.

168 Ibn al-Wazīr, *al-ʿAwāṣim* v, 29–30. The challenge to the argument from the absence of evidence which Ibn al-Wazīr deploys here has been responded to by Ibn al-Malāḥimī; cf. Shihadeh, Argument from Ignorance 188.

169 Ibn al-Wazīr, *al-ʿAwāṣim* v, 34; cf. Yaḥyā b. Ḥamza, *al-Tamhīd* i, 33–34.

170 Ibn al-Wazīr, *al-ʿAwāṣim* v, 34–35; cf. Yaḥyā b. Ḥamza, *al-Tamhīd* i, 34.

What is at issue here again are the means of possessing knowledge and the interdependence of human knowledge and truth. Whereas the opponents argue that valid evidence would have to be found by human reason if it existed, Ibn al-Wazīr is weary of restricting valid evidence to the products of established ways of rational inferences.

> They say that there is no proof for it [an entity], and whatever cannot be proved by an evidence has to be negated. Concerning the explanation for the absence of evidence, they argue for it by rendering the proofs of those who argue for the existence of the entity (*al-shay'*) and then explain their invalidity and weakness. They base the cogency [of evidence] on the restriction [*ḥaṣr*] on certain types of proofs, and then merely explain their nonexistence by the fact that they have not found them. (…) I say: They have no evidence that all proofs must be accounted for by the method of restriction and investigation apart from not finding [what is not accounted for].[171]

To him, it is conceivable that evidence as yet unavailable be found at a later time or by someone else. Accordingly, no certain statement can be made as long as no positive evidence exists for the presence or absence of an entity or state of affairs. Ibn al-Wazīr clearly takes the position that absence of evidence leads to conjectural statements or deferment of judgement:

> The non-existence of that which necessitates certain affirmation does not necessitate certain negation because a third category is possible. This is that no certain resolution is taken at all, rather the judgement is deferred.[172]

It is evident that Ibn al-Wazīr once again opts for ambiguity in the form of a statement of probability rather than claiming certainty based on logical inferences.

171 Ibn al-Wazīr, *al-ʿAwāṣim* v, 31. Ibn al-Wazīr probably refers to a corollary of the argument from the absence of evidence used to establish the *ratio legis* (*ʿilla*) of the original case in an analogy called investigation and disjunction (*al-sabr wa-l-taqsīm*): A restricted yet supposedly comprehensive number of possible solutions (*inḥiṣār*) is discussed; then each of them is refuted until only one remains to be affirmed; cf. Yaḥyā b. Ḥamza, *al-Tamhīd* i, 35; cf. Shihadeh, Argument from Ignorance 192–193.

172 Ibid., v, 37.

Where the divine names are concerned, Ibn al-Wazīr argues that both the Muʿtazila and the Ashʿariyya negate particular names of God in their literal sense. Instead, they find interpretations (*taʾwīl*) for the very reason that they cannot find or agree with evidence that affirms the literal meaning of those names.[173] An example of this would be the above-mentioned rejection of God's purposeful wisdom by the Ashʿariyya, who interpret the divine name of *al-ḥakīm* as the masterful maker (*al-muḥkim li-maṣnūʿātihi*) instead. They do not acknowledge the existence of evidence for the literal meaning of *al-ḥakīm* as the "wisely purposeful" (*lahū fī dhālika l-iḥkām ḥikma*).

> We have to have faith in them [God's names] and firmly believe that they have a meaning that is appropriate to the glory of God, along with our strong conviction that there is none like God, and that He is beyond being subject to anthropomorphism in His entire word. (…) The rational reasoning [behind the opposing view] is that the interpreter is certain that his interpretation of what God intended is true, to the exclusion of any other interpretation. This is erroneous because there is no evidence that no other interpretation might possibly conform to what God intended. At the most, it [the other interpretation] might be a search that does not find. However, not finding the object of the search does not mean that the object itself does not exist. How many scholars provide an interpretation and are then succeeded by others who offer a better interpretation without claiming that their interpretation is equal to what God intended for certain.[174]

In addition, in this context there is the all-pervading concept of divine wisdom to consider. A premise of the argument from the absence of evidence implies that a thing must be proved and known for what it is in itself (*maʿlūm fī nafsihi*).[175] When talking about the wise purposes of the Divine, Ibn al-Wazīr categorically refers to human beings' limitations on knowing a thing for what it really is, namely the content of the wise purpose itself. Although human beings have general necessary knowledge of the goodness of God as well as the moral value of types of actions (*al-taḥsīn wa-l-taqbīḥ al-ʿaqlī*), the goodness of His particular actions and their purposes cannot always be demonstrated. Indeed, human knowledge considers some actions that may be ascribed to God

173 Ibn al-Wazīr, *Īthār al-ḥaqq* i, 123. See also ch. 4 on Ibn al-Wazīr's theological positions below.

174 Ibn al-Wazīr, *al-ʿAwāṣim* viii, 324–325.

175 Taqī l-Dīn al-ʿUjālī, *al-Kāmil* 323.

as reprehensible, as for example intending His servant to do something reprehensible. A distinction is made between the evil in itself (*li-nafsihi*) and that which only appears evil (*li-ghayrihi*). The first kind of evil is known by necessary knowledge to be evil without possibility of there being anything good in it. In contradistinction, that which only appears evil really contains an ultimate good. But this good is beyond human knowledge or evidence. Conjecture as to the contained good is possible, but ultimately no certain evidence is attainable or perceivable. In the section on divine wisdom in chapter 4, it will become evident that the entire reasoning is built on the existence of a purpose that cannot be made evident in detail by human perception or inference, and the entire reasoning hinges on the very hiddenness of that purpose. This reasoning is diametrically opposed to an argument that takes the lack of certain evidence as grounds for necessitating negation.

As in many other cases, Ibn al-Wazīr refers to Shaykh Mukhtār in support of his concept of a divine wisdom that is built on the purposeful limitedness of human knowledge. Ibn al-Wazīr quotes from Shaykh Mukhtār's *Kitāb al-Mujtabā* concerning God's wisdom in intending what appears to be evil. He first outlines the counterargument that reasons with either of two possibilities: If God's intention is born out of wisdom, it would either have to agree with reason or go counter to reason. In the second case it would be no wisdom at all and would have to be rejected. In case of agreement with reason, the *compos mentis* would have to comprehend it. According to Ibn al-Wazīr, Shaykh Mukhtār replies:

> We do not consent [to saying] that if it [the wise purpose] agrees with reason we would have to comprehend it. How many things agree with reason yet the *compos mentis* cannot comprehend them until they are instructed.[176]

In contrast to this, we find yet another support for the initial thesis that Ibn al-Wazīr's thought largely relies on: the limitation of necessary knowledge and the broad space that is left to conjecture in the correlation between the argument from the absence of evidence and Ibn al-Wazīr's concept of divine wisdom. What cannot be known does not need to be known. Instead of negating the unknown, judgment should be deferred and possible further evidence awaited, as occurred in the form of revelation and transmission (*khabar*), for example.[177]

---

176 Ibn al-Wazīr, *al-ʿAwāṣim* v, 301.

177 Ibid., v, 33.

Negation is of course just another way of knowing, namely knowing about non-existence. In contrast, postponing apodictic judgment is tantamount to not knowing, hence to the acknowledgement of ambiguity.

5 Conclusion

The argument from the absence of evidence again shows that one underlying principle of Ibn al-Wazīr's thinking is satisfaction with ambiguity. In many questions, the available positive evidence does not suffice to come to a necessary judgment. The example of the lack of evidence for the existence of God in eternity shows how absurd it seemed to Ibn al-Wazīr to base certain judgments on the absence of evidence. Similarly, and in harmony with Ibn al-Wazīr's perpetual reference to what the common people know as a standard, he refers to all the divine things that the common people cannot prove by evidence. Must we conclude the non-existence of these things accordingly?[178]

Although Ibn al-Wazīr blatantly disregards his opponents' line of argument with this polemic simplification—no Muʿtazili considered a mere ignorance of proofs tantamount to something that could not be proven—his point accords with his own insistence on the negation of the obligation of philosophical speculation, the original human disposition as the means to attain true knowledge, and the knowledge of God's existence as necessary. The common epistemological feature of Ibn al-Wazīr's reasoning in all of these topics is the insistence that true knowledge is that which is "common necessary knowledge," and that all else is conjectural knowledge. Whereas the first is bestowed by God and amounts to substantial intuitional, sensual, experiential, revelational and *tawātur* evidence, the second may be constructed by conscious rational deductions and inferences, but does not amount to apodictic knowledge. As far as Ibn al-Wazīr is concerned, no rational argument and ordering of premises amounts to evidence that is absolutely certain. There is always an element of ambiguity in all knowledge that is not necessary.

In contradistinction to Ibn al-Wazīr's position, if *naẓar* is considered to be the first duty as well as the means of proving God's existence and arriving at certain knowledge, there would of course be no lack of evidence among the common people for the existence of the divine things. This latter train of thought clearly represents Ibn al-Murtaḍā's thinking. In his *al-Durar al-farāʾid*, for example, he requires detailed acquired knowledge of the divine attributes of

178 Ibid., v, 32.

every believer, arrived at by *naẓar*. Accordingly, he does not need to fear that the lack of evidence results in a negation of the attributes. He clearly supports and employs the argument from the absence of evidence in several instances. Similarly, he supports the division of apodictic knowledge into the necessary and the acquired, the knowledge of God as acquired by *naẓar* and the human intellect (*ʿaql*) as the means to actively generate apodictic knowledge. The degree of certainty that can and must be attained in all of these questions is considerably high.

With regard to the historical level, it appears likely that Shaykh Mukhtār, Taqī l-Dīn al-ʿUjālī and Imam Yaḥyā b. Ḥamza[179] represent a development within the school of Abū l-Ḥusayn that moves even further away from Bahshami Muʿtazilism than Abū l-Ḥusayn al-Baṣrī or at least Ibn al-Malāḥimi did. What is evident in the case of the argument from the absence of evidence was already suggested in the case of the proof of God's existence, where Shaykh Mukhtār apparently even went so far as to not require *naẓar* in the sense of philosophical speculation at all. Ibn al-Wazīr again felt much more drawn towards this current within the Muʿtazila than towards the Bahshami variety that was supported by many of his Zaydi contemporaries. Ibn al-Wazīr could frequently invoke these later followers of Abū l-Ḥusayn al-Baṣrī's school in order to support his claim that there had been Muʿtazilis who did not support the trends of his own time. When refuting the argument from the absence of evidence, Ibn al-Wazīr, like Taqī l-Dīn al-ʿUjālī before him, did not mention that Ibn al-Malāḥimī and, at least to a degree, Abū l-Ḥusayn also deployed it.

Ibn al-Murtaḍā could very well have been the person referred to in Ibn al-Wazīr's *Tarjīḥ*, especially in light of what we know about Ibn al-Murtaḍā's teaching on the proof of God's existence, on *naẓar* and the detailed knowledge he required of every believer. On these and related issues, the influential Zaydi scholar represented the Bahshami view that Ibn al-Wazīr contended with in particular.

Ibn Abī l-Qāsim, whom Ibn al-Wazīr argues against in *al-ʿAwāṣim*, did not explain his initial claim that provoked the extensive refutation of the argument from the absence of evidence. However, the fact that Ibn al-Wazīr anticipated the argument together with Ibn al-Murtaḍā's endorsement of it renders it very

179 This is not to say that Yaḥyā b. Ḥamza agreed with Taqī l-Dīn al-ʿUjālī and Shaykh Mukhtār in everything, nor Ibn al-Wazīr with Yaḥyā b. Ḥamza. Yaḥyā b. Ḥamza, for example, supports *naẓar* as the first duty and the only way to know God's attributes; cf. Yaḥya b. Ḥamza, *Kitāb al-Tamhīd* i, 48–58. However, while the influence of Abū l-Ḥusayn on Yaḥya b. Ḥamza has been mentioned, he deviates from Abū l-Ḥusayn in the present case and is more in line with Taqī l-Dīn al-ʿUjālī, Shaykh Mukhtār and indeed Ibn al-Wazīr.

likely that the Bahshami line of argument was still prevalent among Ibn al-Wazīr's Zaydi contemporaries. This supports our thesis that Ibn al-Wazīr's epistemology of ambiguity distinguished him from his contemporary Zaydis, the hallmark of whose epistemology was the attainment of certain knowledge in more than one field or discipline. This may appear to contrast with the initial suggestion that Ibn al-Wazīr's theory of knowledge was his means of harmonization. However, although Ibn al-Wazīr's understanding did contrast with that of his contemporaries, the broadness of his epistemology of ambiguity allowed him to incorporate a wide range of conflicting doctrines into the possible, including those doctrines that resulted from his opponents' theory of knowledge.

CHAPTER 4

Central Concepts of Ibn al-Wazīr's Theological Thought

One characteristic that runs through most of Ibn al-Wazīr's writings is the attempt to demonstrate that the doctrines of contending theological schools—predominantly the Muʿtazila and the Ashʿariyya—were essentially consistent.

The difference between the Muʿtazila and the Ashʿariyya is most pointed in regard to divine unicity and justice.[1] The most predominant and recurrent aspects of God's unicity and justice in Ibn al-Wazīr's theological writings are God's names and attributes (*asmāʾ* and *ṣifāt*) as well as His will (*irāda*) and the question of human actions (*afʿāl al-ʿibād*). Arguably, Ibn al-Wazīr was particularly occupied with these questions for the very reason that harmonization was needed most here. At the outset of Ibn al-Wazīr's harmonization of the "controversial detailed matters" (*al-masāʾil al-tafṣīliyya al-mukhtalafa fīhā*) following the general prolegomena in *Īthār al-ḥaqq*, most of the topics treated are subsumed under one of these three aspects.[2]

The question is how exactly Ibn al-Wazīr's epistemology of ambiguity functions to arrive at a general form of the central Islamic tenets (*jumal*) on which all Muslims supposedly agree, on the one hand, and tolerate ambiguity in matters on which they disagree on the other. How does Ibn al-Wazīr apply his concepts of *al-ʿilm al-ḍarūrī l-ʿadī*, *fiṭra* and *naẓar* to apparently conflicting teachings of different schools? What constitutes the central Islamic

1 The issue of divine justice has been a topic of major interest in research on Muslim theology. A few examples are Heemskerk, *Suffering in the Muʿtazilite Theology*; Vasalou, *Moral Agents and Their Deserts*; Frank, Several Fundamental Assumptions 5–18; Hourani, Divine Justice and Human Reason 73–83. As divine justice (*ʿadl*) was arguably one of the first pillars of Muʿtazili theology, the attempt to justify some of God's actions figures prominently in the majority of books on Muʿtazili doctrine. Although Ashʿari theology does not have as great a need to defend God's actions, the issue received broad attention among Ashʿaris as well. Since it has been a major point of controversy between contending theological schools, scholars who formulated views in contradistinction to the theological schools, like Ibn Taymiyya or Ibn Qayyim, were much occupied with the question as well. For a discussion of the latter two's concept of God's justice, see mainly the research of Hoover, *Ibn Taymiyya's Theodicy*; Hoover, Islamic Universalism 181–209; Hoover, Justice of God 53–75; Hoover, God's Wise Purposes 113–134.

2 Cf. Ibn al-Wazīr, *Īthār al-ḥaqq* 157, 181.

 | DOI:10.1163/9789004381117_006

tenets in their general form? And how do these epistemological concepts structure Ibn al-Wazīr's own views?

Before we get to the how of Ibn al-Wazīr's harmonization, a word on methodology is due. In research, the feasibility of the attempt to harmonize has been discussed. Al-Ṣubḥī praises Ibn al-Wazīr's endeavor which speaks to him of Ibn al-Wazīr's outstanding skill and scholarship. Yet he questions the final result of Ibn al-Wazīr's attempt.[3] The question of whether harmonization of differing theological school doctrines is feasible depends on one's understanding of speculative theology (*ʿilm al-kalām*). We can look at this from two different perspectives. First, we could start from the premises of *ʿilm al-kalām* as an "art of contradiction-making," as Frank suggests (but then rejects).[4] From the perspective of an "elaborate polemics of apology"[5] where the content of an argument is determined in contradistinction to the opponent's intended concept, it would be hard to deny that the difference between the Ashʿariyya and the Muʿtazila goes beyond mere form and expression. However, Ḥajar is persuaded by Ibn al-Wazīr's argumentation and attempts to show that the two schools do not disagree profoundly.[6] If we look at Ibn al-Wazīr's claim from different premises, namely those that object to the necessity and usefulness of the apologetic element of *kalām* as a means of grasping fundamental truths, Ibn al-Wazīr's claim of essential agreement no longer seems so far-fetched. Al-Ṣubḥī writes that Ibn al-Wazīr's uniqueness as a theologian consisted in his ability to "elevate its [*ʿilm al-kalām's*] subject matter from its disputative character unto the character of religious knowledge."[7] Arguably, Ibn al-Wazīr would disagree with Frank who insists that the raison d'être of *kalām* "is a knowing (scientia, *ʿilm*) based on a genuine quest for the true, impl[ying] a love of wisdom."[8] He would likely agree with van Ess, who claims that "nicht selten geht es weniger um die Wahrheit als um Rechthaben, im günstigsten Fall um Überzeugen."[9] Therefore, Ibn al-Wazīr tries to dissociate the content of the theological doctrines from their respective polemic and apologetic elements.[10]

---

3 Al-Ṣubḥī, *al-Zaydiyya* 493.
4 Frank, The *Kalām* 295–309.
5 Ibid., 295.
6 Ḥajar, *Ibn al-Wazīr wa-manhajuhu* 361. His conclusion is that much of modern scholarship would have to be rewritten, based on the uncovering of the essential agreement between the two groups. Although I do agree that some essential agreement can be proved, this only applies as long as the terminology employed in *kalām* debates is not taken in its strict sense.
7 Al-Ṣubḥī, *al-Zaydiyya* 499.
8 Frank, The *Kalām* 295.
9 Van Ess, *Erkenntnislehre* 20.
10 In this, Ibn al-Wazīr is much closer to the philosophers, described by Weiss as relegating

1 God's Wisdom (*ḥikma*) as the Key to Harmonization

In the classical discussions of *kalām*, the concept of divine wisdom did not figure prominently on its own.[11] Its main significance lay in its implications for the doctrines on divine justice and omnipotence so central in Muʿtazili and Ashʿari theology. For Ibn al-Wazir, it occupied a key position in his theological thought:

> They could not find an escape from one of the three calamities in the [religious] sciences except through allegorical interpretation,
> of the wise purpose of the Lord of creation, or His capacity to be gracious, or the consignment of evildoers to eternity [in the Fire].
> Better than this is withholding judgement in [the matter] because we all are definite about the goodness of the judgment of the best Judge.
> That suffices, seeing that the safety of the judicious in the face of fear [of error] is better than the correctness that is [only] possible.[12]

This excerpt from Ibn al-Wazīr's largely lost poem *al-Ijādā fī l-irāda* preserved in *Īthār al-ḥaqq* indicates that engaging in the discussion of the classical questions of *kalām* did not constitute a major interest for Ibn al-Wazīr. His own positions on those classical questions are not given prominence and often remain vague. In the introduction to his elaboration of divine wisdom in *Īthār al-ḥaqq*, Ibn al-Wazīr refers to the results of speculation about the classical questions of *kalām*:

> This ponderous matter [divine wisdom] is devoted to him who knows of *ʿilm al-kalām* and its disagreements, which sicken his heart and inhibit

an inferior position to the art of dialectics within theology, because dialectics are more interested in defeating an adversary than in discovering truth; cf. Weiss, *Search for God's Law* 47.

11 Similar in meaning to the concept of knowledge (*ʿilm*) at the beginning of Islam, *ḥikma* later lagged behind *ʿilm*. However, among the philosophers and Ṣufīs, the concept of *ḥikma* retained more prominence; cf. Rosenthal, *Knowledge Triumphant* 35; Goichon, Ḥikma.

12 For the translation of this part of Ibn al-Wazīr's *Ijāda fī l-irāda*, I mostly rely on Hoover's translation. However, I made minor changes, as for example translating "*ta'awwul*" as "allegorical interpretation" rather than "reinterpretation," because the conflict was between taking a divine name at face value on the one hand, and interpreting it allegorically on the other hand. Furthermore, I interpreted the second part of the last line "*awlā min iṣāba jāza*" as "better than correctness that is [only] possible," rather than "better than correctness of the [overly] decisive," because of the significance of the aspect of chance in it. As Hoover explains: "It is in fact better, Ibn al-Wazīr affirms, to exercise caution than to be rashly and compulsively decisive and per chance get something correct." Hoover, Withholding judgement 235, footnote 99.

> him from attaining the certainty [that comes] by way of belief in the generalities (*al-iʿtiqād al-jumlī*). [It is also for] him in whose heart fanaticism has taken root, so that he cannot avert it without an irrefutable argument, or for him who has gone astray through *taqlīd*.[13]

Apparently, Ibn al-Wazīr considers the concept of God's wisdom to be the solution to many conflicts that arise due to immersion in the subtleties of *kalām*. *Ḥikmat Allāh*[14] is a major component of all topics treated throughout *Īthār al-ḥaqq*. In *al-ʿAwāṣim* the concept is most prevalent in the discussions of volumes 5–7. As a consequence, Ibn al-Wazīr does not merely refer to God's wisdom in his elaboration of other theological issues. Rather, the centrality of the concept of God's wisdom for Ibn al-Wazīr's thought becomes evident in that his own views in this regard are much more pronounced than in any other theological question. He does not merely juxtapose and harmonize positions of other scholars, but explicitly offers his own interpretation.

---

13 Ibn al-Wazīr, *Īthār al-ḥaqq* 181.

14 In this regard, a word on translation is due. Rosenthal tells us that *ḥikma* became a synonym of *ʿilm* and eventually was relegated to a lower place for most Muslims, partly because it was associated with *ḥukm* as 'worldly authority' and lost fame as a consequence.; cf. Rosenthal, *Knowledge Triumphant* 38. This, however, is not the case for Ibn al-Wazīr and scholars like Ibn Taymiyya and Ibn Qayyim al-Jawziyya in whose thought divine wisdom figures prominently. I translated *ḥikma* as "wisdom" in its broadest sense. Scholars such as Hoover who devoted considerable effort to the *ḥikma*-theories of Ibn Taymiyya and Ibn Qayyim al-Jawziyya, referred to *ḥikma* as "wise purposes;" cf. Hoover, *Ibn Taymiyya's Theodicy*; Hoover, God's Wise Purposes 113–134. Others, like Ormsby in his discussion of al-Ghazālī's concept of theodicy, described the concept of *ḥikma* in terms of causality; cf. Ormsby, *Theodicy in Islamic Thought*. In Ibn al-Wazīr's thought, the term *ḥikma* often appears in the sense of a "wise purpose" or a "hidden good" pointing to purposefulness or intentionality, rather than causality. Moreover, Bell translates Ibn Taymiyya's concept of *ḥikma* as "for the sake of wisdom," which Ibn Taymiyya apparently used in contradistinction to the Muʿtazili understanding of *ḥikma* as "purpose." Bell, *Love Theory* 69. This translation likewise suits Ibn al-Wazīr's use of the term *ḥikma*, because it still bears the connotation of "knowledge" (*ʿilm*), which is a constituent of Ibn al-Wazīr's definition of wisdom and which will help us to see the link to epistemology. However, Ibn al-Wazīr makes use of Ashʿari concepts of causality as well as of Muʿtazili concepts of purposefulness in order to prove an essential agreement on the concept of God's wisdom. Therefore, using a variety of translations for *ḥikma* such as "wisdom" or "for the sake of wisdom" as well as "wise purpose" and "hidden good" seems appropriate because it allows for a rapprochement of contending views, which again provides the background of Ibn al-Wazīr's own concept.

1.1 *Ibn al-Wazīr's Harmonization Regarding God's Wisdom*

Regarding divine wisdom, the Ashʿari doctrine appears to be especially in need of rectification in the eyes of Ibn al-Wazīr, whereas the Muʿtazila is already a strong proponent of divine purpose in all of God's acts.[15] However, they also "exaggerate," as we shall see in the paragraph on Ibn al-Wazīr's development of the concept. Al-Ṣubḥī paraphrases Ibn al-Wazīr's view when he writes that "the Muʿtazila went too far in [their concept of] wisdom and neglected the will, whereas the Ashʿariyya exaggerated [the importance] of will and neglected wisdom."[16] Since the Muʿtazila identifies wisdom with a cause, divine wisdom in all actions means that God is dependent on causes, a thought inconceivable to the Ashʿariyya. The supposed exaggeration of the Muʿtazila consists in the claim that human reason is able to know the details of divine wisdom.[17] Ibn al-Wazīr's golden mean insists on God's divine wisdom as the end of all his actions, of which the human being has merely a general knowledge (*ʿilm jumlī*). One line in *al-ʿAwāṣim* well illustrates what we will elaborate in the following: "His [the human being's] general knowledge of His [God's] wisdom is sufficient."[18]

Before we proceed to Ibn al-Wazīr's unique view, common ground needs to be established, namely a doctrine of divine wisdom in a general form that can be agreed upon by all (*jumal*). According to Ibn al-Wazīr, it is in fact common knowledge that everything that proceeds from God does so for a reason. He reconstructs this supposedly common knowledge in the following way: The Ashʿariyya deny that God has a goal in (*gharaḍ*) or motivation for (*dāʿī*) His actions. They deny *ḥikma* because they identify it with such a compelling goal or motivation. The troublesome thought for them is the idea that God could be forced to do something, if anything outside His own will had a causative effect on His decisions. Accordingly, the limitlessness of God's volition and power would appear to be impaired. God would be incapacitated (*taʿjīz*) and imperfect for lack of self-sufficiency.[19] In consequence, Ashʿaris often interpreted the Qurʾānic *al-ḥakīm* as referring to the concept of perfection in acts (*iḥkām*).[20]

---

15 The Ashʿariyya is not the only theological school to deny that divine actions have causes. Similarly, the Māturīdiyya and the Ẓāhiriyya reject the idea of the purposiveness of divine behavior. But Ibn al-Wazīr's discussion mainly involves Muʿtazili and Ashʿari theology. I will therefore refer only to these two positions here.

16 Al-Ṣubḥī, *al-Zaydiyya* 493.

17 Ibn al-Wazīr, *Īthār al-ḥaqq* 182.

18 Cf. Ibn al-Wazīr, *al-ʿAwāṣim* vi, 122.

19 For the view of Ibn Taymiyya, who struggled with the same tension between the Ashʿari and Muʿtazili visions of God, having a different agenda but coming to a similar conclusion, see Hoover, Ibn Tamiyya as an Avicennan Theologian 42.

20 Cf. Bell, *Love Theory* 69.

However, according to Ibn al-Wazīr, it is the very centrality of God's volition and power in Ashʿari doctrine which speaks of purpose. Questioning the Ashʿari interpretation of the divine name *al-ḥakīm*, he writes:

> Expositors of the Beautiful Names who did not understand this danger [of denying God's action a purpose or a motive] have construed *al-ḥakīm* to mean 'the one who acts with perfection' (*al-muḥkim*) (…) What necessarily follows from this is that generosity and the like does not become God more than their opposites, and also that every object of power (*kull maqdūr*) may exist as well as remain in non-existence. One possible thing preponders only through a preponderator, and there is no preponderator other than the motive (*dāʿī*). This means that the ambiguous matters do not need an allegorical interpretation. What follows from this is that those who deny God's wise purposes are unable to affirm the truthfulness of the Exalted and the truthfulness of His noble apostles, peace be upon them, with certainty.[21]

And in response to the Ashʿari reasoning against God's wisdom based on His supposed incapacitation, Ibn al-Wazīr writes:

> This [Ibn al-Wazīr's concept of wisdom] refers causes, motives and wise purposes back to God. The creation of those created beings who are purely good was intended for itself, not for any other meaning or secondary reason. That which is evil was intended for a good that resides in it or that necessarily follows from it or is dependent on it. Human beings' intellect in the state of their original disposition (*fiṭar al-ʿuqūl*) agree and the law asserts that wanting evil because it is evil is reprehensible. But [concluding] the incapacitation of the Lord is a most preposterous error in this. Where is the connection between the negation of the capacity and the negation of the action? God the Exalted has demonstrated this in his Word, {Blessed is He in whose hands is sovereignty and He is able to do all things}. He did not say that He does all things. And we did not say that God is unable to do the futile, trick or act unjustly. But we said that He does not do it and we praised Him for it as He Himself does in His noble book. If He were incapable of doing it, He would not be praiseworthy for not doing it.[22]

21 Ibn al-Wazīr, *Īthār al-ḥaqq* 194.

22 Ibid., 222.

In other words, the fact that God could have acted, but did choose not to act in a futile way is the precondition of the praiseworthiness of His action.[23] This means that the two possibilities of the choice were not even. Otherwise, it would not have been a choice at all. Unevenness implies the existence of something that made the choosing of one side preponderant (*murajjiḥ*). Ibn al-Wazīr here refers to a term coined by Fakhr al-Dīn al-Rāzī, and indeed by Abū l-Ḥusayn al-Baṣrī.[24] Thus, he presumes that such a *murajjiḥ* is much the same as a motive, cause or a wise purpose.[25]

Furthermore, the fact that God made a choice—for example, to create a particular thing in a particular way—shows that He had an intention for his action.[26] God sent the prophets because He intended that humankind should be shown the way. Moreover, He affirmed the truthfulness of the prophets through miracles. The Ashʿariyya generally agree with these statements, which is reason enough for Ibn al-Wazīr to argue that the Ashʿariyya in fact believe that God's actions are not futile (*ʿabathan*).[27]

Interestingly, showing that God's action are not futile was one of the Muʿtazila's major concerns in their line of argument against Ashʿari doctrine.[28]

---

23 This reasoning is again very similar to Ibn Taymiyya's position. Ibn Taymiyya admits that God is able to do evil. The goodness of His action depends on the fact that He did not choose to do the evil action. Had he been unable to choose to do evil He would not have been praiseworthy; cf. Hoover, Justice of God 72.

24 In his *Maṭālib*, Fakhr al-Dīn al-Rāzī explains how we know by necessary knowledge that man makes his choice between two actions based on a preponderator (*murajjiḥ*); cf. al-Rāzī, *al-Maṭālib* ix, 29; Abrahamov, Necessary Knowledge 28. For Abū l-Ḥusayn al-Baṣrī's use of the term, see Yaḥyā b. Ḥamza, *Kitāb al-Tamhīd* i, 123. In fact, Abū l-Ḥusayn was not the first to formulate the thought that motives are unequally strong and that one of them must be preponderant. But ʿAbd al-Jabbār, who discussed the thought before him, did not allow any compelling force to the preponderant motive; cf. Hoover, *Ibn Taymiyya's Theodicy* 142; Madelung, Late Muʿtazila 247–248.

25 However, Ibn al-Wazīr repeatedly states that Fakhr al-Dīn al-Razī got confused and entangled himself in his concept of the preponderator, ending up confirming the Muʿtazili position; cf. Ibn al-Wazīr, *al-ʿAwāṣim* i, 7, 87, 319, 326. For the equation of motive, preponderator and wise purpose, see also Ibn al-Wazīr, *Īthār al-ḥaqq* 193. Al-Ghazālī is one of those Ashʿaris whom Ibn al-Wazīr quotes in order to show the essential agreement. He refers to al-Ghazālī's concept of a motive (*dāʿī*). Of course it is not difficult to associate al-Ghazālī with the doctrine of God's wise purposes; cf. ibid., 194.

26 Obviously, Ibn al-Wazīr does not agree with the view held by some Muʿtazilis that only the evenness of two possibilities renders a choice really free.

27 Ibn al-Wazīr, *Īthār al-ḥaqq* 192. The argument that leading Ashʿaris make the confirmation of the prophets' truthfulness dependent on miracles was already used by Ibn Taymiyya as an argument against the Ashʿari rejection of God's purposeful activity; cf. Hoover, Justice of God 64–65.

28 For the Muʿtazila, an act without purpose would be foolish and absurd, which of course

It is noteworthy that Ibn al-Wazīr refers to a concept Fakhr al-Dīn al-Rāzī apparently took over from Abū l-Ḥusayn al-Baṣrī's school in order to argue for the supposed agreement between the contending theological schools. Yet Ibn al-Wazīr evidently ignored the contrast between the two scholars' conclusions from the same concepts. He did not point out that Fakhr al-Dīn al-Rāzī practically restricted the use of the term *murajjiḥ* to human actions and apparently ignored its implications for his concept of the divine will. Fakhr al-Dīn al-Rāzī ascribed the origin of such a preponderator to God and used it as an argument to prove the divine role in the occurrence of human actions. However, Abū l-Ḥusayn al-Baṣrī used the term to argue for man's role as the originator (*mūjid*) of his actions as well as to describe what being willing means in the case of God, as we shall explore further below.[29] Yet, for Ibn al-Wazīr, the existence of the concept of a preponderator or motive that causes an agent, be it God or man, to choose one action over another was sufficient to claim essential agreement on a general tenet of divine wisdom and purposefulness.[30]

It seems that, due to his intention to find common ground, Ibn al-Wazīr occasionally ignored distinctions between the use of terms and the connotations they carry. The term *gharaḍ*, for example, was rejected not only by the Ashʿariyya but also by explicit supporters of the concept of God's wise purposes like Ibn Taymiyya, because *gharaḍ* connotes need.[31] As another example, Ibn al-Wazīr himself uses the distinction between motive (*dāʿī*) and wise purpose (*ḥikma*) to show the superiority of divine action above human action, as I

cannot be said about God's actions; cf. Ibn al-Murtaḍā, Riyāḍat al-afhām 99; Bell, *Love Theory* 67.

29 Cf. Madelung, Late Muʿtazila 256; Yaḥyā b. Ḥamza, *Kitāb al-Tamhīd* i, 120–123; al-Kamālī, *Imām al-Mahdī* 294; Schmidtke, *Theologie, Philosophie und Mystik* 147.

30 Cf. Ibn al-Wazīr, *al-ʿAwāṣim* vii, 326. The potentially connecting role of the idea of a preponderator has been pointed out already by Ḥajar. However, Ḥajar focused on the link between the *murajjiḥ* and independent intellectual discernment, rather than its link to motive, which seems to have been considered of greater importance in research; cf. Ḥajar, *Ibn al-Wazīr wa-manhajuhu* 364. Ibn Taymiyya is only one example of those who interlinked the concepts of preponderator, motive and wise purpose. However, in contrast to Ibn al-Wazīr, Ibn Taymiyya does not seem to have intended to reveal an essential agreement between the schools; cf. Hoover, Ibn Taymiyya as an Avicennan Theologian 42. Another argument advanced by Ibn al-Wazīr comes from the realm of legal theory. According to him, the widely accepted theory of *uṣūl al-fiqh* as set forth by the Malikite Jamal al-Dīn b. al-Ḥājib (d. 646/1248) builds fundamentally on the validity of causes for the divine stipulations of religious law. In fact, all who agree on analogical reasoning (*qiyās*) as a main instrument of legal interpretation would thus support the idea of purposefulness and intentionality behind divine stipulations; cf. Ibn al-Wazīr, *Īthār al-ḥaqq* 187.

31 Bell, *Love Theory* 67–69.

shall discuss below.[32] This seemingly casual attitude toward details appears to be a natural result of Ibn al-Wazīr's agenda of focusing on and being satisfied with "the general tenets." If mere occupation with one another's concepts and adoption of key terms is argument enough for establishing common ground, Abū l-Ḥusayn and al-Rāzī are indeed good examples for the convergence of Muʿtazili and the Ashʿariyyi doctrine.

1.1.1 Mitigated Rational Discernment and God's Wisdom

A related concept where Ibn al-Wazīr considers the essential agreement of the schools to be evident is that of rational discernment of good and evil independent of revelation (*al-taḥsīn wa-l-taqbīḥ al-ʿaqlī*). Undisputedly, many Ashʿaris expressly reject the objectivism in the notion that human reason can discern whether an action is good (*ḥasan*) or evil (*qabīḥ*) without prior revelation.[33] This refers to God's actions and commands in particular. According to the Ashʿari teaching, it would be meaningless to call a divine action evil on the basis of the human intellect, because the categories of good and evil only acquire meaning through divine command or prohibition.[34] Accordingly, they do not apply to God and His actions and are restricted to the realm of human responsibility. Further, if revelation does not give a reason why a particular divine action or command is good or evil, no reason exists. In contrast, the Muʿtazila generally hold that good and evil are objective categories intrinsic to acts in the human as well as in the divine realm. Sound human reason is endowed with an immediate knowledge of these intrinsic values. It is therefore not only capable of judging human acts independently of revelation, it can also discern whether or not a divine act agrees with the moral principles that human beings are subject to. Accordingly, God's imposition of obligation on His creatures (*taklīf*) as well as His own actions would always have to be comprehensible to the human intellect.[35] The Muʿtazili theory of divine justice rests to a large degree on these objectivistic assumptions, as does the greater part of the differences between Muʿtazili and the Ashʿari theology. Ibn al-Murtaḍā goes so far as to say that agreement in this question would result in agreement in all other questions.[36]

---

32 Ibn al-Wazīr, Īthār al-ḥaqq 183; see also 237 below.

33 For an account of the Ashʿari attitude toward *al-taḥsīn wa-l-taqbīḥ*, see Reinhart, *Before Revelation* 62.

34 Cf. al-Ḥayyī, *al-Muntazaʿ min al-Durar al-farāʾid* f. 69b. Ibn al-Murtaḍā discusses positions of Ashʿari scholars in contrast to his own views as well as that of different Muʿtazili scholars. I therefore used Ibn al-Murtaḍā as a source for Ashʿari views in order to augment Ibn al-Wazīr's depiction of Ashʿari doctrine.

35 Frank, Fundamental Assumptions 16.

36 Cf. al-Ḥayyī, *al-Muntazaʿ min al-Durar al-farāʾid* f. 66a.

Yet Ibn al-Wazīr endeavors to show that the two schools effectively—though not explicitly—assume the same concept concerning speech. He argues as follows: In the context in question, the theological issue of *al-taḥsīn wa-l-taqbīḥ al-ʿaqlī* pertains to seemingly evil or unjust divine acts that are mentioned in the scriptural sources. Many Ashʿaris hold that God's acts are above moral judgement by human reason. Therefore, no one can say that God acts unjustly in these cases. Furthermore, revelation does not usually mention the reasons for God's actions. Accordingly, there is no need to look for some good reason or interpretation of the cause for such actions. However, Ibn al-Wazīr argues that Ashʿaris along with the whole of the Muslim community do assert that God must be taken to be truthful in His speech. A common Ashʿari explanation for this assertion is that lying is an attribute of imperfection. Such attributes of imperfection could never be ascribed to God. One can be sure, for example, that He has not send liars as messengers. Ibn al-Wazīr affirms this:

> This is a sound saying. Yet, [considering] lying to be an attribute of imperfection is rationally tantamount to acknowledging *al-taḥsīn wa-l-taqbīḥ* as well as to proving divine wisdom. If there is consensus that lying is an attribute of imperfection and that it cannot possibly be ascribed to God *because* it is an attribute of imperfection, then the same applies to the punishment of prophets for the sins of their enemies and the rewarding of their enemies for their good deeds on the Day of Resurrection, the Day of Religion, of truth and justice. Rationally and by revelation it is impossible to ascribe these things to God in the same way that lying cannot possibly be ascribed to Him. Whoever claims that there is a difference between the two in regard to the imperfection of the Just and the Wise is wrong. God loves justice, so that sending truthful messengers without liars belongs to the good actions that they [some Ashʿaris] combat and not to the truthful speech that they require.[37]

The knowledge that lying is evil and that God is no liar is a classic instance of *al-taḥsīn wa-l-taqbīḥ* with regard to God's words. This is not limited to Muʿtazili reasoning.[38] Yet Ibn al-Wazīr concludes from the Ashʿari doctrine that God can-

---

37 Ibn al-Wazīr, *Īthār al-ḥaqq* 185.

38 For a discussion of the Muʿtazili view of the objectivity of the evilness of lying, see for example Vasalou, *Moral agents* 15; Hourani, *Islamic Rationalism* 8–14. Ibn Taymiyya also held that the moral value of a lie was necessarily known by reason. However, the moral value of a speech or an action was not determined in the independent nature of the speech

not be a liar based on the nature of a lie, and thus reasons that the Ashʿariyya does hold to *al-taḥsīn wa-l-taqbīḥ*. Their supposedly erroneous distinction between divine speech and divine actions does not dissuade him from the validity of his harmonization.

The result is Ibn al-Wazīr's own view: Man knows in his *fiṭra* what is good and what is evil in a general way. He knows that lying is evil and that punishing sinless human beings is likewise evil. He knows that evil things cannot be ascribed to God because He is perfect. Perfection includes goodness. All these things are known necessarily, they do not need deliberate demonstration or clarification. Yet, this common necessary knowledge does not extend to all the details of divine speech and action. Where practical application of the general knowledge of moral values is concerned, namely in *taklīf* and its legal implications, revelation is still needed.

Besides law, there are those instances where God's action does not seem to agree with the general rational evaluation of moral values. Here the very concept of the ability for *taḥsīn* and *taqbīḥ* itself is helpful. God has created human beings in such a way that they know of God's perfection and goodness. Even where they cannot understand a particular divine action, that knowledge is still valid. There must be some good reason or wise purpose for God's action which reflects His goodness. Ibn al-Wazīr explains his synthesizing view with the Quranic example typically employed to argue for divine wisdom:

> It is conceivable that He has a wise purpose which is hidden to the creatures because of the incompleteness of their knowledge of the things that are possible (*al-umūr al-muḥtamala*). Like when the angels, peace be upon them, asked about the wisdom in creating Adam and his offspring because they assumed that they would all be evil without there being any good in a single one of them—the downright kind of evil which contains no good at all, neither now nor in the future, [the evil] that is abominable to reason. What concerns that kind of evil which contains some good, some praiseworthy purposes or that which may have some of these, [concerning this] no reason can say with certainty that it is abominable. That is why the Exalted replied to them [the angels] "I know things you do not [know]."[39] And He did not say that whatever they or the knowledgeable

---

or action, but by the respective suitability or unsuitability, benefit or harm, pleasure or pain related to it in a given circumstance; cf. Ibn Taymiyya, *al-Radd ʿalā l-manṭiqiyyīn* 424; Hoover, *Ibn Taymiyya's Theodicy* 34–35.

39 Ibn al-Wazīr quotes from Q 2:30, which reads {[Prophet], when your Lord told the angels, 'I am putting a successor on earth,' they said, 'How can You put someone there who will

> people (*al-ʿārifūn*) consider abominable is good with regard to Himself. If God's actions were void of wise purposes, His mentioning of His own knowledge and its surplus beyond their knowledge would have no meaning in this case at all.[40]

In other words, there are divine actions that are not comprehensible to anyone but God. This is so because of His surpassing knowledge. However, that surpassing knowledge is only one of extent, not of moral nature. The essential general idea of goodness or evil remains the same.[41]

The thought expressed here contains two important arguments as to the contention between the schools, answering the Ashʿariyya as well as the Muʿtazila. Responding to the Ashʿariyya, Ibn al-Wazīr insists that the difference between God's and human knowledge is in extent, not in moral assessment. The other argument responds to the Muʿtazila, or rather, to those among the Muʿtazila who "exaggerate" in that they require detailed knowledge of God's actions and their justification.

These arguments are reminiscent of Ibn al-Wazīr's principle of general knowledge and the *jumal*. He refers to the angels' general knowledge of God's goodness, a knowledge they should apply to those of His actions which they do not, and in fact cannot, understand. God's superiority is maintained by the superior extent of His knowledge. The angels' attempt to determine the reason and purpose of God's action in detail would have lead them to false assumptions because there was a lack of knowledge. Of course, God might have told them His reasons. However, that would have required the angels to share in the knowledge of the unknown (*ʿilm al-ghayb*), an important distinctive feature between the superiority of divine and creaturely attributes and abilities.[42]

This is just another way of talking about the unclear, the ambiguous matters (*al-mutashābihāt*). Ibn al-Wazīr refers the detailed understanding to God's superior knowledge. Human beings lack the ability to understand the details. However, the knowledge that they do have, the general knowledge, ensures that there is a best possible interpretation of the unknown. Because God is good, there must be some good and wise purpose behind the incomprehensible action.

---

cause damage and bloodshed, when we celebrate Your praise and proclaim Your holiness?' but He said, 'I know things you do not.'}.

40 Ibn al-Wazīr, *Īthār al-ḥaqq* 345.

41 Cf. ibid., 194.

42 Ibid., 345.

> This 'good' is that which is intended, it is what revelation calls the interpretation of the ambiguous matters (*ta'wīl al-mutashābihāt*), and what the wise call the objective of the objective (*gharaḍ al-gharaḍ*).[43]

Both claims, the Muʿtazili claim that the details of the ambiguous acts can be known and the Ashʿari claim that whatever is not known or understood (e.g. for lack of reasons) of the ambiguous acts does not exist, cause doubt about particular attributes of God. In contrast, if one accepts an epistemology of ambiguity concerning the details, it becomes possible to uphold a literal understanding of all of God's attributes and maintain what Ibn al-Wazīr, in his *Dīwān* and other writings, calls "a good opinion" (*ḥusn al-ẓann*) of God.[44] For Ibn al-Wazīr, an interpretation of the ambiguous theological matters always exists. It must be a positive interpretation, but it can be known by God only.

In short, Ibn al-Wazīr's harmonization can maintain the major Muʿtazili concern to deny all evil in relation to God[45] as well as the Ashʿari desire to keep God's decisions above too much human incursion. The human intellect is able to discern good and evil, but only in a general manner. In contrast, the human being should "omit outright rational discernment of good and evil in some subtle matters where the human intellect may err due to its confusedness and dullness."[46] If God's knowledge does not differ from human knowledge in its moral assessment, one must ask how exactly Ibn al-Wazīr resolves the conflict between the following two concepts by his doctrine of wise purposes: On the one hand, *al-taḥsīn wa-l-taqbīḥ al-ʿaqlī*, on the other hand, the existence of evil in creation besides apparently abominable (*qabīḥ*) acts of God?

---

43 Ibid.

44 A great number of poems in Ibn al-Wazīr's *Dīwān* are devoted to this topic, of which the following is only one example:

"Concerning hope (*raja'*) and the thinking well of God (*ḥusn al-ẓann*).
The good is the first thing that reaches a rank, evil the last to be considered in the classes.
Therefore ease is promised to come after it, so that the purpose of the evil is merely the good, it does not remain.
So all becomes good in reality, unless one's goal ignores the assignment of this good.
Lo! Interpret mercy as preceding wrath, (wrath is) vanquished in the good, as is written in the books."

Ibn al- Wazīr, *Majmaʿ al-ḥaqā'iq* 386; Ibn al-Wazīr, *Dīwān* laq. 34r. See also Ibn al-Wazīr, *Majmaʿ al-ḥaqā'iq* 374; Ibn al-Wazīr, *Dīwān* laqs. 8l; Ibn al-Wazīr, *Īthār al-ḥaqq*, 366, 227.

45 According to Vasalou, all the principles ʿAbd al-Jabbār deals with in his *Mughnī* form part of the same project, namely to deny all evil of God; cf. Vasalou, *Moral agents* 19.

46 Ibn al-Wazīr, *al-Rawḍ al-bāsim* 366.

According to Ibn al-Wazīr, God's knowledge is superior in its extent and must be so in order to be distinguishable from human knowledge. Human reason knows that God's knowledge is superior, and that His actions are perfected by the goodness of their purpose, which is a goodness perceivable by the human intellect. However, some of His actions appear to contradict the rational evaluation of moral goodness. They seem to lack a good purpose or benefit. Why, for example, has God created Iblīs or those human beings of whom He knows that they will end up in hell-fire? Or why do innocent children suffer and die before they can make a choice for or against Islam? These and other commonly asked questions appeal to the issue of God's justice and were therefore the object of much discussion especially in Muʿtazili circles.[47]

According to Ibn al-Wazīr, the explanation lies in a distinction between the relative and the ultimate evil. The relative evil only seems to be such, because of the limitedness of human knowledge. Man fails to see that God is good because he does not know the hidden purpose of the apparent evil: the purpose of the purpose (*gharaḍ al-gharaḍ*) referred to in the quote above, or the "hidden wisdom" (*ḥikma khafiyya*).[48] Referring to al-Ghazālī, Ibn Taymiyya and Ibn Qayyim al-Jawziyya, his predecessors in this particular view, Ibn al-Wazīr explains that God's action has to be evaluated in view of its ultimate purpose. This purpose is aimed at for itself, and not as a means to some other purpose. We find this concept throughout Ibn al-Wazīr's writings: the good for the good itself or the evil for the evil itself. This describes an ultimate value in contradistinction to a relative, instrumental or consequential value. A quote from *al-ʿAwāṣim* illustrates well the link of "the good in itself" to wisdom:

> The good is the primary goal in the action of every wise person. That is, that which is intended for itself. There cannot be evil in the action of the wise person unless it is a means to something else, like cupping is the means to health. Health is the primary goal which is intended for itself. Cupping is the evil that is the secondary goal which is intended for something other than itself. The downright evil can have no part in the action of the wise person. It [the evil] is never intended for itself.[49]

In *Īthār al-ḥaqq*, Ibn al-Wazīr explains how human beings should know whether a particular action considered abominable is so intrinsically, or whether it is

47 A classical illustration of these and similar questions is the dilemma of the three brothers ascribed to Abū ʿAlī l-Jubbāʾī and al-Ashʿari; cf. Gwynne, Three Brothers 132–161.

48 See for example Ibn al-Wazīr, *al-ʿAwāṣim* vi, 122; Ibn al-Wazīr, *Īthār al-ḥaqq* 259.

49 Ibn al-Wazīr, *al-ʿAwāṣim* v, 287.

only an instrument which appears evil. Why not suppose a hidden good in any apparently evil action? Might there not be a hidden good in sending prophets who lie?[50] In response, Ibn al-Wazīr distinguishes between the necessary and the suppositional discernment of evil (*taqbīḥ*). If a thing is known by necessity to contain no good, like lying or violating a promise, no hidden purpose may be sought. In such cases, the intellect can be trusted in not ascribing them to God. Other things are only assumed to be evil, like the cupping in the example above, or if one goes back on his word by cancelling a threat.[51]

However, the criteria for each category appear somewhat vague or arbitrary in their generality, which is typical for Ibn al-Wazīr. Necessary *taqbīḥ* is that which all people possessing sound reason agree to be evil. In contradistinction, *taqbīḥ* is merely suppositional and describes an instrumental or relative evil when disagreement exists due to the different degrees of knowledge and understanding that people have. For example, not all *compos mentis* agree that it is evil for God not to carry out His threat of punishment. While some would consider this to be injustice, others call it forgiveness (*ʿafw*). This disagreement means that this breach (*khulf*) of His word cannot be an ultimate evil.[52]

This principle of an ultimate as opposed to an instrumental value is also key to Ibn al-Wazīr's explanation of the obligation of the impossible (*taklīf mā lā yuṭāq*). A common example in the question of *taklīf mā lā yuṭāq* and determinism is the case of Abū Lahab. Having heard Muhammad's message, Abū Lahab was obliged to believe (*al-taklīf bi-l-īmān*). However, Q 111:1–5 determines that he will be thrown into hell. Was Abū Lahab then obliged to do the impossible since it was already certain that he would not believe? Ibn al-Wazīr uses this example to illustrate the difference between that which is impossible in itself (*al-mumtaniʿ li-dhātihi*)—an ultimate impossibility—and that which is impossible because of another—a consequential impossibility (*al-mumtaniʿ li-ghayrihi*).[53] The intrinsically impossible is called *muḥāl*. Accordingly, Abū Lahab's faith is not impossible in itself. Rather, the statement that his faith is impossible is based on the knowledge that he will not believe. God's knowledge of the unknown, His foreknowledge, discerns that Abū Lahab will not believe.

---

50 Ibn al-Wazīr, *Īthār al-ḥaqq* 224.

51 Revoking one's threat leads to the good of forgiveness. Therefore, this breach of promise only seemingly gives the lie to the initial promise; cf. ibid., 227.

52 Ibid., 224.

53 I call the instrumental the consequential in this case. Both connote a kind of secondary nature. Yet, whereas instrumentality suggests a transitive character, consequentiality denotes an intransitive one.

It was Ibn al-Wazīr's conviction that this foreknowledge did not have an immediate causative effect on actions.[54] Therefore, God did not cause the impossibility, but rather stated that it is impossible for Abū Lahab to believe.[55] The key is God's foreknowledge. In many cases of apparent *taklīf mā lā yuṭāq* or other actions and commands of God that appear abominable to human reason, Ibn al-Wazīr must resort to the principle of "the ultimate" vs. "the consequential" or "the instrumental" to preserve God's ultimate goodness. Often, however, "the ultimate" is only known to God himself. And man is left with the general knowledge that God has knowledge of the ultimate goal and that the purpose of his *taklīf*, his action, command or prohibition intends that very goal. That remains true even if the human being does not know of or perceive anything good in the particular aspect of *taklīf*, action, command or prohibition.

1.1.2 God Is Perfect Through His Wisdom

In *Īthār al-ḥaqq*, Ibn al-Wazīr defines God's wisdom as "a particular kind of knowledge about hidden benefits, praiseworthy reasons and preponderant interests" (*al-manāfiʿ al-khafiyya wa-l-ʿuqūl al-ḥamīda wa-l-maṣāliḥ al-rājiḥa*).[56] He does not explicitly address the question of whether or not the benefits are only geared to the interests of human beings, as the Muʿtazila commonly hold. For the Muʿtazila, the wisdom of God's action usually has human beings' highest benefit (*al-aṣlaḥ*) as its end. Ibn Taymiyya, on the other hand, spent much effort in showing that God also benefits from acting wisely, namely that He gets praised for being wise in His actions.[57] From the following explanation

---

54 Ibn al-Wazīr refers to Shaykh Mukhtār in the latter's *Kitāb al-Mujtabā* to explain that the effect of foreknowledge or knowledge on action is restricted to the motive. It does not have the causative effect that would lead to compulsion; cf. Ibn al-Wazīr, *al-ʿAwāṣim* i, 92; iv, 42; vii, 84 etc.; Ibn al-Wazīr, *Īthār al-ḥaqq* 332.

55 Ibn al-Wazīr, *al-ʿAwāṣim* ix, 52; Ibn al-Wazīr, *Īthār al-ḥaqq* 330–335.

56 Ibn al-Wazīr, *Īthār al-ḥaqq* 181.

57 Hoover, *Ibn Taymiyya's Theodicy* 75; cf. Hoover, Ibn Taymiyya as an Avicennan Theologian 42; Bell, *Love Theory* 69. Ibn al-Wazīr repeatedly refers to Ibn Taymiyya and Ibn Qayyim al-Jawziyya in the contexts of God's wisdom. Of these two, Ibn Taymiyya is known for his doctrine of "the golden mean." Although there are apparent similarities between the Ibn al-Wazīr and Ibn Taymiyya, to my understanding Ibn Taymiyya followed a very different agenda in his quest to find the middle path. Ibn Taymiyya wrote a book called *al-Aqīda al-wāsiṭiyya* where he explains his "golden mean" most concisely and claims it to be the orthodox position; cf. Ibn Taymiyya, *al-ʿAqīda al-wāsiṭiyya*. According to Hoover, Ibn Taymiyya's creed became well known already in his day and has been widely read ever since; cf. Hoover, *Ibn Taymiyya's Theodicy* 119, footnote 78. A comprehensive comparison of Ibn Taymiyya and Ibn al-Wazīr with regard to "the middle path" is beyond the scope of this study. However, the difference most obvious to me is that while Ibn al-Wazīr constantly

of the link between wisdom and perfection, we can conclude that Ibn al-Wazīr held a view similar to Ibn Taymiyya in this case: For Ibn al-Wazīr, all divine attributes go back to the title of "the praiseworthy ruler" (*al-malik al-ḥamīd*). Consequently, they are subsumed under either the title "ruler" or the attribute "praiseworthy." God's being a "ruler" requires that His sovereignty, His power, His omnipotence, His independence and His glory be perfect (*kāmil*). God's being "praiseworthy" comprises His goodness, His mercy, His benevolence, His truthfulness, His justice and His uncovering of harm, in their perfect form (*kāmil*).[58] Hence, it is perfection that distinguishes God from human beings, and the divine attributes from their namesakes among human beings. Yet, by what is this perfection signified?

According to Ibn al-Wazīr, God's wisdom is the foundation of all of His names and attributes, because it is what the perfection of those names and attributes consists of. Subsequent to the explanation of the names, he writes that the greatest state of perfection in all of these names and attributes is signified by their praiseworthy purposefulness that is free of futility.[59] Elsewhere in *Īthār al-ḥaqq*, the reader is told:

> There is neither doubt nor uncertainty that the foundation of perfection in actions is that they proceed from an extensive wisdom that is directed towards a preponderant benefit and praiseworthy result. Whenever this is apparent in them [the actions], it is proof of the wisdom of the agent, [of] his knowledge and the good and praiseworthy character of his choice. Wherever they [the actions] are far from this, they resemble accidental traces and that which results from necessitating causes (*al-ʿilal al-mūjiba*), like the actions of little boys in their games or of madmen in their fantasies. There is nothing more base and more deficient than the actions of little boys and madmen because they are void of wisdom, although they do accord with their desires and are not without purpose. (…) The fundamental reason why Muslims prohibit comparing God's acts to the actions of the rational and the wise in their perfectness and their want of measuring up to them [God's acts] is their [God's acts] excess in perfectness,

points to the common ground between the schools, including them in the golden mean, Ibn Taymiyya focusses more on showing who is outside it. In *Love Theory*, Bell shows how Ibn Taymiyya discusses concepts of God's will and wisdom by showing where Muʿtazilis and Ashʿaris went wrong; cf. Bell, *Love Theory* 46–73. Although Ibn al-Wazīr may have come to similar conclusions about the essence of tenets or "the golden mean," he endeavoured to show that the Muʿtazila and Ashʿariyya do in fact agree on those.

58 Ibn al-Wazīr, *Īthār al-ḥaqq* 186.

59 Ibid., 186.

> and their excess in this [perfectness] reaches a point that the intellects of the smart and wise cannot arrive at. Similarly, the brutish animal with its instinct does not get to know the wisdom of the wise, the compilations of the clever and the learning of the bright. And they cannot know the degree to which they [the wise, smart and bright] are beyond them [the animals]. Accordingly, the wise people do not know the whole of God's wisdom, the Exalted. And they are unable to know how much it exceeds their own wisdom, as is evident in the story of Moses and al-Khiḍr.[60]

In the example of the boy and the madman, the lack of a wise purpose is the reason why their actions are not praised at all, and are far from being called perfect. God's wise purposefulness is then a key concept to understanding Ibn al-Wazīr's view of Him.

As shall be discussed below, Ibn al-Wazīr insists that all divine attributes must be equally affirmed. He criticizes the Ashʿariyya and Muʿtazila profoundly for voiding particular divine names of significance by interpreting them metaphorically, or by negating them altogether for lack of evidence.[61] Nevertheless, it seems that Ibn al-Wazīr himself gives precedence to certain attributes. God's wisdom is a certain kind of divine knowledge: God's knowledge of the best possible benefit as well as the action that goes along with that knowledge. Or, put differently, the excellence of knowledge is in acting according to it.[62] If all of His attributes are made perfect by being geared to that knowledge of the benefit, it is really God's knowledge that takes center stage. The greatest praise that a human being can render to God, therefore, is to praise and honor Him in and for His superior and perfect knowledge.[63]

This explains the continuous reference to God's knowledge and wisdom throughout Ibn al-Wazīr writings. However, as shown above, divine knowledge as opposed to human knowledge is signified by a superiority of quantity or extent. There is no hint of two kinds of knowledge that are distinct as to moral standards. God does not know of another kind of good. Accordingly, the purposes He aims at on the basis of the knowledge that He has are not "wise"

60 Ibid., 183.

61 In a similar way, Ibn Taymiyya criticized the Ashʿariyya for interpreting God's love and not interpreting His will in their equation of will and love; cf. Bell, *Love Theory* 64.

62 Cf. Ibn al-Wazīr, *al-ʿAwāṣim* v, 287.

63 In contradistinction, Ibn Taymiyya, according to Hoover, leaves it unstated and only implies that God is perfect and praiseworthy because of the rationality in the things that He does; cf. Hoover, Ibn Taymiyya as an Avicennan Theologian 43. Hoover shows how Ibn Taymiyya takes God's perfection to rest in His continuous creativity; cf. Hoover, *Ibn Taymiyya's Theodicy* 70–102; Hoover, Perpetual Creativity 3.

according to a different kind of good, even though their moral quality might be beyond the human grasp.

Human beings can (or must, as we shall see) have enough general knowledge of God, His goodness and His wise purposes to praise Him for them and to admit their own lack. The superiority of God's knowledge is not maintained by a difference in moral nature. This principle is also effective when Ibn al-Wazīr responds to the accusation of anthropomorphism in *al-ʿAwāṣim*.[64] There he argues that the affirmation of God's visibility does not require a detailed knowledge of that which is seen (God). Man knows that God can be seen in general, but cannot understand what this entails exactly. How much more important then to uphold this principle with the insistence that the difference is merely one of extent, along with implications that follow for theological as well as legal activity.

1.1.3 The Hiddenness of Wise Purposes

Ibn al-Wazīr requires every believer to know of God's purposefulness in a general way (*jumlatan*). Consistent with his teaching of "the sufficiency of the general tenets" (*kifāyat al-jumal*), Ibn al-Wazīr does not define in much detail what exactly he takes to be God's wise purposes. He provides suggestions of other scholars, albeit with much more reluctance to conclude a meticulously defined and exclusive doctrine. Nevertheless, Ibn al-Wazīr undertakes the discussion of what these wise purposes may look like for two reasons. Firstly, for the sake of refuting those who employ several Quranic verses and Prophetic traditions to argue for the utter inexplicability of God's actions. Of course the explicability must be confirmed, if only in a general sense. Secondly, and more importantly, Ibn al-Wazīr discusses what God's purposes might be in order to point out the reason for their hiddenness.

As part of the elucidation of his *ḥikma*-theory in *Īthār al-ḥaqq*, Ibn al-Wazīr provides a list of wise purposes behind pain and catastrophes. The purposes that he does explain are those supposedly already mentioned in the texts of revelation.[65] Otherwise, the explanations should be understood as possibilities. After all, Ibn al-Wazīr considers the Muʿtazili assumption that the purpose of creating unbelievers is clear (*jalī*) an error.[66]

64 Ibn al-Wazīr discussed this charge on numerous occasions, usually in defense of different Sunni scholars. See for example Ibn al-Wazīr, *al-ʿAwāsim* v, 5.

65 Ibn al-Wazīr, *al-ʿAwāṣim* vi, 124.

66 Ibn al-Wazīr, *al-ʿAwāsim* v, 278–279.

The beginning of the list mostly reflects the educational ends also mentioned by the Muʿtazila as well as other supporters of a concept of God's wisdom, like Ibn Taymiyya and Ibn Qayyim al-Jawziyya.[67] Accordingly, pain and calamitous events in the world are geared towards disciplining the character, teaching patience, moral admonition, engendering a desire for the Hereafter, testing faith and the like.[68] Besides educational and religious ends, there is already an element in this list that indicates the display of God's superior wisdom as an end in itself:

> The human being learns of his own inability and lowliness. He unites his heart towards God and His acceptance of his [the human being's] petition and supplication. He then knows that God will answer his petition, uncover the harmful and increase his certainty.[69]

Hence, in the sorrow of the world there is the good of becoming aware of human limitations and God's superiority. This element becomes more obvious in the explanation of God's creation of sinners, torture in the Hereafter and *taklīf* in spite of the foreordainment of actions. These explanations make use of the principle of the relative and the ultimate end—an apparent evil for the sake of the ultimate good.

The question why God created human beings who would be sinners and unbelievers was of central importance to the question of God's justice. Why did He create people who would sin although He hates and punishes sin? In *Īthār al-ḥaqq*, Ibn al-Wazīr mentions seven aspects of the hidden wisdom behind the creation of sinners, and one general principle (*amr jumlī*) which comprises them all. A very similar list is found in *al-ʿAwāṣim*, albeit in a slightly different order.[70] Significantly, the general principle is phrased in God's statement, "I know what you do not know." In the particular aspects, we see the display of His attributes as an ultimate purpose. However, the purposes are formulated in what seems at first a peculiar fashion, amounting to hardly more than an affirmation of these attributes in spite of a seeming tension. For example, "God, the Exalted, has created sinners for His worship with regard to his command (…)

67 Hoover, God's Wise Purposes 122–127. For the Muʿtazila, see for example Heemskerk, *Suffering in Muʿtazilite Theology* 151–156.

68 Ibn al-Wazīr, *Īthār al-ḥaqq* 211.

69 Ibid., 211.

70 Ibn al-Wazīr, *al-ʿAwāṣim* v, 6–7. Preceding the list, Ibn al-Wazīr remarks that the list is not at all exhaustive.

and for testing with regard to his justice (…).”[71] Aspect five consists in the fact “that He cannot be comprehended in full (*lam yuḥāṭ bi-jamīʿihi*), except that He is Glorified and Exalted with regard to His knowledge and mercy.”[72]

God apparently also created sinners so that just punishment for the unbelief in His favor (*kufr niʿma*) and the denial of His authority may exist. This purpose rests on divine knowledge, choice, foreordainment and His book. In these and other examples, Ibn al-Wazīr does not inform the reader about the content of the wise purposes themselves.[73] Yet, in one way or another they are intended to affirm the different divine names and attributes. How, for example, could God's justice be understood if there was no possibility of doing wrong?

Others, like Ibn Qayyim al-Jawziyya, have used a similar kind of argument in order to explain why God created human beings who would be sinners and unbelievers. Yet, Ibn al-Wazīr went beyond arguing, as for example Ibn Qayyim has done according to Hoover, that the purpose in creating evil is geared towards the display of God's individual attributes.[74] What is more, God's wise purposefulness functions as the glue that makes sense of otherwise potentially conflicting aspects of God's description of Himself. This is well illustrated in aspect seven:

> Aspect seven is the wise purpose that made His punishment preponderant over His pardoning and His justice over His favor in their case [the case of the sinners]. This [wise purpose] signifies the interpretation of the ambiguous matters (*mutashābihāt*). This, in turn, is the good that is the ultimate goal in what appeared to the rationalists to be the intention in what ambiguous matter occurred before. This [according to what the rationalists took to be the intent] is that kind of evil in which no good is known [to exist]. This is the seventh kind which refers to the ultimate hiddenness of His purposes. It is connected to His will and design. It is what is primarily intended. And it is the interpretation of the ambiguous matters which no one knows except Him.[75]

71 Ibn al-Wazīr, *Īthār al-ḥaqq* 261.

72 Ibid., 261.

73 Ibid., 260–262.

74 Hoover, God's Wise Purposes 126. Ibn Qayyim also argued based on the distinction between the relative or instrumental good on the one hand, and the ultimate good on the other hand.

75 Ibn al-Wazīr, *Īthār al-ḥaqq* 262.

Ibn al-Wazīr explains punishment in the Hereafter by a similar reasoning. Accordingly, there is some truth in the fact of punishment that comprises justice and benefit, and that is also the interpretation of the ambiguous matters. Man's lack of detailed knowledge of the exact purposes is a necessity.

> How shall this great Lord not be distinguished by a knowledge of the subtle wise purposes which we do not have. The uniqueness of His knowledge of them [the purposes] necessitates that He alone knows the good that is connected with them as well as its interpretation. That is what opens the breast of the knowledgeable for faith in the ambiguous things and belief in the unknown (*ghayb*).[76]

According to Ibn al-Wazīr, the existence of sinners, torture and *taklīf* serves the end of displaying God's attributes, most of all His wisdom, in one way or another. Ibn al-Wazīr does not go as far as Ibn Qayyim in explicitly stating that evil is a necessary concomitant of the good in order for the good to be displayed. He does not say explicitly that both good and evil necessarily proceed from God's essence.[77] Yet, considering that it is God's wisdom that perfects his attributes, as we have seen in the explanation of the two categories of God's attributes "praiseworthy" and "ruler," and if the difference between God's attributes and man's attributes is perceived by necessity, as we shall see below, the means by which the superiority of God's wisdom is displayed would seem to be necessary as well.

To summarize, the reasoning for God's wisdom points to the concept of wise purposes as the end, rather than a means, of explaining the seemingly inexplicable. The hiddenness of these wise purposes secures God's superiority over human beings and especially over human knowledge. Some things are hidden so that man acknowledges the superiority of God's knowledge and wisdom and consequently commits all his affairs to Him trustingly. Ibn al-Wazīr's *Dīwān* testifies to the centrality of human worship by means of trust in and surrender to God's purposes. Furthermore, the affirmation of God's wise purposefulness is directly connected to the harmonization of God's attributes and names. The limitedness of human knowledge causes human beings to see contradictions between God's attributes. This results in metaphorical interpretations or the

---

76 Ibid., 87.

77 For Ibn Qayyim al-Jawziyya's explanation of the purposes in creating Iblīs, see Hoover, God's Wise Purposes 123–127. For the translation of Ibn al-Qayyim's list of wise purposes in the creation of Iblīs as recorded in his *Kitāb al-Shifāʾ*, see ibid., 127–131.

negation of some attributes, as well as the elevation of some attributes over others. However, that is only the case if the necessity to know in detail is claimed, on the one hand, or if the human ability to understand in terms of moral assessment is denied altogether, on the other. According to Ibn al-Wazīr, all names can be preserved and equally displayed against the background of the limitations of human knowledge. The divine counterpart of the limitations of human knowledge is God's wisdom, His wise purposes. Herein rests His perfection. Ibn al-Wazīr describes the inexplicable, the ambiguous matters, as a means of manifesting God's wisdom. These ambiguous matters are often related to the existence of evil and pain. It stands to reason that Ibn al-Wazīr draws a necessary connection between God's essence and the existence of evil as a means of achieving a greater good, namely the display of God's attributes in toto and the incitement to worship.

Drawing a line from Ibn al-Wazīr's theory of God's wise purposes back to other issues of the theological debate, the question is: How does Ibn al-Wazīr's epistemology of ambiguity as displayed in his concept of God's wise purposes contrast with the concept of God's wisdom held among his Zaydi contemporaries?

1.2 *Ibn al-Murtaḍā's Concept of God's Wisdom*

Ibn al-Murtaḍā discusses issues pertaining to divine wisdom in the context of the divine attribute of justice (*ʿadl*) in *al-Durar al-farāʾid*.[78] According to al-Ḥayyī, Ibn al-Murtaḍā defines a just person as "someone who does not do the evil and does not fail to perform [his] duty, and whose actions are all good."[79] The first two criteria of justice help the reader to understand Ibn al-Murtaḍā's concept of divine wisdom. It is evident that Ibn al-Murtaḍā represents the Bahshami branch of the Muʿtazila, because he holds that God is capable of evil (*min maqdūrātihi*).[80] This distinguishes him clearly from those holding the common Ashʿari view, according to which God's actions are altogether beyond moral assessment. But his view also distinguishes Ibn al-Murtaḍā from those Muʿtazila who equally took God to be incapable of evil, as for example al-Naẓẓām (d. 221/836) and his student al-Jāḥiẓ (d. 255/868).[81] For Ibn al-Murtaḍā,

78 Cf. al-Ḥayyī, *al-Muntazaʿ min al-Durar al-farāʾid* f. 65b.

79 Ibid., f. 65b.

80 For ʿAbd al-Jabbār's definition of divine justice, see for example Peters, *God's Created Speech* 30–33, 224.

81 Cf. Ibn al-Murtaḍā, Kitāb al-Qalāʾid 95. Al-Naẓẓām's student al-Jāḥiẓ apparently shared his teacher's views on this topic. Al-Naẓẓām and indeed al-Jāḥiẓ are worth mentioning, as al-Naẓẓām's theory on God's volition and creation was received by the Baghdadi Muʿtazila

God's actions are not beyond assessment. God is able to do actions that would have to be considered evil for two reasons. Firstly, there is no kind of object of power (*maqdūr*) that He is incapable of.[82] Secondly, the human intellect is capable of discerning good and evil independent of revelation (*al-taḥsīn wa-l-taqbīḥ al-ʿaqlī*). Thus, if God did any evil action, the *compos mentis* would be able to tell, because the evil is intrinsic to the action.[83] What then is the reason that God's actions are never described as evil? How can His justice remain indefeasible? Divine wisdom is the answer to this question. The indefeasibility of God's justice can be maintained by stating that God has no motive (*dāʿī*) to act in an evil way.

> The Muʿtazila and the Zaydiyya hold that God, the Exalted, does not do evil. And we have two proofs for this: We say that He has no motive for doing it. Put clearly, this means that the Exalted has ample deterrents from doing it. He has no motive to do it—neither a motive of need as this [need] cannot be ascribed to him, nor a motive of wisdom, as there is no benefit. And He is not forced to do it, therefore it must be that He does not do it.[84]

The first kind of motive, the motive of need, cannot be ascribed to God, because He is self-sufficient (*ghanī*). This is no point of contention. But the reference to the second kind of motive, the motive of purposefulness, reveals Ibn al-Murtaḍā's Muʿtazili thinking. God does not commit evil actions, because evil actions would not be for the benefit of human beings. And it is a requirement of God's justice to act according to the utmost human benefit (*al-aṣlaḥ*).[85] Thus, wisdom is intricately intertwined with justice. This is emphasized by the fact that Ibn al-Murtaḍā usually mentions the two together: "God, being just and wise."[86]

The doctrine of *al-aṣlaḥ* is one of the most distinctive features of Muʿtazili thinking. Ormsby, in analyzing al-Ghazālī's concept of "the best possible world," suggests that the Muʿtazili doctrine of what he calls "the optimum" (*al-aṣlaḥ*) may have been a major reason for the initial rift between the Muʿtazila and the

---

as well as by Abū l-Ḥusayn al-Baṣrī, albeit in a modified form; cf. Thiele, *Theologie in der jemenitischen Zaydiyya* 82; McDermott, Abū l-Ḥusayn al-Baṣrī on God's Volition 89.

82 Ibid., f. 71b.

83 Ibid., fs. 66b; al-Kamālī, *al-Imām al-Mahdī*, 310–320.

84 Cf. al-Ḥayyī, *al-Muntazaʿ min al-Durar al-farāʾid* fs. 72b–73a.

85 Al-Kamālī, *al-Imām al-Mahdī* 318.

86 For Ibn al-Murtaḍā's refutation of the claim that the argumentation for justice and wisdom by motive is circular, see al-Ḥayyī, *al-Muntazaʿ min al-Durar al-farāʾid* f. 73b.

Ash'ariyya.[87] It requires that the unaided human intellect must be able to assess the divine acts in order to discern what is most beneficial, and thus determine God's duties (*wājib*) towards human beings.[88] After all, the quote above leaves no doubt that performing one's duties is a vital component of justice. Thus, this principle contradicts the Ash'ari belief that God is beyond human assessment. Likewise, Ash'aris generally reject the idea that God would be under any obligation whatsoever.[89]

From Ibn al-Murtaḍā's Muʿtazili perspective, his concept of wisdom and the intellectual ability of moral discernment could be employed to argue for a detailed understanding of God's duties towards human beings. Just after explaining why God does not do anything evil (*qabīḥ*), Ibn al-Murtaḍā proceeds with a list of God's duties towards human beings resulting from this definition of divine justice and purposefulness. Both are aimed at the benefit of the believer. For example, God is obliged to empower the legally responsible human beings (*tamkīn al-mukallafīn*), and He must clarify His speech to the addressees (*bayyān lil-mukhāṭabīn*). This latter duty involves the creation of necessary knowledge and the establishment of evidence from reason and revelation. Consequently, God must clarify his intention in an unambiguous way and in detail. In line with Muʿtazili doctrine, Ibn al-Murtaḍā requires that "the knowledge of this issue is an individual duty (*min furūḍ al-aʿyān*) since the knowledge of God's justice is incomplete without it."[90]

In short, Ibn al-Murtaḍā's concept of divine wisdom is vital for the maintenance of the doctrine of divine justice. The purpose of this justice is the benefit of the believer. And it is a concept that requires the individual to know God's justice in greater detail. Indeed, it guarantees that he can know and understand God's justice, as it signifies the path of God's working for human benefit.

---

87 For a discussion of the origin of the theory of *al-aṣlaḥ*, see Robert Brunschvig, Muʿtazilism et Optimum 5–23; Gwynne, Three Brothers 132–161. According to Gwynne, it was Fakhr al-Dīn al-Rāzī who first identified the doctrine of *al-aṣlaḥ* as the cause of the rift between al-Ash'ari and his teacher Abū 'Alī al-Jubbā'ī and accordingly associated the problem of "the three brothers" with the two scholars' controversy; cf. ibid., Brothers 132.

88 Of course there are different understandings of what this optimum entails. A major difference within the Muʿtazila was that the Baghdadi school obliged God to do what is most beneficial for human beings in this world and in the next, whereas the Basran Muʿtazila generally restricted the necessity of *al-aṣlaḥ* to the next world, hence to what human beings need in order to fulfill their religious duties; cf. Brunschvig, Muʿtazilism et Optimum 17.

89 Ormsby, *Theodicy in Islamic Thought* 21–22. Even though the world that God created is the best of all possible worlds, al-Ghazālī was eager to emphasize that God was under no obligation to do so in the way He did; cf. ibid., 258–260.

90 Al-Ḥayyī, *al-Muntazaʿ min al-Durar al-farāʾid* f. 74a; cf. al-Kamālī, *al-Imām al-Mahdī* 318.

1.3 *Conclusion*

The benefits mentioned by Ibn al-Murtaḍā can be much more easily defined than Ibn al-Wazīr's general and rather vague idea of wise purposes beyond the understanding of human beings. Ibn al-Wazīr, like Ibn al-Murtaḍā, maintains that God's actions must be assessed as good in a general manner. Yet, for Ibn al-Wazīr the purposes are good by virtue of proceeding from divine wisdom, rather than by virtue of benefitting the believer in a manner susceptible to detailed proof. Even more importantly, in Ibn al-Wazīr's thinking this characteristic of being beyond human understanding is essential as it maintains God's uniqueness. Defining the nature and recipient of the benefit is far less important. The affirmation that God is good and wise is enough. According to al-Murtaḍā's understanding of the intellect's ability to discern, and of God's justice and duty to do what most benefits the human being, it is inconceivable that the human intellect should be restrained from achieving a detailed knowledge of God's purposes. In Ibn al-Wazīr's thinking, however, the intellect must always assume the best of purposes behind an apparent evil action.

Ibn al-Murtaḍā's thoughts on these issues render him in line with Bahshami-Muʿtazili thinking.[91] He claims that his view represents the Zaydi position. However, Ibn al-Wazīr refers to Shaykh Mukhtār and Ibn al-Malāḥimī as examples of Muʿtazili scholars who did require of God's justice and purposes the same degree of assessability. Ibn al-Wazīr locates Shaykh Mukhtār's argumentation in his book on justice. Citing Shaykh Mukhtār, Ibn al-Wazīr speaks of a hidden purpose (*ḥikma khafiyya*), whereas the quote from Ibn Malāḥimī's *Kitāb al-Fāʾiq* mentions "a wise purpose not known to anyone but God" behind the creation of a human being with a nature unable to receive benevolence (*luṭf*).[92] Discussing the motive of an action in *al-Awāṣim*, Ibn al-Wazīr ascribes this position to Abū l-Ḥusayn al-Baṣrī himself, as we shall discuss below.[93]

Unfortunately, the original line of argument cannot be verified, as Shaykh Mukhtār's writing is not extant. Yet Ibn al-Wazīr's quote from Ibn al-Malāḥimī's *Kitāb al-Fāʾiq* can be confirmed. Both scholars belong to the school of Abū l-Ḥusayn al-Baṣrī, and both seem to allow for a hidden purpose that is not evident to the human intellect, giving the respective action the appearance of evil (*istiqbāḥ*). Were that purpose to become known, however, its assessment would certainly be positive (*istiḥsān*).[94]

91 Cf. Brunschvig, Muʿtazilism et Optimum 12.

92 Ibn al-Wazīr, *al-ʿAwāṣim* v, 302.

93 Ibid., vi, 123.

94 Ibid., v, 302; cf. Ibn al-Malāḥimī, *Kitāb al-Fāʾiq* 149–156.

In conclusion, Ibn al-Wazīr and Ibn al-Murtaḍā apparently represent the influence of different Muʿtazili schools within the Zaydiyya of the 9th/15th century. Or it may be more accurate to suggest that Abū l-Ḥusayn's school was more conducive to Ibn al-Wazīr's harmonization of conflicting school doctrines and to his epistemology of ambiguity than was the Bahshami school represented by Ibn al-Murtaḍā. So far, this has been made apparent regarding the concept of divine wisdom. In the following this claim will be consolidated as to other theological questions, namely God's names and attributes (*asmāʾ* and *ṣifāt*), God's will (*irāda*), and human actions (*afʿāl*) in relation to Ibn al-Wazīr's concept of wisdom.

2 Harmonized Doctrine: God's Names (*asmāʾ*) and Attributes (*ṣifāt*)

A central topic that occupied the minds of Muʿtazili and Ashʿari scholars in their controversy was God's unicity. How is God different from human beings, and how can this difference be maintained in spite of the human character which all descriptions of divine things have? According to Wensinck, the discussion of the divine attributes representing man's description of God was a result of the problem of anthropomorphism.[95] Ibn al-Wazīr's focus on the question of whether anthropomorphic descriptions in revelation should be interpreted allegorically (*taʾwīl*) would seem to confirm this.

2.1 *Ibn al-Wazīr's Harmonization Regarding God's Names and Attributes*

Apparently, some revelational descriptions of the Divine were more prone to being confused with human attributes than others. Consequently, they were interpreted according to each group's respective doctrine.[96] Ibn al-Wazīr insists that both the Muʿtazila and the Ashʿariyya essentially agree that God's names should not be interpreted allegorically. This agreement manifests in the aversion expressed by both schools towards the allegorical interpretation of a name they themselves take at its face value. Ibn al-Wazīr does not differenti-

95 Wensinck, *Muslim Creed* 68.

96 As mentioned above, Ibn al-Wazīr criticized the Ashʿari interpretation of the divine name *al-ḥakīm* (the All-wise) as well as the Muʿtazili interpretation of the divine name *al-baṣīr* (the Seeing). The Ashʿariyya, theoretically rejecting the idea of purposefulness, emphasized the connotation of "creating masterfully" or "ruling," both contained in the root *ḥ-k-m*. The Muʿtazila, refusing the idea that God has eyes necessary for seeing, interpreted *al-Baṣīr* in terms of "perception."

ate between the divine attributes. On the one hand, he rebuffs the charge of anthropomorphism (*tashbīh*) brought forward against the traditionists as well as the Ashʿaris. On the other hand, Ibn al-Wazīr argues that it was only the "extremists" of the Muʿtazila who denied God the power to act by divesting Him of His attributes (*taʿṭīl*) in order to forestall anthropomorphism.[97] In Ibn al-Wazīr's view, both groups are guilty of interpreting one or the other divine attribute more or less arbitrarily. For him, there can be no allegorical interpretation of any of the attributes, and therefore no subordination of one attribute to another. All alike are affirmed (*ithbāt*).[98] The negation of anthropomorphic meanings of God's names and attributes should never lead to the negation of the attributes themselves. God's transcendence consists in that His attributes are free (*tanzīh*) of the insufficiencies and deficiencies which human beings' attributes feature.

> Concerning the explanation of the inability to comprehend the true meaning of the knowledge of God, His names and sublime attributes (…). However you understand the meaning of the similitude (*mumāthala*) that must not be ascribed to God the Exalted, you know that nothing is like Him (*annahu lā mithlahū shayʾ*). It is not desirable for you to assume that participating in the same expression necessitates similitude. Do you not see that the two [God and man] are so distinct from one another that more of a contrast could not be imagined. They have many descriptions in common, just as black and white share in being accidents, in being perceptible, in being colors etc.[99]

And elsewhere in *Īthār al-ḥaqq*, Ibn al-Wazīr notes:

> Names of praise by which human beings are called in different manners necessarily entail an imperfection, and [the names of praise by which] God is called in different manners necessarily entail perfection. These are the attributes of knowledge, power, mercy, life and the like. They are applied to God, the Exalted, in the way of perfection. They apply [to Him] free of the imperfection of creatures which befall them for reasons particular to them, unlike Him the Exalted.[100]

97 Ibn al-Wazīr, *al-ʿAwāṣim* vii, 122; cf. Ibn al-Wazīr, *Īthār al-ḥaqq* 103.
98 Ibn al-Wazīr, *al-ʿAwāṣim* iii, 339.
99 Ibn al-Wazīr, *Īthār al-ḥaqq* 177.
100 Ibid., 165.

Ibn al-Wazīr does not specify here how these attributes and names apply to God other than in their perfect meaning (*akmal maʿānīhā*). This knowledge is restricted to the only one to whom they apply, God (*lā yuḥīṭ bi-ḥaqīqatahu illā llāh taʿālā*).[101] In that sense, the *bi-lā kayf* of the middle course applies to all of God's attributes: they should be described "without qualifying God in a way only to be applied to His creation."[102] The true meaning of things must be surrendered to God's knowledge. But the literal meaning of the names must not be denied just because their true sense cannot be affirmed in detail.

Ibn al-Wazīr justified the use of the same descriptions for God and human beings by referring to the difference between perfection and imperfection.[103] Using anthropomorphic descriptions for God does not necessarily mean putting Him on a level with human beings. No metaphorical explanations should be found for God's attributes. Rather, it is the human equivalents of those terms that are to be understood in an allegorical way. As in the example of a child that asks about the characteristics of marriage and is told that marriage is as sweet as sugar, human beings get an idea of how God describes Himself by using concepts that exist in the human world as well.[104] Yet human beings possess their attributes in an imperfect way. As discussed above, perfection is characterized by the wisdom of the purpose behind an action or an attribute. Consequently, God's perfection consists in the wise purposefulness of all of His attributes, names and actions. Therefore, Ibn al-Wazīr can refer not only to God's knowledge and wisdom for the true meaning of attributes, names and actions, but also to God's wise purposes behind the ambiguities that accompany the divine attributes, as they are the benchmark for the distinction between God and man. Ibn al-Wazīr can thus justify a literal reading of the anthropomorphic descriptions in the texts without exposing himself to the charge of anthropomorphism. The difference between the divine and the human description is self-evident.[105]

Hoover, his insightful article on the duration of hell-fire has shown how Ibn al-Wazīr's "agnosticism"—what I call his epistemology of ambiguity—allowed him to include different and conflicting positions on the question. Beyond

101 Ibid., 166.

102 Van Ess describes this as "the middle course between a literal acceptance of the anthropological statements in the Scripture (*takyīf tashbīh*) on one side, and their metaphorical interpretation in the Muʿtazili sense (*taʾwīl* = *taʿṭīl*) on the other." Even Ibn Taymiyya adopted this attitude; cf. van Ess, Tashbīh wa-Tanzīh.

103 Cf. Ibn al-Wazīr, *Īthār al-ḥaqq* 277.

104 Ibn al-Wazīr, *Īthār al-ḥaqq*, 177–180.

105 Cf. Ibn al-Wazīr, *al-ʿAwāṣim* i, 208.

being a point in argument for the present thesis, Hoover's argument underlines the conclusions from this sub-chapter. How it does so is best illustrated in the concluding part of Ibn al-Wazīr's poem *al-Ijāda fī l-irāda*:

> Laud and do not exclude anything from laudation,
> and let innovations be like the muddles of a dreamer.
> Fear neither impotence nor ignorance of wise purposes,
> neither the exasperation of the oppressed nor the tyranny of the oppressor,
> and [think] not that He in His beneficence is not powerful and mighty,
> and not that He in His might is not merciful,
> and not that He in His judgement is not just, wise and knowing
> what creatures do not know.[106]

Ibn al-Wazīr's epistemology of ambiguity not only allows him to include a number of possible explanations for the ambiguous matters like the duration of hell-fire, it also allows him to affirm all divine names equally, without having to deny or find an allegorical interpretation of one or more of them as a result of a particular explanation of ambiguous matters.

Yet, with all of Ibn al-Wazīr's desire to equally affirm God's attributes, he seems to have neglected one aspect. He himself has elevated one divine attribute over the rest: God's wisdom, His wise purposes, is defined as "a type of knowledge." Ultimately then, it is God's superior knowledge in which the perfect nature of His names and attributes consists.

2.2 *Ibn al-Murtaḍā's Concept of God's Names and Attributes*

In comparison, the views expressed by Ibn al-Murtaḍā in his *al-Durar al-farāʾid* bespeak the views Ibn al-Wazīr ascribes to the Basran Muʿtazila. Just as Ibn al-Wazīr has criticized, Ibn al-Murtaḍā puts much emphasis on a particular knowledge of God's attributes according to a specific order of evidence. Essential attributes are ascribed to God because of their identity with His essence. For example, God is not able by virtue of an ability (*qudra*), but rather by virtue of an essential ableness (*qādiriyya*).[107] Apart from devoting long passages to the

---

106 Ibn al-Wazīr, *Īthār al-ḥaqq* 204. Again I used Hoover's very apt translation; cf. Hoover, Withholding Judgement 26.

107 Cf. al-Ḥayyī, *al-Muntazaʿ min al-Durar al-farāʾid* f. 22b. This doctrine was developed early in the history of Muʿtazili *kalām* in order to maintain both God and man as autonomous and freely choosing agents, while yet preserving a distinction between God and the human being; cf. Thiele, *Theologie in der jemenitischen Zaydiyya* 83.

demonstration of the true nature (*ḥaqīqa*) of each divine attribute like ableness or knowingness (*ʿālimiyya*), Ibn al-Murtaḍā insists that many descriptive Quranic statements about God must be interpreted allegorically. In a passage concerned with countering invalid similitude (*tamāthul*) between human and divine attributes, Ibn al-Murtaḍā rejects the anthropomorphism implied in a number of Quranic verses:

> The intellect refuses to understand them [the verses] in their apparent meaning (*ʿalā ẓāhirihā*). Where that [meaning] allows that He [God] has a body, they [the verses] must be interpreted as figurative expressions.[108]

This contrasts with Ibn al-Wazīr's reasoning. According to Ibn al-Murtaḍā, it is God's side of the equation that has to be interpreted with the goal of defining its meaning. Whereas Ibn al-Wazīr leaves the precise nature of the difference between divine attributes and their human equivalents largely unknown, Ibn al-Murtaḍā explains the difference in detail:

> He is equally capable of all types of objects of creative power (*jamīʿ ajnās al-maqdūrāt*), and it is impossible to restrict it [God's ableness] to some object of power (*maqdūr*) and not another. That which limits the object of power to a type or number is the ability (*qudra*). The Creator, the Exalted, is able by His essence not by an ability. (…) It is established that His ableness (*qādiriyyatuhu*) is transcendent. It is impossible to prove that it is limited to one type but not to another, or one number but not another in contradistinction to our ability, for it is limited to its object of power.[109]

The difference between the divine and the human attribute is that God is able by His essence, whereas the human being is able by an ability. According to Ibn al-Murtaḍā, this doctrine is a knowledge item that every believer must know in detail, based on the evidence and the order of evidence established by the theologians, just as a detailed knowledge of the true meaning of every divine attribute is required of him.[110]

108 Al-Ḥayyī, *al-Muntazaʿ min al-Durar al-farāʾid* f. 38b.
109 Ibid., f. 22b.
110 Ibid., fs. 3a, 5a.

2.3 *Conclusion*

Ibn al-Murtaḍā's reasoning for allegorical interpretation as well as his requirement for detailed knowledge of the meaning contrasts sharply with Ibn al-Wazīr's argument. According to Ibn al-Wazīr, the difference between divine and human attributes consists in the self-evident perfection-imperfection divide. Furthermore, it contrasts with Ibn al-Wazīr's broad concept of the difference as to the particular attributes. Ibn al-Wazīr leaves this difference to God's wisdom and knowledge, and he leaves human beings with cognitive uncertainty of it. Whereas Ibn al-Murtaḍā's claim to detailed understanding requires that some attributes be interpreted allegorically, Ibn al-Wazīr's broad understanding as to the actual difference between the divine and the human attributes allows him to affirm all of God's attributes. He maintains the ambiguity as to their precise meaning.

3 Harmonized Doctrine: God's Will (*irāda*)

Ibn al-Wazīr's concept of divine will and his harmonization of conflicting ideas again underlines the central role the concept of God's wisdom plays in Ibn al-Wazīr's thinking. He challenges the widely accepted assessment that the Muʿtazili idea of a God who wills only what is just is essentially contrary to the Ashʿari doctrine of a God who wills all that occurs.

3.1 *Ibn al-Wazīr's Harmonization Regarding God's Will*

Ibn al-Wazīr's understanding of the divine will is characterized by a similar harmonization of Muʿtazili and the Ashʿari positions as in the case of divine attributes. At the heart of these issues is the execution of the Divine volition. The conflicting concepts are illustrated by the question of why disobedience exists in the face of God's omnipotence. Does God will it or not? And if He does not, why does it occur? Does not God have the power, for example, to guide the disobedient to obedience? Or does He lead them into disobedience? The significance this question had for Ibn al-Wazīr is especially tangible in *Īthar al-ḥaqq* and *al-Ijāda fī l-irāda*,[111] or in *al-Āyāt al-mubīnāt* where he treats Q 16:93.[112] However, it recurs throughout his writings and in the context of different questions, indicating its key role in Muslim thought about God.

111 Ibn al-Wazīr, *Īthār al-ḥaqq*, 186 (in the context of elevating one divine name above another), 201–204 (in the context of the negation of divine wisdom), 352 (in the context of the question of the duration of hell-fire); cf. Hoover, Withholding Judgement 21–27.

112 Cf. Ibn al-Wazīr, *al-Āyāt al-mubīnāt* 289.

Ibn al-Wazīr acknowledges that the gap between the two schools of thought, i.e. the Muʿtazila and the Ashʿariyya, appears to be particularly great with regard to this question. Yet, he insists that ultimately all Muslim groups agree that God can and does guide disobedient human beings in spite of seeming contradiction:

> It [the fifth study] is the most precious of all and sufficient for it [the question of agreement]: The apparent meanings of the expressions of Muʿtazila and Ashʿariyya in this question [right guidance for sinners] show the utmost incompatibility. But a close examination of their positions necessitates that their words agree concerning the power of God, the Exalted, to guide whomever He wills by benevolence and making easy (*taysīr*). [They also agree] that God the Exalted, does not will disobedience and shameful deeds. This is truly astonishing. One can hardly believe it unless one has conducted sincere research and profound examination.[113]

Ibn al-Wazīr establishes the common ground:

> It [God's will] is the command (*amr*) by which the action of the freely choosing agent occurs according to different aspects of good or evil, different degrees of much or little, and the rest of shapes and forms like speed and slowness, according to purpose or against it in different points of time.[114]

A paraphrase of Ibn al-Wazīr's explanation reads as follows: As the Muʿtazila hold, God hates disobedience. By no means does He love it. This, however, does not mean that disobedience happens in contravention of the divine will, as

113 Ibn al-Wazīr, *Īthār al-ḥaqq* 251. In the preceding discussion, Ibn al-Wazīr traces the reasonings of prominent scholars of both sides. For the Muʿtazili side, he traces Abū ʿAlī al-Jubbāʾī's position, who tried to justify the limitedness of God's power to right guidance by limiting divine knowledge. According to Ibn al-Wazīr's presentation of the argument, this "excuse of the limiting of God's power by another error" was merely a result of the attempt to object to the Ashʿari insistence on the limitlessness of God's power. Hence, Ibn al-Wazīr considers this example appropriate to show that disagreement is restricted to the play with and the entanglement of words, expressions and concepts. Ibn al-Malāḥimī represents the return to the essential point of agreement with the Ashʿariyya; cf. ibid., 252–253. For the question of divine guidance, see also Ibn al-Wazīr, *al-Āyāt al-mubīnāt* 289.

114 Ibn al-Wazīr, *Īthār al-ḥaqq* 228.

He has the power to realize whatever He wills.[115] Disobedience is within God's will, as the Ashʿariyya hold. Yet, that disobedience is not intended for itself. The Ashʿari doctrine that God is to be praised for the completeness of His power and for the fulfillment of His will can be upheld. But the Muʿtazili appeal to God's justice does not have to be surrendered either. God wills that the agent chooses in what characteristic the action occurs. This choice is rewarded or punished according to the agent's deserts.

3.1.1 Will and Love

Beyond what seems like an affirmation of apparently conflicting statements and their integration into one general tenet, Ibn al-Wazīr's concept of divine wisdom appears in the shape of "the relative or instrumental" vs. "the ultimate:" something apparently evil may be willed, yet not for its own sake. After insisting that some Muʿtazila affirm God's ability to make the sinner a recipient of guidance, Ibn al-Wazīr quotes from the Quran and explains:

> {And there are others who are waiting for God's decree, either to punish them or to show them mercy. God is All-Knowing and All-Wise.} [Q 9:106] Therein is an argument for the establishment of the wise purposefulness of God, the Exalted, concerning their guidance which the intellect knows to be good, and [concerning] the omission of guidance in spite of the capacity to do so. Of these [latter] things, the intellect does not know the goodness.[116]

The apparent conflict between the effective execution of God's will (*irāda*) on the one hand, and His aversion (*karāha*) to disobedience and evil on the other, can be resolved by reference to God's wise purposes. In cases where His demand or decree effectuates an apparent evil or a seeming contradiction to other important values and concepts, it cannot be for the sake of the apparent evil. There must be an ultimate goal that is entirely good. The assurance of the good as the ultimate purpose of the apparent evil maintains the integrity of God's will, even if that particular good is not within human comprehension. Thus, the execution of God's will is assured and God's justice is maintained by the assurance of purposefulness.

For the above distinction between what is willed ultimately and what is willed relatively, Ibn al-Wazīr takes refuge in a distinction between will (*irāda*)

115 Ibid., 228.
116 Ibid., 252.

and love (*maḥabba*). This distinction was made before Ibn al-Wazīr by Ibn Taymiyya and a number of Ashʿaris, albeit with different conclusions. It is also discussed in Muʿtazili literature.[117] Ibn al-Wazīr claims that it originates in the apparent text of the Scripture:

> Resorting to belief in the general tenet is more prudent and preferable, namely that God *hates* evil actions and *does not love* them; and that He is capable of all things. If he wanted He could have rightly guided all people. Verily, He has an effective wise purpose in all that He does, and omits, and decrees and ordains. And this is not contradictory.[118]

According to Ibn al-Wazīr's understanding, the Quranic text is clear that God does not love evil. In order to maintain that God's will is always executed, it must be something other than love. God's will and aversion refers to another's actions only in a relative way, whereas love (*maḥabba*) and wrath (*sukhṭ*) refer to another's actions in an ultimate way. Elsewhere, Ibn al-Wazīr explains that this means that will in its literal meaning does not refer to another's action at all; although it is used metaphorically for that purpose. Love, in contrast, refers to the act of another in a literal way.

> This part is the clearer one of the two [parts] on wise purposes. I mean the part on those creatures that receive mercy. Apparently, the above-quoted verse [Q 6:125][119] means that He wills that the straying from the right path occurs through Him, although it [the straying] is a hateful disobedience according to the text of the divine saying {The evil of all these actions is hateful to your Lord}[Q 17:38]. (…) The will is not connected with the action of another, rather it is love called will metaphorically which is connected with it [the action of another]. This whole book is built on [the principle] that we do not exchange the apparent meaning with the text.

117 Cf. ibid., 250. For a discussion of this distinction among Ashʿari theologians prior to Ibn Taymiyya, see Bell, *Love Theory*, 50–60; and on Ibn Taymiyya's thought and refutation of the Ashʿari concepts, see ibid., 60.

118 In the preceding passage, Ibn al-Wazīr explains Ibn Taymiyya's distinction between God's existential will (*al-irāda al-kawniyya*) and His prescriptive will (*al-irāda al-sharʿiyya*). Although much of what Ibn al-Wazīr holds resembles Ibn Taymiyya's view on the matter, Ibn al-Wazīr cannot verify Ibn Taymiyya's distinction because his terminology is not confirmed either in scripture or by the righteous forefathers; cf. Ibn al-Wazīr, *Īthār al-ḥaqq* 249, italics mine. For Ibn Taymiyya's distinction, see Bell, *Love Theory* 67.

119 The quoted part of Q 6:125 reads {when He [God] wishes to lead them astray, He closes and constricts their breast}.

> Do you not see that His misguidance, of which the clear text says that it is His will, can only be construed to mean that God does good things that coincide (*yaqaʿa ʿindahā*) with hateful sins on their part. Like what God, the Exalted, says about the extension of provision in many verses and prophetic traditions: It does not mean what they have stipulated, because it is possible that the intention (*murād*) of such good actions which are means to the most excellent morals in this world and the next, is forgiveness (*ʿafw*) after offense and charity towards the offender (…), like His will in the creation and eternal life of unbelievers in spite of His aversion of them. There is no contradiction between the two.[120]

In other words, God may do something according to His will that correlates with another's evil act which He abhors, but for the sake of some ultimate good He may yet do it. Accordingly, God may will the evil action of a sinner for the good of something else, never for its own sake. God's will, either relative or ultimate, is always executed. In contradistinction, not all that God loves comes into being, and not everything that comes into being is loved by God.[121]

According to Ibn al-Wazīr's understanding of the general tenet of the divine will, the God-given rational original nature (*fiṭra*) of all human beings is receptive to the benevolence (*luṭf*) of God's guidance. God loves obedience and His power to guide is not limited.[122] But the question remains as to why some particular human beings happen to be rightly guided in the end, whereas others are not. The answer to this question has to be surrendered to God's hidden wisdom (*ḥikma*) in particular cases.[123] He may abhor the action of the disobedient

120 Ibn al-Wazīr, *Īthār al-ḥaqq* 242. Ibn al-Wazīr discusses several Ashʿari scholars who distinguish between God's will and His love, prominent among them al-Shahrastānī; cf. ibid., 277.

121 Cf. Ibn al-Wazīr, *al-ʿAwāsim* v, 382.

122 Ibn al-Wazīr does admit, though, that the Muʿtazila presuppose that a change of the human constitution (*binya*) be effected by God before a disobedient human being can be receptive to God's guiding benevolence. Other schools, on the other hand, do not require this. But this difference does not affect the essentials as understood by Ibn al-Wazīr; cf. Ibn al-Wazīr, *Īthār al-ḥaqq* 251–252. Ibn al-Wazīr is careful to use the word *binya* and not *fiṭra* when talking about the Muʿtazili position. *Fiṭra* may imply a moral, rational as well as a pre-existential dimension. Ibn al-Wazīr's distinction allows that *binya* is the post-natal disposition which varies between people, whereas all mankind has the same *fiṭrā*. On *fiṭra*, see MacDonald, Fiṭra. According to Ibn al-Wazīr, the *fiṭra* can be corrupted, but does not change or is not created with the inability to receive divine guidance. He can therefore use *fiṭra*, when talking about his own view of the entity that is always receptive to benevolence. This *fiṭra* would not be changed, like the *binya*, but only healed.

123 Ibn al-Wazīr, *Īthār al-ḥaqq* 229, 278.

human being, yet does not choose to guide him rightly because of some hidden wise purpose. Note that the knowledge of the ultimate end in the quote above, i.e. forgiveness in spite of sin, was only a possible, never a certain option.

3.1.2 Will and Motive

Another question that was much debated in the context of God's will was whether or not God's will is identical to His motive (*dāʿī*). The concept of a motive is closely linked to the concepts of a wise purpose as referred to above. In the theological debates, the question was significant because a motive could be understood as a factor that determines God's will.[124]

It is especially in this context that Ibn al-Wazīr refers to the understanding of divine will among theologians of Abū l-Ḥusayn al-Baṣrī's school, and it seems that Abū l-Ḥusayn's school once again helps to establish what Ibn al-Wazīr takes to be an essential agreement. In one instance, Ibn al-Wazīr argues that Abū l-Ḥusayn defines will as "the preponderant motive (*al-dāʿī al-rājiḥ*) that arises from the knowledge of what results from the action."[125] Although the majority of the Muʿtazila as well as the Ashʿariyya apparently reject this idea, Ibn al-Wazīr sees a uniting factor in Abū l-Ḥusayn's equation of will and motive.[126] The conflict Ibn al-Wazīr refers to is that between the Muʿtazili doctrine that God's will is contingent, and the Ashʿari doctrine that it is eternal. Arguing from Abū l-Ḥusayn's equation of will and motive, Ibn al-Wazīr writes that "this leads to something like the Ashʿari position concerning the eternity of the will (*qidam al-irāda*)."[127]

The conflict takes shape, for example, in the question of how the Quranic term "God's misguidance" (*iḍlāl*) is to be understood in terms of His will to punish. Is His will eternal, thereby excluding that anything but what He wills occurs? Or is it contingent, coming into being in the moment the intended thing (the punishment) is justified by the occurrence of sin? Ibn al-Wazīr rescues the concept of an eternal will from injustice by defining the implied predetermination (*qadar*) as "knowledge, recording, and willing the punishment that

---

124 I referred to this problem above, when discussing Ibn al-Wazīr's attempt to prove the agreement between the Muʿtazila and the Ashʿariyya by referring to the concept of the preponderator (*murajjiḥ*).

125 *"Al-dāʿī al-rājiḥ al-rājiʿ ilā l-ʿilm li-mulāzamat al-fiʿl li-dhālika wa-li-mulāzamat al-irāda lahu"*; Ibn al-Wazīr, *Īthār al-ḥaqq* 267.

126 The rejection of the equation of will and motive is well documented, see for example Ibn al-Malāḥimī, *Kitāb al-Muʿtamad* 240; Ibn al-Murtaḍā, Kitāb al-Qalāʾid 58; al-Ḥayyī, *al-Muntazaʿ min al-Durar al-farāʾid* fs. 74b; al-Kamālī, *al-Imām al-Mahdī* 226; McDermott, Abū l-Ḥusayn al-Baṣrī on God's Volition 89.

127 Ibn al-Wazīr, *Īthār al-ḥaqq* 267.

is deserved by action."[128] Ibn al-Wazīr takes Abū l-Ḥusayn's equation to mean that he defines will as knowledge. After all, it is the knowledge of the results that determines the motive and the will accordingly. And whoever holds to such a definition cannot reject the idea of the eternity of the divine will, according to Ibn al-Wazīr.[129]

It is relatively well documented that Abū l-Ḥusayn al-Baṣrī equated God's will with His motive.[130] Accordingly, Ibn al-Malāḥimī could argue that evil could not be part of God's will because, being wise, He could have no motive to do evil.[131] Motive, according to Ibn al-Malāḥimī, is the knowledge of the benefit of the action.[132] His and probably Abū l-Ḥusayn's definition of motive resembles Ibn al-Wazīr's definition of *ḥikma*. Ibn al-Wazīr's concept of *ḥikma* describes "the knowledge of the most excellent of actions and the action according to that knowledge."[133] Both concepts are determined by the knowledge of the result of the action.[134] In God's case, His perfect knowledge ensures the best of motives, and the wisest of purposes.

Ibn al-Wazīr concludes that will is knowledge according to Abū l-Ḥusayn. Therefore being willing to punish, or talking of "leading astray" before it is deserved, neither causes the punishment nor is it unjust.[135] This understanding fits well with Ibn al-Wazīr's understanding of the wise purpose that is intended by a seeming evil action or command on God's part, the purpose being an absolute good that only God knows of. Hence, if God does something apparently evil, it is the wisest action in reaction to His foreknowledge of what will happen. He wills this, His own action, for a relative purpose, thereby determining

128 Ibid., 244.

129 Besides Abū l-Ḥusayn, Ibn al-Wazīr mentions the Baghdadi branch of the Muʿtazila as examples of the same view; cf. ibid. Ibn al-Wazīr probably refers to Abū Isḥāq al-Naẓẓām, Abū ʿUthmān al-Jāḥiẓ and Abū l-Qāsim al-Kaʿbī al-Balkhī, who are known to have held corresponding views; cf. Ibn al-Malāḥimī, *Kitāb al-Muʿtamad* 240. According to Ansari, Madelung and Schmidtke, the association of Abū l-Ḥusayn al-Baṣrī's school with Abū l-Qāsim al-Balkhī and the Baghdadis was apparently not uncommon among Zaydi; cf. Ansari et al., Yūsuf al-Baṣīr's Rebuttal 36.

130 This is true of those who endorse Abū l-Ḥusayn's theological doctrine, see Taqī l-Dīn al-ʿUjālī, *al-Kāmil* 284; Ibn al-Malāḥimī, *al-Muʿtamad* 240; Yaḥyā b. Ḥamza, *al-Tamhīd* i, 223, 228–232, as well as those who mostly opted for the Bahshami position; cf. al-Ḥayyī, *al-Muntazaʿ min al-Durar al-farāʾid* f. 74b.

131 McDermott, Abū l-Ḥusayn al-Baṣrī on God's Volition 90.

132 Cf. Ibn al-Malāḥimī, *Kitāb al-Muʿtamad* 241, 248.

133 Ibn al-Wazīr, *Īthār al-ḥaqq* 181.

134 The motive does not necessarily need to be good, although of course it is where God is concerned; cf. Ibn al-Malāḥimī, *Kitāb al-Muʿtamad* 247–248.

135 Ibn al-Wazīr, *Īthār al-ḥaqq* 244.

the human action which He hates for itself, yet which He knows will happen. Accordingly, Ibn al-Wazīr can claim Muʿtazili support for his thesis that God could have guided the disobedient differently—for example by giving them another constitution (*binya*)—but did not for some good reason only known to himself:

> After mentioning that the Muʿtazila agree with *ahl al-sunna*, Ibn al-Malāḥimī basically says: "If it is asked 'What do you mean by the creation of one who is disobedient according to a constitution that is not receptive to benevolence in spite of God's power to create them according to a constitution that is receptive to benevolence, or even to infallibility?', we say that God has a wise purpose in a general way [*ʿalā sabīl al-ijmāl*], but that we do not know its details." So, after asserting that the obvious meanings of [the texts of] Quran, Sunna and the traditions of the righteous forefathers are ignominious, and [after] embarking on everything difficult and base in their allegorical interpretation, the Muʿtazila returned to what the *ahl al-sunna* began with. If only I knew what the difference is supposed to be between the Muʿtazili admission of this unknown wise purpose and the admission that God, the Exalted, wills the occurrence of the sins of disobedient humans and omits to guide them rightly in spite of His power to do so for some wise purpose that we do not know, rather than because of the evil aspect for which it [the disobedience] is called evil and is hated. Even if some Muʿtazila disagree in this, we are content to gather from this that the *ahl al-sunna* occupy a position that Muʿtazila like Abū l-Ḥusayn and his followers approve of.[136]

We are not interested here in Ibn al-Wazīr's interpretation of the Muʿtazili concept of *binya*. Rather, we are interested in the agreement with his own thinking that Ibn al-Wazīr spots in Abū l-Ḥusayn al-Baṣrī's concept of *binya* and divine guidance: the divine knowledge of an absolute good unknown to human beings that is tantamount to God's will to permit or to do something apparently evil or unjust in spite of His power to act in a way that appears good and just.

Ibn al-Wazīr argues that the concept of God's wisdom exists in the contending schools albeit in different forms. Accordingly, he could call it one of the general tenets (*jumal*). He achieved this basically by equating the concepts preponderator (*murajjiḥ*), motive (*dāʿī*) and wise purposes (*ḥikam*) behind

136 Ibn al-Wazīr, *al-ʿAwāṣim* vi, 19, 123. See also Ibn al-Wazīr, *Īthār al-ḥaqq* 251–252, in the context of the divine will.

actions. However, as pointed out earlier, Ibn al-Wazīr himself did distinguish between a motive and wisdom, for example to point out the difference between a divine action and that of a common human being or a madman. The fact that Ibn al-Wazīr ascribes a motive to the madman and distinguishes between motive and wise purpose is another point supporting the thesis that he favored Abū l-Ḥusayn's teachings.[137] Where Ibn al-Wazīr equated the preponderator, the motive and the wise purposes, he referred to God's will and actions. In contrast, where he distinguished between motive and wisdom, he referred to human beings. Similarly, Abū l-Ḥusayn equates motive and will where God is concerned, and allows that will is something additional to motive where human beings are concerned.[138]

The reason for the distinction, according to Ibn al-Wazīr, would be that God knows what is really the best outcome, something human beings do not know. Their motive does not require rationality and awareness, they might not be guided by wisdom, or their knowledge of what would be best and most beneficial is limited. Not so for God. For that reason, human beings often do not know what God intends in particular nor exactly what the wise purpose.[139]

3.2 *Ibn al-Murtaḍā's Concept of God's Will*

Ibn al-Murtaḍā discusses God's will as part of divine justice especially in his *Kitāb al-Qalāʾid* and its commentary *al-Durar al-farāʾid*, and to a lesser degree in his *Riyāḍat al-afhām*.[140] Ibn al-Murtaḍā clearly holds that God does not will evil and that He cannot guide the disobedient. Indeed, He would have to, if He could.[141] Rather, according to Ibn al-Murtaḍā, God "wills that which is better done than left undone"[142] as opposed to the position of what he calls the compulsionists (Mujbira), according to whom God wills everything that hap-

137 Abū l-Ḥusayn al-Baṣrī, according to Ibn al-Malāḥimī, made even an unconscious or unreflected action dependent on a motive, albeit to a minor degree. Madelung showed how this altered the Muʿtazili theory of act and responsibility, as consciousness and rational reflection no longer delimitated the concept of motive and knowledge; cf. Madelung, Late Muʿtazila 251.

138 Cf. Ibn al-Malāḥimī, *Kitāb al-Muʿtamad* 240.

139 Ibn al-Wazīr, *Īthār al-ḥaqq* 267. In fact, Abū l-Ḥusayn argued in a similar way. This is one of the few points in which Ibn al-Malāḥimī apparently disagreed with his master. Ibn al-Malāḥimī equated will and motive in the divine as well as the human realm; cf. Ibn al-Malāḥimī, *Kitāb al-Muʿtamad* 241. Ibn al-Murtaḍā, in his discussion of the different positions on *irāda*, notes the disagreement; cf. al-Ḥayyī, *al-Muntazaʿ min al-Durar al-farāʾid* f. 74b.

140 Ibn al-Murtaḍā is sure to have treated the subject elsewhere as well.

141 Cf. al-Ḥayyī, *al-Muntazaʿ min al-Durar al-farāʾid* f. 74a.

142 Ibn al-Murtaḍā, Kitab al-Qalāʾid 58.

pens. Ibn al-Murtaḍā, and with him most of the Muʿtazila and Zaydiyya (as he claims), does not distinguish between God's will and His love or approval (*riḍā*) of an action. In *Riyāḍat al-afhām* he writes:

> Love, hatred, anger, displeasure, wrath and approval are names for will and antagonism that occur in different manners. We say, that love is the will to benefit the beloved and antagonism his harm. There is no other meaning apart from this. (...) Approval of an action is to will it and [approval] of the agent is to will his aggrandizement.[143]

Similarly in *al-Durar al-farāʾid*, Ibn al-Murtaḍā clarifies that God does not will anything He does not love or approve of.[144] We can conclude from this that Ibn al-Murtaḍā could not envision God willing anything like the disobedience of a sinner for some good purpose without approving of the sin itself. Neither could He will to refrain from giving sinners right guidance based on some unknown wisdom, and thereby fail to do His duty. In both cases, God's justice would be violated in an inconceivable way. No unknown purpose could justify divine love for something obviously evil.

As mentioned above, God's justice requires that He does not will anything evil. One of Ibn al-Murtaḍā's arguments for this, and indeed a common Muʿtazili one, is that God is wise. God's wisdom provides that He acts from a motive (*dāʿī*), and since He has no motive for evil actions, He does not commit such actions. So far, this does not seem any different from Abū l-Ḥusayn al-Baṣrī's and Ibn al-Malāḥimī's position. It must be asked then how Ibn al-Murtaḍā answered the question of whether God's will is identical to His motive. The later Bahshami theologians, and along with them Ibn al-Murtaḍā, held that God's will is not identical to motive. Ibn al-Murtaḍā answers this question more extensively for the human side. However, the Bahshami Muʿtazila often argue based on an analogy between God and human beings (*qiyās al-ghāʾib ʿalā l-shāhid*). This allows us to illustrate Ibn al-Murtaḍā's understanding of God's will by quoting from a passage on human will.[145] Ibn al-Murtaḍā cites four positions on the issue of the quiddity (*māhiyya*) of the will, with Abū l-Ḥusayn al-Baṣrī's

143 Ibn al-Murtaḍā, Riyāḍat al-afhām 143.

144 Al-Ḥayyī, *al-Muntazaʿ min al-Durar al-farāʾid* f. 78a.

145 According to al-Ḥayyī, Ibn al-Murtaḍā himself argues thus after a long passage on the human will in *al-Durar al-farāʾid*: "He [God] is willing in the true sense which means that an attribute of willingness (*murīdiyya*) can be established for Him according to the definition that has been established for us. And it is in His case additional to motive and deterrent, as it is in our case." Al-Ḥayyī, *al-Muntazaʿ min al-Durar al-farāʾid* f. 75a.

view of the identity of will and motive in the unseen world as the fourth one. A little later, Ibn al-Murtaḍā writes:

> The method by which it was established that they [*irāda* and *karāha*] are additional to desire and aversion (*al-shahwa wa-l-nafra*) is the same by which it is established that they [*irāda* and *karāha*] are additional to motive and deterrent. Do you not see that the hungry person has ample motives for eating, yet may not intend to take food because it belongs to someone else or the like. Hence, the motive is not the will.[146]

Although Ibn al-Murtaḍā negates the equation of will and motive, he does acknowledge that a knowing person has a motive or an effect that renders the action preponderant over non-action. Yet this motive or effect is only a relative (*iʿtibārī*) requisite of the action that influences the will to do the action.[147]

For Abū l-Ḥusayn al-Baṣrī and Ibn al-Malāḥimī, the will is identical to the preponderant motive. Therefore the knowledge of the outcome may be taken to determine what God wills.[148] This is a problem that was pointed out by Fakhr al-Dīn al-Rāzī and resulted in charging Abū l-Ḥusayn al-Baṣrī with determinism, as McDermott, Madelung and Gimaret have shown.[149] Ibn al-Murtaḍā demonstrates Fakhr al-Dīn al-Rāzī's determinism based on the latter's adoption of Abū l-Ḥusayn al-Baṣrī's concept of the preponderant motive as the determinant of action.[150] But if God's will is equated with His motive and hence as determin-

146 Ibid., f. 74b.

147 Ibid., f. 73b.

148 This charge could be extended to the matter of human will and action for all those who draw an analogy between the seen and the unseen world in general, or in this question in particular. Abū l-Ḥusayn, in contrast to his follower Ibn al-Malāḥimī, does not apply the identity of motive and will to the human realm. As Madelung has shown, it was rather Fakhr al-Dīn al-Rāzī himself whose "argument of the preponderator involved him in insoluble problems while trying to defend the Muslim belief in a freely choosing creator God against the philosophers' view of God as the necessitating cause of the world." Madelung, Late Muʿtazila 256. It seems that Fakhr al-Dīn al-Rāzī solved the problem by ignoring his own requirement of motives for God analogous to human actions. He asserted that God's will itself is the preponderator.

149 Gimaret, *Théories de l'acte humain* 34; McDermott, Abū l-Ḥusayn on God's volition 68, footnote 1; Madelung, Late Muʿtazila 246. Madelung questions Gimaret's concession to Fakhr al-Dīn al-Rāzī's accusation that Abū l-Ḥusayn holds to determinism, and rightly so. Of course, Fakhr al-Dīn al-Rāzī's main argument refers to the determination of human acts, but Abū l-Ḥusayn's concept of the preponderant motive as determining the action holds true for divine as well as human actions.

150 Cf. al-Ḥayyī, *al-Muntazaʿ min al-Durar al-farāʾid* f. 73b; al-Kamālī, *al-Imām al-Mahdī* 294–296.

ing His action according to Abū l-Ḥusayn al-Baṣrī, what reasons does God have for his will to act according to a particular motive in Ibn al-Murtaḍā's view? Although this question is not answered explicitly by Ibn al-Murtaḍā in any of the consulted texts, his argument for God's justice is telling: God cannot will or do evil, as we were told above. For Ibn al-Murtaḍā, this necessarily means that God must fulfill a duty (*siḥḥa wujūb al-wājib*).[151] Or, to be more precise, God is obliged to a set of duties that follow from His justice and His acting according to the highest benefit (*al-aṣlaḥ*) of human beings.

It appears that obliging God to do what is most beneficial for the human being (*al-aṣlaḥ*) in order to maintain His justice does not determine God's will in any less significant way, even if God's will should be something additional to His motive. Whereas God seems obliged to act according to His preponderant motive according to Abū l-Ḥusayn and those who follow him, God is obliged to act according to man's highest benefit according to Ibn al-Murtaḍā and other Bahshami Muʿtazila.

The determining factor in Abū l-Ḥusayn al-Baṣrī's view seems somewhat vague. McDermott suggests that "Abū l-Ḥusayn has God willing, it seems, for no reason."[152] I would add, '[for no reason] other than the existence of a preponderant motive.' But this vagueness goes very well with Ibn al-Wazīr's concept of the hidden purpose behind God's actions that is often unknown to human beings: God intends, for example, not to guide some sinners to paradise, although He could have given them a new *binya*, because He knows something that human beings do not know. This is not arbitrary, let alone evil. The reason for this particular "willing" is merely not known. Claiming to know the wise purpose behind this is erroneous.[153]

3.3 *Conclusion*

Ibn al-Wazīr would not have agreed with Fakhr al-Dīn al-Rāzī's charge of determinism toward Abū l-Ḥusayn al-Baṣrī because of the latter's concept of motives. Ibn al-Wazīr has shown this, for example, in his juxtaposition of Abū l-Ḥusayn al-Baṣrī and Fakhr al-Din al-Rāzī in *Masʾalat al-ikhtilāf*. In his view, and supposedly that of Abū l-Ḥusayn al-Baṣrī, God's will is determined by some wise purpose—or preponderant motive—that is hidden to human understanding. But the existence of this purpose does not forestall freedom of will on God's part. The exact purpose and the way it comes about is uncertain, yet certainly wise and good. It is the role played by ambiguity in Abū l-Ḥusayn's thought that

151 Cf. al-Ḥayyī, *al-Muntazaʿ min al-Durar al-farāʾid* f. 74a.

152 McDermott, Abū l-Ḥusayn on God's volition 92.

153 Ibn al-Wazīr, *al-ʿAwāṣim* v, 277.

seems to render him favorable for Ibn al-Wazīr's harmonization, as well as supportive of his own thinking.

Ibn al-Murtaḍā's concept of God's will and His action, although proved not to be evil by his insistence on God's wisdom, is determined by God's justice and the human knowledge of what this justice entails in particular instances. If God failed to lead some to paradise by withholding guidance or a change of constitution, this would have to be proved as being just and for human benefit. Since it cannot be proved to be such, God cannot will or do such a thing. The same is true of man's disobedient actions.

Whereas God's will is determined by His justice in Ibn al-Murtaḍā's thinking, Ibn al-Wazīr—and, it seems, Abū l-Ḥusayn al-Baṣrī—has it determined by His superior knowledge. In contrast to Ibn al-Wazīr's concept of a hidden purpose behind God's will that is unknown but sure to be wise and good, Ibn al-Murtaḍā has human beings able to determine with certainty what God wills in general as well as in particular instances. This, of course, renders it easy to judge the conclusions on God's will that other scholars or scholars of other schools draw. Ibn al-Wazīr's lack of certainty concerning what exactly God wills leaves room for a number of probable conclusions. However, since certain answers as to what exactly God wills and why cannot be given, the different answers must be accepted as equally probable. The question remains ambiguous.

4 Harmonized Doctrine: Human Actions (*afʿāl al-ʿibād*) and Free Will (*ikhtiyār*)

Closely related to the doctrine of God's will is the doctrine of human actions (*afʿāl al-ʿibād*) and free will (*ikhtiyār*). The debate is especially intense with regard to the question of responsibility for evil human actions. Who is the agent of these actions and therefore responsible for them? Are these actions compelled or do they happen in violation of God's will? As is the case with God's will, the Muʿtazila are concerned with maintaining God's justice, whereas the Ashʿariyya attempt to champion God's omnipotence. Here as above, Ibn al-Wazīr's position on the question of human responsibility for actions is manifest in his description of an agreement between the Muʿtazila and the Ashʿariyya.[154]

154 Ibn al-Wazīr's description of the agreement excludes two extreme positions. On the extreme side of predetermination is the what Ibn al-Wazīr calls the "Jahmiyya" or "pure Jabriyya (*al-Jabriyya al-khāliṣa*)" or "the extremist Jabriyya (*ghulāt al-Jabriyya al-khāliṣa*)." These groups claim that human will and power have no effect on human action whatsoever, and do not acknowledge the self-evident distinction between a voluntary action

Accordingly, Ibn al-Wazīr defends both notions: Human actions are not compelled (*jabr* or *iljāʿ*) but happen according to human beings' free choice. Yet every human action occurs according to God's will and power.

4.1 *Ibn al-Wazīr's Harmonization Regarding Human Actions and Free Will*

According to Ibn al-Wazīr, the points of agreement between Muʿtazila and Ashʿariyya consist in the two major notions above, albeit expressed in different, complicated and often ostensibly contradicting terminology.[155] Both God and man play their very distinct parts in the occurrence of human actions. This is masterfully illustrated in Ibn al-Wazīr's *Masʾalat al-ikhtilāf* with regard to human faith. In *al-ʿAwāṣim*, Ibn al-Wazīr distinguishes between "the obvious side" (*al-ṭaraf al-jalī*) and "the hidden side" (*al-ṭaraf al-khafī*) of human actions. All apparently agree that, on the obvious side, human actions are dependent on human choice and motive. This renders it possible for man to be responsible for his actions. He is responsible, because he wills an action to occur in a particular way and thus performs it.[156] The hidden side refers to the existence of actions in their essential form (*ḥaqīqat afʿāl al-ʿibād ʿalā jihat al-taʿyīn wa-l-tamyīz lahā ʿan sāʾir al-ḥaqāʾiq*). In this regard, they originate with God in one way or another.[157] According to Ibn al-Wazīr, agreement exists between the schools that an essential part of the action is beyond human power, or that it happened with some kind of help (*iʿāna*) from God. Hence, man does not perform his action completely independently (*mustaqill*).[158] God's part, in contrast, cannot be defined with equal certainty.

(*ḥarakat al-mukhtār*) and an involuntary action (*ḥarakat al-maflūj wa-l-masḥūb*). The other extreme is represented by the extreme Qadariyya. They are said to hold that God has neither influence on nor foreknowledge of human actions, or future events for that matter. Ibn al-Wazīr excludes both groups from the discussion, as they either no longer exist or are rejected by the entirety of the Muslim community; cf. Ibn al-Wazīr, *al-ʿAwāsim* vii, 6, 73 (where he refers to Shaykh Mukhtār for this distinction.); Ibn al-Wazīr, *Īthār al-ḥaqq* 287.

155 Ibn al-Wazīr, *Īthār al-ḥaqq*, 285–286. Ḥajar agrees with Ibn al-Wazīr that it is virtually impossible to clearly charge one entire group with believing in predestination; cf. Ḥajar, *Ibn al-Wazīr wa-manhajuhu* 344. Al-Kamālī, discussing Ibn al-Murtaḍā's thought, repeatedly states how complicated and extensive the conflict about this topic has been, especially on the question of acquisition, without "ever arriving at real results." Al-Kamālī, *al-Imām al-Mahdī* 286–287.

156 Ibn al-Wazīr, *al-ʿAwāṣim* vii, 28.

157 Ibn al-Wazīr, *Īthār al-ḥaqq* 281–283, 294, 308, quote 282.

158 See for example Ibn al-Wazīr, *al-ʿAwāṣim* vii, 13.

In contrast to what Ibn al-Wazīr illustrates, Zaydis influenced by Bahshami-Muʿtazili doctrine do in fact hold that it is possible, and indeed imperative, to define the exact nature of the essence of human action.[159] The difference between Ibn al-Wazīr's attempt to harmonize conflicting understandings of human actions based on his epistemology of ambiguity on the one hand, and the Zaydi-Muʿtazili attempt to define correct doctrine in detail by means of unimpeachable inferences on the other, is especially prominent in two central notions of the concept of human actions, namely capacity (*qudra*) and motive (*dāʿī*).

4.1.1 Action and Capacity

Ibn al-Wazīr has no difficulty in upholding God's creation of acts (*khalq*) as well as real human responsibility. True to type, he again maintains the "golden mean" also ascribed to Ibn Taymiyya.[160] The Ashʿari idea of appropriation (*kasb*)[161] is no absurdity to him: God creates the essence of an act. This essence does not have the attribute of good or evil. Rather, God's agency may be taken to signify the transfer of the act from non-existence to existence. Human beings appropriate the act by performing it in a way that renders it praiseworthy or reprehensible.

> The essence [of the act] that is dependent on the power of the Lord cannot be described as evil (*qabḥ*) as the two sides, Muʿtazila and Ashʿariyya, agree. Rather, it [the act] is described as evil by the admission of all, because it occurs according to different aspects and additional relative manners (*iʿtibārāt iḍāfiyya*). And it [the act] does not occur according to these by the power of the Lord, as all agree as well, because these aspects are no real entities (*ashiyāʾ ḥaqīqiyya*), according to all. That which is ascribed to God, the Exalted, of human acts is the move of the essence of the acts that are real entities from non-existence to existence. The capacity of human beings effect that the essences of the acts occur according to different aspects. And because they occur according to these only by the capacity of human beings, they [the acts] deserve names that could not be ascribed to God at all, like worship, obedience and disobedience. If these

159 See also Hajar, *Ibn al-Wazīr wa-manhajuhu* 348.

160 Hoover, *Ibn Taymiyya's Theodicy* 173.

161 I tend towards the translation of *kasb* as "appropriation" used first by Watt, as it seems to express the active part of "performing something" or "doing something" (*iktasaba*) more strongly than either of those two terms. For Ibn al-Wazīr, the human beings' activity in their own actions cannot be overemphasized; cf. Watt, The Origin 237.

> aspects happened by the power of God, the Exalted, He would have to be called worshipping, disobeying, praying, fasting and the like. And whereas these names cannot be attributed to Him—rather, He is called Creator, Originator and Producer—this indicates that that which is dependent on the power of Him, the Glorified, is that from which His Beautiful Names are derived. And that which is derived from one word differs according to its different aspects.[162]

Ibn al-Wazīr incorporates concepts into this discussion that are also used in the question of *al-taḥsīn wa-l-taqbīḥ al-ʿaqlī* without much differentiation. In this latter context, the "way" or "aspect" or "respect" is referred to as "*wajh*" or "*jiha*" by some Muʿtazili scholars, or as referring to the "state" (*ḥāl*), manner (*ʿayn*) or attribute (*ṣifa*) of the action by others.[163] In the context of the Ashʿari concept of acquisition, this concept of the non-essential part of actions is also expressed by the idea of "relativity" (*iʿtibār*).[164] Elsewhere, Ibn al-Wazīr calls this way or aspect the "particular form" (*hayʾa makhṣūṣa*).[165] Whichever name is given to the morally assessable aspect of the action, the human being is its real agent, because he has a will and a motive that corresponds to the action in its state of moral assessability. The action that human beings perform is the side (*ṭaraf*) of it that deserves praise or punishment, although God has a part in the creation of the action.[166] Several ideas exist among the Muʿtazila that

162 Ibn al-Wazīr, *al-ʿAwāṣim* vii, 28.

163 The goodness or evil of an action is not essential but rather refers to the condition (*ḥāl*) of the action; cf. al-Kamālī, *al-Imām al-Mahdī* 319–320. In *Īthār al-ḥaqq*, Ibn al-Wazīr writes that will "is that by which the action of a freely choosing agent occurs in its different aspects (or literally: manners—*wujūh*) as to good and evil, its different degrees as to plenty and scarcity etc." He claims consensus for this definition as far as it goes; cf. Ibn al-Wazīr, *Īthār al-ḥaqq* 228. For ʿAbd al-Jabbār and the aspects or *aḥwāl* that render something obligatory etc., see also Brunschvig, Muʿtazilism et Optimum 14–15. According to Peters, the Muʿtazili position represented by ʿAbd al-Jabbār discerns the point where an act becomes morally assessable in "the way" it is brought into existence; cf. Peters, *God's Created Speech* 415. However, according to Omari, Abū l-Qāsim al-Balkhī held the view that an act is called good or evil because of its attributes (*ṣifātihi*) and manner (*ʿaynihi*), but this was refuted by the Basran Muʿtazila; cf. Omari, The Theology of Abū l-Qāsim al-Balkhī 72. For Ibn al-Wazīr's concept of *jumal*, this would make no difference. The distinctions between the terms and even between the different understandings of the same terms as described, for example, by Frank are effectively ignored by Ibn al-Wazīr; cf. Frank, Ḥāl.

164 Cf. Ibn al-Wazīr, *al-ʿAwāṣim* vii, 13.

165 Ibn al-Wazīr, *al-Rawḍ al-bāsim* 362.

166 Ibn al-Wazīr, *Īthār al-ḥaqq* 282. In *al-Rawḍ al-bāsim* 361, Ibn al-Wazīr has an Ashʿari affirm the apparent agreement on the general doctrine of the human action: "We say that human beings have no effective power on the essence of their actions. The Muʿtazila consider this

Ibn al-Wazīr interprets to the effect that there is a side to human action that is beyond human power. Many Muʿtazila would not ascribe the creation of the essence of action to God. They take it to have a real existence in pre-eternity (*thābita fī l-azal*), without being an object of God's power.[167] However, according to Ibn al-Wazīr, some of those Muʿtazilis who ascribe creation to human beings take this creative act to refer to the attribute of existence of the essence (*ṣifat al-wujūd*) rather than the essence itself.[168] In both cases, the essence of the act could be understood as being beyond the realm of immediate human influence. And this is precisely what Ibn al-Wazīr attempts to show in order to furnish proof for his harmonization efforts.

Put thus, it seems that Ibn al-Wazīr accepts the concepts of *kasb* and "one object of power for two wielders of power" (*maqdūr bayna qādirayn*). In some passages in *al-ʿAwāṣim*, he employs this terminology in his discussion of human actions.[169] This, however, should be seen as a means of harmonization rather than as Ibn al-Wazīr's own terminology.[170] In the above-mentioned passage in

---

sound. We say that human beings have an effective power on the attributes of good and evil. This also is considered sound by the Muʿtazila. The majority of the Muʿtazila have established that actions are not good or bad in their essence. Rather, [they become such] by occurring in a certain manner or regard. This is because the essences of humans beings' actions are all one."

167 This thought is part of the Muʿtazili theory of substances. It says that in non-existence (*ʿadam*) all essences are alike (*tamāthul*); cf. Ibn al-Wazīr, *Īthār al-ḥaqq* 282–283. *Azal* (pre-eternity) must be distinguished from *qidam* (eternity) in that *azal* has no beginning, whereas *qidam* has neither beginning and nor end. Non-existence (*ʿadam*) can apply to both; cf. R. Arnaldez, Ḳidam. However, according to Bahshami-Muʿtazili teaching, the essence of the act that exists in pre-eternity is not subject to God's power (*ghayr maqdara li-llāh*); cf. Ibn al-Wazīr, *al-ʿAwāsim* v, 270; vi, 14.

168 Ibn al-Wazīr, *al-Rawḍ al-bāsim* 361–362. For a list of eight Muʿtazili and four Ashʿari positions on the question, see Ibn al-Wazīr, *al-ʿAwāṣim* vii, 10–14. ʿAbd al-Jabbār, for example, distinguishes between the neutral act that has no other attributes but existence, and acts with moral value that have further attributes added to the attribute of existence. An example of the first would be an act performed while sleeping. An example of the second kind of act would be lying. These added attributes then are the entitative ground for the characteristic of an act; cf. Ghaneabassiri, Epistemological Foundations 81.

169 God's power (*qudra*) effects that the neutral essence of the action comes into existence. Man's power (*qudra*) effects (*yuʾaththir*) the assessable aspect of the action (*wujūh al-ḥusn wa-l-qabḥ*); cf. Ibn al-Wazīr, *al-ʿAwāṣim* vii, 32.

170 In other instances, Ibn al-Wazīr questions the expression of *maqdūr bayna qādirayn*. This, I think, can be explained by Ibn al-Wazīr's claim that God's and man's actions do not really refer to the same aspect of the object of power (*maqdūr*). Indeed, man's part in the action cannot really be called creation; cf. ibid., vii, 24. For the corresponding Muʿtazili discussion of the term creation (*khalq*), see for example al-Ḥayyī, *al-Muntazaʿ min al-Durar al-farāʾid* f. 86b.

al-ʿAwāṣim, Ibn al-Wazīr seeks to demonstrate that not all Muʿtazilis rejected the concept of appropriation outright,[171] and some even endorsed the idea of *maqdūr bayna qādirayn*.[172] Again, it is Abū l-Ḥusayn al-Baṣrī and his disciples who function as examples of a supposed agreement.

> Abū l-Ḥusayn has permitted what the inquirer has prohibited, [namely] that the physical essence [of the action] (*al-dhāt al-jismiyya*) is an action of God, the Exalted, and that its [the physical essence's] attributes which are generated according to different respects (*ṣifātuhā l-kawniyya fī l-jihāt*), are the actions of human beings. He [Abū l-Ḥusayn al-Baṣrī] has done enough to refute him who considers this impossible. Whoever wants to, let him study his [Abū l-Ḥusayn al-Baṣrī's] books and the books of his adherents like Maḥmūd b. al-Malāḥimī, and beyond that [the books] of Mukhtār, author of *al-Mujtabā*, and of [Imam] Yaḥyā b. Ḥamza.[173]

Although this does not mean that Abū l-Ḥusayn al-Baṣrī defends the Ashʿari concept of *kasb*, it does substantiate Ibn al-Wazīr's claim that there are Muʿtazilis who do not consider it altogether irrational (*ghayr maʿqūl*).[174] The same could be said of Ibn al-Wazīr. Two pages later, Ibn al-Wazīr explicitly says that he shares the views of Abū l-Ḥusayn al-Baṣrī and his followers on the question.[175] The explicitness of this endorsement (*al-mukhtār ʿindī qawl Abī l-Ḥusayn*) is rather significant, as Ibn al-Wazīr refrains from positioning himself with any group apart from what he ascribes to the righteous forefathers in most cases.

The background for Ibn al-Wazīr's utilization of Abū l-Ḥusayn al-Baṣrī is the latter's theory of the states (*aḥwāl*) of essences and bodies which was described above in the argument for God's existence. According to Abū l-Ḥusayn al-Baṣrī, the accidents of substances are not real entities (*dhawāt, maʿānī*) with an inde-

---

171 The often-cited Shaykh Mukhtār is again an example of a Muʿtazili who gives the Ashʿari position the benefit of the doubt and does not dismiss the matter of *kasb* as outright irrational; cf. Ibn al-Wazīr, *al-ʿAwāṣim* vii, 56. For an account of the possible origin of the theory along with the different definitions, see Watt, The Origin. He shows that the concept was neither originated by al-Ashʿarī nor restricted to the Ashʿariyya, but rather was connected with the early Muʿtazila, especially the school of Baghdad. This supports Ibn al-Wazīr's emphasis on the similarities between the Ashʿariyya and the Muʿtazila.

172 Yaḥyā b. Ḥamza confirms this for Abū l-Ḥusayn; cf. Yaḥyā b. Ḥamza, *al-Tamhīd* i, 138–141.

173 Ibn al-Wazīr, *al-ʿAwāṣim* vii, 70; see also ibid., 56–57.

174 When claiming this, Ibn al-Wazīr often refers to Shaykh Mukhtār as a representative of Abū l-Ḥusayn's school, see also ibid., 56, 66.

175 By his own admission, Ibn al-Wazīr does not hold to *kasb*, rather "his choice" (*al-mukhtār ʿindī*) is that of Abū l-Ḥusayn; cf. Ibn al-Wazīr, *al-ʿAwāṣim* vii, 72.

pendent existence, but rather states (*aḥwāl*) or characteristics (*aḥkām*).[176] For the question of human agency, this theory is important as it means that human beings can only affect the characteristics of substances, bodies or essences (actions in this case),[177] without negating the self-evident nature of human agency.[178] In fact, Ibn al-Wazīr must have meant Abū l-Ḥusayn al-Baṣrī when he spoke of Muʿtazilis who thought that man did not really produce the essence of the action, but rather the non-entitative aspects that render an action good or evil, obedient or disobedient. In *Īthār al-ḥaqq*, Ibn al-Wazīr ascribes this very position not only to Abū l-Ḥusayn al-Baṣrī and his disciples, but to Imam Yaḥyā b. Ḥamza and "the majority of *ahl al-bayt.* (...) And this is what is contained in the original disposition of every *compos mentis* whose *fiṭra* has not been changed with a change of teachers."[179] In other words, it needs no philosophical speculation to know that human beings' capacity to bring about their actions bears upon that part of the actions that deserves praise or blame, leaving room for a less defined influence of God on the actions. Attempts such as the Ashʿari *kasb*-theory or Abū l-Ḥusayn al-Baṣrī's *aḥwāl*-theory to define the details of this necessary knowledge may or may not be employed, according to Ibn al-Wazīr, but they should certainly not be condemned as they fall within the realm of possible explanations. In fact, Abū l-Ḥusayn al-Baṣrī's teachings prove once again a helpful tool for Ibn al-Wazīr to argue for an essential agreement in a way that was acceptable in a context where Muʿtazili doctrine was highly esteemed.

The significance of this last statement for Ibn al-Wazīr's thinking also determines his means of harmonization concerning another central aspect of human responsibility, namely the motive.

4.1.2 Action and Motive

Besides the question of essence and capacity, human responsibility finds expression in the question of free choice (*ikhtiyār*). According to Abrahamov, a theory of actions and freedom must include something on the role that motives play.[180] As should be clear by now, Ibn al-Wazīr affirms that human beings have free will. Reminiscent of the Muʿtazili doctrine, man is by no means com-

176 For Abū l-Ḥusayn, existence (*wujūd*) was tied to essence. Nothing non-essential could exist independently; cf. al-Ḥayyī, *al-Muntazaʿ min al-Durar al-farāʾid* fs. 6b, 26b; Madelung and Schmidtke, *Rational Theology* 5; Schmidtke, *The Theology of al-ʿAllāma al-Ḥillī* 181–184.

177 Madelung and Schmidtke, *Rational Theology* 5–7.

178 See for example Yaḥyā b. Ḥamza, *al-Tamhīd* i, 120–122.

179 Ibn al-Wazīr, *Īthār al-ḥaqq* 285, 295.

180 Abrahamov, A Re-Examination 215.

pelled (*jabr*) to do anything he does not also will to do or for which he has no motive.[181] Human beings choose whether to perform or omit an action in concrete circumstances that are related to command or prohibition. This choice renders an action either an act of obedience or of disobedience. And this choice determines whether or not human beings deserve praise or blame, reward or punishment. As became evident, for example, in Ibn al-Wazīr's *Āyāt al-mubīnāt* where he interprets a verse often used to defend the doctrine of predestination, God does not "lead astray" (*iḍlāl*) before this is deserved in one way or another.[182] The choice is not unaided, as for example there may be a motive, which God may influence.[183] But it is man's choice nevertheless, and therefore his own act and his own merit.[184]

Generally, motives are considered to be under divine influence.[185] So even if opinions differed on the degree of divine influence on motives, Ibn al-Wazīr was able to claim agreement between the schools in the sense that human beings do not perform their part of the action entirely independently. God could influence their choice in a certain direction. Yet, when and to what degree He does so is to be left within the realm of uncertainty.[186] Again the question of guidance is used as an example: Guidance is understood by Ibn al-Wazīr as

181 ʿAbd al-Jabbār argued that man is responsible for his actions because it is his own will and his own motive that causes him to perform these actions. Motives consist in the knowledge, presumption or belief that performing a particular act is beneficial or averts harm; cf. Madelung, Late Muʿtazila 246. However, according to ʿAbd al-Jabbār, the act is not necessitated by the preponderant motive. For the difference between ʿAbd al-Jabbār's concept of motive and that of Abū l-Ḥusayn al-Baṣrī as rendered by Ibn al-Malāḥimī see especially Madelung, Late Muʿtazila 250–257; al-Kamālī, *al-Imām al-Mahdī* 270.

182 See for example Ibn al-Wazīr, *al-Āyāt al-mubīnāt* 285.

183 For example, motivation is influenced by all kinds of knowledge, including necessary knowledge. Necessary knowledge is created by God in man. However, man still has to decide between items of knowledge and motives, according to ʿAbd al-Jabbār; cf. Gimaret, *Théories de l'acte humain* 48–49; Madelung, Late Muʿtazila 246.

184 Ibn al-Wazīr, *al-Rawḍ al-bāsim*, 359.

185 In the case of Bahshami theologians like ʿAbd al-Jabbār, such an example for a motivation created by God would be the warner (*khāṭir*) who initiates the first duty of philosophical reflection (*naẓar*). For the connection between motive and warner in ʿAbd al-Jabbār's thought, see Ghaneabassiri, Epistemological Foundation 83–84. Furthermore, it is God who creates the necessary knowledge, as I discussed above. "God could be seen to be directly responsible, thus, for the basis of all motivation of action and for the actuality of that which leads man to seek God, viz., the desire, knowledge, and fearful concern that impel man to seek the locus of his ultimate well-being, as also He furnishes the material evidence that will lead to the knowledge thus sought and the possibility of understanding them." Frank, Fundamental Assumptions 13.

186 Ibid., 13.

the creation of incentives to do good. This is called *luṭf*, *hidāya*, *ʿiṣma* or *taysīr* in different contexts. In the context of the point in question, Ibn al-Wazīr calls it *taysīr* in the sense that God makes the righteous path easier by providing motives. The strength of the motives He creates, or whether He omits to guide in particular cases, is determined by God's wise, yet unknown purposes.[187]

The discussion of an action's motive is yet another point for Ibn al-Wazīr to argue for harmonization, and one where Abū l-Ḥusayn al-Baṣrī's school again proves conducive to the task. Abū l-Ḥusayn held that there is no action without a motive and that the preponderant motive is a necessitating cause of the action—a concept that was adopted by Fakhr al-Dīn al-Rāzī, as discussed above in the case of divine will.[188] However, for Fakhr al-Dīn al-Razī the preponderant motive is caused by God. Accordingly, he deployed the concept as a means to prove determinism.[189] In contrast, Abū l-Ḥusayn al-Baṣrī used the concept to prove that man is truly responsible for his actions. He argued that man's actions are known to be his by necessity (*ḍarūratan*). According to him, it is self-evident to man that his own actions occur according to his motives. Furthermore, all *compos mentis* know intuitively that it is good to praise one who does good or reprimand an evildoer. Or if one asks another to do something, he knows by necessity that the other is the producer (*muḥdith*) of the respective action.[190]

This necessity by which the ascription of the action to the agent and the resulting responsibility is known suits Ibn al-Wazīr's initial statement that the point of agreement—human responsibility—is evident. For Ibn al-Wazīr, this is the general tenet that is known in the natural human disposition (*fiṭra*). Although Ibn al-Wazīr affirms that God has an influence on human motiva-

187 Ibn al-Wazīr, *al-ʿAwāsim* vi, 116–117.

188 Madelung takes this information on Abū l-Ḥusayn's position from Ibn al-Malāḥimī. Abū l-Ḥusayn not only holds that the action occurs according to a motive, as the Bahshamiyya do; according to him, the motive necessitates the action and there is no action without a motive. Ibn al-Malāḥimī apparently somewhat mitigated this strict stance to a very high probability; cf. Madelung, Late Muʿtazila 249–250. This is confirmed by Ibn al-Wazīr's rendering of Abū l-Ḥusayn; cf. Ibn al-Wazīr, *Masʾalat al-ikhtilāf* 368; Ibn al-Wazīr, *al-Rawḍ al-bāsim* 363.

189 For Ashʿaris like Fakhr al-Dīn al-Rāzī, God's responsibility for causing a preponderator was so clear that "denying that acts require a preponderator is tantamount to denying the Creator," as Hoover put it; cf. Hoover, *Ibn Taymiyya's Theodicy* 144.

190 Cf. al-Ḥayyī, *al-Muntazaʿ min al-Durar al-farāʾid* f. 81b. Ibn al-Wazīr argues that the Muʿtazila and the Ashʿariyya all agree on the coexistence of necessitating motive (*talāzum al-dāʿī fī-l-afʿāl*) and free choice (*ikhtiyār*); cf. Ibn al-Wazīr, *al-ʿAwāṣim* vii, 78–79. Again Ibn al-Wazīr claims that Abū l-Ḥusayn ascribes the creation of motive to God, without negating free choice (*ikhtiyār*); cf. ibid., vi, 120.

tion, the self-evidence of human responsibility for human action takes center stage as compared to the more elusive divine influence on the preponderant motive in the choice of particular action.[191]

Summing up this discussion, the human part does not pertain to the essence of the action. But it is this human part which belongs to the "clear side" rather than the "hidden side" that causes the conflict and mutual charge of unbelief. This focus on the clear side, where the ascription of actions to human choice and performance is obvious, leaves the hidden side in the realm of the ambiguous. Focussing on the clear side means focussing on the agreement, whereas requiring detailed understanding of the hidden side may result in mutual charges of unbelief. And the clear side suffices to absolve God of the false suspicion of injustice. This suits Ibn al-Wazīr's rejection of probing into matters beyond the reach of human understanding. Rather, what needs to be known can be known by the *fiṭra* that all human beings have in common.[192]

On the hidden side, the modes of origination are less clear and less agreed upon because they are beyond what can be said with certainty.[193] Therefore the opinions concerning them cannot be an issue of mutual *takfīr*. It is impossible to verify their exact nature, as they belong to the realm of things deferred to God's knowledge and purposes.[194] What is important and also agreed upon, is the fact that God does play a part. Yet, the part that He plays consists neither in the sinfulness of a given act, nor in any kind of coercion exercised on the human being against his will. As a crucial consequence, nothing intrinsically evil can be ascribed to God.

Ibn al-Wazīr's own understanding of God's part in the occurrence of human action attests to the epistemology of ambiguity he is known for. The term in question is *khalq* (creation): "The conviction that they [human actions] are created (*makhlūqa*) in the sense that they are foreordained (*muqaddara*) is sufficient. And it is considered sound by all."[195]

A little earlier in *Īthār al-ḥaqq*, while expounding on the divine name "the Afflictor" (*al-Ḍārr*), Ibn al-Wazīr explains what he means by foreordainment and correlates it with divine wisdom: "However, what concerns God's fore-

191 In response to the question of how God would invalidate the excuse of sinners if He was the one to create motives, Ibn al-Wazīr replies: "If the argument is grounded on the proof of God, His justice and His wisdom, there is no further need to remove any of the futile excuses that they insist on." Cf. ibid, 116–136, quote 122.

192 Ibn al-Wazīr, *Īthār al-ḥaqq* 323.

193 Cf. Hajar, *Ibn al-Wazīr wa-manhajuhu* 356.

194 The minor importance ascribed to understanding this hidden side is also said to be the reason why the *salaf* did not mention this side; cf. Ibn al-Wazīr, *Īthār al-ḥaqq* 281.

195 Ibid., 324.

ordainment of it [the evil action] according to human choice out of a wise purpose, this is like His foreknowledge (*sābiq al-ʿilm*) of it."[196]

But how could God permit a sinner to sin eventually and thereby violate His will, unless He could not keep the disobedient from sinning? Or could the sinner do nothing but sin, and has God commanded something impossible? This issue of *taklīf mā lā yuṭāq* requires explanation with regard to the role of divine guidance in human action. For Muʿtazilis, it is one of God's duties to provide right guidance (*luṭf*) wherever it is possible. Given that the sinner does not accept guidance, it must be concluded that God could not have given him guidance. For Ashʿaris, it would be inconceivable that the sinner could refuse something that God wanted executed (i.e. guidance). Hence, God must have wanted to the sinner to go astray.

For Ibn al-Wazīr, God's wisdom again serves as a means to defer understanding of the inexplicable element of the idea, with the purpose of maintaining harmony with His other names and attributes as well as upholding the harmonization of different doctrines. The only way in which Ibn al-Wazīr would concede to calling God the creator (*khāliq*) of human actions is in the sense of foreordainment (*taqdīr*) and prescience (*sābiq al-ʿilm*).[197] In this sense, God could have brought forth the neutral part of the human action that He knew the human being would choose and appropriate, and then choose His own action according to some wise, often hidden, purpose that takes into consideration what He knew of the human being's choice. But this is not predictable by human beings in particular cases and goes beyond the requirements of justice. In *al-ʿAwāṣim*, Ibn al-Wazīr concludes a section on the foreordainment of evil actions with the following statement:

> We conclude all this with a subtle point, which is the secret of all this speech and its core: Punishment merely because of merit takes the rank of the indifferent (*mubāḥ*), which really means futility where God, the Exalted, is concerned, because it does not become preponderant [on either side] except out of a desire or whim. It cannot occur on God's part unless in reference to a wise purpose. Hence, one must say that the punishment that certainly happens to the unbelievers is preponderant because of a wise purpose other than sin.[198]

196 Ibid., 174.

197 Cf. ibid., 311. The concept of *taqdīr* as foreknowledge or even as will or a synonym of creation (*khalq*) is not new to the Muʿtazila; cf. al-Ḥayyī, *al-Muntazaʿ min al-Durar al-farāʾid* fs. 86b–87b.

198 Ibn al-Wazīr, *al-ʿAwāṣim* vi, 151.

Foreordainment of evil actions and punishment is thus taken beyond justice. Thereby, Ibn al-Wazīr can go beyond the certainty that dictates knowledge of divine actions determined by the requirements of divine justice.

This would provide an answer to the great mystery of the creation of unbelievers. Accordingly, God could have created people of whom He knew that they would choose disobedience, and foreordain this disobedience by bringing into existence the action that they would choose in a manner rendering it disobedience. Though playing a part in the occurrence of the sinful action, God is not the agent. His creative task consists in establishing what He knew would occur. Establishing this occurrence instead of preventing it aims at a good end and happens out of a wise purpose. His foreordainment of what would effectively be a sin on the part of the disobedient human being is not aimed at the sin for its own sake.

The above mentioned story of Abū Lahab is an example.[199] God commanded something relatively—not absolutely—impossible when He commanded Abū Lahab to do something He knew Abū Lahab would not do (i.e. to believe, in accordance with Islam), and that He knew Abū Lahab would be punished for. He could have forestalled His own judgment by giving him more guidance. Yet He did not, because of a wise and just purpose unknown to human beings.

In the section above on Ibn al-Wazīr's concept of wisdom, I referred to Abū l-Ḥusayn al-Baṣrī's position on the inexplicability of God's decision not to give the sinner a constitution (*binya*) receptive to divine guidance. Abū l-Ḥusayn and his followers apparently agreed that an unknown purpose may be the reason why God did not give a different constitution to one He knew would sin. Although this does not conform to Ibn al-Wazīr's understanding of the human *fiṭra*—which is always receptive to guidance in its original state—it leaves the aspect of God's reasons for lack of guidance among His hidden purposes and hence beyond the realm of human understanding.

In conclusion, Ibn al-Wazīr can claim agreement on the question of human responsibility which concerned theologians of all different schools. The uncertainty about God's own part in the account, deferred to divine wise purposes, forestalls a mutual charge of unbelief for representatives of different opinions.[200] What Ibn al-Wazīr achieves by all this is that, on the one hand, God's actions and will is not beyond human assessment in a general way—God does not do anything evil in itself—yet they are beyond assessment in many particular cases on the other: if a certain action appears evil, this is because human beings do not know what good lies behind it. This is true for God's own actions

199 See 212–213 above.

200 Ibn al-Wazīr, *Īthār al-ḥaqq* 376.

as well as for the influence He has on the actions of human beings. And if a particular interpretation of the hidden side appears to result in a conclusion not accepted by one school or scholar, the impossibility of certainty in this question must be invoked.

Once again, it is the Muʿtazili school of Abū l-Ḥusayn al-Baṣrī that is conducive to finding common ground between the theological schools that vie for influence in the Yemeni Zaydiyya of Ibn al-Wazīr's day. And once again it is the positions of this theological school among the Muʿtazila that come closest to Ibn al-Wazīr's own concepts.

4.2 *Ibn al-Murtaḍā's Concept of Human Actions*

Al-Kamālī states that Ibn al-Murtaḍā paid more attention to the question of human actions than to any other theological issue.[201] And indeed, if understood in the wider context of human responsibility, the question receives considerable attention in *Kitāb al-Qalāʾid* and its commentary *al-Durar al-farāʾid* due to its close link to the concept of divine justice. For Ibn al-Murtaḍā, human actions are clearly brought into existence (*iḥdāth*) by human beings. God cannot will evil actions, neither His own nor those of human beings.[202] Even less could He be the creator of them. Like the famous leader of the Bahshami Muʿtazila, ʿAbd al-Jabbār, Ibn al-Murtaḍā argues that human actions must be ascribed to human agents because they happen according to their motives.[203] In contrast, God, being just and wise, cannot have a motive to do evil. Human free will is expressed in the choice between various motives. Praise and blame follow according to this choice. Indeed, that is how one knows that human actions originate from them.[204] Motives do play a role and God does have an influence on them; however, the role of motives is merely a relative one (*iʿtibārī*).[205] Acts do not necessarily occur according to a preponderant motive in Ibn al-Murtaḍā's thinking. Thus God cannot be said to determine actions through the creation of motives.[206]

---

201 Al-Kamālī, *al-Imām al-Mahdī* 287.

202 Cf. Ibn al-Murtaḍā, Kitāb al-Qalāʾid 59–60; al-Ḥayyī, *al-Muntazaʿ min al-Durar al-farāʾid* f. 78b. For an in-depth discussion of causality in the Yemeni Zaydiyya prior to Ibn al-Murtaḍā, see Thiele, *Theologie in der jemenitischen Zaydiyya* 59–116.

203 On the defense of ʿAbd al-Jabbār's concept of human actions against the charge of determinism based on the relationship between action and motive, see Madelung, Late Muʿtazila 245–248.

204 Ibn al-Murtaḍā, Kitāb al-Qalāʾid 61.

205 Cf. al-Ḥayyī, *al-Muntazaʿ min al-Durar al-farāʾid* fs. 81a–b.

206 Cf. Ibid., fs. 81a–b. This again agrees with ʿAbd al-Jabbār's reasoning; cf. Madelung, Late Muʿtazila 247–248.

In line with Bahshami teaching, Ibn al-Murtaḍā considers capacity (*qudra*) as the necessary element for an action's occurrence.[207] It is in this regard that God plays a part in human actions, because it is God who creates the power that the human being needs in order to perform an act. Yet it also illustrates the Muʿtazili idea of the autonomy of the human agent, since God's act is restricted to creating a neutral power of which the human being can dispose according to his choice.[208] The verb *aqdara* is used to describe God "caus[ing] man to have a capacity."[209] As a vital constituent of this concept of capacity, it always relates to an action and its contrary, and thus leaves the possibility of either action or non-action. Hence, the existence of capacity does not necessitate the occurrence of the act (*al-qudra mūjiba lil-maqdūr*) as it does in the teachings of what Ibn al-Murtaḍā calls "the later generations of Ashʿaris."[210]

Ibn al-Murtaḍā does not explicitly state that acts in their neutral form exist in non-existence in any of the consulted material on the question of human actions. However, a number of points indicate that he follows Bahshami teaching on this question. For one thing, his view on the intellect's ability to discern good and evil independently shows that he considers the aspect that implies either blame or praise to be merely an attribute or accident of the act.[211] According to Ibn al-Murtaḍā, as conveyed by al-Ḥayyī, an act is evil because of "its occurrence in a certain manner" (*li-wuqūʿihi ʿalā wajh*).[212] Thus, Ibn al-Murtaḍā fits into Ibn al-Wazīr's general tenet of the "not independent" responsibility of the human being. Nevertheless, his support of the *akwān*-theory discussed above clearly bespeaks the fact that accidents are real entities in Ibn al-Murtaḍā's thinking, which human beings would bring into existence, thus becoming the autonomous agents and creators of their acts. Accordingly, Ibn al-Murtaḍā, along with the Bahshami Muʿtazila, insists that human beings are truly the agents who bring actions into existence (*iḥdāth, ījād*). God is not connected to human acts themselves by an act of creation (*khalq*). Although

---

207 Cf. Frank, Fundamental Assumptions 10.

208 Ibn al-Murtaḍā, Riyāḍat al-afhām 125.

209 For this translation of *aqdara*, see Abrahamov, A Re-Examination 210.

210 According to al-Ḥayyī, Ibn al-Murtaḍā admits that al-Juwaynī, al-Ghazālī and Fakhr al-Dīn al-Rāzī concede an effect to human capacity. However, they deny that the deployment of that capacity is truly at the disposal of human beings' will and free choice; cf. al-Ḥayyī, *al-Muntazaʿ min al-Durar al-farāʾid* fs. 81a–b. What Ibn al-Murtaḍā ascribed to these later Ashʿaris was already part of the teaching of al-Ashʿarī himself; cf. Frank, The Structure of Created Causality 30. According to Abrahamov, al-Ashʿarī never explicitly denied that *qudra* has effective influence on actions, cf. Abrahamov, A Re-Examination 212.

211 Cf. al-Kamālī, *al-Imām al-Mahdī* 311.

212 Ibn al-Murtaḍā, Kitāb al-Qalāʾid 59; cf. al-Ḥayyī, *al-Muntazaʿ min al-Durar al-farāʾid* f. 67b.

He admittedly has power over all objects of power, this does not extend to all particular actions (*ʿalā aʿyānihā*).[213] As a logical consequence, Ibn al-Murtaḍā, supposedly along with the Muʿtazila and the Zaydiyya, rejects the ideas of *maqdūr bayna qādirayn* and *kasb* outright.[214] *Maqdūr bayna qādirayn* is inconceivable to him, because one object of power cannot be related to two powers, as the object of power in question (the action) could possibly exist and not-exist (*mawjūdan maʿdūman*) at the same time. This is so because according to Bahshami teaching, only one agent can be the cause of an event.[215] Furthermore, an action is performed according to the will of the agent. Thus, of two agents (*qādirān*) one may will the action while the other may not will it.[216]

Kasb is similarly inconceivable to Ibn al-Murtaḍā.[217] The theory of *kasb* presupposes another concept of power. According to this concept, the power to act is created by God and appropriated after the choice and in the moment of action. After the creation of the power, the human being has no further opportunity to act otherwise. Opponents of *kasb* like Ibn al-Murtaḍā claim that such a human being could not be described as 'able' at all, since ableness (*qādiriyya*) correlates with an act as well as its opposite, and an act must be ascribed to someone who has the ability to perform it.[218] Accordingly, a human being thus described could not be held responsible.[219] Ibn al-Murtaḍā holds this view even against those of the Ashʿariyya whose position he considers closest to his own, in that they concede an effective causality (*taʾthīr*) to power or capacity. Again, he takes issue with their claim that this effective causality renders the occurrence of the action inevitable.[220]

But beyond such ontological consideration of *maqdūr bayna qādirayn* and *kasb*, Ibn al-Murtaḍā is more concerned with the ethical implication of both

213 In *Riyāḍat al-afhām*, Ibn al-Murtaḍā writes that "the Eternal is capable of all kinds of objects of power, every kind and at all times without end. Yet, it is not said '[capable] of them [objects of power] in their particular occurrences,' because of the impossibility of 'one object of power for two wielders of power'." According to Ibn al-Murtaḍā, there are ten kinds of objects that are within human power and thirteen kinds that are exclusively within God's power; cf. Ibn al-Murtaḍā, Riyāḍat al-afḥam 126–127.

214 Cf. al-Hayyī, *al-Muntazaʿ min al-Durar al-farāʾid* f. 83b.

215 Cf. Frank, Structure of Created Causality 25.

216 Ibn al-Murtaḍā, Kitāb al-Qalāʾid 59; al-Ḥayyī, *al-Muntazaʿ min al-Durar al-farāʾid* f. 84a.

217 Ibid., f. 84b.

218 Ibn al-Murtaḍā, Kitāb al-Qalāʾid 59–60; al-Ḥayyī, *al-Muntazaʿ min al-Durar al-farāʾid* f. 80b.

219 Ibid., f. 84a.

220 Apparently, Ibn al-Murtaḍā also discusses other concepts of *kasb* even more inconceivable to him, as for example that of al-Ashʿarī; cf. al-Ḥayyī, *al-Muntazaʿ min al-Durar al-farāʾid* fs. 84a–86b; al-Kamālī, *al-Imām al-Mahdī*; on the later Ashʿari theory referred to above, see al-Ḥayyī, *al-Muntazaʿ min al-Durar al-farāʾid* f. 85b.

concepts. He rejects them because, to him, they imply divine responsibility for evil human actions. Neither the idea of *maqdūr bayna qādirayn* nor of *kasb* could be maintained without jeopardizing God's justice. Both concepts are part of Ibn al-Murtaḍā's theory of God's justice in general and of man's independent rational discernment (*taḥsīn wa-taqbīḥ*) which we identified as a major key to the understanding of different concepts of divine justice and wisdom. In Ibn al-Murtaḍā's thought, justice must always be comprehensible. Hence God's actions and human actions must be explicable and manifestly distinct from one another in order to discern good and evil in them.

4.3 *Conclusion*

In sum, for Ibn al-Murtaḍā it is crucial to determine God's involvement in the act exactly in line with the typical Muʿtazili agenda of championing God's justice. The principle of God's just purposes is the end and goal of the argument. Ibn al-Murtaḍā aims to prove that God is just and can therefore not be attributed with any part in the evil acts of human beings. Justice and wisdom, or rather God as being just and wise, is almost always mentioned in the same breath and used to argue for the certainty of the results of Ibn al-Murtaḍā's reasoning.

This stands in contrast to Ibn al-Wazīr, who uses the concept of God's wisdom in order to keep God's particular actions outside the realm of certain human knowledge. Besides leaving God's exact role on the ontological level of the action unexplained, Ibn al-Wazīr defers God's particular decisions as to when and how He influences a human agent to God's wisdom and His wise purposes. Justice is not the final end. Yet, since independent rational discernment is maintained as a vital part of the concept of wisdom, God's goodness is preserved without violating the human ability to discern the moral value of God's or man's actions per se.

The fact that Ibn al-Murtaḍā restricts the divine part to a creating capacity indicates two things: firstly, God's part is more clear than in Ibn al-Wazīr's theory of human actions; and secondly, God's part is more restricted than in Ibn al-Wazīr's thinking (as it must conform to the conditions of human knowledge and principles of good and evil). For Ibn al-Murtaḍā, knowing precisely what role God plays is not as unimportant as Ibn al-Wazīr would have it. After all, it has a considerable effect on defining God's justice. The fact that God's part is restricted to creating the human being's power is something every individual must know (*farḍ ʿayn*).[221]

221 Cf. ibid., f. 83a.

This alone would be a case in point for the thesis that Ibn al-Wazīr attempts to restrict the realm of certainty, namely of theology, and extend the realm of the probable, namely law. To him, it suffices to know that human beings are responsible for their actions. He sees no need to speculate about what God does, with the result that they stand in opposition to one another on these points.

5 Conclusion

According to Frank, the systems of the central figures of the Basran Muʿtazila and Ashʿariyya, Abū ʿAlī al-Jubbāʾī and Abū l-Ḥasan al-Ashʿarī, are too distinct for dialogue, because neither conceded validity to the fundamental assumptions of the other.[222] Ibn al-Wazīr, in contrast, seeks to demonstrate precisely the opposite, namely that they—or at least their later adherents—do agree in their most basic assumptions. What belongs to these assumptions and what does not—that is, what unites the Muslim community and what separates them—occupied much of Ibn al-Wazīr's thinking and writing. Ḥajar, in his analysis of Ibn al-Wazīr's theology, was convinced that Ibn al-Wazīr was right to assume agreement.[223]

As a final comment on Ibn al-Wazīr's theology, a reference back to al-Ṣubḥī's statement about Ibn al-Wazīr's unique role in the theological discourse is due. Al-Ṣubḥī writes that Ibn al-Wazīr's contribution to *kalām* consisted in its elevation from a polemic to the nature of a religious science (*ʿilm dīnī*). A major feature of the way Ibn al-Wazīr practiced this "religious science" is the harmonization of apparently conflicting concepts in order to arrive at general doctrines agreed upon by all. Much of this harmonization and broadening was made possible by Ibn al-Wazīr's concept of God's wisdom. It is then really Ibn al-Wazīr's concept of God's wise purposefulness filling the gap left open by the superiority of God's knowledge that effected the shift from a polemic to a religious science. The superiority of this knowledge is kept in the realm of human understanding by asserting a general morality shared by God and human beings. God's purposes do not need to be known in order to assert the wisdom and goodness behind them.

Ormsby, in analyzing al-Ghazālī's concept of "the best possible world," suggests that the Muʿtazili doctrine of optimistic purposefulness (*al-aṣlaḥ*) may

222 Frank, Structure of Created Causality 75.

223 Hajar, *Ibn al-Wazīr wa-manhajuhu* 395–396.

have been a major reason for the initial rift between the Muʿtazila and the Ashʿariyya.[224] Ibn al-Wazīr's doctrine of divine purposefulness again represents a middle way. In line with Muʿtazili thinking, human beings can expect every divine act or command to have a purpose that would ultimately have to be called good in itself according to human standards of good. Yet, this purpose is usually beyond human knowledge or understanding in its particular occurrence. In conclusion, it appears that Ibn al-Wazīr constructed his theological views around his concept of God's wise purposefulness in order to arrive at a doctrine supposedly acceptable by Muʿtazilis, Ashʿaris and really all who are endowed with the original disposition (*fiṭra*) given by God.

The concept of *ḥikma* allows Ibn al-Wazīr to leave a considerable part of doctrine in the realm of ambiguity. This is highly expressive of his own view of God beyond mere harmonization. He counteracts systematization as well as mutual charges of unbelief by referring the particular implications and effects of general doctrines and theological tenets to divine wisdom. Indeed, Ibn al-Wazīr's theology culminates in the concept of the hiddenness of God's wise purposes as the end of the theological endeavor. The goodness of God's purposes behind His actions and the human inability to know more than their goodness expresses the difference between the perfection of divine knowledge and the limitedness of human knowledge.

The juxtaposition of Ibn al-Wazīr's theological thought with that of Ibn al-Murtaḍā—and therefore that of the Bashamiyya—has revealed a considerable difference between their concepts of divine wisdom. Although the concept is present throughout the whole theological reasoning in both cases, it performs a different function in each. Ibn al-Murtaḍā's concept of divine wisdom is tantamount to his concept of divine justice. Thus it is used to prove the correctness of his Zaydi-Muʿtazili doctrine in great detail. In contrast, for Ibn al-Wazīr the concept is linked to God's superior knowledge and the inability of human beings to penetrate it in great detail. It is the variable that "interprets the ambiguous" (*taʾwīl al-mutashābihāt*), as he states repeatedly. Thus it is used to incorporate a great number of different doctrines into one general tenet. Whereas the Muʿtazili concept of wisdom brings greater theological certainty, Ibn al-Wazīr's concept of wisdom preserves theological ambiguity. Whereas Ibn al-Murtaḍā's concept paints a detailed picture of a just God, Ibn al-Wazīr's concept paints a vague picture of a good God. Whereas Ibn al-Murtaḍā's concept can be employed to exclude many theological schools and trends from

224 Ormsby, *Theodicy in Islamic Thought* 21–22.

the correct doctrine, Ibn al-Wazīr's concept can be employed to include many theological schools and trends into one correct doctrine.

Furthermore, the thought of Abū l-Ḥusayn al-Baṣrī was the teaching most conducive to harmonization from among the Muʿtazila. Ibn al-Wazīr often referred to it in order to argue for essential agreement. Examples are Abū l-Ḥusayn al-Baṣrī's equation of will and preponderant motive, his notion of motive as a determining force for action, of the possibility that one action be ascribed to two agents or of the necessary nature of the knowledge that man is responsible for his actions. With Abū l-Ḥusayn al-Baṣrī as a support for his own thinking, Ibn al-Wazīr could not be blamed as easily for abandoning the Muʿtazila-dominated realm of Zaydi theology entirely. He seems to have represented a current within the Zaydiyya that favored the Muʿtazili school of Abū l-Ḥusayn al-Baṣrī over the prevalent Bahshami Muʿtazila which had great influence on contemporaries like Ibn al-Murtaḍā. This does not mean that Ibn al-Wazīr should be considered either a Zaydi or a Muʿtazili, but rather that he made use of a school of thought that seemed conducive to harmonization with other schools, yet was also acceptable to his contemporaries in light of the Zaydi entrenchment in Muʿtazili teaching. In contrast, Ibn al-Murtaḍā endorsed the Bahshami focus on the human ability to have certain knowledge not only of generalities but also of details of the nature and moral value of things and actions, along with the ensuing expectation to define the truth of doctrines in all its intricacies. Inferring from God's justice a non-negotiable understanding of God's role in human action is only one example. In this case, the detailed reach of human knowledge forestalls divine wisdom from going beyond what the human intellect knows to be just. And with divine justice as a central feature of the theological system, it would be hard to imagine how a different understanding of God's role in human action could coexist. Thus, amplifying the role of particular theological doctrines in defining the Zaydi identity and hierarchically relating them to different versions of these doctrines naturally works towards an increased distance between the Zaydiyya and other theological as well as legal schools that increasingly shared their regional, political and intellectual horizon.

CHAPTER 5

The Structure of Legal Authority in Ibn al-Wazīr's Thought

Ibn al-Wazīr maintains that he was initially prompted to conduct extensive studies across schools by two doctrines prevalent in the Zaydi and Muʿtazili teachings he grew up with. According to those two doctrines, emulation was prohibited in doctrinal matters (*lā taqlīd fī-l-uṣūl*) as well as for persons capable of legal interpretation, because "every *mujtahid* is correct" (*kull mujtahid muṣīb*) in legal matters.[1] While the first doctrine played a central role in his investigation of the theological teachings and sources of his contemporaries and led him to claim that the coexistence of different interpretations of a number of merely probable secondary doctrines was a given, his understanding of the second doctrine allowed him to widen the scope of probability in Islamic law.

1 The Theory of Infallibilism and the Probability of *Ijtihād*

The probable nature of the results of a *mujtahid*'s endeavor is at the root of both the theory and the practice of *ijtihād*. The interpretation of legal indicators leads a *mujtahid* to a conclusion about rules for cases not explicitly stipulated by the source texts. The conclusion the *mujtahid* arrives at is what he has to adopt and apply, as it is built on what seems to him to comprise the highest probability of being correct. Applying that which is conjectural is the *mujtahid*'s certain duty.[2] Scholars or schools like the Twelver-Shiʿa and the Ẓāhiriyya who have rejected the aspect of probability in Islamic law at one point or another have consequently also rejected *ijtihād* in the process of the interpretation and application of law.[3] Where probability is admitted, other

1 See for example Ibn al-Wazīr, *Kitāb al-Qawāʿid* f. 93a.

2 In fact, as Ibn al-Wazīr puts it in *al-ʿAwāṣim*, "All the deeds of rational people are built on suppositions and the weighing out of those that contradict each other." Cf. Ibn al-Wazīr, *al-ʿAwāṣim* iii, 397.

3 Cf. Zysow, *Economy of Certainty*. This is also illustrated in a number of dissertations. See for example Osman, The History and Doctrine of the Ẓāhirī *Madhhab*; Tobgui, The Epistemology of *Qiyās* and *Taʿlīl*.

 | DOI:10.1163/9789004381117_007

issues arise. While one scholar arrives at a ruling based on the interpretation of the conjectural signs that seem most probable to him, other scholars come to different conclusions. But those different rulings are likewise based on conclusions from indicators that seem most likely to them. A number of questions have arisen early in the history of Islamic law as a result of this theory: How shall the underlying concept be interpreted? And how shall the process and result of the scholars' endeavors be evaluated from an epistemological viewpoint? Two major trends have prevailed throughout the centuries, one assuming that "every *mujtahid* is correct" (*kull mujtahid muṣīb*) and the other that only one *mujtahid* finds the truth (*al-ḥaqq maʿa wāḥid*). The theory of *ijtihād* became so central in Muslim legal theory that al-Ghazālī went so far as to say that one who did not hold to a particular theory of *ijtihad*—that of infallibility in his case—was no *mujtahid* at all.[4] Far from being cohesive groups, the representatives of the first theory are called infallibilists (*muṣawwiba*), and those of the second are termed fallibilists (*mukhaṭṭiʾa*). Bernand, referring to ʿAbd al-Jabbār and al-Shāfiʿī, names the Muʿtazila-affine ʿUbayd Allāh b. al-Ḥasan al-ʿAnbarī (d. 168/785) from Basra as being the first to formulate the principle of infallibilism.[5] Names of early Muʿtazili representatives of fallibilism frequently mentioned in the sources are Abū Bakr al-Aṣamm (d. 201–202/816–7),[6] Ismāʿīl b. ʿUlayya (d. 218/833–834)[7] and Bishr al-Marīsī (d. 218/833–834).[8]

The most extensive analysis of the theories on fallibility or infallibility of *ijtihād* in the context of epistemology has been undertaken by Zysow.[9] Bernand's helpful discussion treats the different theories in relation to a particular con-

4 Likewise al-Bāqillānī; cf. Zysow, *Economy of Certainty* 276.

5 Ibn al-Wazīr mentions him only once, and in the context of using another scholar's books if the handwriting is ascertained; cf. Ibn al-Wazīr, *al-ʿAwāṣim* i, 345. Ibn al-Murtaḍā quotes al-ʿAnbarī as one who claimed that even in the rational questions every *mujtahid* is correct; cf. Ibn al-Murtaḍā, Miʿyār al-ʿuqūl 194. On al-ʿAnbarī in the context of *ijtihād*, see also Zysow, *Economy of Certainty* 263; Ṣārim al-Dīn, *al-Fuṣūl al-luʾluʾiyya* 281, 289; Bernand, L'*Ashbah* 154–155. Ibn Taymiyya rejects the claim that al-ʿAnbarī supported infallibility in the *uṣūl*; cf. Ibn Taymiyya, *Fatāwā* xviii, 138; similarly the editor of Ṣārim al-Dīn, *al-Fuṣūl al-luʾluʾiyya* 377, footnote 1.

6 On al-Aṣamm, see Madelung, *Der Imām al-Qāsim b. Ibrāhīm* 42–43; Aḥmad b. Yaḥya b. al-Murtaḍā, *Ṭabaqāt al-Muʿtazila* i, 76–77. Ibn al-Murtaḍā mentions 225/840 as the date of his death.

7 On Ibn ʿUlayya see Zysow, *Economy of Certainty* 26, 246.

8 Cf. Zysow, *Economy of Certainty* 265; Ṣārim al-Dīn, *al-Fuṣūl al-luʾluʾiyya* 377; Ibn al-Murtaḍā, *Minhāj al-wuṣūl* 766–767; Bernand, L'*Ashbah* 158. On al-Marīsī see Zysow, *Economy of Certainty* 265.

9 Zysow, *Economy of Certainty* 463–492.

cept penetrating those theories, namely that of verisimilitude (*al-ashbah*).[10] The significance for the present question pertains to the consequences of the different theories for the system of legal schools. Zysow has claimed that supporting the theory of infallibilism threatened the institutionalized legal schools because it individualized the legal process. This is so, because infallibilism necessitates that each scholar who performs *ijtihād* and applies the results of this *ijtihād* is correct by means of his performance. The correctness is based on the compliance with the certain duty of *ijtihād*. For lack of independent objective standards to evaluate the result, the only measurement for the correctness of his ruling is the quality of his performance of *ijtihād*. His *ijtihād* is valid if it complies with the rules of analogy. This is because the interpretative process of the theory of infallibilism in its classical form is brought into the realm of certainty—and therefore stability—by the *mujtahid*'s application of the rules of analogy in his *ijtihād*.[11] As Zysow puts it: "When it comes to extending the law, the only rule that is certain is the obligation of analogy. By applying this rule, the jurist can be certain that his result is valid."[12] The correctness of the ruling itself cannot be known. Yet, the ruling is to be followed by the *mujtahid* himself and by those emulating him. The absence of an outward standard is counterbalanced by the inner standard of the *mujtahid*: he must follow what seems most probable to him.

Infallibilism was introduced to and adopted in Zaydi legal methodology under the influence of al-Mahdī Abū ʿAbdallāh al-Dāʿī (d. 360/970). In the Caspian Zaydiyya, the followers of Imam al-Qāsim b. Ibrāhīm al-Rassī (d. 246/860) and Imam al-Nāṣir b. Utrush (d. 304/917) had developed into two groups of legal schools that were divided by legal differences. Because of those differ-

---

10 Verisimilitude is defined as something that has 'the quality of seeming real;' cf. "verisimilitude," *Merriam-Webster.com*. In this context, it should be described as something that has most similarity to the truth. To my knowledge, it was first introduced to the discussion of *al-ashbah* by Bernand; cf. Bernand, L'*Ashbah* 151. Bernand's discussion contains an aspect of *al-ashbah* not mentioned by Zysow, namely in terms of analogy between different existing rulings where *al-ashbah* is equated with "the most likely evidence." Bernand, L'*Ashbah* 167–170; cf. Zysow, *Economy of Certainty* 267–269.

11 This is not so for al-Bāqillānī in his radical infallibilism (*al-muʾammima fī l-taswīb*), who maintained that there is no special method of identifying the cause and that "the relation between any evidence and the subjective probability of the jurist was purely fortuitous." Cf. Zysow, *Economy of Certainty* 261.

12 For the most helpful explanation of *ijtihād* and its former equation with *qiyās*, see Zysow, *Economy of Certainty* 260–261. Scholars who widely reject analogy usually reject the theory of infallibilism as a consequence. An example in our context would be the Yemeni scholar al-Shawkānī; cf. Haykel, Dissolving the *Madhāhib* 350.

ences they condemned each other (*yukhṭiʾū baʿḍuhum baʿḍan*). Al-Mahdī Abū ʿAbdallāh al-Dāʿī succeeded in uniting the two groups by introducing the principle that the scholars of both groups were correct.[13] A similar effort is ascribed to an imam of the Yemeni Zaydiyya, namely al-Mutawakkil ʿalā llāh Aḥmad b. Sulaymān (d. 566/1170). Imam al-Mutawakkil was active not only in the theological exchange between the Caspian and the Yemeni Zaydiyya, but also in the spread of the idea that correctness was not restricted to the Hādawiyya, i.e. the school of the founder of the Yemeni Zaydiyya, al-Hādī ilā al-Ḥaqq Yaḥyā b. al-Ḥusayn.[14] Consequently, Yemeni *mujtahids* acknowledged imams and *mujtahids* of the Caspian Zaydiyya. Subsequently and only with rare exceptions, the doctrine of *kull mujtahid muṣīb* has theoretically been supported by all scholars of Zaydi legal methodology.

1.1 *Ibn al-Wazīr's Concept of Infallibilism and* al-Ashbah

The most explicit discussion of infallibilism in the writings of Ibn al-Wazīr is found in *al-ʿAwāṣim*. But throughout all of his writings Ibn al-Wazīr leaves no doubt that the infallibility of *ijtihād* is among the central doctrines of his thought. Ibn al-Wazīr's name became so closely linked with the doctrine of *kull mujtahid muṣīb* that al-Iryānī claims Ibn al-Wazīr to be its only defender in his time.[15] For example, Ibn al-Wazīr insists that the *mujtahid*'s duty is to follow his own *ijtihād* based on his own conjecture wherever he defends the prohibition that one *mujtahid* practice emulation (*taqlīd*) of another. Acting according to the most probable conjecture is considered good by reason, where no apodictic certainty can be attained.[16] Most often the infallibility of conclusions based on conjectural proofs is brought forth to counter his opponents' tendency to shift to the realm of certainty (*qaṭʿ*) what is really a matter of probability (*ẓann*). Whereas disagreement in the former results in mutual accusation of unbelief and division, differences in the latter are natural and intended by God because of the way he made the world. Ibn al-Wazīr illustrates this point in *Īthār al-ḥaqq*:

> [Concerning] the *furūʿ*-books where every *mujtahid* is correct or rewarded, and the books of Arabic linguistics and the like: [In those] it is impossible to remove the differences about issues similar to those on

13 Madelung, Zaydiyya; al-Akwaʿ, *al-Zaydiyya* 40; Ṣārim al-Dīn, *al-Fuṣūl al-luʾluʾiyya* 283; Ibn al-Murtaḍā, Kitāb al-milal wa-l-niḥal 40.

14 Ṣārim al-Dīn, *al-Fuṣūl al-luʾluʾiyya* 283; see also introduction.

15 Cf. al-Iryānī (intr.), *al-Burhān al-qāṭiʿ* 5.

16 *"Al-ʿamal bi-l-ẓann ḥasan ʿaqlan."* See for example Ibn al-Wazīr, *al-ʿAwāṣim* iii, 403.

> which Moses and al-Khiḍr were in disagreement, or Solomon and David, and concerning which the heavenly hosts argued, because it is what God intends.[17]

The elevation of those sciences (*ʿulūm*) in which rational evidence allows for only one truth, and the obligation to attain those proofs, not only causes confusion for the little experienced; even more so, it causes the community to fall apart. On the other hand, the occasions for applying the maxim that "action according to conjecture is good" (*al-ʿamal bi-l-ẓann ḥasan ʿaqlan*) are quite extensive. On all levels of legal activity, the legally responsible subject is bound to seek merely what seems most probable to him. He must then act in accordance with it, irrespective of whether or not others come to the same conclusion. Thus, Ibn al-Wazīr explains in *al-ʿAwāṣim*:

> This does not contradict the doctrine of the 'correctness of all of the *mujtahidūn*.' This is so because it is said that it pertains to what God requires of them, since God, the Exalted, requires them to expend their highest efforts in the quest for what is correct (*ṭalab al-ṣawāb*), not in the meeting of the same (*iṣābatihi*).[18]

After comparing the *mujtahid* to a rifleman, Ibn al-Wazīr explains that God could not expect either *mujtahid* or rifleman to hit their goal with certainty, because that lies outside their abilities.

> Yet, they have met the goal of God which is the expending of the highest effort in the quest to hit [the goal]. They have not hit the goal that they sought for, which is the hitting [itself]. The one who inquires after the *qibla* is like the one who shoots at the unbelievers in strife [for God's cause] (*jihād*), he hits and he misses. In both, his hitting and his missing, he meets what God intends by seeking the correct.[19]

This is the point at which Ibn al-Wazīr locates two things to be sought, and to be potentially hit or missed: One is what God requests, the other one is what the *mujtahid* searches for. God wants the *mujtahid* to attempt to find the truth (*ṭalab al-iṣāba lil-ḥaqq lā sawāʾ*), the *mujtahid* wants to hit the very truth itself,

17 Ibn al-Wazīr, *Īthār al-ḥaqq* 35.
18 Ibn al-Wazīr, *al-ʿAwāṣim* iii, 401.
19 Ibid.

the thing that he is commissioned to search for. The commonly used example of the Kaʿba and the recess for prayer (*qibla*) helps to explain this idea. Whereas God wants the *mujtahid* to search for the direction in which the Kaʿba lies rather than the Kaʿba itself, the *mujtahid* searches for the Kaʿba itself.[20] Thus, it becomes evident that Ibn al-Wazīr belongs to the infallibilists, like the majority of his fellow Zaydi scholars. What God commissioned the scholar to do is the practice of *ijtihād*. The scholar has lived up to this commission once he has expended great efforts to reach an opinion concerning a particular question of law. Although the result of his *ijtihād* is conjectural, the performance of his duty renders him correct in the compliance with the commission. That is the reason for the correctness of every *mujtahid* who performs his duty of *ijtihād*. He is obliged to reach an opinion by the most probable interpretation of the indicators (*amārāt*). And he is obliged to follow through with this opinion, because it is built on the highest likelihood as it appears to him.

The correct performance of *ijtihād* is what renders the *mujtahid* certainly correct. This, however, does not say anything about the likelihood of the opinion itself. Ibn al-Wazīr does not explicitly mention the term *al-ashbah*, which is used for the ruling that most resembles the decree that would have been sent down by God, had he chosen to do so. Yet, the wording that he uses indicates that he did support the idea of the one correct rule pre-existent with God, even though the *mujtahid* could not be expected to discover it or to know whether he has discovered it. He can only try:

> But to say that there is no particularly appointed object of research (*lā maṭlūb muʿayyan*) is inconceivable because the search needs an object to be sought for that precedes the searching and with which conjecture is connected, like the Kaʿba in the investigation of the *qibla*.[21]

Although Ibn al-Wazīr declares that he has not elsewhere come across the short explanation he himself gave for the issue,[22] his wording very much resembles the phrasing used by al-Manṣūr bi-llāh ʿAbdallāh b. Ḥamza to present the opinion of the supporters of the idea of *al-ashbah*:

---

20 Ibid., iii, 402.

21 Ibid., iii, 402.

22 Ibn al-Wazīr finally found the same thought expressed in the same concise way in Ibn Baṭṭāl's *Sharḥ ṣaḥīḥ al-Bukhārī*. Abū l-Ḥasan ʿAlī b. Khalaf b. Baṭṭāl alias Ibn al-Lajjām (d. 449/1057) was a Maliki scholar in Cordoba and among the first to write a commentary of al-Bukhārī's hadith compilation; cf. al-Dhahabī, *Siyār aʿlām* xviii, 47.

> Those holding to the first opinion [that of the existence of *al-ashbah*] argue that the *mukallaf* is a seeker. There must inevitably be a particular object of pursuit for the seeker. Hence, the search for a thing that is not specifically designated is inconceivable. Accordingly, we know that the inquirer into the direction of the *qibla* necessarily needs a direction which, if he finds it, he has found the truth, yet is excused if he misses it.[23]

The key idea is the pre-existence of the object of seeking (*maṭlūb*). Ibn al-Wazīr acknowledges that hitting the goal is beyond the capability of *mujtahids* (*lā ṭarīq lahum wā-lā ṭāqa*), but the goal must exist by all means, so as not to render the search devoid of meaning. This is similar to the argument of those who hold to the theory of verisimilitude. Here, the "most similar" is sometimes called *al-ashbah* or *al-aṣwab* with respect to God (*ʿinda llāh*), which may be hit or missed.[24]

Elsewhere, we find further indication that Ibn al-Wazīr was not as thorough in the idea of the true correctness of all *mujtahids* as he cared to explain. On one occasion, he compares the kind of correctness attributed to consensus, on the one hand, with that ascribed to the *mujtahid*, on the other. Ibn al-Wazīr shows that the correctness of a *mujtahid* does not go beyond being infallible in the performance of the task given by God. By means of the application of the rules of *ijtihād* he is incapable of committing an obvious (*ẓāhir*) error. Yet, this does not render him exempt from the possibility of falling into a hidden error. That is why his opinion is not authoritative (*ḥujja*) in the way that consensus is. The *mujtahid* does what God wants from him in his *ijtihād*. Whether he hits the goal and finds the correct ruling is beyond his influence. This does not preclude the possibility of God revealing to someone else something—the content of a ruling—that is hidden to the first *mujtahid*. From this, one can deduce that there is a truth that is revealed to some but not to others through no fault of their own. Ultimately, the true knowledge can only be bestowed by God in the manner of necessary knowledge. All *mujtahids* are correct. One of them can only be more correct than the other because of what God reveals.

---

23 ʿAbdallāh b. Ḥamza, *Ṣafwat al-ikhtiyār* 370.

24 Ṣārim al-Dīn, *al-Fuṣūl al-luʾluʾiyya* 283. Different definitions of the term are mentioned by Bernand, Zysow and others: 'that for which the signs are the strongest,' 'the one that has most reward,' 'the ruling that comes closest to the one God would have sent down had he done so,' 'that which can be described by nothing but the most similar (*al-ashbah*);' cf. Zysow, *Economy of Certainty* 267–269; Ṣārim al-Dīn, *al-Fuṣūl al-luʾluʾiyya* 283; Bernand, L'*Ashbah* 169.

Further support for this understanding of *muṣīb* comes from Ibn al-Wazīr's interpretation of Q 21:79, which reads {And [We] made Solomon understand the case [better]; though We gave sound judgment and knowledge to both of them. We made the mountains and birds celebrate Our praises with David—We did all these things.} Here, the difference of opinion is linked to the different degrees of understanding given to both Solomon and his father David. Although both are prophets, commended by God and correct in what they stipulate, the correctness of their understanding differs. But Ibn al-Wazīr does not go so far as to call either of the two *mujtahids* or of the two prophets wrong.[25] He did not make his point very strongly, although he must have known that this very Quranic verse was one much used to argue for the "one true ruling" theory of fallibilism. In this case, God is said to acknowledge the one that has "hit" the correct goal, namely Solomon.

However, the position Ibn al-Wazīr takes on *al-ashbah* does not effect his stance towards the legal schools. It only illustrates once more how Ibn al-Wazīr located the main scope of human intellectual activity in the realm of conjecture, while at the same time affirming the absolute truth of the revelational ideal. The knowledge of the one correct ruling is beyond human access, beyond the access of every single *mujtahid*. God alone knows the truth, but this truth exists. Whether or not God bestows it on one of the *mujtahids*, and if so, then on which, is likewise beyond human knowledge. No *mujtahid* is more likely than another to hit the one correct goal based on any merit of his own.

1.2 *Ibn al-Murtaḍā's Concept of Infallibilism and* al-Ashbah

Ibn al-Murtaḍā dedicated ten pages of one of his most important works on legal theory, *Minhāj al-wuṣūl*, to the question of infallibility. He leaves no doubt that the doctrine of infallibility is central to his legal thinking. However, Ibn al-Murtaḍā does not agree with the above explanation of Q 21:79, neither in support of fallibilism nor of the common take on the theory of *al-ashbah*.

Verisimilitude in the form of *al-ashbah* was an answer that could not be endorsed by many Muʿtazilis like Abū l-Ḥusayn al-Baṣrī or ʿAbd al-Jabbār.[26] It was argued that, according to the theory of verisimilitude, God has commanded the *mujtahids* to find something for which He had not given clear signs. This would be tantamount to a Muʿtazili anathema, namely that God commanded the impossible (*taklīf mā lā yutāq*) in violation of His justice. If,

25 Ibn al-Wazīr, *al-ʿAwāṣim* i, 217–218, 244.

26 Former leaders of the Bahshami branch of the Muʿtazili school like Abū Hāshim and Abū ʿAlī al-Jubbāʾī, having a different understanding of *al-ashbah*, apparently endorsed it; cf. Bernand, L'*Ashbah* 167.

however, signs were given and the scholar who failed to make correct conclusions on their basis was excused, God's justice would likewise be infringed.[27]

Ibn al-Murtaḍā does not fail to treat the challenge to the theory of infallibilism, mentioned by Ibn al-Wazīr and al-Manṣūr bi-llāh ʿAbdallāh b. Ḥamza, according to which the object of seeking had to exist for any search to be valid. However, for Ibn al-Murtaḍā the idea of *al-ashbah* needed only little attention as an argument against infallibility.[28] It was in another context that Ibn al-Murtaḍā's understanding of the term stands out. In his reply to the challenge that some of the companions insisted that any mistake in interpretation would be ascribed to them whereas the correct conclusion would be ascribed to God, Ibn al-Murtaḍā argues:

> It is possible that ʿAlī [b. Abī Ṭālib], Peace be upon him, when he said that 'they have made a mistake' meant that they had missed the strong indicator (*al-amāra al-qawiyya*) because of distraction and negligence in their investigation. Undoubtedly, there are strong and weak signs in the process of evidencing. And if the *mujtahid* is led to the weak [sign] by his *ijtihād* without being deliberately negligent in the searching, then he hits upon that which God wanted, which is that he acts according to his conjecture after he has arrived there by his searching.[29]

A little later in this argumentation, Ibn al-Murtaḍā refers to Abū l-Ḥusayn al-Baṣrī. Abū l-Ḥusayn al-Baṣrī was one of those infallibilists who strongly opposed the notion of a pre-existing ruling abiding with God. Consequently, he must have been opposed to the notion of an external standard in approximation or resemblance to which the correctness of a particular *ijtihād* could be evaluated (*al-ashbah*).[30] To preserve some kind of a benchmark for evaluating *ijtihād* nevertheless, Abū l-Ḥusayn al-Baṣrī redefined the idea of verisimilitude and the meaning of *al-ashbah*. According to him, *al-ashbah* was that which is most likely (*ghālib al-ẓann*) to be the strongest evidence in the mind of the respective *mujtahid*. The *mujtahid* is required to find what is most probably the

---

27 Ibn al-Murtaḍā says that the scholars could not have failed to see the signs most similar to the truth, had they not erred or failed in the performance of *ijtihād*; cf. Ibn al-Murtaḍā, *Minhāj al-wuṣūl* 768–770.

28 Ibn al-Murtaḍā, *Minhāj al-wuṣūl* 774–775.

29 Ibn al-Murtaḍā first mitigates the argument by saying that the reports about it are not *mutawātir* and therefore only probable evidence, unable to have an effect on principles of legal methodology like the question of infallibilism; cf. Ibn al-Murtaḍā, *Minhāj al-wuṣūl* 776.

30 Abū l-Ḥusayn al-Baṣrī, *al-Muʿtamad* ii, 298–299, 396.

reason that dictated the ruling of an original case on the basis of the strongest evidence, so that he can draw his conclusions for a present case. The "most probable" comes to signify the most probable or strongest sign (*ashbah al-amārāt*), rather than the most probable or strongest result. It is important to note that the *mujtahid* is only obligated to find what is the most probable and strongest evidence in his mind, not to find evidence that necessitates the same result for all similar rulings. This latter would be certain evidence, which applies only in the realm of doctrine.[31] Hereby the focus on the process rather than the result in evaluating the *mujtahid*'s endeavor—so central to the doctrine of infallibilism—can be preserved. The meaning of *al-ashbah* is transferred from signifying 'the result most similar to the objectively correct result which cannot be known but is present with God' (*al-ashbah 'inda llāh*), to signifying 'the process most similar to the ideal process somewhat present in the *mujtahid*.'[32]

From the above-mentioned argument used by Ibn al-Murtaḍā it becomes clear that he adopted Abū l-Ḥusayn's idea that the following of the strongest signs becomes the basis of evaluating the *mujtahid*'s efforts (and results). Ibn al-Murtaḍā supports this idea also when he responds to what he considers the strongest argument against infallibilism. He follows up with Abū l-Ḥusayn's idea of the stronger and weaker evidence as a standard when he defines the term mistake (*khaṭa'*). A mistake, according to Ibn al-Murtaḍā, means failing to hit the stronger evidence due to negligence. In this case, the discernment of the weaker and stronger signs requires thorough and serious *ijtihād* so as to avoid negligence and hence a less probable result. But as there is no objective standard for evaluating the result, the likelihood of the accurateness of the *mujtahid*'s ruling depends on his capabilities in performing *ijtihād*. Beyond this general level of discussing the standard for evaluating a scholar's *ijtihād*, Ibn al-Murtaḍā brings another element into the debate:

> It is possible that [Muḥammad], peace be upon him and upon his family, when he said 'If he fails, he will have one reward,' meant that if he [the judge] unwittingly ruled in disagreement with his school, he then has the reward of having settled the dispute without getting the reward of having hit the goal of his school. And if he hits upon it, he has two rewards, one for settling [the dispute] and one for meeting the ruling of his school.[33]

31 Ibid., ii, 371, 373, 395.

32 Bernand also shows how Fakhr al-Dīn al-Rāzī took over this notion; cf. Bernand, L'*Ashbah* 168.

33 Ibn al-Murtaḍā, *Minhāj al-wuṣūl* 776.

It should be noted that the evaluation of the result of the scholar's *ijtihād* could be provided by the framework of a school of law according to this reasoning. Hence, the lack of stability resulting from the subjective nature of the infallibilists' notion of *ijtihād* would be counterbalanced by a new standard of evaluation: the school's doctrine and set of principles. It can be imagined that the framework of a school with its doctrines, principles and existing rulings could substantiate a standard for evaluating the subjective enterprise of the *mujtahid*. Then, beyond the *mujtahid*'s knowledge of the rules of interpreting revelation, it would be his knowledge of the rules and doctrines of the school by which the likelihood of the accurateness of his *ijtihād* could be evaluated. The theory of verisimilitude provides a theoretical frame for this evaluation.

Ibn al-Murtaḍā's identification of *al-ashbah* with *ghālib al-ẓann* speaks in favor of the notion that there is a difference in the strength of indicators that goes beyond what seems most likely in the individual scholar's mind. External factors like the school's principles and doctrines could be the ideal in approximation to which the strength and probability of a scholar's signs could be measured. As Ibn al-Murtaḍā suggests when he writes about the two rewards: 'hitting' the correct ruling is tantamount to arriving at a conclusion in line with the doctrine of the legal school. Consequently, a scholar would not be required to arrive at the ruling that is as close as possible to the one that 'is present with God.' Rather, he would be required to arrive at a ruling as close as possible to the one that is present within the principles and rulings of his school.

In conclusion, the differences between Ibn al-Wazīr's and Ibn al-Murtaḍā's understanding of the principle that 'every *mujtahid* is correct' are not significant at first sight. Both defend the doctrine of infallibilism. That is also why both are confronted with the results that the doctrine has on the system of the legal schools. But while Ibn al-Murtaḍā attempts to counterbalance the disseminating effect of the doctrine by a narrowing and consolidating of the legal identity of the Zaydiyya, Ibn al-Wazīr strives to open up the field of legal interpretation to a wider circle in order to transcend the school boundaries. Ibn al-Murtaḍā's explanation of the possibility of "hitting" and the two rewards, as well as his interpretation of *al-ashbah*, can be seen as the theoretical framework for the narrowing down of the scope of legal interpretation. It shows how an external standard can be introduced into the realm of equally probable rulings by means of a legal school. For Ibn al-Wazīr, the probable nature implied in the doctrine of infallibilism does not allow for qualification by an external standard. Although some results of *ijtihād* may be closer to the truth than others, this truly remains beyond human grasp—in terms of knowledge as well as in terms of obligation. Hence we can affirm that epistemological considerations concerning the extent and source of knowledge are manifest in the background of each scholar's response to the problem of infallibilism.

2 The Possibility of *Ijtihād* and the Existence of *Mujtahids*

Two questions of significance for the existence and structure of legal schools have long occupied Muslim authors on legal theory, as well as subsequent western researchers. The first question, discussed by Muslim scholars since the 5th/11th century, was whether there could be an age without *mujtahids*. Secondly, the distinct question of whether "the gate of *ijtihād*" was closed became prominent from the 10th/16th century onwards. Among western scholars, Schacht and Hallaq were the most prolific of those working on these questions. However, they, like Muslim scholars throughout history, took opposing sides.[34]

The discussion of the second question as to whether or not "the gate of *ijtihād*" was closed in the course of the development of Islamic law is largely determined by the respective definitions of the term *ijtihād*. The debate between Schacht and Hallaq suggests that the gate was closed in one sense, but not in another. If one speaks of an *ijtihād* that draws exclusively and directly from the texts of revelation by means set down in the classical manuals of *uṣūl al-fiqh*, the gate appears to have been more or less shut since the mid-4th/10th century. However, if the term is understood to mean any kind of interpretative activity of religious texts including legal opinions of earlier scholars, the gate can hardly said to be closed. Calder agrees with Schacht that the gate was closed around the end of the 3rd/beginning of the 10th century in that the Muslim community embraced the principle of school affiliation about that time. He writes that "Hallaq will be correct in asserting that the gate of *ijtihād* did not close, if he distinguishes clearly the two types of *ijtihād*—independent and affiliated."[35] What this effectively means is that all the interpretative activity henceforth took place within the confines of the legal school and refers to the texts and principles supposedly laid down by the founding imam. According to Calder, subsequent works on the hermeneutical structure of legal reasoning were written to justify and consolidate the structure of the legal school based on the authority of the founding *mujtahid*. They were not, for the most part, handbooks on how to arrive at independent judgements in supposedly new cases.[36]

34 See especially Hallaq, On the Origins; Schacht, *An Introduction*.

35 Calder, Al-Nawawī's Typology 157.

36 Ibid., 158.

To my knowledge, none of the debates around this question in modern western research includes the Zaydiyya. An important Zaydi doctrine says that no time can be without a *mujtahid* from among the *ahl al-bayt*.[37] According to al-Akwaʿ the Zaydi *madhhab* distinguishes itself from the Sunni legal schools by "opening the gate of *ijtihād*." Interestingly, he does not merely use the term Zaydiyya in this context, but rather speaks of the "Zaydi-Hādawī *madhhab*" referring to Imam al-Hādī ilā l-ḥaqq.[38] This raises the question: To what kind of *ijtihād* was the gate opened—independent or affiliated? Al-Kibsī claims that the generations following the early imams were absolute *mujtahids* who merely agreed on the principles of their predecessors.[39] Zysow and Haykel show how the structure of the Zaydiyya provided that its authority was not officially based on the legal rulings of one single founder, in contrast to the Sunni schools. Rather, it was the principles (*qawāʿid*) which guided the legal interpretations of a number of early imams of *ahl al-bayt* to which later Zaydi scholars owed their authority.[40] Consequently, later scholars could produce a legal opinion that was not directly based on an existing opinion. Rather, it was based on principles that a particular set of later scholars (*muḥassilūn*) had recognized in the background of a multitude of opinions of preceding imams. Another version of school identity locates it in the affiliation with the theological doctrines of the early Zaydi imams.[41] In either case, the claim to the continuance of *ijtihād* cannot justifiably be said to refer to absolute and independent *ijtihād*.[42] It should be remembered how the infallibilism theory was introduced into the Caspian as well as the Yemeni Zaydiyya, as touched upon above. In both cases there were currents within the Zaydiyya that associated themselves with different scholars based on the latters' legal doctrine. An independent or absolute *mujtahid* is unlikely to do either, associating himself with a particular school or a particular set of legal principles. Consequently, the answer to the question whether or not *ijtihād* exists is largely determined by the concept of *ijtihād* that is held by a particular school or scholar.

---

37 ʿAbd al-Allāh b. Ḥamza, *Ṣafwat al-ikhtiyār* 377; Ibn al-Wazīr, *al-ʿAwāṣim* ii, 120; Ibn al-Murtaḍā, Kitāb al-Intiqād; Ibn al-Murtaḍā, *al-Baḥr al-zakhkhār* xvi, 92.

38 Al-Akwaʿ, *al-Zaydiyya* 40.

39 Al-Kibsī, *al-Furūq al-wāḍiḥa* 84.

40 Haykel and Zysow, What Makes a *Madhhab*? 338. The imams usually meant in this context are al-Qāsim b. Ibrāhīm al-Rassī (d. 246/860), his son Muḥammad b. al-Qāsim (d. 2), his grandson al-Hādī ilā l-Ḥaqq Yaḥya b. al-Ḥusayn (d. 298/911) and the latter's two sons Muḥammad (d. 310/922) and Aḥmad (d. between 315/927 and 322/934).

41 Haykel and Zysow trace this idea of school identity back to Imam al-Manṣūr ʿAbdallāh b. Ḥamza in his *Kitāb al-Shāfī*; cf. ibid., 335–336.

42 Strothmann, *Staatsrecht* 70.

2.1 *Ibn al-Wazīr's Position on the Existence of* Ijtihād

Ibn al-Wazīr's main argument for the existence of *ijtihād* is that *ijtihād* is a collective duty which has to be performed at all times. If Muslims were no longer able to do so they would be charged with the impossible (*taklīf mā la yutāq*). Next to the explicit duty of *ijtihad*, Ibn al-Wazīr's views are driven by the identification of knowledge with the science of the religious law. *Fiqh* is knowledge (*ʿilm*) even though the results of *ijtihād* belong into the realm of the conjectural (*ẓannī*). Hence it is what Ibn al-Wazīr calls conjectural knowledge which can be called knowledge in some respects, as explained above. In the preamble of his *Kitāb al-Qawāʿid* as well as in several instances in *al-Rawḍ al-bāsim* and *Īthār al-ḥaqq*, Ibn al-Wazīr connects the absence of *mujtahids* with a well known tradition according to which the demise of knowledge occurs only in connection with the disappearance of scholars.[43] The feared demise of knowledge is clearly identified with the demise of *ijtihād*. The duty to know can thus be identified with the duty to practice *ijtihād*. Accordingly, legal opinions not proceeding from *ijtihād* are equivalent to *fatwās* not based on knowledge (*yuftī man laysa bi-ʿilm*).[44]

Hallaq suggests that the question of whether there could be an age without a *mujtahid* is mainly determined by eschatological discussions around the approaching of the end of times. In his view, the discussion was mainly theological and only received attention in law as a consequence.[45] To my mind, the reasoning in this question seems rather to reveal whether theology or law should be the main field of human activity in a scholar's thinking. Johansen describes the increasing distance between *fiqh* scholars and theologians from the 4th/10th century onwards as a correlation of the different practical functions that the respective groups had in the Muslim community. Whereas theology is occupied with the rational justification of religious truths, with possible implications for political legitimacy, "*fiqh* serves as a normative reference for

43 The tradition reads as follows: "Verily, God does not remove knowledge entirely, but he takes away knowledge along with the scholars. So that, when no scholar remains, people will take ignorant men as leaders who will then give legal opinions without knowledge, thereby falling in error and leading others astray." Ibn al-Wazīr, *al-Rawḍ al-bāsim* 64. For other instances where Ibn al-Wazīr connects the idea of the absence of *ijtihād* with the demise of knowledge in the sense of the prophetic traditions, see for example ibid., 77; Ibn al-Wazīr, *Īthār al-ḥaqq* 141–142; Ibn al-Wazīr, *Kitāb al-Qawāʿid* f. 62b. The preamble of one copy of *al-Rawḍ al-bāsim* also refers to traditions in connection with the demise of *ijtihād*. However, the preamble is not quoted here because I did not obtain the copy which contained it.

44 Ibn al-Wazīr, *al-ʿAwāṣim* iii, 121.

45 Hallaq, On the Origins 140–141.

a universally valid system of justice."[46] Whereas theologians argue for the general authority of their doctrines based on the concept of the conclusive power of human reason's demonstrative proofs, legal interpretation merely claims to find probable translations of religious truth into the particular cases of individuals. Locating the reasoning with regard to the question of the existence of *mujtahids* therefore indicates which field is considered the most appropriate for human intellectual activity.

Among the Zaydiyya, the question of the existence of *mujtahids* is typically discussed in the context of the theory of the imamate, one of the principle Zaydi theological tenets. Accordingly, there must be a candidate who qualifies for the position at all times, and *ijtihād* is a major requirement for qualification.[47] Explanations according to which *ijtihād* may cease to exist "because God takes away knowledge along with the scholars at the end of times" are refuted by the belief that one group in the Muslim community will preserve the truth until the day of judgment.[48] Ibn al-Wazīr refers to this Zaydi belief as well. Acquiring legal knowledge cannot be impossible, because knowledge cannot be taken away until the day of judgement.[49] Yet, for Ibn al-Wazīr, this is not tied to the imamate or the *ijtihād* of an imam, but rather to the practice of *ijtihād* per se. Consequently, the conclusions he draws from the decrease of knowledge is neither the concession to a wide permissibility of *taqlīd* of earlier imams or contemporary scholars who judge according to their principles, nor to doctrinal and political affiliation.

Ibn al-Wazīr's contemporary and teacher in his early years, ʿAlī b. Muḥammad b. Abī l-Qāsim, seems to have denied the possibility of *ijtihād* altogether. Unfortunately, his letter that provoked Ibn al-Wazīr's most extensive defense of *ijtihād* is lost. Therefore Ibn Abī l-Qāsim's views can only be reconstructed tentatively from the quotes and insinuations of his opponent Ibn al-Wazīr.[50] Apparently, Ibn Abī l-Qāsim thought *ijtihād* to be exceedingly difficult (*taʿadhdhara, taʿassara*) in his day. So difficult, indeed, that it could no longer be performed. To him, the *taqlīd* of the early imams was the only remaining chance

46 Johansen, *Contingency* 26.

47 Cf. Abū Zahra, *al-Imām Zayd* 331; Ibn al-Murtaḍā, *al-Baḥr al-zakhkhār* xvi, 92; i, 110; al-Kamālī, *al-Imām al-Mahdī* 453–459; Madelung, *Imam al-Qāsim* 141; Strothmann, *Staatsrecht* 4, 70.

48 Ibn al-Murtaḍā, Kitāb al-Intiqād. This explanation was part of the well received legal methodology of the Maliki Ibn al-Ḥājib (d. 646/1248–1249).

49 Ibn al-Wazīr, *al-ʿAwāṣim* ii, 118–119.

50 Sometimes Ibn al-Wazīr quotes from his former teacher's letter. At other times, he takes the position of his opponent for granted and then draws conclusions from it that his opponent cannot agree with in the typical *ilzām* style.

to preserve legal knowledge and be rightly guided.[51] Although it is not certain exactly how Ibn Abī l-Qāsim understood the terms *taʿadhdhara* and *taʿassara*, he obviously concluded the necessity of emulating the dead scholars (*taqlīd al-amwāt*).[52] In contrast, Ibn al-Wazīr's conclusion from the decrease of knowledge is the necessity to strive for individual *ijtihād*:

> He [Ibn Abī l-Qāsim] says that it [*ijtihād*] is exceedingly difficult and impossible. That implies that he believes that there are no *mujtahids* in this time, because if there was a *mujtahid* in this time, its [*ijtihād*] impossibility would no longer be in question and the ability [to perform *ijtihād*] would have to be confirmed with certainty. His—may God strengthen him [Ibn Abī l-Qāsim]—words indicate that the time is without *mujtahids*. But he—may God strengthen him—disregards what follows from this. What follows is that striving for *ijtihād* is an individual duty upon him and upon us together, because that is the rule if a collective duty is not performed.[53]

The apprehension toward the decrease of knowledge in the Muslim community is faced in two different ways: On the one hand, Ibn al-Wazīr's contemporaries refer to the doctrine of the imamate and affiliation with the doctrines and principles of the founding imams to preserve knowledge. Ibn al-Wazīr, on the other hand, intends to achieve that goal by expanding the activity of legal interpretation.

Notably, Ibn al-Wazīr frequently asks Ibn Abī l-Qāsim why he does not think the common believer or scholar is capable of arriving at conjectural knowledge in legal interpretation, while requiring him to arrive at a detailed and certain knowledge of God, his attributes and many other doctrinal questions without *taqlīd*.[54] Although we do not know what Ibn Abī l-Qāsim would have replied, the answer to that question lies at the heart of the epistemological difference between Ibn al-Wazīr and his Zaydi-Muʿtazili contemporaries: Whereas Ibn al-Wazīr's Zaydi-Muʿtazili contemporaries locate the most important area of human intellectual activity in the realm of what they consider objective

---

51 See for example Ibn al-Wazīr, *al-ʿAwāṣim* i, 345–346.

52 See Ibn al-Wazīr, *al-ʿAwāṣim* i–iii, for example i, 346; cf. Ibn al-Wazīr, *al-Rawḍ al-bāsim* 73. Ibn al-Wazīr discusses what the term *taʿadhdhara* may imply. Aḥmad b. al-Ḥasan b. Yaḥyā l-Qāsimī (d. 1375/1955), in his later refutation of *al-Rawḍ al-bāsim* and defense of Ibn Abī l-Qāsim, insists that the latter does not mean utter impossibility (*muḥāl*).

53 This is only one of many instances in which Ibn al-Wazīr adduces this argument; cf. Ibn al-Wazīr, *al-ʿAwāṣim* i, 263.

54 Ibid., i, 271–272; 276.

certainty, Ibn al-Wazīr locates it in the realm of individual conjecture. It will be remembered that he divides knowledge into the necessary and the conjectural. Legal knowledge to him is no less significant than doctrinal knowledge arrived at by inference. Consequently, the affiliation with the doctrines of the early Zaydi imams could be of no greater importance than any *ijtihād* per se. Loyalty to those doctrines and principles would not secure more knowledge or higher epistemic value than individual *ijtihād* based on methods accepted by the whole of the Muslim community. As became clear in preceeding chapters, Ibn al-Wazīr warns against spending extensive efforts in the attempt to acquire certain and detailed knowledge of what cannot be known in the realm of doctrine and theology. To him, the realm where knowledge should be acquired is the realm of law, where probability is all that can be achieved. Once again, the space he leaves for the individual to acquire knowledge, albeit conjectural knowledge, is greater than what his contemporaries in their focus on doctrine allow for.

2.2 *Ibn al-Murtaḍā's Concept of the Existence of* Ijtihād

Ibn al-Murtaḍā is a known defender of *ijtihād.* While this topic is singled out in some sources as one on which Ibn al-Wazīr and Ibn al-Murtaḍā were united against Ibn Abī l-Qāsim, others portray them as opponents even in this respect.[55] Yet a brief look at Ibn al-Murtaḍā shows that even his defense of *ijtihād* was limited and thus differs from Ibn al-Wazīr's position.

Ibn al-Murtaḍā claims in his *al-Munya wa-l-amal* that in contradistinction to adherents of the Sunni legal schools, the Zaydis do not draw their affiliation to the Zaydiyya from following in the *furūʿ*. Rather, it is supposed to be the commitment to the legal and theological doctrine of the early imams which constitutes the Zaydi identity.[56] On the other hand, there is a statement in Ibn al-Murtaḍā's major work on *uṣūl al-fiqh, Minhāj al-wuṣūl,* that the "Zaydiyya applies the sayings of their imams" like the Shafiʿiyya and other Sunni schools apply (*taʿmal bi-*) the opinions of al-Shāfiʿī, Abū Ḥanīfa etc. According to Ibn al-Murtaḍā, "the schools have been established" so that no one issues

55 According to Ibn Abī l-Rijāl in *Maṭlaʿ al-budur* iv, 148–149, the dispute of the two scholars evolved around theological matters, whereas they agreed concerning *ijtihād*; similarly Aḥmad b. ʿAbdallāh, *Taʾrīkh Banī l-Wazīr* 33. In contrast, al-Iryānī in his introduction to *al-Burhān al-qāṭiʿ* renders the practice of *ijtihād* as the only distinctive feature between the two scholars, Ibn al-Wazīr being the one practicing and promoting it, unlike Ibn al-Murtaḍā; cf. al-Iryānī (intr.), *al-Burhān al-qāṭiʿ* 7.

56 Ibn al-Murtaḍā, *al-Munya wa-l-amal* 96; see also Haykel and Zysow, What Makes a *Madhhab*? 336.

opinions based on original inference (*istinbāṭ*) from the evidence in the revelational sources anymore. Yet that does not mean that *ijtihād* is entirely impossible (*taʿadhdhara bi-l-marra*). It only means that it is largely not needful in its independent form.[57] It is likely that Ibn al-Murtaḍā expresses a common opinion of his time, confirming what Calder says about the function of writings on the basic hermeneutical instruments. After all, Ibn al-Murtaḍā authored what remains to this day one of the greatest one of the greatest compendia of Hādawī-Zaydi *fiqh*. Similarly, Ibn al-Wazīr's brother al-Hādī insists on the Zaydi norm of knowing the imam of the time, with *ijtihād* as requirement of the imamate. Yet he praises the early *ahl al-bayt*, notably al-Hādī ilā l-Ḥaqq, and insists on the adherence to their school to a degree that renders the possible *ijtihād* of a contemporary *mujtahid* of little weight. Indeed, the *ijtihād* of a contemporary *mujtahid* is valid only as far as it agrees with the opinions of Imam al-Hādī ilā l-ḥaqq and other *ahl al-bayt*:

> If a *mujtahid* who is not from among them, agrees with one of their *mujtahids* in his *ijtihād*, there is no obstacle to having recourse to him in this question, because he in his ruling is like one referring back to them, boarding the ship[58] and not leaving it. If someone does not agree with them, he opposes the command to resort back to the agreement with them and to walk in their path (*al-sulūk fī madhhabihim*) in accordance with what has been shown above: their consensus is authoritative, must be followed and must not be opposed.[59]

Ibn Abī l-Qāsim seems to have gone yet further. Unlike Ibn al-Murtaḍā and al-Hādī, he does not refer to the sufficiency or the excellence of what legal interpretation already exists. Rather, to him the lack of independent *ijtihād* was caused by the supposed incapability of acquiring sufficient information about the sources so as to judge on their reliability and applicability in a given question. Throughout the first three volumes of *al-ʿAwāṣim*, Ibn al-Wazīr exerts himself to refute his former teacher's claims. Ibn Abī l-Qāsim apparently holds that neither the legal verses of the Quran (*āyāt al-aḥkām*), the traditions (*aḥādīth*), the truthfulness of transmitters, nor the Arabic language along with other required source material can be known any longer to a sufficient degree for the performance of *ijtihād*. Such thinking is rationalized by general legal max-

57 Ibn al-Murtaḍā, *Minhāj al-wuṣūl* 797.

58 The whole of *ahl al-bayt* was often depicted as a ship that ensures safe travels across the water.

59 Al-Hādī b. al-Wazīr, *Hidāyat al-rāghibīn* 94.

ims (*qawāʿid*) of the Zaydiyya such as one listed in the commentary on Ibn al-Murtaḍā's *fiqh* compendium *Kitāb al-Azhār* by Aḥmad b. Ṣalāḥ al-Sharafī, "When *ijtihād* is exceedingly difficult, *taqlīd* is permissible (*idhā taʿadhdhara l-ijtihād jāza l-taqlīd*)."[60]

It is quite evident that Ibn al-Wazīr's contemporaries do not mean the independent *ijtihād* when they use the term for the contemporary activity. Yet, they do not distinguish the one from the other with different terms. Ibn al-Wazīr does not use any distinctive terms either. But he apparently considers all kinds of *ijtihād* possible. Yet the main point of controversy is the independent *ijtihād*. The challenges expressed by Ibn Abī l-Qāsim and the replies of Ibn al-Wazīr focus on the legal verses, prophetic traditions and the Arabic language. Many passages begin with such phrases as:

> "The *sayyid* [Ibn Abī l-Qāsim]—may God strengthen him—mentioned that *ijtihād* is built on the knowledge of the required exegesis of the Quran and he states that this is exceedingly difficult (…)." "Then, he [Ibn Abī l-Qāsim] renders the knowledge of the traditions exceedingly difficult for the *mujtahid* (…)." "Then, he doubted in the knowledge of linguistics and of Arabic, which are the foundation of the exegesis of Quran and Sunna."[61]

The two scholars do not primarily discuss whether the opinions of earlier imams can be understood or whether the principles behind their opinions can be known.[62] These latter questions would have to be at issue if Ibn al-Wazīr and his teacher were concerned with the affiliated *ijtihād*. However, Ibn al-Wazīr and his teacher discuss the requirements for independent *ijtihād*. Ibn al-Wazīr insists that everything that is needed for *ijtihād* on every level is available and employable. Indeed, the access and employment of the sources and instruments for *ijtihād* on the highest, the independent level are the basis for *ijtihād* on the lower, the affiliated level as well as for *taqlīd*. For Ibn al-Wazīr, *ijtihād* is possible and *mujtahids* must always exist.

---

60 Cf. al-Kibsī, *al-Furūq al-wāḍiḥa* 62.

61 Cf. Ibn al-Wazīr, *al-ʿAwāṣim* i, 276, 300; Ibn al-Wazīr, *al-Rawḍ al-bāsim* 62–63. For similar examples see Ibn al-Wazīr, *al-ʿAwāṣim* i, 150; iii, 88–89.

62 The practice of extrapolating the legal principles called *takhrīj* is a major task of affiliated *mujtahids* as well as the basis for subsequent affiliated *ijtihad*, as shall be discussed in ch. 5 sec. 6 below.

3 *Taqlīd* and Concepts of Following

The term *taqlīd* is often translated as "following" or "emulation." An early definition of the term was coined by ʿAbd al-Jabbār (d. 415/1025) but may have existed before. He defined *taqlīd* as "the acceptance of the saying of another without evidence" (*qubūl qawl al-ghayr min ghayr ḥujja*),[63] a definition that prevailed in the literature on theology and legal theory beyond the Muʿtazila.[64]

In the broadest sense, the term refers to a so-called *muqallid* who follows a scholar in rational conclusions, or interpretation of the source texts to render a judgement on a given question. In the legal context, *taqlīd* is an essential element of the system of law schools as the counterpart to *ijtihād*. Accordingly, a legal school is structured by the interpretation of one or a few scholars and the following of many laymen.

The correlation of the consolidation of the *madhhab*-system and the prevalence of *taqlīd* is commonly agreed upon in modern research.[65] The different uses of the concept of *ijtihād*, the diachronic development of the concept and the different ranks of the *mujtahids* in relation to the school system have received considerable attention—less so the different nuances of the concept of *taqlīd*.[66]

3.1 *Ibn al-Wazīr's Concept of* Taqlīd *and Following*

It became clear that Ibn al-Wazīr and Ibn al-Murtaḍā both assert the infallibility doctrine as well as the existence of *mujtahidūn*, albeit with different meanings. Starting with Ibn al-Wazīr's notion of *taqlīd*, a considerable part of *al-ʿAwāṣim* as well as *al-Rawḍ al-bāsim* is devoted to the discussion of *ijtihād* and *taqlīd*.

---

63 Cf. Ibn al-Malāḥimī, *Kitāb al-Muʿtamad* 25.

64 For the same definition used by other scholars, see for example Weiss, *Search for God's Law* 717, which investigates the legal methodology of the Shafiʿi Sayf al-Dīn al-al-Āmidī (d. 631/1233). Al-Āmidī adds "compelling" (*mulzima*) to the "evidence." According to Calder, the term was initially defined by the Ashʿari theologian and Shafiʿi jurist Abū Isḥāq al-Shirāzī (d. 476/1083); cf. Calder, Taqlīd. See also Wiederhold, Legal Doctrines in Conflict 243. However, Ibn al-Malāḥimī (d. 536/1141) attests the above definition already for ʿAbd al-Jabbār (d. 415/1025). It is likely to have been in use beforehand because emulation in doctrinal matters (*uṣūl al-dīn*) was already discussed before the 5th/11th century. See for example Omari on Abū l-Qāsim al-Balkhī's (d. 319/931) acceptance of *taqlīd* in doctrinal issues; Omari, The Theology of Abū l-Qāsim 170.

65 Hallaq, *The Origins and Evolution*; Hallaq (ed.), *The Formation of Islamic Law*; Hallaq, *Authority, Continuity and Change*; Hallaq, *A History of Islamic Legal Theories*; Melchert, *The Formation of the Sunni Schools of Law*; Jackson, *Islamic Law and the State*; Fadel, The Social Logic of *Taqlīd*; Aghnides, *Mohammedan Theories*.

66 See footnote above and Calder, al-Nawawī's Typology of *Muftīs* 137–164.

The focus is especially on whether or not *ijtihād* is possible. A more distinct picture of the different nuances of *taqlīd* presents itself in Ibn al-Wazīr's *Kitāb al-Qawāʿid*, in which the reader learns that Ibn al-Wazīr distinguishes between prohibited and permitted kinds of *taqlīd*.

Ibn al-Wazīr's thinking is determined by two duties. First, the duty to attain knowledge and second, the duty to follow the Prophet. For the first duty, it needs to be remembered that Ibn al-Wazīr equated knowledge with *ijtihād*. This is not an unusual equation. Sunni scholars like al-Shāfiʿī or Imām al-Ḥaramayn al-Juwaynī equated *ʿilm* (knowledge in general) with *fiqh* (knowledge of the religious law). In the first two centuries of the history of Islam, knowledge was often identified with tradition (*ḥadīth*) and transmission. It only gained entry into the prolegomena of religious writings as a means of distinguishing religious information in the 3rd/9th century, and in the sense of philosophical or theological knowledge only in the 4th/10th century.[67] But, as we have seen in the section on epistemology, Ibn al-Wazīr backs his equation of knowledge and the performance of *ijtihād* with a philosophical distinction between necessary knowledge on the one hand, and knowledge tantamount to preponderant conjecture on the other. According to Ibn al-Wazīr, the realm of the preponderant conjecture applies in secondary matters of theology as well as in law. In matters of theological doctrine, *taqlīd* is not permitted by the great majority of schools. Most scholars exclude information based on *taqlīd* from the definition of knowledge, even if the content corresponds to reality. Ibn al-Wazīr extends this definition of knowledge to the legal realm of probability, as we have seen above. Although he does not explicitly reject the permissibility of uninformed *taqlīd* for the utter layman that Ibn al-Murtaḍā permitted, he does so implicitly in that he insists on every *mukallaf*'s ability to discern between scholars and gain a basic understanding of their rulings. After all, "*taqlīd* without weighing the evidence is impermissible."[68] This is because the duty to know, as well as the duty to act upon conjecture, applies to all believers. *Taqlīd* in the strict sense of uninformed emulation precludes the performance of this duty on every level—the level of apodictic knowledge as well as of conjectural knowledge—because *taqlīd* in the strict and prohibited sense assumes ignorance of evidence.[69]

The second duty that determines Ibn al-Wazīr's thinking is the duty to follow the Prophet. The charge that seems to have been frequently brought against Ibn al-Wazīr was that he forsook the school of *ahl al-bayt* and therefore, according

67 Cf. Hallaq, Origins of the Controversy 130–131; Rosenthal, *Knowledge Triumphant* 72–96, 210.

68 Ibn al-Wazīr, *Kitāb al-Qawāʿid* f. 94a.

69 Cf. ibid., f. 71a.

to Zaydi thinking, the command of the Prophet Muḥammad to adhere to *ahl al-bayt*. A major incentive in writing the *Kitāb al-Qawāʿid* was to show that he did not violate this Zaydi doctrine.[70] A three-fold division in the introduction is supposed to illuminate the true sense of following (*ittibāʿ, iqtidāʾ*) as grounds for understanding Ibn al-Wazīr's rejection of *taqlīd*. One human being can follow another a) in form (*fī l-ṣūra*), b) in meaning (*fī l-maʿnā*), or c) in form and meaning (*fī l-ṣūra wa-l-maʿnā*).[71] Whereas the latter two correspond to the true sense of following, a mere formal adherence in the sense of outward emulation does not comply with the true sense of following:

> Following the example means that you do something the way your model has done it. That is why the *uṣūlīs* require that agreement exists even in the intention. If the Prophet prayed two *rakʿas* with the intention of complying with a duty, and we prayed the two [*rakʿas*] with the intention of a supererogatory performance, we would not be taking him as an example. There is a subtle point here, which is that 'taking as an example' is unlike *taqlīd*. (…) Even if we supposed that *ahl al-bayt* permitted the *taqlīd* of the dead and someone complied with it [the permission], he would not be taking them as an example, because they never emulated the dead nor promoted it [emulation of the dead].[72]

Thus, outward compliance with the sayings and rulings of *ahl al-bayt* tantamount to emulation of the dead would actually be the very opposite of following the *ahl al-bayt*. Accordingly, striving for the performance of *ijtihād* in order to gain knowledge accords not only with the duty of *ijtihād* itself, but also with the Zaydi claim to adherence to the Prophet's progeny. Therefore, emulation could never be seen as a valid form of complying with the duty to follow in Ibn al-Wazīr's view.

Furthermore, Ibn al-Wazīr distinguishes between the permissibility and impermissibility of *taqlīd* based on three elements involved in the practice: the process of *taqlīd* itself, the emulator (*muqallid*); and the one emulated (*muqallad*).

Firstly and in line with the above-mentioned definition, the prohibition of *taqlīd* applies when someone accepts the judgement of another without asking for proofs. The permitted kind of *taqlīd*, on the other hand, occurs when someone accepts the judgement of another after having received and understood

70 See for example ibid., f. 62b.
71 Ibid., f. 64b.
72 Ibid., fs. 72a–b.

the indicators for the judgment. This refers to the judgement itself as well as to the *muqallid*'s choice of a *mujtahid* to follow. The decision concerning which *mujtahid* to follow must be based on the strongest indicators leading to the highest probability. Strictly speaking, this may not be termed *taqlīd* because indicators are provided.[73] Effectively, however, it is used that way nevertheless. In his attempt to strengthen the legal subject's identity beyond *madhhab* boundaries, Ibn al-Wazīr is therefore majorly concerned with the first kind of *taqlīd*. Indeed, he often refers to the second kind of *taqlīd* as a kind of *ijtihād* in defending the possibility of interpreting sources and weighing indicators in general, and of switching from the compliance with the *fatwā* of one *mujtahid* to that of another in particular. As Weiss points out when discussing Sayf al-Dīn al-Āmidī's (d. 631/1233) *al-Iḥkām fī uṣūl al-aḥkām*, emulation in the prohibited sense is unlike the consultation of a jurisconsult (*istiftāʾ*).[74] Accordingly, Ibn al-Wazīr admits a distinction between qualified *mujtahids* and laymen. An utter layman (*ʿāmmī*) may have to consult a *mujtahid* in a legal issue and then follow his opinion. But he must build his decision to comply with the *fatwā* of a scholar on indicators that speak in favor of the aptness of scholar as well as of the soundness of the *fatwā*. He may not merely follow a *mujtahid* unquestioningly on the grounds that he belongs to a particular legal school. Rather, he must search out the indicator for each scholar's judgement, both in cases of disagreement between scholars and concerning the abilities of the different scholars.[75] Ibn al-Wazīr concedes a degree of understanding and of the ability to weigh indicators and determine preponderance (*tarjīḥ*) to every believer.[76] He does not seem to allow the prohibited kind of *taqlīd* to even the plainest of *compos mentis*. This becomes sufficiently clear in his lamentations at the outset of his *Kitāb al-Qawāʿid*. Although the five "menaces" (*āfāt*) that hinder the understanding of indicators and arguments are not primarily aimed at utter laymen, the claim Ibn al-Wazīr puts on all believers is evident:

> The second calamity is represented by a contemplator who is convinced of his own insufficiency and goes beyond the limit in belittling his own ability. When he hears the correct proof to which his reason leads him

73 Ibn al-Malāḥimī points this out in his definition of *taqlīd*; cf. Ibn al-Malaḥimī, *Kitāb al-Muʿtamad* 25.

74 Weiss, *Search for God's Law* 717–718.

75 For the weighing that needs to be performed by the *muqallid* in case of disagreement, cf. Ibn al-Wazīr, *al-ʿAwāṣim* iii, 125, 137, 140. For the search of indicators (*ṭalab amarāt*) for the scholars' ability to perform *ijtihād*; cf. ibid., iii, 128.

76 Weiss's translation of *tarjīḥ* as "determination of preponderance" expresses the concept most accurately; cf. Weiss, *The Search for God's Law* 730.

> as well, and his heart is compelled to know (…) because of the puniness of his knowledge and the weakness of his understanding, he is convinced that, if the emulated imam were alive, he would have given him an answer. That is a great error which befalls *muqallids* in particular. If they contemplated, they would know that if their reason had reached this degree of inability in discerning, then *taklīf* would no longer apply to them. They would be neither obliged to practice *ijtihād* nor *taqlīd*. If that were not so, what security would a *muqallid* have when he with all the smallness of his knowledge and weakness of understanding chooses the *madhhab* of his imam.[77]

It is very likely that whenever Ibn al-Wazīr speaks of the kind of *taqlīd* permitted to the laymen, he speaks of that kind which includes the acquaintance with the *mujtahid*'s arguments or has substantiated reasons for complying with the ruling of a particular *mujtahid*. Although Ibn al-Wazīr concedes that a certain kind of *taqlīd* is permissible for laymen, he does make it sufficiently clear that this permissibility is merely an exception from an otherwise general prohibition of *taqlīd*.

> The generals (*ʿumūmāt*) prohibit *taqlīd* entirely. There is for example the divine saying [Q 2:166] {when those who have been followed disown their followers}. This is a general verse. (…) These generals can only be particularized by a revelational text or consensus, but there is no text that particularizes it. (…) That consensus is concluded from the action of some of them and the silence of the rest. And it is a consensus on the *taqlīd* of the living in the practical questions of the *furūʿ*. Accordingly *taqlīd* must be permitted in those things only.[78]

Ibn al-Wazīr's reasoning is based on the assumption that *taqlīd* does not constitute knowledge. According to Zaydi-Muʿtazili doctrine, *taqlīd* would have to be prohibited wherever the attainment of knowledge is commanded. Ibn al-

---

77 Ibn al-Wazīr, *Kitāb al-Qawāʿid* f. 63b.

78 Ibid., fs. 65a–b. A practical as well as a tacit consensus merely results in probable particularization. That is why the general impermissibility expressed in the clear Quranic texts remains valid. Ibn al-Wazīr generally rejects tacit consensus. According to him, there are many reasons for a *mujtahid* to be silent other than that he agrees. The absence of evidence for his disagreement is not proof of his agreement. This is another example of Ibn al-Wazir's rejection of the "argument from the absence of evidence;" cf. ibid., fs. 76a–b. For the connection between tacit consensus and a corollary of the argument from the absence of evidence, the "argumentum e silentio," see van Ess, *Erkenntnislehre* 376.

Wazīr refers to the Quranic verse often used to argue in favor of *taqlīd*, namely Q 16:43 which reads: {[Prophet], all the messengers We sent before you were simply men to whom We had given the Revelation: you [people] can ask those who have knowledge if you do not know.}:

> From the word of the Exalted {if you do not know} it must be understood that the wise purpose in asking them [those who have knowledge] is to leave ignorance behind and enter into knowledge. That is why one cannot use it to argue for *taqlīd*. Firstly, because that [leaving ignorance behind] is the understanding that comes to mind most readily to everyone, which no one denies except for lack of tasting the sound. If someone said 'Drink, if you are thirsty!' it would be understood that the intention is to drink water that quenches thirst. (…) Secondly, *taqlīd* does not make one leave ignorance and enter into knowledge. That is why *taqlīd* is prohibited in questions that require the acquisition of knowledge.[79]

It must be borne in mind that Ibn al-Wazīr considers legal knowledge to be a kind of knowledge and *ijtihād* the preservation of knowledge.

Ibn al-Wazīr's second distinction within the term *taqlīd* refers to the emulator himself. Whereas a kind of *taqlīd* is permitted to the utter layman, it ceases to be so once a believer has attained the ability to practice a basic *ijtihād* in one or more questions or disciplines.

> They did not conclude a consensus that *taqlīd* is permitted to the discerning student who is occupied with seeking knowledge and capable of searching the indicators. That is why al-Mu'ayyad bi-llāh stipulated in the *Ziyādāt* that the discerning one must investigate and research the indicators until he has arrived at preponderant probability concerning what he must do.[80]

The case of a student who is able to investigate and discern an issue's evidence necessitates a distinction. Both titles rendered to such a one by Ibn al-Wazīr indicate a high level of activity: "discerning student" (*ṭālib al-ʿilm al-mumayyiz*) or "one aspiring to *ijtihād*" (*mutaḥarrī l-ijtihād*).[81] The distinction thus made is between a layman, on the one hand, who is not occupied with the search for knowledge at all and is therefore permitted to inquire of a scholar, and on

79 Ibid., f. 71a.
80 Ibn al-Wazīr, *Kitab al-Qawāʿid* f. 70b.
81 See for example ibid., fs. 70b, 74b.

the other hand, a layman who is occupied with the memorization of Quran and Sunna as well the analysis of the contained meanings and proofs. Beyond mere acknowledgement, the latter scrutinizes legal opinion of the *mujtahids* as to their proofs until his supposition (*ẓann*) concerning the soundness of an argument reaches overwhelming probability (*rujḥān*). He thereby reaches the rank of a *mujtahid* in a particular question and later in a whole discipline. He remains a student in other areas until the rank of a *mujtahid* is attained in all disciplines.[82]

Ibn al-Wazīr bases this distinction between the two kinds of laymen on the permissibility of *taqlīd* under certain conditions. The permissibility of emulation applies to laymen of the first kind. The general impermissibility of *taqlīd* mentioned in the first distinction, i.e. between the informed and the uninformed process of *taqlīd*, encompasses all other cases and hence prohibits *taqlīd* to laymen and students who have advanced beyond the capabilities of an uneducated layperson.

Ibn al-Wazīr, who knows himself to have the qualities of the "discerning student," is not permitted to practice *taqlīd* at all. In turn, the differentiation within the "discerning student" between being a *muqallid* in some and a *mujtahid* in other areas exposes two possibilities: initially there is the following of a scholar by way of *taqlīd* followed by the information about the evidence and indicators; secondly the student investigates the sources and the contained indicators himself and reaches a judgement.

The third distinction within *taqlīd* refers to the one emulated (*muqallad*). The point at issue is whether the emulated *mujtahid* is alive. Ibn al-Wazīr commits the major part of his *Kitāb al-Qawāʿid* to demonstrating that the emulation of dead scholars (*taqlīd al-amwāt*) is prohibited. Besides arguments from the revelational texts and opinions of scholars,[83] Ibn al-Wazīr provides a consequentialist argument: Emulation of the dead has detrimental effects on the performance of the duty of *ijtihād* in the present times and on the incentive to attain the rank of a *mujtahid*. However, the performance of *ijtihād* is incumbent on the Islamic community at large.

---

82 See for example ibid., fs. 72b, 74a, 84b. The importance this distinction has in Ibn al-Wazīr's thinking becomes obvious from the frequency with which it is iterated.

83 Ibn al-Wazīr repeatedly refers to Zaydi scholars like the Caspian imam Abū Ṭālib al-Hārūnī, the Yemeni imam Yaḥyā b. Ḥamza or the *faqīh* ʿAbdallāh b. Zayd al-ʿAnsī. See for example ibid., fs. 64b or 65b. Ibn al-Wazīr is to date the only known reference for al-ʿAnsī's work on Zaydi legal theory, called *al-Durar al-manẓūma fī uṣūl al-fiqh*, cf. Ansari and Schmidtke (eds., intr.), *Zaydī Theology in the 7th/13th Century Yemen* 11.

> In the *taqlīd* of the dead, there is a great cause of corruption because it is thereby made easy for the *mukallafūn* to omit a certain duty agreed upon to be a duty. This [duty] is *ijtihād* at all times. And there is no doubt that the *taqlīd* of the previous generations is among the strongest reasons for the omission of this duty and the greatest agents of the abolishment of the religious law. (…) If students (*ṭalabat al-ʿilm*) are allowed to practice *taqlīd*, it will be a factor for them to leave *ijtihād*. (…) When seekers of knowledge resort to *taqlīd, ijtihād* will be omitted and the knowledge of the religious law will dwindle away.[84]

Furthermore, Ibn al-Wazīr warns that the emulation of dead scholars often leads to the contradiction of prophetic traditions, based on the unquestioning adherence to their sayings:

> You find that every group (*ṭāʾifa*) prefers an opinion to the clear text in some issues. They imagine that this text is weak or that it needs to be interpreted. (…) The reason is their partisanship for the saying of the dead. If that dead [person] were alive, he would reject what they are doing and prefer the tradition to his [own] opinion. An example [for this] is the preference the Malikiyya gives to feeding a slave as an atonement for sexual intercourse during Ramaḍān in spite of what God's Prophet stipulated and what has been affirmed as sound.[85]

The mere fact that Ibn al-Wazīr spent such a great effort (40 of 75 folios in his *Kitāb al-Qawāʿid*) on demonstrating the impermissibility of this kind of emulation reveals his attitude toward the school system most clearly. As has been made sufficiently clear in research, the formation and consolidation of, as well as affiliation with, a legal school hinges precisely on some manner of emulation of the founders. A scholar's authority as an influential part of a legal school is derived from his reference to the person and application of the rulings of the dead eponym.[86] Most instances in which this issue is discussed refer to the structure of legal authority. Must someone who issues legal opinions (i.e. a mufti) be a *mujtahid*, or can he be a *muqallid* issuing rulings based on the opin-

84 Ibn al-Wazīr, *Kitāb al-Qawāʿid* fs. 72b–73a.

85 Ibid., f. 70a.

86 Hallaq, *Authority, Continuity and Change* 24–120; Fadel, The Social Logic of Taqlīd 193–233; Jackson, *Islamic Law and the State*, especially introduction and 69–83; Jackson, Legal Scaffolding 165–192.

ions of dead scholars? Ibn al-Wazīr clearly rejects the latter idea.[87] Although Ibn al-Wazīr claims wide agreement on the impermissibility of *taqlīd al-mayyit*, support for his prohibition does not seem to abound.

It is evident in Ibn al-Wazīr's threefold distinction within the notion of *taqlīd* that he does not altogether ignore the fact that legally responsible individuals are at different levels of legal knowledge or have different abilities of legal interpretation requiring them to seek legal consultation in some but not in all matters. However, such consultation should happen irrespective of legal affiliation. It involves knowledge of the textual sources and an increase of such knowledge on every level. It follows that religious law is the field of intellectual activity of every legally responsible individual.

3.2 *Ibn al-Murtaḍā's Concept of* Taqlīd *and Following*

Concerning Ibn al-Wazīr's first distinction (i.e. the process of *taqlīd*), it is evident that Ibn al-Murtaḍā is less confident of the layman's ability to evaluate a *mujtahid* or understand the indicators he provides. Although the one seeking legal advice must inquire into the condition of the *mujtahids* and choose an imam to follow, Ibn al-Murtaḍā nevertheless does not think that a *muqallid* needs to or even can understand the arguments for a *mujtahid*'s opinion. One argument provided by the Baghdadī Muʿtazila for the prohibition of unquestioning *taqlīd* refers to the duty to gain knowledge. Ibn al-Murtaḍā responds to this as follows:

> They say: 'The layman is capable of knowledge, therefore he is commissioned with it like the scholar, as is the case with doctrine.' We say: 'As the *mujtahid knows* that his way is *ijtihād*, likewise the layman *knows* for certain that his way is to refer back to the scholar.'[88]

Hence, for Ibn al-Murtaḍā the duty to know does not refer to the knowledge item—the legal ruling—but rather to the duty itself. As became clear in the chapter on epistemology above, Ibn al-Murtaḍā defends every believer's duty to gain certain knowledge in doctrinal matters. To him, the exclusion of *taqlīd* is a vital part of the very definition of knowledge—the knowledge of the indicators and evidence as much as the knowledge that results from these. *Taqlīd* is not permitted in any of these fields of knowledge. It is interesting that Ibn al-Murtaḍā should have denied the common believer the ability to

---

87 Ibn al-Wazīr, *Kitāb al-Qawāʿid* fs. 67a–69a.

88 Ibn al-Murtaḍā, *Minhāj al-wuṣūl* 781.

know the indicators and evidence in the legal realm. This position is explicable by the need for certain knowledge. Ibn al-Murtaḍā stipulates that the layman knows his duty by apodictic proof (*ʿilm qāṭiʿ*). The knowledge that Ibn al-Wazīr would require the layman to arrive at by understanding his *mujtahid*'s arguments would merely be conjectural knowledge because it refers to the judgement itself, which always remains in the realm of the probable. In contrast, the emphasis on the duty to follow without understanding the proof leaves the layman in the realm of the certain. But it also keeps him within the limits of his school because an advancement of his own understanding and striving for independent interpretation of the sources is constrained by the duty to follow. He must follow by implementing a ruling he himself has not investigated at all. In contrast, Ibn al-Wazīr concedes a greater ability to the common believer in the realm of the probable. The kind of *taqlīd* that Ibn al-Wazīr permits is one that leaves room for the development of the layman's ability to discern for himself instead of consolidating the structure of the legal school.

Ibn al-Murtaḍā's stance towards the second distinction (i.e. the emulator) is tantamount to his stance towards the discerning student (*al-ṭālib al-mumayyiz*) discussed below. Therefore, that discussion will merely be anticipated here by stating that Ibn al-Murtaḍā, like Ibn al-Wazīr, requires the *mujtahid* to act upon his *ijithād* once reached, but has less confidence in the ability of the discerning student to do so.

As to Ibn al-Wazīr's third distinction (i.e. the emulated), Ibn al-Murtaḍā's position marks the strongest contrast. He concedes that the emulation of a living scholar is preferable to the emulation of a dead scholar. Nevertheless, he permits *taqlīd al-mayyit* and even endorses it as a common practice:

> We know of a consensus among the Muslims of today that *taqlīd* of the dead scholar is not denied and that it is permitted to emulate him in all of the Muslim regions without pretense or hesitation.[89]

The notion that *taqlīd* of the living is merely preferable to *taqlīd* of the dead was apparently widespread among the Zaydiyya of his time. Ibn al-Wazīr mentions this as a particularly erroneous defense of *taqlīd al-mayyit*, as it rests on the idea that dead scholars need to be emulated because of the absence of qualified living *mujtahids*.[90] Ibn al-Murtaḍā explains that original derivation of legal

89 Ibn al-Murtaḍā, *Minhāj al-wuṣūl* 797–798, quote 798.
90 Cf. Ibn al-Wazīr, *Kitāb al-Qawāʿid* f. 72b.

rulings (*istinbāṭ*) tantamount to original *ijtihād* no longer takes place. The *ijtihād* that occurs in his time is rather

> an agreement with the *ijtihād* of his imam in [the way that] he establishes the questions and indicators. (...) *The mujtahid* of a later generation is no *muqallid*, rather his *ijtihād* agrees with the one whose *madhhab* he has taken hold of, like al-Shāfiʿī.[91]

Ibn al-Murtaḍā argues for the permissibility of *taqlīd al-mayyit* with the unrestricted consensus of Muslims at large. As referred to above, *ijtihād* is no longer to be understood in the independent but only in the restricted sense, namely within the legal school. The parallel drawn between the Zaydiyya and the established Sunni legal schools is telling. In contrast, Ibn al-Wazīr in his consequentialist line of argumentation considers the threat of the absence of *mujtahid* as all the more reason to leave *taqlīd* and strive for *ijtihād* in order to fulfill the collective duty. He refutes the consensus argument based on its composition. The consensus Ibn al-Murtaḍā speaks of apparently consists of the agreement of common people, many of whom are *muqallids* themselves. But according to Ibn al-Wazīr, such a consensus is not valid in matters that belong to the principles (*uṣūl*) of legal theory, like the question of the permissibility of *taqlīd*.[92]

It stands to reason that the attitude taken towards the emulation of dead scholars had a central function in each scholar's vision of the structure of the legal enterprise. Where the *ijtihādāt* of early *mujtahids* and founding imams are prioritized and *taqlīd* of them permitted, the school structure is consolidated and the impetus for *ijtihād* diminished. Where legal interpretation is informed by the sources, even if it be along with proofs and arguments advanced by other scholars, the interpreter is not confined to a particular school.

To conclude, it must be said that Ibn al-Wazīr's claim that the eponyms of a particular legal school insisted that their rulings not be followed or even recorded is not unique. Traditionists like Aḥmad b. Ḥanbal (d. 241/855) are not the only ones said to have rejected *taqlīd*. But this does not alter the effect of claims such as Ibn al-Wazīr's on a legal school and the system of schools as a whole. It would seem extremely difficult to determine what the intentions were behind sayings of early *ahl al-bayt*, and therefore what following in meaning would signify in each particular case. There is much less certainty, and tolerating ambiguity seems inevitable. This is true at least on an objective level,

91 Ibid., f. 72b.

92 Ibid., f. 66a.

especially since Ibn al-Wazīr discourages the use of mechanisms for the extrapolation of such meanings (*takhrīj*) as we shall see below. In contrast, *taqlīd* of the dead as well as unquestioning *taqlīd* in general, both endorsed by Ibn al-Murtaḍā, render it much easier to find a common application of the sayings of the early imams. This would be an application the adherents of a school could emulate in order to fulfill their duty of following.

4 The Requirements (*shurūṭ*) for *Ijtihād*

The changes in what is required of a scholar issuing legal opinions (i.e. a mufti) in Sunni legal theory have been considerable.[93] Hallaq has identified four positions that emerged more or less subsequently one after the other. The first position, represented by scholars of the 2nd/8th–5th/11th centuries, holds that a mufti has to have an encompassing knowledge of the Quran, prophetic Sunna, Arabic language, questions of consensus and *qiyās*. *Qiyās* was later included in the requirement of mastery of legal methodology in general. These were also the requirements a *mujtahid* had to fulfill. In fact, no explicit distinction was made between a mufti and a *mujtahid*. This resulted in the conviction that a mufti had to be a *mujtahid* capable of deriving principles from the main sources and of manifesting them in rulings in new cases. Authors of foundational works on legal theory like the Muʿtazili Abū l-Ḥusayn al-Baṣrī (d. 436/1044) and the Ashʿari Imām al-Ḥaramayn al-Juwaynī (d. 478/1085), whose theories served as standards for later scholarship throughout the different schools, clearly promoted this view: A mufti was to follow his own opinion arrived at by his own legal reasoning and no *muqallid* was allowed to issue legal opinions.[94] The second position, according to Hallaq, resulted from a change in the 6th/12th century. This position claims to concede to the exigencies of reality, namely that non-*mujtahids* do issue, and have indeed issued fatwas, without being prohibited from doing so. Accordingly, a restricted *ijtihād* is allowed for scholars who use the texts and principles of their legal school as sources. The agent of such a practice is called a *mujtahid*, among other things, within the legal schools (*mujtahid fī l-madhhab*).[95] The two other positions emerged from the mid-8th/14th

93 Hallaq, *Iftāʾ* and *Ijtihād* 332.

94 Examples of this first position begin with the definition of al-Shāfiʿī (d. 204/820) and are also documented for al-Shirāzī (d. 476/1083), al-Bāqillānī (d. 402/1013) and al-Ghazālī (d. 505/1111).

95 Hallaq, *Iftāʾ* and *Ijtihād* 36, 41. Examples for this position are numerous. Prominent among them are al-Āmidī (d. 631/1233), Ibn al-Ḥājib (d. 646/1248–1249) and Ibn al-Ṣalāḥ al-

century and either allowed for a *muqallid* to issue fatwas, if there was no *mujtahid* present, or accepted *iftā'* by a *muqallid* without restriction.[96]

Parallel to these positions, a categorization of the ranks of *mujtahids* developed. Whereas throughout the first two and a half centuries of Islamic history (i.e. 1st/7th to mid-3rd/9th century) no scholar seems to have been deprived of the right to conclude legal positions, two to seven different ranks of *mujtahids* were apparently recognized from the 5th/11th century onward.[97] The need for these categorizations was at least partly caused by the tension between the high standard of what was required of a *mujtahid* on the one hand, and the continuous request for legal opinions with which unqualified jurists effectively complied on the other hand.

4.1 *Ibn al-Wazīr's and Ibn al-Murtaḍā's Concepts of the Requirements for* Ijtihād

The first comprehensive list of such requirements was set down in Abū l-Ḥusayn al-Baṣrī's *al-Muʿtamad fī uṣūl al-fiqh* and, with minor changes, adopted by most scholars of legal methodology afterwards.[98] From the writings of Ibn al-Wazīr as well as of Ibn al-Murtaḍā it is obvious that they were both well aware of the debate preceding them. However, neither explicitly adopts any of the previous categorizations of different ranks of *mujtahids*. Ibn al-Wazīr alludes to the existence of the different ranks (*marātib*) without further specification in his *Kitāb al-Qawāʿid*.[99] The kind of categorization used in the Zaydiyya was still another, with less explicit steps.[100] Yet classical positions as that of al-Ghazālī, Fakhr al-Dīn al-Rāzī and Imām al-Ḥaramayn al-Juwaynī are often quoted for the support of an argument. The widespread notion of a differentiation between an independent *mujtahid* and one practicing *ijtihād* within the scope of other scholars' legal opinions was an intrinsic part of the discussion.

Ibn al-Wazīr's and Ibn al-Murtaḍā's lists of requirements read as follows:

Shahrazūrī (d. 643/1245), Ibn ʿAbd al-Salām (d. 660/1261), Tāj al-Dīn al-Subkī (d. 771/1369). Ibn al-Ḥājib is of special interest as he was the model upon which Ibn al-Murtaḍā admittedly fashioned much of his own legal theory.

96 Hallaq, *Iftā'* and *Ijtihād* 41.

97 Cf. Hallaq, Was the Gate Closed? 18; 84; Kamali, *Principles* 333. Al-Ghazālī is said to have been the first to divide *ijtihād* into two kinds: that which refers directly to the sources on the one hand, and that which elaborates and implements the law developed within the context of the school on the other.

98 Hallaq, Was the Gate Closed? 5; Kamali, *Principles* 322.

99 Ibn al-Wazīr, *Kitāb al-Qawāʿid* f. 84b.

100 Cf. Haykel and Zysow, What Makes a *Madhhab*? 340–341.

Ibn al-Wazīr mentions in his *Kitāb al-Qawāʿid*: theology (*ʿilm al-kalām/uṣūl al-dīn*), knowledge of the Quran, knowledge of prophetic traditions (*ḥadīth*), Arabic linguistics (*al-ʿarabiyya*), knowledge of legal methodology (*uṣūl al-fiqh*) and stylistics and imagery (*ʿilm al-maʿānī wa-l-bayān*).

Ibn al-Murtaḍā's list of requirements in the introduction (*Muqaddima*) to his *Kitāb al-Baḥr al-zakhkhār* is as follows: legally relevant Quranic verses, prophetic traditions (*ḥadīth*), consensus (*ijmāʾ*), legal methodology (*uṣūl al-fiqh*), theology (*kalām*/*uṣūl al-dīn*).[101] In the introduction to his *Kitāb al-Azhār*, Ibn al-Murtaḍā furthermore considers explicit and implicit rectitude (*ʿadl taṣrīḥ wa-taʾwīl*) as an indispensable requirement of a *mujtahid*. In *Minhāj al-wuṣūl*, he determines three sciences as the bases of the *mujtahid*'s activity, namely theology (*ʿilm al-kalām*), Arabic linguistics (*ʿilm al-ʿarabiyya*) and knowledge of the laws (*ʿilm al-aḥkām*).[102]

Ibn al-Murtaḍā's lists in *Kitāb al-Azhār*, the introduction to *Kitāb al-Baḥr al-zakhkhār* and in *Minhāj al-wuṣūl* differ. The commentary (*sharḥ*) of the *Kitāb al-Azhār* written by the second generation student of Ibn al-Murtaḍā, ʿAbdallāh b. Abī l-Qāsim b. Miftāḥ (d. 877/1472), provides a digest of the different lists with subsequent elaboration. Ibn Miftāḥ divides Ibn al-Murtaḍā's requirements into two types: Firstly, a *mujtahid* needs to be able to derive the legal rulings from their sources and proofs. In order to be capable of this, he needs to have proficiency in Arabic linguistics (*lugha*), legally relevant Quranic verses (*āyāt al-aḥkām*), prophetic traditions (*ḥadīth*), cases of consensus (*ijmāʾ*) and legal methodology (*uṣūl al-fiqh*). Secondly, the *mujtahid* needs to have an untainted rectitude (*ʿadāla*).[103]

The first set of requirements, i.e. Quran, prophetic traditions, legal methodology, consensus, Arabic linguistics and stylistics and imagery, is generally less controversial than the requirements of theology and rectitude. There is little to no disagreement, neither between Ibn al-Wazīr and his contemporaries nor between Islamic scholars in general, about the centrality of the Quran in legal reasoning. Most scholars of *uṣūl al-fiqh* agree that a *mujtahid* needs to know those verses of the Quran from which legal rulings are derived (*āyāt al-aḥkām*).[104] This is likely to be the reason why Ibn al-Wazīr spends so little time on the issue. However, other issues like the number of *āyāt al-aḥkām*

101 Ibn al-Murtaḍā, *Muqaddima* 30–31. In Ibn al-Murtaḍā's own words, all the above-mentioned sciences are provided in the books contained in the *Muqaddima* as a basis for understanding the subsequent legal compendium *al-Baḥr al-zakhkhār*.

102 Ibn al-Murtaḍā, *Minhāj al-wuṣūl* 213.

103 Ibn Miftāḥ, *Sharḥ al-Azhār* i, 7–11.

104 Pakatchi and Harris, Āyāt al-aḥkām.

and how thoroughly a scholars needs to know them were answered differently. The majority of scholars take those *āyāt al-aḥkām* to number 500.[105] Ibn al-Wazīr would only grant that number if the counting involved every "saying" (*kalām*) in accordance with the custom of the grammarians to call individual verses as well as sentences *kalām*. If verses are meant in the strict sense, Ibn al-Wazīr counts only around 200 verses.[106] This reduces what is expected of a *mujtahid* considerably. And those verses do not even need to be known by heart (*ḥifẓ ghayb*). What is required is the ability to know their place in the text in order to refer back to them with ease when necessary. Further, one needs to know how they came to be in the place where they are (*asbāb al-nuzūl*). Considering Ibn al-Wazīr's strong emphasis on the authoritative texts, it is striking that he should require of a jurist so little knowledge of the Quran.[107]

Ibn al-Murtaḍā, in the introduction to *al-Baḥr al-zakhkhār*, requires a little more. There are 500 verses relevant for legal issues. Yet, of these, only their place in the text needs to be known.[108] In his *Kitāb al-Intiqād lil-āyāt al-muʿtabara lil-ijtihād*, it becomes clear, however, that Ibn al-Murtaḍā also allowed for the number of 500 only if what was meant by verse (*āya*) was one phrase, or two phrases connected by a conjunction and expressing one meaning.[109] Concerning the requirements of knowledge of the Quran, therefore, the difference between the two scholars is not wide.

The requirement of prophetic traditions shows a slightly larger degree of variation. Just as the Quran contains parables and narratives without immediate connection to legal rulings, the prophetic Sunna comprises reports about

105 According to Abū l-Ḥusayn, the scholar must have a full grasp of the *āyāt al-aḥkām* including knowledge of their interpretation (*tafāsīr*). Ibn ʿArabī, al-Ghazālī and others agree that it must be 500 verses; cf. Kamali, *Principles*, 251, 321; al-Ghazālī, *Mustaṣfā* ii, 102; Ṣārim al-Dīn, *al-Fuṣūl al-luʾluʾiyya* 372.

106 Al-Shawkānī agrees with him in challenging the number of 500. Interestingly, however, Shawkānī does not restrict the number further, as Ibn al-Wazīr does, and so lowers the requirements of *ijtihād*. Al-Shawkānī, in *Irshād al-fuḥūl*, even widens the scope by saying that a scholar can also derive rules from the parables and narratives contained in the larger part of the Quran; cf. al-Shawkānī, *Irshād al-fuḥūl* 250–251.

107 This is indeed also what his brother al-Hādī b. al-Wazīr remarks about him, as quoted in *Taʾrīkh Banī l-Wazīr*. Aḥmad b. ʿAbdallāh al-Wazīr cites: "In spite of all the intense study (of the book) he only read a fourth of it and did not add to it, so that he was very familiar with the verses of the rules (*āyāt al-aḥkām*), the reasons for revelation, what was abrogated and what was not, the repeated and the unrepeated (…)." Aḥmad al-Wazīr, *Taʾrīkh Banī l-Wazīr* 28.

108 Ibn al-Murtaḍā, *Muqaddima* 30.

109 Ibn al-Murtaḍā, Kitāb al-Intiqād 476.

the Prophet Muḥammad or other prophets' biographies, about Quranic exegesis or details of heaven and hell, etc. Not all of these are relevant for legal reasoning and therefore not all need to be known.[110] Ibn al-Wazīr contents himself with a compilation like al-Tirmidhī's (d. 279/892) *Jāmiʿ* or Abū Dāwūd's (d. 275/889) *Sunna*. Most importantly, a *mujtahid* must be firm in those legally relevant traditions (*aḥādīth al-aḥkām*) which distinguish the sound from the weak and the authentic from the spurious.[111]

Seen in the wider context of Islamic scholars, the difference of opinion in the case of prophetic traditions is greater than concerning the Quranic verses. Al-Ghazālī and most legal theorists, like Ibn al-Wazīr, restricted the required amount to one of the dominant collections. Yet, there were others like Aḥmad b. Ḥanbal (d. 241/855), who according to al-Shawkānī, required a thorough acquaintance with 500,000 traditions.[112] Ibn al-Wazīr was content with less:

> I mentioned these books as a guide and support, not as an obligation. After all, to occupy oneself with the chanting of the Quran, the refining and examination of the soul, with restraining oneself from evil, from sophism and inquisitiveness without much occupation with hadiths is better than high regard of hadiths while transgressing in respect to what is precedent to all these things and what bears more resemblance to the example of the companions and followers.[113]

Merely as a piece of advice, Ibn al-Wazīr suggests to the more eager student commentaries on the hadith books or discussions of the legally relevant traditions. But again his strong emphasis on the low benchmark of requirements is made in reference to the early generations. To require comprehensive knowledge of numerous prophetic traditions could not be shaped on the practice of the forefathers, as they modeled an *ijtihād* that could draw on only a few traditions in contrast to what was written down later. To underline this point, Ibn al-Wazīr recounts the reluctance of a number of very knowledgable companions and *anṣār* to transmit sayings of the Prophet. Ibn al-Wazīr not only infers that few hadiths are prerequisites for *ijtihād*, he also finds that the practice and

110 There is little disagreement among scholars of legal reasoning concerning this issue; see for example al-Ghazālī, *Mustaṣfā* ii, 101.
111 Ibn al-Wazīr, *Kitāb al-Qawāʿid* f. 95a.
112 Al-Shawkānī, *Irshād al-fuḥūl* ii, 208. However, al-Shawkānī and Aḥmad b. Ḥanbal did not require that the traditions be known by heart.
113 Ibn al-Wazīr, *Kitāb al-Qawāʿid* f. 95 a.

attitude of the early generations in respect to transmission speaks for a greater emphasis on acts of piety and soul-searching (*muḥāsabat al-nafs*). The little significance Ibn al-Wazīr appears to concede to prophetic traditions here appears striking, but his emphasis on piety and mysticism is clear. In contrast to a laudible occupation with prophetic traditions, he laments the existence of a quest for reports (*ṭalab al-ḥadīth*) more occupied with the accumulation of names and titles than with the essential meaning (*māhiyya*) of the traditions. Hence, the quantity of memorized hadiths does not determine the status of a *mujtahid*, nor the piety of a believer. The model of the early generations emphasizes this point.[114]

For Ibn al-Murtaḍā, the required knowledge of prophetic traditions is little specified. Of course the traditions that refer to legal issues are of utmost importance: those that contain reference to duty and recommendation, permission, reprehensibility and prohibition. Similar to Ibn al-Wazīr, he contents himself with one of the hadith compilations like the *Sunan* of Abū Dāwūd or al-Amīr al-Ḥusayn b. Badr al-Dīn's (d. 662/1264) *Shifāʾ al-uwām* for the Zaydi *madhhab*. According to Ibn Miftāḥ, it suffices for Ibn al-Murtaḍā to have received the license for the respective compilation through one way of transmission.[115] Ibn al-Murtaḍā's mention of one of the Six Sunni hadith compilations, i.e. Abū Dawūd's *Sunan*, bespeaks the inclusion of some non-Zaydi sources on the basic level. However, unlike Ibn al-Wazīr, Ibn al-Murtaḍā mentions these elements in addition to Zaydi sources.

The requirement of a thorough knowledge of legal methodology for *ijtihād* need hardly be mentioned. Ibn al-Wazīr does not offer an exception to the general notion that *uṣūl al-fiqh* is the science at the heart of *ijtihād*. Suffice it to quote his wording that finds its equivalent in most other treatises discussing the indispensable requirements for *ijtihād*:

> *Uṣūl al-fiqh* is its [*ijtihād*'s] stem and its head, its root and its foundation so that Abū l-Ḥusayn al-Baṣrī mentioned that all requirements for *ijtihād* are unequal to this one. This is so, because the *uṣūlīs* have taken everything or most of what the *mujtahid* needs from the other disciplines [and made it available to them], so that some scholars of stylistics and imagery (*ʿilm al-maʿānī wa-l-bayān*) complain that the *uṣūlīs* have stolen their art from

114 Ibid., f. 95a.

115 The strongest of the four ways of receiving the authority to transmit a certain writing is if the teacher reads to his student or *vice versa*, followed by the assertion of the teacher that he has either heard his student read the book or that he has made him hear it; cf. Ibn Miftāḥ, *Sharḥ al-Azhār* i, 9.

> them. Likewise they have transmitted what issues the *mujtahid* needs [to know] from the Arabic language.[116]

This is to show what a central role the science of *uṣūl al-fiqh* occupied in the interplay of different arts. Ibn al-Wazīr, like many scholars, was aware of it, and, as can be seen throughout his writings, made ample use of it outside the strictly legal framework. Ibn al-Wazīr does not specify what exactly he includes in the requirement of *uṣūl al-fiqh*. Other scholars of legal methodology of the Zaydiyya and other schools of law have listed *qiyās* and abrogation as separate items. It is very likely that Ibn al-Wazīr gives them as high a priority as he gives the knowledge of legal methodology.

Ibn al-Murtaḍā does not differ much from him in this regard. He mentions the whole of the characteristics of consensus, the conditions of *qiyās* and the rules of abrogation as indispensable parts of *uṣūl al-fiqh*, without the knowledge of which *ijtihād* is impossible. Furthermore, *uṣūl al-fiqh* comprises what needs to be known of the general and the particular, the comprehensive and the explicit (*al-mujmal wa-l-mubayyan*), what results from command and prohibition as to incumbency, repetition, immediacy of performance as well as the rules and validity of various instances of consensus and analogy.[117] Ibn al-Murtaḍā's *Miʿyār al-ʿuqūl* forms that part of the *Muqaddima* of *al-Baḥr al-zakhkhār* that is devoted to this requirement for *ijtihād*.[118]

According to Ibn Miftāḥ's reading of Ibn al-Murtaḍā, proficiency in legal methodology is the second skill that renders *ijtihād* immensely difficult.[119] In the introduction to *Kitāb al-Baḥr al-zakhkhār*, Ibn al-Murtaḍā states:

> The fourth [discipline]: Legal methodology and the investigation of the questions of its different sections. It is a matter of consensus that these things must be considered [as required part of *ijtihād*], and there is no disagreement that the deterioration of these would mean the distortion of the greater *ijtihād*.[120]

What is interesting in this brief statement is that Ibn al-Murtaḍā links the lack of knowledge of *uṣūl al-fiqh* to the distortion of the "greater *ijtihād*." "Greater *ijtihād*" can be understood as absolute *ijtihād*, allowing the possibility of another

116 Ibn al-Wazīr, *Kitāb al-Qawāʿid* f. 96b.
117 Cf. Ibn al-Murtaḍā, *Minhāj al-wuṣūl* 212.
118 Ibn al-Murtaḍā, Miʿyār al-ʿuqūl 159–204.
119 Ibn Miftāḥ, *Sharḥ al-Azhār* i, 10.
120 Ibn al-Murtaḍā, *Muqaddima* 31.

kind, a 'lesser' *ijtihād* or an *ijtihād* within the *madhhab* that is possible without scholarship in legal methodology, as we shall discuss below. In comparison to Ibn al-Wazīr, Ibn al-Murtaḍā puts a higher emphasis on the difficulty of *uṣūl al-fiqh* and consequently of attaining the rank of a proper *mujtahid*.

In the preceding four issues, the differences between Ibn al-Wazīr's and Ibn al-Murtaḍā's requirements of a *mujtahid* are not significant, although they already indicate different emphases. However, the differences become more evident where Arabic linguistics and theology are concerned.

All the sources for legal reasoning are written in the Arabic language. It is therefore not surprising that familiarity with Arabic linguistics (*maʿrifat al-ʿarabiyya/al-lugha*) is a commonly agreed upon prerequisite for *ijtihād*. However, the required degrees of understanding vary. Ṣārim al-Dīn al-Wazīr (d. 914/1508) in *al-Fuṣūl al-luʾluʾiyya*, writing a century after Ibn al-Wazīr and Ibn al-Murtaḍā, is very unspecific on this issue. He only states that to derive rulings from the sources, a scholar needs to be firm in the different fields of linguistics.[121]

As can be expected, Ibn al-Wazīr is among those scholars who require little knowledge of Arabic linguistics. But what does that little knowledge include? And how does Ibn al-Wazīr explain why so little is required, given that all the sources are composed in Arabic? Ibn al-Ḥājib's *Muqaddima* is a book Ibn al-Wazīr suggests as a sufficient source for the study of Arabic. According to Ibn al-Wazīr, what needs to be known is that which is vital to grasp the meaning of a word or phrase. Ibn al-Wazīr concludes from the common experience of Arabic speakers that most do not know, for example, why the agent in a sentence is expressed in the nominative (*limā irtafaʿa l-fāʿil*). Yet Arabic speakers do understand the meaning of the sentence without desinential inflection. However, some rules must be known: Arabic grammar determines that the relationship between the exception (*istithnāʾ*) and that from which it is excepted can be direct (*muttaṣil*) or indirect (*munqaṭaʿ*). This is indispensable in order to understand the purport of the statement. Understanding the purport does not, however, depend on knowing which final vowel (*iʿrāb*) the exception carries. Ibn al-Wazīr supports this argument based on common experience with a prophetic tradition. The Prophet is reported to have said that "one does not need to know that [the term] 'actions' is in the nominative in order to know what is meant by the phrase 'actions are based on intentions'."[122]

121 Ṣārim al-Dīn, *al-Fuṣūl al-luʾluʾiyya* 373.

122 Ibn al-Wazīr, *Kitāb al-Qawāʿid* f. 96a.

Furthermore, the respective understanding of the language of the sources is of interest here. Ibn al-Wazīr considers only the Quran to leave room for multiple meanings, whereas the prophetic Sunna is supposedly clear (*ẓāhir* or *jalī*) in almost everything it conveys. A layman can read and understand the prophetic traditions without a thorough study of grammatical rules. He should be able to read and understand a mufti's legal ruling in a similar way. The danger of misunderstanding, though it exists, is but negligible. For one thing, it rarely occurs because the meaning is not contained in grammatical subtleties. If the meaning is clearly conveyed, there is no danger of misreading. But if there should be ambiguity (*ishkāl*), the layman turns to a specialist of language to be informed about what rules he needs to know for a correct understanding. Thereby his own understanding is enhanced.

This example can be understood in almost direct parallel to the progress a *mujtahid* makes in understanding and interpreting the textual sources. The correspondence with the doctrine of divisibility of *ijtihād*, to be discussed below, is obvious. A *mujtahid* must master Arabic only to the degree that enables him to inquire into the evidence in a given field or question. The common knowledge accessible to all is sufficient as a basis for understanding. In the process of inquiring into a question and acquiring the needed knowledge, he widens the range of fields in which he is entitled to practice *ijtihād*. An independent *mujtahid* of all fields (*mujtahid muṭlaq*) would have to know Arabic grammar in its entirety. However, because every *mujtahid* starts as a student or a layman, and because the major sources do not require much for basic understanding, mastery is not necessary.[123] Ibn al-Wazīr's understanding can be comprehended more easily if contrasted with the reasoning of supporters of the indivisibility of *ijtihād*: It rests on the common notion that *ijtihād* means formulating a particular supposition (*ẓann*) concerning a legal question. Those who oppose divisibility start from the premise that only a *mujtahid* has the intellectual capability to formulate that kind of supposition. This capability grants him the confidence he needs to be sought as a *mujtahid*. To form an opinion in a particular case involves reaching overwhelming conjecture on the evidence and being able to ascertain that no conflicting evidence exists. This, it is thought, is the case because all the sciences and legal issues are interrelated.[124] For scholars

123 Ibid., f. 96a.

124 The science of inheritance (*ʿilm al-farāʾiḍ*) is taken to be independent from the other sciences. Some opponents of the divisibility of *ijtihād* allow for an exception in this case. Accordingly, there may be scholars that practice *ijtihād* exclusively in the science of inheritance.

who hold to the indivisibility of *ijtihād*, thorough mastery of Arabic linguistics would therefore be a necessity from the outset of any legal investigation.

Although Ibn al-Murtaḍā does not support the indivisibility of *ijtihād*, as we shall see, the degree of grasp a *mujtahid* should have of Arabic linguistics reveals the different standard both scholars set for a *mujtahid*. Ibn al-Murtaḍā is most likely one of the Zaydi contemporaries to whom Ibn al-Wazīr refers in his criticism of the central position that Arabic linguistics occupy in the requirements for *ijtihād*.[125] First of all, Ibn al-Murtaḍā was widely known for his profound linguistic skill and literary productivity. Additionally, Ibn al-Murtaḍā does not even consider the mastery of Arabic linguistics as a separate requirement in his *al-Baḥr al-zakhkhār*, because of the obviousness of the matter. Mastery of Arabic linguistics is not listed there explicitly, because it is a precondition even to the requirements for *ijtihād*. Twice in his introduction—before and after he lists the sciences required for *ijtihād*—Ibn al-Murtaḍā insists that these sciences are only worth considering "after the mastery of the arts (*funūn*) of the Arabic language."[126] According to Ibn Miftāḥ, proficiency in the different sub-disciplines of Arabic linguistics (*'ilm al-'arabiyya*), syntax (*naḥw*), morphology (*taṣrīf*), lexicography (*lugha*) as well as stylistics and imagery (*'ilm al-ma'ānī wa-l-bayān*) is required explicitly. A little later he adds: "The hardest of them [the five prerequisite sciences for *ijtihād*] are Arabic linguistics, because one cannot reach the degree of precision except after much time and devotion."[127] Designating Arabic linguistics as one of the three sources of the practice of a *mujtahid* in *Minhāj al-wuṣūl* leaves little doubt of the central position that the discipline occupied in Ibn al-Murtaḍā's concept of the requirements for *ijtihād*.[128]

Ibn al-Wazīr, in turn, questions this requirement. *Ijtihād*, he argues, pertains only to those questions that are neither necessary nor obvious. Accordingly, the result does not go beyond probable knowledge. He argues that questions of necessary knowledge that every believer needs to know from revelation include the promise and the threat, the imamate, the caliphate, stipulations of the state of a human being as an unbeliever (*takfīr*) or grave sinner (*tafsīq*). Some of these the Zaydiyya takes to be concluded from the hidden meaning of the texts (*khafī*), as for example the imamate of 'Alī b. Abī Ṭālib. The hidden mean-

---

125 Ibid., f. 96a.
126 Ibn al-Murtaḍā, *Muqaddima* 30–31.
127 Ibn Miftāḥ, *Sharḥ al-Azhār* i, 10.
128 Cf. Ibn al-Murtaḍā, *Minhāj al-wuṣūl* 213.

ing of the text would require a deeper understanding of the Arabic language. However, this deeper understanding of the Arabic language is no obligation for every *mukallif*, even though every *mukallif* is obliged to support ʿAlī b. Abī Ṭālib's imamate according to Zaydi teaching.[129] How then, Ibn al-Wazīr asks, would the thorough comprehension of the rules of language be required of one who is only commissioned to reach probable knowledge in particular legal questions?[130]

A comparison of the two scholars on the question of language shows that Ibn al-Wazīr's method of calling for *ijtihād* is manifest not only in the low degree of requirements for an *ijtihād* based on a direct investigation of the main sources, but also in his challenge of the unevenness between supposed abilities of every common believer in the realm of certain knowledge (in doctrine) compared to his abilities in the realm of conjecture (in law). At the outset of the legal enterprise, Ibn al-Wazīr requires hardly more of the Arabic language than what is common knowledge. Furthermore, the high degree of probability in the whole enterprise of *ijtihād* renders those fields in which the high requirements were fixed questionable to him. Ibn al-Murtaḍā, in turn, requires a high degree of knowledge (Arabic in this case), much beyond what was required of a common Muslim, for the production of only probable, legal opinions.

Ibn al-Wazīr mentions as a separate requirement a discipline that is subsumed by most other scholars under Arabic linguistics, namely stylistics and imagery (*ʿilm al-maʿānī wa-l-bayān*). As in the case of Arabic linguistics, scholars disagree concerning the degree of mastery required of a *mujtahid*. The *mujtahid*, according to Ibn al-Wazīr, does need *ʿilm al-maʿānī wa-l-bayān* in some questions and therefore should have a basic knowledge of it. But if little is required, and it is generally part of Arabic linguistics anyway, why does Ibn al-Wazīr mention it as a separate requirement at all?

To understand this, one must keep in mind Ibn al-Wazīr's constant ambition to emphasize the unifying and simplifying concepts of Islamic law and doctrine. According to him, the scholars of *uṣūl al-fiqh* have listed most of the things that are required. The requirements they have mentioned differ. However, this is apparently only the case because of the variety of expressions that are used. Ibn al-Wazīr indicates that to know the real meaning of a number of different statements, it is necessary to understand how things can be expressed in different ways. Otherwise one is led to see contradictions where none exist. Knowledge of imagery and stylistics are therefore required insofar as they are

129 Ibn al-Wazīr, *Kitāb al-Qawāʿid* f. 96a.

130 Ibid., f. 96a.

needed to illuminate the real meaning of what is postulated by scholars.[131] For Ibn al-Murtaḍā, stylistics and imagery belong to Arabic linguistics and need not be discussed separately.

Let us turn to the question of theology as a requirement for *ijtihād*. The first requirement Ibn al-Wazīr discusses in his *Kitāb al-Qawāʿid* concerns the question of whether a *mujtahid* must be educated in theology, the order of the premises of evidence (*tartīb al-adilla*, or *tartīb al-muqaddimāt*) and the analysis of what he calls the science of the Greek. All of the potential requirements are subsumed under *ʿuṣūl al-dīn* or *ʿilm al-kalām* in this context. Although this question is treated in the context of legal reasoning, it goes to the very heart of the controversy about what knowledge is required for a person to be qualified as a believer. Furthermore, the status that theology is given among the requirements of a *mujtahid* indicates the relationship between the possibilities of a layman and those of a *mujtahid*.

As was discussed in chapter 3 sections 2.1. and 2.2., not all Muʿtazilis conditioned the state of a believer on the duty of speculation. Yet with the duty of *naẓar* as a prominent doctrine among Zaydi scholars who, like Ibn al-Murtaḍā, favor Bahshami-Muʿtazili doctrine, it is understandable why *ʿilm uṣūl al-dīn* figures first in the discussion of requirements and why Ibn al-Wazīr asserts his deep and lasting occupation with the issue.[132] Ibn al-Wazīr obviously disagrees with Ibn al-Murtaḍā's notion of the first duty of every believer, let alone of a *mujtahid*. Stating his position about the requirement of *ʿilm al-kalām* in his *Kitāb al-Qawāʿid*, Ibn al-Wazīr writes:

> They [his detractors] made *ʿilm al-kalām* a requirement, but the scholars established that it is no condition of *ijtihād*. Rather, those who say that [it is a requirement of *ijtihād*] condition upon it the correctness of doctrine. The truth is that this is meaningless, because the first generation relied upon before there was literature and teaching or even classification and foundational work, did practice *ijtihād*. In the rational nature (*gharāʾiz al-ʿuqūl*) there is that which is sufficient for the later generations as it was sufficient for the earlier generations. (…) How can it be sound to say that whoever is like the first generation in that he does not know

131 Ibid., f. 96b.

132 Ibn al-Wazīr "disputed with the *mutakallimūn*" on this issue and came to a conclusion which yet again reveals his constant effort to harmonize. He concluded that the source of this indeed extremely reprehensible innovation was not to be sought among the *mutakallimūn* themselves, but resulted from the intrigues of the heretics; cf. Ibn al-Wazīr, *Kitāb al-Qawāʿid* f. 95a.

> *kalām*, the ordering of the premises of evidence (*tartīb muqaddimāt al-burhān*) and how to investigate the subtleties of sciences of the Greek, is an unbeliever?[133]

Although Ibn al-Wazīr does not explicitly mention his definition of a believer in the *Kitāb al-Qawāʿid*, he refers to an early Muʿtazili authority, namely Shaykh Mukhtār, who required only the two testimonies (*shahāda*) for a person to be considered a Muslim.[134] Furthermore, as discussed in chapter 5 sections 2 and 3, Ibn al-Wazīr considers it every believer's duty to perform a degree of *ijtihād*. *Ijtihād* belongs to the realm of probability, whereas philosophical speculation is supposed to inform certain knowledge. This supports Ibn al-Wazīr's refusal to require that a *mujtahid* be educated in the art of speculation and the order of principles of proofs. For Ibn al-Wazīr, it is the common experience of having a rational nature (*gharāʾiz al-ʿuqūl*) and sound understanding (*ṣiḥḥat al-afhām*) which makes it possible for all generations to draw conclusions from evidence. Ibn al-Wazīr's use of *gharāʾiz al-ʿuqūl* indicates synonymity with the *fiṭra* or *fiṭar al-ʿuqūl* we encountered in a more strictly theological context in preceding chapters. He argues that the principles of speculation and evidencing were not known to the first generations of scholars either. But those were the scholars who lay down the foundations for legal reasoning. Having the same raw material to draw from as later generations valorizes the effort and achievement of the early generations.

Interestingly, in Ibn al-Murtaḍā's earlier *Kitāb al-Azhār* neither speculative theology nor *al-uṣūl al-dīn* is explicitly mentioned as a requirement. However, as we shall see below, theological doctrine forms a rather important albeit implicit requirement even in *Kitāb al-Azhār*.[135] In his list of what is required of a *mujtahid* in the introduction to *al-Baḥr al-zakhkhār*, Ibn al-Murtaḍā men-

133 Ibn al-Wazīr, *Kitāb al-Qawāʿid* f. 94b.

134 However, Ibn al-Wazīr does say that although this is the opinion of the *mutakallimūn*, it only concerns the status in this world. If the "two testimonies" are sufficient, the judgement in the Hereafter remains a point of disagreement. Yet, according to Ibn al-Wazīr, this should be left to God; ibid., f. 94b.

135 This has led at least one commentator to drop the importance of the knowledge of *uṣūl al-dīn* in the context of *ijtihād* for Ibn al-Murtaḍā altogether. In al-ʿAnsī's *Tāj al-mudhhab*, Ibn al-Murtaḍā's opinion of the importance of *uṣūl al-dīn* is not mentioned. Of course, al-ʿAnsī's is a much later commentary and one of his aims, as he states explicitly, is to render the *Kitāb al-Azhār* easier to understand in comparison to Ibn Miftāḥ's *Sharḥ al-Azhār*. Nevertheless, al-ʿAnsī neglected a vital point of Ibn al-Murtaḍā's thinking by omitting this requirement, because he neglected an important element of Ibn al-Murtaḍā's Muʿtazili thinking; cf. al-ʿAnsī, *al-Tāj al-mudhhab* 4, 7–8.

tions theology (*ʿilm al-uṣūl al-dīn*) as number five of the five fields of knowledge (*ʿulūm*) a *mujtahid* has to master. Although it is not first on the list, Ibn al-Murtaḍā does say that the knowledge of *uṣūl al-dīn* is among the most important skills, because "the correctness of the deduction of evidence from revelation is dependent on its [*uṣūl al-dīn*'s] implementation."[136] By this he means that correct inference from revelation for the formulation of rulings can only be realized if a scholar knows the ways evidence is to be established in general. Beyond the initial list, more than a third of Ibn al-Murtaḍā's *Muqaddima* is devoted to theological matters, which speaks clearly of the importance theology has for a *mujtahid* according to Ibn al-Murtaḍā. After all, the *Muqaddima* is supposed to provide systematically and comprehensively (*intiẓām shāfin*) what the *mujtahid* needs for his endeavor.[137] Furthermore, Ibn al-Murtaḍā makes *ʿilm al-kalām* in *Minhāj al-wuṣūl* a condition for the practice of a *mujtahid* because of the supposed interdependence between legal proofs and principles and, for example, the knowledge of God.[138] The controversial nature of the knowledge of God and the way it was arrived at were shown in chapter 2 sections 3 and 2 above. Accordingly, restricting valid *ijtihād* to those who practice *ʿilm al-kalām* would restrict the number of acceptable *mujtahids* considerably.

Hence, the comparison between the doctrinal foundations and ways of deriving them required by each of the two scholars shows a considerable degree of deviation. Ibn al-Wazīr expects much less of a full-fledged *mujtahid* than does Ibn al-Murtaḍā. Even if professional occupation with theology was not explicitly required by Ibn al-Murtaḍā, as the *Kitāb al-Azhār* seems to indicate, the mere rational nature common to all Muslims was not enough to know how to derive rulings from the sources, nor for proper understanding of those derivations. That Ibn al-Murtaḍā, at least at a later stage, did require a thorough knowledge of *uṣūl al-dīn* for the qualification of a *mujtahid* further confirms the difference in the expectations the two scholars had of a jurisconsult. For Ibn al-Wazīr, however, the general rational nature and sound understanding of a human being is sufficient, not only to practice *ijtihād*, but also to reconstruct the ways an inference from revelation was conducted.

As concluded by Ibn Miftāḥ, Ibn Murtaḍā's requirements of one who can be emulated is two-tiered. While the first tier is concerned with the ability to draw conclusions from the sources, the second is concerned with the scholar's recti-

136 Ibn al-Murtaḍā, *Muqaddima* 31.

137 Ibid.

138 Ibn al-Murtaḍā, *Minhāj al-wuṣūl* 213.

tude (*ʿadāla*). The issue of a *mujtahid*'s rectitude is not explicitly raised by Ibn al-Wazīr in his list of requirements. However, throughout his *magnum opus* and most comprehensive presentation of his thinking, i.e. *al-ʿAwāṣim*, the issue of a scholar's standing in relation to his rectitude has a rather potent role in the argumentation. But the discussion includes all kinds of scholars, not only the *mujtahids*, and is indeed mostly occupied with the transmitter's integrity. But since the train of thought is the same—the *mujtahid*'s and the transmitter's rectitude rather being two aspects of the same idea—it seems reasonable to let the quantity of questions dedicated to this topic speak for the importance that Ibn al-Wazīr attaches to a *mujtahid's* rectitude. Additionally, Ibn al-Wazīr himself compares the two—*mujtahids* and transmitters. In the wider context of the argument for the acceptance of a transmitter whose doctrinal integrity is impaired (*kāfir* or *fāsiq taʾwīl, ahl al-taʾwīl*), Ibn al-Wazīr argues that such a one is accepted generally and by Zaydi scholars in particular. With support from a number of traditions and opinions (*anẓār*) he establishes the following concept of the rectitude of scholars:

> They perform the five pillars of Islam and avoid grave sins and those iniquities that are a sign of vileness. They elevate the sanctity of Islam and do not take liberty with God by lying intentionally. (…) The occupation with [their] discipline is evident in them. For even if the traditionist makes a mistake in Arabic or the jurist with hadith, that does not concern us in [the question of] acceptance. Rather, what we mean is that the traditionist is accepted based on his discipline, and that he outwardly appears not to err in it or be mistaken. These things are the indicators of rectitude.[139]

In a quotation from al-Manṣūr bi-llāh ʿAbdallāh b. Ḥamza's *Ṣafwat al-ikhtiyār*, it becomes clear that Ibn al-Wazīr (like al-Manṣūr bi-llāh ʿAbdallāh b. Ḥamza here) considers rectitude as being determined by moral and religious integrity and most of all by professional skill rather than supposedly certain theological matters. According to al-Manṣūr bi-llāh ʿAbdallāh b. Ḥamza, the conditions for issuing legal opinions rests solely on one idea, namely, the most probable assumption of the seeker of legal advice (*yaghlib ẓann al-mustaftī*) that the one he addresses is from among the scholars and *mujtahids*. This assumption is reached when the layman in need of a legal opinion is almost certain that the appointed mufti is a pious man capable of *ijtihād*.[140] In other words, the out-

139 Ibn al-Wazīr, *al-ʿAwāṣim* i, 315.

140 Ibid., i, 316; al-Manṣūr bi-llāh ʿAbdallāh b. Ḥamza, *Ṣafwat al-ikhtiyār* 381–382. Ibn al-Wazīr

ward appearance of the general Muslim faith and the skill of a scholar—what Johansen calls the *forum externum*[141]—is sufficient to evaluate his rectitude. Ibn al-Wazīr states frequently that it is impossible to know what is in the heart of a scholar (or anyone else).[142]

Another example is given in *al-ʿAwāṣim*. The companion Abū Hurayra is considered to be one of the *ahl al-taʾwīl* by the Muʿtazila and Shīʿa because of his position as governor in Medina in the days of Muʿāwiya. In spite of this, Ibn al-Wazīr does not see his authority impaired, because of the effectiveness of his pious conduct.

> Because the man was religious (*mutadayyin*) and assiduous (*mutaḥarrī*) he did not intend to perpetrate the forbidden. The most that can be said is that he [Abū Hurayra] sinned on the basis of wrong interpretation. But this neither invalidates his transmission nor his *ijtihād* according to what I will elucidate in its proper place, God willing. Anyway, it [his sinning by interpretation] does not degrade his religiosity or his reign for a number of reasons.[143]

As stated above, opinions on what the *mujtahid* must be known for besides the professional qualities come within the wider discussion of a scholar's rectitude in general. Ibn al-Wazīr argues that what must be known of a scholar in order to be accepted as a transmitter, mufti, grammarian or indeed anyone bearing any kind of knowledge (*ḥāmil al-ʿilm*), is his professionalism in his discipline. To this is added the outer appearance of a pious and religious life which is taken as rectitude until evidence to the contrary should appear.[144] This principle is commonly known in the science of transmitter criticism. But Ibn al-Wazīr elevates it

---

refers to Abū l-Ḥusayn al-Baṣrī to the same effect; cf. Abū al-Ḥusayn al-Baṣrī, *al-Muʿtamad* ii, 363–364.

141 "The *forum internum* is the instance of the religious conscience, the seat of the relation between God and the individual, of veracity and of absolute identity between truth on the one hand, rights and obligations on the other. The *forum externum* is an instance of contingent decisions which are legally valid and whose assertions about the facts of the cases are probable. (…) The tragical conflicts which may arise from this necessary and unbridgeable hiatus between the *forum externum* which has to rely on probable enunciations and the *forum internum* which combines a sure knowledge of facts and motivations with the absolute ethical obligation to follow truth engage the individiuals ethical responsibility." Johansen, *Contingency* 36–37.

142 See for example Ibn al-Wazīr, *al-ʿAwāṣim* viii, 322; Ibn al-Wazīr, *Qubūl al-bushra* 335.

143 Ibn al-Wazīr, *al-ʿAwāṣim* ii, 77.

144 To support this point of view, Ibn al-Wazīr invokes influential witness from among the Zaydiyya like Imam al-Manṣūr bi-llāh in *Hidāyat al-mustarshidīn*, ʿAbdallāh b. Zayd in

to a general principle. Thereby he can argue that a *mujtahid*'s rectitude consists in outward appearance of religiosity and skill without referring to soundness of belief or any other criteria beyond the *forum externum* and within the realm of certainty to which the human being has no access. The implications for the structure of legal authority are evident: The one seeking legal advice can go to whoever seems most knowledgable in his trade irrespective of doctrinal, let alone legal affiliation, as long as he displays the basic sign of Islamic religiosity.[145]

Ibn al-Murtaḍā defines more closely in which sense rectitude is expected of a *mujtahid*. This second tier of requirements for *ijtihād* is to him of no less importance than the first tier, which discussed the details of professional requirements. In *Sharh al-Azhār*, Ibn al-Miftāḥ defines Ibn al-Murtaḍā's and the supposedly widespread notion of rectitude as religious modesty, piety, manliness, freedom from innovation, eschewing grave sins and not holding on to any kind of rebelliousness.[146] Ibn al-Murtaḍā goes beyond this in that he requires the upright scholar not to commit any of the lesser sins and even abstain from some of what is indifferent (*baʿḍ al-mubāḥāt*).[147] Visible evidence of moral and religious integrity is a common requirement to be deemed worthy of *iftāʾ*, not only for *mujtahids*.[148] However, what differs between Ibn al-Wazīr and Ibn al-Murtaḍā is the measure of visible sinlessness required, as well as the degree to which the layman is obliged to investigate a scholar's rectitude. Whereas Ibn al-Wazīr's stance as to objective signs of integrity does not go beyond outer appearance, Ibn al-Murtaḍā's expectation reflects the claim, widespread in the Zaydiyya, that moral and religious integrity in terms of practical piety and doctrine is indeed attainable. This reflects the idea that the *forum internum* is an integral part of the legal realm. An illustration of this conviction is the doctrine of the immaculacy of *ahl al-bayt*. According to Ibn al-Wazīr's brother al-Hādī b. Ibrāhīm for example, the *ahl al-bayt* are the ones most worthy of *taqlīd* for the very reason that they are deemed impeccable in conduct, piety *and* doc-

---

al-Durar al-manzūma, Abū Ṭālib al-Hārūnī in *Jawāmiʿ al-adilla fī l-uṣūl* and *al-Mujzī* among others; cf. Ibn al-Wazīr, *al-ʿAwāṣim* i, 308.

145 The implications for the acceptance of transmitters and traditions are also considerable and of great importance in the thought of Ibn al-Wazīr. But a study of the science of *hadīth* goes beyond the scope of this study.

146 Ibn Miftāḥ, *Sharḥ al-Azhār* i, 12.

147 Ibn al-Murtaḍā, *al-Bahr al-zakhkhār* xvi, 94.

148 See for example the discussion of the rectitude of witnesses, Ibn al-Murtaḍā's chapter "Kitāb al-Shihādāt" in *al-Baḥr al-zakhkhār* xiii, 13, 97; and of transmitters, Ibn al-Wazīr, *al-ʿAwāṣim* i, 280–281, 325–326; Ṣārim al-Dīn, *al-Fuṣūl al-luʾluʾiyya* 218–219.

trine.[149] It is hence easy to pursue this train of thought to the higher standard of morality and doctrine represented in Ibn al-Murtaḍā's expectations of a *mujtahid*.

For Ibn al-Wazīr, it is purely an assumption that not following the scholar deemed trustworthy would lead to harm (*fī mukhālafatihi muḍirra maẓnūna*). Ibn al-Wazīr often refers to the human reality that no legal opinion or transmission could be accepted if one awaited proof of flawless conduct or absolute congruence of doctrine.[150] Ibn al-Wazīr is aware that a degree of probability is always retained. He counterbalances this with a professionalism in the *mujtahids*' and each scholar's respective field of study. In contrast to that, Ibn al-Murtaḍā seeks to counterbalance the probability with affiliation. In quoting Ibn al-Murtaḍā, Ibn Miftāḥ writes:

> What concerns those great sins that are not explicitly called great sins in the Book of God, or Sunna of His Prophet or the consensus relied upon, yet upon which there is no disagreement as to its meaning but that it is interpreted as unbelief or great sin because of what necessarily follows from it: whoever does such is called an unbeliever by interpretation (*kāfir taʾwīl*) like a determinist, or a grave sinner (*fāsiq taʾwīl*) by interpretation like the ones who strove against ʿAlī. Upon those our judgement is like that upon the explicit sinners in that it is forbidden to emulate them. This is what we meant to point out by our statement 'explicitly and implicitly upright,' meaning that rectitude pertains to both.[151]

In *Kitāb al-Azhār*, Ibn al-Murtaḍā merely mentioned that the *mujtahid* needs to be 'implicitly and explicitly upright.' One reason why he considered *ahl al-bayt* most worthy of being emulated was the assurance that their doctrine was free of such things as "the vision [of God]" (*al-ruʾya*), which means that they were not guilty of sin by wrong interpretation (*taʾwīl*).[152] Accordingly, it does not suffice to gather evidence on the *mujtahid*'s qualification by the outward signs of his religiosity, and the fact that he occupies the position of a mufti effectively. To remain with the common example of the traveling layman: According to Ibn al-Murtaḍā, evidence of the *mujtahid*'s doctrinal rectitude must be given by a trustworthy witness which can be a righteous imam or other authority in the

149 Al-Hādī b. al-Wazīr, *Nihāyat al-tanwīh* 224–269.
150 See for example Ibn al-Wazīr, *al-ʿAwāṣim* i, 383.
151 Ibn Miftāḥ, *Sharḥ al-Azhār* i, 12.
152 Ibn al-Murtaḍā, *Kitāb al-Azhār* i, 1.

respective country, as long as they do not permit that a *fāsiq ta'wīl* may be the object of emulation. Another way of justifying emulation of an unknown *mujtahid* would be to refer to some who "count as more than one in the justification [of scholars]," referring to imams of the Prophet's progeny.[153] If these things are not given, *taqlīd* is not permissible. The restriction this places on the scope of scholars from which to accept opinions is obvious.

It is not assumed here that either Ibn al-Wazīr or the earlier Zaydi scholars he refers to did not care about a *mujtahid's* uprightness.[154] But a number of scholars who list requirements for *ijtihād* at least do not discuss rectitude in terms of doctrinal affiliation as a precondition, even if *ahl al-bayt* are considered most deserving of *taqlīd* as, for example, in Imam Yaḥyā b. Ḥamza's thinking.[155] Drawing a conclusion to the effect that those earlier scholars were indifferent to the doctrinal affiliation of a scholar would be premature. After all, those scholars clearly counted themselves as belonging to the Zaydi *madhhab* and upheld the notion of the central role of the *ahl al-bayt* and Zaydi imams. But as far as those among them who merely prefer the *taqlīd* of the living without prohibiting *taqlīd al-mayyit* are concerned, it is not clear whether they would have permitted a layman to ask a *mujtahid* for a legal opinion—say on a journey—without being certain that the said scholar was of sound doctrine, or in the event that he belonged to another school of law. At least the question of rectitude in terms of a *mujtahid's* soundness of doctrine has not reached the importance that it seems to have held for Ibn al-Murtaḍā. After all, Ibn al-Murtaḍā considered doctrinal rectitude and the need of the *mustaftī* to know about it important enough to constitute the second tier of his two-tier categorization of requirements. The increasing importance of this criteria should be seen as another indication for a stronger inroad of theology on law and the subsequent and intended consolidation of the Zaydiyya as a legal school on theological foundations, to the exclusion of *mujtahids* of other schools.

Most likely, the requirement of doctrinal soundness is only a consequence of requiring the aspiring *mujtahid* to master the art of theology. Gimaret has

153 Ibn Miftāḥ's example of someone like that is al-Hādī ilā l-ḥaqq; cf. Ibn Miftāḥ, *Sharḥ al-Azhār* i, 13.

154 The notion that *ijtihād* as a divine commission can only be entrusted to the upright is a general one. See for example al-Ghazālī, al-*Mustaṣfā* ii, 101; al-Shawkānī, *Irshād al-fuḥūl* 252.

155 See for example al-Manṣūr bi-llāh 'Abdallāh b. Ḥamza, who only mentions professional skills as requirements and supports the above-mentioned way for a layman to discern the qualification of a scholar for *ijtihād* or *iftā'*; cf. 'Abdallāh b. Ḥamza, *Ṣafwat al-ikhtiyār* i, 381–382; ii, 357–359. See also Yaḥyā b. Ḥamza, *Kitāb al-Intisar* i, 198–199.

pointed out that the study of *uṣūl al-dīn* does not merely designate the study of the sources of religion or the sources of theological judgments, as the term might indicate. Rather, *uṣūl al-dīn* focuses on the judgements—hence the doctrines—themselves.[156] Assuming the validity of Gimaret's position, it must be concluded that the requirement of a mastery of *uṣūl al-dīn* is equal to requiring the belief in a particular set of theological doctrines. This confirms our conclusions from what Ibn al-Murtaḍā's requires of a *mujtahid*. In writings where Ibn al-Murtaḍā does not explicitly mention it as a required discipline, he does determine it at a stage that is much closer to the person of the *mujtahid*, namely, at the stage of his personal rectitude. Before the *ijtihād* of a *mujtahid* can be accepted, it must be ascertained that the *mujtahid* is not one of the *fussāq* or *kuffār taʾ wīl*. Being considered a *fāsiq* or *kāfir taʾwīl* effectively means holding different beliefs in one or more of the theological questions that belong to the realm of certain yet acquired knowledge.

In contrast to Ibn al-Murtaḍā's reference to correct, i.e. Zaydi-Muʿtazili, theology as the standard for the person of the *mujtahid*, Ibn al-Wazīr's frame of reference is a time before the existence of theological and legal schools. At the very beginning of the fourth principle in Ibn al-Wazīr's *Kitāb al-Qawāʿid*, called "the requirements for *ijtihād*," two guiding notions are given as the platform for subsequent categorization.[157] First, he advocates the superiority of the early generations. Secondly, he insists on the capability of later generations to perform *ijtihād* with a relatively low degree of difficulty. The two notions are linked in that the former facilitates the latter. It was the scholars of the early generations (*salaf*) who travelled to numerous scholars of hadith even before the Prophet's traditions were written down. For the rules of Arabic needed for interpretation they sought out the masters of language, i.e. Beduin, in their widely scattered wadis. The science of speculation (*ʿilm al-naẓar*) was not yet elaborated so as to impose guidelines in the method of conclusion and inference. Their efforts then resulted in the elaboration of methods, systemization and authoring of sources. The early scholars' achievements are what makes it possible for later scholars to perform their duty of *ijtihād*. Their capability of performing it rests not on a higher degree of education or higher intelligence, but on the efforts of their predecessors and the human nature (*gharīza*) or original disposition (*fiṭra*) that all share. Acknowledging this is equal to acknowledging God's grace in enabling his subjects and in rendering the performance of their duty easy to them (*rafʿ al-ḥaraj*, literally "removal of hardship").[158] It is from

156 Gimaret, Uṣūl al-Dīn.

157 Ibn al-Wazīr, *Kitāb al-Qawāʿid* fs. 94a–b.

158 Ibid., f. 94a.

general values like *rafʿ al-ḥaraj* and the "right kind of following" (i.e. *fī l-maʿnā*) that Ibn al-Wazīr sought to establish guidelines for the legal interpretation of revelation. Thus, he retained a level of subjectivity of the scholar's opinion and probability in the interpretation not conducive to stability in institutionalized law.

The rectitude of *mujtahids* bears on three issues which are important for the present question: First, the moral standing of a *mujtahid* has an effect on how high the benchmark for *mujtahid*s is set. Secondly, the determining factors for the required moral standing also determine what doctrinal orientation a *mujtahids* represents, as rectitude is not exclusively concerned with practical moral piety and integrity but also with doctrinal purity. Lastly, the concern with rectitude is again an indication for questions regarding the major realm of human activity. In explaining the gap between jurists and theologians with regard to the role contingency plays for them, Johansen shows how the field of activity for *fiqh* scholars is what he called the *forum externum*. The *forum externum* is concerned with the actions of an individual. Thus, a jurist would judge an individual's outward conduct in terms of legal norms of a probable epistemological nature. Theologians, on the other hand, are concerned with the *forum internum* "that decides conflicts in the light of the absolute criteria which govern the relationship between the individual and God."[159] This inner forum of belief and conscience, concerned with questions of absolute truth, would be a realm which the jurist would not dare to judge, since this realm can only be truly known to God and remains within the responsibility of the ethical conscience of the individual. Coming to legal decisions and interpretations based on doctrinal convictions would mean penetrating the *forum internum* which is supposedly beyond the realm of human assessability. Consequently, Ibn al-Wazīr's and Ibn al-Murtaḍā's positions in the issue of rectitude yet again reveal the comparative levels of certainty that each scholar considered attainable.

The differences between Ibn al-Wazīr's and Ibn al-Murtaḍā's requirements seem to be most apparent in the *uṣūl al-dīn* as well as in Arabic linguistics, with repercussions in what is required in the field of legal methodology. The emphasis on both speculative theology and Arabic linguistics is widespread in Muʿtazili circles. Ultimately, it is not general negation of attainability that provides the grounds for contrasting Ibn al-Murtaḍā's thought with that of Ibn al-Wazīr. That would be the case with Ibn al-Wazīr's opponent in *al-ʿAwāṣim* and *al-Rawḍ al-bāsim*, Ibn Abī l-Qāsim. The open question between Ibn al-

159 Johansen, *Contingency* 36.

Wazīr and Ibn al-Murtaḍā seems rather to be to what group of people *ijtihād* is restricted and how large the group may be.

To sum up: the probable nature of the interpretative process and outcome of Islamic law was especially salient in the notion of the infallibility of all *mujtahidūn*. This rendered a high degree of instability to the legal institutions and institutionalization of law in legal schools (*madhāhib*). Restricting the scope of those capable of legal interpretation to a group with a certain set of skills restores stability, as the scope of possible results is likewise restricted. Additionally, the kind of restriction is of interest: those fit to be *mujtahids* must have a firm grasp of theology. Hence more stability is gained for Ibn al-Murtaḍā—and many other Zaydis—by restricting *ijtihād* and its outcome to those strongly influenced by a particular theological outlook on law. This buttresses the tendency Zysow has indicated, namely that a shift to those sciences where certainty was available was made by many scholars who were occupied with the interpretation of divine law. To my mind, the consolidation of the Zaydi *madhhab* was Ibn al-Murtaḍā's strategy on the level of law. And he represented a view supported by many Zaydis during his time and after.

Ibn al-Wazīr's reaction to the probable nature of Islamic law was different. He argued for a low standard in the set of requirements. Not much is needed that is not required of any Muslim, rendering *ijtihād* within reach for many if not all legal subjects to one degree or another. For Ibn al-Wazīr, the requirements for *ijtihād* had little to do with the certain knowledge of doctrine beyond what is commonly known by all Muslims' *fiṭra*. This is uniquely manifest in the position Ibn al-Wazīr and Ibn al-Murtaḍā take towards rectitude as a separate requirement. The aspect of the exigencies of rectitude alone would not suffice to argue for a step in the process of consolidation of the Zaydi *madhhab*. But as part of a whole, it points to a delimitation of school identity which provided Zaydi-Muʿtazilis with grounds for rejecting elements of other schools (opinions or *mujtahids*) on the basis of affiliation, as well as for defining the relationship between the schools in a hierarchical manner. In this regard, a scholar like Ibn al-Wazīr struggled against the effects of three things: first of all, the stringent requirements confronting every scholar aspiring to *ijtihād*; secondly, the ease with which laymen and scholars could refer to existing products of legal inference from the sources; and thirdly, the narrowing down of the scope of scholars from whom to receive legal knowledge to only those within certain limits of doctrinal affinity. We encounter this latter issue also in the discussion of the acceptance of transmitters. Here as there, Ibn al-Wazīr insists on outward criteria of professionalism rather than affiliation with a school or a set of doctrines that draws from the *forum internum*. The infallibility of *ijtihād* had a destabilizing effect on the theory of the institutionalization of legal schools. As Zysow suggested, the centrality of law was replaced by theology, by means of which other groups in the legal arena could be excluded, defined as inferior or marginalized. Given the correctness of all jurists, this was impossible on the basis of their legal rulings per se. However, it was not impossible on the basis of their doctrinal or methodological affiliation (theology and *uṣūl al-fiqh*), because certainty was required in these issues. The more certainty is required, the more grounds for excluding the other and elevating one's own school are retained. Ibn al-Wazīr's set of requirements for *ijtihād* theoretically set the Zaydi *mujtahids* on a par with scholars of other schools, thereby delineating a syncretistic model of the structure of legal authority reinforced by referring to a supposed original state before the emergence of schools. All this once again substantiates Ibn al-Wazīr's high tolerance of ambiguity.

5 Divisibility (*tajazzu*ʾ) of *Ijtihād* and the Discerning Student (*al-ṭālib al-mumayyiz*)

The debate around the requirements for *ijtihād* indicates that different scholars expected qualifications in different disciplines, as well as different levels of erudition in these disciplines. Similarly, scholars differed as to the scope in which *ijtihād* was possible as a consequence of such qualification. Whereas some thought that the qualification for *ijtihād* was comprehensive once reached, others held that *ijtihād* could be divided according to qualification and discipline. Kamali states that indivisibility was the majority opinion among Muslim scholars.[160] However, this was not the case among the Zaydi scholars and those scholars from other schools from which Ibn al-Wazīr and Ibn al-Murtaḍā drew.[161] Ibn al-Murtaḍā does speak of the majority of scholars of *uṣūl al-fiqh* in his argument for divisibility (*tajazzu*ʾ). Yet he claims that Imam al-Manṣūr

160 He names Abū l-Ḥusayn al-Baṣrī, al-Ghazālī, Ibn Taymiyya, Ibn Qayyim al-Jawziyya and al-Shawkānī beside "some Maliki, Hanbali and Ẓāhirī ulema" as exceptions to the doctrine of indivisibility; cf. Kamali, *Principles* 326.

161 Ibn al-Wazīr and Ibn al-Murtaḍā defend the divisibility of *ijtihād* as the opinion of the majority of scholars of legal theory in general, and the Zaydiyya in particular; cf. Ibn al-Wazīr, *Kitāb al-Qawāʿid* f. 93a. According to Ṣārim al-Dīn, the doctrine of divisibility was supported by a number of Zaydi authorities like al-Muʾayyad bi-llāh Yaḥyā b. Ḥamza, al-Manṣūr bi-llāh ʿAbdallāh b. Ḥamza, next to al-Ghazālī, Fakhr al-Dīn al-Rāzī and others; cf. Ṣārim al-Dīn, *al-Fuṣūl al-luʾluʾiyya* 279. It is important to him to point out that the one practicing partial *ijtihād* is restricted to those issues on which opinions already exist. He is not entitled to come to an independent opinion.

bi-llāh ʿAbdallāh b. Ḥamza was one example among a number of Zaydi scholars who rejected the notion.[162] Furthermore, Ibn al-Wazīr's defense against his critic in *Kitāb al-Qawāʿid* shows that divisibility was rejected among a number of his Zaydi contemporaries.[163] But what does the doctrine of the divisibility of *ijtihād* entail? And how does it affect the matter of school identity?

The editor of *al-ʿAwāṣim*, al-Arnaʾūṭ, conforms with what al-Shawkānī and also later scholarship say, namely that the indivisibility of *ijtihād* is a doctrine of a minority.[164] The argument that al-Shawkānī refers to for those who support divisibility is much the same as that which Ibn al-Murtaḍā uses, as we shall see. However, al-Shawkānī provides some insight on the argumentation of those negating it:

> They say: (…) but most of the sciences of *ijtihād* are interdependent and have a claim on one another (*yaʾkhudh baʿḍuhā bi-ḥujza baʿḍ*). Especially in respect to what is established of the sciences [of *ijithād*] originating in the endowment (*al-malaka*) [of *ijtihād*].[165]

It is known that a scholar is not allowed to perform *ijtihād* on the basis of evidence, unless he is assumed to have reached the degree of preponderant probability that he has acquired all that is required, and that nothing has inhibited him (*ʿadam al-mānīʿ*) from finding the relevant evidence. According to the deniers of divisibility, this assumption can only be reached by one holding the abilities of an absolute *mujtahid*.[166] The interdependence argument suggests that whoever claims to know everything that is necessary in one question regardless of other questions cannot have reached the necessary degree of probability. It is still possible that someone could inform him of something he did not know. The wording used by al-Shawkānī to portray the opinion of the deniers of divisibility sounds very much like what al-Arnaʾūṭ ascribed to Abū

162 Ibn al-Murtaḍā claims that Imam al-Manṣūr bi-llāh ʿAbdallāh b. Ḥamza rejected the divisibility of *ijtihād*, because of the interdependence between the different legal issues; cf. Ibn al-Murtaḍā, *Minhāj al-wuṣūl* 763.

163 Ibn al-Wazīr, *Kitāb al-Qawāʿid* f. 84b.

164 Of all the Sunni, Muʿtazili and Imami scholars, it is said only of Abū Ḥanīfa that he prohibited partial *ijtihad*. The reason for ascribing this position to Abū Ḥanīfa may be a rooted in a mere difference in wording, as the prohibition was concluded by Abū Ḥanīfa's transmitters from Abū Ḥanīfa's definition of a *faqīh* as "one who is gifted with the ability of deriving (a rule—*instinbāṭ*) in everything." Ibn al-Wazīr, *al-ʿAwāṣim* ii, 30, footnote 2. See also al-Ghazālī, *al-Mustaṣfā* ii, 354–453; Abū l-Ḥusayn, *al-Muʿtamad* ii, 929.

165 Al-Shawkānī, *Irshād al-fuḥūl* ii, 217.

166 Ibid.

Ḥanīfa.[167] In both cases it is an endowment (*malaka*) of practicing *ijtihād* that characterizes the *mujtahid*.

5.1 *Ibn al-Wazīr's Position on the Divisibility of* Ijtihād

In *al-ʿAwāṣim*, Ibn al-Wazīr mentions divisibility once. The context is that of the fighters (*mujāhidūn*) among the companions who were called scholars (*mutafaqqihūn*). They were allowed to give legal opinions in questions where they have heard or seen the Prophet do or say something. However, as Ibn al-Wazīr reasons, "they were no *mujtahids* in issues that they neither saw nor heard. (…) This is one of the proofs for the divisibility of *ijtihād*."[168]

The commonly accepted rule says that a *mujtahid* must act according to his *ijtihād*. The question that arises is: when is the conclusion arrived at to be considered *ijtihād*? The reference to the Prophetic traditions at a time when the Prophet and his companions were still alive suggests a very basic level. This is echoed in Ibn al-Wazīr's *al-Ḥusām al-mashhūr* in which he defends the legitimacy of al-Manṣūr's imamate. His legitimacy was doubted because of his supposed deficiency in the professional abilities needed for *ijtihād*.[169] Ibn al-Wazīr repudiates this charge by arguing that the imam does indeed possess what knowledge and capability is required for partial *ijtihād*:

> When methods began to differ and creatures started feuding with each other, those who were occupied with kinds of knowledge (*ʿulūm*) other than that of the forefathers (*salaf*) deemed those who were [occupied with it] to be void of knowledge. Just as those engaged with the knowledge of the forefathers knew those ignorant of it to be void of the true knowledge. Thus, the ignorant ones identified the vilest [kind of] ignorance with the highest levels of knowledge. How terribly strange is the way they consider knowledge what really is ignorance, and they discredit our Lord, Commander of the Faithful, peace be upon him, for not being occupied with what they consider knowledge. The truthful answer to those who speak such evil things has a number of aspects. First of all, their certainty about the non-existence of his [capability of] *ijtihād* is merely a

167 See al-Arnaʾūṭ (intr., ed.), *al-ʿAwāṣim* ii, 30, footnote 2.

168 Ibn al-Wazīr, *al-ʿAwāṣim* ii, 30.

169 In *al-Ḥusām al-mashhūr*, Ibn al-Wazīr's major argument does not evolve around *ijtihād*, but rather around the question of whether or not *ijtihād* is the most important function of an imam. He argues that whereas the sources mention the necessity of a just imam repeatedly, little is said about the necessity of being the most learned imam; cf. Ibn al-Wazīr, *al-Ḥusām al-mashhūr* fs. 111a–112b.

> false accusation since the least [form of] *ijtihād* is a hidden thing about the interpretation, easiness or difficulty of which there is severe disagreement between the scholars of Islam. It is not something that can be perceived by the senses, nor does it belong to those things that are known in the intellect by necessity or by analogous inference.[170]

In this passage, Ibn al-Wazīr indicates only what he considers the most important aspect of *ijtihād*, namely the knowledge of that which the *salaf* knew. It is obvious from the emphasis put on Imam al-Manṣūr's mastery of Quran and the prophetic Sunna throughout the writing that this "knowledge of the *salaf*" means the texts of revelation.[171] In this context, Ibn al-Wazīr lists the variety of definitions of *ijtihād*, including smaller and greater *ijtihād* as well as partial and absolute *ijtihād*.[172] According to him, the lowest form of *ijtihād* is possible on the basis of the mastery of the texts of Quran and Sunna. Accordingly, Imam al-Manṣūr does qualify as a scholar and *mujtahid*, although he is a *muqallid* in many areas.

The case of Imam al-Manṣūr is a very vivid manifestation of Ibn al-Wazīr's understanding not only of *ijtihād*, but also of what is to be considered knowledge, as discussed in chapter 3. Ibn al-Wazīr emphasizes the ambiguity as to the starting point from which the legal interpretation can be called *ijtihād*. Elaborating on the question of when probable conclusions on legal questions can be considered *ijtihād* suggested itself to Ibn al-Wazīr as part of his rebuttal of the idea that it is permissible to emulate dead scholars. The distinction between the layman and the discerning student (*al-ṭālib al-mumayyiz*) was a crucial element in the distinction between the permitted and the prohibited kind of *taqlīd* in terms of the emulator. Ibn al-Wazīr knows himself to have the qualities of the discerning student who is not permitted to practice *taqlīd*. This last point seems to be aimed primarily at defending Ibn al-Wazīr against the often repeated accusation that he is not following the early Zaydi imams. The true meaning of following, i.e. following in meaning (*al-ittibāʿ fī l-maʿnā*), taken together with the impermissibility of *taqlīd* for the distinguishing student, ren-

170 Ibn al-Wazīr, *al-Ḥusām al-mashhūr* f. 103b.

171 Elsewhere in the work Ibn al-Wazīr asks how, after considering the concession to the *ijtihād* of *muqallids* by a number of Zaydi scholars, it is possible that some claim consensus to the effect that people like Imam al-Manṣūr are neither *mujtahids* nor scholars in spite of their profound studies of the knowledge of divine law in Quran and Sunna; cf. ibid., f. 104a.

172 The full list of what the term *ijtihād* comprises is given in ibid., f. 103b. As Zysow remarked, it is difficult to frame a satisfactory definition of *ijtihād* in the juridical sense; cf. Zysow, *Economy of Certainty* 260.

der the study of indicators and subsequent independent judgement incumbent on him. The doctrine of divisibility provides an explanation and a solution to the tension in which scholars like Ibn al-Wazīr found themselves.[173] In turn, the differentiation within the discerning student between being a *muqallid* in some and a *mujtahid* in other areas exposes two possibilities: initially, there is the following of a scholar by way of *taqlīd* succeeded by attaining information about the evidence and indicators; secondly, the student investigates the sources and the contained indicators himself and reaches an independent judgement.

Furthermore, Ibn al-Wazīr responds to the interdependence-argument. His answer runs as follows: Different books treat different disciplines. Besides that, books are divided into chapters in which each chapter treats a question along with the related evidence separately. Accordingly, one can rationally grasp and become professional in a certain field, like Arabic grammar, without having to know everything pertaining to, for example, the theological question of predestination. Yet, in a linguistic question, the word of a grammarian is more heeded than what great imams of *ijtihād* hold true. To become informed in another field, a man turns to scholars of that field for information without losing his status as a scholar of his own field. If he could not rationally grasp one field because of its interdependence with another, teaching and learning would be pointless. Neither does his turning to another scholar for information make him a *muqallid*, because it would then not be knowledge which he attains. This is because a *muqallid* is defined by the lack of knowledge of and evidence for an issue. What guides the process of *ijtihād* is the conclusion on the basis of what seems most probable to the scholar after he has studied the evidence of a specific question—be he an absolute *mujtahid* or a discerning student practicing *ijtihād* in a particular field.[174]

In *al-Rawḍ al-bāsim*, Ibn al-Wazīr describes the context in which the doctrine of indivisibility becomes manifest:

> But now to our question concerning one who follows the opinions of the majority and considers it sound: If, after extensive study of the writings of the scholars that contain the indicators according to topics and that mention disagreements and arguments fairly and completely, some opinions seem to him more likely because they comply with the sound texts (*li-muwāfaqat al-nuṣūṣ al-ṣaḥīḥa*), [and if] he fears to have become a *mujtahid* in that question even if he is no *mujtahid* but a *muqallid* practicing

173 Ibn al-Wazīr, *Kitāb al-Qawāʿid* f. 93a.

174 Ibid., fs. 84b–93a, 85b.

> *tarjīḥ* without there being in his mind the slightest partisanship (*dukhān al-ʿaṣabiyya*) which would lead him to follow the less excellent and to act according to the less likely (*al-marjūḥ*), [about such a one] there is disagreement as to his duty [to follow his conclusions], not as to whether or not this is permitted or desirable.[175]

Ibn al-Wazīr points to the probable nature of *ijtihād* in the defense of its divisibility. *Ijtihād* itself is not abolished because of the possibility of its indicators being out-weighted (*marjūḥ*) in any given matter, as long as there are no concrete indicators that are indeed stronger than those that led to a given judgment initially. *Ijtihād* is based on conjecture (*ẓann*)—the scholar is driven by the evidence to assume a particular conclusion. This is as true for the *muqallid* practicing *ijtihād* in particular areas as it is for the *mujtahid* of all disciplines.[176] But the context manifest in the question at hand indicates that those who prohibit the divisibility of *ijtihād* would also be wary of allowing a *muqallid* to search out the indicators and arguments and to come to his own conclusion instead of following an imam, *mujtahid* or school irrespective of indicators. However, the major disagreement exists in the question as to whether this practice of looking for indicators is a duty, rather than whether or not it is permissible. Ibn al-Wazīr says that "concerning those who hold to divisibility, it is obvious." By "obvious" he means that among supporters of divisibility, unlike those who reject divisibility, the duty of the *muqallid* to act according to what he assumes to be the correct position irrespective of who expressed that opinion is taken for granted.[177]

5.2 *Ibn al-Murtaḍā's Position on the Divisibility of* Ijtihād

Ibn al-Murtaḍā was likewise a supporter of the doctrine of divisibility. However, he spent much less effort on the defense of his views. His appellation of someone practicing partial *ijtihād* has nothing of the active connotation found in Ibn al-Wazīr's elaboration. In his words, partial *ijtihād* sounds rather unlike an active part of the interpretative legal process: namely "one (yet) unable to reach the stage of *ijtihād* (*al-qāṣir ʿan rutbat al-ijtihād*)."[178] In *Minhāj al-wuṣūl*, Ibn al-Murtaḍā's definition of the general and the particular *ijtihād* at the beginning of the chapter on *ijtihād* is directly followed by a discussion of its divisibility.

---

175 Ibn al-Wazīr, *al-Rawḍ al-bāsim*, 217.

176 Ibid., 216; similarly al-Ghazālī, *al-Mustaṣfā* ii, 353.

177 Ibn al-Wazīr, *al-Rawḍ al-bāsim* 217. The wider context of the above quote involves the possibility of *ijtihād* during the lifetime of the Prophet.

178 Ibn al-Murtaḍā, *Minhāj al-wuṣūl* 763.

According to Ibn al-Murtaḍā, *ijtihād* in a certain discipline or question is just as possible to someone yet incapable of absolute *ijtihād* as it is to the absolute (*kāmil*) *mujtahid*, in as far as both are confined to a given question that is not dependent on another question or discipline. Both equally have to investigate all the indicators (*amārāt*) that pertain to that particular question according to their understanding. Since the restricted one (*qāṣir*) is limited in his investigation to what a *mujtahid* provides for him in terms of proofs and signs, both start from the same premises. Responding to a critic who rejects the divisibility of *ijtihād*, claiming that the restricted scholar might not know all the signs relevant to his question, Ibn al-Murtaḍā writes:

> If absolute *ijtihād* in all disciplines were a requirement—meaning that the *mujtahid* would not be ignorant of a single source of any question—it would necessarily follow that he [such a *mujtahid*] would not be ignorant of anything pertaining to all the questions of *ijtihād*, because of his complete cognizance of the source (*ma'khadh*) of every single question. If not, he would be a restricted one (*qāṣir*).[179]

In short, the absolute *mujtahid* does not have complete knowledge of all the sources and indicators. An unfinished *mujtahid* is allowed to practice *ijtihād* in his limited field because the absolute *mujtahid* does likewise. An absolute *mujtahid* does not become restricted because of ignorance in certain questions. This is demonstrated by a tradition about Mālik b. Anas. When Mālik is asked forty questions, he can only answer four and says of the remaining ones that he does not know the answer. Where Mālik is concerned, apparently no one questions his rank of an absolute *mujtahid*, nor did anyone dispute his ability to give answers to the said four questions.[180] If it was possible in these questions that their indicators did not relate to the questions of which he did not know the answer, this would likewise be possible in the case of a *muqallid* who is a *mujtahid* only in some respects (here called *qāṣir*). Hence, the *qāṣir* is guided and restricted by the same principles as the *mujtahid*. He is to act on the assumption gained by the indicators he knows to be independent of indicators unknown to him. If the restricted one were not allowed to practice his partial *ijtihād*:

179 Ibid., 763.

180 The example of Mālik b. Anas was commonly used in support of divisibility. See for example Ibn al-Wazīr, *al-Ḥusām al-mashhūr* f. 103b; Ibn al-Murtaḍā, *al-Baḥr al-zakhkhār* ii, 292; al-Shawkānī, *Irshād al-fuḥūl* 255; cf. Kamali, *Principles* 326.

> It would contradict duty. The duty is to acquire all indicators that he assumes to pertain to that question—either by adopting from a *mujtahid* or after the imams have established the indicators and categorized them according to classes. If that is so, the possibilities mentioned by you do not invalidate the conjecture about the ruling. Hence, he has to act according to it.[181]

According to this reasoning, the only, yet very significant, difference between the restricted and the absolute *mujtahid* is that the former refers to and is limited by the evidence provided by a *mujtahid* or the early imams, whereas the latter refers to and is limited by the revelational sources.

In comparison, Ibn al-Wazīr and Ibn al-Murtaḍā both support the divisibility of *ijtihād* based on the principle common to all kinds of *ijtihād*, namely preponderant conjecture (*ghālib al-ẓann*). However, there is a difference in what they allow as source material for the *qāṣir* in the production of *ijtihād*-decisions. The source material determines the scope within which the scholar is allowed to issue his rulings; perhaps that of a particular discipline or science. In this case the *qāṣir* would not be restricted to drawing from the texts and proofs of his own school, although that could be the first stage. Rather, a discerning student could directly draw from the source texts that are concerned with this question, informed about the methodology of inference and reasoning from his studies. He would hence be a student and *muqallid* in numerous areas of law, but a *mujtahid* in one field. Another possibility would be that a *muqallid* practices legal interpretation of the existing texts of his school or imams in certain fields. He would then be a *mujtahid* within the school of law (*mujtahid fī l-madhhab*) in the sense of affiliation.

The implications are obvious: If, on the one hand, partial *ijtihād* is to mean that the texts of the school can be interpreted, then the concept of partial *ijtihād* supports the idea of narrowing down the scope within which a scholar can act in his interpretation of the sources. The school identity is more consolidated and the relationship to other interpretations and schools defined. If, on the other hand, partial *ijtihād* is to mean that the aspiring *mujtahid* is fit to consult the original sources and produce opinions in particular fields, the case lies differently. This by no means narrows down the scope the scholar has for legal reasoning, but rather leaves open the possibility of extension and growth

181 Ibn al-Murtaḍa, *Minhāj al-wuṣūl* 763. Parts of the quote are taken from the glosses of Ibn al-Murtaḍā's *Miʿyār al-ʿuqūl*, of which *Minhāj al-wuṣūl* is a commentary.

with the aim of achieving complete and independent *ijtihād*. The boundaries between schools are given little significance, if any at all.

In Ibn al-Murtaḍā's partial *ijtihād*, the student weighs the sources provided within the realm of the school. In contrast, partial or restricted *ijtihād* in Ibn al-Wazīr's defense of Imam al-Manṣūr does not mean that *ijtihād* is to be practiced within the confinements of the school's texts. It rather means that *ijtihād* is possible from the moment of access to the revealed sources. This echoes the example Ibn al-Wazīr gave in *al-ʿAwāṣim* of the *ijtihād* of some of the companions. There the initial moment for the process of interpreting law was the unmediated access to one of the sources of law, a deed or saying of the Prophet. There was no justification for actively drawing conclusions from that which the respective companion had not witnessed. But the lack of access to some sources—sayings or actions of Muḥammad—did not necessitate the obstruction of *ijtihād* in other cases.[182]

This idea of the divisibility of *ijtihād* goes considerably beyond what seems to have been the prevalent notion a century after Ibn al-Wazīr (and most likely also earlier). Ṣārim al-Dīn, in his systematic exposition of the legal methodology of the Prophet's progeny, states about the restricted *mujtahid*: "He is a *mujtahid* in those things in which disagreement exists. It is not permissible for him to reach an independent opinion in any question in contradistinction to the absolute *mujtahid*."[183] Although Ibn al-Wazīr does not exclude such cases, he does not restrict partial *ijtihād* to them. Of course, no discourse preceded the alleged *ijtihād* of the companions. But they could have consulted each other.

Both assertions of divisibility, i.e. that of Ibn al-Wazīr as well Ibn al-Murtaḍā's, argue with *ghālib al-ẓann*. On the one hand, the conjecture upon which the partial *mujtahid* is to act according to Ibn al-Murtaḍā (and most other Zaydis of temporal proximity) is framed by the conjecture of the absolute *mujtahid* or else the *mujtahids* the *qāṣir* learns from. The *mujtahid* provides the probable evidence from among which the *qāṣir* can choose. In contrast, Ibn al-Wazīr's understanding of partial *ijtihād* is determined by the probable nature of probability itself. Since it is only probability that needs to be reached, anyone at any stage is able to do just that, irrespective of other positions. His reference point are the texts of revelation. This is illustrated in *Kitāb al-Qawāʿid*:

> *Ijtihād* has different stages. We do not say that he [the aspiring *mujtahid*] has reached the most elevated one, but we say that he has reached *ijtihād* in some of its aspects. He has come to have tranquility of the soul

182 Cf. Ibn al-Wazīr, *al-ʿAwāṣim* ii, 30.
183 Ṣārim al-Dīn, *al-Fuṣūl al-luʾluʾiyya* 279.

> (*sukūn al-nafs*). [Even] in the matters of certainty the Bahshamiyya has only made tranquility of the soul incumbent, not that the result is necessary (*ḍarūra*). They allowed for doubt and uncertainty concerning conclusive evidence. Likewise, conjecture (*ẓann*) does not cease only because of doubts. Even if the great *mujtahid* should argue with him [the aspiring *mujtahid*], he will not change his assumption. His assumption only changes by way of contextual evidence that outweighs what he himself holds.[184]

Ibn al-Wazīr makes the tranquility of the soul a criteria of *ijtihād*. It will be remembered that for Bahshami Muʿtazilis like ʿAbd al-Jabbār and with him Ibn al-Murtaḍā, the tranquility of the soul was the single most important criteria for certain knowledge. But Ibn al-Wazīr applies it here to conjecture. If one's soul has reached the state of tranquility as to the highest likelihood of the result of one's own legal interpretation, the practice is performed and one needs to hold on to the result. For many Muʿtazila, and Ibn al-Murtaḍā as a Zaydi representative, the main importance of *sukūn al-nafs* referred to acquired knowledge. According to them, this distinguished it from *taqlīd* in doctrinal questions. But Ibn al-Wazīr did not consider acquired knowledge to be certain knowledge in the strict sense. In the criteria of tranquility of the soul for the completion of *ijtihād* it becomes evident once again that Ibn al-Wazīr identified the most probable conjecture in the field of legal theory with the secondary theological positions based on so-called acquired knowledge. In both cases, the position of the individual is determined by what seems most probable, even if this position contrasts with that of other potentially more erudite scholars or *mujtahids* in a broader spectrum of disciplines. His own informed assumption in a particular matter instead of that of a higher ranking *mujtahid* is standard because he himself is able to discern the sources in this particular matter. Both opinions, i.e. that of the discerning student as well as that of an absolute *mujtahid*, are equally based on the subjective standard of the most probable interpretation of the textual sources. This leaves little room for hierarchical definitions of relationships within or between schools even on these lower levels of partial *ijtihād*. The contrasting position that locates partial *ijtihād* within the school system thereby consolidates school identity and relates to other schools in a hierarchical manner. The meaning and impact of such partial *ijtihad* is best illustrated by the practice of *takhrīj*, or extrapolation of principles.

184 Ibn al-Wazīr, *Kitāb al-Qawāʿid* f. 85b. For a discussion of the circumstantial evidence (*qarāʾin*), see Hallaq, Notes on the Term *qarīna* 475–478.

6 Extrapolation of Principles (*takhrīj*)

Takhrīj means inferring legal principles (*qawāʿid, uṣūl, ḍawābiṭ*) from a scholar's judgements in particular cases. Individual rulings of an earlier authority are put in relation to the supposedly underlying principles. Thereby the guiding principles for the *madhhab* of the early authority are established. These principles are then applied in cases where no explicit ruling of the scholar exists.[185]

Hallaq laments that the practice and its significant role in the shaping of the schools of law has been neglected in western scholarship.[186] Although he says this in the context of the formation of the Sunni schools of law, it is even more true in respect to the development of the Zaydiyya as a legal school. Hallaq excludes Jackson's analysis of the role of the Malikī legal theorist Shihāb al-Dīn al-Qarāfī (d. 684/1285) who advanced the idea of a corporate status of the *madhhab* in the time of the then well established "regime of *taqlīd*."[187] In the Zaydi context, one has to exclude from this lack of investigation the treatise of Haykel and Zysow concerning the identity of the Zaydi *madhhab*.[188] Hallaq relates the practice of *takhrīj* to the establishment of the doctrine of a school associated with an eponym.[189] *Ijtihādāt* of scholars that came after the schools' eponyms needed to be related to the supposed founders in order to bear authority—hence the ascription of principles to the founders, which would then be applied to later scholars' legal interpretations.[190] Jackson shows how *takhrīj* was crucial in a schools' transition from loose association with a broad set of principles to adherence to a fixed body of positive rules. He describes the state of affairs in Ayyūbid-Mamlūk Cairo of the late 7th/13th century where Shafiʿi scholars widely dominated the four schools: Being affiliated with one of the schools and adhering to its legal doctrine was more important than the content of the respective doctrine. It was a means to preserve school identity.[191] The growing attitude that a school's doctrine or the supposed doc-

185 *Takhrīj* in the context of legal methodology and the development of a school doctrine is not to be confused with its namesake in the science of hadith. *Takhrīj* or *istikhrāj* in the science of hadith signifies the tracking back of a particular tradition to its origin, sometimes through an *isnād* other than what is recorded in one of the tradition compilations. Ibn al-Wazīr addresses this kind of *takhrīj* in his *Tanqīḥ al-anẓār* 40.

186 Hallaq, Early *Ijtihād* 336. Aḥmad in his doctoral thesis affirms this state of affairs; cf. Aḥmad, Structural Interrelations of Theory and Practice 18, 24.

187 Jackson, *Islamic Law and the State* 57.

188 Haykel and Zysow, What Makes a *Madhhab*? 332–371.

189 Hallaq, Early *Ijtihād*, 336.

190 Hallaq, Takhrīj 320, 333.

191 Jackson, *Islamic Law and State* 225–229.

trines of the eponym should not be violated is manifest in the development of the so called *qawāʿid* genre. *Qawāʿid* works are collections of legal precepts that delineate a school's body of subject matter. Jackson locates the beginning of that genre, and hence the tightening of a scholar's range of legal reasoning, somewhere in the 7th/13th century.[192]

Although Zaydi scholars evidently practiced a form of *takhrīj*—those scholars are often called *muḥaṣṣilūn* (i.e. those who infer [a principle]) in the Zaydi context[193]—as early as the 5th/11th century, a list of principles reflecting the previous endeavors is known to have been set down in Ibn Miftāḥ's *Sharḥ al-Azhār*, written in the 9th/15th century.[194] Ibn Miftāḥ's commentary addresses Ibn al-Murtaḍā's own commentary on his famous *fiqh* work *Kitāb al-Azhār*, which has thenceforward served as a major source for Zaydi *fiqh*. Haykel and Zysow, following al-Sayāghī, count Ibn al-Murtaḍā among the first and most important of the so-called *mudhākirūn*. The term *mudhākirūn* describes scholars after the period of the *muḥaṣṣilūn*, who further established their school's principles and collated them with the opinions of former imams as well as new cases on the basis of the principles they extracted from Quran and Sunna. Both studies locate the beginning of period of the *muḥaṣṣilūn* with the two Caspian Zaydi imams and brothers, Aḥmad b. al-Ḥusayn al-Hārūnī (d. 411/1020) and al-Nāṭiq Abū Ṭālib Yaḥyā b. al-Ḥusayn al-Hārūnī (d. 424/1032).[195] The last Zaydi imam to practice *takhrīj* was probably al-Manṣūr bi-llāh ʿAbdallāh b. Ḥamza (d. 640/1217).[196]

192 Ibid., 94. According to Hajjī Khalīfa, the first one to write a *qawāʿid* work was a certain Shafiʿi Muʿīn al-dīn Abū Ḥamīd Muḥammad b. Ibrāhīm al-Jajīrmī (d. 613/1216). However, al-Mikhlāfī locates the origin of the occupation with principles in the Hanafiyya. Yet the first one to discuss the principles in technical terms is said to have been the Shafiʿi Ibn ʿAbd al-Salām al-Sulamī (d. 660/1262). Al-Mikhlāfī's study, like Jackson's, shows that the Shafiʿi school of law was most active in the field of *qawāʿid*; cf. al-Mikhlāfī, *al-Wajīz fī-l-qawāʿid* 18–19.

193 Al-Siyāghī also calls the *muḥaṣṣilūn* "*mujtahidū l-madhhab*;" cf. al-Siyāghī, *Uṣūl al-madhhab* 13–16, 14.

194 Ibn Miftāḥ, *Sharh al-Azhār* i, 46–48.

195 See also al-Hādī b. al-Wazīr, *Hidāyat al-rāghibīn* i, 343–344. Al-Hādī b. al-Wazīr especially mentions them as having established (*taqrīr*) the *madhhab* of al-Hādī ilā al-ḥaqq, the eponym of the Hādawiyya.

196 Haykel and Zysow, What Makes a *Madhhab*? 10. Al-Manṣūr bi-llāh ʿAbdallāh b. Ḥamza, however, does not discuss the term *takhrīj* in his major work on legal methodology, *Ṣafwat al-ikhtiyār*. What he does mention is the method of ascribing an opinion to a scholar in terms of drawing an analogy. Al-Manṣūr bi-llāh ʿAbdallāh b. Ḥamza's context is the difference of opinion among the *mujtahids* and the infallibility of *ijtihād*; cf. ʿAbdallāh b. Ḥamza, *Ṣafwat al-ikhtiyār* 364–365.

According to al-Sayāghī, scholars began to establish the principles of the Zaydi imams when the name Zaydiyya started to signify a legal school, between the early 4th/10th and late 5th/11th century.[197] Interestingly, this period coincides with dates given by other researchers for the establishment of the principles of the four Sunni schools of law. This time of "the formation of a *madhhab*" in the Sunni schools was succeeded by a greater confinement of a scholar's *ijtihād* to the borders of his own *madhhab*. This is manifest in a development of the meaning of *ijtihād* (and *mujtahid*) from the absolute to the affiliated, as well as in an increase in the importance of *taqlīd*.[198]

6.1 *Ibn al-Wazīr's Concept of* Takhrīj

In *Kitāb al-Qawāʿid*, Ibn al-Wazīr addresses *takhrīj* as part of the first principle because it was employed to justify emulating dead scholars.[199] Ibn al-Wazīr is accused of inhibiting students of law and religion from practicing *taqlīd* based on his alleged contempt for the early imams and righteous forefathers. In response, Ibn al-Wazīr scrutinizes the practice of *takhrīj* and concludes that it does not represent the following of the forefathers, in contrast to what is claimed. According to him, the way *takhrīj* is practiced is to be eyed with caution, as it is often substantiated with wrong assumptions and practiced without knowledge of the criteria of *takhrīj*. The wrong assumption based on which *takhrīj* is justified is its supposed equivalence to analogical reasoning from the Prophet's sayings (*naẓīr al-qiyās*). This is manifest, for example, in the parallel between the activity of the absolute and that of the restricted *mujtahid* (*qāṣir*) as drawn by Ibn al-Murtaḍā above: The absolute *mujtahid* infers his rulings from the texts of revelation—Quran and Sunna—and performs his *ijtihād* by drawing analogies from them. The restricted *mujtahid* performs his (restricted) *ijtihād* by drawing analogies from the texts of absolute *mujtahids*.[200] However, for Ibn al-Wazīr, there is a major difference between the justification for *qiysā* and the justification for *takhrīj*:

> The permissibility [of *qiyās*] is neither derived from an analogy which says that the basis of *qiyās* should be the Prophet's sayings, nor do we ascribe to the Prophet that on which the analogy is based and then say he allowed a certain thing or prohibited it.[201]

---

197 Al-Siyāghī, *Uṣūl al-madhhab* 14–15.

198 Jackson, *Islamic Law and the State* 91, 227; Hallaq, Early *Ijtihād* 334–344.

199 Ibn al-Wazīr, *Kitāb al-Qawāʿid* f. 83a.

200 On the similarities and differences between inferring rulings from the texts of revelation and the sayings of absolute *mujtahids*, see Weiss, *Search for God's Law* 709–710.

201 Ibn al-Wazīr, *Kitāb al-Qawāʿid* f. 74b. These words are quoted from Imam Abū Ṭālib's *al-*

In other words, there is an explicit command to draw analogies from prophetic traditions. Ibn al-Wazīr contrasts this with the reference to earlier scholars. To use their sayings as a basis for analogy, i.e. *takhrīj*, in terms of extrapolating the principle behind their judgement as a counterpart of a effective cause (*ʿilla*) is neither explicitly commanded nor explicitly permitted.

> Analogical reasoning (*qiyās*) on the basis of words of the scholars is not permissible, because we were not commanded to do so. It is not our duty to do so, in fact we are not empowered to do so and it is not permitted.[202]

In short, an explicit command exists and is the foundation of *qiyās* from prophetic traditions. This contrasts with the extraction of principles from the sayings of earlier scholars in order to issue judgements accordingly. In this latter case, the permissibility is only based on vague similarities between it and analogical reasoning on the basis of the Prophet's stipulations. Even if the similarities between the two practices were enough to justify *takhrīj* by analogy to the Prophet's sayings, it would remain probable knowledge and could not be translated into permissibility as a general rule, in contradistiction to *qiyās*.

Imam Abū Ṭālib Yaḥyā l-Hārūnī (d. 424/1033) in his *Mujzī fī uṣūl al-fiqh* lists three conditions that render *takhrīj* permissible in a particular case. The first group of permissible sources for *takhrīj* are those in which the original case is identical, in its apparent form, to the new issue. No possible ambiguity is allowed, as for example in the case of a male slave who is informed of his freedom and then actually set free and a female slave who is equally informed of her freedom. The two cases are identical. She likewise should be set free.[203] Both Ibn al-Wazīr and Ibn al-Murtaḍā support this criterion. Ibn al-Murtaḍā refers to Abū l-Ḥusayn al-Baṣrī who mentioned the case "of a clear text of which the corresponding cases are exact equivalents."[204] Other cases where *takhrīj* is permissible are those where the text of the scholar represents a general statement, the rule of which pertains to all the particulars included in it. In all the new particular cases, the ruling of that general statement can be applied in reference to the principles of the late scholar. Hence, if a scholar says that all kinds of intoxicating liquids are prohibited, it can be concluded that he considers for

---

Mujzī. Ibn al-Wazīr extensively quotes from him in this section. In some points he agrees with him, in others not.

202 Ibid., f. 74b.

203 This example is not given by Imam Abū Ṭālib. Ibn al-Wazīr refers to an undefined group of scholars of *uṣūl*.

204 Ibn al-Murtaḍā, *Minhāj al-wuṣūl* 801.

example *muthallath* (boiled grape juice) prohibited.[205] In *al-ʿAwāṣim*, Ibn al-Wazīr considers this the highest and soundest form of *takhrīj*.[206] A third group of cases in which Imam Abū Ṭālib permits *takhrīj* is rejected by Ibn al-Wazīr but endorsed by Ibn al-Murtaḍā: If a scholar mentions an effective cause and is not among those who practice the particularization of the *ʿilla* (*takhṣīṣ al-ʿilla*), it is permissible to apply that ruling to a new case with an identical *ʿilla*. If, for example, a scholar has stipulated that quantitive disparity is prohibited in the sale of wheat in exchange for wheat because of the congruence in kind and value, and it is moreover known that his opinion is likewise where barley is concerned, it is correct to infer his position (*madhhab*) from either case.[207]

There are a number of reasons why Ibn al-Wazīr does not consider the third condition a valid ground for *takhrij*. Firstly, the mentioned *ʿilla* might be considered an *ʿilla* that pertains only to certain cases, like the reason for shortening the prayer during a journey (*ʿilla qāṣira*).[208] Furthermore, there might be contradicting or equally valid *ʿilal* in other rulings of the said scholar. The scholar might have made a general statement or specific stipulation that invalidates the analogy drawn from this singular case. Hence, no general principle of his *madhhab* can be inferred from a singular case. It is impossible to reach that level of certainty about the scholar's *madhhab* that is required for general principles and rules. To this Ibn al-Wazīr adds that this third group of cases cannot function as the grounds for *takhrīj*, since all scholars of early generations apparently considered *takhṣīṣ al-ʿilla* permissible. Accordingly, every *ʿilla* mentioned by said scholars may have been such a case of particularization, rendering it impossible to use it in another case.[209]

Though Ibn al-Wazīr concedes a limited space for *takhrīj*, the warning against it is not grounded in contempt for the early scholars and *ahl al-bayt*. Ibn al-Wazīr claims that neither they nor other early Zaydi authorities practiced that kind of inference in actual fact. The *ahl al-bayt*, for example, apparently

---

205 This example is taken from Abū l-Ḥusayn al-Baṣrī as quoted by Ibn al-Murtaḍā. Abū l-Ḥusayn al-Baṣrī mentions this type of inference of a scholar's *madhhab* as the second, after the clear textual stipulation (*naṣṣ ṣarīḥ*): cf. Ibn al-Murtaḍā, *Minhāj al-wuṣūl* 801. For *muthallath* see Wensinck, Khamr.

206 Ibn al-Wazīr, *al-ʿAwāṣim* iii, 130.

207 This example is likewise taken from Abū l-Ḥusayn al-Baṣrī, as quoted in Ibn al-Murtaḍā, *Minhāj al-wuṣūl* 801.

208 The restricted *ʿilla* is theoretically not equal to the particularization of the *ʿilla*. Whereas in the latter case, a generally applicable *ʿilla* might not pertain to a number of particular cases, a restricted *ʿilla* pertains only in a few cases without being related to a general rule. In effect, the difference is negligible.

209 Ibn al-Wazīr, *Kitāb al-Qawāʿid* f. 74b.

did not practice *takhrīj* from the stipulations of ʿAlī b. Abī Ṭālib in spite of the high standing he had among them.[210] This means that they were neither his *muqallids* nor *mujtahids* within his *madhhab*. Although *takhrīj* can be considered permissible in a few particular cases, this permissibility is not based on following the early generations in the true meaning of the word, namely true to the intention of what they said, did and stipulated.

According to Ibn al-Wazīr, the limited understanding of when *takhrīj* is permitted and how it is to be performed produces weak results of *takhrīj*. These—Ibn al-Wazīr again agrees with Imam Abū Ṭālib here—have been and are often the cause for reprehensible innovation (*bidʿa*). These innovations are then justified by the back-projection to a school's eponym or the early generations.

An example of a supposedly weak result of *takhrīj* is found in Ibn al-Wazīr's *al-ʿAwāṣim*. In a discussion about the acceptance or rejection of *mutaʾawwilūn*, Ibn al-Wazīr's opponent Ibn Abī l-Qāsim argues that the principle (*aṣl*) of the early imams al-Hādī ilā l-ḥaqq and al-Qāsim b. Ibrāhīm was to reject them. This principle was ascribed to the two imams by Abū Jaʿfar al-Daylamī.[211] The counterargument is supported by a transmission of Qadi Abū Muḍar (d. 5th/11th c.),[212] according to whom both imams would have accepted *mutaʾawwilūn*.[213] But Ibn Abī l-Qāsim does not explain the origin of this *takhrīj* and expects that its authority should be convincing. According to Ibn al-Wazīr, such an approach to *takhrīj* is reminiscent of the prohibited kind of *taqlīd*. It is impossible to know whether the three requirements of Imam Abū Ṭālib (or the two that Ibn al-Wazīr accepts) apply here, because Ibn Abī l-Qāsim does not specify how *takhrīj* was effectuated in this case. Whereas Ibn Abī l-Qāsim does not explain how the process and result of his alleged *takhrīj* came about, Ibn al-Wazīr lists two proofs for a *takhrīj* of Imam Abū Ṭālib which conform with the transmis-

210 Ibid., f. 75a.

211 On Abū Jaʿfar b. ʿAlī al-Daylamī, see al-Wajīh, *Aʿlām* 285. Al-Muʾayyidī mentions Abū Jaʿfar as a transmitter of al-Muḥsin b. Karrāma (al-Ḥākim) al-Jishumī; cf. al-Muʾayyidī, *Lawāmiʿ al-anwār* ii, 14–15.

212 Qadi Abū Muḍar was also known as "the commentator (*sharrīḥ*) of al-Muʾayyad," referring to his famous commentaries on the books of the Caspian imam al-Muʾayyad bi-llāh al-Hārūnī (d. 411/1020), like the *Sharḥ al-Ziyādāt* to which Ibn al-Wazīr refers in his reasoning. Abū Muḍar's father was a judge at the court of al-Muʾayyad bi-llāh. He played a significant role in consolidating the Zaydi *madhhab* by establishing its legal principles. In turn, his commentaries became the object of super-commentaries once they reached Yemen; cf. Ibrāhīm b. al-Qāsim, *Ṭabaqāt al-Zaydiyya* i, 485–486; al-Wajīh, *Aʿlām* 478–479. Abū Muḍar himself was a teacher of Qadi Jaʿfar b. ʿAbd al-Salām, who played a crucial role in the spread of the Bahshami teaching among Yemeni Zaydis. However, apparently Qadi Jaʿfar was not an immediate student of Abū Muḍar; cf. al-Muʾayyidī, *Lawāmiʿ al-anwār* ii, 28.

213 Ibn al-Wazīr, *al-ʿAwāṣim* ii, 147; cf. Ibn al-Wazīr, *Kitāb al-Qawāʿid* f. 96b.

sion of Abū Muḍar as well as the required criteria of *takhrīj*. Although Ibn al-Wazīr does refer to *takhrīj* and explains its process in detail (what principle was extrapolated from which sayings), he qualifies the significance of the *takhrīj* by juxtaposing the alleged *takhrīj* with the transmission of Abū Muḍar.[214] The argument of Abū Muḍar in favor of acceptance of *muta'awwilūn* is not based on *takhrīj* but on transmission, which has precedence over *takhrīj*. Abū Muḍar's credibility as a transmitter is uncontested. The opposing Ibn Abī l-Qāsim would need an uninterrupted *isnād* for his *takhrīj* of Abū Jaʿfar, much as Abū Muḍar does for his transmission, so both could be weighed against each other.[215]

The supposedly wrong understanding of *takhrīj*, ascribed here to Ibn Abī l-Qāsim by Ibn al-Wazīr, leads to other aberrations with a similar tendency: an unquestioning adoption of principles supposedly ascribed to authorities of the school. In the same way that opinions are taken over by way of unquestioning *taqlīd*, principles are ascribed to authorities without the elucidation of the process of extrapolation. Ibn al-Wazīr seeks to counterbalance this by elevating the direct consultation of the primary sources. This, of course, would challenge the school structure which is rendered relatively stable by reference to its authorities' opinions and alleged principles.

Ibn al-Wazīr's opponent in his *Kitāb al-Qawāʿid* also argues for the permissibility of emulating the dead (*taqlīd al-mayyit*) by referring to *takhrīj*. Although Ibn al-Wazīr allows for *takhrīj* under particular conditions, he leaves no room for justification of *taqlīd al-mayyit* on its basis. Earlier scholars of yet later generations than the eponyms, such as Imam Abū Ṭālib, were much occupied with the study of the rulings of the school's authorities and the discernment of the respective *ʿilla* (i.e. *taʿlīl*). They were indeed occupied with defining the *madhhab* itself. Yet Ibn al-Wazīr claims that they did not practice *taqlīd* of the given scholar in the process. Imam Abū Ṭālib, as demonstrated repeatedly in *Kitāb al-Qawāʿid*, was himself a staunch assailant of *taqlīd al-mayyit*. The fact that he nevertheless practiced *takhrīj* especially from the opinions of Imam al-Hādī ilā l-ḥaqq is for Ibn al-Wazīr argument enough to show that the two—*taqlīd al-mayyit* and *takhrīj*—cannot be equated. The study of previous scholars' opinions had other reasons. They were studied in order to understand their opinions and derive principles from them (*istinbāṭ minhum*). Yet those principles had to be elaborated and should not be the object of the kind of *taqlīd* that adopts

214 Ibn al-Wazīr, *al-ʿAwāṣim* ii, 149.

215 Ibn al-Wazīr also argues based on consensus: What if two results of *takhrīj* are equal in their trustworthiness yet contradictory, one negating acceptance of *kuffār ta'wīl* and one affirming it? The acceptance has precedence because a group of Zaydi imams says that there is consensus about it. Such a consensus would have to include al-Qāsim b. Ibrāhīm and al-Hādī ilā l-ḥaqq.

principles unquestioningly. Additionally, a scholar investigating consensuses and disagreements could extend his understanding of such only if he knew the opinions of the earlier scholars.[216]

As a result of the former, Ibn al-Wazīr does not ascribe to *takhrīj* the persuasiveness of a general rule that it has for others. Significantly, he rejects *takhrīj* in terms of *qiyās* even where the reason for the initial ruling is stated in the source text of the authoritative scholar. This restricts the scope of *takhrīj* considerably, since principles arrived at by *qiyās* constitute a great part of the legal doctrine ascribed to early authorities.[217]

The example of Ibn Abī l-Qāsim indicates that he used *takhrīj* in a manner similar to *taqlīd*, where it did not seem necessary to give evidence for the process and result of the extrapolation. Similarly, the opponent's line of argumentation in Ibn al-Wazīr's *Kitāb al-Qawāʿid*: *takhrīj* is compared to *taqlīd al-mayyit* and used as its justification. Ibn al-Wazīr counters that with transmission as the more accountable method: transmission from the Prophet irrespective of what, for example, Imam al-Hādī ilā l-ḥaqq says; or transmission from Imam al-Hādī ilā l-ḥaqq so that one knows what he stipulated in a particular case (not his alleged principles) and can weigh the evidence employed by him.[218]

6.2 *Ibn al-Murtaḍā's Concept of* Takhrīj

The question of the legal opinion of people other than *mujtahids* was of much interest in the literature of legal methodology in the early 9th/15th century. Two positions already existed in the Zaydi context: On the one hand, there were those who permitted the reproduction of a *mujtahid*'s position unrestrictedly (*iftāʾ al-muqallid bi-madhhab imāmihi muṭlaqan*), even without a thorough investigation of the origin of the *mujtahid*'s ruling (*maʾkhadh*), the knowledge of the rules of *takhrīj* or how to weigh rulings and their *ʿilal* against each other. Reproduction of a position would be transmission, just as one transmits a prophetic tradition.[219] On the other hand, there were those who did not permit

216 Ibn al-Wazīr, *Kitab al-Qawāʿid* f. 82b.

217 Jackson describes how the relationship of the *mukharrij* to the texts of his imam is analoguous to the relationship of the imam to the texts of divine revelation. The *mukharrij* must be thoroughly familiar with *uṣūl al-fiqh* in order to apply it to the rulings of his imam; cf. Jackson, *Islamic Law and the State* 94–95.

218 Ibn al-Wazīr's position here is echoed, for example, in what the much later al-Qāsim b. Muḥammad (d. 1029/1620) demanded: Unclear questions and opinions should be put in relation to the primary sources; cf. Haykel and Zysow, What Makes a Madhhab? 17–18; al-Qāsim b. Muhammad, *al-Irshād* 105.

219 In Hallaq's *Continuity and Change*, it becomes evident that this discussion had already existed for some time. It is uncertain, so far, when it was introduced to the Zaydiyya.

takhrīj at all. Anyone who is capable of *ijtihād* must stipulate his own judgements. He himself is a scholar and need not extract another scholar's principles let alone transmit the position of another.[220] Ibn al-Murtaḍā agrees with neither position. By his time, consensual practice of scholars of all schools—Sunni and Zaydi—had already established the distinction between what utter laymen reproduce of their *mujtahids*, and what rulings full-blown *mujtahids* issue on their own accord.[221] In other words, *takhrīj* was a prevalent practice. Ibn al-Murtaḍā briefly discusses *takhrīj* in the chapter on *ijtihād* and *taqlīd* in his *Minhāj al-wuṣūl*. The background question is: Can a layman issue a legal opinion on the basis of the principles he derives from rulings of a *mujtahid* or his imam?

According to Ibn al-Murtaḍā, *takhrīj* is permissible when the following requirements are fulfilled: the man in question must be able to investigate the sources (*ma'khadh*); he must be conversant with the evidences of speech (*dalālat al-khiṭāb*), what of it is dropped (*al-sāqiṭ ʿanhu*) and what of it is used (*al-maʿmūl bihi*); furthermore he must know how to trace a judgement back to a principle; what the ways of the *ʿilla* are and what to do if two *ʿillas* contradict each other, as well as how they are measured out against each other. This is because *takhrīj* is based exclusively on the implicit meaning of speech (*mafhūm al-khiṭāb*) and on analogy. It is possible, says Ibn al-Murtaḍā, that the agent of this *takhrīj* be someone other than a *mujtahid*, if he has already become a student of the sources and is qualified for reasoning (*ahlan lil-naẓar*).[222]

Further material indicative of Ibn al-Murtaḍā's stance towards *takhrīj* can be found in the chapter on "the mufti and the *mustaftī*" in his *Miʿyār al-ʿuqūl*.[223] On what basis, the question goes, is one entitled to ascribe an opinion to a particular scholar?

> The opinion (*madhhab*) of a scholar can be known either from his explicit text (*bi-naṣṣihi l-ṣarīḥ*), from a comprehensive general statement (*ʿumūm shāmil*), a text that resembles the present case or from another text of his where he reasoned on the basis of an explicit *ʿilla*, even if he is one who supports the particularization of the *ʿilla*.[224]

The first three of these four scenarios are congruent with what Ibn al-Wazīr holds. When discussing the necessary features of a scholarly position from

220 Ibn al-Murtaḍā, *Minhāj al-wuṣūl* 795.
221 Ibid., 795.
222 Ibid., 794–795.
223 Ibn al-Murtaḍā, Miʿyār al-ʿuqūl 197.
224 Ibid., 197.

which to infer a legal principle in *Minhāj al-wuṣūl*,[225] Ibn al-Murtaḍā elaborates his stance in the last scenario: *takhrīj* based on the analogical application of an *ʿilla*. The background for his argumentation is *qiyās* on the basis of legal statements in Quran and Sunna. If the *mujtahid* has explicitly determined an *ʿilla* in a certain text, that *ʿilla* can be considered effective in all cases in which that *ʿilla* occurs. Consequently, the rulings effected by the *ʿilla* can be understood as the *mujtahid*'s opinions by way of *takhrīj*. A reference to the comparison with analogical deduction from rulings in Quran and Sunna is not missing. Where these contain rulings with an *ʿilla* that is only implicitly indicated (*nabbaha*), this *ʿilla* can still be effective in an analogy. If a scholar only hints at his *ʿilla*, on the other hand, it cannot be indisputably concluded that he would have ruled based on the same *ʿilla* in a parallel case: his *madhhab* for the new case cannot be inferred. Analogy does not apply in the same way here, because of the possibility of error on one side (that of the scholar in his reasoning) and the impossibility of it on the other (God and the Prophet in their decreeing). Where the *ʿilla* of the scholar is explicitly stated, however, it is similar enough to the reasoning in the Quran and Sunna. Hence the scholar's *ʿilla* in a stipulated case is effectively attributed to him as his *ʿilla* in all cases where it occurs, analogously to an *ʿilla* in Quran or Sunna.[226]

Ibn al-Murtaḍā explains why particularization of the effective cause does not impair the analogical application of the explicit *ʿilla*, even if the scholar in question supports the practice. Unless the scholar positively designates the *ʿilla* of the ruling in question to be one special case, it can be taken as generally applicable. The case is different in Quran and Sunna. In these two sources, almost all generals are particularized somewhere. Hence a scholar cannot achieve highest probability unless he has scrutinized the sources extensively for particularizations. However, in the case of a scholar Ibn al-Murtaḍā writes:

> We speak about his research in a question in which he pronounces a general statement. It is most probable that he would only have pronounced that general statement after *ijtihād* has fully discharged of its duty in the investigation of the regular forms of the question, not finding any causes for particularization (*mukhaṣṣiṣ*) in Quran, Sunna, consensus, analogy or reason. If he has found none, the case could be called general without restriction.[227]

225 Cf. Ibn al-Murtaḍā, *Minhāj al-wuṣūl* 801.
226 Ibid., 801.
227 Ibid., 802.

Using the opinions of scholars who allowed for particularization of the *ʿilla* as a source of analogy thus widens the scope of sources for *takhrīj* even further.

That *takhrīj* was a common practice in the Zaydiyya at the beginning of the 9th/15th is evident. Ibn al-Murtaḍā consolidates the idea of a *madhhab* with a somewhat more fixed body of rulings expressing the manifestation of what principles his predecessors, i.e. the *muḥaṣṣilūn*, extrapolated from the founding imams. This notion is further supported by his own introduction to *al-Baḥr al-zakhkhār*, a work that is still considered one of the major *fiqh*-works of the Yemeni Zaydiyya today. Ibn al-Murtaḍā's explanation of the abbreviations used by him show that the results of *takhrīj* from the opinion of particular scholars are considered important enough to deserve a whole category of specific symbols. Thereby the body of rulings produced indirectly through *takhrīj* is added to the corpus of what rulings already exist, expanding it considerably. Hardly a century later, Ṣārim al-Dīn al-Wazīr does not even mention that there is disagreement as to the acceptance of *takhrīj* in general, although he is known for having created "an encyclopedia compiling the opinions of the scholars from different schools and directions."[228]

What Ṣārim al-Dīn does mention is the disagreement concerning what part of the speech should be used as the source for *takhrīj*: can anything be deduced from the implicit meaning (*mafhūm*) of the text or can only the explicit meaning (*lafẓ al-khiṭāb*) function as source? Ibn al-Murtaḍā did not leave any doubt that *takhrīj* could be based on the implicit meaning (*mafhūm al-khitāb*). Ibn al-Wazīr's insistence on the explicit texts (*al-naṣṣ al-ṣarīḥ*) shows that he rejected the implicit as a source. But according to Ṣārim al-Dīn, most Zaydi scholars, including himself and Ibn al-Murtaḍā, allow the result of *takhrīj* from the implicit meaning of a scholar's ruling to be ascribed to him. The distinction from his own explicit statements has to be made clear, however, by reference to *takhrīj*.[229]

In his list of requirements for *takhrīj*, Ṣārim al-Dīn calls a person who is entitled to practice *takhrīj* a *mujtahid muqayyad*, i.e. restricted *mujtahid*. This is tantamount to what was called a *mujtahid fī l-madhhab* above, locating the focus of the legal enterprise clearly within the legal school. Ibn al-Wazīr, in contrast, focuses on the conditions that make a case or statement fit for *takhrīj*.

In the sources investigated for this study, al-Hādī b. Ibrāhīm does not discuss the concept of *takhrīj* explicitly. However, in his *Nihāyat al-tanwīh*, praise of the whole of the Prophet's progeny and especially of Imam al-Hādī ilā l-ḥaqq is

---

228 Editor-comment, Muhammad ʿIzzān in: Ṣārim al-Dīn, *al-Fuṣūl al-luʾluʾiyya* 64.

229 Ibid., 392.

ample. Many chapter headings attest to al-Hādī b. al-Wazīr's attempt to demonstrate the superiority of the Zaydiyya above other schools.[230] Although al-Hādī, like Ibn al-Murtaḍā, concedes that *taqlīd* of a living imam is preferable to *taqlīd* of a dead imam, one gets the impression that a contemporary imam would, in al-Hādī b. Ibrāhīm's view, hardly carry enough authority and knowledge to stand a chance against Imam al-Hādī ilā l-ḥaqq's views. After all, his arrival in Yemen and his crucial role in bringing justice had, according to al-Hādī b. al-Wazīr, been especially prophesied by Muḥammad and ʿAlī b. Abī Ṭālib.[231] In fact, later *mujtahids* may only be emulated by virtue of the congruity between their and the early imam's ruling. In other words, the authority of later scholars feeds on their relation to the eponym:

> Our imams of the later generations have chosen the *madhhab* of [Imam] al-Hādī, they have established it, relied upon it, refined it and built it up. This [al-Hādī's *madhhab*] was what the scholars of Yemen and the knights of duty and Sunna executed.[232]

Al-Hādī b. al-Wazīr's choice of words to describe the role of the later Zaydi scholars hardly allows for any other interpretation than the thorough endorsement of *takhrīj*. This is confirmed by his above-quoted statement in *Hidāyat al-rāghibīn* where the criteria of following anyone apart from the members of the Prophet's family is that his *ijtihād* agree (*wāfaqa*) with theirs.[233] In effect, and although al-Hādī b. al-Wazīr theoretically affirms that *taqlīd* of the living is preferable to *taqlīd* of the dead, he considers the opinions of *ahl al-bayt* to be the highest authority. Consequently, *taqlīd* as well as *takhrīj* of their opinions is preferable to any other frame of reference. This corresponds to what Haykel and Zysow suggest, namely that al-Hādī b. al-Wazīr seeks to establish al-Hādī ilā l-ḥaqq's authority over the authority of later imams.[234]

This brief survey of the opinions of Ibn al-Wazīr and two of his contemporaries, Ibn al-Murtaḍā and al-Hādī b. al-Wazīr, indicates that *takhrīj* had already become a common practice in the early 9th/15th century. However, the degree of discussion only anticipated the debate around *takhrīj* that would emerge

---

230 The chapters carry titles such as "The Preponderance of the *Madhhab* of the Imams, Peace Be Upon Them, Over Others," "The Preponderance of the *Madhhab* of the Prophet's Progeny Based on Theoretical Proof," "Some Excellent Qualities of al-Hādī [ilā l-ḥaqq]." Cf. al-Hādī b. Ibrāhīm, *Nihāyat al-tanwīh* 237, 262, 268.

231 Ibid., 268–271.

232 Ibid., 276.

233 See 277 above.

234 Haykel and Zysow, What Makes a *Madhhab*? 338.

two centuries later, as Haykel and Zysow's article illustrates.[235] Yet the tension between those who practiced and endorsed *takhrīj* like Ibn al-Murtaḍā, al-Hādī b. al-Wazīr and Ibn al-Wazīr's opponents, as mentioned in *Kitab al-Qawāʿid* and *al-ʿAwāṣim*, on the one hand, and those wary of it like Ibn al-Wazīr on the other hand, is clearly palpable. It is as conspicuous as the connection between the first position and the consolidation of the *madhhab* on the one hand, and the second position and the more subjective, revelatory text-based legal reasoning on the other hand. Where *takhrīj* constitutes the main source for the body of rulings as well as for the authority of rulings produced by active subjects in the legal interpretation subsequent to the founding imams, the main focus of activity is within the legal school. In contrast, where *takhrīj* is only permitted, yet not limited to a particular authority, it is not the underlying principles of the founding imams, but rather those of the revelational texts that function as the benchmark for later rulings.

Ibn al-Murtaḍā concedes a much wider scope of application to *takhrīj* than Ibn al-Wazīr. This is especially evident where the sources for *takhrīj* are discussed. Whereas Ibn al-Wazīr does not allow for *takhrīj* based on the *ʿilla* of a scholar's ruling, Ibn al-Murtaḍā considers this the most important source for *takhrīj*. Moreover, Ibn al-Murtaḍā permits the employment of the implicit meaning of a scholar's text or of the *ʿilla* of a scholar known to have supported the particularization of the *ʿilla*. The way *takhrīj* is practiced, however, is clearly the activity of a restricted *mujtahid*, or a *qāṣir*. In consequence, Ibn al-Murtaḍā's wide acceptance of *takhrīj* and application of the resulting *madhhab* principles had a consolidating impact on the legal identity of the Zaydiyya—unlike Ibn al-Wazīr, whose wariness of *takhrīj* left the *mujtahid*'s interpretation largely independent of school principles.

In the legal interpretation described by Ibn al-Wazīr, *ijtihād* in terms of the consultation of the revelational sources still forms the main part of the activity of the legal interpreter. And even where he consults the texts of earlier scholars or foundational imams, it is by collation with the texts of revelation that rulings are weighed and applied. The activity of *takhrīj* itself cannot be equated with *taqlīd*. Yet, the way such results of *takhrīj* are apparently accepted resembles the impermissible *taqlīd* of mere opinions of earlier scholars. Thus the significance of *takhrīj* furthermore represents a concession to the practice of *taqlīd* in Ibn al-Wazīr's context.

Takhrīj has the potential to complicate and widen the activity of a *mujtahid* within the *madhhab* considerably, as well as to render the task of such a one by

235 Ibid., 347.

no means inferior in interpretative skill to complete *ijtihād*. In a way, it gives him more freedom in his interpretation than the mere weighing out of the evidence provided by *mujtahids* of a higher rank. The interpretative freedom within the school increases. At the same time, *takhrīj* as a well defined practice has the potential to fix the school's teaching and extend its scope of influence to a degree that mere weighing out of existent opinions does not have.[236] This is because, if the alleged principles of the school's founders are established, the opinions inferred from the principles have the ability to reach posthumously into all questions and realms of law that might emerge in the future. Those alleged opinions then have an authority beyond any opinion a later *mujtahid* may conclude from the sources independently. The body of subject matter to which the members of a school are liable would thus be considerably more extensive, yet would be more restricted by its reference to the authority of the founding figures. The delimitation of school identity by principles of founding figures and their superiority above interpretations that draw directly from the texts of revelation counterbalances the instability that follows from the infallibility doctrine. In contrast, retaining the texts that all schools share as the major source of legal interpretation theoretically emphasizes the common legal identity and practically preserves the conjecture of the individual *mujtahid* as the decisive factor for legal practice.

7 The *Muqallid*'s Commitment to a Legal School (*iltizām*)

Ramifications of the theory of infallibility are also tangible in the realm of affiliation and adherence. As the *mujtahid* cannot be certain that his ruling is correct, neither can the layman be entirely sure that he chose the correct *mujtahid* or legal ruling. If every *mujtahid* is correct in the way he interprets the probable evidence of scripture, whom then should a layman refer to? What are the criteria for adherence? And what is its scope? And if there is no such thing as a correct or a wrong ruling, on what basis should he choose a *mujtahid*, and why should he abide by his choice and commit (*iltazama*) himself exclusively to one *mujtahid* or school?[237]

---

236 In that case, opinions independent of the school would still have to be arrived at in all new cases.

237 *Iltizām*—which shall here be translated as commitment, exclusive commitment and adherence to the school of a *mujtahid*—has no technical connection to either *iltizām* in literary theory (*lazam mā lā yalzam*), or *iltizām* in the context of the Ottoman and Egyptian tax-reform. Ṣārim al-Dīn defines *iltizām* as "the acceptance of the saying of another

It is clear from Ibn al-Wazīr's as well as Ibn al-Murtaḍā's writings that Zaydi scholars of *uṣūl al-fiqh* were by no means ignorant of the issue of adherence and the destabilizing consequences that infallibility could have on that very issue. In writings on legal theory, this topic is usually discussed in the chapter on the mufti and the *mustaftī*.

7.1 *Ibn al-Wazīr's Concept of* Iltizām

Ibn al-Wazīr's major concern in the question of adherence is that the *muqallid* should choose the *mujtahid* based on his professional skill evident in the products of his legal interpretation. Consequently, Ibn al-Wazīr does not agree with the above-mentioned analogy between the *mujtahid*'s choice of a particular ruling based on the textual indicators on the one hand, and the *muqallid*'s choice of *mujtahid* based on his person on the other. The major task of the *mujtahid* is to deduce a ruling for a new case from the textual sources, which may lead to an independent unprecedented opinion. The *muqallid*, on the other hand, determines preponderance (*tarjīḥ*) from between existing rulings or between the *mujtahids* that already have an opinion. Indeed, both are commanded to act according to what seems most probable in their mind, and thus to apply the most probable evidence. Yet, whereas the *mujtahid's* effort manifests something new, the *muqallid*'s effort does not.[238] Hence Ibn al-Wazīr, like Ibn al-Murtaḍā, urges the search for the most probable and prohibits turning to what is unlikely. According to Ibn al-Wazīr, adherence to the opinion of the chosen *mujtahid* is incumbent if it appears to the *muqallid* that his chosen *mujtahid* is most likely to be the one most learned. But if the scholar whose opinion was chosen in one case does not produce an opinion that appears very likely in another, the *muqallid* has to look elsewhere. Every case requires a renewed choice.[239]

For Ibn al-Wazīr, the principle of seeking and following the strongest conjecture (*ṭālib ghālib al-ẓann*) carries the strength of argument against the preference of a particular person. Apparently not wanting to disqualify al-Manṣūr bi-llāh ʿAbdallāh b. Ḥamza as a point of reference, Ibn al-Wazīr argues that al-Manṣūr bi-llāh ʿAbdallāh b. Ḥamza's position implicates the principle of *ghālib*

---

without asking for its proofs. If that applies to all the issues [treated by the other] it is called *iltizām*, otherwise it is not. Hence, every *multazim* is a *muqallid* but not the reverse." Ṣārim al-Dīn, *al-Fuṣūl al-luʾluʾiyya* 289. The discussion shows that *iltizām* was also used in the context of one single question. In such cases, the question was whether or not a *muqallid* must adhere to the answer he got from a *mujtahid* in response to his own question.

238 Ibn al-Wazīr, *al-Rawḍ al-bāsim* 228.

239 Ibn al-Wazīr, *al-ʿAwāṣim* iii, 128–129.

al-ẓann. In the attempt to invalidate Ibn Abī l-Qāsim's claim that al-Manṣūr bi-llāh ʿAbdallāh b. Ḥamza prohibited the transfer from one *mujtahid* to another (*tanaqqul*), Ibn al-Wazīr identifies Ibn Abī l-Qāsim's underlying assumptions as erroneous:

> The first view: He [Ibn Abī l-Qāsim] forbade the *muqallid* to practice *tarjīḥ* in every question. He assumes that al-Manṣūr [bi-llāh ʿAbdallāh b. Ḥamza] and Shaykh al-Ḥasan [al-Raṣṣāṣ] prohibited that because they made it incumbent to adhere to the *madhhab* of a particular imam. But it is not as the sayyid [Ibn Abī l-Qāsim] erroneously imagined. There is an obvious difference between the two questions because al-Manṣūr [bi-llāh ʿAbdallāh b. Ḥamza] made it incumbent to adhere to the opinion of the most learned and excellent for the reason that conjecture about the soundness of his saying is strongest. Al-Manṣūr [bi-llāh ʿAbdallāh b. Ḥamza] said verbatim "Whenever the learned and the *mujtahids* agree on a legal ruling, the *mustaftī* has to accept it without contradiction. If they disagree, we oblige him to practice *ijtihād* of the most learned and the most pious among them. And he has to search for evidence on that because he is able to do it and thereby strengthens his conjecture."[240]

Ibn Abī l-Qāsim in his concentration on exclusive commitment supposedly overlooked the fact that al-Manṣūr obliged the *muqallid* to adhere to his *mujtahid* only *after* he has practiced his own form of restricted *ijtihād*. According to Ibn al-Wazīr, Ibn Abī l-Qāsim's position is tantamount to following al-Manṣūr bi-llāh ʿAbdallāh b. Ḥamza's opinion in its literal form, or simply "in form" (*fī l-ṣūra*). This stands in contrast to following "in meaning" (*fī l-maʿnā*), as Ibn al-Wazīr claims himself to practice vis-à-vis al-Manṣūr bi-llāh b. Ḥamza. This contrastive pair of following "in form" or "in meaning" is a way of working with the general and the particular here, closely related to the practice of *takhrīj*. In Ibn Abī l-Qāsim's conclusion, following "in form" arises from inferring a general rule out of a particular statement of al-Manṣūr bi-llāh ʿAbdallāh b. Ḥamza. This is equal to a form of *takhrīj* which was labelled invalid by Ibn al-Wazīr, where the possibility of particularizing the effective cause (*ʿilla*) is not heeded. Furthermore, the prevalence of the ruling taken from a general statement is neglected. Ibn al-Wazīr, in contrast, insists that he agrees with al-Manṣūr bi-llāh ʿAbdallāh b. Ḥamza in meaning; namely he agrees with a principle that al-Manṣūr bi-llāh ʿAbdallāh b. Ḥamza expressed in a general statement, accord-

240 Ibid., iii, 128.

ing to which "it is incumbent to act according to the preponderant conjecture and it is forbidden to act according to the weakest conjecture."[241]

For Ibn al-Wazīr, it is important that a scholar is followed because of the high probability of the correctness of his ruling. This conjecture is informed by the evidence the scholar provides as well as by his occupation with a certain topic, or skill in a certain discipline. Doctrine, school affiliation or inherent personal qualities should have no effect on the degree of probability of the outcome. After all, "determination of preponderance is unlike preference because of superiority (*fa-l-tarjīḥ ghayr al-tafḍīl*)."[242] Determination of preponderance (*tarjīḥ*) is thus not to be confused with preference (*tafḍīl*), and neither should it be substituted by it. Whereas the former pertains to indications of skill, the latter pertains to excellence in other disciplines than the legal one in general, or than the one at question in particular.[243] Ibn al-Wazīr juxtaposes *tarjīḥ* and *tafḍīl* throughout his writings. Thus he challenges the justification of the structure of the Zaydi-Hādawī legal school in particular.

As mentioned above, Ibn al-Wazīr also endorses inquiry into the evidence before the transfer from one scholar to another. Yet he does not consider the degree of certainty that is needed for the transfer unattainable. On the contrary, in *Kitāb al-Qawāʿid*, he explains that weighing up the indicators is the very thing that makes a certain kind of *taqlīd* permissible; *taqlīd* without it is impermissible (*al-taqlīd min ghayr tarjīḥ lā yajūz*).[244] In Ibn al-Wazīr's thinking, the *mujtahid*'s person is not insignificant in terms of outward appearance of proficiency and piety, but doctrinal affiliation is of no interest whatsoever. In *Kitāb al-Qawāʿid*, he laments that some people adhere exclusively to one school, even though it is possibly weak.[245] Similarly, he writes in *Qubūl al-bushrā*:

> It is strange beyond measure that when one of the jurists who practice *taqlīd* comes across the weakness of his imam's sources and is unable to rebut the weakness, he still emulates [the imam] in the issue and ignores the witnesses in Quran and Sunna. He is so fixed on emulating the *madhhab* of his imam that he concocts invalidations of the apparent

241 Ibid., iii, 130.

242 Ibid., ii, 417.

243 Ibid., ii, 418. In the passage discussed, Ibn al-Wazīr is occupied with the defense of the reports of an innovator over those of a sound Muslim. But, as is his habit, he extends the principle and also mentions *taqlīd* of a *mujtahid's* opinion along with acceptance of a report.

244 Ibn al-Wazīr, *Kitāb al-Qawāʿid* f. 94a.

245 Ibid., f. 94a.

> meanings of [the texts of] Quran and Sunna and exchanges them with far-fetched and futile interpretations in defense of the one he emulates.[246] We have seen them gathered in their circles. If one of them remarks something of his own conjecture, they are utterly bewildered. They do not even take a breath to look at the evidence because of what is written down of the *madhhab* of their imam, thinking that this alone is where truth can be found. If they reflected upon the issue, they would first of all be bewildered concerning the *madhhab* of their imam. With people like them, discussion is a lost matter which leads to the breaking of relationships and opposition without benefit. I have not seen one who withdrew from the opinion of his imam when truth was presented to him from elsewhere. Rather, he would insist on the said opinion in spite of his knowledge of its weakness and remoteness (*buʿduhu*). It is better to stop the discussion with those who say, if they cannot comprehend the *madhhab* of his imam, 'Maybe my imam found a proof that I did not find.'[247]

In other words, evidence is not being weighed in each question before deciding whom to follow, because the *muqallid* considers that to be beyond his abilities. In contrast, Ibn al-Wazīr grants the intellectual interpretative endeavor of the individual on every level ample space in the conjectural realm.

7.2 *Ibn al-Murtaḍā's Concept of* Iltizām

In *Minhāj al-wuṣūl*, Ibn al-Murtaḍā explicitly treats the tension between exclusive commitment (*iltizām*) and the doctrine of the correctness of all *mujtahids*. He first presents the other extreme: transfer without renewed weighing of evidence. Those who endorse this argue as follows:

> They said: We say that every *mujtahid* is correct. Revelation forbids us only to transfer from the correct (*ṣawāb*) to the wrong (*khaṭaʾ*), rather than from the correct to the correct. Likewise the *muqallid*, if he emulates a *mujtahid* and then turns to follow another *mujtahid*, is like one who starts out with one kind of atonement and then prefers to practice a second kind of it. As he is not prohibited to do so, neither is the *muqallid* if he goes over [to another *mujtahid*]. This is only prohibited, if one holds that truth is only with one [*mujtahid*] and that the one disagreeing is in error. They say: As the *muqallid* is allowed to choose whatever *madhhab* he wants at

246 Apparently, this is attributed to Ibn ʿAbd al-Salām al-Sulamī (d. 660/1262) and his *Qawāʿid al-aḥkām*, as is some of what follows; cf. al-Yāfiʿī, *al-Tamadhhub* 131.

247 Ibn al-Wazir, *Qubūl al-bushrā* 315–316.

> the beginning—without this being disagreed upon—because of the correctness of the *mujtahids*, [accordingly] we hold on to the initial status as long as there is no new command (*istiṣḥabnā al-ḥāl*) after his *taqlīd* of one of them [the scholars], because no new stipulation prohibits him [from doing] this.[248]

In Ibn al-Murtaḍā's quote, those permitting transfer (*tanaqqul*) do not draw the common analogy between the *muqallid*'s and the *mujtahid*'s choice, whereas Ibn al-Murtaḍā considers it definitive and indeed a certain one (*qiyās qaṭʿī*).[249] In support of his position, Ibn al-Murtaḍā quotes al-Manṣūr bi-llāh ʿAbdallāh b. Ḥamza along with al-Ḥasan al-Raṣṣāṣ as the strongest Zaydi supporters of the impermissibility of transferring from *taqlīd* of one imām to that of another. Their argument is built on the comparison between the layman's choice of a *mujtahid* based on the most persuasive sign (*arjaḥ al-amārāt*) on the one hand, and the *mujtahid*'s choice in his reliance on the most persuasive signs for his ruling on the other. In the *muqallid*'s decision the *mujtahid* becomes equal to the strongest evidence in the *mujtahid*'s decision, and the results of that *mujtahid*'s *ijtihād* become tantamount to a single ruling of the *mujtahid*. As the *mujtahid* is not allowed to turn away from the evidence that he considers strongest, the *muqallid* is not permitted to turn away from his imam, once chosen.[250] It should be noted that, as to the *muqallid*'s choice, this analogy hinges on the person of the *mujtahid*, rather than on the individual rulings.

Interestingly, Ibn al-Murtaḍā mentions Ibn Abī l-Qāsim, next to Abū Muḍar and Imam Yaḥyā b. Ḥamza, as among those who permit transfer of following. Throughout *al-ʿAwāṣim* and *al-Rawḍ al-bāsim*—both said to be written in response to Ibn Abī l-Qāsim—one gets a very different impression of Ibn Abī l-Qāsim's position. In the two writings, Ibn al-Wazīr defends the legal opinions and even more prominently the transmissions of scholars not belonging to those in complete compliance with Zaydi doctrines. It is in this context that the adherence to one scholar is discussed. Therefore, it is likely that Ibn Abī l-Qāsim, as Ibn al-Murtaḍā indicates, allowed for the "unqualified transfer" of *taqlīd* among the *mujtahids* of *ahl al-bayt* only.[251] This observation, far from

248 Ibn al-Murtaḍā, *Minhāj al-wuṣūl* 803.

249 Ibid., 803. For the acceptance of the analogy, see Weiss, *The Search for God's Law* 703. Ibn al-Wazīr's opponents in *al-ʿAwāṣim, al-Rawḍ al-bāsim* as well as in *Kitāb al-Qawāʿid* draw it as well.

250 Ibid., 807.

251 "Unqualified transfer" here signifies a transfer of *taqlīd* without preceding investigation

complicating the matter, rather speaks in favor of the thesis that Ibn al-Wazīr attempts to open up legal interpretation beyond the schools while his contemporaries strove to consolidate the legal identity of the Zaydiyya. Accordingly, Ibn Abī l-Qāsim did not oppose transfer of commitment to a different scholar's opinion as such and for the sake of the correctness of the opinion itself. He rather opposed some kind of transfer of commitment to a different scholar, because he wanted to preserve the commitment to the scholar's person and affiliation. Investigation of the evidence for the different scholars' rulings was not needed. Indeed, it could not have a place in the decision because Ibn Abī l-Qāsim, more so even than Ibn al-Murtaḍā, considered it beyond the abilities of a layman to weigh the evidence and determine preponderance. *Tarjīḥ*, according to him, was a characteristic and requirement of a *mujtahid*.[252] As long as the transfer happened within the group of the *ahl al-bayt*, no doctrinal soundness was threatened and no evidence needed to be weighed because the rulings were all equally correct.

Ibn al-Murtaḍā and Ibn Abī l-Qāsim both concluded from the words of al-Manṣūr bi-llāh ʿAbdallāh b. Ḥamza and al-Ḥasan al-Raṣṣāṣ that their command to adhere to the *madhhab* of a certain *mujtahid* necessitated the prohibition of reconsidering and weighing the evidence anew in every question. To my mind, this interpretation of the statement of al-Manṣūr bi-llāh ʿAbdallāh b. Ḥamza is based on the elevation of the authority of the person above the authority of the indicators.[253] The likelihood is determined by who the person is, rather than what skills he has. In the Zaydiyya, this takes the shape of preferring the rulings of *ahl al-bayt* qua *ahl al-bayt* over the rulings of other *mujtahids* because of a certain superiority (*faḍl*) that was ascribed to them.[254]

---

of the evidence up to the point of preponderance. This indeed could result in a more or less arbitrary and inconsistent following, irrespective and unheeding of any kind of evidence other than the unfounded belief in the correctness of the *mujtahids* of *ahl al-bayt*. Such decisions based on the originator rather than the content of legal opinions, or any productivity in the realm of law and religion for that matter, is the very thing Ibn al-Wazīr intends to caution believers against. "The experts recognize men by the truth, rather than the truth by the men." Ibn al-Wazīr, *Kitāb al-Qawāʿid* f. 63a.

252 Ibn al-Wazīr, *al-Rawḍ al-bāsim* 228.

253 Weiss discusses the different levels on which authority operates: on the level of indicators, of the texts, of methodologies for deriving the rules from the texts, of applying rules to concrete situations and finally of the *mujtahids* themselves; cf. Weiss, *Search for God's Law* 700–701.

254 The corresponding preference (*tafḍīl*) may be put more suggestively here as 'considering as superior.' Both terms are regularly used to refer exclusively to the Prophet's progeny.

Al-Manṣūr bi-llāh ʿAbdallāh b. Ḥamza's argument for exclusive commitment, as quoted by Ibn al-Murtaḍā, identifies a conclusion concerning the probability of one individual ruling of a scholar with a conclusion concerning the probability of all his rulings. Accordingly, al-Manṣūr bi-llāh ʿAbdallāh b. Ḥamza assumes that the complete program of legal interpretation of a *mujtahid* (*maslak al-ijtihād*) is represented in a single ruling. Ibn al-Murtaḍā quotes him:

> It is impermissible for one who requests a legal opinion in a certain case from a scholar to act according to the opinion of another in another case, even if the opinion of that other scholar is more cautious (*aḥwaṭ*) than the opinion of his imam. The 'more cautious' has no meaning for one who is certain about the correctness of the *mujtahids*.[255]

Accordingly, no new investigation into a scholar's opinions on other questions, let alone issues of other disciplines, would be necessary or even allowed. Once the conclusion is reached concerning a scholar's method of interpretation, along with the decision to adhere to that scholar or school, no further investigation is necessary. The link to a strong school affiliation and even more so to an affiliation with the Zaydiyya, because of the status of the Zaydi imams from among the Prophet's progeny, is not far fetched. As part of the doctrine of the Zaydiyya, the imams of the *ahl al-bayt* are attributed with particular inherent qualities and, of course, sound doctrine. A quote from Ibn al-Wazīr's brother al-Hādī b. al-Wazīr duly illustrates the understanding of superiority common among Zaydis of Ibn al-Wazīr's time and beyond:

> Truly, the one who knows what we know concerning the superiority (*faḍl*) of the *ahl al-bayt*, and if his mind is aware of what we have mentioned about their knowledge, their asceticism and their piety, about the special status they have through their noble prerogatives and outstanding ranks, about their doctrinal soundness in the articles of faith, their distinct position concerning the correctness (*iṣāba*) in the way they proceed in matters of opinion, [knows that] this is a noble particularity none of the other Muslim groups has. This has been indicated by Imam Yaḥyā b. Ḥamza, peace be upon him, as we have mentioned in the transmission of him. These particularities number ten in total. We will conclude our

255 Ibn al-Murtadha does not specify from which writing of al-Mansur bi-llāh he quotes; cf. Ibn al-Murtaḍā, *Minhāj al-wuṣūl* 807.

> words about their [the *ahl al-bayt*'s] superiority and the preponderance of their *madhhab* with [mentioning] them.[256]

Tellingly, the first particularity of the *ahl al-bayt* mentioned subsequently by al-Hādī b. al-Wazīr is their doctrinal soundness in the articles of faith. This doctrinal soundness finds expression in the idea of a personal rectitude (*ʿadāla*). Next to abstention from sins and obedient performance of duties, this personal rectitude is defined, according to al-Hādī b. al-Wazīr, by what beliefs they hold.[257] Ibn al-Murtaḍā argues similarly in the introduction of *Kitāb al-Azhār*. According to him there are two reasons why the *ahl al-bayt* are yet the preferable *mujtahids* to be followed:

> The famous ones among the *ahl al-bayt*, peace be upon them, are more worthy [of being emulated] because the soundness of their beliefs and their freedom from wrong doctrines is *tawātur*.[258]

In *Sharḥ al-Azhār* this is explained further:

> (…) because there is no *tawātur* report about any of the famous among them according to which he has committed the wrong of predeterminism or anthropomorphism or any such error in doctrine. By that and by their texts also we know that their faith comprises [divine] justice and unicity in its complete form.[259]

Hence, a reason to prefer the *mujtahids* of *ahl al-bayt* is the certainty one can have about the soundness of their doctrine and belief, free of doctrinal errors—unlike the eponyms of the four other schools, for example.

Ibn al-Murtaḍā is not as staunch an opponent of the transfer of one's legal loyalty as he understands al-Manṣūr bi-llāh ʿAbdallāh b. Ḥamza and al-Ḥasan al-Raṣṣāṣ to be. Although he admits to being impressed by their above-cited argument and does not refute it, neither does he impose exclusive commitment to the *madhhab* of one scholar without exception. Should the *muqallid* discover that the *mujtahid* he follows is deficient in his uprightness (*ʿadāla*), he

256 Al-Hādī b. al-Wazīr, *Hidāyat al-rāghibīn* 373. Interestingly, this is the same scholar, namely Imam Yaḥyā b. Ḥamza, that Ibn al-Wazīr quotes in the context of his distinction between weighing up (*tarjīḥ*) and preference (*tafḍīl*); cf. Ibn al-Wazīr, *al-ʿAwāṣim* ii, 418.

257 Al-Hādī b. al-Wazīr, *Hidāyat al-rāghibīn* 374.

258 Ibn al-Murtaḍā, *Kitāb al-Azhār* i, 1.

259 Ibn Miftāḥ, *Sharḥ al-Azhār* i, 15.

is allowed to transfer to one who is more complete (*al-akmal*). As we have seen above, rectitude of a particular, i.e. Zaydi, molding is widely considered to be a requirement for *ijtihād*. If this rectitude is infringed, the *muqallid* must transfer his *taqlīd* to another opinion, even if the legal opinion of his initial imam was correct.[260]

> Among the things because of which relocation of one's following is expedient, for example, [becomes clear in the case of] a *muqallid* of al-Shāfiʿī. If he continues to follow him, then he adheres to a false doctrine like determinism and anthropomorphism. Yet, if he goes over to following someone else he transfers to justice and unicity (*tawḥīd*). In this case, the *mujtahid* of the ʿAdliyya is permitted to command him [the *muqallid*] to transfer. He can issue a legal opinion to that effect because of the religious benefit.[261]

In a number of cases, the weighing of the indicators can lead the layman to transfer to another scholar. But this weighing of indicators means tracing all the signs and proofs that led the scholar to the very ruling (*istīfāʾ ṭuruq al-ḥukm*). Arriving at that point is a highly uncertain matter, and necessitates that the layman be capable of philosophical speculation (*ahl al-naẓar*) and know the rulings of the other scholars as well:

> Among them [the conditions for transfer] is that the *muqallid* knows the arguments of the different scholars on the case, and he must be from among the *ahl al-naẓar*. (…) Furthermore, among them [the conditions for transfer] is that he [the *muqallid*] discovers a deficiency in his imam's rectitude or his *ijtihād*.[262]
>
> After commitment (*iltizām*), transfer (*intiqāl*) from whom he has committed himself to is forbidden, unless he himself determines preponderance (*tarjīḥ nafsihi*) after exhaustive treatment of all the ways of the ruling that he inquires into.[263]

260 Cf. ibid., i, 20.

261 Ibn al-Murtaḍā, *Minhāj al-wuṣūl* 806. The term ʿAdliyya refers to those who defend God's justice, i.e. the Muʿtazila.

262 Ibid., 805–806.

263 Ibn al-Murtaḍā, *Kitāb al-Azhār* i, 2.

As we have seen in chapter 5 section 5 on the divisibility of *ijtihād*, Ibn al-Murtaḍā is wary of conceding the ability of determining preponderance to laymen. Hence, shifting from one *mujtahid* to another would occur rather seldom. Ibn al-Murtaḍā considers *taqlīd* by a *muqallid* the strongest of all kinds of *ijtihād* (*ka-ijtihād aqwā min ijtihād*). *Ijtihād*, of course, must here be understood in the wider sense of great effort expended in reaching a conclusion. Ibn al-Murtaḍā thought of it in the context of a *muqallid* weighing up the indicators for the probability of a scholar's or his ruling's correctness. To him, this weighing—and especially for a second time—is a task almost too difficult for the *muqallid*. It would be of little religious benefit (*maṣlaḥa dīniyya*) to him.[264] Consequently, Ibn al-Murtaḍā considered transfer of a *muqallid*'s adherence only of religious benefit when done on the grounds of the *mujtahid*'s doctrine. In the cases of Ibn al-Murtaḍā, al-Hādī b. al-Wazīr and Ibn Abī l-Qāsim, *tarjīḥ* based on case-specific evidence is substituted (or circumvented) by *tafḍīl* based on doctrine, affiliation or inherent qualities. Again we see how the realm of certain knowledge in the form of the *mujtahid*'s doctrine bears heavily on the realm of probable knowledge, i.e. of indicators and preponderance. Furthermore, it is a case in point of Ibn al-Murtaḍā's desire to maintain the cohesion of the *madhhab*, whereas Ibn al-Wazīr transgresses its boundaries.

8 Conclusion

The question of exclusive commitment to one school or imam (*iltizām*) reveals once again what had already become evident in the discussions around *taqlīd* and the concepts of following, the requirements (*shurūṭ*) of *ijtihād*, the divisibility (*tajazzu'*) of *ijtihād* and the extrapolation of principles (*takhrīj*): The stability that had been lost due to the theory of infallibilism was regained by shifting to the realm of certainty, namely theological doctrine. Unrestricted transfer of commitment and following as a consequence of infallibilism was tempered by elevating a specific theological doctrine as the main criteria for the permissibility of that transfer. One of the Zaydiyya's major doctrines is the

264 However, Ibn al-Murtaḍā considers the adherence to a ruling or school of much religious benefit, even if it went contrary to one's own immediate benefit, because it was equal to the battle against one's own soul. He discusses the case of changing one's *madhhab* because of a thrice uttered repudiation and the subsequent regret of the change, and concludes by saying: "This [the change of *madhhab*] is not permissible where I am concerned. Rather, it is imposed upon him to battle with his soul for the sake of the improvement of its religion (*mujāhadat nafsihi fī ṣalāḥ dīnihā*)." Ibn al-Murtaḍā, *Minhāj al-wuṣūl* 806.

superiority (*faḍl*) of *ahl al-bayt*. But since it could hardly be upheld for its own sake in the legal realm of probability, another factor was needed—beyond the probability in the legal realm, yet with an effect on that very probability.

The certainty to be attained in doctrinal issues was also introduced into the question of *iltizām* in another way. Ibn Abī l-Qāsim allowed unqualified transfer of *taqlīd* within the group of the *ahl al-bayt* in matters of disagreement. Ibn al-Murtaḍā required sound theological doctrine, certainly present with the *ahl al-bayt*. Al-Hādī b. al-Wazīr allowed transfer to anyone outside of that group as long as he agreed with the whole of the *ahl al-bayt*. Some Zaydis applied the prophetic report on the "clasping" (*tamassuk*) to the individual *ijtihādāt* of each member of the *ahl al-bayt* in general, and thereby interpreted it as the duty to emulate them. Ibn al-Wazīr argues that this report pertains to the consensus, not to *ijtihādāt* of the *ahl al-bayt*.[265] According to him, the choice of *mujtahid* was independent of the *mujtahid*'s legal or theological affiliation. Rather, it was based on preponderant conjecture (*ghālib al-ẓann*) concerning the soundness of a particular ruling provided by a *mujtahid*, said ruling being informed by the underlying scriptural indicators and arguments in line with the permitted kind of *taqlīd*. In this sense, every legally responsible person is capable of a kind of *ijtihād*, supported by the notion of the divisibility of *ijtihād*. Being able to discern what *mujtahid*, ruling, argument or textual indicator is most probably preponderant (*tarjīḥ*) in any given question, and on any level of legal interpretation, enforces the duty to act upon such conjecture irrespective of the origin of the *mujtahid*, ruling, argument or textual indicator (as to who provided it).

Zysow writes that while "infallibilism precluded a direct attack on a legal school at the level of its rules of law, this was not true for methodology."[266] Even though Zysow speaks of *uṣūl al-fiqh* here, while Zaydi contemporaries of Ibn al-Wazīr like Ibn al-Murtaḍā, Ibn Abī l-Qāsim and al-Hādī b. al-Wazīr argue on the level of theological beliefs, the discussion yet remains in the realm of *uṣūl al-fiqh*. This is because doctrinal and theological matters enter into the realm of *uṣūl al-fiqh* in the form of requirements for *ijtihād*. We can see a clear tendency toward what Zysow called "the elevation of those sciences where one truth was available."[267]

---

265 He mentions this in the context of *taqlīd* of the dead, where unqualified and uninvestigated adherence is a similar issue; cf. Ibn al-Wazīr, *Kitāb al-Qawāʿid* f. 72a. Ibn al-Wazīr strengthens this argument by pointing out that the Caspian imam Abū Ṭālib did not mention the report in the context of *taqlīd*.

266 Zysow, *Economy of Certainty* 482.

267 Ibid., 481.

The doctrine of infallibilism also had a challenging effect on the Zaydi aggrandizement of the *ahl al-bayt*. If the soundness of their legal opinions could not be distinguished from that of others' by evaluating the legal opinions themselves, then other reasons had to be found to justify the relationship between the Zaydis and their dead imams. Thus the uncertainty about the *ahl al-bayt*'s distinct correctness in probable matters of *fiqh* was counterbalanced by the certainty about their alleged soundness in the certain matters of theology.

The investigation of Ibn al-Murtaḍā's position concerning *iltizām* to one scholar introduces an aspect that is neither inherent in the process nor the result of *ijtihād*. Yet, it is said to bear on the probability of both. There is something in the person of the *mujtahid* that enhances the probability of the soundness of both the process and the result of *ijtihād*. The *muqallid*, in his choice of an imam, is to follow his conjecture. He is—like the *mujtahid*—obliged to act according to what seems most probable to him. That is what God wants of him, and this is what he will be held responsible for—not the result or the correctness of his *mujtahid*'s ruling. But Ibn al-Murtaḍā feared deterioration (*tahawwur*) and ensuing instability.[268] The stabilizing aspect introduced into the system by him, his Zaydi contemporaries and predecessors does not result from, but bears on, the result and process of *ijtihad*, i.e. the person of the *mujtahid*. The independent standard included in the evaluation is informed by sciences in which truth can be determined with certainty: doctrine and theology. It can indeed be easily explained by the theory of the imamate and the importance that Zaydis generally render to the Prophet's family. Without going into these theories in detail, their subtle ramifications must be pointed out: Ibn al-Murtaḍā is a staunch defender of infallibilism. He explained it by the notion of *ghālib al-ẓann*, which is informed by the quest for the strongest indicators (*aqwā l-amārāt*). But additionally, there is an element of doctrinal soundness inherent in one certain group more than in others. The notion of school doctrine influences *ghālib al-ẓann* in the case of the *mujtahid*, as we have seen above. This is even more so in the case of a *muqallid*, where the school affiliation and doctrinal soundness are a better measure of probability than the indicators pertaining to a particular case. It is easier for the layman to reach the point of overwhelming probability based on the certainty of the doctrine held by the *mujtahid*, than based on the merely probable evidence that leads to a particular ruling.

268 Ibn al-Murtaḍā, *Minhāj al-wuṣūl* 804.

Ibn al-Wazīr also supports *ghālib al-ẓann* as the basis for the choice of *mujtahid*, as well as for the successful performance of what the *muqallid* is commissioned with. However, for Ibn al-Wazīr, reaching overwhelming probability primarily consists in two characteristics which Ibn al-Murtaḍā does not emphasize: First, *ghālib al-ẓann* is arrived at exclusively by investigating the indicators and tracing the process that led to a ruling. The person of the *mujtahid* is only of interest in terms of his skill and experience in the discipline in question. Secondly, it is quite possible for the layman to arrive at that degree of probability that allows him to make a decision, renew it or change it.

Interestingly, this difference in the abilities conceded to a layman is similar to that noted by Weiss between the orthodox view and that of "some Baghdadī Muʿtazilis." The orthodox view, represented by the Shafiʿi al-Āmidī (d. 631/1233), held that all commoners are obliged to consult a legal interpreter because of the laymen's lack of understanding. In contrast, the Baghdadī Muʿtazila ascribed to the commoner the ability and even the duty to inquire into the *ijtihādāt* of a *mujtahid* before they adopt his opinion.[269] In both cases, where laymen are not thought capable of much, they are to base their choice of *mujtahid* on the authority of the person: in the case of Sunni orthodoxy on his prestige and influence, and in the case of Zaydis on his doctrinal affiliation or family.

The significance of this for the present study's thesis is clear: If the theological standing of a *mujtahid* bears on the probability of the otherwise equal correctness of all *mujtahids*, it is the theological standing that will in the end determine to which *mujtahid* (or group of *mujtahids*) a *muqallid* turns. This is because the *muqallid* still has the duty to act according to what seems most probable to him. Of course in this case, the probability is not exclusively determined by what lies in the realm of probability itself—the results or process of *ijtihād*. The difficulty of discerning the correct ruling or opinion from within the legal system is mitigated by reference to an independent factor where certainty is available. Doctrinal affiliation as the determinant for initial as well as permanent legal affiliation could function as a counterbalance to the restricted abilities of laymen, as well as the instability of the legal system wrought by the doctrine of infallibilism.

Ibn al-Wazīr's reaction to the consequences which the theory of infallibility imposes on the legal system does not seem to be one of counterbalancing at all,

269 Weiss, *The Search for God's Law* 221–222. Weiss discusses this issue in the context of legal consultation (*istiftāʾ*). For al-Āmidī, all laymen irrespective of the knowledge they have in different areas are obliged to consult their superiors in rank (*mujtahidūn*) in all legal issues. According to him, the impermissible kind of *taqlīd* refers only to consultation of a peer, be it layman by layman or *mujtahid* by *mujtahid*.

as he considers conjecture independent of all but each particular set of indicators to be the basis of all action. For him, the attainment of this conjecture is within the abilities and even within the responsibility of laymen at large. The legal realm in which probability reigns is the main field of activity of individuals on all levels of learning—inquiring *muqallid* as much as full-fledged *mujtahid*. The barely restricted reign of probability allows for pluralism in legal interpretation and little room for organization into schools. In contrast, an inroad of the theological realm of certainty into the legal realm restricts that pluralism and consolidates the structure of the authority of schools.

CHAPTER 6

Conclusion

The primary goal of the present study was to shed light on the role played by the Yemeni scholar Muḥammad b. al-Wazīr (d. 840/1438) in a development that has been called the "Sunnisation of the Zaydism"[1] by Cook, Haykel, Schwarb, Schmidtke and others who have investigated the developments of the Yemeni Zaydiyya. Most studies refer to Ibn al-Wazīr as the first Yemeni traditionist and initiator of a "Sunnisation" that climaxed in Muḥammad b. ʿAlī al-Shawkānī (d. 1250/1834) and has a strong bearing on the identity of Zaydi Yemenis even today. We investigated Ibn al-Wazīr's thought in the intellectual milieu in which it developed, in order to determine the factors that shaped his thought as well as expose the fundamental conceptional differences between his own and his Zaydi contemporaries' approach to questions of theological and legal diversity and affiliation. The resulting image of the fundamental concepts of Ibn al-Wazīr's thought provides a means for comparison of Ibn al-Wazīr's influence on the "Sunnisation of Zaydism" with that of later scholars associated with this process, in order to advance our understanding of the process itself.

In the introduction, I explained that Ibn al-Wazīr lived in the intellectual environment of the 8th/14th–9th/15th century Yemeni Zaydiyya, which became increasingly exposed to a variety of theological and legal alternatives on the level of textual sources as well as teacher-student relationships and scholarly exchange within and outside the Zaydi community. From within the Zaydi community, several Muʿtazili schools had vied with one another for prevalence in Zaydi theology from the time of its inception. At the time of Ibn al-Wazīr there were two surviving Muʿtazili schools: the predominant Bahshamiyya and the less prominent school of Abū l-Ḥusayn al-Baṣrī (d. 436/1044). Ashʿari texts had been studied by Zaydi theologians for at least one and a half centuries before Ibn al-Wazīr. At the end of the 8th/14th century, the use of the Sunni hadith compilations was promoted by Zaydi imams in order to bolster Zaydi positions in theology and law. Similarly, the first Zaydi-Sufi school was founded in the late 8th/14th century. Outside the Zaydi community, Ashʿarism was thriving among the Zaydis' Rasulid neighbors, who also endorsed the spread of

1 Initially coined by Cook in reference to the development of the duty to command right and forbid wrong in the Zaydi context, the term "Sunnisation of Zaydism" was subsequently used to refer to the Zaydi accommodation to Sunni texts and doctrines in general; cf. Cook, *Commanding Right* 247–251.

 | DOI:10.1163/9789004381117_008

different Sufi orders in lower Yemen. The formerly Zaydi sharifs of Mecca had turned to Sunnism, yet Mecca continued to be sought out for religious studies and scholarly exchange by Yemeni Zaydis.

As seen above in the biographical chapter, Ibn al-Wazīr acknowledged the increasingly multilayered intellectual and religious landscape in a way the scholarly elite of his time did not. After initial confusion in the face of the diversity, Ibn al-Wazīr took an epistemological approach that allowed for the inclusion of most theological and legal schools into the Muslim community without conceding exclusive correctness to any of them. However, his biography does not show a significant difference to those of his contemporaries, such as Aḥmad b. Yaḥyā b. al-Murtaḍā who represented the predominant current of Zaydi-Muʿtazili doctrine. Ibn al-Wazīr spent a significant time during his early years with Zaydi scholars who promoted the use of the Sunni hadith collections or who showed strong affinities to Sufism. But so did Ibn al-Murtaḍā. Later Ibn al-Wazīr intensified his knowledge of Sunni hadith with Sunni teachers in lower Yemen and Mecca. Although Ibn al-Murtaḍā apparently never travelled to Mecca, he did have exposure to Sunni thought and texts in lower Yemen as well. Similarly, Ibn al-Wazīr's brother al-Hādī shared Ibn al-Wazīr's experience to a large degree, yet he was a champion of Muʿtazili Zaydism and the Zaydi-Hādawī school of law.

Ibn al-Wazīr acknowledged the theological and legal diversity that encroached on the Zaydi community in Yemen, incorporated it into his thinking and reacted by formulating an integrative epistemological approach to theology and law that took a basic understanding of the Quran and the prophetic Sunna as its common source, but provided little fixed structure beyond that. Contemporaries like Ibn al-Murtaḍā acknowledged the diversity as well, and likewise drew their conclusions. However, these conclusions led Ibn al-Murtaḍā to confirm and consolidate the Zaydiyya as a superior theological and legal entity, which is as evident in his extensive textual heritage as it is in the reception of his works by his students. The consequences of the two different approaches were already manifest during the lifetime of these two scholars. Political choices relating to the imamate made early on in their relationship foreshadowed a long intellectual controversy which revealed profound epistemological differences and their ramifications in various religious disciplines. While Ibn al-Wazīr endeavored to establish common ground by defining common sources that had validity for Zaydis as well as other theological and legal schools, he was criticized for his disregard for supposedly uniquely Zaydi doctrines and often retreated from the public sphere to the more individualistic religiosity of Sufism. In contrast, Ibn al-Murtaḍā, after his political career had ended, became an important link in a chain of scholars who shaped the identity of the Zaydiyya as a legal and a theological school. While research on the following centuries shows that the practical consequences Ibn al-Wazīr drew from the theological and legal diversity would gain momentum and only indirectly forward the so-called Sunnisation, Ibn al-Murtaḍā's immediate influence on his students and the identity of the Yemeni Zaydiyya is more dominant. Although a degree of inclusion of Sunni texts cannot be denied, it is limited to the hermeneutical inclusivism which, according to Grünschloss, is almost inevitable whenever the determination of one's own position in a religiously pluralistic environment is required.[2]

In the chapter on Ibn al-Wazīr's works (ch. 2), Ibn al-Wazīr's epistemological approach is apparent in his early *al-Burhān al-qāṭiʿ*, where he proved the sufficiency of the knowledge of God gained from the primary sources Quran and Sunna, as well as general knowledge common to all believers (*al-ʿilm al-ḍarūrī l-ʿādī*). The same concern is also evident in his brief *Masāʾil shāfiyāt*. Along these lines, Ibn al-Wazīr defended the imamate of Imam al-Manṣūr billāh ʿAlī b. Ṣalāh al-Dīn (d. 840/1436) against charges of insufficient erudition, based on the imam's profound familiarity with the *tawātur* knowledge of scriptural revelation, in his *al-Ḥusām al-mashhūr*.

In Ibn al-Wazīr's most famous reaction to the criticism of one of his teachers, *al-ʿAwāṣim wa-l-qawāṣim* and its later abridgment *al-Rawḍ al-bāsim*, Ibn al-Wazīr defended the doctrine of many Sunni theologians and traditionists in order to vindicate the validity of their contribution to the transmission of the prophetic Sunna. Here and in his last known work, *Īthār al-ḥaqq*, Ibn al-Wazīr claimed to have revealed an essential harmony between contending theological schools, employing scholars from both Muʿtazila and Ashʿariyya to prove his point. The attempt to illustrate an essential harmony and its delimitation in commonly accepted general tenets (*jumal*) is also evident in shorter theological treatises such as *Masʾalat al-ikhtilāf*, *Taḥrīr al-kalām* and expositions of Quranic verses like his *al-Āyāt al-mubīnāt*.

Moreover, *Tarjīḥ asālīb al-Qurʾān* was written as a defense of Ibn al-Wazīr's epistemological choices. One main goal was to disclose and invalidate those theological proofs and epistemological modes of reasoning which are not based on the unifying sources, and which therefore result in recriminations between schools of thought. Similar to the discussion of the general tenets in other theological writings, Ibn al-Wazīr employed positions of Muʿtazili scholars to show his contemporaries that he could claim positions from among their own group to support his views. More than any other writing, Ibn al-Wazīr's col-

2 Grünschloss, *Der eigene und der fremde Glaube* 313.

lection of panegyrical poems *Majmaʿ al-ḥaqāʾiq* is replete with poetical attestations to Ibn al-Wazīr's Sufi leanings and his reliance on theological concepts like *tawakkul* (perfect trust in God's plan) and *ḥusn al-ẓann* (thinking well of God) which focus on the believer's individual relationship to God rather than his duty towards a particular set of school doctrines. Records of dreams and visions contained in this collection attest to Ibn al-Wazīr's application of such Sufi concepts. Similarly, his *al-Amr bi-l-ʿuzla* discusses the benefits of retreat and focus on individual spirituality instead of involvement in the contentious debates of contemporary scholarship. The poems contained in *Muthīr al-aḥzān* treat the emotional occupation of the individual with the ritual practices during the month of fasting.

However, Ibn al-Wazīr's *magnum opus*, *al-ʿAwāṣim* along with its later abridgment *al-Rawḍ al-bāsim*, not only argued for essential harmony between theological schools but also stand out as multi-genre works in which Ibn al-Wazīr argued for the almost unrestricted validity and applicability of *ijtihād* by referring to well-known principles and early authorities that supposedly all legal schools have in common. In these two works as well as in his *Kitāb al-Qawāʿid*, referring to the principles of *ijtihād*, and the shorter treatise *Masāʾil arbaʿa*, Ibn al-Wazīr's emphatic rejection of *taqlīd* obviously reveals the attempt to eradicate the phenomenon of dividing the Muslim community into several legal schools. Ibn al-Wazīr again referred extensively to the textual sources and early authorities that all schools have in common, bolstering his positions with the opinions of scholars from several legal schools. Of Ibn al-Wazīr's works on legal theory, his *Manẓūma shiʿriyya* is the only one that treats the classical topics of legal theory apart from the structure of legal authority in a systematic (albeit brief) form. Ibn al-Wazīr's *Qubūl al-bushrā* is essentially an argument for the leniency of Islamic law and the divine intention to render it easy for human beings, as well as an argument for claiming the misrepresentation of the law of the founder of the Yemeni Zaydiyya resulting from *taqlīd*.

Ibn al-Wazīr is not known to have written a large number of legal opinions (*fatāwā*). However, those he did issue feature proofs from the main sources, the Quran and Sunna, and also refer to a variety of scholarly opinions in line with Ibn al-Wazīr's promotion of individual *ijtihād*. For example in *al-Istiẓhār*, it was Ibn al-Wazīr's expressed goal to enable the legal inquirer to form his own opinion rather than emulate Ibn al-Wazīr or the decision of any other scholar or school. Even though Ibn al-Wazīr also emphasized this goal in *Takhṣīṣ āyāt al-jumʿa* concerning the Friday noon prayer and provided proofs accordingly, his own conclusions from the sources would have set him at odds with many of his Zaydi contemporaries, who would hardly welcome the Friday prayer without a righteous, i.e. Zaydi, imam.

Ibn al-Wazīr's works on the science of traditions, *Tanqīḥ al-anẓār* and *Mukhtaṣar mufīd fī ʿulūm al-ḥadīth*, combine terms and principles in the Zaydi as well as the Sunni science of traditions.

These and other works mentioned in chapter 2 bespeak a coherent, yet not systematically presented construct of thoughts, linked together by epistemological principles that restrict cognitive certainty to a minimum and champion the acceptance ambiguity in many respects. In chapter 3, on epistemology, it was shown how Ibn al-Wazīr's principles contrast with the principles underlying the dominant doctrine among contemporary Zaydis, who did not seek such an integrative approach. Central in Ibn al-Wazīr's thinking is that he restricts what can properly be called certain knowledge to what occurs necessarily in the original human disposition (*fiṭra*) of every legally responsible subject. Such necessary knowledge (*ḍarūrī*) comprises *a priori* knowledge, sense perception, experience and, importantly, information that meets the conditions of a *tawātur* like the Quran, the prophetic Sunna or other information that is based on a high number of sources. According to Ibn al-Wazīr, this kind of knowledge comprises the central tenets of Islam in their most general form (*jumal*). The second category of certain knowledge determined by most speculative theologians is that of acquired or inferred knowledge (*muktasab*, *istidlālī*) which is arrived at by philosophical speculation (*naẓar*). Ibn al-Wazīr rejected this category and equated it with conjectural knowledge. This equation allowed him to deplete a great many secondary or detailed theological doctrines that had resulted from inference of their binding force, thus rendering the divergence between different schools of thought less significant. In contrast, Ibn al-Wazīr's colleague and representative of Bahshami-Muʿtazili theology, Ibn al-Murtaḍā, endorsed the classical division into necessary and acquired knowledge and claimed certainty for many of the prevalent doctrines of his school that were generated by inference according to a particular order of premises (*tartīb al-muqaddimāt*). This notion of *naẓar* was seen as a major means of possessing knowledge in speculative theology. For Ibn al-Wazīr, *naẓar* was mainly a means of contemplating what was known already by necessity, rather than a conscious inference from a particular order of premises. According to him, the occurrence of knowledge may correlate with the practice of *naẓar*, but correct *naẓar* does not generate (*tawallud*) certain knowledge and therefore could not be used to argue for the exclusive validity of a particular set of secondary doctrines. Ibn al-Wazīr could refer to a later follower of Abū l-Ḥusayn al-Baṣrī, Shaykh Mukhtār b. Maḥmūd (d. 658/1260) to ensure support for his notion of *naẓar* from the Muʿtazili camp. In effect, Ibn al-Wazīr declared the insistence on *naẓar* among speculative theologians like Ibn al-Murtaḍā to be the cause of division and mutual charge of unbelief (*takfīr*) between contending theological schools. For him, the means of possessing knowledge was the God-given original disposition (*fiṭra*) that all human beings share. The common aspect of this *fiṭra* ensured that knowledge about the necessary aspects of God and religion would not be reserved to a particular school or conditioned by a particular rational exercise like *naẓar*. Hence, commonality effectively became an essential, though not exclusive, criterion for certain knowledge.

In many respects, Ibn al-Wazīr's concept of *fiṭra* resembles the concept of the human intellect (*ʿaql*) among speculative theologians of the Muʿtazila. Both concepts represent the place where knowledge occurs and in both concepts, necessary knowledge constitutes the initial body of knowledge. However, while *fiṭra* in Ibn al-Wazīr's thinking embodies the disposition to possess necessary knowledge, *ʿaql* to Ibn al-Murtaḍā's and other Muʿtazilis' minds already comprises necessary knowledge. Moreover, whereas *fiṭra* needs revelation and *tawātur* information to extend its knowledge and particularize what it knows in general according to Ibn al-Wazīr, *ʿaql* comprises the knowledge of the duty and the ability of *naẓar* to generate more and detailed knowledge according to Ibn al-Murtaḍā.

This difference becomes apparent in the proof of God's existence. In this regard, Ibn al-Wazīr persistently contrasts two lines of argument that had become the epitomes of the rift between the Bahshami Muʿtazila and Abū l-Ḥusayn al-Baṣrī's school. The *akwān*-proof of the Bahshamiyya, echoed by Ibn al-Murtaḍā, argues for God's existence on the basis of a multi-tiered line of inferences starting from the temporality of the entitative accidents (*aʿrāḍ*) of bodies. The starting point of such *naẓar* is the state of *not* knowing of God's existence, rendering *naẓar* a kind of speculation. Because the existence of God must ultimately be known by every believer, such speculation was made incumbent on every believer by Muʿtazili theologians like Ibn al-Murtaḍā. The *aḥwāl*-proof coined by Abū l-Ḥusayn al-Baṣrī considers such accidents (*aʿrāḍ*) mere adjectives or states of the bodies they characterize. For him, the general knowledge of God occurs by necessity and needs no multi-tiered line of inferences. Ibn al-Wazīr applies the *aḥwāl*-proof to the states and circumstances of creation as well as to the lives of the prophets in a generalizing manner. Dispensing with the speculation and multi-tiered inferences which signify the *naẓar* of speculative theologians, pondering the states and circumstances of creation and revelation commonly coincides with the necessary knowledge of God in the human *fiṭra* according to Ibn al-Wazīr. Yet it is neither a necessary condition for such knowledge nor does it generate knowledge. It is obvious that such concepts of *fiṭra* and *naẓar* allowed Ibn al-Wazīr to render differences in (secondary) doctrines less significant, as well as to devalue speculative theology that required every believer to concern himself with the subtleties of derived knowledge. To Ibn al-Wazīr, *naẓar* in the speculative sense was not a duty because every believer would know of God's existence and none need get involved in the controversies about detailed inferences that separate the various schools of thought and that are little more than conjectural doctrines.

How profoundly Ibn al-Wazīr's acceptance of ambiguity in secondary theological issues differed from the approach of his Muʿtazili contemporaries is manifest in an underlying principle of reasoning, i.e. the argument from the absence of evidence (*al-istidlāl bi-l-ʿadam*). This argument was applied in the Bahshami Muʿtazila as well as by the earlier representatives of Abū l-Ḥusayn al-Baṣrī's school. It was also used by Ibn al-Murtaḍā, although he does not make it a separate topic of discussion. This argumentative principle purports that whatever fact or entity cannot be proved decisively must be denied, as for example attributes of God beyond those demonstrated in most treatises on systematic theology. However, Ibn al-Wazīr argues, along with some later representatives of Abū l-Ḥusayn al-Baṣrī's school and in line with his attitude towards ambiguity in secondary matters, that absence of decisive conclusions results in deferment of judgement rather than in certain negation of the issue. Hence, many things about God and the unseen world are yet unknown and uncertain and remain possibly existent until positive evidence becomes effective.

Returning to Ibn al-Wazīr's context of theological and legal diversity, the underlying principles of what I term his epistemology of ambiguity fulfill their purpose in the harmonization of different theological schools. In chapter 4, it was demonstrated how Ibn al-Wazīr's understanding of necessary knowledge occurring in the human *fiṭra* enabled him to argue for essential agreement among Islamic schools of thought concerning the major Islamic tenets in their general form, and ambiguity concerning a great number of details. The school that the contemporary Zaydiyya, with their predominantly Bahshami theology, grappled with was increasingly the Ashʿariyya. Hence, Ibn al-Wazīr's attempt to reveal essential agreement was focused on those theological aspects that seemed like an unbridgeable divide between the Muʿtazila and the Ashʿariyya.

His own key to harmonization was his concept of God's wisdom (*ḥikma*), which defined the uniqueness of God by His superior knowledge of the hidden purposes of all His commands and actions. Human beings could only know of God's actions and their purposes in a general form, and realize only their essential goodness. This idea of Ibn al-Wazīr's went beyond the Muʿtazili equation of *ḥikma* with God's justice, and took up all forms of causality, instrumentality or motive present in Ashʿari thought in order to argue for agreement on the general tenet of God's wisdom. Whereas Ibn al-Murtaḍā clearly echoes the Bahshami doctrine that God's justice must gear His actions to the utmost human benefit (*al-aṣlaḥ*) in a comprehensible way, Ibn al-Wazīr referred to Abū l-Ḥusayn al-Baṣrī's followers to convince his contemporaries that some Muʿtazilis left God's purposes in the realm of ambiguity like he himself did. Similarly, the details of God's names and attributes beyond the general affirmation (*ithbāt*) of what the human *fiṭra* knows from revelation was said to belong to the ambiguous matters (*mutashābihāt*) of which God's wisdom was the interpretation. To Ibn al-Wazīr, the difference between descriptions of God and descriptions of human beings was so self-evident to the *fiṭra* that the absence of detailed knowledge need not lead to fear of an illicit equation between the two (*tamāthul*), neither does it require metaphorical interpretation (*ta'wīl*) as occurred in both Muʿtazili and Ashʿari theology. Ibn al-Wazīr held that, contrary to common opinion, only the extremists of both groups denied God's attributes altogether (*taʿṭīl*) or literarily equated them with human attributes (*tashbīh*). Ibn al-Wazīr's reference to God's wisdom as the interpretation of ambiguous descriptions of God, as well as of conflicting implications from different names and attributes, allowed the inclusion of multiple, albeit only conjectural doctrines and again served his aim to harmonize various schools of thought. By contrast, Ibn al-Murtaḍā's expositions of God's attributes required a particular understanding of many detailed issues, invalidating conclusions that did not agree with his own school's system of certain doctrines.

Furthermore, Ibn al-Wazīr's concept of *ḥikma* allowed him to define a general tenet of God's will (*irāda*) that affirms different statements in revelation and incorporates Muʿtazili as well as Ashʿari concerns. According to Ibn al-Wazīr, the general tenet conceived by the human *fiṭra* purports that no human action can contravene God's will, yet God's justice in what He wills, does and commands is never impaired. Whenever God expresses His will or a command that appears unjust or evil, this must be understood as a relative instrument to something ultimately good. However, where this ultimate good is beyond human understanding or conflicts with the human conception of good and evil, Ibn al-Wazīr refers it to God's knowledge of the good end. Whereas God wills or commands an apparent evil for the sake of a hidden good, He wills and loves the ultimate good for its own sake. Referring to Abū l-Ḥusayn al-Baṣrī for Muʿtazili support, Ibn al-Wazīr employs his concept of *ḥikma* to establish a general doctrine of God's will in another way: *ḥikma* signifies God's knowledge of the good but often hidden end of an action or a command, which then determines what He wills. This is similar to Abū l-Ḥusayn al-Baṣrī's equation of God's will with His motive, which did not clearly delineate what determines this motive, other than God's knowledge of the outcome. According to Ibn al-Wazīr, the eternity of God's knowledge thus corresponds to the eternity of God's will in Ashʿari thinking. In contrast, Ibn al-Murtaḍā, as a typical Bahshami theologian, insists that God wills according to a comprehensible standard of right and wrong. This standard is manifest in God's obligation to act for the highest benefit of human beings (*al-aṣlaḥ*) which must be determined in a way that is comprehensible to human understanding in general, but also in particular cases.

In the closely related question of human actions, Ibn al-Wazīr established the general tenet of a choosing, yet not independently acting human agent, which is again evident to the human *fiṭra*. Abū l-Ḥusayn al-Baṣrī's doctrine of the states (*aḥwāl*) supports this understanding in that it provides that the moral aspect of an action for which human beings are responsible, and on the grounds of which they are judged, is not a separate entity that the human being brings into existence independently. Human beings have the capacity to effect this aspect according to the choice they make out of a particular motive. Thus the human responsibility is self-evident. In line with Ibn al-Wazīr's concept of *ḥikma*, God's intervention into the act and the motive accords with His knowledge of the ends, which is often unknown to the human being beyond its ultimate goodness. This differs from Ibn al-Murtaḍā's view that human beings have indeed the power to bring actions into existence and are alone responsible for their choice. Far from being satisfied with a self-evident general responsibility, human beings must be able to argue along these lines to preserve a detailed understanding of God's justice.

In chapter 5, we discussed how Ibn al-Wazīr's discouragement of preoccupation with theology beyond the self-evident general tenets of the Islamic religion is balanced by his encouragement of broad participation in legal interpretation. Revealing the essential agreements of theological schools in matters of certainty, as well as the merely probable nature of matters of disagreement, achieved an important goal for Ibn al-Wazīr: traditionalists of theological schools whose transmissions had heretofore been rejected on the grounds of theological error could now be vindicated. As a matter of course, this allowed for a new and different approach to their transmissions, namely the Sunni hadith compilations. Although Sunni hadith compilations had been used as a basis for consolidating Zaydi doctrine from the 6th/12th century onwards, historiography reports an increased endorsement of Sunni hadith in Ibn al-Wazīr's and shortly before. Ibn al-Wazīr's justification of their use as equal or superior in value to genuinely Zaydi sources was new, and had the potential to change the legal landscape entirely. Since the theological doctrine of the transmitters became an insignificant criteria for him, their professional skill could occupy centre stage. An extension of the range of textual sources meant that the results of interpreting these sources would be extended as well.

The transformative potential of Ibn al-Wazīr's justification of the Sunni hadith compilations was amplified by the theory of infallibilism. This theory provided that the ruling of every legal interpreter (*mujtahid*) would be considered correct as long as it was arrived at by a designated process of *ijtihād* in light of the probable nature of all results of *ijtihād*. The theory of the infallibility of all *mujtahids* had been a vital part of Zaydi legal doctrine since the 6th/12th century. With regard to the increasing level of legal diversity in the context of the 8th/14th and 9th/15th century Zaydiyya, a consistent application of the doctrine would have required that Zaydis be allowed to resort to scholars of other schools for legal advice. Ibn al-Wazīr followed through with the theory and concerned himself with the sources, arguments and legal rulings of all schools of Islamic law. The parallel trend in the contemporary Zaydiyya counteracted the ramifications of the theory of infallibilism in a legally and theologically diverse landscape by consolidating the legal identity of the Zaidiyya. This consolidation was based not on legal decisions per se, but on an inroad of theology into the structure of legal authority and therefore legal interpretation. This inroad meant that theological matters of supposed certainty were introduced into the legal realm of probability. Its effects can be traced in various questions of the structure of legal authority.

Concerning the theory of infallibilism itself, a comparison between Ibn al-Wazīr and Ibn al-Murtaḍā reveals that, although both endorsed this theory, the scope of ambiguity they allowed with regard to the various rulings differed. Ibn al-Wazīr held that, while there may be one ruling among many that bears verisimilitude (*al-ashbah*) to a singular correct ruling that God envisions, human beings have no possible way of knowing which one it is. Every scholar must adhere to what seems most probable to him (*ghālib al-ẓann*). Although the concept of *ghālib al-ẓann* likewise runs through Ibn al-Murtaḍā's argumentation, his notion that school doctrine could be the benchmark for the most probable ruling or the evidence "verisimilar" (*al-ashbah*) to the most probable evidence put a restriction on the range of probable results of *ijtihād*.

As to the possibility of *ijtihād* and the existence of *mujtahids*, Ibn al-Wazīr's position contrasts most with that of his teacher Ibn Abī l-Qāsim, who apparently held that *ijtihād* was no longer possible, wherefore scholars and laymen had to resort to the early imams of the Zaydiyya. Ibn al-Murtaḍā, for his part, was a defender of the possibility of *ijtihād*, yet he effectively referred to an *ijtihād* within the legal school (*ijtihād fī l-madhhab*) that used the existing rules of the founding imams along with their principles as a source for legal interpretation. According to him, there was no need for original inference of rulings (*istinbāṭ*) from the revelational sources after the establishment of the schools, including the Zaydiyya. The extrapolation of the founding imams' principles (*takhrīj*) and their subsequent application to new cases, though a highly sophisticated activity, did not provide for legal interpretation beyond the realm of the Zaydi school. Ibn al-Murtaḍā's affirmative attitude is manifest in his foundational legal compendia *Kitāb al-Azhār* and *al-Baḥr al-zakhkhār*, which would be major sources for Zaydi *fiqh* for centuries to come. In contrast, Ibn al-Wazīr largely rejected the practice of *takhrīj*. The insistence on the duty of *ijtihād* beyond school affiliation became a distinctive mark of his concept of legal interpretation, and the supposed absence of scholars capable of *ijtihād* all the more cause to encourage the practice of *ijtihād*.

The counterpart of the insistence on *ijtihād* was Ibn al-Wazīr's prohibition of emulation (*taqlīd*). In his three-tiered analysis of the practice of emulation, the emulator and the emulated scholar, Ibn al-Wazīr distinguished a permitted from a prohibited kind of following. *Taqlīd* of the prohibited kind is identified with an unquestioning adoption of a ruling without understanding the arguments and textual indicators that led to it. For his part, Ibn al-Wazīr grants the laymen the ability to comprehend and weigh arguments and indicators and to subsequently act according to what seems most probable, similar to the triggering factor of the *mujtahid*'s decision. This freedom of action in the realm of the probable allows for the choice of any *mujtahid* as well as any ruling to follow, along with a subsequent transfer (*intiqāl*) to another *mujtahid* according to the state of evidence. By implication, in Ibn al-Wazīr's view, the active participation in the legal enterprise is relatively broad on all levels of legal responsibility: layman, discerning student (*al-ṭālib al-mumayyiz*) and *mujtahid*. The doctrine of the divisibility of *ijtihād* (*tajazzuʾ*) as understood by Ibn al-Wazīr further enhances this participation. According to this view the legal subject can aspire to a form of *ijtihād* not only on the level of different disciplines, but also on the level of individual questions.

As compared to Ibn al-Wazīr, Ibn al-Murtaḍā is more hesitant to grant laymen the ability to weigh evidence and determine preponderance (*tarjīḥ*). For him, the choice of a *mujtahid* is largely determined by the person of the *mujtahid* and the soundness of his beliefs, and less by the evidence for the rulings. Accordingly, commitment (*iltizām*) to an authority, be it a *mujtahid* or a school, is understood to be stable, and transfer is mainly justified on the grounds of the authority's rectitude and doctrinal soundness. This restricted confidence in the layman's participation in interpretative activity correlates with a practice that formed the strongest contrast between Ibn al-Wazīr and many of his contemporary Zaydis, namely the emulation of dead scholars (*taqlīd al-amwāt*). Ibn al-Murtaḍā's endorsement of the practice of emulating the founding Zaydi imams and *ahl al-bayt* would have had a strong effect on the restriction of legal activity to the confinements of the Zaydiyya as a legal school. The certainty about the soundness of the *ahl al-bayt*'s theological doctrine rendered the results of their *ijtihād* most worthy to be followed. The same criteria became the distinctive mark between Ibn al-Wazīr's and Ibn al-Murtaḍā's requirements (*shurūṭ*) of a *mujtahid*. Ibn al-Murtaḍā's requirements with regard to scientific disciplines were slightly higher in general, and in the field of Arabic linguistics (*lugha*) in particular. However, the decisive difference was that Ibn al-Murtaḍā conditioned the qualification for being emulated on theological doctrine, both in terms of the practice of theology (*uṣūl al-dīn* or *ʿilm al-kalām*) as a discipline and in terms of the profession of certain Zaydi-Muʿtazili beliefs as a vital part of the *mujtahid*'s personal rectitude (*ʿadāla*). Consequently, Ibn al-Murtaḍā's position would restrict legal inquiry to Zaydi *mujtahid*'s with Muʿtazili leanings. In contrast, Ibn al-Wazīr's requirements were restricted to professional skill and disregarded doctrine beyond belief in the general tenets (*jumal*). Consequently, any legally responsible person could seek advice from any *mujtahid* irrespective of legal or doctrinal affiliation, as long as the *mujtahid*'s outward appearance testified to his Islamic faith and his arguments were convincing.

For Ibn al-Wazīr, the only kind of following (*ittibāʿ*) of the (dead) founding Zaydi imams and the *ahl al-bayt* was what he termed "following in meaning" (*fī l-maʿnā*). To him, this kind of following was central and the reference to the first few generations of Islamic history, the *salaf*, highly recurrent. However, this kind of following pertained to the intentions that the first generations had in their general approach to Islamic law and the structure of legal authority, and therefore remained rather vague.

The image of Ibn al-Wazīr that presents itself on the basis of his life and thought is that of a man who sought to acknowledge the different theological and legal currents that existed in his social context without committing himself to any single one thereof. Starting from the genuinely Zaydi basis of the theory of infallibilism and the prohibition of emulation in doctrinal matters, Ibn al-Wazīr followed through with what other Zaydi scholars had started—the Sufism of his teacher Ibn Abī l-Khayr and Ibrāhīm al-Kaynaʿī, the dissemination of Sunni hadith compilations by Imam al-Nāṣir and his son Imam al-Manṣūr, and the endorsement of Abū l-Ḥusayn al-Baṣrī's Muʿtazili school by Imam Yaḥyā b. Ḥamza (d. 614/1217). Furthermore, Ibn al-Wazīr incorporated the Sunni law and Ashʿari theology that was present in his wider non-Zaydi context in lower Yemen and the Hejaz. Ibn al-Wazīr's original contribution to these ongoing developments was his formulation of a consistently integrative approach to theological and legal diversity. This approach was based on an epistemology that claimed cognitive certainty only for agreed upon theological tenets, and relegated intellectual disagreements and the main realm of religious activity to fields in which conjecture was a central systematic feature, namely positive law, or that were not concerned with rationally demonstrable knowledge, like Sufism. These latter fields were only touched upon here and await further research, the main focus in the present work having been on how Ibn al-Wazīr's epistemological approach shaped his theology and determined his outlook on law with regard to the structure of legal authority. Similarly, Ibn al-Wazīr's intellectual productivity was focused on theology and the structure of legal authority as this was where he perceived the greatest need for rectification, so that individual activity could shift to the realms of law and Sufism.

The thesis of an "epistemology of ambiguity" may appear to contradict Ibn al-Wazīr's own quest for certainty, which was only satisfied when he acknowledged the authoritativeness of the Sunni hadith compilations. Moreover, this quest for certainty and its attainment in the Sunni hadith compilations has been pointed out as a distinctive feature of the Yemeni traditionists and patronizers of the "Sunnisation" process.[3] While this indeed holds true for Ibn al-Wazīr as well, it does so only with regard to the *scope* of the sources. Although Haykel's identification of epistemology at the heart of traditionism and the process of "Sunnisation" is plausible, and the quest for a higher degree of certainty did determine the choice of sources, this did not lead to a higher degree of certainty in the *application* of theological doctrine and legal interpretation in the case of Ibn al-Wazīr. In the interpretation and actual application of the sources in the context of the Islamic community, Ibn al-Wazīr's thought is dominated by concepts of conjecture and ambiguity in that multiple interpretations coexist, and the highest probability (*ghālib al-ẓann*) that the individual can arrive at determines the way he relates to those who support other interpretations as well as his own action. Compared to his contemporaries, Ibn al-Wazīr's certainty was greater because of the objective standard that went along with the commonality of knowledge as to the core of his religion. Yet, he was satisfied with ambiguity in a large number of matters which he located in the realm of subjective and individual interpretation. His certainty even about the sources of revelation did not spring from rational proof his individual mind could produce—indeed, this would have invalidated his doubt in reason's reliability—but from the certainty that allegedly occurred in the minds of all Muslims without much effort. Furthermore, Ibn al-Wazīr was not primarily occupied with the inner state of the knowing person, in the manner of scholars like al-Ghazālī in his study of the

3 Cf. Haykel, *Revival and Reform* 10.

different degrees of certainty in terms of *yaqīn*, but rather with the scope of items of certain knowledge.

At the same time, the choice of sources does have an effect on the theological and legal interpretations of a scholar. Hence Ibn al-Wazīr's vindication of the Sunni hadith compilations is correctly identified as a decisive element in the process of the "Sunnisation" of the Zaydiyya. However, the present study showed that Ibn al-Wazīr's epistemology provided a basis for accrediting all schools with validity—including the Hādawī-Zaydi school, albeit not to the exclusion of other schools and not by virtue of its authority as a school. The same was true for the Sunni schools of law, even though Ibn al-Wazīr's own legal interpretations led to results that differed from those of his Zaydi contemporaries and at times were more in line with Sunni rulings. This is why he was often thought to be a Sunni. However, with regard to how he arrived at his interpretations, Ibn al-Wazīr indeed seems well described by the words of his contemporary Aḥmad b. Muḥammad al-Azraqī (d. around 850/1446), who, when asked which school Ibn al-Wazīr follows, apparently said "[he follows] the evidence (*warā' al-dalīl*)."[4] This is true regarding both theological and legal affiliation.

Although Ibn al-Wazīr played a decisive role in the "Sunnisation of Zaydism," Sunnisation should not be seen as an inevitable result of Ibn al-Wazīr's thought. To my mind, Ibn al-Wazīr's epistemological approach to theology and legal theory might just as well have been employed for a "Sufisation" of the Zaydiyya, had socio-political developments within and outside Yemen been different. Why Zaydi theological and legal doctrine were less receptive to, and the politics in the Zaydi imamate less open for, a "Sufisation" than they were for a "Sunnisation" is a question for further study.[5] What Ibn al-Wazīr's approach certainly encouraged was a devaluation of the Hādawī-Zaydi identity, because he discouraged "madhhabisation" in theological as well as in legal terms and valorized the intellectual effort and the religious experience of the individual in a universalistic manner. Although at the core of religion the commonality of the religious experience largely determined and defined its epistemic value as absolutely certain, this core was rather restricted. Hence, Ibn al-Wazīr's epistemology of ambiguity encouraged an individualization of the religious experi-

---

4 Quoted in Ibn Abī l-Rijāl, *Maṭlaʿ al-budūr* iv, 145.

5 Throughout the greater part of its history, the Yemeni Zaydi imamate was hostile to Sufism. Interestingly, the anti-Sufi polemics reached one of its peaks during the reign of the first imam of the Qāsimī dynasty (11th/17th–14th/20th century) and persisted throughout the later Qāsimī rule that was greatly influenced by al-Shawkānī's teachings; cf. Madelung, Zaydī Attitudes 138–139; Madelung, Introduction. Part VI: Theology 457.

ence, as well as interpretation with a minimum set of certain doctrine to unite individuals into the same religion, and thus resembles a rather modern feature of religiosity.

Furthermore, Ibn al-Wazīr's approach discouraged the Bahshami-Muʿtazili epistemology of contemporaries like Ibn al-Murtaḍā who participated actively in the consolidation of the theological and legal identity of the Zaydiyya. Ibn al-Wazīr did so because this epistemology interfered with Islamic universalism as he saw it. In this context, the sources chosen by Ibn al-Wazīr to support his harmonization between theological schools are of particular interest. In a number of theological questions, Ibn al-Wazīr resorted to epistemological and ontological concepts shaped by Abū l-Ḥusayn al-Baṣrī or his followers in order to strengthen his own position as well as his claim of an essential agreement between the Muʿtazila and the Ashʿariyya. In other theological questions, like the existence of miracles, Abū l-Ḥusayn's doctrine may also have been more in line with Ibn al-Wazīr's doctrine than the Bahshami counterparts, but Ibn al-Wazīr did not explicitly mention him in that context. Even though Ibn al-Wazīr should not be seen as a follower of Abū l-Ḥusayn al-Baṣrī as long as other central aspects of Abū l-Ḥusayn's thought have not been compared with Ibn Wazīr's notions, Abū l-Ḥusayn's doctrine could evidently be used to harmonize Muʿtazili and Ashʿarī doctrine and, having thus played an important role in the "Sunnisation of Zaydism," should be the object of further study in this context.[6]

Likewise, more research has to be done on Ibn al-Wazīr's positions on other aspects of legal theory, positive law, Sufism and method of hadith criticism in his religious and socio-political context. But while such research would provide much needed insight, on the one hand, into the relationship between the 9th/15th century Zaydiyya and other schools and trends in Islam and increase the points of comparison with later (or earlier) actors in the process of "Sunnisation" like al-Shawkānī, I expect that it would, on the other hand, only confirm my findings as to Ibn al-Wazīr's epistemology of ambiguity and its focus on commonality as an essential criterion for certain knowledge in a minimal set of core doctrines, as well as on the intellectual and spiritual activity of the individual in secondary matters. Take, for example, the case of Ibn al-Wazīr's *Qubūl al-bushrā*, which is concerned with legal principles (*qawāʿid fiqhiyya*) at the intersection of legal theory and positive law. *Qubūl al-bushrā* is devoted to demonstrating that opting for the lenient ruling (*rukhṣā*) is preferable in many

6 A comprehensive comparison between the thought of Ibn al-Wazīr and Abū l-Ḥusayn al-Baṣrī would have to include an investigation of Imam Yaḥyā b. Ḥamza's teaching as well as an investigation of the difference between Ibn al-Wazīr and Ibn al-Murtaḍā in their use of Abū l-Ḥusayn's teachings in the realm of legal theory.

cases of textual ambiguity (*mutashabihāt*). The counterposition defended by followers of the Hādawī-Zaydi school systematically insists on the severe ruling (*ʿazīma*) based on the notion that it represents the most prudent choice (*al-aḥwaṭ*) in cases of ambiguity. In contrast to his stance on ambiguity in theological matters, where the interpretation of ambiguous texts or statements is left to God's wisdom, Ibn al-Wazīr holds that cases of legal ambiguity must be decided by each individual scholar and may vary according to the *mujtahid*'s understanding of the indicators and the state of the one that asks for the legal ruling.

This study was primarily concerned with the thought of Ibn al-Wazīr and not with any other of the Yemeni traditionists. Whether or not what was argued with regard to Ibn al-Wazīr's thought vis-á-vis the "Sunnisation" of the Zaydiyya also applies to other contemporaries or later traditionists is a question that only further study can answer. Although al-Shawkānī, for example, identifies with Ibn al-Wazīr, his epistemological approach to theological and legal diversity is likely to differ considerably from that of Ibn al-Wazīr. A first indication of this is the fact that al-Shawkānī vehemently rejected the theory of infallibilism, which was a major component of Ibn al-Wazīr's notion of the structure of legal authority.[7]

Besides contrasting Ibn al-Wazīr's concepts with those of other Yemeni traditionists and patronizers of the "Sunnisation" process like al-Shawkānī, comparing Ibn al-Wazīr's thought with that of Ibn Taymiyya and Ibn Qayyim al-Jawziyya promises to be most insightful. Parallels between them were already noted throughout chapter 4 on central concepts of Ibn al-Wazīr's theological thought. But what is more important, Ibn Taymiyya and to a lesser degree Ibn Qayyim al-Jawziyya were monopolized by a variety of intellectual and spiritual trends, just as might be the case for Ibn al-Wazīr as well, because his thought incorporates Zaydi, Sufi, traditionist, Sunni and Salafi elements.

A Salafi claim, broad and diverse as the term Salafi is, to Ibn al-Wazīr is well worth considering, given the frequency with which Ibn al-Wazīr refers to the *salaf* and the authoritativeness of prophetic traditions in contradistinction to school doctrines, beside other similarities between them such as the rejection of *taqlīd* and the easy attainability of legal knowledge for the individual. In contrast, the Salafi emphasis on theological issues where only one understanding is correct, along with the related notions of *takfīr* and the only victorious group saved in the Hereafter (*firqa najiyya*)—ideas that Ibn al-Wazīr's epistemology left no room for—should induce a circumspect comparison.[8]

---

7 Cf. Haykel, *Revival and Reform* 96.

8 Cf. Brown, *Canonization* 314, who ascribes a "Salafi spirit" to Ibn al-Wazīr. For an illustration

As a consequence of all this, one could challenge the view that the ongoing struggle that Ibn al-Wazīr is identified with, regarding the identity of the Yemeni Zaydiyya, is best described by the term "Sunnisation." Bonnefoy has recently called this term into question in the modern context of the struggle between Shiʿi Zaydism and Sunni Shafiʿism, which, according to him, has resulted in the polarization of identities on the one hand, and individualization of the religious experience and practice on the other hand, rather than in a "Sunnisation" of Zaydism in particular and of Islam in Yemen in general.[9] Though one must keep in mind that almost 600 years of history have passed since the time of Ibn al-Wazīr, the reactions to the tension that accompanies theological and legal diversity may yet be similar. In this sense, Ibn al-Wazīr's "epistemology of ambiguity," which considers a minimal body of fixed certain doctrine and leaves ample room for multiple interpretations, provides an answer to the challenge of theological and legal diversity that is even more compelling today than it was at Ibn al-Wazīr's lifetime.

---

of the unifying and dividing elements of different Salafi currents, see Haykel, Nature of Salafī Thought. Haykel refers to Ibn al-Wazīr via al-Shawkānī in the explanation of the Salafi rejection of legal schools and thus confirms the Salafi claim on Ibn al-Wazīr; cf. ibid., 44.

9 Bonnefoy, Les identités religieuses 207, 213.

Bibliography

Consulted Manuscripts

al-Ḥayyī, Dāwūd b. Aḥmad Ṣārim al-Dīn, *Kitāb Sharḥ al-Qalā'id al-muntazaʿ min al-Durar al-farā'id fī sharḥ Kitāb al-Qalā'id fī taṣḥīḥ al-ʿaqā'id*, Berlin, Glaser 202 (1057/1647), http://digital.staatsbibliothek-berlin.de/werkansicht/PHYS (September 2014).

Ibn al-Amīr al-Ṣanʿānī, Muḥammad b. Ismāʿīl, *Fatḥ al-khāliq fī sharḥ Majmaʿ al-ḥaqā'iq wa-l-raqā'iq fī mamādiḥ Rabb al-khalā'iq*, Sanaa, Mu'assasat al-Imām Zayd b. ʿAlī al-thaqāfiyya, CD 412 (1353/1934).

Ibn al-Wazīr, Muḥammad b. Ibrāhīm, *al-Amr bi-l-ʿuzla fī ākhir al-zamān*, Sanaa, Maktabat Muḥammad al-Kibsī, coll. s.n. (1035/1626).

Ibn al-Wazīr, Muḥammad b. Ibrāhīm. *al-Amr bi-l-ʿuzla fī ākhir al-zamān*, Sanaa, Maktabat Muḥammad al-Kibsī, coll. s.n. (1350/1932).

Ibn al-Wazīr, Muḥammad b. Ibrāhīm. *Āyāt al-aḥkām al-sharʿiyya*, Sanaa, Maktabat Muḥammad al-Kibsī, coll. s.n. (1034/1625).

Ibn al-Wazīr, Muḥammad b. Ibrāhīm. *al-Āyāt al-mubīnāt li-qawlihi taʿālā "yuḍill man yashā' wa yahdī man yashā'"*, Sanaa, Maktabat Muḥammad al-Kibsī, coll. s.n. (1035/1626).

Ibn al-Wazīr, Muḥammad b. Ibrāhīm. *al-Burhān al-qāṭiʿ fī ithbāt al-ṣāniʿ wa-jamīʿ ma jā'at bihi al-sharāʾiʿ*, Sanaa, Dār al-Makhṭūṭāt, coll. 3133 (1158/1745).

Ibn al-Wazīr, Muḥammad b. Ibrāhīm. *al-Burhān al-qāṭiʿ fī ithbāt al-ṣāniʿ wa-jamīʿ ma jā'at bihi al-sharāʾiʿ*, Sanaa, Maktabat Muḥammad al-Kibsī, coll. s.n. (1350/1931), Mu'assasat al-Imām Zayd b. ʿAlī al-thaqāfiyya, CD coll. 1407.

Ibn al-Wazīr, Muḥammad b. Ibrāhīm. *Dīwān Muḥammad b. Ibrāhīm al-Wazīr*, Sanaa, s.l. (1247/1832).

Ibn al-Wazīr, Muḥammad b. Ibrāhīm. *al-Ḥusām al-mashhūr fī l-dhabb ʿan al-Imām al-Manṣūr*, Sanaa, Dār al-Makhṭūṭāt, coll. 3158 (n.d.).

Ibn al-Wazīr, Muḥammad b. Ibrāhīm. *al-Ḥusām al-mashhūr fī l-dhabb ʿan al-Imām al-Manṣūr*, Sanaa, Dār al-Makhṭūṭāt, coll. 3313 (1158/1745).

Ibn al-Wazīr, Muḥammad b. Ibrāhīm. *al-Istiẓhār bi-l-dalīl al-samʿī fī ʿadam wuqūʿ al-ṭalaq al-bidʿī*, Sanaa, Maktabat Muḥammad al-Kibsī, coll. s.n. (1350/1932).

Ibn al-Wazīr, Muḥammad b. Ibrāhīm. *al-Istiẓhār bi-l-dalīl al-samʿī fī ʿadam wuqūʿ al-ṭalaq al-bidʿī*, Sanaa, Maktabat Muḥammad al-Kibsī, coll. s.n. (1032/1622).

Ibn al-Wazīr, Muḥammad b. Ibrāhīm. *Īthār al-ḥaqq ʿalā l-khalq fī radd al-khilāfāt ilā l-madhhab al-ḥaqq min uṣūl al-tawḥīd*, Sanaa, Dār al-Makhṭūṭāt, MS 579 (846/1443).

Ibn al-Wazīr, Muḥammad b. Ibrāhīm. *Kitāb al-Qawāʿid*, Sanaa, Dār al-Makhṭūṭāt, coll. 3158 (n.d.).

Ibn al-Wazīr, Muḥammad b. Ibrāhīm. *Majmaʿ al-ḥaqāʾiq wa-l-raqāʾiq fī mamādiḥ rabb al-khalāʾiq*, Sanaa, Muʾassasat al-Imām Zayd b. ʿAlī al-thaqāfiyya, CD 279 (1035/1626).

Ibn al-Wazīr, Muḥammad b. Ibrāhīm. *Manẓūma shiʿriyya fī uṣūl al-fiqh*, Sanaa, Muʾassasat al-Imām Zayd b. ʿAlī al-thaqāfiyya, CD 1407 (1350/1931).

Ibn al-Wazīr, Muḥammad b. Ibrāhīm. *Masāʾil arbaʿa tataʿallaq bi-l-muqallid wa-l-mustaftī*, Sanaa, Maktabat Muḥammad al-Kibsī coll. s.n. (1032/1622).

Ibn al-Wazīr, Muḥammad b. Ibrāhīm. *Masāʾil shāfiyāt wa-maṭālib wāfiyāt fīma yataʿallaq bi-āyāt karīma qurʾāniyya tadullu ʿalā llāh al-mabʿūd wa-ṣidq anbiyāʾihi*, Sanaa, Dār al-Makhṭūṭāt, coll. 3133 (around 1158/1745).

Ibn al-Wazīr, Muḥammad b. Ibrāhīm. *Masʾalat ikhtilāf al-Muʿtazila wa-l-Ashʿariyya fī ḥamd Allāh ʿalā l-imān*, Sanaa, Dār al-Makhṭūṭāt, coll. 2990 (n.d.).

Ibn al-Wazīr, Muḥammad b. Ibrāhīm. *Masʾalat ikhtilāf al-Muʿtazila wa-l-Ashʿariyya fī ḥamd Allāh ʿalā l-imān*, Sanaa, Maktabat Muḥammad al-Kibsī, coll. s.n. (1035/1626).

Ibn al-Wazīr, Muḥammad b. Ibrāhīm. *Mukhtaṣar mufīd fī ʿulūm al-ḥadīth*, Sanaa, Maktabat Muḥammad al-Kibsī, coll. s.n. (1334/1625).

Ibn al-Wazīr, Muḥammad b. Ibrāhīm. *Mukhtaṣar min Kitāb al-Qawāʿid*, Sanaa, Dār al-Makhṭūṭāt, coll. 3088 (n.d.).

Ibn al-Wazīr, Muḥammad b. Ibrāhīm. *Muthīr al-aḥzān fī wadāʿ shahr Ramaḍān*, Sanaa, Maktabat Muḥammad al-Kibsī, coll. s.n. (1359/1940).

Ibn al-Wazīr, Muḥammad b. Ibrāhīm. *Qawāʿid min qadīm*, Sanaa, Muʾassasat al-Imām Zayd b. ʿAlī al-thaqāfiyya, CD 620 (1204/1799).

Ibn al-Wazīr, Muḥammad b. Ibrāhīm. *Qubūl al-bushrā bi-l-taysīr lil-yusrā*, Sanaa, Dār al-Makhṭūṭāt, coll. 3133 (1158/1745).

Ibn al-Wazīr, Muḥammad b. Ibrāhīm. *Qubūl al-bushrā bi-l-taysīr lil-yusrā*, Sanaa, Muʾassasat al-Imām Zayd b. ʿAlī al-thaqāfiyya, CD 3 (1151/1738).

Ibn al-Wazīr, Muḥammad b. Ibrāhīm. *Taḥrīr al-kalām fī masʾalat al-ruʾya wa-tajwīdihi wa-dhikr mā dāra bayna l-Muʿtazila wa-l-Ashʿariyya*, Sanaa, Dār al-Makhṭūṭāt, coll. 3133 (1185/1745).

Ibn al-Wazīr, Muḥammad b. Ibrāhīm. *Taḥrīr al-kalām fī masʾalat al-ruʾya wa-tajwīdihi wa-dhikr mā dāra bayna l-Muʿtazila wa-l-Ashʿariyya*, Sanaa, Maktabat Muḥammad al-Kibsī, coll. s.n. (1034/1625).

Ibn al-Wazīr, Muḥammad b. Ibrāhīm. *Takhṣīṣ āyāt al-jumʿa*, Sanaa, Maktabat Muḥammad al-Kibsī, coll. s.n. (1035/1626).

Ibn al-Wazīr, Muḥammad b. Ibrāhīm. *Tarjīḥ asālīb al-Qurʾān ʿalā asālīb al-Yunān*, Sanaa, Muʾassasat al-Imām Zayd b. ʿAlī al-thaqāfiyya, CD 314 (1204/1790).

al-Murtaḍā, al-Ḥasan b. Aḥmad b. Yaḥyā, *Kanz al-ḥukamāʾ wa-rawḍat al-ʿulamāʾ*, Maktabat Muḥammad al-Kibsī, s.n. (1063/1653), http://arks.princeton.edu/ark:/88435/z890rv53n (February 2015).

al-Wazīr, Muḥammad b. ʿAbdallāh, *Tarjamat Muḥammad b. Ibrāhīm al-Wazīr*, Sanaa, Dār al-Makhṭūṭāt, 3002 (n.d).

Consulted Edited Sources

ʿAbd al-Jabbār, *Sharḥ al-uṣūl al-khamsa*, ed.ʿA.K. ʿUthmān, Cairo 1996.

ʿAbd al-Jabbār. *al-Mughnī fī abwāb al-tawḥīd wa-l-ʿadl*, eds. M. al-Khuḍayrī and M.M. Qāsim, 14 vols., Cairo 1965.

Abū l-Ḥusayn al-Baṣrī, *Kitāb al-Muʿtamad fī uṣūl al-fiqh*, ed. K. al-Mays, Beirut 1983.

al-ʿAnsī, A.Q., *Tāj al-mudhhab li-aḥkām al-madhhab. Sharḥ matn al-Azhār fī fiqh al-aʾimma l-aṭhār*, Sanaa 1993.

al-ʿAshʿarī, *Kitāb Maqālat al-islamiyyīn wa-ikhtilāf al-muṣallīn*, ed. H. Ritter, Istanbul 1929–1933.

al-Ghazālī, *al-Mustaṣfā min ʿilm al-uṣūl*, 2 vols., Beirut 1990.

Ibn al-Amīr, *Tawḍīḥ al-afkār li-maʿānī Tanqīḥ al-anẓār*, ed. A.ʿA.-R. Awīḍa, Beirut 1997.

Ibn Fanad, *Maʾāthir al-abrār fī tafṣīl mujmalāt Jawāhir al-akhbār*, Amman 2002.

Ibn al-Malāḥimī, *Kitāb al-Muʿtamad fī uṣūl al-dīn*, ed. W. Madelung, Tehran 2012.

Ibn al-Malāḥimī, *al-Tajrīd fī uṣūl al-fiqh. Legal Methodolgy in the 6th/12th Century Khwarazm* eds. H. Ansari and S. Schmidtke, Tehran 2011.

Ibn al-Malāḥimī, *Tuḥfat al-mutakallimīn fī l-radd ʿalā l-falāsifa*, eds. H. Ansari and W. Madelung, Tehran 2008.

Ibn al-Malāḥimī, *Kitāb al-Fāʾiq fī uṣūl al-dīn*, eds. W. Madelung and M. McDermott, Tehran 2007.

Ibn Mattawayh, *An anonymous commentary on Kitāb al-Tadhkira by Ibn Mattawayh. Facsimile edition of Mahdavi Codex 514 (6th/12th Century)*, ed. S. Schmidkte, Tehran 2006.

Ibn Miftāḥ, *Kitāb al-Muntazaʿ al-mukhtār min al-Ghayth al-midrār al-mufattiḥ li-kamāʾim al-Azhār fī fiqh al-aʾimma al-athār*, Cairo 1914.

Ibn al-Murtaḍā, *Minhāj al-wuṣūl ilā Miʿyār al-ʿuqūl fī ʿilm al-uṣūl*, ed., intr. A.ʿA. al-Mākhidhī, Sanaa 1996.

Ibn al-Murtaḍā, *Muqaddimat al-Baḥr al-zakhkhār al-jāmiʿ li-madhāhib ʿulamāʾ al-amṣār*, ed. ʿA.ʿA.-K.M. al-Faḍīl, Sanaa 1986.

Ibn al-Murtaḍā, Kitāb al-Intiqād lil-āyāt al-muʿtabara lil-ijtihād, in Ibn al-Murtaḍā, *Muqaddimat al-Baḥr al-zakhkhār al-jāmiʿ li-madhāhib ʿulamāʾ al-amṣār*, Sanaa 1988.

Ibn al-Murtaḍā, Kitāb al-Qalāʾid fī taṣḥīḥ al-ʿaqāʾid, in Ibn al-Murtaḍā, *Muqaddimat al-Baḥr al-zakhkhār al-jāmiʿ li-madhāhib ʿulamāʾ al-amṣār*, Sanaa 1988.

Ibn al-Murtaḍā, Riyāḍat al-afhām fī latīf al-kalām, in Ibn al-Murtaḍā, *Muqaddimat Kitāb al-Baḥr al-zakhkhār*, Sanaa 1988.

Ibn al-Murtaḍā, *Ṭabaqāt al-Muʿtazila*, ed. S. Diwald-Wilzer, Beirut 1961.

Ibn al-Murtaḍā, *Bāb dhikr al-Muʿtazila min Kitāb al-Munya wa-l-amal fī sharḥ Kitāb al-Milal wa-l-niḥal*, ed. T.W. Arnold, Leipzig 1902.

Ibn al-Wazīr, *al-ʿAwāṣim wa-l-qawāṣim fī l-dhabb ʿan sunnat Abī l-Qāsim*, ed. S. Arnaʾūṭ, 9 vols., Beirut 1992.

Ibn al-Wazīr, *al-Burhān al-qāṭiʿ fī ithbāt al-ṣāniʿ wa-jamīʿ mā jāʾat bihi al-sharāʾi*, ed. M.ʿA.-K. al-Khaṭīb, Beirut: 1988.

Ibn al-Wazīr, *al-Burhān al-qāṭiʿ fī ithbāt al-ṣāniʿ wa-jamīʿ mā jāʾat bihi al-sharāʾi*, Cairo 1931.

Ibn al-Wazīr, *Īthār al-ḥaqq ʿalā al-khalq: fī radd al-khilāfāt ilā al-maḏhab al-ḥaqq min usūl al-tawḥīd*, Beirut 1987.

Ibn al-Wazīr, *al-Rawḍ al-bāsim fī l-ḍabb ʿan sunnat Abī l-Qāsim*, ed. ʿA.M. al-ʿAmrān, Mecca 1998.

Ibn al-Wazīr, *Tanqīḥ al-anẓār fī maʿrifat ʿulūm al-athār*, eds. M. Ṣubḥī et al., Beirut 1999.

Ibn al-Wazīr, *Tarjīḥ asālīb al-Qurʾān ʿalā asālīb al-Yunān*, Cairo 1931.

Ibn Taymiyya, *al-ʿAqīda al-wāsiṭiyya*, Cairo 1973.

Ibn Taymiyya, *Majmūʿ fatāwā*, eds. ʿA.-R. Ibn Qāsim et al., Riyad 1995.

Ibn Taymiyya, *al-Radd ʿalā l-manṭiqiyyīn*, ed. M.H.M.H. Ismāʿīl, Beirut 2003.

al-Jāḥiẓ, *al-ʿIbar wa-l-iʿtibār*, ed. Ṣ. Idrīs, Cairo 1994.

al-Jāḥiẓ, al-Masāʾil wa-l-jawābāt fī l-maʿrifa (al-risāla al-thālitha ʿashara), in *Rasāʾil al-Jāḥiẓ Abī ʿUthmān ʿAmr b. Baḥr b. Maḥbūb al-mutawaffī sanat 255 h.: al-fuṣūl al-mukhtāra min kutub al-Jāḥiẓ*, ed. M.B.ʿU. al-Sawd, Beirut 2000, 33–47.

al-Juwaynī, *al-Shāmil fī uṣūl al-dīn*, eds. A.S. Nashshār et al., Alexandria 1969.

al-Manṣūr bi-l-llāh ʿAbd al-Allāh b. Ḥamza, *Ṣafwat al-ikhtiyār fī uṣūl al-fiqh*, eds. I.Y. Darsī and H.Ḥ.Ḥ. Ḥamzī, Saʿda 2002.

al-Muʿayyad bi-l-llāh Yaḥyā b. Ḥamza, *Kitāb al-Tamhīd fī sharḥ maʿālim al-ʿadl wa-l-tawḥīd*, ed. H.Ḥ. Sayyid, Cairo 2008.

al-Muʿayyad bi-l-llāh Yaḥyā b. Ḥamza, *Kitāb al-Intiṣār ʿalā ʿulamāʾ al-amṣār fī taqrīr al-mukhtār min madhāhib al-aʾimma wa-aqāwīl ʿulamāʾ al-umma*, 4 vols., eds. ʿA.-W.ʿA. al-Muʾayyad and ʿA.A. al-Mufaḍḍal, Amman 2002.

al-Qāsim b. Muhammad, *al-Irshād ilā sabīl al-rashād*, ed. M.Y.S. ʿIzzan, Sanaa 1996.

al-Qāsimī, A.H.Y., *al-ʿIlm al-wāsim fī l-radd ʿalā hafawāt al-Rawḍ al-bāsim*, Saʿda 2001.

Fakhr al-Dīn al-Rāzī, *al-Arbaʿīn fī uṣūl al-dīn*, eds. A. Hijāzī and M. Saqqā, Beirut 2004.

Fakhr al-Dīn al-Rāzī, *Kitāb Maʿālim uṣūl al-dīn*, ed. S. Dughaym, Beirut 1992.

Fakhr al-Dīn al-Rāzī, *al-Maṭālib al-ʿāliyya min al-ʿilm al-ilahī*, eds., A. Ḥijāzī and M. Saqqā, Beirut 1987.

al-Samāwī, M.Ṣ.H., *al-Ghaṭamṭam al-zakhkhār al-muṭahhir li-riyāḍ al-Azhār min āthār al-Sayl al-Jarār*, ed. M.Y.S. ʿIzzān, Amman 1994.

al-Shahrastānī, *al-Milal wa-l-niḥal*, 3 vols., ed. M. Kaylānī, Beirut 1984.

al-Shawkānī, *Irshād al-fuḥūl ilā taḥqīq al-ḥaqq min ʿilm al-uṣūl*, ed. A.Q. al-ʿAbbādī, Cairo 1937.

Taqī l-Dīn al-ʿUjālī, *al-Kāmil fī l-istiqṣāʾ fīmā balaghanā min kalām al-qudamāʾ*, ed. M. al-Shāhid, Cairo 1999.

al-Wazīr, A.ʿA.A., *Taʾrīkh al-sāda l-ʿulamāʾ al-fuḍalāʾ wa-l-aʾimma banī l-Wazīr ʿulamāʾ al-Zaydiyya* (*Tāʾrīkh Banī l-Wazīr*), ed. Z.ʿA. al-Wazīr (forthcoming).

al-Wazīr, Ḥ.I., *Hidāyat al-rāghibīn ilā madhhab al-ʿitra l-ṭāhirīn*, ed. ʿA.-R.M. Ḥajar, Saʿda 2002.
al-Wazīr, Ḥ.I., *Nihāyat al-tanwīh fī izhāq al-tamwīh*, eds. A.D. Ḥawriyya and I.M.-D. al-Muʾayyidī, Saʿda 2000.
al-Wazīr, Ḥ.I., *Thabat Banī l-Wazīr*, ed. Z.ʿA. al-Wazīr, (forthcoming).
al-Wazīr, Ṣ-D.I., *al-Fuṣūl al-luʾluʾiyya fī uṣūl fiqh al-ʿitra l-zakiyya wa-iʿlām al-umma al-muḥammadiyya*, ed. M.Y.S. ʿIzzān, Beirut 2001.
Yaḥyā b. al-Ḥusayn, *Ghāyat al-amānī fī tāʾrīkh al-quṭr al-yamānī*, ed. S.ʿA.-F. ʿĀshur, Cairo 1968.

Consulted Catalogues

Ahlwardt, W., *Die Handschriften-Verzeichnisse der Königlichen Bibliothek zu Berlin. Verzeichniss der arabischen Handschriften*, 10 vols., Berlin 1899.
al-ʿĪsawī, A.M. et al., *Fihris al-makhṭūṭāt al-Yamaniyya li-Dār al-makhṭūṭāt wa-l-maktaba al-gharbiyya bi-l-Jāmiʿ al-kabīr Sanaa*, 2 vols., Qom 2005.
Muʾassasat al-Imām Zayd b. ʿAlī al-thaqāfiyya (ed.), *al-Fihris al-makhṭūṭāt al-raqmiyya bi-Muʾassasat al-Imām Zayd b. ʿAlī al-thaqāfiyya*, Sanaa 2012.
al-Ruqayḥī, A.A.R. et al., *Fihrist Makhṭūṭāt Maktabat al-Jāmiʿ al-kabīr*, 4 vols., Sanaa 1984.
al-Wajīh, ʿA.S., *Maṣādir al-turāth fī l-maktabāt al-khāssa fī l-Yaman*, 2 vols., Sanaa 2002.

Consulted Bio- and Bibliographical Reference Works

ʿAfīf, A.J. et al., *al-Mawsūʿa l-yamaniyya*, 4 vols., Sanaa2003.
al-Akwaʿ, I.ʿA., *Hijar al-ʿilm wa-maʿāqiluhu fī l-Yaman*, Beirut/Damaskus 1995–2003.
al-Dhahabī, M.A., *Siyār aʿlām al-nubalāʾ*, eds. S. Arnaʾūt and B. ʿAwwād, Beirut 2001.
al-Fāsī, M.A., *al-ʿIqd al-thamīn fī taʾrīkh al-balad al-amīn*, 8 vols., Beirut 1986.
al-Ḥibshī, ʿA.-A.M., *Maṣādir al-fikr al-islāmī fī l-Yaman*, Abū Dhabī 2004.
al-Ḥibshī, ʿA.-A.M., *Muʾallafāt ḥukkām al-Yaman*, ed. E. Niehwöhner-Eberhard, Wiesbaden 1979.
al-Ḥusaynī, S.A., *Muʾallafāt al-Zaydiyya*, 3 vols., Qum 1992–1993.
Ibn Abī l-Rijāl, A.S., *Maṭlaʿ al-budūr wa-majmaʿ al-buḥūr fī tarājim rijāl al-Zaydiyya*, eds. ʿA.-R.M. Ḥajar and M.-D. al-Muʾayyidī, 4 vols., Saʿda 2004.
Kaḥḥāla, U.R., *Muʿjam al-muʾallifīn. Tarājim muṣannifī l-kutub al-ʿarabiyya*, 15 vols., Beirut 1985.
al-Muʾayyidī, M.-D.M., *Lawāmiʿ al-anwār fī jawāmiʿ al-ʿulūm wa-l-āthār wa-tarājim ūlī l-ʿilm wa-l-anẓār*, 2 vols., Saʿda 1993.

al-Sakhāwī, M.ʿA.-R., *al-Ḍawʾ al-lāmiʿ li-ahl al-qarn al-tāsiʿ*, 12 vols., Beirut 1992.
al-Sabḥānī, J., *Buḥūth fī l-milal wa-l-niḥal. Dirāsa mawḍūʿiyya muqārina lil-madhāhib al-islāmiyya*, Qom 1997.
Sayyid, A.F., *Maṣādir taʾrīkh al-Yaman fī l-ʿaṣr al-islāmī/Sources de l'histoire du Yémen à l'epoque musulmane*, Cairo 1974.
al-Shahārī, I.Q., *Ṭabaqāt al-Zaydiyya al-kubrā*, ed. ʿA.-S. al-Wajīh, 3 vols., Amman 2001.
al-Shawkānī, M.ʿA., *al-Badr al-ṭāliʿ bi-maḥāsin man baʿd al-qarn al-sābiʿ*, ed. M.M. Zabāra, 2 vols., Cairo 1929.
al-Wajīh, ʿA.-S., *Aʿlām al-muʾallifīn al-Zaydiyya*, Amman 1999.
Zabāra, M.M., *Aʾimmat al-Yaman*, Taʿizz 1952.
al-Ziriklī, K.-D., *al-Aʿlām. Qāmūs tarājim li-ashhar al-rijāl wa-l-nisāʾ min al-ʿarab wa-l-mustaʿribīn wa-l-mustashriqīn*, 10 vols., Beirut 2002.

Consulted Secondary Literature

Abdel Haleem, M.A.S., *The Qur'an*, New York 2005.
Abdeljelil, J.B., Eine Islamische Annäherung zur Gottesfrage sowie dem Wesen Gottes und seinen Attributen—Von der Apologie zur Epistemologie, in *Zeitschrift für Islamische Studien* 2.4 (2012), 16–21.
Abrahamov, B., *Al-Qāsim b. Ibrāhīm on the Proof of God's Existence. Kitāb al-Dalīl al-Kabīr*, Leiden/New York/Kopenhagen/Köln 1990.
Abrahamov, B. (ed.), *Anthropomorphism and the Interpretation of the Qur'ān in the Theology of al-Qāsim b. Ibrāhīm Kitāb al-Mustarshid*, Leiden/New York/Köln 1996.
Abrahamov, B., Necessary Knowledge in Islamic Theology, in *British Journal of Middle Eastern Studies* 20.1 (1993), 20–32.
Abrahamov, B., Ibn Taymiyya on the Agreement of Reason with Tradition, in *MW* 82. 3–4 (1992), 256–273.
Abrahamov, B., A Re-Examination of al-Ashʿarī's Theory of *'Kasb' 'Kitāb al-Lumaʿ'*, in *JRAS* 2 (1989), 210–221.
Abrahamov, B., al-Kāsim ibn Ibrāhīm's Theory of the Imamate, in *Arabica* 34 (1987), 80–105.
Abrahamov, B., al-Kāsim ibn Ibrāhīm's Argument from Design, in *Oriens* 29–30 (1987), 259–284.
al-ʿAbsī, M.R., *Aqwāl al-Imām Muḥammad b. al-Wazīr (775–840) fī-l-tafsīr min awwal Sūrat al-Fātiḥa ilā ākhir Sūrat al-Aʿrāf*, PhD diss., University of Umm al-Qurra 2012.
Abū Zahra, M., *al-Imām Zayd. Ḥayātuhu wa-ʿaṣruhu, ārāʾuhu wa-fiqhuhu*, Cairo 2005.
Adang, C., Islam as the Inborn Religion of Mankind: The Concept of *Fiṭrah* in the Works of Ibn Hazm, in *Qantara* 21 (2000), 391–410.
Aghnides, N.P., *Mohammedan Theories of Finance with an Introduction to Mohammedan Law and a Bibliography*, Lahore 1961.

Ahmad, A.A., *Structural Interrelations of Theory and Practice in Islamic Law: A Study of* Takhrīj al-Furūʿ ʿalā al-Uṣūl *Literature*, PhD diss., Harvard University 2005.

al-Akwaʿ, I.ʿA., *al-Zaydiyya. Nashʾatuhā wa-muʿtaqadātuhā*, Beirut 2000.

al-Akwaʿ, I.ʿA., Les Hijras et les Fortresses du Savoir au Yémen, in *Les Cahiers du* CFEY 2 (1996).

al-Akwaʿ, I.ʿA. (intr.), al-Imām Muḥammad b. Ibrāhīm al-Wazīr wa-kitābuhu al-ʿAwāṣim wa-l-qawāṣim, in M.I. al-Wazīr, *al-ʿAwāṣim wa-l-Qawāṣim fī l-dhabb ʿan sunnat Abī l-Qāsim* i, Beirut 1992.

Ali-Karamali, S.P. and F. Dunne, The *Ijtihād* Controversy, in *Arab Law Quarterly* 9.3 (1994), 238–257.

Ansari, H., Ketab al-Kamil Saʿed b. Aḥmad al-Uṣūlī ketabī dar dānesh-e kalām muʿtazilī, http://ansari.kateban.com/post/1829 (08 September 2014).

Ansari, H., Maḥmūd al-Malāḥimī al-Muʿtazilī fī l-Yaman, http://ansari.kateban.com/post/1382 (09 January 2013).

Ansari, H. et al., Yūsuf al-Baṣīr's Rebuttal of Abū l-Ḥusayn al-Baṣrī in a Yemeni Zaydī Manuscript of the 7th/13th Century, in *The Yemeni Manuscript Tradition*, eds. D. Hollenberg et al., Leiden/Boston 2015, 28–65.

Ansari, H. and S. Schmidtke, The Literary-Religious Tradition among 7th/13th-Century Yemeni Zaydīs (II): The Case of ʿAbdallāh b. Zayd al-ʿAnsī (d. 667/1269), in *The Yemeni Manuscript Tradition*, eds. D. Hollenberg et al., Leiden/Boston 2015, 101–154.

Ansari, H. and S. Schmidtke, The Muʿtazilī and Zaydī Reception of Abū l-Ḥusayn al-Baṣrī's *Kitāb al-Muʿtamad fī Uṣūl al-Fiqh*: A Bibliographical Note, in *Islamic Law and Society* 20.1–2 (2013), 90–109.

Ansari, H. and S. Schmidtke, The Literary-Religious Tradition among 7th/13th Century Yemeni Zaydīs: The Formation of the Imām al-Mahdī li-Dīn Allāh Aḥmad b. al-Ḥusayn b. al-Qāsim (d. 656/1258), in *Journal of Islamic Manuscripts* 2 (2011), 165–222.

Ansari, H. and J. Thiele, MS Berlin, State Library, Glaser 51: A Unique Manuscript from the Early 7th/13th-Century Bahshamite Milieu in Yemen, in *The Yemeni Manuscript Tradition*, eds. D. Hollenberg et al., Leiden/Boston 2015, 66–81.

al-ʿAnsī, ʿA.-A., *Zaydī theology in the 7th/13th century Yemen. Facsimile edition of* Kitāb al-Maḥajja al-bayḍāʾ fī uṣūl al-dīn *of Ḥusām al-Dīn ʿAbd Allāh b. Zayd al-ʿAnsī (d. 667/1269)*, ed., intr. H. Ansari and S. Schmidtke, Tehran 2015.

ʿĀrif, A.ʿA.-A., *al-Ṣila bayna l-Zaydiyya wa-l-Muʿtazila. Dirāsa kalāmiyya muqārina li-ārāʾ al-firqatayn*, Sanaa 1987.

Arnaldez, R., Ḳidam, in *EI*² online (14 January 2015).

Bakar, O., *History and Philosophy in Islamic Science*, Cambridge 1999.

Bell, J.N., *Love Theory in Later Ḥanbalite Islam*, Albany Press 1979.

Bencheikh, J.E., Marwān al-Akbar b. Abī Ḥafṣa and Marwān al-Aṣghar b. Abī ʿl-Janūb, in *EI*² online (13 February 2014).

Bernand, M., Le Problème de L'*Ashbah* ou les Implications Ontologiques de la Règle Juridico-Religieuse, in *Arabica* 37 (1990), 151–172.

Bernand, M., Ḥanafī *Uṣūl al-Fiqh* through a Manuscript of al-Jaṣṣāṣ, in *JAOS* 105.4 (1985), 623–635.

Bernand, M., La Notion de *ʿilm* chez les Premiers Muʿtazilites, in *SI* 36 (1972), 23–45.

Bernand, M., Des Critères de la Certitude: Un Opuscule de Ḥasan Ibn Sahl, in *JA* 1–2 (1969), 95–124.

Blackburn, J.R. et al., Al-Mahdī li-Dīn Allāh Aḥmad, 2., in *EI*² online (15 February 2014).

Bonebakker, S.A. and B. Reinert, al-Maʿānī wa-l-Bayān, in *EI*² online (10 January 2014).

Bonnefoy, L., Les identités religieuses contemporaines au Yémen: convergence, résistances et instrumentalisations, in *REMMM* 121–122 (2008), 199–203.

Brown, J., *The Canonization of al-Bukhārī and Muslim. The Formation and Function of the Sunni Hadith Canon*, Leiden/Boston 2007.

Brunschvig, R., *Études d'Islamologie*, Paris 1976.

Brunschvig, R., Mutazilism et Optimum (*al-aṣlah*), in *SI* 39 (1974), 5–23.

Brunschvig, R., Pour ou Contre la Logique Grecque chez les Théologiens-Juristes de l'Islam: Ibn Ḥazm, al-Ghazālī, Ibn Taymiyya, in *Convegno Internazionale 9–15 Aprile 1969. Oriente e Occidente nel Medioevo: Filosofia e Scienze* (*Convegno Volta*), Rome 1971, 185–209.

Brunschvig, R., Rationalité et Tradition dans l'Analogie Juridico-Religieuse chez le Muʿtazilite ʿAbd al-Jabbār, in *Arabica* 19 (1972), 213–221.

Calder, N., al-Nawawī's Typology of *Muftīs* and its Significance for a General Theory of Islamic Law, in *Islamic Law and Society* 3.2 (1996), 137–164.

Calder, N., Taqlīd, in *EI*² online (22 September 2014).

Cook, M., *Commanding Right and Forbidding Wrong in Islamic Thought*, Cambridge 2000.

Dahlén, A.P., *Islamic Law, Epistemology and Modernity. Legal Philosophy in Contemporary Iran*, New York/London 2003.

Eissa, M.A., Abū l-Ḥusayn al-Baṣrī's Use of Reason in *ʿIlm al-Kalām* and *Uṣūl al-Fiqh*, in *al-Shajarah Journal of The International Institute of Islamic Thought and Civilization* 16.1 (2011), 1–46.

Elshahed, E., *Das Problem der transzendenten sinnlichen Wahrnehmung in der spätmuʿtazilitischen Erkenntnistheorie nach der Darstellung des Taqīaddīn an-Nağrānī*, Berlin 1983.

Fadel, M., The Social Logic of *Taqlīd* and the Rise of the *Mukhtaṣar*, in *Islamic Law and Society* 3.2 (1996), 193–233.

Fakhry, M., Some Paradoxical Implications of the Muʿtazilite View of Free Will, in *MW* 43.2 (1953), 95–109.

Fierro, M., Local and Global Hadith Literature. The Case of al-Andalus, in *The Transmission and Dynamics of the Textual Sources of Islam: Essays in Honour of Harald Motzki*, eds. N.B. van der Voort et al., Leiden 2011.

Frank, R.M., *Beings and Their Attributes: The Teaching of the Basrian School of the Muʿtazila in the Classical Period*, Albany 1978.

Frank, R.M., Knowledge and *Taqlīd*. The Foundations of Religious Belief in Classical Ashʿarism, in *JAOS* 109 (1989), 37–62.

Frank, R.M., Several Fundamental Assumptions of the Baṣra School of the Muʿtazila, in *SI* 33 (1971), 5–18.

Frank, R.M., The *Kalām*, an Art of Contradiction-Making or Theological Science? Some Remarks on the Question, in *JAOS* 88 (1968), 295–309.

Frank, R.M., The Structure of Created Causality According to al-Ashʿarī: An Analyses of the *'Kitāb al-Lumaʿ'*, §§ 82–164, in *SI* 25 (1966), 13–75.

Frank, R.M., Ḥāl, in *EI*² online (15 January 2015).

Gardet, L., al-Djubbāʾi, *EI*², i, 569–570.

Gardet, L., al-Ḳaḍāʾ wa 'l-Ḳadar, in *EI*² online (01 April 2014).

Ghaneabassiri, K., The Epistemological Foundation of Conceptions of Justice in Classical *Kalām*: A Study of ʿAbd al-Jabbār's *al-Mughnī* and Ibn al-Bāqillānī's *al-Tamhīd*, in *JIS* 19 (2008), 71–96.

al-Gharāwī, S., *al-Zaydiyya bayna al-Imāmiyya wa-ahl al-sunna. Dirāsa taʾrīkhiyya tahlīliyya fī nashʾatihā wa-ẓuhūrihā wa-ʿaqāʾidihā wa-firaqihā*, Beirut 2006.

Gibb, H.A.R., The Argument from Design. A Muʿtazilite Treatise Attributed to al-Jāḥiẓ, in *Ignaz Goldziher Memorial I*, eds. S. Löwinger and J. Somogyi, Budapest 1948, 150–162.

Gimaret, D., *Théories de l'Acte Humain en Théologie Musulmane*. Paris/Leuven 1980.

Gimaret, D., Un Problème de Théologie Musulmane: Dieu Veut-Il les Actes Mauvais? Thèses et Arguments: III. Les Arguments Muʾtazilites (Suite et Fin), in *SI* 41 (1975), 63–92.

Gimaret, D., Taklīf, in *EI*² online (28 January 2014).

Gimaret, D., Muʿtazila, in *EI*² online (20 August 2013).

Gimaret, D., Ruʾyat Allāh, in *EI*² online (25 February 2014).

Gimaret, D., Uṣūl al-Dīn, in *EI*² online (5 September 2013).

Gleave, R., *Inevitable Doubt: Two Theories of Shīʿī Jurisprudence*, Leiden/Boston/Köln 2000.

Gobillot, G., *La Fiṭra: La Conception Originelle, ses Interprétations et Fonctions chez les Penseurs Musulmans*, Cairo 2000.

Gochenour, D.T., *The Penetration of Zaydī Islam into Early Medieval Yemen*, Phd diss., Harvard University 1984.

Gochenour, D.T., A Revised Bibliography of Medieval Yemeni History in Light of Recent Publications and Discoveries, in *Der Islam* 63 (1986), 309–322.

Goichon, A.M., Ḥikma, in *EI*² online (8 January 2013).

Griffel, F., Al-Ghazālī's Use of 'Original Human Disposition' (*Fiṭra*) and Its Background in the Teachings of al-Farābī and Avicenna, in *MW* 102.1 (2012), 1–32.

Grünschloss, A., *Der eigene und der fremde Glaube. Studien zur interreligiösen Fremdwahrnehmung in Islam, Hinduismus, Buddhismus und Christentum*, Tübingen 1999.

Guenther, S., Al-Jāḥiẓ and the Poetics of Teaching. A Ninth Century Muslim Scholar on Intellectual Education, in *Al-Jāḥiẓ: A Muslim Humanist for Our Time*, eds. J.L. Meloy et al., Beirut 2009, 17–26.

Gutas, D., Certainty, Doubt, Error: Comments on the Epistemological Foundations of Medieval Arabic Science, in *Early Science and Medicine* 7 (2002), 276–289.

Gwynne, R., Al-Jubbā'ī, al-Ash'arī and the Three Brothers: The Uses of Fiction, in *MW* 75 (1985), 132–161.

Haider, N., *Shīʿī Islām: An Introduction*, New York 2014.

Ḥajar, R., *Ibn al-Wazīr al-Yamānī wa-manhajuhu al-kalāmī*, Jedda 1984.

Hallaq, W.B., *The Origins and Evolution of Islamic Law*, Cambridge 2005.

Hallaq, W.B., *Authority, Continuity and Change in Islamic Law*, Cambridge/New York 2001.

Hallaq, W.B., *A History of Islamic Legal Theories. An Introduction to Sunnī Uṣūl Al-Fiqh*, Cambridge 1997.

Hallaq, W.B., *Ibn Taymiyya against the Greek Logicians*, New York 1993.

Hallaq, W.B., *Takhrīj* and the Construction of Juristic Authority, in *Studies in Islamic Legal Theory*, ed. B. Weiss, Leiden/Boston/Köln 2002, 317–335.

Hallaq, W.B., Inductive Corroboration, Probability, and Certainty, in *Islamic Law and Jurisprudence*, ed. N.L. Heer, Seattle/London 1990, 3–31.

Hallaq, W.B., *Ifta'* and *Ijtihad* in Sunni Legal Theory: A Develomental Account, in *Islamic Legal Interpretation. Muftis and Their Fatwas*, eds. B. Messick et al., Cambridge/London 1996, 33–43.

Hallaq, W.B., Ibn Taymiyya on the Existence of God, in *AO* 52 (1991), 49–69.

Hallaq, W.B., Notes on the Term *Qarīna* Islamic Legal Discourse, in *JAOS* 108.3 (1988), 475–480.

Hallaq, W.B., The Development of Logical Structure in Islamic Legal Theory, in *Der Islam* 64.1 (1987), 42–67.

Hallaq, W.B., On the Origins of the Controversy about the Existence of *Mujtahids* Gate of *Ijtihād*, in *SI* 63 (1986), 129–141.

Hallaq, W.B., Was the Gate of *Ijtihād* Closed?, in *IJMES* 16.1 (1984), 3–41.

al-Ḥarbī, ʿA.ʿA., *Ibn al-Wazīr wa-arāʾuhu al-iʿtiqādiyya wa-juhūduhu fī l-difāʿ ʿan al-sunna al-nabawiyya*, Jedda 2009.

Harris, R. and A. Pakatchi, Āyāt al-aḥkām, in *Encyclopaedia Islamica*, Brill online (16 March 2014).

Haykel, B., *Revival and Reform in Islam. The Legacy of Muḥammad al-Shawkānī*, Cambridge 2003.

Haykel, B., Reforming Islam by Dissolving the *Madhāhib*: Shawkānī and his Zaydī Detractors in Yemen, in *Studies in Islamic Legal Theory*, ed. B. Weiss, Leiden/Boston/Köln 2002, 337–364.

Haykel, B., The *Ahl al-Ḥadīth* Scholars among the Zaydīs of Yemen, in *al-Masār* 2 (2001).
Haykel, B., Al-Shawkānī and the Jurisprudential Unity of Yemen, in *REMMM* 67.1 (1993), 53–65.
Haykel, B. and A. Zysow, What Makes a *Madhhab* a *Madhhab*: Zaydī Debates on the Structure of Legal Authority, in *Arabica* 59 (2012), 332–371.
Heinrichs, W.P., Ḳawāʿid Fiḳhiyya, in *EI*² online (20 January 2014).
Heinrichs, W.P., al-Sakkakī, in *EI*² online (08 January 2013).
Heemskerk, M.T., *Suffering in the Muʿtazilite Theology. ʿAbd al-Jabbār's Teaching on Pain and Divine Justice*, Leiden 2000.
al-Ḥibshī, ʿA.-A., *al-Ṣūfiyya wa-l-fuqahāʾ fī l-Yaman*, Sanaa 1976.
Hodgson, M.G.S., Bāṭiniyya, in *EI*² online (14 September 2014).
Holzmann, L., Human Choice, Divine Guidance and the *Fiṭra* Tradition, in *Ibn Taymiyya and His Times*, eds. Y. Rapoport and S. Aḥmad, Karachi 2010, 163–188.
Hoover, J., *Ibn Taymiyya's Theodicy of Perpetual Optimism*, Leiden/Boston 2007.
Hoover, J., Withholding Judgement on Islamic Universalism: Ibn al-Wazīr (d. 840/1436) on the Duration and Purpose of Hell-Fire, in *Locating Hell in Islamic Traditions*, ed. C. Lange, Leiden 2016, 208–237.
Hoover, J., God's Wise Purposes in Creating Iblīs. Ibn Qayyim al-Jawziyyah's Theodicy of God's Names and Attributes, in *A Scholar in the Shadow: Essays in the Legal and Theological Thought of Ibn Qayyim al-Jawziyya*, eds. C. Bori and L. Holtzman, *Oriente Moderno* 90.1 (2010), 113–134.
Hoover, J., Islamic Universalism: Ibn Qayyim al-Jawziyya's Salafī Deliberations on the Duration of Hell-Fire, in *MW* 99.1 (2009), 181–201.
Hoover, J., The Justice of God and the Best of All Possible Worlds. The Theodicy of Ibn Taymiyya, in *Theological Review of the Near East School of Theology* 27.2 (2006), 53–75.
Hoover, J., Ibn Taymiyya as an Avicennan Theologian: A Muslim Approach to God's Self-Sufficiency, in *Theological Review of the Near East School of Theology* 27.1 (2006), 34–46.
Hoover, J., Perpetual Creativity in the Perfection of God: Ibn Taymiyya's Hadith Commentary on God's Creation of this World, in *JIS* 15 (2004), 287–329.
Hourani, G.F., *Islamic Rationalism: The Ethics of ʿAbd al-Jabbār*, Oxford 1971.
Hourani, G.F., Divine Justice and Human reason in Muʿtazilite Ethical Theology, in *Ethics in Islam*, ed. G. Hoviannisian, Malibu 1985, 73–83.
Ibn ʿĀshūr, M.Ṭ, *Ibn ʿĀshūr: Treatise on Maqāṣid al-Sharīʿa*, trans. M.Ṭ. al-Misawī, London/Washington 2006.
Ibrahim, A.F., *School Boundaries and Social Utility in Islamic Law: The Theory and Practice of* Talfīq *and* Tatabbuʿ al-Rukhaṣ *in Egypt*, PhD diss., Georgetown University 2011.
ʿIzzān, M.Y.S., Dawr al-Zaydiyya fī takrīz manhaj al-tasāmuḥ al-madhhabī, http://www.yemenhrc.com (21 March 2013).

al-ʿIzzī, ʿA.-A.Ḥ., *ʿUlūm al-ḥadīth ʿinda l-Zaydiyya wa-l-muḥaddithīn*, Saʿda 2001.

Jackson, S.A., *Islamic Law and the State. The Constitutional Jurisprudence of Shihāb al-Dīn al-Qarāfī*, Leiden/New York/Köln 1996.

Jackson, S.A., *Taqlīd*, Legal Scaffolding and the Scope of Legal Injunctions in Post-Formative Theory *Muṭlaq ʿāmm* of Shihāb al-Dīn al-Qarāfī, in *Islamic Law and Society* 3 (1996), 165–192.

Jaques, R.K., *A Muslim History of Islamic Law: Qāḍī Shuhbah's* Ṭabaqāt al-Fuqahāʾ al-Shāfiʿiyyah (*the Generations of the Shāfiʿī Jurists*), PhD diss., Emory University 2001.

al-Jirāfī, ʿA.-A., *al-Muqtaṭaf min taʾrīkh al-Yaman*, Beirut 1987.

Johansen, B., *Contingency in a Sacred Law. Legal and Ethical Norms in the Muslim Fiqh*, Leiden/Boston/Köln 1999.

Johansen, B., Signs as Evidence: The Doctrine of Ibn Taymiyya (1263–1328) and Ibn Qayyim Al-Jawziyya (D. 1351) on Proof, in *Islamic Law and Society* 9 (2002), 168–193.

Kamali, M.H., *Principles of Islamic Jurisprudence*, Cambridge 1991.

al-Kamālī, M.M., *al-Imām al-Mahdī Aḥmad b. Yaḥyā b. al-Murtaḍā wa-atharuhu fī l-fikr al-islāmī siyāsiyyan wa-iʿtiqādiyyan*, Sanaa 1991.

Khān, M.Ṣ.Ḥ., *al-Tāj al-mukallal li-jawāhir maʾāthir al-ṭirāz al-akhīr wa-l-awwal*, Qatar 2007.

al-Kibsī, M.A., *al-Furūq al-wāḍiḥa l-bahiyya bayna l-firaq al-Imāmiyya wa-bayna l-firqa l-Zaydiyya*, Sanaa 2009.

King, J.R., Zaydī Revival in a Hostile Republic: Competing Identities, Loyalties and Visions of State in Republican Yemen, in *Arabica* 59 (2012), 404–445.

Kohlberg, E., Some Zaydī Views on the Companions, in *BSOAS* 39 (1976), 91–98.

Krawietz, B., Transgressive Creativity in the Making. Ibn Qayyim al-Jawziyyah's Reframing within Ḥanbalī Legal Methodology, in *A Scholar in the Shadow: Essays in the Legal and Theological Thought of Ibn Qayyim al-Jawziyya*, eds. C. Bori and L. Holtzman, *Oriente Moderno* 90.1 (2010), 47–66.

Kruse, H., *Takfīr* und *Jihād* bei den Zaiditen des Jemen, in *WI* 23–24 (1984), 424–457.

von Kügelgen, A., The Poison of Philosophy. Ibn Taymiyya's Struggle for and against Reason, in *Islamic Theology, Philosophy and Law. Debating Ibn Taymiyya and Ibn Qayyim Al-Jawziyya*, eds. G. Tamer and B. Krawietz, Berlin/Boston 2013, 253–328.

Lamotte, V., Ibn Taymiyya's Theory of Knowledge, PhD diss., McGill University 1994.

Laoust, H., *Essai sur les Doctrines Sociales et Politique de Taḳī-d-Dīn Aḥmad b. Taymiyya*, Cairo 1939.

Leaman, O.N.H., Luṭf, in *EI*² online, (10 January 2014).

Masud, M. et al., Muftis, Fatwas and Islamic Legal Interpretation, in *Islamic Legal Interpretation. Muftis and Their Fatwas*, eds. B. Messick et al., Cambridge/Massachusetts/London 1996, 3–32.

Maʿṣūmī, M.Ṣ.Ḥ., *Ijtihād* through Fourteen Centuries, in *Islamic Studies* 21.4 (1982), 39–70.

Macdonald, D.B., Fiṭra, in *EI*² online (20 May 2014).

Madelung, W., *Arabic Texts concerning the History of the Zaydī Imāms of Tabaristān, Daylamān und Gīlān*, Beirut 1987.

Madelung, W., *Der Imām al-Qāsim Ibn Ibrāhīm und die Glaubenslehre der Zaiditen*, Berlin 1965.

Madelung, W., Introduction. Part VI: Theology, in *The Study of Shīʿī Islam. History, Theology and Law*, eds. F. Daftary and G. Miskinzoda, London 2014, 455–463.

Madelung, W., Abū l-Ḥusayn al-Baṣrī's Proof for the Existence of God, in *Arabic Theology, Arabic Philosophy. From the Many to the One: Essays in Celebration of Richard M. Frank*, ed. J.E. Montgomery, Leuven/Paris/Dudley 2006, 273–280.

Madelung, W., Zaydī Attitudes to Sufism, in *Islamic Mysticism Contested. Thirteen Centuries of Controversies and Polemics*, eds. F. de Jong and B. Radtke, Leiden/Boston/Köln 1999, 124–144.

Madelung, W., The Origins of the Yemenite Hijra, in *Religious and Ethnic Movements in Medieval Islam*, ed. W. Madelung, Aldershot 1992, 25–44.

Madelung, W., The Late Muʿtazila and Determinism: The Philosopher's Trap, in *Yād-Nāma in Memoria di Allessandro Bausani*, Rome 1991, 245–258.

Madelung, W., Islam im Jemen, in *Jemen: 3000 Jahre Kunst und Kultur des Glücklichen Arabien*, ed. W. Daum, Innsbruck/Frankfurt 1987, 172–176.

Madelung, W., Elsayed Elshahed: Das Problem der transzendenten sinnlichen Wahrnehmung in der spätmu'tazilitischen Erkenntnistheorie nach der Dartellung des Tagīaddīn an-Nağrānī (review), in *BSOAS* 48 (1985), 128–129.

Madelung, W., Abū l-Ḥusayn al-Baṣrī, in *EI*² online (16 July 2014).

Madelung, W., Djafar b. Abī Yaḥyā, Shams al-Dīn Abū l-Faḍl, in *EI*² online (15 January 2014).

Madelung, W., ʿAbd al-Ḥamīd b. Abū l-Ḥadīd, in *EIr*, i, 108–110.

Madelung, W., Jaʿfar b. Abī Yaḥyā, Shams al-Dīn Abū l-Faḍl, in *EI*² online (14 February 2014).

Madelung, W., Ibn Mattawayh, in *EI*² online (21 July 2014).

Madelung, W., Murdji'a, in *EI*² online (30 January 2014).

Madelung, W., Muṭarrifiyya, in *EI*² online (08 January 2013).

Madelung, W., al-Zamakhsharī, in *EI*² online (03 April 2014).

Madelung, W., al-Zaydiyya, in *EI*² online (20 January 2013).

Madelung, W. and S. Schmidtke, *Rational Theology in Interfaith Communication. Abū l-Ḥusayn al-Baṣrī's Muʿtazilī Theology among the Karaites in the Fatimid Age*, Leiden/Boston 2006.

al-Maḥaṭwarī, M.Z., *Uṣūl al-fiqh—al-Ḥukm al-sharʿī wa-mutaʿallaqātuhu*, Sanaa 2008.

Manning, J.F., Textualism and Legislative Intent, in *Virginia Law Review* 91. 2 (1995), 419–450.

Mansurnoor, I.A., Shawkānī and the Closed Door of *Ijtihād*, in *Hamdard Islamicus* 11. 2 (1988), 57–65.

McDermott, M.J., Abū l-Ḥusayn al-Baṣrī on God's Volition, in *Culture and Memory in Medieval Islam. Essays in Honour of Wilferd Madelung*, eds. J.W. Meri and F. Daftary, London/New York 2003, 86–93.

Meisami, J.S. and P. Starkey (eds.), *Encyclopedia of Arabic Literature*, 2 vols., London/New York 1999.

Melchert, C., *The Formation of the Sunni Schools of Law, 9th–10th Centuries C.E.* (SILS 4), Leiden/New York/Köln 1997.

al-Mikhlāfī, B.S., *al-Wajīz fī l-qawāʿid al-fiqhiyya*, Sanaa 2004.

Mir-Hosseini, Z., *Marriage on Trial: A Study of Islamic Family Law*, New York 2000.

Mirza, M.H., The Quest for Knowledge: Birūnī's Method of Inquiry, PhD diss., Yale University 2010.

Mortel, R.T., Zaydī Shiʿism and the Ḥasanid Sharīfs of Mecca, in *IJMES* 19 (1987), 455–472.

Muslim, *Ṣaḥīḥ Muslim*, trans. ʿA.-Ḥ. Ṣiddīqī, New Delhi 1984.

Nasir, S.A., The Epistemology of *Kalām* of Abū Manṣūr Al-Māturīdī, in *JIS* 43.2 (2005), 349–365.

el-Omari, R.M., *The Theology of Abū l-Qasim al-Balkhī/al-Kaʿbī (d. 319/931): A Study of Its Sources and Reception*, PhD diss., Yale University 2006.

el-Omari, R.M., Abū l-Qāsim al-Balkhī al-Kaʿbī's Doctrine, in *A Common Rationality. Muʿtazilism in Islam and Judaism*, eds. S. Schmidtke et al., Würzburg 2007, 39–57.

Ormsby, E.L. *Theodicy in Islamic Thought. The Dispute over al-Ghazālī's "Best of All Possible Worlds"*, Princeton 1984.

Osman, A., The History and Doctrine of the Ẓāhirī *Madhhab*, PhD diss., Princeton University Press 2010.

Peters, J.R.T.M., *God's Created Speech. A Study in the Speculative Theology of the Muʿtazilī Qāḍī l-Quḍāt Abū l-Ḥasan ʿAbd al-Jabbār b. Aḥmad al-Hamadhānī*, Leiden 1976.

Powers, D.S., Wael B. Hallaq on the Origins of Islamic Law: A Review Essay, in *Islamic Law and Society* 17 (2010), 127–157.

Rahman, F., Functional Interdependence of Law and Theology, in *Theology and Law in Islam*, ed. G.E. von Grunebaum, Wiesbaden 1971, 89–98.

Rapoport, Y., Ibn Taymiyya's Radical Legal Thought: Rationalism, Pluralism and the Primacy of Intention, in *Ibn Taymiyya and His Times*, eds. Y. Rapoport and S. Ahmed, Oxford 2010, 191–226.

Reinhart, A.K., *Before Revelation. The Boundaries of Muslim Moral Thought*, Albany 1995.

Reinhart, A.K., Like the Difference between Heaven and Earth: Ḥanafī and Shāfiʿī Discussions of *Farḍ* and *Wājib* in Theology and *Uṣūl*, in *Studies in Islamic Legal Theory*, ed. B. Weiss, Leiden/Boston/Köln 2002, 205–234.

Reinhart, A.K., Taḥsīn wa-Taḳbīḥ, in *EI²* online (02 February 2014).

Rispler, V., Toward a New Understanding of the Term *Bidʿa*, in *Der Islam* 68 (1991), 320–328.

Rosenthal, F., *Knowledge Triumphant. The Concept of Knowledge in Medieval Islam*, Leiden 1970.

Rudolph, U., Ratio und Überlieferung in der Erkenntnislehre al-Ashʿarīs und al-Māturīdīs, ZDMG 142.1 (1992), 72–89.

Schacht, J., *An Introduction to Islamic Law*, Oxford 1964.

Schallenbergh, G., Ibn Qayyim al-Jawziyya's Manipulation of the Sufi Terms Fear and Hope, in *Islamic Theology, Philosophy and Law. Debating Ibn Taymiyya and Ibn Qayyim Al-Jawziyya*, eds. G. Tamer and B. Krawietz, Berlin 2013, 94–122.

Schmidtke, S. (ed., trans.), *A Muʿtazilite creed of az-Zamakhshari*, Stuttgart 1997.

Schmidtke, S., *Theologie, Philosophie und Mystik im zwölferschiitischen Islam des 9.15. Jahrhunderts. Die Gedankenwelten des Ibn Abī Jumhūr al-Aḥsāʾī (um 838/1434–1435—nach 906/1501)*, Leiden 2000.

Schmidtke, S., *The Theology of al-ʿAllāma al-Ḥillī*, Berlin 1991.

Schmidtke, S., The History of Zaydī Studies. An Introduction, in *Arabica* 59 (2012), 185–199.

Schmidtke, S., The Sunnī transmission of Abū l-Ḥusayn al-Baṣrī's theological thought, (forthcoming).

Schwarb, G., MS Munich, Bavarian State Library, Cod. arab. 1294: A Guide to Zaydī Kalām-Studies during the Ṭāhirid and Early Qāsimite Periods (Mid-15th to Early 18th Centuries), in *The Yemeni Manuscript Tradition*, eds. D. Hollenberg et al., Leiden/Boston 2015, 155–202.

Schwarb, G., Muʿtazilism in a 20th Century Zaydī Qurʾān Commentary, in *Arabica* 59 (2012), 371–402.

Schwarb, G., Muʿtazilism in the Age of Avarroes, in *In the Age of Avverroes: Arabic Philosophy in the 6th/12th* Century, ed. P. Adamson, London 2011, 251–282.

Schwarb, G., *Handbook of Muʿtazilite Works and Manuscripts*, Leiden (forthcoming).

Schwarz, M., Who Were Maimonides *Mutakallimūn*? Some Remarks on Guide of the Perplexed Part 1, in *Maimonides Studies* 2 (1991), 159–209.

Serjeant, R.B. and R. Lewcock (eds.), *Sanaa. An Arabian Islamic City*, London 1983.

Sezgin, F., *Taʾrīkh al-turāth al-ʿarabī*, Riyadh 1991.

Shahid, I., Thamūd, in EI² online (10 March 2014).

Shihadeh, A., The Argument from Ignorance and Its Critics in Medieval Arabic Thought, in *Arabic Sciences and Philosophy* 23 (2013), 171–220.

al-Siyāghī, Ḥ.A., *Uṣūl al-madhhab al-Zaydī l-Yamanī wa-qawāʿiduhu*, Sanaa 1984.

Smith, G.R., Politische Geschichte des islamischen Jemen bis zur ersten türkischen Invasion (1–945 Hidschra = 622–1538 n. Chr.), in *Jemen: 3000 Jahre Kunst und Kultur des Glücklichen Arabien*, ed. W. Daum, Innsbruck/Frankfurt 1987, 136–154.

Smoor, P., al-Maʿarrī, in EI² online (03 April 2014).

Spevack, A., *The Archetypical Sunni Scholar: Law, Theology, and Mysticism in the Synthesis of al-Bājūrī*, PhD diss., A.L.B., Harvard University 2008.

Stern, S.M., ʿAbd al-Djabbār b. Aḥmad, in *EI*² online (21 July 2014).

Strothmann, Rudolf, *Das Staatsrecht Der Zaiditen*, Strassburg 1912.

Syed, M.U., *Coercion in classical islamic law and theology*, PhD diss., Princeton University 2011.

al-Ṣubḥī, A.M., *al-Zaydiyya*, Alexandria 1984

Thiele, J., *Theologie in Der Jemenitischen Zaydiyya: Die Naturphilosophischen Überlegungen Des Al-Ḥasan Al-Raṣṣāṣ*, Leiden/Boston 2013.

Thiele, J., Muʿtazilism in the VIth/XIIth Century Zaydiyya: The Role of al-Ḥasan al-Raṣṣāṣ, in *Arabica* 57 (2010), 536–558.

Thiele, J., The Jewish and Muslim Reception of ʿAbd Al-Jabbār's *Kitāb Al-Jumal wa-l-ʿuqūd*: A Survey of Relevant Sources, in *Intellectual History of the Islamicate World* 2 (2014), 101–121.

el-Tobgui, C.S., The Epistemology of *Qiyās* and *Taʿlīl* between the Mutazilite Abū l-Ḥusayn al-Baṣrī and Ibn Ḥazm al-Ẓāhirī, in *UCLA Journal of Islamic and Near Eastern Law* 2 (2003), 281–354.

Tritton, A.S., Theory of Knowledge in Early Muslim Theology, in *Woolner Commemoration Volume* (*in Memory of the Late Dr. A.C. Woolner*), ed. M. Shafi, Lahore 1940, 253–256.

Tritton, A.S., Muʿtazilī Ideas about Religion in Particular about Knowledge Based on General Report, in *BSOAS*. 3 (1952), 612–622.

van Arendonk, C., *Les Debuts de l'Imamat Zaidite au Yemen*, Leiden: Brill 1960.

van Donzel, E., al-Manṣūr bi-llāh, in *EI*² online (10 June 2012).

van Ess, J., *Der Eine und das Andere. Beobachtungen an islamischen häresiographischen Texten*, 2 vols., Berlin 2010.

van Ess, J., *Theologie und Gesellschaft im 2. und 3. Jahrhundert Hidschra: Eine Geschichte des religiösen Denkens im frühen Islam*, 6 vols., Berlin 1991–1997.

van Ess, J., *Zwischen Hadith und Theologie. Studien zum Entstehen Prädestinatianischer Überlieferung*, Berlin: De Gruyter 1975.

van Ess, J., *Die Erkenntnislehre des Addudadin al-Ici: Übersetzung und Kommentar des ersten Buches seiner Mawaqif*, Wiesbaden 1966.

van Ess, J., Al-Jāḥiẓ and Early Muʿtazilī Theology, in *Al-Jāḥiẓ: A Muslim Humanist for Our Time*, eds. J.L. Meloy et al., Beirut 2009, 3–15.

van Ess, J., Early Islamic Theologians on the Existence of God, in *Islam and the Medieval West. Aspects of Intercultural Relations*, ed. K.I. Semaan, Albany 1980, 64–81.

van Ess, J., Tashbīh wa-Tanzīh, in *EI*² online (21 January 2015).

van Gelder, G.J.H., Yaḥyā b. Ḥamza al-ʿAlawī, in *EI*² online (05 March 2013).

Vasalou, S., *Moral Agents and Their Deserts. The Character of Mutazilite Ethics*, Princeton 2008.

vom Bruck, G., *Islam, Memory and Morality. Ruling Families in Transition*, New York 2005.

vom Bruck, G., Regimes of Piety Revisited: Zaydī Political Moralities in Republican Yemen, in *WI* 50 (2010), 186–223.

Watt, W.M., The Origin of the Islamic Doctrine of Acquisition, in *JRAS* 75 (1943), 234–247.

Watt, W.M., D̲j̲ahm b. Ṣafwān, in *EI*² online (11 February 2014).

Weiss, B., *The Spirit of Islamic Law*, Athens/Georgia 1998.

Weiss, B., *The Search for God's Law. Islamic Jurisprudence in the Writings of Sayf al-Dīn al-Āmidī*, Salt Lake City: University of Utah Press 1992.

Weiss, B., Knowledge of the Past: The Theory of "*Tawātur*" According to Ghazali, in *SI* (1985), 81–105.

Weiss, B., Exotericism and Objectivity in Islamic Jurisprudence, in *Islamic Law and Jurisprudence*, ed. N. Heer, Washington 1990, 53–71.

Weiss, B., Interpretation of Islamic Law: The Theory of *Ijtihād*, in *The American Journal of Comparative Law* 26.2 (1978), 199–212.

Weiss, B., Uṣūl-Related Madhhab Differences Reflected in Āmidī's *Iḥkām*, in *Studies in Islamic Legal Theory*, ed. B. Weiss, Leiden/ Boston/Köln 2002, 293–313.

Wensinck, A.J., *The Muslim Creed. Its Genesis and Historical Development*, New York 1965.

Wensinck, A.J., Khamr, in *EI*² online (10 July 2013).

Wiederhold, L., Legal Doctrines in Conflict. The Relevance of *Madhhab* Boundaries to Legal Reasoning in the Light of an Unpublished Treatise on *Taqlīd* and *Ijtihād*, in *Islamic Law and Society* 3.2 (1996), 234–304.

Wiederhold, L., Spezialisierung und geteilte Kompetenz. Sunnitische Rechtsgelehrte über die Zulässigkeit von *ijtihād*, in *WO* 28 (1997), 153–169.

al-Yāfiʿī, ʿA.-F.Ṣ., *al-Tamadhhub. Dirāsa taʾṣīliyya muqārana li-masāʾil wa-aḥkām al-tamadhhub*, Beirut: 2006.

Zayd, ʿA.M., *Muʿtazilat al-Yaman. Dawlat al-Hādī wa-fikruhu*, Sanaa 1981.

Zysow, A., *The Economy of Certainty. An Introduction to the Typology of Islamic Legal Theory*, Atlanta 2013.

Zysow, A., Muʿtazilism and Māturidism in Ḥanafī Legal Theory, in *Studies in Islamic Legal Theory*, ed. B. Weiss, Leiden 2002, 235–265.

Index of Pre-modern Authors

ʿAbd al-Jabbār al-Hamadhānī 3n15, 13n, 24, 27, 47, 51n196, 52, 53, 96n222, 115n338, 118n354, 145, 152, 159n30, 162, 171n86, 172, 173n94, 175n104, 177, 204n24, 210n45, 220n80, 244n163, 245n168, 248n181, 248n183, 248n185, 253, 261, 267, 279, 321
Abū ʿAlī al-Jubbāʾī 30n76, 211n47, 222n87, 230n113, 257, 27n26
Abū Bakr b. al-ʿArabī 19n23, 151n2
Abū Dāwūd 294, 295
Abū Ḥāshim al-Jubbāʾī 4, 5n22, 30, 171
Abū l-Ḥusayn al-Baṣrī 5, 7, 11, 12n55, 13n, 29, 109n303, 110n317, 111n320, 118–119, 175n104, 177–178, 179n121, 181–183, 185n143, 187n151, 190, 196, 204–206, 221n81, 223–224, 234–241, 246–249, 252–253, 259, 267–269, 290–291, 293n105, 295, 305, 312n160, 313n164, 325–326, 350, 354–358, 361, 364
Abū l-Qāsim al-Balkhī 65n25, 90n165, 93n189, 113n329, 152n7, 235n129, 244n163, 279n64
Aḥmad b. ʿAbdallāh al-Wazīr 16
Aḥmad b. Ḥanbal 67, 131n435, 289, 294
Aḥmad b. ʿĪsā b. Zayd b. ʿAlī 24n53, 27, 145n519
Aḥmad b. Sulaymān b. Muḥammad b. al-Muṭahhar 27
al-Āmidī, Sayf al-Dīn 279n64, 282, 290n95, 348
al-Amīr ʿAlī b. al-Ḥusayn 22n39, 46n155
al-Amīr al-Ḥusayn b. Badr al-Dīn 87, 295
al-Anbarī, ʿUbayd Allāh b. al-Ḥasan 261
al-ʿAnsī, ʿAbdallāh b. Zayd 7n35, 103n255, 285n83, 302n135
al-Aṣamm, Abū Bakr 261
al-Ashʿarī, Abū l-Ḥasan 6, 95n207, 211n47, 222n87, 246n171, 254n210, 255n220, 257

al-Baqillānī, Abū Bakr Muḥammad 119, 185n142, 187n149, 261n4, 262n11, 290n94
Bishr al-Marīsī 261
al-Bukhārī, Muḥammad b. Ismāʿīl 25, 47, 66, 132, 141, 167n67, 265n22

al-Dhahabī, Muḥammad b. Aḥmad 33, 265n22

al-Fāsī, Muḥammad b. Aḥmad 16, 34, 40n125, 129n423

al-Ghazālī, Abū Ḥāmid Muḥammad 4, 13n, 79n106, 95, 161n38, 168, 201n14, 204n25, 211, 221–222, 254n210, 257, 261, 290–291, 293–294, 308n154, 312n160, 312n161, 313n164, 317n176, 362

al-Hādī b. Ibrāhīm al-Wazīr 15–23, 25, 32–33, 37–38, 40, 42n137, 45, 110n314, 136–137, 148, 150, 277, 293n107, 306–307, 323n195, 332–334, 342–343, 345–346, 351
al-Hādī ilā l-ḥaqq Yaḥyā b. al-Ḥusayn 4, 5, 34–35, 51, 54n213, 59, 127, 188, 263, 272, 277, 308, 323n195, 327–329, 332–333
al-Ḥākim al-Jishumī 51–52, 96n224, 144, 327n211
Ḥanash, Muḥammad b. Aḥmad 27, 53
al-Ḥasan b. Aḥmad b. Yaḥyā al-Murtaḍā 44, 53
al-Ḥayyī, Dāwūd b. Aḥmad 50n182, 177, 220, 238n145, 254
al-Ḥillī, al-Ḥasan b. Yūsuf 82n124
Ḥumaydān b. Yaḥyā 5, 24, 26, 134n455
al-Ḥumaydī, Muḥammad b. Abī Naṣr 33

Ibn Abī l-Ḥadīd, ʿAbd al-Ḥamīd 93n189, 147, 181
Ibn Abī Ḥafsa, Marwān b. Sulaymān 150
Ibn Abī l-Khayr, ʿAlī b. ʿAbdallāh 23–26, 28–30, 47, 113n328, 136, 361
Ibn Abī l-Qāsim, ʿAlī b. Muḥammad 31–32, 35–38, 42, 56–57, 63, 70, 129, 131–133, 135, 196, 274–278, 310, 327–329, 337, 340–341, 345–346, 359
Ibn Abī l-Rijāl, Aḥmad b. Ṣāliḥ 16, 18–19, 22n37, 30–31, 36, 42n137, 57, 61n6, 63n16, 72, 76, 87n148, 103–105, 121n364, 123n371, 124, 126, 129, 141, 143, 148, 276n55
Ibn Afkānī, Muḥammad b. Ibrāhīm 90

Ibn al-Amīr, Muḥammad b. Ismāʿīl 1, 105, 109, 141, 150n561
Ibn al-ʿArabī, Muḥyī al-Dīn 6, 91n171, 109
Ibn al-Athīr, ʿAlī b. Muḥammad 33
Ibn Baṭṭāl, ʿAlī b. Khalāf 265n22
Ibn Fanad 47n169
Ibn Ḥajar al-ʿAsqalānī 16n6, 20, 64n17, 123–124
Ibn al-Ḥājib, Muḥammad b. ʿAbdallāh 25, 31, 47, 79n106, 83n124, 95n207, 119n358, 149, 205n30, 274n48, 290n95, 291n95, 297
Ibn Ḥazm, ʿAlī b. Aḥmad 33, 155n18
Ibn al-Malāḥimī, Maḥmūd b. Muḥammad 5n23, 29, 151n5, 152n7, 162n42, 165–166, 170, 172n90, 177–178, 181–182, 187, 189n158, 190–191, 196, 230n113, 234–235, 237–239, 246, 248n181, 249n188, 279n64, 282n73
Ibn Mattawayh 27, 47, 181, 190n164, 191
Ibn Miftāḥ, ʿAbdallāh b. Abī l-Qāsim 48, 292, 295–296, 299, 302n135, 303, 306–307, 308n153, 323
Ibn al-Qāsim, Yaḥyā b. al-Ḥusayn 22, 23n43, 41n133, 46, 76–77
Ibn Qayyim al-Jawziyya 149, 185, 198n1, 201n14, 211, 213n57, 217–219, 312, 365
Ibn Sīnā, Abū ʿAlī l-Husayn 109
Ibn Taymiyya 68, 129, 149, 170n80, 185, 198n1, 201n14, 202n19, 204n23, 204n27, 205, 207n38, 211, 213–215, 217, 226n102, 232, 243, 261n5, 312n160, 365
Ibn Ẓahīra, Muḥammad b. ʿAbdallāh 19, 34–35, 108, 129
Ismāʿīl b. ʿUlayya 261

Jaʿfar b. ʿAbd al-Salām 28, 80, 327n212
al-Jāḥiẓ, Abū ʿUthmān 92n178, 152n8, 156n23, 165–167, 180n124, 183–184, 220, 235n129
al-Jalāl, al-Ḥasan 1n2
al-Juwaynī, ʿAbd al-Malik b. ʿAbdallāh 13n, 111, 119, 153n9, 179n106, 187, 254n210, 280, 291, 300

al-Kaynaʿī, Ibrāhīm b. Aḥmad 25n59, 25n60, 28n72, 30n78, 361

al-Maʿarrī, Abū l-ʿAlāʾ 125–126
al-Mahallā, al-Nāṣir b. ʿAbd al-Ḥāfiẓ 143
al-Mahdī Abū ʿAbdallāh al-Dāʿī 262–263
al-Mahdī l-Husayn b. al-Qāsim al-ʿIyānī 134
al-Mahdī Muḥammad b. al-Muṭahhar 27
Mālik b. Anas 67, 318
al-Manakdim, Aḥmad b. al-Ḥusayn 47, 53, 118
al-Manṣūr bi-llāh ʿAbdallāh b. Ḥamza 5, 17n10, 25, 68, 110n316, 113n328, 124, 139n489, 265, 268, 272n41, 304, 305n144, 308n155, 312–313, 323, 336–337, 340–343, 352
al-Maqbalī, Ṣāliḥ b. al-Mahdī 1n2, 62n8
al-Mizzī, Yūsuf b. ʿAbd al-Raḥmān 33
al-Mu'ayyad bi-llāh Yaḥyā b. Ḥamza 5, 46n155, 68, 78n106, 113n329, 124, 139n489, 145, 181, 182n128, 188, 190–191, 196, 246–247, 285n83, 308, 312n161, 340, 342, 343n256, 361, 364n6
al-Mu'ayyad bi-llāh Yaḥyā b. al-Ḥusayn al-Ḥārūnī 46n155, 83n124, 90n164, 92n178, 115n338, 129n489, 145, 159n30, 165, 284, 327n212
al-Muḥallī, al-Qāsim b. Aḥmad 47
Muḥammad b. ʿAbdallāh b. al-Hādī al-Wazīr 15, 25, 42
Muḥammad b. al-Mufaḍḍal al-ʿAfīf al-Wazīr 17, 110
Muḥammad b. ʿAlī al-ʿAlawī al-Ḥasanī 24, 144
Muḥammad b. al-Ḥusayn b. al-Qāsim 75
Mukhtār b. Maḥmūd 96n224, 145–147, 165–166, 170, 181–182, 187–188, 194, 196, 213n54, 223, 242n154, 146, 174, 302, 354
al-Murādī, Muḥammad b. Manṣūr 24, 93n189, 97n226, 144
al-Mutanabbī, Abū Ṭayyib 108, 109n303
al-Mutawakkil ʿalā llāh Aḥmad b. Sulaymān 4, 263, 28n71

Nafīs al-Dīn al-ʿAlawī 19, 32–33, 47
al-Najrī, ʿAbdallāh b. Muḥammad 48
al-Najrī, ʿAlī b. Muḥammad 48
al-Nāsir lil-ḥaqq al-Ḥasan b. ʿAlī al-Utrush 86n137, 262
al-Nāṭiq bi-l-ḥaqq Abū Ṭālib al-Ḥarūnī 25, 110n316, 115n338, 145, 285n83, 306n144, 323, 324n201, 325n203, 326–328, 346n265

al-Naẓẓām, Abū Isḥāq 79, 220, 235n129

al-Qarāfī, Shihāb al-Dīn 322
al-Qāsim b. Ibrāhīm al-Rassī 34, 68, 180, 262, 272n40, 327, 328n215

al-Raṣṣāṣ, Aḥmad b. al-Ḥasan 19n23, 22n39, 24, 27, 46, 53, 118, 171n86
al-Raṣṣāṣ, Aḥmad b. Muḥammad 22n39, 24, 47, 50, 53, 113n328
al-Raṣṣāṣ, al-Ḥasan b. Muḥammad 5n23, 28n71, 113n328, 124, 337, 340–341, 343
al-Rāzī, Fakhr al-Dīn 5n22, 13n, 77–79, 95, 118–119, 149, 151, 187–188, 190–191, 204–206, 222n87, 239–240, 249, 254n210, 269n32, 291, 312n161

al-Sakhāwī, Muḥammad b. ʿAbd al-Raḥmān 16, 18n12
Ṣārim al-Dīn b. Ibrāhīm al-Wazīr 110n316, 297, 312n161, 320, 332, 335n237
al-Shahārī, Ibrāhīm b. al-Qāsim 16, 18n15, 19n24, 22n37, 27n67, 40, 42n137
al-Shahrastānī, Muḥammd b. ʿAbd al-Karīm 50n181, 136–137, 233n120
al-Shahrazūrī, Ibn al-Ṣalāḥ 290n95
al-Shawkānī, Muḥammad b. ʿAlī 1, 3, 9, 16, 19n27, 22n39, 24, 42n139, 44n145, 44n146, 61, 64, 77, 88, 140, 143, 293n106, 294, 312n160, 313, 350, 363n5, 364–365, 366n8
al-Shirāzī, Abū Isḥāq 279n64, 290n94
al-Subkī, Tāj al-Dīn 291n95

al-Tirmidhī, Muḥammad b. ʿIsā 151n2, 294

al-ʿUjālī, Taqī l-Dīn 178n116, 181, 187, 189, 196, 235n130

Yaḥyā b. Manṣūr b. al-ʿAfīf b. Mufaḍḍal 25, 68n45
Yūsuf b. Aḥmad b. ʿUthmān 46, 55

al-Zamakhsharī, Abū l-Qāsim Maḥmūd 109
Zayd b. ʿAlī 27–28, 98, 115n338, 145n519

Index of Geographical Names

Alhān Ans 44

Bayt Baws 45

Dhamar 41, 44–45

Ḥajja 46, 54
Hejaz 6, 16, 20, 58–59, 361

Ibb 39

Jabal Miswar 46, 53–54, 56
Jabal Saḥammur 39n119

Kawkabān 41

Mecca 6, 16, 19–20, 23, 32–34, 38, 39n122, 40, 59, 122–123, 153, 351

Nuqum 39

Saʿda 7n, 18, 21–23, 30n78, 45, 81
Sanaa 6, 18, 22–23, 27, 30–31, 39, 41n131, 42–45, 59, 61, 76, 81n116, 89, 98–99, 104, 105n273, 120, 131, 143

Taʿizz 19, 32–33, 42, 47
Thulāʾ 41n131, 45, 53–56

Yarīm 39n119

Ẓafīr 46, 54
Ẓahrawayn 17, 21

Index of Pre-modern Books

Al-ʿAḍb al-ṣārim 130
Al-ʿAlam al-shāmikh 62n8
Amālī 24n53, 27
al-Amr bi-l-ʿuzla 38, 39n118, 41, 61–63, 353
al-ʿAqīda al-wāsiṭiyya 213n57
al-Arbaʿīn 77, 78n101, 151
al-ʿAwāṣim wa-l-qawāṣim 8, 24, 31, 32n91, 35, 37–38, 40–41, 54–56, 60, 63–72, 77, 81, 88, 103n257, 106, 116, 127, 129–132, 141–144, 149, 163, 168–169, 188, 190, 196, 201–202, 211, 216–217, 223, 242, 245–246, 251, 260n2, 263–264, 277, 279, 304–305, 310, 313–314, 320, 326–327, 340, 352–353
Āyāt al-aḥkām al-sharʿiyya 74–76
al-Āyāt al-mubīnāt 60, 72–74, 120n362, 121n365, 229, 248, 352
Kitāb al-Azhār 48–51, 53, 54, 174, 278, 292, 302–303, 307, 323, 343, 360

al-Badr al-ṭāliʿ 16
al-Baḥr al-zakhkhār 48–54, 292–293, 299, 302, 306n148, 332, 360
Bayān al-ḥikma fī l-ʿadhāb al-akhrawī 149
al-Burhān al-qāṭiʿ 32–33, 54, 76–80, 151, 154, 159, 174, 178, 276
al-Burhān fī uṣūl al-fiqh 13n

K. al-Dalīl al-kabīr 180n124
K. al-Dalīl al-ṣaghīr 180n124
Dāmigh al-awhām 50, 53
al-Ḍawʾ al-lāmiʿ 16
Dīwān shiʿr 39, 88n150, 104–110, 150, 165, 210, 219 (see also *Majmaʿ al-ḥaqāʾiq*)
al-Durar al-farāʾid 49n179, 50, 53–54, 164, 166, 188, 195, 220, 227, 237–238, 253
al-Durar al-kāmina 16n6
al-Durar al-manẓūma 103n255, 306n155, 285n83
al-Durr al-kāmin 16n6, 16n7

Fāʾiqat al-uṣūl 50, 53
K. al-Fāʾiq fī uṣūl al-dīn 165n57, 172n90, 177, 223
Fatḥ al-bārī 64
Fatḥ al-khāliq 105
al-Fuṣūl al-luʾluʾiyya 110n316, 297

Ghāyat al-afkār 50n182, 53
Ghāyat al-amānī 22, 81
al-Ghiyāṣa sharḥ al-Khulāṣa 27, 53
al-Ghurar wa-l-ḥujūl 47

Ḥadī l-arwāḥ 149
Hidāyat al-mustarshidīn 305n144
Hidāyat al-rāghibīn 19n23, 323n195, 333
al-Ḥusām al-mashhūr 32, 41n133, 80–84, 156, 158, 314, 352

al-ʿIbar wa-l-iʿtibār 165, 184
al-Iḥkām 282
al-Ijāda fī l-irāda 149, 200, 227, 229
Iklīl al-tāj 54
al-ʿIlm al-wāṣim 130
K. al-Intiqād 293
K. al-Intiṣār 46n155
al-ʿIqd al-thamīn 16, 34n97, 34n100, 40n125, 129n423
Irshād al-fuḥūl 293
Irshād al-qāṣid 90n169
Irshād al-sālikīn 32n88
al-Istibṣār 46n155
al-Istiẓhār 84–87, 353
Īthār al-ḥaqq 21, 40–41, 64, 87–98, 103, 106, 149, 151, 168–169, 198, 200–201, 211, 213, 216–217, 225, 229, 244n163, 247, 250, 263, 273, 352

Jamʿ bayn al-Ṣaḥīḥayn 33
Jamʿ al-jawāmiʿ 158
al-Jāmiʿ al-kāfī 24n53, 25, 144
Jawāb Muḥammad b. Ibrāhīm ʿalā fuqahāʾ 150
Jawāb al-nāṭiq 38n113
Jawāmiʿ al-adilla 110n316, 306n144
Jawharat al-uṣūl 22n39, 24, 47, 50, 53
Jumal al-islām 68n45
al-Jumla wa-l-ulfa 24n53, 97n226, 144

K. al-Kāmil fī l-istiqṣāʾ 181n126
Kanz al-ḥukamāʾ 44, 52, 53

al-Kashshāf 47
al-Kawkab al-ẓāhir 52
al-Khulāṣa al-nāfiʿa 19n23, 22n39, 24, 27, 46, 53, 118
al-Lumaʿ fī fiqh ahl al-bayt 22n39, 46n155

al-Maḥṣūl 13n
Majmaʿ al-ḥaqāʾiq 104–109, 352
Majmūʿ Zayd b. ʿAlī 27
Manẓūma shiʿriyya 109–112, 353
Masāʾil arbaʿa 100, 112–116, 353
Masāʾil mustakhrajāt 120
Masāʾil shāfiyāt 120–122, 123n378, 352
Masāʾil sharīfa 122–123
Masʾalat ikhtilāf al-Muʿtazila wa-l-Ashʿariyya 116–119, 240, 242, 352
al-Maṭālib al-ʿāliyya 204n24
Maṭlaʿ al-budūr 16, 20n32, 27, 121n364, 125, 276n55
al-Minhāj al-jalī 28
Minhāj al-wuṣūl 11, 47, 50, 53, 267, 276, 292, 299, 303, 317, 319n181, 330–331, 339
Mirqāt al-anẓār 48n173
Mishkāt anwār al-ʿuqūl 25
Miʿyār al-ʿuqūl 50, 53, 296, 319n181, 330
al-Milal wa-l-niḥal 51
al-Muḥīṭ 47
K. al-Mujtabā 96n224, 145, 147, 165, 181n126, 188, 194, 213n54, 246
al-Mujzī 25, 110n316, 306n144, 324n201, 325
Mukhtaṣar fī ʿilm al-maʿānī wa-l-bayān 150
Mukhtaṣar mufīd fī ʿulūm al-ḥadīth 121, 123–124, 140n496, 354
Mukhtaṣar Muntahā l-suʾl 25, 83n124
Muntahā l-marām 75
al-Munya wa-l-amal 51, 276
Muqaddimat al-Baḥr al-zakhkhār 48–49, 50n182, 51, 292, 296, 303
al-Mustaṣfā 13n
K. al-Muʿtamad fī uṣūl al-dīn 28n73, 152n7, 162n42, 166, 177, 178n115, 182n130, 234n126, 235n134, 237n139
K. al-Muʿtamad fī uṣūl al-fiqh 12n55, 13n, 29n73, 47, 291, 305n140
Muthīr al-aḥzān 124–125, 353
Nahj al-balāgha 144, 147n538, 181
Nihāyat al-aqdām 136–137
Nihāyat al-tanwīh 19n23, 332, 333n230
Nihāyat al-ʿuqūl 118, 191n167
Nukhbat al-fikr 123
Nuṣrat al-aʿyān 125–126

K. al-Qalāʾid 49–50, 52–54, 176, 188, 237, 253
al-Qamar al-nawwār 52, 54, 56, 127
al-Qāmūs al-fāʾiḍ 54
K. al-Qawāʿid 24, 61, 98–103, 127, 237, 280–282, 285–286, 291–292, 301–302, 309, 313, 320, 324, 328–329, 334, 338, 340n249, 342n251, 346n265, 353
Qawāʿid al-aḥkām 339n246
al-Qisṭās al-mustaqīm 54
Qubūl al-bushrā 57, 99, 100, 126–129, 338, 353, 364

K. al-Radd ʿalā ṣāḥib al-Nihāya wa-l-Maḥṣūl 148–149
al-Rawḍ al-bāsim 35, 37–38, 64, 73, 121n365, 129–135, 244n166, 273, 275n52, 279, 310, 316, 340, 352, 353
Risāla jalīla 149
Risāla fī zakāt al-fiṭr 149
Riyāḍat al-afhām 50, 54, 152n7, 156n23, 163n46, 166n63, 170, 172n90, 176, 182, 188, 205n28, 237–238, 255n213

Ṣafwat al-ikhtiyār 25, 110n316, 304, 308n155, 323n196
Sharḥ al-Azhār 48, 53, 302n135, 306, 323, 343
Sharḥ al-Najrī 48
Sharḥ Nukat al-ʿibādāt 28
Sharḥ al-Nukhba 64n17
Sharḥ al-Qalāʾid al-muntazaʿ min al-Durar al-farāʾid 48, 50n182, 119n358, 177n112, 251n197, 254n210
Sharḥ al-Uṣūl al-khamsa 24, 27, 46, 53
Sharḥ ʿUyūn al-masāʾil 51, 96n224, 144
Sharḥ al-Ziyādāt 327n212
al-Sirāj al-wahhāj 28

Ṭabaqāt al-Muʿtazila 52
Ṭabaqāt al-Zaydiyya 16, 27, 47
Tadhhīb Tahdhīb al-kamāl 33
al-Taʾdīb al-malakūtī 135–136

al-Tadhkira 27, 47, 181, 190n164
Taḥrīr al-kalām 136–138, 352
K. fī l-tafsīr 103
Tahdhīb al-kamāl 33
al-Tāj al-mudhhab 302n135
Tāj ʿulūm al-adab 54
Tajrīd al-Kashshāf 31n84
Takhṣīṣ āyāt al-jumʿa 138–140, 353
Talkhīṣ al-ḥabīr 64
K. al-Tamhīd 145, 188, 196n179, 204n24
Tanqīḥ al-anẓār 38, 140–142, 322n185, 354
Taʾrīkh Banī l-Wazīr 15, 16n2, 18n15, 18n19, 19n22, 20n31, 20n32, 34n99, 38, 39n122, 42n139, 56n221, 57, 110n314, 129, 293n107
Tarjamat Muḥammad b. Ibrāhīm al-Wazīr 15n1, 16, 56n221, 129n425
Tarjīḥ asālīb al-Qurʾān 39–40, 54, 75, 88, 142–148, 168–169, 174–175, 180, 183, 190, 196, 352
Taṣaffuḥ al-adilla 187, 190n161
Tawḍīḥ al-afkār 141
Taysīr al-ʿibādāt 129
Thabat Banī l-Wazīr 15n1, 18n15, 20n31
Thamarāt al-akmām 52
al-Tuḥfa al-ṣafiyya 148

ʿUlūm Āl Muḥammad 24
K. al-ʿUmad 13n
ʿUqūd al-ʿuqyān 27
Usūl al-aḥkām 27

Wāḍiḥat al-manāhij 80–81

al-Ziyādāt 46n155, 83n124, 90n164, 284

Index of Quran Citations

2 (Baqara) 75
- 2:7 73
- 2:30 208n39
- 2:144 122
- 2:166 283
- 2:230 87

3 (Āl ʿImrān)
- 3:7 147

4 (Nisāʾ)
- 4:94 118
- 4:95 63n15

5 (Māʾida)
- 5:3 118

6 (Anʿām)
- 6:125 232

7 (Aʿrāf)
- 7:143 137

9 (Tawba)
- 9:36 63
- 9:41 63
- 9:91 63
- 9:106 231

11 (Hūd)
- 11:6 122

13 (Raʿd)
- 13:9 120

14 (Ibrāhīm)
- 14:4 72n71, 73

16 (Naḥl)
- 16:43 284
- 16:93 72–73, 229

17 (Isrāʾ)
- 17:38 232

21 (Anbiyāʾ)
- 21:79 267

30 (Rūm)
- 30:30 167

39 (Zumar)
- 39:57–59 74

41 (Fuṣṣilat)
- 41:17 74

49 (Ḥujurāt)
- 49:17 118

60 (Mumtaḥina)
- 60:10 158

62 (Jumʿa)
- 62:9 139

72 (Jinn)
- 72:26–27 123

92 (Layl)
- 92:7 126

100 (ʿĀdiyyāt)
- 100:11 74

108 (Kawthar) 75

111 (Masad)
- 111:1–5 212

Index of Arabic Terms

ʿadāla 78, 132, 142, 292, 304, 343, 361
ʿadam 169, 185n143, 190, 245n167, 313, 356
ʿadiyyāt 79
ʿadl 94, 98n1, 220, 292
ʿAdliyya 344
afʿāl (sg. *fiʿl*) 94, 198, 224, 241–242, 249n190
ʿafw 96, 107, 212, 233
aḥad (pl. *āḥād*) 79, 124, 154
aḥkām (sg. *ḥukm*) 128, 178, 201n14, 247, 292, 344
  aḥādīth al-aḥkām 294
  āyāt al-aḥkām 75–76, 277, 292–293
ahl al-bayt 19–20, 35–36, 46, 59, 65–68, 71, 83, 95, 97n226, 98, 101, 114–115, 145, 247, 272, 277, 280–281, 289, 306–308
ahl al-ḥadīth 67 (see also *muḥaddithūn*)
ahl al-maʿārif 152n8, 165–166, 183–184
ahl al-sunna 94, 96, 236
aḥwāl (sg. *ḥāl*) 78, 80, 122, 147, 175, 177–182, 244, 246–247, 355, 358
aḥwaṭ 102, 127–128, 342, 365 (see also *iḥtiyāṭ*)
ajsām (sg. *jism*) 190, 246
ʿajz 179
akwān 146–147, 174–177, 178n115, 180–181, 254, 355
ʿālimiyya 228
amāra (pl. *amārāt*) 265, 268–269, 282n75, 318, 340, 347
ʿāmm (pl. *ʿumūm*) 65, 111, 282–283, 330
ʿaql (pl. *ʿuqūl*) 12, 69, 78, 94–95, 149, 153, 165, 167, 169–174, 193, 196, 203, 206–207, 210, 221, 244, 263n16, 264, 301–302, 355
aʿrāḍ 146, 175–177, 355
asbāb al-nuzūl 293
ashbah 262–270, 359
aṣlaḥ 213, 221, 222n87, 222n88, 240, 257, 357–358
asmāʾ 90, 198, 224
aṣwab 266
ʿayn (pl. *aʿyān*) 222, 244, 255–256
azal 191, 245

badīhī 153
barāʾa 96
bayyān 222
bidʿa (pl. *bidaʿ*) 85–86, 327
bi-lā kayf 68, 190, 226
binya 233n122, 236, 240, 252
burhān (pl. *barāhīn*) 106, 302

dāʿī 70, 202–203, 204n25, 205, 221, 234, 236, 238, 243, 249n190
ḍaʿīf 141
dalāla 91, 147, 185, 187, 330
dalīl (pl. *adilla*) 111, 115, 161–163, 170, 173, 177, 188, 190–191, 301, 363
  dalīl al-āfāq 147, 167
  dalīl al-anfus 147, 167
  dalīl al-mawāniʿ 188n155, 189
ḍarūrā 119, 178, 249, 321
ḍarūrī 78, 90, 97, 152, 155, 160, 198, 352, 354
dhāt (pl. *dhawāt*) 78, 93, 212, 246

faḍl 134, 341–342, 346
farʿ (pl. *furūʿ*) 48, 111, 126, 263, 276, 283
farḍ (pl. *furūḍ*) 31, 222, 256
fāsiq taʾwīl (pl. *fussāq taʾwīl*) 66, 102, 135, 304, 307–309
fiqh 7, 21–22, 24–25, 27–28, 32n88, 34, 42n137, 49–51, 53–54, 127, 139, 273, 277–278, 280, 310, 323, 332, 347, 360
firqa nājiyya 365
fisq 93, 97
fiṭrā (*pl. fiṭar*) 12, 89, 90, 96, 148, 167–174, 180, 183–184, 198, 203, 208, 233, 247, 249–250, 252, 258, 302, 309, 311, 354–358

gharaḍ 202, 205, 210–211
gharāʾiz (sg. *gharīza*) 301–302, 309
ghayr 101, 194, 212, 245–246, 279, 338

Hādawiyya 54, 87, 263, 323n195
ḥadd (pl. *ḥudūd*) 98, 116
ḥakīm 73, 193, 202–203, 224n96
ḥaqīqa 111, 226, 228, 242
ḥaqīqī 243
hayʾa 244
ḥaẓar wa-ibāḥa 111
hidāya 249

ḥikma (pl. *ḥikam*) 94, 107, 193, 200–202, 205, 211, 216, 223, 233, 235, 258, 356–358
ḥissī 78, 153
ḥudūth 177
ḥujja 266, 279
ḥaqq (pl. *ḥuqūq*) 82, 114, 261
ḥusn 119, 245n169

iʿāna 242
iḍlāl 234, 248
iḥdāth 253–254
iḥkām 146, 193, 202
iḥtiyāṭ 102, 114, 128
ʿijāz 68
ijāza 22–23, 25–29, 31, 33, 41, 46n155, 47n168, 48, 83, 124
ijmāʿ 111, 114–115, 117, 292
ijmāl 91, 236
ijtihād (pl. *ijtihādāt*) 5, 9n42, 13, 30, 35–36, 57, 61, 65–66, 82–84, 101–102, 111–112, 114–115, 132–133, 140, 142, 157, 260–263, 265–266, 268–287, 289–291, 293–306, 308–309, 311–324, 330–331, 333–335, 337, 340, 342, 344–348, 353, 359, 360–361
ikhtiyār 69, 117, 241, 247, 249n190
ilāhiyya (pl. *ilāhiyyāt*) 105, 109
ʿilla (pl. *ʿilal*) 192n171, 214, 325–326, 328–332, 334, 337
ʿilm (pl. *ʿulūm*) 3–4, 60, 82, 90–92, 111, 151, 152n7, 157, 160, 199, 200n11, 201n14, 202, 234n125, 257, 264, 303, 314
  al-ʿilm al-ḍarūrī al-ʿadī 151, 155, 160, 198, 352
  ʿilm al-ghayb 209
  al-rāsikhūn fī l-ʿilm 147
  sābiq al-ʿilm 251
  ṭālib al-ʿilm (pl. *ṭalaba*) 284, 286
iltizām 113–114, 116, 335–337, 339, 344–347, 360
ilzām 64, 131, 274n50
Imāmiyya 86–87, 145
intifāʾ 163n46
intiqāl 344, 360
irāda 69, 94, 198, 224, 229, 231, 232n118, 234, 237, 239 (see also *mashīʾa*)
irjāʾ 69–70, 96, 133–134
iṣāba 264, 342, 200
ishkāl 298
ʿiṣma 67, 249
isnād 142, 322n185, 328
istidlāl 175
  istidlāl bi-l-ʿadam 185, 356
  istidlālī 119, 152, 155, 176, 354 (see also *muktasab*)
istiḥsān 223
istiḥqāq 73
istinbāṭ 277, 289, 328, 359
istiqbāḥ 223
istiṣḥāb 86, 111, 340
ithbāt 91, 174, 188, 225, 357
iʿtibār 165–166, 239, 243–244, 253
iʿtiqād (pl. *iʿtiqādāt*) 31, 121, 152, 156, 201
iṭmiʾnān 121
ʿitra 106
ittibāʿ 101, 115, 281, 361
  ittibāʿ fī l-maʿnā 101, 281, 310, 315, 337, 361
  ittibāʿ fī l-ṣūra 101, 281, 337
Ittiḥādiyya 91

jabr 68, 70, 94, 119, 133–134, 242, 248
Jabriyya 94, 117–118, 241n154
jahl 90, 111, 159, 163
Jahmiyya 241n154
jāʾir 83, 139
jalī 216, 242, 298
jarḥ 124
jazm 151–152, 163
jiha 242, 244, 246
jihād 63, 264
jismiyya 190, 246
jumal (sg. *jumla*) 65, 68–69, 95, 147, 160–161, 165–166, 169–170, 180, 198, 202, 216, 236, 244n163
  ahl-jumal 67, 168
  iktifāʾ bi-l-jumal 72, 168
  kifāyat al-jumal 145, 216
jumlī 201–202, 217

kāfir (pl. *kuffār*)
  kāfir taʾwīl (pl. *kuffār taʾwīl*) 66, 97, 102, 135, 304, 307, 309, 328n215
  kāfir ṣarīḥ 97
kalām 18, 21–22, 25n57, 26, 28–29, 32, 34, 46, 48–49, 52–53, 58, 64, 67, 69, 71, 72n74, 80n115, 89–90, 93n189, 102, 111, 133–135, 145, 166, 172, 179, 181, 188–189, 199–201, 227n107, 257, 292–293, 301–303, 361

kāmil 214, 318
karāha 231, 239
karāmāt 38, 39n122
kasb 70, 243, 245–247, 255–256
khabīr 74
khafī 83, 211, 213, 223, 242, 299
khalaf 140
khalq 122, 146, 243, 245n170, 250, 251n197, 254
khāṣṣ 65n24, 111
khāṭir 172, 248n185
khiṭāb 330, 332
khulf 212
khurūj 84, 139
kufr 69, 93, 97, 134–135, 218

lafẓ 117, 332
lugha 21, 34, 138, 292, 297, 299, 361
luṭf 74n81, 176, 223, 233, 249, 251

madhhab (pl. *madhāhib*) 34, 43, 51, 54, 100, 102, 106, 112n325, 115, 272, 277, 279, 282–283, 289–290, 295, 297, 308, 311, 319, 322–324, 326–334, 337–339, 341, 343, 345, 359, 363
madlūl 70, 161
mafāsid 62
mafhūm 330, 332
maḥabba 232
māhiyya 238, 295
majāz 71, 111
maʿjūz 179
majhūl 102, 124, 132
maʾkhadh 318, 329, 330
makhlūq (pl. *makhlūqāt*) 114, 146, 250
makrūh 128
malaka 313–314
maʿnā (pl. *maʿānī*) 175n104, 177n112, 178, 226, 246
  al-maʿānī wa-l-bayān 21, 34, 102, 292, 295, 299–300
maqdūr (pl. *maqdūrāt*) 203, 220–221, 228, 254
  maqdūr bayna qādirayn 245–246, 255–256
maqṣad 63
marjūḥ 158, 317
mashīʾa 69, 94 (see also *irāda*)
maṣlaḥa (pl. *maṣāliḥ*) 62, 157, 213, 345
matn 142
mithl 225 (see also *mumāthala*)
muʿaddilūn 133
muʿjizāt 78
muʿassirūn 65
muʾawwal 111
mubayyan 111, 296
mubham 92–93
mubtadiʿūn 105
mudhākirūn 323, 46n155
muḥaddithūn 1, 67 (see also *ahl al-ḥadīth*)
muḥāl 212, 275n52
muḥaṣṣilūn 115n340, 272, 323, 332
muḥdith 177, 249
muḥkam (pl. *muḥkamāt*) 92, 148
muḥkim 193, 203
muḥtamal 208
mujāhidūn 314
mūjib 158, 214, 254
mūjid 205
mujmal 111, 183, 296
mujtahid 7, 35n102, 36, 43, 45, 66, 82–83, 97, 112–113, 260–279, 282–312, 323n196, 324n200, 327, 329–331, 333–349, 359–361, 365
  mujtahid fī-l-madhhab 290, 319, 323n193, 332
  mujtahid muṭlaq 298
mukallaf (pl. *mukallafūn*) 62, 84, 154, 164, 166, 170, 176, 222, 266, 280, 286
mukhaṣṣiṣ 331
mukhaṭṭiʾa 261
mukhtār 242n154, 246
muktasab 152, 354 (see also *istidlālī*)
mulāzama 137, 234n125
mumāthala 92, 225 (see also *mithl*)
mumtaniʿ 212
muqaddar 250
muqallad 112, 281, 285 (see also *mujtahid*)
muqallid 84, 112, 114, 116, 128, 279, 281–283, 285–287, 289–291, 315–319, 327, 329, 335–337, 339–340, 343–345, 347–349
muqarribāt 106
murād 94, 233
murajjiḥ 204–205, 234n124, 236
murīdiyya 238
Murjiʾa 69, 96, 135
mursal 102, 124, 132

muṣaḥḥiḥūn 115–116
muṣawwiba 261
muṣīb 267
kull mujtahid muṣīb 4, 260–263
mustaftī 111–112, 304, 308, 330, 336–337
mustaḥabb 128
mustaḥīl 137
mustaqill 242
muta'awwilūn 97, 102, 134, 327–328 (see also *ahl al-taʾwīl*)
mutābaʿa 101 (see also *ittibāʿ*)
muṭābaqa fī l-khārij 151, 156, 163
mutakallimūn 188, 301n132, 302n134
mutashābih (pl. *mutashābihāt*) 71, 92, 128, 144, 147–148, 209–210, 218, 258, 357, 365
mutawātir 97, 124, 161n38, 171n85
muṭlaq 86, 329
muyassirūn 65

nafy 137–138, 185, 188, 191
nafra 239
nafs 193–194, 295, 345n264
sukūn al-nafs 100, 151n5, 152, 156, 163, 321
nahy 111
naqṣ 92–93, 169
Nāṣiriyya 86–87
naskh 111
naṣṣ (pl. *nuṣūṣ*) 92, 111, 140, 316, 326n205, 330, 332
naẓar 12, 63, 66, 80, 89–90, 113, 115, 145, 154–155, 161–167, 172–174, 176, 178–179, 182, 184, 186, 189, 195–196, 198, 248n185, 301, 309, 330, 344, 354–356

qabḥ 119, 243, 245n169
qadar 69, 234
Qadariyya 242n154
qadīm 191
qādir 160, 245–246, 255–256
qadīr 166
qādiriyya 188, 227–228, 255
qidam 234, 245n167
qalb 165
qarīna (pl. *qarāʾin*) 65, 78–79, 115, 154, 321n184
qaṣd 79
qāṣir 317–320, 324, 326, 334

qaṭʿ 71, 97, 163, 263
qaṭʿī 114, 156, 340
qāṭiʿ (pl. *qawāṭiʿ*) 97, 127, 162, 288
qawāʿid 127, 177, 272, 278, 322–323, 364
qawwām 118
qiyās 111, 205, 262n12, 290, 296, 324–325, 329, 331, 340
qiyās al-ghāʾib ʿalā l-shāhid 176, 238
qudra 119, 227–228, 243, 245n169, 254
quwwa 173 (see also *qudra*)

rafʿ al-ḥaraj 309–310
rajāʾ 69, 71, 96, 106–107, 210n44
rājiḥ 62–63, 133, 157–158, 213, 234
riḍā 107, 238
riwāya 93, 135
rubūbiyya 91, 144
rujḥān 155, 285 (see also *tarjīḥ*)
rukhṣa 128, 364
ruʾya 68, 136, 138

al-sabr wa-l-taqsīm 138
ṣaḥīḥ 84n128, 133, 141, 316
salaf 68, 94–95, 97n226, 116, 140, 145, 250n194, 309, 314–315, 361, 365
ṣawāb 264, 339
shahwa 239
shakk 111, 114, 162
sharʿī 138, 232n118
sharṭ (pl. *shurūṭ*) 102, 165–166, 290, 345, 361
shayʾ 192, 225
ṣifa (pl. *ṣifāt*) 182, 198, 224, 244–245
shukr 107
sukhṭ 232

taʿadhdhara 274–275, 277–278
taʿassara 274–275 (see also *taʿadhdhara*)
taḍarruʿ 107
taʿdīl 124
tafḍīl 338, 341n254, 343n256, 345
tafṣīl 92–93, 198
tafsīq 114, 299
tafsīr (pl. *tafāsīr*) 21, 34, 93, 103, 293n105
tafwīḍ 40, 107
taḥsīn 149
al-taḥsīn wa-l-taqbīḥ 69, 94–96, 149, 153, 193, 206–208, 210, 221, 256
tajazzuʾ 101, 312, 345, 360

taʿjīz 202
tajrīd 165
tajsīm 67, 70, 190
tajwīz 186
takfīr 65, 68–69, 93, 96–97, 114
takhrīj 278n62, 290, 321–335, 337, 345, 360
takhṣīṣ 111, 326
taklīf 84, 95, 166, 170–171, 173, 176, 184, 206, 208, 212–213, 217, 219, 283
  taklīf mā lā yuṭāq 70, 95, 97, 134, 212–213, 251, 267, 273
takyīf 226n102
ṭālib mumayyiz 101, 284, 288, 312, 315, 360
tamadhhub 92
tamassuk 346
tamāthul 191, 228, 245, 357
tamkīn 222
tanaqqul 100, 114, 337, 340 (see also *intiqāl*)
tanzīh 225
taqbīḥ 212 (see also *al-taḥsīn wa-l-taqbīḥ*)
taqdīr 94, 122, 251
taqlīd 13, 25n56, 34, 36, 66, 72, 82–83, 84n128, 85, 90, 100–101, 111, 113–114, 116, 126, 132–133, 152, 163, 176, 201, 260, 263, 274–275, 278–290, 308, 315–316, 322, 324, 327–330, 333–334, 338, 340, 344–346, 348n269, 353, 360, 365
  taqlīd al-mayyit (pl. *al-amwāt*) 101, 275, 285, 287–289, 308, 328–329, 360
tarjīḥ 85, 115, 133, 140, 282, 317, 336–338, 341, 343n256, 344–346, 360
tarkīb 147, 180
tartīb al-adilla 111, 301
tartīb al-muqaddimāt 162n42, 164–166, 182, 301–302, 354
taṣarruf 93
taṣawwuf 25, 61
taṣdīq 121
tashābuh 2
tashbīh 67, 225, 226n102, 357
taṣḥīḥ 141
tashkīk 151, 161, 163
taskīn 156
taṣwīb 262n11
taʿṭīl 225, 226n102, 357
tawakkul 40, 106–108, 353
tawallud 162, 165, 354
tawaqquf 186
tawātur 78–79, 97–98, 153–154, 157–158, 161n38, 171, 183, 195
tawḥīd 91, 144, 344
taʾwīl 71, 147–148, 193, 210, 224, 226n102, 258
  ahl al-taʾwīl 66–68, 97, 102n255, 304–305 (see also *mutaʾawwilūn*)
taʿyīn 182, 242
taysīr 230, 249
thabāt ʿinda l-tashkīk 151, 161, 163
thubūt 90, 185n143

ʿudhr 63
ʿurf 138
uṣūl 53, 173, 260, 261n5, 289, 322, 325n203
  uṣūl al-dīn 21, 36, 55, 93n189, 175, 279n64, 292, 301–303, 309–310, 361
  uṣūl al-fiqh 21–22, 25, 28–29, 34, 46–47, 49, 58, 111–113, 142, 205n30, 271, 276, 292, 295–297, 300, 312, 329n217, 336, 346
  uṣūlān 21, 24, 29, 31
ʿuzla 38, 61–62

al-waʿd wa-l-waʿīd 70–71, 93, 96
Waʿīdiyya 96
wājib 185, 222, 240
wajh (pl. *wujūh*) 244, 245n169, 254
walāya 96
wijāda 141
wujūd 190, 245, 247
wuqūʿ 254

yaqīn 3–4, 90, 154, 363

ẓāhir (pl. *ẓawāhir*) 85–86, 92, 97, 111, 144, 228, 298
Ẓāhiriyya 86–87, 202, 260
ẓann 92, 97, 111, 115, 152n7, 155–157, 159
  ghālib al-ẓann 159, 268, 270, 304, 319–320, 336–337, 346–348, 359, 362
  ḥusn al-ẓann 96, 100, 106–108, 210, 353
ziyāda (pl. *ziyādāt*) 92–93, 169